RESISTANCE, REBELLION, AND CONSCIOUSNESS
IN THE ANDEAN PEASANT WORLD,
18TH TO 20TH CENTURIES

This volume is the product of a project in Andean history and anthropology organized and sponsored by the Social Science Research Council.

Resistance, Rebellion, and Consciousness
in the
Andean Peasant World, 18th to 20th Centuries

Edited by

STEVE J. STERN

The University of Wisconsin Press

Published by
The University of Wisconsin Press
2537 Daniels Street
Madison, Wisconsin 53718

3 Henrietta Street
London WC2E 8LU, England

10   9   8   7   6   5   4   3

Printed in the United States of America
Publication of this volume has been made possible in part by a grant from the
Cyril B. Nave Fund of the University of Wisconsin-Madison.

Cover illustration: Túpac Amaru triumphant at the Battle of Sangarará in 1780.
Túpac Amaru's uniform corresponds not to the 1780s, but to the Independence
battles of the 1820s. Detail from a painting on goatskin, early nineteenth
century. Artist: Tadeo Escalante (?). Reproduction and analysis in Pablo
Macera, *Retrato de Túpac Amaru* (Lima: Universidad Nacional Mayor de San Marcos,
1975).

Library of Congress Cataloging-in-Publication Data
Resistance, rebellion, and consciousness in the
  Andean peasant world, 18th to 20th centuries.
  Includes bibliographies and index.
  1. Indians of South America—Andes Region—Government
relations. 2. Peasant uprisings—Andes Region.
3. Indians of South America—Andes Region—Ethnic
identity. 4. Andes Region—History. I. Stern,
Steve J., 1951-
F2230.1.G68R47   1987   980'.004'98   87-40152
ISBN 0-299-11350-7
ISBN 0-299-11354-X (pbk.)

For my parents,
and in memory of A. Eugene Havens

Contents

Maps

Preface

This book is the product of a collective effort initiated by the Joint Committee on Latin American Studies of the Social Science Research Council (SSRC) and the American Council of Learned Societies (ACLS). In 1981, the Joint Committee invited Brooke Larson and me to write a working document for a meeting to be held in October for the purpose of designing a project on Andean history. At the October meeting were Carlos Sempat Assadourian, José María Caballero, Magnus Mörner, John V. Murra, Silvia Rivera, Karen Spalding, Enrique Tandeter, Larson, and myself. The outcome was a framework for three interrelated conferences intended to develop new hypotheses and conclusions based on recent advances in Andean history and anthropology, and to chart directions for future research. One conference was to focus on market penetration and Andean responses to the market over the course of the sixteenth to twentieth centuries. Results from that symposium, held in Sucre in 1983, will be available shortly in Olivia Harris, Brooke Larson, and Enrique Tandeter, eds., *Participación indígena en los mercados surandinos. Estrategias y reproducción social, siglos XVI–XX* (Cochabamba: CERES, 1987). A second conference was to focus on the more endogenous and elusive processes by which native Andean societies defended and reproduced themselves since the time of the Spanish conquest, and the internal transformations engendered by such strategies. This, the most experimental of the three conferences, took place in Quito in July 1986. A third conference was to look specifically at the history of Andean resistance and rebellion from the eighteenth to twentieth centuries, with emphasis on (1) analyzing moments of violent collective action as transitions or ruptures within a long-term trajectory embracing varied forms of resistance, and (2) assessing the ideological and cultural dimensions of domination, political legitimacy, and rebellion. That conference was held in Madison in April 1984, and provided an initial set of materials subsequently reworked and revised into this book. The topic of each conference intentionally blended into the topics of the other meetings; this, as well as the overlap of participants and various consultations among conference coordinators, has helped make the symposia related efforts toward a common agenda. Together and individually, the symposia seek to analyze the varied ways Andean peoples have participated in and responded to the macrolevel social, economic, cultural, and political worlds into which they are inserted, as well as to draw out the more endogenous motivations and dynamics of Andean historical experience.

Gratefully, then, I acknowledge the support of the many people who had a hand in shaping the overarching project on the Andes, and the rebellions project in particular. These individuals include the participants at the October 1981 meeting mentioned above, the authors of chapters that appear in this volume, and the following people who contributed research findings and commentaries to the 1984 conference in Madison: Manuel Burga, Víctor Hugo Cárdenas, John Coatsworth, Michael Gonzales, Rosalind Gow, Friedrich Katz, and Scarlett O'Phelan. I owe a special thanks to Brooke Larson for her collaboration in our role as co-coordinators of the general project, and for her work as Staff Associate at the SSRC; and to Silvia Rivera and Karen Spalding for their work when we drafted the specific agenda and rationale for the rebellions conference. Eric R. Wolf and an anonymous reader reviewed the entire manuscript when it was under consideration by the University of Wisconsin Press, and made many suggestions which improved the book. The book also benefitted from the editorial advice of Elizabeth Steinberg, Chief Editor at the University of Wisconsin Press, and from Jack Kirshbaum's careful editing. My colleagues Florencia Mallon and Thomas Skidmore have provided good general and specific advice along the way, as did Joan Dassin, Staff Associate at the SSRC. George Reid Andrews deserves thanks for launching the idea of the project during his tenure as Staff Associate at the SSRC. All these people have played an important role in shaping this book, and its role in the larger project of which it is a part.

Others who deserve thanks include the staff at the Ibero-American Studies Program of the University of Wisconsin (UW) and Cindy Hummel, who helped in the organization of the 1984 conference; the staff of the Latin America and Caribbean section at the SSRC, for all kinds of administrative help and advice at every step along the way; the staff of the Department of History at the UW, especially Anita Olson and Paula Pfannes, for conscientious and efficient work typing editorial letters and sometimes messy manuscripts; and my friends and colleagues at the University of Wisconsin Press. Hunter Fite co-translated Chapters 7, 8, and 11; Lianne Werlein-Jaén co-translated Chapter 12. Our procedure was as follows: they provided me with draft translations, which I subsequently reworked into a final draft. The translations were the product of our joint efforts, but I assume final responsibility for their accuracy. The Cartography Laboratory at the University of Wisconsin has provided generous and meticulous service in producing the maps; for this, I am especially grateful to David Dibiase, Paula Robbins, and Onno Brouwer. Gregory Crider undertook the arduous task of compiling an index with care and grace.

Research, conferences, and books cost money. Funds for the 1984 meetings at Madison, and for subsequent editorial costs, were provided by the Joint Committee on Latin American Studies of the SSRC and ACLS, and the Anonymous Fund and Cyril B. Nave Fund of the University of Wisconsin–Madison. Research grants from the National Endowment for the Humanities and the University of Wisconsin Graduate School Research Committee also provided me opportunities for research incorporated into this book.

Chapter 1 synthesizes the lines of inquiry and perspectives which unify this book into a "whole" larger than the sum of its parts, and assesses the implications of the Andean case studies for the study of peasants more generally. The division of the rest of the book into four major sections, each with an editorial introduction, will serve to orient the reader to the book's contents. Foreign terms are defined upon first usage, and the index records the location of definitions. Scholars differ in the spelling of certain Andean terms; in general, this book uses a uniform spelling for words that recur frequently in various essays, and inclines toward the spelling that will be familiar both to English and Spanish readers. One exception to uniform spelling appears in Chapter 12, when "Túpac Katari" is changed to "Tupaj Katari" out of deference to current usages in the political movement analyzed in that essay. Maps 1 and 2 will serve as general maps for the book. (Readers should bear in mind that the names of many late colonial districts identified in Map 2 have persisted well beyond the colonial period, in some instances to this day.) Other maps, pertinent to specific chapters, appear within the chapters themselves.

I have taken the liberty of dedicating this book to my parents, in their own way masters of survival and examples of the complexity of human consciousness; and to the memory of A. Eugene Havens, a colleague and friend who had much to say about resistance, rebellion, and consciousness in the Andean peasant world.

Madison, Wisconsin   SJS
January 1987

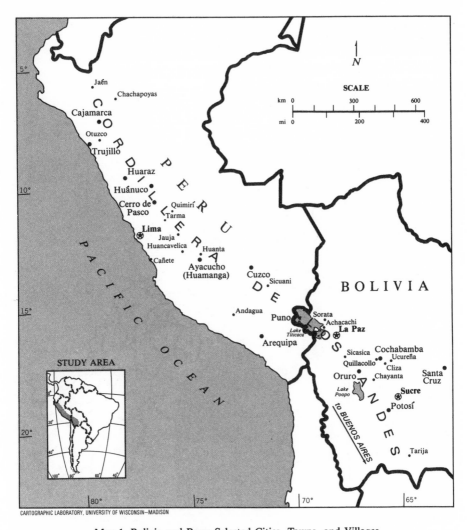

Map 1. Bolivia and Peru: Selected Cities, Towns, and Villages

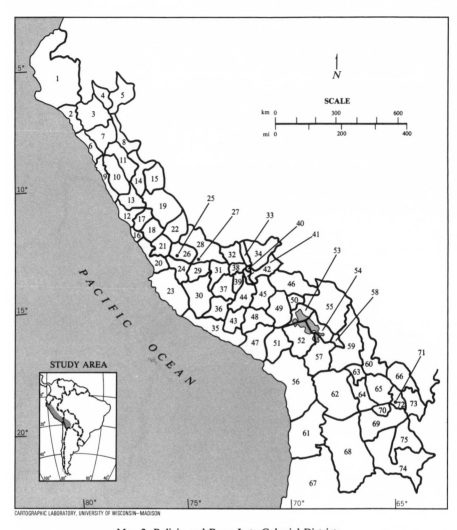

Map 2. Bolivia and Peru: Late Colonial Districts

xvi

LATE COLONIAL DISTRICTS

Alphabetical list

Abancay (38)
Andahuaylas (31)
Angaraes (26)
Arequipa (47)
Arica (56)
Atacama (67)
Aymaraes (37)
Azángaro (50)
Cajamarca (3)
Cajamarquilla (8)
Cajatambo (13)
Calca y Lares (33)
Camaná (35)
Canta (17)
Cañete (20)
Carabaya (46)
Carangas (62)
Castrovirreyna (24)
Caylloma (48)
Chachapoyas (5)
Chancay (12)
Chayanta (65)
Chílquez y Mázquez (41)
Chucuito (52)
Chumbivilcas (44)

Cochabamba (60)
Conchucos (11)
Condesuyos (43)
Cotabambas (39)
Cuzco (40)
Huamachuco (7)
Huamalíes (14)
Huamanga (27)
Huancavelica (25)
Huanta (28)
Huánuco (15)
Huarochirí (18)
Huaylas (10)
Ica (23)
Jauja (22)
La Paz (58)
La Plata (71)
Lambayeque (2)
Lampa (49)
Laraceja (55)
Lima/Cercado (16)
Lipes (68)
Lucanas (30)
Luya y Chillaos (4)
Misque (66)

Moquegua (51)
Omasuyo (54)
Oruro (63)
Pacajes (57)
Paria (64)
Parinacochas (36)
Paucarcolla (53)
Paucartambo (34)
Pilaya y Paspaya (75)
Piura (1)
Porco (69)
Potosí (70)
Quispicanchis (42)
Santa (9)
Sicasica (59)
Tarapacá (61)
Tarija y Chichas (74)
Tarma (19)
Tinta (45)
Tomina (73)
Trujillo (6)
Urubamba (32)
Vilcashuaman (29)
Yamparaez (72)
Yauyos (21)

Numerical list

1) Piura
2) Lambayeque
3) Cajamarca
4) Luya y Chillaos
5) Chachapoyas
6) Trujillo
7) Huamachuco
8) Cajamarquilla
9) Santa
10) Huaylas
11) Conchucos
12) Chancay
13) Cajatambo
14) Huamalíes
15) Huánuco
16) Lima/Cercado
17) Canta
18) Huarochirí
19) Tarma
20) Cañete
21) Yauyos
22) Jauja
23) Ica
24) Castrovirreyna
25) Huancavelica

26) Angaraes
27) Huamanga
28) Huanta
29) Vilcashuaman
30) Lucanas
31) Andahuaylas
32) Urubamba
33) Calca y Lares
34) Paucartambo
35) Camaná
36) Parinacochas
37) Aymaraes
38) Abancay
39) Cotabambas
40) Cuzco
41) Chílquez y Mázquez
42) Quispicanchis
43) Condesuyos
44) Chumbivilcas
45) Tinta
46) Carabaya
47) Arequipa
48) Caylloma
49) Lampa
50) Azángaro

51) Moquegua
52) Chucuito
53) Paucarcolla
54) Omasuyo
55) Laraceja
56) Arica
57) Pacajes
58) La Paz
59) Sicasica
60) Cochabamba
61) Tarapacá
62) Carangas
63) Oruro
64) Paria
65) Chayanta
66) Misque
67) Atacama
68) Lipes
69) Porco
70) Potosí
71) La Plata
72) Yamparaez
73) Tomina
74) Tarija y Chichas
75) Pilaya y Paspaya

Introduction

New Approaches to the Study of Peasant Rebellion and Consciousness: Implications of the Andean Experience

STEVE J. STERN

The non-European world exploded after World War II, and the combined effects of decolonization, revolution, and the Cold War provoked a torrent of studies on agrarian unrest and political mobilization.[1] The new pre-occupation—in certain respects a "rediscovery"—was especially evident among social scientists in the United States.[2] After all, it was the United States that assumed leadership of the West in the Cold War, financed a huge and expanding university system, and agonized over policy failures in China, Cuba, and Vietnam.

By the 1960s, as scholars struggled to understand the turbulence of the non-European world, and wrestled with their own political consciences, the agrarian question came to assume an ever more prominent place in our understanding of modern world history. Normally irrelevant or second-ary to the contemporary political life of industrialized societies such as the United States, England, and (to a lesser extent) France, the "tradi-tional" agrarian classes—landlords and peasants—suddenly played pivotal roles on the stage of contemporary history. Students of modernization and political mobilization, for example, saw in the Third World the final death throes of archaic classes and values as once traditional societies awakened painfully to contemporary urban values and expectations. The agrarian sector nurtured the historic values, traditions, and social relations that held non-Western societies back from a more rapid modernization of their economies and political institutions, and that made the transition to modern life more difficult and politically explosive.[3] Those who took a more critical stance toward the industrialized West discovered that the agrarian question was central to an understanding of the Western and non-Western worlds alike. Barrington Moore (1966) demonstrated that contemporary political cultures, whether democratic or authoritarian, rested on a historical foundation of agrarian violence and transformation. It was in an earlier world of lords, peasants, and nascent bourgeois strata, and in the political paths their societies took to revamp the agrarian sector, that Moore found the keys to the "democratic" or "authoritarian" features of political life in contemporary England, France, Germany, the United States, China, and Japan. Eric R. Wolf (1969) focused more pointedly on the "Third World" and argued that the great revolutions of the twentieth century were fundamentally "peasant wars." In various parts of the world, peasantries — subsistence-oriented agricultural producers subjected to the authority and economic exactions of a state, or a landed class of overlords, or both — faced the destructive advance of capitalist relations and values. Capitalism's advance undermined the peasants' access to the land, resources, and sociopolitical mechanisms they normally needed to sustain their way of life. In Mexico, Russia, China, Vietnam, Algeria, and Cuba, peasantries rose up in great defensive mobilizations that made revolution both necessary and possible. (In fairness to Wolf, his superb analysis of specific case studies illuminated the limits and variations that qualify the general interpretation. See, for example, his handling of the idiosyncrasies of the Cuban case.) The irony was that, in shattering the old order, the peasants facilitated the rise to power of revolutionary groups, political parties, and states whose interest in social transformation might, in the end, hasten the peasants' own destruction or subjugation.[4]

By the 1970s, the study of peasantries and agrarian conflict had become a well-established and vital field of scholarly inquiry. The field is now sufficiently mature and self-sustaining to produce theoretically and empirically interesting work for decades to come. Whether the issue is the impact of "modernization" on peasants, the transition to capitalism in the countryside, the structural causes of agrarian rebellion and its role in regime breakdown and revolution, or the internal differentiation of the peasantry into strata of varying economic welfare and political proclivities, we can now point to a cluster of studies rich in sophistication.[5] Within peasant studies, the subject of agrarian rebellion continues to command the attention of talented intellectuals, and the more interesting attempts to generalize about "peasants" often focus implicitly or explicitly on agrarian conflict and rebellion. To the list of early classics by Hobsbawm (1959), Moore (1966), and Wolf (1969), we can now add more recent landmark works by Scott (1976), Paige (1975), Tilly (1978), Popkin (1979), and Skocpol (1979). And these are simply works that aspire to high levels of generalization. Any area studies specialist could easily add a list of pioneering efforts for his or her culture area.

The study of peasants and agrarian conflict is a field too sophisticated, diverse, and politically charged to descend into stale uniformity. Yet, despite notable dissents (to be discussed later), one can identify several widespread assumptions and assertions that shape our overall image of peasants and agrarian rebels. First, most scholars now agree that the incorporation of predominantly peasant territories into the modern capitalist world economy had a destructive impact on peasant life, at least in the medium run. Even those who see "modernization" as ultimately beneficial would now be inclined to concede that it first exacts a heavy price (see, for example, Clark and Donnelly 1983: 11). Traditional values and social relations come under assault; local institutions that once provided a measure of economic security and income redistribution become ever more precarious; time-tested political strategies vis-à-vis lords or the state prove increasingly obsolete. The net result breaks down the viability of an earlier way of life, and provokes political unrest and mobilization. Second, scholars tend to agree that the penetration of capitalism accentuates the internal differentiation of peasant society into rich and poor strata. More precisely, capitalism breaks down institutional constraints that pressured wealthy peasants and villagers to channel their resources into "redistributive" or prestige-earning paths that blocked the free conversion of wealth into investment capital. In the most extreme cases, such a process polarizes peasant society into bourgeois farmers and proletarianized paupers, and subjects the remaining "middle peasants" to an insecure and problematic future. Political analysis of agrarian movements requires explicit attention to internal differentiation among the peasantry. Third, the political resolution of agrarian conflict and crisis is held to have had a strong, sometimes decisive, impact on the modern political history of countries with an important peasant tradition. In these countries' histories, the "agrarian question" looms large in the structural breakdown of colonial and *ancièn regime* states. The essays in this book do not by and large challenge the three assertions mentioned thus far, although they complicate the picture by offering evidence of greater peasant capacities to resist, ameliorate, or survive the destructive effects of capitalism than might be expected from the literature.

Fourth, and most questionable in view of this book's essays, are the assumptions about peasants as political actors. Peasants are frequently depicted as parochial and defensive "reactors" to external forces, and their political behavior, in this view, tends to reflect their objective "structural" position in society. Agrarian rebels "react" to changes dictated by forces outside the peasant sector itself — price cycles in the world market, the spread of capitalist plantations, the policies of the landed upper class or the state, and so on. Their economic base and social relations fragment the peasantry into separate and highly localized "little worlds"—the parochial world of a community, or a landed estate—and frequently pit peasants against one another as competing clients of the state's or lords' patronage. Limited in their political horizons, structurally divided amongst themselves, unable to understand national-level politics, let alone forge effective political strategies beyond the immediate locale, peasants succumb to the appeal of a millenarian redemption when searching for a means to transform society as a whole. To the extent that peasants either develop or benefit from effective political initiatives at the national level, such successes reflect not the peasants' historic capacity to analyze and respond to national-level politics, but instead rather recent changes: the peasants' political modernization; the leadership and influence of urban groups, rural-to-urban migrants, and intellectuals allied with the peasants; the ability of revolutionaries to channel rural mobilization against foreign invaders into a national political movement.

In short, when peasants rebel, they are held to do so in reaction to changes determined by all-powerful external forces or "systems." Their modes of consciousness, even in rebellion, are generally seen as quite limited and predictable, and logically derivative from their "structural" position in society. These assumptions about peasants as political actors are not simple figments of intellectuals' imagination. Enough evidence exists to demonstrate that the "parochial reactor" phenomenon is not only real, but that it also represents at least one powerful tendency in peasant political life. The problem, in view of this book's essays and the argument made later in this introduction, is that a tendency which is partial and in many cases offset by other tendencies has been taken to represent *the* essential character of peasant political behavior and consciousness.

The four sets of assumptions and assertions mentioned above do not exactly add up to a unified theory of agrarian conflict and peasant rebellion, nor do they command uniform consensus among scholars. The literature includes explicit dissents from these views. Popkin (1979), for example, presents a sweeping challenge to assertions about the destructive impact of capitalism on peasants, and their alleged mobilization to defend the crumbling "moral economy" associated with a precapitalist way of life. Macfarlane's (1978) portrait of rural folk in medieval and early modern England likewise stresses their individualism and calculating entrepreneurship—although his typically British preoccupation is not to challenge our theoretical notions of "peasants" so much as to establish "peculiarities" that set England apart from truly peasant regions of the world. The weight of population and life cycle trends in analyzing the causes and limits of internal differentiation is a subject of some dispute rooted in the distinctive perspectives of Chayanov (1986) and Lenin (1964) (cf. Shanin 1972). More recent and ongoing researches into "everyday forms of peasant resistance" (Scott 1985, *JPS* 1986; cf. Cooper 1980, Isaacman et al. 1980, Isaacman 1985) will undoubtedly drive us to reconsider our views of peasants as political actors, and is at least partly compatible with the approaches to peasant resistance and consciousness taken in this book. Nonetheless, the dissenters swim upstream against a formidable tide, and the new areas of inquiry are only beginning to recast deeply held assumptions and interpretations. The images sketched above—the destructive impact of capitalism, the boost given by capitalism to the internal differentiation of peasant strata into rich and poor, the major impact of the agrarian question on national political life more generally, and the parochial character of peasants as political actors—continue to constitute a common core of "prevailing wisdoms" that permeate both general theory and particular case studies.

The experience of native Andean peoples in the highlands of Peru and Bolivia is highly relevant to the literature on peasants and agrarian rebellion. In highland Peru-Bolivia, large majorities of the population have historically earned their sustenance as peasant cultivators. Andean peoples have for centuries been sharply affected by the North Atlantic economies in the vanguard of world capitalist transition and development. The ethnic division between Andean "Indians" and creole "nationals" has made the assumption of peasant parochialism pervasive and intense. Moreover, Andean rebellions of varying scope and ambition have erupted frequently since the eighteenth century—first in relation to the breakdown of the Spanish colonial order in the late eighteenth and early nineteenth centuries, later in relation to creole attempts at nation-building during the late nineteenth and twentieth centuries. These Andean rebellions provide a thick set of historical materials with which to reconsider the paradigms and methods we use to understand agrarian and peasant unrest more generally.

Yet despite the pertinence of the Andean experience, it has not played an important role in developing or evaluating general theory on peasants and peasant rebellion. Although research in Andean history and anthropology has crackled with intellectual innovation and excitement in recent decades, the sense of *implication* drawn from such research has been largely restricted to the Andean culture area itself. (For important exceptions, however, see Orlove and Custred 1980.) At least three factors account for this somewhat insular sense of implication. First, within the Andean field, specialists have struggled to liberate the Andean experience from the shadow of other culture areas and political discourses. In an earlier era, and even to this day, some writers have viewed the ancient Incas and their contemporary descendants as examples of the virtues or defects of socialism, welfare states, or totalitarianism, or as mere variations on a general theme such as "irrigation civilizations." To discover the real nature of Andean civilization and its achievements it has been necessary to react against earlier manipulations and superficiality by emphasizing unique aspects of the Andean experience not easily subsumed under general categories. John V. Murra's pioneering and influential interpretations of Andean "verticality" and Inca-peasant political relations may be understood in these terms.[6] Second, outside the Andean field, political events in Bolivia and Peru have not generated the kind of sustained political obsessions provoked by political conflicts in China, Cuba, Vietnam, and Chile. The Bolivian revolution of 1952 and the Peruvian revolution of 1968 each provoked intellectual interest and valuable studies, but each defied the usual Cold War categories, each erupted at times when other revolutions and upheavals loomed larger in political debate (China and Korea in the early 1950s, Vietnam and Chile in the late 1960s and early 1970s), and each fizzled to a murky denouement that reduced political interest. Finally, the ethnic issue is unavoidable in the Andean agrarian experience, and introduces complicating and awkward complexities to general discussions of "peasants." Uncertainty about the role that indigenous, ethnic, and racial issues should have in theoretical debates about "peasantry" — a category usually defined and theorized in ethnic-blind terms — has probably impeded explicit intellectual dialogue between Andean specialists and students of peasantry in general.

The articles in this book largely avoid explicit engagement of theory, yet they add up to something more than an original contribution to Andean history and studies. Of course, the Andean world is a worthy scholarly subject in its own right. Moreover, any serious attempt to analyze the Andean experience must address its singular, even idiosyncratic, features. The essays in this book contribute provocative findings and reevaluations to problems in the history of Andean rebellion and consciousness. In doing so, they add depth to and substantially revise, sometimes radically revise, the historiography of Andean peoples. This contribution alone justifies the publication of this collection, and each of the book's four sections will include brief introductory remarks highlighting the essays' specific significances for the history of Andean rebellion and resistance. The remainder of this general introduction will focus not on this book's contributions to Andean historiography as such, but rather on its implications for the study of "peasants" and agrarian unrest in general.

Taken as a whole, the essays in this book plead for a rethinking of assumptions and paradigms in four areas: the role of peasants as continuous initiators in political relations; the selection of appropriate time frames as units of analysis in the study of rebellion; the diversity of peasant consciousness and political horizons; and the significance of ethnic factors in explaining "peasant" consciousness and revolt. In each of these four areas, I will point to essays and findings in this book that recast our perspectives during three different Andean historical conjunctures: the late colonial crisis of the eighteenth century, political conflicts and wars of the nineteenth-century republics, and agrarian conflict and political mobilization in Bolivia since the 1940s. I will also suggest why the perspectives taken in these essays apply broadly, not to the Andean cases alone. And finally, in each of these four areas, I will conclude with a methodological suggestion that illustrates the practical implications of these essays for students of peasant rebellion more generally.

Let us begin with peasants as *continuous initiators* in political relations among themselves and with nonpeasants. For all the advances made in the field of agrarian studies, we are still only beginning to understand the manifold ways whereby peasants have continuously engaged their political worlds—in apparently quiescent as well as rebellious times, as initiators of change as well as reactors to it, as peoples simultaneously disposed to "adapt" to objective forces beyond their control and to "resist" inroads on hard-won rights and achievements. Peasant political action tends still to be reduced to its most dramatic and abnormal moments— moments of rupture, defensive mobilization against harmful change, collective violence against authority. Although the literature recognizes that peasants have placed their own stamp on the political histories of their regions and countries, it shrinks such impact to moments of crisis leading to rebellion. During more "normal" times, peasants recede from the political picture. Politically speaking, they are an inert force—dormant, traditional, or ineffectual. This reductionism fits nicely with the image of peasant rebels as parochial "reactors" to external forces, and with the assumption that such defensive and limited political behavior is largely inherent in the objective, "structural" condition of peasants.

The problem with this approach is not only that it fails to understand peasant politics during "normal" or quiescent times, but also that it leads to superficial explanations of the causes of rebellion. Such is the case, at least, for Andean history. For the late colonial period, for example, my essay and that by Mörner and Trelles demonstrate the danger of attempts to deduce insurrectionary behavior from "structural" variables, or to explain insurrection as defensive reactions to destructive external forces. Significantly, my essay's attempt to propose an alternative explanation of late colonial insurrection requires that we look seriously at the evolution of *preexisting* patterns of "resistant adaptation" that entailed innovative political engagement of the state by peasants. In this perspective, the relevant question becomes not why a politically dormant and traditionalist peasant mass suddenly became insurrectionary, but rather why, at specific moments, ongoing peasant resistance and self-defense increasingly took the form of collective violence against established authority. In this context, Campbell's vivid discussion of Andean political splits and choices during the wars of the 1780s analyzes not a sudden effort by peasants to forge effective political relations and strategies, but rather the continuation of such efforts in a new and insurrectionary context.

Similarly, this book's essays on republican history point to the importance of peasants' ongoing and sometimes innovative political involvement. Platt's and Mallon's analyses of nineteenth-century politics invert our conventional understanding of peasant-state relations. For Bolivia, Platt shows how peasants tried, with mixed results, to *impose* their conception of peasant-state relations on state officials, and explains rebellion in terms of the history of this peasant initiative. For Peru, Mallon shows how a particular group of peasants developed a "national project" of their own, one sufficiently vital to sustain the creation of an independent "peasant republic" and sufficiently threatening to oligarchical state-building to invite repression. In the perspective of these essays, the political dilemmas and decisions faced by Bolivian peasant rebels since the 1940s take on new meaning. The Andean political strategies and evaluations studied by Albó and by Dandler and Torrico for the contemporary period represent not a sudden "awakening" of political consciousness, but the continuing experimentation and accumulation of experience by peasants in their political relations with the state and with nonpeasants.

For the modern as well as colonial periods, it is when we assume a prior history of "resistance" and peasant self-defense — a history that embraces apparently tranquil periods and that places peasants in a position of active, sometimes innovative political engagement — that we are able to arrive at a more profound appreciation of the moments when peasants turned to outright rebellion. It is when we study the bases of apparent and real accommodations to authority, consider the patterns of resistant assertion and self-protection incorporated into such accommodations, the ways such "resistant adaptation" made accommodation partial and contingent, and the values and ongoing political evaluations that lay behind partial accommodations, that we discern more clearly why peasants sometimes became rebels or insurrectionists.

The essays in this book study native Andean peoples in terms that see them as continuously involved in the shaping of their societies, sometimes in a role as political initiators, not mere reactors, and often exerting an important limiting impact on their local superiors and on "external" actors or systems. This perspective, in turn, serves as a prerequisite for under-

standing the causes and character of political unrest in the Andes. Although
such an approach has not yet made much of an impact on theory, a growing body of area studies literatures on peasants and slaves suggest the applicability of this perspective to rural culture areas beyond the Andean
region.[7] Our first methodological suggestion follows directly from this
perspective: *explicit analysis of preexisting patterns of "resistant adaptation" is an essential prerequisite for any adequate theory or explanation
of peasant rebellion.* Only by asking why, during what period, and in what
ways earlier patterns of "resistance" and defense proved more compatible
with and "adaptive" to the wider structure of domination, and perhaps
even its partial legitimation, do we understand why resistance sometimes
culminated in violent collective outbursts against authority. (In some cases,
"resistant adaptation" may have included occasional acts of violence, and
the necessary analysis would therefore include study of transformations
in the uses of violence, rather than imply a pure or simple transition from
nonviolent to violent forms of resistance.) Successful analysis of the "resistant adaptation" that preceded the outbreak of rebellion or insurrection requires, in turn, that one see peasants as continuously and actively
engaged in political relations with other peasants and with nonpeasants.

This approach views rebellion as a short-term variant within a long-
term process of resistance and accommodation to authority, and therefore raises our second area of rethinking: the selection of time frames as
units of analysis. Whether studying a local rebellion or a full-scale insurrection of regional or supraregional proportions, how far back in time
need the analyst go to discern correctly the causes and internal dynamics
of the rebellion?

Again and again, the Andean case studies in this book suggest that we
must look at multiple time frames simultaneously—relatively short time
frames ("conjunctural" and "episodic") to understand the recent changes
that make rebellion or insurrection more likely and possible, and to appreciate dynamic changes that emerge during the course of violent conflicts;
and longer time frames spanning centuries to understand the historic
injustices, memories, and strategies that shape the goals, consciousness,
and tactics of the rebels. For the colonial period, the essays by Salomon
and Szemiński and the ongoing researches of Manuel Burga (discussed
in the Introduction to Part II), demonstrate that a deep familiarity with
pre-eighteenth-century culture history and memory is essential if we are
to grasp the categories and concepts of late colonial rebels. My essay's
speculation on the breakdown of "resistant adaptation" makes seventeenth-
century history an indispensable building block, not mere "background,"
in the explanation of civil war in the 1780s. Similarly, despite notable differences between them, Bonilla, Platt, and Mallon all invoke continuities

and legacies from distant colonial times to explain, in part, the character of nineteenth-century rebellions. And for modern Bolivia, Albó demonstrates that politically engaged Aymara peoples and their opponents think in terms of memories spanning two centuries' time. In each of these cases, limiting the relevant historical unit of analysis to a forty- or fifty-year period preceding rebellion is perilously myopic, and violates the historical memory and consciousness of the rebels themselves.

Obviously, the need to incorporate long time frames into the relevant units of analysis does not imply that short-term events and changes are irrelevant. Campbell's account of tupamarista-katarista relations during the civil war of the 1780s, Mallon's study of the unfolding of peasant nationalism in the midst of war and foreign occupation, and Dandler and Torrico's close account of the commitment established between President Villarroel and Cochabamba's peasants, provide eloquent and convincing proof that so-called episodic events matter enormously, above all in fluid moments of crisis and rebellion. The challenge faced by scholars is not to *replace* short- or medium-term units of analysis with the *longue durée*, a procedure that risks burying real changes, moments of fluidity and rupture, and their causes under a picture of long continuities and glacially paced change. The challenge is, rather, to develop an analysis that successfully incorporates multiple time scales into its vision of rebellion and its causes.

Unfortunately, social scientists and theoreticians are somewhat disposed to look at the shorter time frames alone and to restrict "history" to decades rather than centuries. If long-term phenomena are mentioned, they may be presented as mere historical "background" to orient the reader, not as a source of explanatory tools explicitly incorporated into the analysis. Whether the long-term view is omitted altogether, or included pro forma, the resulting myopia can lead to erroneous, even absurd conclusions. As Theda Skocpol (1979: 41) has noted for studies of the Chinese Revolution: "it seems remarkably shortsighted in historical terms to regard it as a new-nation-building revolution of the mid-twentieth century. China had an imperial Old Regime with a cultural and political history stretching back many hundreds of years." Peasants, almost by definition, interact with state structures and overlords, and in many culture areas this political inheritance embraces centuries and partly defines the issues at stake in rebellion. When the Mexican revolutionary Emiliano Zapata was asked why he and his peasant armies were fighting, he pointed to a box of old colonial land titles.[8] For the peasants of revolutionary Morelos, the relevant time scales included not only the changes introduced under the recent rule by Porfirio Díaz (1876–1910), not only the immediate policies of their Constitutionalist contemporaries, who betrayed the peasants' version of the revolution, but also a centuries-long struggle over land that defined the peasants' aspirations and understandings of proper rights and obligations in their relations with the state.

Our second practical suggestion, then, is that *the method used to study peasant rebellion should incorporate long-term frames of reference explicitly into the analysis.* The precise definition of the relevant long-term frame of reference will depend on the particular case at hand, but it should at least include the period considered relevant in the rebels' own historical memory, and the period during which the last enduring strategy of "resistant adaptation" was developed. It is difficult to imagine a time scale less than a century long that meets these criteria. A method which studies multiple time scales, including long-term ones, will not only explain better the causes and ideological characteristics of particular rebellions and insurrections. It will also enable the student to distinguish more clearly between genuinely new patterns of collective violence and grievance, and repetitions of historic cycles of resistance and accommodation that occasionally included some forms of collective violence.

We have already attached importance to the historical memory of peasants, but historical memory is itself but a slice of the larger pie called peasant consciousness. In this area, too, this book calls for a reassessment of common theoretical assumptions. For the Andean case, the expectations of ideological parochialism and predictability do not stand up under scrutiny. The forms of consciousness and the breadth of political horizons uncovered in this book's essays are too diverse and flexible to fit into the usual straitjacketed category of "peasant consciousness" described earlier in this essay. The peasants' aspirations and ideological commitments go beyond narrow obsessions with local land, subsistence guarantees, or autonomy (i.e., the desire simply to be left alone). Nor can we say that the peasants' material experience, social connections, and political understandings were largely bounded by the "little worlds" of communities and haciendas. For the late colonial period, both directly and through intermediaries, peasants moved in social, economic, and ideological orbits that stretched considerably beyond their principal locales of residence and work. Mobilization to install a new Inca-led social order reflected not a simple yearning for local subsistence and autonomy, but an effort to forge a new macrolevel polity that blended more successfully local peasant needs and aspirations with supraregional political order. True, one could dismiss the struggle for an Inca-led Andean renaissance as an example of the "prepolitical" millenarianism to which peasants desperate to overcome their fragmentation are prone. But in this case, one would have to confront Alberto Flores Galindo's inversion of our usual assumptions. Flores shows that the search for an Inca liberator was not an aspiration confined only to peasants or Indians. The dream of an Inca-led resurgence was a political idea whose appeal was so compellingly "universal," in the late colonial Andean world, that it fired the imagination of more "cosmopolitan" individuals, and made it possible for Andean peasants to envision a social order that allied them with nonpeasants and nonindigenous peoples under Inca auspices.

Similarly, our nineteenth- and twentieth-century materials depict an awareness of political worlds beyond the immediate locale, a willingness to deal with states, and a flexibility of consciousness far more complex than the predictable parochial obsessions with land, subsistence, or autonomy. Platt introduces notions of peasant-state reciprocities; Mallon argues for a bottom-up peasant nationalism *before* a bourgeoisie imposes "nationalism" on a citizenry integrated by an internal market; Dandler and Torrico provide eloquent testimony of peasant interest and commitment to populist political pacts; Albó explores the painful reevaluations that led Aymara peasants, in particular, to reject paternal political pacts, and to search for new forms of *national-level* political action. In all these depictions, Andean peasants are no more inherently parochial than other political actors; their consciousness does not conform to a priori assumptions; their political behavior is nurtured by a long historical experience dealing with states and macrolevel political forces; and their ideological history is an important variable in its own right in the explanation of rebellious activity.

The particular values, memories, and vision of the world that define the content of Andean rebel consciousness may be in important respects uniquely Andean, but the same cannot be said of the failure of Andean peasant consciousness to conform to a priori categories. One must recall that most peasantries have had long experience with states and with nonpeasants. Moreover, most peasantries have resided in well-defined "culture areas" (Mesoamerica, Mediterranean Europe, Islamic North Africa, China, Indochina, etc.) with complex internal histories defining cultural notions of social identity and aspiration, order and disorder, justice and vengeance, continuity and change, and the like. These cultural notions are products of a history shaped by both peasants and nonpeasants; more important, their spread has not been restricted only to nonpeasant elites, even if peasants have imposed their own partial variation on broad cultural themes.[9] Under these circumstances, deducing from the general "structural" features of peasantries their characteristic form(s) of consciousness is hopelessly one-dimensional and ahistorical. Deducing, in addition, that peasants are characteristically parochial, backward, and defensive merely adds insult to injury. It is quite instructive that sensitive students of *particular* peasantries find the history and complexity of their consciousness far richer than our theoretical postures would imply. Frances Fitzgerald's analysis of "Marxism-Leninism in the Vietnamese Landscape" (1973: 284–304; based in good measure on Mus 1952), for example, is a stunning example of the way specific historical traditions and values in Vietnamese culture provided a foundation for a rebel-peasant consciousness compatible with Marxist notions of revolution and justice. To take a more narrowly defined example, Arturo Warman found that Mexican peasants' resistance, in the 1970s, to state attempts to "collectivize" the management of their communal lands (*ejidos*) did not reflect the ignorance, parochialism, and traditionalism intellectuals commonly used to explain the peasants' "reactionary" stance. On the contrary, the peasants shrewdly recognized that behind the rhetorical masks of progress and material reward lay an attempt by the state to organize and control modern agrarian enterprises in ways that would destroy economic options the peasants needed to survive (Warman 1980: 61–83).[10] The peasants were neither ignorant about macrolevel politics, nor inherently opposed to "progress" or to collective forms of economic organization.

Our third methodological suggestion, then, is that studies of peasant rebellion *should treat peasant consciousness as problematic rather than predictable, should pay particular attention to the "culture history" of the area under study, and should discard notions of the inherent parochialism and defensiveness of peasants.* From this perspective, parochialism and defensive obsessions with local rights may indeed prevail among particular rebellious peasantries at particular times and places, but these patterns could not be explained away as a near-universal phenomenon inherent in the situation of being a peasant threatened by external overlords, state authorities, or markets. This perspective also allows the analyst to assess more dynamically the interplay of material and ideological variables (since the latter do not always "reflect" the former in simple or direct ways), and to consider in what ways explicit attention to peasant consciousness changes our understanding of the causes and issues at stake in rebellion. It will encourage us, too, to develop the new theoretical tools needed to explain the multiple contours peasant consciousness can take. Mallon's theoretical explanation of the development of nationalist consciousness before the consolidation of a dominant bourgeoisie and internal market is an instructive and exciting example.

If one takes peasant consciousness seriously in the Andes, one must immediately weigh the significance of ethnicity in "peasant" consciousness and revolt. Here, too, the Andean experience provokes a reassessment of assumptions and paradigms. By ethnicity, I mean the use of presumed cultural and physical attributes (race or color, biological or cultural ancestry, religion, language, work habits, clothing, etc.) — attributes considered to adhere strongly to the persons involved rather than to be easily renounced, adopted, or transferred — to draw social boundaries that place people into distinctive groupings within the larger world of social interaction. To the extent that ethnic boundaries do *not* coincide with class boundaries, ethnic relations and identification may serve to link the grievances and world views of peasants and nonpeasants. Such was the case, for example, in the insurrectionary mobilizations that sought to install an Inca-led order in the late colonial Andes. A shared sense of ethnic identification and grievance served as a bridge, in at least some areas, uniting the loyalties of native Andean peasants, and Andean elites whose class privileges (ownership of haciendas, investment in mercantile enterprises, participation in tribute incomes, etc.) sharply distinguished them from peasants. To the extent, on the other hand, that ethnic boundaries *do* coincide with class boundaries, the language, ideology, and causes of peasant rebellions are difficult to understand in ethnic-blind terms. An ethnic component is built into the oppressions, patterns of adaptation and resistance, sense of grievance, and aspirations that will loom large in the explanation and analysis of revolt. Such ethnic bases of revolt are particularly important, for example, in the rebellions studied by Salomon and Platt for the eighteenth and nineteenth centuries. (Cf. the research of Gonzales, discussed in the Introduction to Part III.) It is precisely the ethnic dimension of Andean peasant consciousness in Peru that leads Bonilla to dismiss Mallon's finding of peasant nationalism in Peru's central highlands as atypical at best. In most other areas, Bonilla argues, the ethnic question loomed larger and would have made peasant nationalism impossible.

Clearly, the ethnic dimension is unavoidable in any broad discussion of rebellion and consciousness by Andean peasants. This has held true, for the Andean area, in regions and time periods when ethnic and class boundaries virtually coincided, and when they have not. The findings of Dandler and Torrico, Albó, and Cárdenas (Cárdenas is discussed in the Introduction to Part IV) make emphatically clear both how significant ethnicity is in contemporary peasant politics, and also how easily it has tripped up those who perceive Bolivian class conflicts in ethnic-blind terms.

But is the weight of ethnic-racial issues in Andean peasant history peculiar and atypical? If so, the tendency to theorize and explain peasant revolts in ethnic-blind terms is not seriously mistaken. The ethnic question, however, has sharply affected the history and probably the consciousness of many peasantries. Especially in the Third World, the spread of North Atlantic capitalism has been closely associated with various forms of colonial domination — formal colonial rule, warfare and informal rule, missionary religion, and so on. The assault on the material underpinnings of peasant life has inevitably brought with it the divisions of language, religion, culture, and race that nurture ethnic relations and consciousness. Under these conditions, we should be surprised if an ethnic-national component does *not* loom significantly in peasant rebellion and consciousness. European peasants may be the exception rather than the rule in this instance, even though one need only look to British Ireland, or to the Christian "reconquest" of Islamic Spain, to find analogies in the European experience.

In addition, even when the division between colonizer and colonized is set aside, internal ethnic matters may be indispensable to any serious analysis of peasant politics, consciousness, or rebellion. Campbell's discussion of late colonial insurrection shows clearly that Andean insurrectionaries were internally divided amongst themselves, and that intra-Andean ethnic boundaries figured significantly in such divisions. Anyone remotely familiar with the religious question in Ireland, or the historic stereotypes that North and South Vietnamese have used to characterize their differences (see Fitzgerald 1973: 64–66), or the tendency of many peasant communities to turn "inward" and claim an identity and interest distinctive from that of rival communities as well as that of nonpeasants (Wolf 1957; Stern 1983), will appreciate the potential significance of ethnic conflicts and consciousness among peasants.

Finally, even when obvious ethnic divisions are not applicable, the protagonists of class conflict may tend to attach more subtle sorts of ethnic accouterments to themselves or to other social classes. (This process is sometimes described as "classism.") The Zapatista peasants of Morelos, for example, were mainly mestizos, not Indians, and they were in any event relatively "acculturated" compared to peasants from other parts of Mexico. Nonetheless, landowners and urban elites could not help but attach a derogatory ethnic label to their class enemies, and considered the Zapatistas barbaric "Indians" engaged in wild and destructive race war. Even urban workers were influenced by the tendency to ascribe ethnic characteristics to other social classes. When the Zapatistas occupied Mexico City, workers were stunned and to some extent alienated by the respectful social style and evident religiosity of the peasants. The characteristics that adhered to the peasants *as a distinctive kind of people* introduced an ethnic element into the controversial decision of the workers to reject a peasant-worker coalition with the Zapatistas, and to ally instead with the peasants' Constitutionalist enemies (Hart 1978: 131–33). It would be naive to believe that the tendency of nonpeasants to dismiss the peasants as barbaric, ignorant, or superstitious did not have an important hand in the peasants' own sense of grievance and aspiration.

If, as I have argued, the significance of ethnic factors in peasant consciousness and revolt is not peculiar to the Andes, we are in a position to make a fourth methodological suggestion. In theory as well as particular studies of peasant revolt, even when ethnic matters are not obviously relevant (as they are, say, in Ireland or Peru), *ethnic-blind analysis should be justified rather than used as a point of departure*. In some cases and for some purposes, ethnic variables may not be important to the understanding of rebellion. But this needs to be demonstrated explicitly. Ethnic-blind categories are probably a mistake for many parts of the Third World in recent centuries, and may seriously limit the usefulness of general theory.

This essay has sought to break with the tendency of Andean historians and anthropologists to restrict the sense of implication we draw from Andean case studies. It also issues a challenge to theorists and to students of other peasantries to incorporate the Andean experience into their paradigms and methodologies. The specific purposes of this introductory essay should not be taken to detract, however, from the importance of the Andean experience in its own right. Each of the essays that follow offers an original and significant twist on one or another theme essential to the history of Andean rebellion. Taken together, they offer eloquent testimony of the varied ways in which Andean peasants have struggled to better their lot, transform aspiration into reality, even take destiny into their own hands. To this history we now turn.

NOTES

1   This assertion is almost self-evident to anyone who has studied the literature on peasants, agrarian revolution, or political mobilization. See, for example, the dates of the literature on peasants and on revolution reviewed by Clark and Donnelly (1983) and by Skocpol (1979: 3–33), or the works cited in notes 3–5. A content analysis of articles published in major scholarly journals, and of the subject areas of new journals (such as *Journal of Peasant Studies* or *Peasant Studies*), would almost certainly support the same assertion.

2   I borrow the term "rediscovery" from Shanin (1971a: 11). As Shanin points out, the late 1950s and 1960s hardly witnessed the rise of the *first* significant scholarly or political interest in peasants and agrarian issues. Debate in Germany and Russia in the late nineteenth and early twentieth centuries, for example, provoked classic works by Chayanov (1986; orig. 1923), Kautsky (1974; orig. 1899), and Lenin (1964; orig. 1899). The weight of agrarian issues in the history and political polemics of particular countries such as France, England, and Mexico, moreover, produced important historical literatures on agrarian matters well before the 1960s, even though these literatures tended not to generalize or theorize beyond the particular country's experience. And, of course, Mao Zedong's great political innovation was to place peasants and agrarian conflict at the heart of the theory and praxis of the Chinese revolution.

Nonetheless, it was the late 1950s and 1960s that witnessed a resurgence of interest in peasants and political mobilization in the Western scholarly world, especially the United States, and an emphasis on theoretical and comparative perspectives facilitating broad generalization. It is no accident that it was precisely during the 1960s and 1970s that "old" classics were rediscovered and reprinted in Western editions.

3   See, for somewhat varied examples of the literature on modernization and political mobilization, Black 1960, 1976; Deutsch 1961; Eisenstadt 1966; Huntington 1968; C. Johnson 1964, 1966; J. Johnson 1958; Lambert 1967; Landsberger 1969; Lipset 1967; Rogers 1969; Shanin 1971b. Influential works by Parsons (1951) and Smelser (1963) had an important impact on much of the literature cited above. For a perceptive critical review of theories of revolution – a literature which partly overlaps that on modernization and political mobilization – see Aya 1979.

4   For influential works critical of the industrialized West, and bearing significant similarities to the perspectives of Moore (1966) and Wolf (1969), see Hobsbawm 1959; Polanyi 1957; Scott 1976; Skocpol 1979; Stavenhagen 1975; Thompson 1971; Wallerstein 1974; Worsley 1968.

5   The characterization of the literature in this and the following four paragraphs draws on the literature cited in notes 1 to 4, my own familiarity with the extensive literature for Latin America, and the following major works not emphasizing Latin America: Adas 1979; Alroy 1966; Blum 1961, 1978; Chesneaux 1973; Cohn 1970; Cooper 1980; Dunn 1972; C. Johnson 1962; Migdal 1974; Paige 1975; Shanin 1966, 1972; Stinchcombe 1961; Tilly 1978; Wolf 1966. Those readers wishing further orientation to the literature on Latin American peasants are advised to consult such journals as *Latin American Research Review* and *Latin American Perspectives*, or to consult the following recent works: Bauer 1979; de Janvry 1982; Duncan and Rutledge 1978; Mallon 1983; and Roseberry 1983. See also Landsberger 1969; Stavenhagen 1970.

6   See Murra 1975: esp. 23–115, 193–223; cf. Murra 1956. For an extensive and recent consideration of Murra's ideas, and Murra's own retrospective, see Masuda et al. 1985.

7   For Latin American and Caribbean cases, see Larson 1983; Mintz 1977; Mintz and Price 1976; Stern 1981. For Africa, see Isaacman and Isaacman 1977; Isaacman et al. 1980; Isaacman 1985. For the U.S. South, see Genovese 1974; Hahn 1983. For Southeast Asia see Scott 1985; *JPS* 1986.

8   The incident was first recounted and explained by Sotelo Inclán (1943: 201–3), and subsequently the subject of further perceptive discussion by Womack (1969: 371–72) and Fuentes (1969). I am very grateful to Eric R. Wolf for graciously drawing my attention to the "scholarly genealogy" of this event.

9   For example, one could argue that in Mesoamerican cultures, the notion that human sacrifice to the gods was necessary to sustain the cosmos served elite interests and was most fully elaborated by ruling priests and intellectuals. Note, for example, Padden's charge (1967) that the Aztecs encouraged and manipulated such beliefs as part of their imperial strategy. Nonetheless, it is also clear that such notions of the relation between humans, gods, and the continuity

of life were long diffuse in Mesoamerican cultures, and that peasants shared
such notions, even if they did not always draw the same conclusions as elites
regarding the necessity and effects of particular sacrificial practices and institutions. Similarly, in Vietnam, the cultural notion that real social transformation could only occur under a "mandate from heaven" might have been
elaborated by Vietnamese elites, but peasants could also partake of such
notions, might bend them to suit peasant needs and understandings, and in
some instances resist or attack elites under the auspices of a heavenly mandate. To cite another example, in Mediterranean Europe, peasants might
absorb much of the paternal values inculcated by the Catholic Church, but
use their "religiosity" to forge special bonds with patron saints so uniquely
responsible to the peasants' communities that the saints seemed to overshadow
Jesus. In each of these examples, the peasants' rebelliousness or lack thereof
might be affected by values and understandings shaped by nonpeasants as
well as peasants, and the nature of the peasants' consciousness and political
proclivities could not be derived exclusively from "structural" variables (community peasant versus hacienda serf, independent yeoman farmer versus
sharecropper or tenant, hacienda peon versus plantation laborer, and so on).
10   Cf. the remarkably complex and sensitive interpretation of peasant consciousness in Mexico in Meyer 1973. Scott's recent book (1985) is also extremely
provocative in this regard.

REFERENCES

ADAS, MICHAEL
1979   *Prophets of Rebellion: Millenarian Protest Movements Against the
          European Colonial Order.* Chapel Hill: University of North Carolina
          Press.
ALROY, GIL CARL
1966   *The Involvement of Peasants in Internal Wars.* Princeton: Center of
          International Studies.
AYA, ROD
1979   "Theories of Revolution Reconsidered: Contrasting Models of Col-
          lective Violence." *Theory and Society: Renewal and Critique in Social
          Theory* 8 (Elsevier-Amsterdam, July): 39–99.
BAUER, ARNOLD J.
1979   "Rural Workers in Spanish America: Problems of Peonage and Op-
          pression." *Hispanic American Historical Review* 59 (Feb.): 34–63.
BLACK, CYRIL E., ed.
1960   *The Transformation of Russian Society: Aspects of Social Change
          since 1861.* Cambridge: Harvard University Press.
1976   *Comparative Modernization: A Reader.* New York: Free Press.

BLUM, JEROME
1961   *Lord and Peasant in Russia: From the Ninth to the Nineteenth Century.* Princeton: Princeton University Press.
1978   *The End of the Old Order in Europe.* Princeton: Princeton University Press.

CHAYANOV, A. V.
1986   *The Theory of Peasant Economy.* Originally published 1923. Madison: University of Wisconsin Press.

CHESNEAUX, JEAN
1973   *Peasant Revolts in China, 1840–1949.* Translated by C. A. Curwen. New York: W. W. Norton & Company.

CLARK, SAMUEL, AND JAMES S. DONNELLY, JR.
1983   "General Introduction." In Clark and Donnelly, eds., *Irish Peasants: Violence and Political Unrest, 1780–1914* (Madison: University of Wisconsin Press). Pp. 3–21.

COHN, NORMAN
1970   *The Pursuit of the Millennium: Revolutionary Millenarians and Mystical Anarchists of the Middle Ages.* Rev. ed. New York: Oxford University Press. Original edition published in 1957.

COOPER, FREDERICK
1980   *From Slaves to Squatters: Plantation Labor and Agriculture in Zanzibar and Coastal Kenya, 1890–1925.* New Haven: Yale University Press.

DE JANVRY, ALAIN
1982   *The Agrarian Question and Reformism in Latin America.* Baltimore: Johns Hopkins University Press.

DEUTSCH, KARL W.
1961   "Social Mobilization and Political Development." *American Political Science Review* 55 (Sept.): 493–514.

DUNCAN, KENNETH, AND IAN RUTLEDGE, eds.
1978   *Land and Labour in Latin America: Essays on the Development of Agrarian Capitalism in the Nineteenth and Twentieth Centuries.* Cambridge: Cambridge University Press.

DUNN, JOHN
1972   *Modern Revolutions: An Introduction to the Analysis of a Political Phenomenon.* Cambridge: Cambridge University Press.

EISENSTADT, S. N.
1966   *Modernization: Protest and Change.* Englewood Cliffs, N.J.: Prentice-Hall.

FITZGERALD, FRANCES
1973   *Fire in the Lake: The Vietnamese and the Americans in Vietnam.* New York: Vintage Books.

FUENTES, CARLOS
1969   "Viva Zapata." *The New York Review of Books* (13 March): 5–11.

GENOVESE, EUGENE D.
1974   *Roll, Jordan, Roll: The World the Slaves Made.* New York: Random House.

HAHN, STEVEN
1983   *The Roots of Southern Populism: Yeoman Farmers and the Transformation of the Georgian Upcountry, 1850–1890.* New York: Oxford University Press.

HART, JOHN M.
1978   *Anarchism and the Mexican Working Class, 1860–1931.* Austin: University of Texas Press.

HOBSBAWM, ERIC J.
1959   *Primitive Rebels: Studies in Archaic Forms of Social Movement in the 19th and 20th Centuries.* Manchester: Manchester University Press.

HUNTINGTON, SAMUEL P.
1968   *Political Order in Changing Societies.* New Haven: Yale University Press.

ISAACMAN, ALLEN
1985   "Chiefs, Rural Differentiation and Peasant Protest: The Mozambican Forced Cotton Regime, 1938–1961." *African Economic History* 1, 4: 15–56.

ISAACMAN, ALLEN, AND BARBARA ISAACMAN
1977   "Resistance and Collaboration in Southern and Central Africa, ca. 1850–1920." *International Journal of African Historical Studies* 10, 1: 31–62.

ISAACMAN, ALLEN, ET AL.
1980   " 'Cotton is the Mother of Poverty': Peasant Resistance to Forced Cotton Production in Mozambique, 1938–1961." *International Journal of African Historical Studies* 13, 4: 581–615.

JPS
1986   *Journal of Peasant Studies* 13 (Jan.): Special Issue on "Everyday Forms of Peasant Resistance in South-East Asia."

JOHNSON, CHALMERS A.
1962   *Peasant Nationalism and Communist Power: The Emergence of Revolutionary China, 1937–1945.* Stanford: Stanford University Press.
1964   *Revolution and the Social System.* Stanford: Hoover Institution.
1966   *Revolutionary Change.* Boston: Little, Brown, and Company.

JOHNSON, JOHN J.
1958   *Political Change in Latin America: The Emergence of the Middle Sectors.* Stanford: Stanford University Press.

KAUTSKY, KARL
1974   *La cuestión agraria.* Mexico City: Ediciones de Cultura Popular. Originally published in 1899.

LAMBERT, JACQUES
1967   *Latin America: Social Structure and Political Institutions.* Berkeley: University of California Press. Originally published in French in 1963.

LANDSBERGER, HENRY A., ed.
1969   *Latin American Peasant Movements.* Ithaca, N.Y.: Cornell University Press.

LARSON, BROOKE
1983   "Shifting Views of Colonialism and Resistance." *Radical History Review* 27: 3–20.

LENIN, V. I.
1964   *The Development of Capitalism in Russia.* Moscow: Progress Publishers. Originally published in 1899.

LIPSET, SEYMOUR MARTIN
1967   "Values, Education, and Entrepreneurship." In Lipset and Aldo Solari, eds., *Elites in Latin America* (New York: Oxford University Press). Pp. 3–60.

MACFARLANE, ALAN
1978   *The Origins of English Individualism: The Family, Property, and Social Transition.* New York: Cambridge University Press.

MALLON, FLORENCIA E.
1983   *The Defense of Community in Peru's Central Highlands: Peasant Struggle and Capitalist Transition, 1860–1940.* Princeton: Princeton University Press.

MASUDA, SHOZO, ET AL.
1985   *Andean Ecology and Civilization.* Tokyo: University of Tokyo Press.

MEYER, JEAN
1973   *La cristiada.* 3 vols. Mexico City: Siglo XXI.

MIGDAL, JOEL S.
1974   *Peasants, Politics, and Revolution: Pressures Toward Political and Social Change in the Third World.* Princeton: Princeton University Press.

MINTZ, SIDNEY
1977   "The So-Called World System: Local Initiative and Local Response." *Dialectical Anthropology* 2: 253–70.

MINTZ, SIDNEY, AND RICHARD PRICE
1976   "An Anthropological Approach to the Afro-American Past: A Caribbean Perspective." Occasional Paper in Social Change No. 2, Institute for the Study of Human Issues (ISHI). Philadelphia: ISHI.

MOORE, BARRINGTON, JR.
1966   *Social Origins of Dictatorship and Democracy: Lord and Peasant in the Making of the Modern World.* Boston: Beacon Press.

MURRA, JOHN V.
1956   "The Economic Organization of the Inca State." Ph.D. diss., University of Chicago. Also available as *La organización económica del estado Inca.* Mexico City: Siglo XXI, 1978.
1975   *Formaciones económicas y políticas del mundo andino.* Lima: Instituto de Estudios Peruanos.

24 STEVE J. STERN

MUS, PAUL
1952 *Viêt-Nam: Sociologie d'une guerre.* Paris: Editions du Seuil.
ORLOVE, BENJAMIN S., AND GLYNN CUSTRED, eds.
1980 *Land and Power in Latin America: Agrarian Economies and Social Processes in the Andes.* New York: Holmes & Meier Publishers, Inc.
PADDEN, R. C.
1967 *The Hummingbird and the Hawk: Conquest and Sovereignty in the Valley of Mexico, 1503–1541.* Columbus: Ohio State University Press.
PAIGE, JEFFREY M.
1975 *Agrarian Revolution: Social Movements and Export Agriculture in the Underdeveloped World.* New York: Free Press.
PARSONS, TALCOTT
1951 *The Social System.* Glencoe, Ill.: Free Press.
POLANYI, KARL
1957 *The Great Transformation.* Boston: Beacon Press.
POPKIN, SAMUEL L.
1979 *The Rational Peasant: The Political Economy of Rural Society in Vietnam.* Berkeley: University of California Press.
ROGERS, EVERETT M.
1969 *Modernization Among Peasants: The Impact of Communication.* New York: Holt, Rinehart and Winston, Inc.
ROSEBERRY, WILLIAM
1983 *Coffee and Capitalism in the Venezuelan Andes.* Austin: University of Texas Press.
SCOTT, JAMES C.
1976 *The Moral Economy of the Peasant: Rebellion and Subsistence in Southeast Asia.* New Haven: Yale University Press.
1985 *Weapons of the Weak: Everyday Forms of Peasant Resistance.* New Haven: Yale University Press.
SHANIN, THEODOR
1966 "The Peasantry as a political factor." *Sociological Review* 14: 5–27.
1971a "Introduction." In Shanin 1971b: 11–19.
1971b (Ed.) *Peasants and Peasant Societies.* Baltimore: Penguin Books.
1972 *The Awkward Class: Political Sociology of Peasantry in a Developing Society: Russia, 1910–1925.* Oxford: Clarendon Press.
SKOCPOL, THEDA
1979 *States and Social Revolutions: A Comparative Analysis of France, Russia, and China.* New York: Cambridge University Press.
SMELSER, NEIL J.
1963 *Theory of Collective Behavior.* New York: Free Press of Glencoe.
SOTELO INCLÁN, JESÚS
1943 *Raíz y razón de Zapata.* Mexico City: Editorial Etnos.
STAVENHAGEN, RODOLFO
1970 (Ed.) *Agrarian Problems and Peasant Movements in Latin America.* New York: Doubleday and Anchor.

1975　　*Social Classes in Agrarian Societies.* New York: Doubleday and Anchor.

STERN, STEVE J.

1981　　"The Rise and Fall of Indian-White Alliances: A Regional View of 'Conquest' History." *Hispanic American Historical Review* 61 (Aug.): 461–91.

1983　　"The Struggle for Solidarity: Class, Culture, and Community in Highland Indian America." *Radical History Review* 27: 21–45.

STINCHCOMBE, A. L.

1961　　"Agricultural Enterprise and Rural Class Relations." *American Journal of Sociology* 67 (Sept.): 165–76.

THOMPSON, E. P.

1971　　"The Moral Economy of the English Crowd in the Eighteenth Century." *Past & Present* 50 (Feb.): 76–136.

TILLY, CHARLES

1978　　*From Mobilization to Revolution.* Reading, Mass.: Addison-Wesley.

WALLERSTEIN, IMMANUEL

1974　　*The Modern World-System: Capitalist Agriculture and the Origins of the European World-Economy in the Sixteenth Century.* New York: Academic Press.

WARMAN, ARTURO

1980　　*Ensayos sobre el campesinado en México.* Mexico City: Nueva Imagen.

WOLF, ERIC R.

1957　　"Closed Corporate Peasant Communities in Mesoamerica and Central Java." *Southwestern Journal of Anthropology* 13: 1–18.

1966　　*Peasants.* Englewood Cliffs, N.J.: Prentice-Hall.

1969　　*Peasant Wars of the Twentieth Century.* New York: Harper and Row.

WOMACK, JOHN, JR.

1969　　*Zapata and the Mexican Revolution.* New York: Alfred A. Knopf.

WORSLEY, PETER

1968　　*The Trumpet Shall Sound: A Study of 'Cargo' Cults in Melanesia.* 2d ed. New York: Schocken Books.

PART I

From Resistance to Insurrection:
Crisis of the Colonial Order

Introduction to Part I

A great Civil War rocked the Andean highlands of southern Peru and Bolivia during the years 1780–1782. Two and a half centuries earlier, the Spanish conquistadores had wrested control of the Inca Empire, displaced its nobility, and proceeded to govern the Incas' former subjects — the peoples of a diverse array of ethnic kingdoms and communities, called "Indians" by the new colonizers. The overwhelming majority of these local Andean peoples were peasants, that is, subsistence-oriented agricultural producers in effective possession of lands but subject to claims by overlords and a state, and it was largely on the base of peasant tribute and labor that the colonizers built their mercantile economy and legendary silver mines. In the 1780s, many of these very peasant peoples rushed to join insurrectionary armies that assaulted the Old Regime and proclaimed the coming of a new era to be governed by Indian kings, in some regions kings considered descendants of the ancient Incas. As one might expect, the peasants supplied the bulk of the fighting force on both sides of the Civil War that ensued.

In its violence, mobilization of common rural folk, high political drama, and far-reaching consequences, the great insurrection ranks with its more well-known late colonial counterpart, the Haitian Revolution (1791–1804). Much as the slave insurrection in Haiti looms over the interpretation of slave societies in the Caribbean and nearby regions in the eighteenth and nineteenth centuries, so it is that the interpretation of the Andean Civil War casts a long shadow over the history of Peru and Bolivia. Any deeplevel consideration of the course of native Andean history must come to grips with the causes and meaning of the great insurrection. And because the insurrectionaries succeeded in mobilizing tens of thousands of peasants, controlling a "liberated territory," and propagating a vision of a just society, their movement provides particularly dramatic and salient material for the comparative and theoretical study of peasant movements.

This book, a collective effort to study the history of resistance and rebellion in the Andean world since the eighteenth century, begins appropriately with the great Civil War. The three essays in Part I reexamine the basic ways we have used to interpret the causes and internal political relations of the insurrectionary mobilization, and point the way to new hypotheses.

My essay introduces the pertinent historiography and attempts a broad reappraisal of the "Age of Andean Insurrection." The essay questions the commonly accepted chronology and geography of insurrectionary movements in the eighteenth century. These chronological and geographical boundaries are critical to a leading methodological trend in the historiography, the use of "spatial analysis" to correlate specific socioeconomic characteristics with the presence or absence of insurrection in major Andean regions, and to interpret the causes and character of the Andean Civil War on the basis of such correlations. My essay argues that a serious insurrectionary threat emerged in the highlands well *before* the 1770s and 1780s (the period emphasized in the historiography), that highland areas previously considered relatively pacific actually erupted in rebellion, and that the insurrectionary utopias that inspired peasants in southern Peru and Bolivia in the 1780s had similar appeal in central-northern Peru as early as the 1740s and 1750s. These findings, if correct, undermine the data base and assumptions used in previous works, render the spatial analyses practiced thus far highly misleading, and, indeed, sharply revise the nature of the problem historians seek to explain and understand. For now the problem becomes *not* how to explain why the peasant peoples in the southern highland provinces were uniquely driven or disposed to rebel in the 1780s, but rather to understand a series of new questions: why the late colonial order contended with insurrectionary threats across a wide territory that embraced central and perhaps northern highland regions, as well as the south; why such conjunctures emerged as early as the 1740s; why pan-Andean notions of a great transformation to be led by a "returned" or "revived" Inca force exerted such great appeal among peasants across otherwise diverse highland regions during much of the eighteenth century; and why, finally, one of several insurrectionary conjunctures actually culminated in prolonged insurrectionary warfare in a particular time and area.

In this perspective, the problem of the insurrectionary movements that exploded in the south in the 1780s becomes a subset of a larger and more long-term problem, and it is to that larger problem that we must address new interpretations and develop new methodologies if we wish to understand the causes of the Andean Civil War. My essay presents the beginnings of an alternative interpretation, offered as a hypothesis, that reaches back into the seventeenth century to understand patterns of "resistant adaptation" by native Andean peoples, and explores the subsequent changes in political economy, demography, and state policies that undermined earlier peasant strategies, eroded the foundations of colonial authority and legitimacy, and generally provoked Andean peoples to greater reliance on collective violence to assert their perceived rights. The essay also proposes several methodological perspectives that might illuminate the specific issues and enigmas raised by these new findings. Particularly important are focused attention on the interplay between moral consciousness and material exploitation; and the use of multiple time scales explicitly concerned with the dynamic interplay of structural, conjunctural, and episodic levels of analysis.

Despite its dangers, spatial analysis of the socioeconomic correlates of insurrectionary and loyalist politics gains in promise as it moves toward more finely grained microlevel analysis that tries to account for local differences *within* a generally rebellious (or loyalist) region. In the hands of scholars thoroughly immersed in the geography and history of a region, careful spatial analysis serves as a source of new hypotheses, as well as a check testing the limits of macrolevel interpretations. The essay by Mörner and Trelles, who study the local geography and correlates of insurrectionary and loyalist activity within the Cuzco region, represents an important advance in several respects. Their painstaking parish-level analysis questions the value, for the Cuzco region, of earlier interpretations correlating insurrectionary activity with the varying percentage of *forasteros* (migrant Indians alienated from their ancestral communities and kin groups) among the total Indian population, and with the varying rates of exploitation imposed by the *reparto de mercancías* (forced distribution of commodities) on Indian peasants. Their findings underscore the significance, at the local level, of variables heretofore less prominent in macrolevel analysis concerned mainly with differences *between* larger regions. Mörner and Trelles find greater insurrectionary sympathy in those Cuzco parishes with fewer (in absolute numbers) non-Indians, fewer haciendas, and smaller proportions of Indians resident on haciendas. Not surprisingly, these parishes experienced more stagnant population growth over the previous century, and tended to be situated at higher altitudes less propitious for commercial agriculture. These findings point to the significance of higher degrees of social "space" or "shielding" from the day-to-day influence of non-Indian patrons and authority figures for successful insurrectionary mobilization. They are consistent with the contention in my essay that the presence or absence of insurrectionary activity may owe as much to geographically varied patterns of social control and repression, as to varying rates of economic exploitation, or structural socioeconomic differences between regions.

As Mörner and Trelles proceed, they discover a striking correspondence between the ancient divisions of the Inca Empire, *Tawantinsuyu*, into four parts, or *suyu*, and the geography of Indian insurrection and loyalism. This apparent correspondence does not necessarily imply a simple "carry-over" of ethnic and political organization from Inca times. But at the very least, the authors' discussion of possible explanations of this finding reminds us that in the history of great insurrectionary mobilization by peasants, the local map of grudges, ethnic distinctions, political alliances, and kin networks *among* the oppressed are a significant part of the on-the-ground equation that tilts a given community or district toward revolt or loyalism.

Leon G. Campbell's essay draws us further into internal Andean matters that gave rise not only to splits between Andean rebels and loyalists, but also to organizational strife and political factionalism among Andean peoples theoretically unified in a common insurrection. Campbell's particular innovation is to study closely the relationship between preexisting Andean belief systems and symbols, Andean political and ethnic fragmentation, and political appeals and manipulations by rival rebel leaders. His analysis illuminates the paradoxical and contradictory role of the unifying symbols propagated by Andean rebel leaders, and the obstacles to unity even among rebel Indians alone. The Inkarrí myth, which envisioned the return of an Andean Creator to set an unjust world right, was a necessary and powerful unifying symbol used by rebel leaders to unite native peoples divided by geography, ethnic-kin boundaries, fragmentary political organization, and the like. But it was also a divisive symbol, insofar as it embodied Andean claims to rule in a specific Quechua Inca from Cuzco whose legitimacy among the Aymara peoples of the altiplano of Bolivia and the extreme south of Peru was at least questionable. Even in Cuzco, many conservative Inca nobles considered Túpac Amaru a fraudulent "upstart" rather than a true redeemer.

The simultaneous rise of rival leaderships — the tupamaristas centered in Cuzco, and the kataristas centered in the Bolivian altiplano — led to a sharpened sense of Aymara ethnicity, as well as significant splits over political program and tactics. In general, the tupamarista version of Andean revolution relied more heavily on recruiting leaders among established native Andean elites and wealth, and seeking coalitions with sympathetic mestizos and creoles; the kataristas more willingly upset local Andean political alignments by raising commoners to leadership positions, and moved more readily to a sense of Aymara racial solidarity that excluded not only non-Indians, but also rebel Quechua peoples. Significantly, the unraveling of the 1781 siege of La Paz, a crucial turning point in military terms, may have had as much to do with these internal Andean tensions as with Spanish military prowess.

Taken together, the essays in this section suggest the outlines of a new interpretation of the transition from native Andean resistance patterns, embracing behaviors as diverse as flight, legal battles, and local riots, to the outbreak of insurrectionary war seeking to transform the colonial Andean world in fundamental ways. My essay stretches the temporal and geographical boundaries of the insurrectionary ferment and episodes we seek to explain, proposes an alternative hypothesis on the causes of the great insurrection, and suggests methodological approaches by which we may more fully understand the long-term transition from "resistant adaptation" to insurrectionary conjunctures. The studies by Mörner and Trelles and by Campbell bring into focus the more finely grained "internal" views indispensable to a deeper understanding of the causes and character of the great war in the 1780s. Mörner and Trelles highlight the significance of new variables, not easily subsumed under macrolevel distinctions in social structure or economic exploitation rates, to explain parish-level behavior in favor of or against the uprising. Campbell demonstrates that a full interpretation of the great insurrection requires explicit analysis of competing political and ideological tendencies *within* the great insurrectionary mobilization. All three essays support the notion that the insurrectionary mobilization as a whole, and the competing tendencies within it, cannot be well understood or explained apart from studies of consciousness and belief systems that served to legitimate or undermine both the colonial authorities, and the Andean leaders who arose to challenge them. We will turn to a more extended study of consciousness in Part II of this volume. Let us turn first, however, to a broad reexamination of the crisis of colonial rule in Andean South America.

CHAPTER 2

The Age of Andean Insurrection, 1742–1782: A Reappraisal

STEVE J. STERN

Well over a hundred times during the years 1720–1790, the native Andean peoples of Peru and Bolivia, sometimes accompanied or led by dissident *castas* (mixed racial groups) and whites, rose up in violent defiance of colonial authorities.[1] In the eighteenth century, far more than in previous times, a colonial who assumed the post of *corregidor de indios* (local magistrate) knowingly risked death for the right to exploit the Indian countryside.

Two moments in this tense century of rebellion stand out. The first was the messianic insurrection launched by Juan Santos Atahualpa from the jungle zone bordering Peru's central highlands in 1742. A self-proclaimed Inca descendant who announced his imminent recapture of the Kingdom of Peru, Juan Santos led disaffected jungle peoples and *serrano* (high-lander) migrants in repeated military assaults that drove the colonizers out of the subtropical *montaña* on the eastern Andean slopes. During ten years of intermittent fighting, the colonial authorities did not once gain victory over Juan Santos's jungle-based guerrilla armies. After several humiliating defeats costing hundreds of lives, the colonial state finally settled on a military fort system designed to prevent the spread of the insurrection to the highlands. The second outstanding moment was the major civil war that engulfed the vast highland territory of southern Peru and Bo-

The author gratefully acknowledges support from the National Endowment for the Humanities and the University of Wisconsin Graduate School Research Committee for the research and writing of this essay. He also wishes to thank participants at the original conference for criticisms and suggestions, and especially the following individuals: Friedrich Katz, Brooke Larson, Florencia E. Mallon, Thomas E. Skidmore, William B. Taylor, and Barbara Weinstein.

livia from 1780 to 1782. The insurrectionaries, predominantly but not exclusively Indian peasants, were inspired and, for a time, led by José Gabriel Condorcanqui, Tomás Katari, and Julián Apasa (who took the name Túpac Katari). Condorcanqui, a moderately wealthy *kuraka* (Andean lord) of the Tungasuca district of Cuzco, was the now famous Inca descendant who adopted the name Túpac Amaru II, and became in many regions the leading name and symbol of the insurrection.[2] Like Juan Santos Atahualpa before him, Túpac Amaru II projected the image of a disinherited Indian noble reclaiming rightful sovereignty over *Tawantinsuyu* (the Inca Empire), and thereby liberating his followers of grievous colonial oppressions. As the mass Indian mobilization drove creole and mestizo sectors out of the insurrectionary coalition, neo-Inca messianism took on increasing importance. This time, the colonial authorities won a decisive victory. But two years of intense warfare cost perhaps 100,000 lives (out of a total population of approximately 1,200,000 in the territory directly affected),[3] and traumatized Indian and white consciousness well into the nineteenth century (Flores G. 1976b: 305-10; 1981: 263-64; Macera 1977: 2:319-24).

Together, these two moments define an era we may legitimately call the Age of Andean Insurrection. During the years 1742-1782,[4] the colonial authorities contended with more than the local riots and abortive insurrectionary conspiracies of earlier years. They now contended with the more immediate threat or reality of full-scale civil war, war that challenged the wider structure of colonial rule and privilege. Local violence and conflict might, under the banner of a messianic Inca-King, mushroom into a regional or supraregional insurrection mobilizing the support of tens of thousands. Túpac Amaru II's civil war galvanized the best hopes of native Andean peoples, and turned into reality the worst nightmares of the colonial elite. As far away as Mexico, it warned colonial officials to take conciliatory measures to prevent village riots from turning into regional insurrection (Taylor 1979: 120).[5] In Peru, the legacy included an assault on the memory of the Inca past, a reorganization of late colonial mechanisms of social control, a bitter hardening of social fears and tensions, and a strong creole tendency toward royalism during the Wars of Independence (Mendiburu 1874-1890: 8:417-18; Rowe 1954: 35-36, 51-53; Fisher 1976; Flores G. 1976b: 305-10; *Mercurio Peruano* 1791-94: 10:255-80, letter and commentaries of Nov. 26, 1793 and April 20-27, 1794; Macera 1977: 2:319-24; Lynch 1973: 157-70). This decisive moment of colonial Andean history has provoked an extensive and sometimes perceptive historical bibliography (see Campbell 1979; Flores G. 1976a). Yet we are only beginning to probe the causes, scope, and consequences of Túpac Amaru's failed revolution.

The purpose of this essay is to use new and old data, both published and unpublished, to critique directions taken by recent study of the Túpac Amaru insurrection, and to suggest tentatively some lines of reappraisal. My argument will be that current interpretation of the causes and scope of the civil war of 1780–1782 is marred by:

(a) too narrow a focus on the southern territory directly involved in the insurrection itself;

(b) too mechanical a methodology for explaining why some regions participated in revolt, while others did not; and

(c) too easy a dismissal of the significance of the eighteenth-century tradition of revolt and Inca-inspired messianism in Peru's central-northern highlands.

A rather extended reexamination of the repercussions of Juan Santos Atahualpa's movement in the highlands will, in this context, prove rewarding. Such study will at once call into question the alleged gap between the propensity toward insurrection in the southern versus the central-northern highlands, and provide clues for explaining why the Túpac Amaru revolution was, indeed, confined to the southern territory. We need first, however, to review briefly the historiographical picture.

THE HISTORIOGRAPHY OF THE ANDEAN INSURRECTIONS

A wide gulf divides the modern historiography of the two major eighteenth-century insurrections. One can, to be sure, discern certain shared patterns. The *indigenismo* of the 1920s and 1930s, for example, gave rise to a celebratory rediscovery of Andean revolt, and of individual heroes, that encompassed both cases. Indeed, most of the documentation currently available on the Juan Santos movement was published by Francisco A. Loayza (1942), who in the 1930s embarked on a major research and publications effort to revindicate the lost Andean past. The nationalist tendency, since the 1940s, to search for "precursors" of independence has incorporated both movements as examples of the inexorable march to national consciousness and anti-Spanish patriotism (Valcárcel 1946; Vallejo F. 1957; García R. 1957; Cornejo B. 1954, 1963; Campbell 1979: 17, 19–21). Yet if one wishes to interpret the significance of the two insurrections as manifestations of the crisis of Spanish colonial authority in Peru-Bolivia, one encounters a sharp contrast in the historiographical literature.

In the case of Juan Santos Atahualpa's mobilization, the most perceptive and substantive studies either focus on Juan Santos's significance for the lowland peoples and serrano migrants who inhabited the central montaña, or study the movement in the context of Franciscan missionary work on the frontiers of colonial settlement (Varese 1973; Lehnertz, n.d., 1974, 1972, 1970; Valcárcel 1946: 47–69; Amich 1771: esp. 179–206; Izaguirre 1922–1929:

2:107-296). On the repercussions of the insurrection in the highlands—the heartland of the colonial economy and polity—the literature on rebellion splits. One group of interpreters views Juan Santos Atahualpa as a figure who established important sierra ties and influence, and thereby contributed to the rising tide of eighteenth-century highland revolt (Vallejo F. 1957; Cornejo B. 1963: 47-129, esp. 62-86; Valcárcel 1946: esp. 155-65; Castro A. 1973: esp. 156-57; Chirif and Mora 1980: 257-58). The most careful proponent of this view (Castro A. 1973) takes note of the serrano clientele that joined Juan Santos Atahualpa in the lowland montaña, and of the apparent links and influence established by the insurrectionaries among highland peoples and conspirators. The problem is that thin evidence (given source limitations), neglect of *systematic* discussion of highland links and their implications, and a tendency toward hyperbole all make it rather easy to dismiss this approach. Most serious students of eighteenth-century Andean rebellion have, in fact, been impressed by the failure of the peoples of the neighboring central sierra provinces (Jauja and Tarma) to join the insurrectionary movement along their eastern perimeter. They therefore view the Juan Santos movement as a frontier insurrection, rather marginal in its practical political consequences. However important the movement's "Indian nationalist" ideology, or its military achievements, it has limited relevance to the larger history of Andean revolt and insurrection in the settled colonial territory of highlands and coast (Metraux 1942; Kubler 1946: 385; Loayza 1942: xi; Vargas U. 1966-71: 4:208-10; Rowe 1954: 40-42; Cornblit 1970: 11; Campbell 1979: 6; O'Phelan 1985).[6] Even Lehnertz (n.d.), who carefully argues that the Juan Santos movement drew on an increasingly serrano social base, does so by focusing on multiethnic highlander renegades who fled to the montaña frontier. Juan Santos's Indian-mestizo guerrilla bands failed to mobilize the sierra itself (see Lehnertz n.d.: Chapter 6).

The net result of the literature is that we are on sound footing when assessing the Juan Santos movement as a case study in lowland frontier history, but on shakier turf when assessing its highland repercussions. Careful scholars acknowledge sierra links but deem them relatively inconsequential; dissenting students tend to exaggerate loosely and face severe source limitations. We contend with a rather shallow historiography, insofar as it deals with the significance of the Juan Santos movement in the history of highland insurrection.

By contrast, the Túpac Amaru revolution, arguably the most important highland event since the age of Spanish Conquest, has generated a huge literature. An earlier era took a panoramic view and asked sweeping questions. The results included a magisterial study of the struggle for social justice and its continental repercussions (Lewin 1957; cf. Valcárcel 1946);

a significant and continuing debate on the "loyalist" or "separatist" character of the insurrection (Cornejo B. 1954; Valcárcel 1947, 1960; García R. 1957; L. Fisher 1966; cf. Szemiński 1976: 201-4; Campbell 1979: 19-21; Choy 1976; Bonilla and Spalding 1972); and a pioneering study of the rise of an "Inca nationalist movement" among dissident Andean nobles of the eighteenth century (Rowe 1954; cf. Rowe 1951; Spalding 1974: 147-93). These works left dangling, however, an explanation of the insurrection's timing and geography, its ideological complexities and contradictions, and its inability to recruit the support of most Andean kurakas. More recent work, politically critical of the search for popular bases of creole independence (Bonilla et al. 1972), and perhaps influenced by recent methodological trends in social and quantitative history, has strived for a more precise view of the insurrection's internal dynamics and causes. On the one hand, a series of ongoing researches look meticulously at the events of rebellion itself to probe the insurrection's multiple ideological strains, its precarious multiethnic composition, its leadership and organizational patterns, its Andean and non-Andean opposition, and its changing internal character as the civil war itself unfolded (Manuel Burga, personal communication, 1982; Campbell 1976, 1978, 1979, 1981, Chapter 4 in this volume; Flores G. 1976b, 1977, 1981; Hidalgo 1982, 1983; Larson 1979; O'Phelan G. 1979, 1982, 1985: 209-56; Szemiński 1976, 1980, 1982, 1984). On the other hand, several students look closely at the timing and geography of late colonial unrest to assess its structural causes and regional social bases (Cornblit 1970; Golte 1980; Flores G. 1981: 254, 262; Mörner 1978: 110-22, 128, 155; Mörner and Trelles, Chapter 3 in this volume; O'Phelan 1985; on regionalism, cf. Fisher 1979; Campbell 1979: 25-26).[7]

Indeed, the geographical scope of the insurrection has become *the* leading issue in recent innovative work on the causes of the Túpac Amaru revolution. The "real issue," as one influential scholar puts it, is "why the revolt inflamed only one portion of the provinces rather than all of them" (Golte 1980: 176). Oscar Cornblit (1970) pioneered this approach in a study of "Society and Mass Rebellion in Eighteenth-Century Peru and Bolivia." Cornblit, like others before and since (see Humphreys and Lynch 1965; Lynch 1973; Phelan 1978), argued that the Bourbon reforms threatened a variety of established interests and thereby sparked multiethnic dissidence in the late eighteenth century. This explained why elite rebels might wish to lead a revolt, but not how they might mobilize a mass following. Despite widespread "permanent resentment" (Cornblit 1970: 39) and local riots in eighteenth-century Andean America, only some rural Indian regions participated in the general insurrection of 1780-1782. Cornblit found that the insurrectionary territory of southern Peru and Bolivia included among its Indian population a large percentage of *forasteros*, displaced migratory natives alienated from their ancestral *ayllus* (Andean kin groups) and communities. The forastero population accounted for 40–60 percent (sometimes even 80 percent, according to Golte) of the Indian tributary population in the insurrectionary regions of the south, but constituted a far lesser proportion, often less than 20 percent, in the noninsurrectionary regions of the center-north (Cornblit 1970: 27, 38–39, 42–43; cf. Golte 1980: maps 5, 27). This regional variation made sense, since the forastero population was in Cornblit's view largely the result of flight and demographic displacement caused by the colonial labor drafts (*mitas*) to the great silver mines of Potosí in Bolivia.[8] Cornblit concluded — on the basis of the regional forastero distributions, contemporary accounts on the volatile and erratic "character" of these Indian floaters, and his own sociological theories of political behavior by displaced and "unintegrated" populations — that dissident leaders found in the forasteros an easily mobilizable mass following. The Túpac Amaru revolution was, in large measure, an outburst of violent vengeance by displaced Indians vulnerable to the charisma of José Gabriel Condorcanqui (see Cornblit 1970: 27, 38–39, 42–43).

Cornblit's conclusions have failed to stand up under scholarly scrutiny, but his methodological innovation has flourished. More finely graded studies of the varying percentages of forasteros in the smaller *corregimiento* districts of the highlands fail to predict which regions and subregions supported the great insurrection (see Mörner 1978: 118; Golte 1980: 182–83, maps 5, 27).[9] But the use of spatial variables to test apparent causes and to explain the geographical scope of the Túpac Amaru revolution has left a strong methodological mark on recent work (Mörner 1978: 91, 110–22, 128, 155; Golte 1980; Flores G. 1976b: 275–78, 285–95; 1981: 262; Mörner and Trelles, Chapter 3 in this volume).

Indeed, the most ambitious recent study of the causes and scope of the general insurrection makes extensive and refined use of the spatial method. In a detailed study of population, economy, and revolt in the eighteenth century, Jürgen Golte (1980) seeks to demonstrate the critical role of the *reparto de mercancías* (forced distribution of goods) in the Túpac Amaru insurrection. The reparto, managed by corregidores acting as monopoly merchants in their Indian districts, was the classic mechanism of surplus extraction in the eighteenth-century Andes (see Tord N. 1974; Lohmann V. 1957: 126–31; Moreno C. 1977; Larson and Wasserstrom 1983; Montero 1742: 45–47; Feyjoó 1778: 338–40). Increasingly, the *limeño* commercial bourgeoisie and its agents, the local corregidores, relied on the reparto to expand artificially the internal market, and simultaneously drain commodities and labor-time from indebted Indian "consumers." The Crown legalized the reparto in 1754, and set up a schedule of permissible — and therefore taxable — quotas in each corregimiento district. In Golte's view, the intensification of the reparto, which he believes tripled after midcentury, made it more than a method to siphon a large "surplus" from Indian peasants. The insatiable demands of the corregidor-reparto system in some regions reached the point of pillaging the very subsistence base of Indian peasants, and expropriating the income of some of the kurakas, mestizos, small merchants, and hacendados who formed small provincial bourgeoisies. The reparto, in conjunction with Bourbon taxation policies and several secondary variables (pp. 151-53), created a ripening conjuncture favoring multiethnic revolt, led by Andean kurakas, in the 1760s and 1770s. In the final analysis, "the attitudes of the population, especially the Indian [population], towards the general insurrection [of 1780-1782] can be explained on the basis of their economic capacity to meet the demands of the corregidores" (p. 182).

To demonstrate this point, Golte engages in an ingenious but flawed spatial study of the reparto's destructive impact on the Indian population on the eve of the Túpac Amaru revolution.[10] By calculating, district by district, the per capita burden of the reparto on Indians, and per capita income, Golte charts regional variation in the estimated ability of Indians to meet their reparto and tribute burdens (pp. 100-114, 176-83, maps 27, 28). The results are striking. The area where ability to pay exceeded reparto-tribute taxation by 20 pesos or less (sometimes falling into negative amounts, meaning that Indians could not meet reparto-tribute taxation) "coincides almost exactly with the regions in revolt during Túpac Amaru's rebellion" (p. 178). The area where the difference did not exceed 35 pesos "coincides with the area of expansion of the general insurrection" (p. 179).

Several exceptions to this general rule appear, but Golte explains these successfully within the terms of his argument. In the southern territory, such anomalies occur because significant economic particularities neglected in his general calculating formula distorted the estimated per capita carrying capacity in some provinces. These provinces turn out, then, not to be anomalies at all when the distortions of the general formula are corrected. In the northern highlands, sheer distance from the insurrectionary territory itself prevented several provinces with an otherwise strong propensity to revolt from joining the Túpac Amaru revolution. The isolation of the north derived, in large measure, from the comparative stability of most provinces in the central sierra during the crisis of the 1780s (see Map 3 of this book). By Golte's formula, the central districts of Huanta, Angaraes, Jauja, Tarma, and Huánuco were singularly disposed *not* to revolt. Their carrying capacity exceeded reparto-tribute burdens by 55-249 pesos (p. 180); it is therefore logical that all failed to join the insurrection of 1780-1782, and that all except Huanta failed to experience local revolts

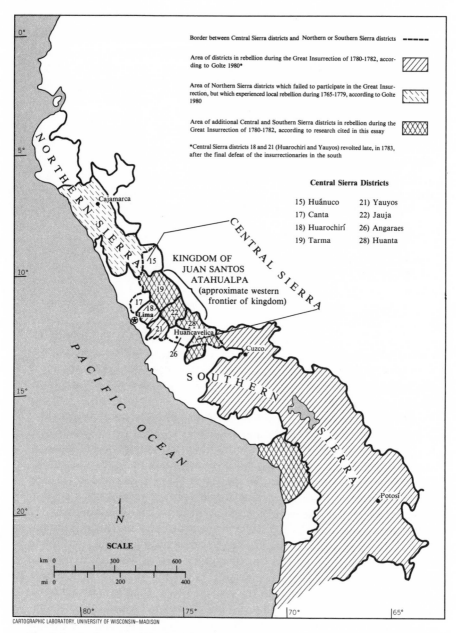

Border between Central Sierra districts and Northern or Southern Sierra districts ━ ━ ━ ━

Area of districts in rebellion during the Great Insurrection of 1780-1782, according to Golte 1980*

Area of Northern Sierra districts which failed to participate in the Great Insurrection, but which experienced local rebellion during 1765-1779, according to Golte 1980

Area of additional Central and Southern Sierra districts in rebellion during the Great Insurrection of 1780-1782, according to research cited in this essay

*Central Sierra districts 18 and 21 (Huarochiri and Yauyos) revolted late, in 1783, after the final defeat of the insurrectionaries in the south

Central Sierra Districts

15) Huánuco	21) Yauyos
17) Canta	22) Jauja
18) Huarochirí	26) Angaraes
19) Tarma	28) Huanta

NORTHERN SIERRA

Cajamarca

CENTRAL SIERRA

15

KINGDOM OF
JUAN SANTOS
ATAHUALPA
(approximate western
frontier of kingdom)

19

17 18
Lima 22

21 28
Huancavelica

26

Cuzco

SOUTHERN SIERRA

PACIFIC OCEAN

Potosí

N

SCALE

km 0 ____ 300 ____ 600

mi 0 ____ 200 ____ 400

0°

5°

10°

15°

20°

80° 75° 70° 65°

CARTOGRAPHIC LABORATORY, UNIVERSITY OF WISCONSIN–MADISON

Map 3. South, Center, and North Distinctions and the Geography of Late Colonial Rebellion

41

during 1765–1779 (maps 26, 27). In two central provinces, Huarochirí and Yauyos, revolt in the name of the Túpac Amaru cause did flare up in 1783. But these seem to confirm Golte's interpretation, since carrying capacity in Huarochirí and Yauyos exceeded reparto-tribute taxation by only 21 and 20 pesos respectively (see Table 2.1).

Table 2.1. Propensity toward Stability or Revolt in the Central Sierra, according to Golte's Model

Central Sierra District	Surplus of Carrying Capacity Over Reparto-Tribute Tax
Huánuco	249
Tarma	212
Huanta	178
Jauja	94
Angaraes	55
Canta	29
Huarochirí	21
Yauyos	20

Source: Golte 1980: 180.

To summarize Golte's complex argument: the reparto, the central instrument in the economic project of Lima's commercial bourgeoisie, unleashed regionally varied destruction and conflict that led, in the more intensely pillaged southern territory, to a multiethnic but Indian-dominated insurrection.

The spatial perspective pioneered by Cornblit and refined considerably by Golte has acquired critical importance to students of eighteenth-century Andean insurrection. It is for this very reason that the marginalization of Juan Santos Atahualpa from serious study of highland insurrection is especially unfortunate. To the extent that we continue to view the Juan Santos movement largely as a frontier episode without much implication for sierra history, we will continue to focus on explaining why the southern highlands exploded while the central sierra remained dormant. But close study of new and old sources raises troubling questions about the assumptions behind this line of inquiry. For as we shall see: (1) the insurrectionary appeal of a messianic Inca-King such as Juan Santos Atahualpa was far greater, in the central sierra, than usually acknowledged; (2) Indian violence and revolt *did* flare up in the central sierra during the era of Túpac Amaru II, although it did not expand territorially or "hook up" with the southern insurrection; and (3) the failure of the central sierra revolts of the 1780s to mushroom into full-scale insurrections had less to do with the comparative welfare or acquiescence of the region's population, than it did with the unusual strength of a repressive military apparatus in the central sierra. These findings should, I believe, recast our interpretation of the Age of Andean Insurrection. But before we jump ahead of our story, let us take a rather extended look at the movement led by Juan Santos Atahualpa.

THE SIERRA THREAT POSED BY AN INCA-KING, 1742–1752

When Juan Santos Atahualpa "Apu-Inca" ("Inca Lord") appeared in the central montaña in May 1742, he proclaimed the start of a new era (see for the following, Loayza 1942: 1–7; Amich 1771: 180–81). Juan Santos, a highlander descended from the murdered Inca Emperor Atahualpa, had come to reclaim his ancestral kingdom and vassals. The new Inca-King, Jesuit-educated and sent by God to set the world right, divided that world into three sovereign kingdoms: Spain for Spaniards, Africa for Africans, and America for "his children the Indians and mestizos" (Amich 1771: 182).[11] The new order would liberate the Indians of their oppressions, and bring prosperity to the Inca's American vassals. The cataclysm would begin in the jungle, spread to the highlands, and culminate with the coronation of the new Inca-King in Lima itself. Within days, message and messenger drew Indians away from the colonial missions and pueblos settled in the early eighteenth century. Thus began a reversal of Franciscan and commercial penetration that would keep much of the subtropical lowland frontier "off limits" to colonizers for over a century.[12]

The military history of this indigenous reconquest is well known (see Varese 1973: 190–204; Castro A. 1973; Loayza 1942; Amich 1771: 179–206; Izaguirre 1922–29: 2:107–64, 291–96), and here we need only to review its broad outlines. The authorities, using both trained soldiers sent from Callao (Lima's port, and Peru's chief military center) and local militia forces recruited in the central sierra districts of Tarma and Jauja, launched major military expeditions in 1742, 1743, 1746, and 1750. All failed. The most crushing blow, perhaps, came in 1746. A new viceroy experienced in the Indian wars of Chile (Campbell 1978: 11), José Antonio Manso de Velasco, Count of Superunda (1745–1761), sent up a new military commander, General José de Llamas, to lead a force of 850 troops against Juan Santos Atahualpa. Llamas, the most prestigious military officer of Peru, had commanded the 12,000 troops mobilized to defend the coast in the recent imperial war with England. But Llamas could work no miracles against Juan Santos Atahualpa. As usual, the survivors of the expedition returned to the sierra exhausted, frustrated, and demoralized. One detects during these years a recurring cycle in the military attitudes of viceregal authorities and local commanders (see esp. Izaguirre 1922–29:

2:129, 133–34; Loayza 1942: 57–67, 111–14, 120–23, 230, 233–34; Fuentes 1859: 3:382–83; 4:102–5). Invariably, such officials first voiced contempt toward presumptuous jungle "savages," and confidence that military might would quickly prevail. The air of disdain then gave way to demoralization and grudging respect. Finally, officials retreated to a strategy of defensive containment designed to seal off the sierra from the rebels. At this stage, contempt for the rebels, if expressed, would focus on their "cowardly" unwillingness to meet colonial troops in open battle in the sierra.

By the 1750s, when indigenous reconquest of the jungle territory was complete, the central sierra districts of Tarma and Jauja had become something of an armed camp. Five companies of trained infantry and cavalry, assisted by local militia forces, staffed several forts in the sierra and along its perimeter with the jungle. A moving sentry patrol would take special care to intercept contact between sierra and selva. In addition, the viceroy would staff the corregidor posts of Tarma and Jauja with trained military officers, even if a civilian had bought title to the corregidor position in Spain (Moreno C. 1977: 140–41).[13] The colonials could not find or defeat Juan Santos Atahualpa in the jungle, but they would at least bar him from threatening the sierra heartland. (On the militarization of Tarma-Jauja between the 1740s and 1780s, see Varese 1973: 190–204; Campbell 1978: 11–13, 17, 38–39, 83–84; Mendiburu 1874–90: 5:106, 140–41; 8:273; Loayza 1942: 13, 57–58, 66–67, 111–14; Amich 1771: 190–91, 197, 202–3; Fuentes 1859: 4:104–5; Moreno C. 1983: 60–61, chart between 390–91, 420, 447; Bueno 1764–79: 47; Amat 1776: 306–7, 392–94, 399; Ruíz L. 1777–88: 1:92; 2:plate 12.)

The central issue, for eighteenth-century contemporaries and for us, was whether Juan Santos Atahualpa's messianic message would rally support in the sierra. And as we have seen, it is precisely on this point that we contend with unsystematic historiography, inadequate evidence, and the undeniable failure of central sierra peoples to mount an insurrection. Let us review first the evidence regarding sierra support, real or potential, of Juan Santos Atahualpa, then turn later to an explanation of the apparently dormant politics of highland Jauja and Tarma. Some of the evidence of sierra attitudes and behavior is available in known but sometimes obscure sources; other evidence draws on heretofore unused criminal cases against alleged spies and agents of Juan Santos Atahualpa.[14]

Juan Santos led a multiethnic and multiracial movement composed in part of highlanders living in the central montaña. For both economic and political reasons, the central montaña bordering Huanta, Jauja, Tarma, and Húanuco had for centuries witnessed considerable contact among sierra and selva peoples. For highlands peoples, trade or colonization in the central montaña provided access to coca leaf, fruit, wood, salt, cotton, and other valued resources (Murra 1975: 62–71; Varese 1973: 115–17, 187; Lehnertz n.d.: chap. 2, 10–12; Chirif and Mora 1980: 230–31). When the Incas occupied the "eyebrow of the jungle" (*ceja de selva*), the deeper jungle came also to serve as a "refuge zone" for dissident highlanders (Chirif and Mora 1980: 232). Spanish colonization intensified the sierra-selva mix. On the one hand, missionaries and landowners brought serrano servants and laborers to staff the missions and haciendas of the central montaña. These serranos, predominantly but not exclusively Indian, formed significant population clusters in the early eighteenth century (Lehnertz n.d.: chap. 3, 15–19; Ortíz 1975–76: 1:132). On the other hand, the *limits* of colonization made the central montaña an important "refuge zone" for dissident Indians, blacks, and castas fleeing an oppressive life in the highlands.[15] Seventeenth- and eighteenth-century sources repeatedly confirm that a mixed population of indigenous selva peoples and highlander émigres, the latter and their descendants probably numbering in the thousands, populated the central montaña (see Lehnertz n.d.: chap. 2, 24–26, chap. 3, 33–34; Fuentes 1859: 3:141; Izaguirre 1922–29: 2:294–95; 7:323, 325; Ortíz 1975–76: 1:127–29; Juan and Ulloa 1826: 250; Moreno C. 1977: 236–37; Varese 1973: 188).

In the montaña frontier itself, therefore, Juan Santos's potential clientele included considerable numbers of disaffected highlanders whose sierra contacts and know-how magnified the movement's insurrectionary threat. The authorities had good reason to fear Juan Santos's ability to organize a network of spies and propagandists in the highlands (see Loayza 1942: 27–28; Eguiguren 1959: 1:319; Amich 1771: 188). Moreover, the messianic vision and military exploits of the movement further expanded its serrano constituency within the montaña. Hundreds of serranos fled to join the Inca-King (see Amich 1771: 189), and the rebels raided the sierra for additional recruits (AGN 1752: 15v, 19v, 20r, 22v; Loayza 1942: 156, 207). An array of rituals brought such prisoners directly to the presence of the Inca Lord, and when successful, integrated the Inca's new "children" into the work, celebrations, and religious life of the new society (AGN 1752: 14v–24r; Loayza 1942: 207). The montaña kingdom of Juan Santos Atahualpa appeared to function as a grand confederation of peoples and chiefs. One set of peoples normally lived apart from the Inca camp, in accordance with their preexisting tribal life, but could be mobilized, coordinated, and called together as needed. Another set of peoples and chiefs, more serrano in flavor and of more recent creation, appeared to live under the more immediate sway of the Inca (AGN 1752: 15v–16v, 19–20, 22r–24r).[16] The mestizo followers alone probably numbered several hundred strong (Lehnertz n.d.: chap. 6, n. 43).

The social composition of the rebel military forces confirmed the presence of a significant serrano minority in the movement. The reports we have available preclude a precise calculation, but give the impression that a fighting force of 400–500 guerrillas might include as many as 100 serranos (see, for examples, the reports from 1743 and 1752 in Loayza 1942: 27–28, 37–38, 43, 44; AGN 1752: 20v). As early as 1743, Juan Santos's serrano following justified organization of a separate fighting unit of some 50 serrana women, captained by one "Doña Ana," a *zamba* (mixed Indian-black) from Tarma (Loayza 1942: 28). As in the runaway slave communities of Brazil and Spanish America, fugitive men may have considerably outnumbered fugitive women (see Price 1979: 18–19; AGN 1752: 20r [sex composition of captured prisoners/recruits]).

But what of the sierra itself? One could, after all, argue that the Juan Santos movement drew away from the sierra precisely the most defiant and restless individuals. Once we turn our focus away from the Inca's active serrano following in the montaña, do we find substantial evidence of latent support among highlanders who remained in the central sierra? Five strands of evidence suggest that Juan Santos Atahualpa's vision and exploits exerted considerable appeal in the sierra, and that under some circumstances such sympathy might lead to more active support.

Let us turn, first, to Indian serranos pressed into duty on colonial expeditions. Forced to play an active role in the conflict, at least some experienced difficulty submitting to their assigned function. On at least two occasions, these tensions led serranos to switch sides. The 1743 expedition against Juan Santos Atahualpa requisitioned the services of Indian *arrieros* (muledrivers) from Huarochirí to transport food, munitions, and other supplies. Probably, the authorities used these arrieros to *avoid* betrayal by arrieros from Tarma or Jauja, the highland districts in the immediate vicinity of the insurrection. (For the availability of arrieros in Tarma-Jauja, see Ruíz L. 1777–88: 1:84.) If so, the precaution proved worthless. After celebration of mass on October 17, the Spanish returned to camp only to discover that the entire arriero contingent had fled (Loayza 1942: 22). The commander of the force organized a new mule train, but arriero desertions continued to plague the expedition (ibid.: 40).

A similar betrayal prefigured the massacre of a small colonial group in 1747. The failure of the military campaign of 1746 had given new impetus to Franciscan efforts to pacify the montaña through Christian persuasion rather than violence (ibid.: 121–22; Ortíz 1969: 1: Appendix, Document 5). One such mission sought to convert the Indians of Acón, a coca zone in the montaña just south of Juan Santos Atahualpa's core area of influence. The Indians of the area had known of Juan Santos Atahualpa since at least 1743, when they had also killed a local priest-hacendado (Izaguirre 1922–29: 2:295, 294). They were now alleged to have requested peace and Christian missionaries. Three Franciscans, accompanied by ten Spanish soldiers and twenty Indian porters, left the Huanta highlands in mid-March of 1747. Two weeks later, the Indian serranos fled under the cover of night. The next morning, a mass of selva Indians — possibly including acculturated highland fugitives — surrounded the colonials and killed them in a "rain of arrows" (Amich 1771: 199; Izaguirre 1922–29: 2:143–44, 291–96).[17] The suspect loyalty of Indian porters, concluded Tarma's corregidor Alfonso de Santa in 1747, would always handicap forays into the jungle (Loayza 1942: 122).

We can gain a second clue to sierra sympathies by asking how serrano Indians responded to the messages and military raids of the newly proclaimed Inca liberator. The rebel forces made several incursions into highland territory during the years 1742–1743, and the most daring penetrated deeply enough to jeopardize their line of retreat into the jungle.[18] Such exposure required that the guerrilla bands — like Hobsbawm's "social bandits" (1965: 16) — count on a certain minimal level of diffuse sympathy. In 1743, Juan Santos Atahualpa began a serious drive to reverse colonial penetration of the interior jungle frontier. On August 1, Juan Santos and a force of 2,000 followers occupied the Quimirí mission. They soon sent word to the nearby Chanchamayo Valley that Friar Lorenzo Nuñez should skip his usual Sunday visit to Quimirí. Chanchamayo, a subtropical zone on the eastern slopes of Tarma, drafted laborers for its haciendas from the Tarma sierra rather than the jungle interior (Ortíz 1975–76: 1:132). Nuñez sent two messengers, one of them an Indian, to Quimirí. Juan Santos Atahualpa interviewed the Indian, refused to rescind the ban on Nuñez's Sunday visits, and sent the visitors back to Chanchamayo with an important message to serrano Indians. ". . . As news spread that the Inca meant no harm to the serranos, the Indians of Chanchamayo held grand celebrations, dances, and drinking that night, celebrating like the Chunchos jungle Indians the coming of their Inca, singing that they would drink chicha beer from the skull of the priest . . ." (Amich 1771: 189; cf. Izaguirre 1922–29: 2:128–30). As dawn broke on the Chanchamayo River Monday, August 5, a large force of selva Indians massed on its banks and triumphantly moved toward the Chanchamayo haciendas. Nuñez and company fled to the high sierra (Amich 1771: 189). It was, in fact, the alarming news of sierra sympathy for the insurgents that convinced the Lima authorities to send more troops and arms to Tarma and Jauja in 1743, and to launch the disastrous military campaign of October–November (Juan and Ulloa 1826: 183–85; Loayza 1942: 57–58).

Numerous serrano Indians might welcome the triumphant conquests of a self-proclaimed Inca liberator, and some might flee to join the Inca in the montaña. But in the absence of a triumphant Inca-led expedition, would serranos dare to challenge the colonial power structure in the sierra itself, where lines of authority and social control were deeply entrenched? Flight by a small minority to the montaña, and diffuse but passive sympathy among the majority left behind, by themselves imply little about the insurrectionary potential of the Juan Santos movement in the sierra. In the absence of conflicting evidence, the apparent tranquility of political life in the central sierra would justify the historiographical tendency to marginalize the montaña movement as a frontier insurrection.

We must, therefore, assess a third and poorly understood area of evidence: the degree to which colonial authorities faced, in the central sierra of the mid-eighteenth century, a genuine threat of violent mobilization by a rebellious populace. One such threat—in the Huarochirí highlands overlooking Lima—is already well known.[19] The Indians of Huarochirí earned a reputation for violent defiance in the eighteenth century (see Loayza 1942: 169; Cangas 1780: 316; *Relaciones* 1867–72: 3:168; Carrió de la Vandera 1782: 47–48). Revolts broke out in 1750, ca. 1758, and 1783, and all three superseded purely local tensions. The first two were related to conspiracies to destroy Spanish rule in Lima itself; the 1783 rebellion belatedly raised the banner of Túpac Amaru II. The 1750 revolt broke out in the aftermath of a round-up of Indian conspirators in Lima. The would-be rebels, partly inspired by a prophecy predicting a restoration of Indian sovereignty in 1750 (Loayza 1942: 165), planned a general insurrection to return Indian Peru to its rightful masters. During their two years of planning, the conspirators sought contact with Juan Santos Atahualpa, and some favored naming him the new Inca-King (Fuentes 1859: 4:97; Loayza 1942: 166, 172). Equally significant, when violence did erupt in Huarochirí, the rebels eagerly embraced a fabricated message assuring them that Juan Santos Atahualpa would send a liberating army of 4,000 from Tarma (Spalding 1984: 287).

Huarochirí experienced violent mobilization and its peoples viewed Inca saviors such as Juan Santos Atahualpa and Túpac Amaru II with considerable positive interest. But when set in the more general central sierra context, is Huarochirí the proverbial exception that proves the rule? After all, historians have long acknowledged Huarochirí's record of violent resistance *without* concluding that the central sierra presented an important insurrectionary threat.[20] Huarochirí's position near Lima and the Pacific coast gave its politics a special cast,[21] and also rendered the area uniquely vulnerable to military repression. Once we return to the more interior heartland of the central sierra, do we not find little insurrectionary potential? As long as Tarma, Jauja, and Huanta—the highland districts which descended directly into the central montaña—remained peaceful and indifferent, the colonials had little to fear.

But as the authorities in the thick of the action understood too well, the interior central highland districts constituted anything but an island of peace between the stormy montaña on the east, and Huarochirí on the west. Although we need more historical digging to clarify a somewhat hazy picture, my own research and that of others now suffice to demonstrate a volatile state of political affairs. A genuine threat of violent mobilization loomed in the 1742–1752 period. At certain moments, only vigilant action by agents of the colonial power structure kept such threats under control and restored an uneasy social peace.

The evidence in the case of Huanta is the least clear. But Lorenzo Huertas (1976: 89; 1978: 8, 10; personal communication, July 1981) has already made two exciting findings: an outright revolt in support of Juan Santos Atahualpa, and a declaration of loyalty to the new Inca-King by alleged Inca descendants. Indeed, the combined researches of Huertas, Patrique Husson (personal communications, 1977, 1981), and Florencia Mallon (personal communication, 1981) establish a tradition of recurring revolts in Huanta spanning the eighteenth and nineteenth centuries.

In Tarma, evidence of secret serrano sympathy for Juan Santos Atahualpa had already alarmed authorities in 1743. The failed military campaign of October–November (and recall, here, the desertion of the arrieros) did little to reassure nervous colonials. As Holy Week (April 6–12) approached in 1744, the tension thickened into nightmarish scenarios. Colonials in the sierra—and even the viceroy in Lima—seemed to expect the week's festivities to provide the occasion for Indians to launch a massive insurrection. On Monday of Holy Week, the anxiety struck hard in places as distant as Lima and Cuzco. In Lima, the viceroy inquired about a possible revolt in Jauja, and about the state of mind of Indians in the Cuzco region (Moreno C. 1977: 171). In the city of Cuzco, the corregidor rounded up the caciques of the Indian parishes and a mysterious foreigner, said to be English, who carried with him a list naming various caciques. The scare blew over, but not before it had "agitated the city and sparked a meeting, watch guard, and other precautions, because of the rumors flying about [Juan Santos Atahualpa] and [about] the provinces east of this city" (Esquivel y Navia ca. 1750: 2:300).

In Tarma, however, the scare did not blow over. Instead, violence broke out. The defects in our sources obscure the details. Some official sources, whether to avoid embarrassment or because other events loomed larger at the time that the documents were written,[22] either omit comment altogether or refer only obliquely to the events of 1744. Others exaggerate.

By the time word of the revolt reached Cuzco, on April 16, 1744, the em-
bellished news had it that the Indians had killed Tarma's corregidor,
Alfonso de Santa y Ortega. Santa, went the story, had apparently tried
to collect on Indian debts owed him from his earlier reparto of unwanted
goods at inflated prices. Those who could not or would not pay Santa,
he tried to take prisoner, prompting them to take refuge in a church. A
rock-throwing mob later killed Santa (ibid.: 2:301). We know from Santa's
later correspondence in 1747 (Loayza 1942: 116–29; cf. Esquivel y Navia
ca. 1750: 2:328–29) that he in fact survived the revolt. But the other details ring true. Corregidores commonly used major celebrations drawing
together crowds as a convenient time to collect on reparto debts, and local
disturbances often broke out at precisely these moments (Golte 1980:
147–49). Santa had, in an earlier term as corregidor in Azángaro (Puno),
provoked an important Indian revolt, probably because of the way he had
handled the reparto (see Esquivel y Navia ca. 1750: 2:295, 261; Zudaire
1979: 258; Loayza 1942: 123–24). Several contemporary sources independently confirm that the reparto produced a strong sense of grievance
in the Tarma-Jauja area in the 1740s, and that recurrent conflicts during
1744–1745 destroyed Santa's authority as corregidor (Juan and Ulloa 1826:
250; Loayza 1942: 75, 81; Fuentes 1859: 4:102; Vallejo F. 1957: 271; see
also Esquivel y Navia ca. 1750: 2:301, 328–29).[23] The disturbances of
1744–1745 came on the heels of evidence that local Indians might welcome an Inca-led liberation. In addition, some evidence suggests that colonial authorities discovered a conspiracy to organize a full-fledged insurrection within Tarma itself.[24] The threat of violent mobilization in the
sierra was real, and demanded a response.

We know of at least three actions taken to restore an uneasy social peace
to the central highlands. In 1744, the viceregal authorities granted Tarma
an exemption from its quota of mita laborers to the Huancavelica mercu-
ry mines (Zavala 1978–80: 3:52–53). Viceroy Villagarcía (1736–1745)
bluntly labeled the act a "means to encourage tranquility" (Fuentes 1859:
3:383).[25] The Huancavelica suspension remained in effect at least until 1761
(Mendiburu 1874–90: 5:179), and perhaps well beyond. As late as 1772,
for example, Tarma's Indians were not pressed to provide a mita quota
to the important local silver mines of Lauricocha (Zavala 1978–80: 3:59).
I suspect that the same was true in the case of Huancavelica; Tarma is
conspicuously absent on the list of districts obligated to Huancavelica in
1782 (Fisher 1977: 92). In 1745, the newly arrived Viceroy Superunda took
two further measures. First, Tarma's corregidor, like an overseer who had
outlived his usefulness on a slave plantation, would have to be replaced.
Superunda quickly recalled the disgraced Santa to Lima (Loayza 1942:
75, 125; Esquivel y Navia ca. 1750: 2:329). Second, the state would have

to signal its ability and intention to quell dissidence. Superunda sent 100 trained troops and Peru's leading general, José de Llamas, to replace Santa. This began a military build-up whose explicit purpose would now be to intimidate serranos as well as to defeat or isolate Juan Santos Atahualpa (Loayza 1942: 75). Troops would be garrisoned not only in forts on the jungle perimeter, but in principal sierra sites as well (see Amich 1771: 203; Ruíz L. 1777–88: 1:92; 2:plate 12; Amat 1776: 399; Mendiburu 1874–90: 5:141; 8:273). By 1760, over half the 421 trained fixed troops theoretically assigned to the Infantry Batallion of Callao actually served in Tarma and Jauja (Campbell 1976: 36, esp. n. 2; 1978: 17). The combination of trained troops and an expanded auxiliary militia (see Campbell 1978: 60–63), both supervised by veteran officers, not only strengthened the state's repressive apparatus in Tarma and Jauja. It also, as we shall see later, allowed these districts, especially Tarma, to serve as a staging area from which to put down disturbances in *other* highland provinces.

The central sierra of the mid-eighteenth century, then, offered no respite from the volatile politics of the montaña frontier. The violence in Huarochirí was, in this sense, but a dramatic local manifestation of a much broader threat. Over the course of the 1740s, central sierra people demonstrated a touchy readiness, if properly provoked or inspired, to mount a violent challenge to established lines of authority. When Alfonso Santa — following the failure of General Llamas to defeat Juan Santos Atahualpa — was reinstated as Tarma's corregidor and military commander in 1747, he avoided the costly mistakes of the past. Wiser by bitter experience, Santa knew not to press his luck too far in exploiting the reparto, and appears to have experienced considerable financial difficulties partly because the reparto could no longer supply him large revenues. Santa pinned his material hopes instead on the possibility that successful termination of the Juan Santos affair would lead to a handsome reward from the Crown (see Loayza 1942: 116–29, esp. 118–19, 123–24, 128).

With good reason, then, colonial officials acted vigorously to choke off the sierra's insurrectionary potential, and to seal it from further seditious influence by Juan Santos and his emissaries. With the defeat of the Huarochirí rebellion and Lima conspiracy in 1750, and the further build-up of forces in Tarma-Jauja (Varese 1973: 199), the central sierra seemed safe from subversion.

But this leads us to a fourth area of evidence: the response of serranos to Juan Santos Atahualpa's audacious invasion of the highlands in 1752. By this time, the division of military control seemed clear. The selva peoples had recovered their lost montaña territory, but colonial forces ruled with authority in the highlands. In August, fully ten years after his initial declaration of Inca sovereignty over Peru, Juan Santos Atahualpa sought

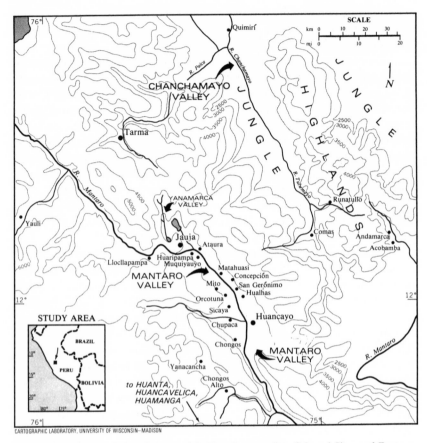

CARTOGRAPHIC LABORATORY, UNIVERSITY OF WISCONSIN–MADISON

Map 4. Tarma-Jauja during the Age of Andean Insurrection: Selected Sites and Features

to break the colonials' grip on the highlands. He would invade the Comas
region of Jauja, establish a sierra beachhead there, wait several months
as sierra provinces declared for his cause, then finally move out to conquer the highlands and take Lima (AGN 1752: 12r, 16v, 20v). Comas, and
its "annexes" Andamarca and Acobamba, lay in a semi-isolated highland
zone east of the Mantaro Valley system along which most pueblos and
traffic of Tarma-Jauja clustered (see Map 4; Amich 1771: 31–32). In the
nineteenth century, peasant guerrillas armed during the War of the Pacific
(1879–1883) established and defended an independent "peasant republic"
in the Comas area from 1888 until 1902 (Mallon 1983: 80–122, esp. 111–21;
and Mallon, Chapter 9 in this volume). Within the Comas area, Andamarca was the last sierra outpost on the highland route to Jauja's montaña.
Extreme topography made the transition between sierra and selva abrupt

rather than gradual. One had first to climb up to cross Andamarca's cold marshy *punas* (high tablelands) before dropping steeply into the subtropical montaña (Amich 1771: 32, 36).

In this difficult but somewhat isolated terrain, Juan Santos Atahualpa made his sierra stand. The rebel forces easily took Andamarca on August 3, but Jauja's corregidor rapidly deployed a force to counterattack. Forewarned by a serrano-turned-spy, Juan Santos left Andamarca before the colonial troops could arrive (Loayza 1942: 183-205; Vallejo F. 1957: 285-86). The occupation had lasted only two full days. On the surface, Juan Santos Atahualpa appeared to have engineered yet another dramatic victory — another guerrilla raid that eluded the colonial forces. In reality, given the Inca's original intentions, the raid marked a disappointing turning point — the failure to establish a permanent liberated territory in the sierra. As if accepting the status quo, neither side launched a military raid against the other after 1752.

Juan Santos Atahualpa's flight from Andamarca underscored the formidable obstacles to sierra insurrection. Such obstacles carried all the more significance if, as Stefano Varese has argued (1973: 183-85, 203), Juan Santos hoped to launch a new era without resorting to major bloodshed (cf. note 29 below).

Most important for our purposes, however, the 1752 invasion demonstrated that the vision of an Inca-led liberation still exerted a powerful popular appeal. The Franciscan historiography obscures this point by presenting the image of a frustrated and vengeful impostor unable to find serrano followers. As Amich put it: "The tyrant Juan Santos did not stay long in Andamarca before recognizing that the serranos were not devoted to him. For they did not render him obedience, and he sacked the town and set it on fire before leaving . . ." (1771: 205; cf. Izaguirre 1922-29: 2:163, 181-82). Upon careful reading, even the letters and testimonies published by Loayza (1942: 183-231, esp. 204-5, 208, 215, 229) contradict this mythology. When Juan Santos and his forces arrived, the defense preparations organized by Andamarca's respectable "citizens" fell apart. Only two shots were fired before an Indian voice shouted: "This is our Inca, come over here" (Loayza 1942: 208). Juan Santos then peacefully entered, marched toward the plaza, and accepted the homage of his new vassals. As a horrified eyewitness later recalled, the Indians and mestizos who betrayed Andamarca's defense "kissed the Rebel's hands and feet" (ibid.: 204). The fire set by Juan Santos Atahualpa, far from a frustrated outburst, appears to have targeted selected houses and symbols, including the local church (ibid.: 215).

More revealing than Loayza's documentary collection, however, are contemporary criminal records against alleged agent-spies of Juan Santos

(AGN 1752). For it is in these records, composed in the immediate aftermath of the August invasion, that the contemporary sense of shock,
urgency, and insurrectionary threat leap to life. The heresy of much of
Andamarca's Indian-mestizo populace scandalized and terrified Crown
loyalists. Just as important, Juan Santos Atahualpa's followers and sympathizers could not easily let go the memory of several dramatic days when
a transforming cataclysm seemed possible and imminent. In short, life
did not "return to normal" with Juan Santos Atahualpa's departure.

Amidst this jittery state of affairs, on August 17, three serrano Indians
wandered into the Comas area asking directions to the whereabouts of
their Inca Lord. The three were food carriers for Juan Santos left behind
in the montaña during the Andamarca invasion. Lost, ill informed, and
eager to find the Inca in Andamarca, they stumbled upon three mestizos
at Runatullo. Fearful for their safety, the mestizos feigned sympathy, acted
as guides to Andamarca, and led the trio—not to Andamarca, but Comas,
where the Indians were promptly jailed. Three weeks later, on September
9, the Indians hung dead. Their heads and limbs were distributed the next
day for symbolic display on tall stakes "in the appropriate places and spots
of these frontiers and on the roads of the pueblos of this said province
[Jauja], where they might serve as an example and warning" (AGN 1752:
41v). Jauja's corregidor, the Marquis of Casatorres, tried the three initially
for spying as well as treason. The hurried investigation demonstrated that
the prisoners were anything but spies and organizers for Juan Santos Atahualpa. The most incriminating testimonies exposed them as rather hap-
less and disoriented citizens of the Inca's montaña kingdom whose misfortune it was to stray into the wrong place at the wrong time. As the
judicial proceedings unfolded, the accusation of spying fell by the way-
side. (See ibid.: 26r–29r.) But the charges of devotion to Juan Santos Atahualpa remained. This treason alone required capital punishment, the
prosecutor explained, "because it is clear that the land demands a speedy
example, with notorious display, in the areas that appear appropriate, of
the bodies or heads of the prisoners, so that horrified and intimidated by
the punishment, the Indians [as well as] those who are not [i.e., castas
and dissident whites] abandon any thought that their vile inclination may
have suggested . . ." (ibid.: 28v). The corregidor agreed. Julián Auqui,
Blas Ibarra, and Casimiro Lamberto were classic scapegoats.

But why? Casatorres's decision was no light matter, and he knowingly
risked trouble with higher authorities. A legal counsel had warned the
corregidor (ibid.: 41r) that under colonial law, he should temporarily sus-
pend capital sentences while submitting the matter to the royal *audiencia*
(high court) in Lima for approval. Earlier, in August, Casatorres *had*

indeed followed normal procedure. He passed on to Lima the cases against three other alleged spies—two Indians and a mestizo—for final hearings and sentencing (ibid.: 43r, 46v; AGN 1756: 1r, 5r–v). All three, especially the mestizo Joseph Campos, had played far more direct and threatening roles in the Andamarca invasion than had the scapegoats Auqui, Ibarra, and Lamberto (see AGN 1752: 46v; AGN 1756; Loayza 1942: 204–5). Casatorres knew that pushing through a speedy trial and execution of Auqui, Ibarra, and Lamberto on his own authority would embroil him in a jurisdictional dispute with the audiencia. Why, then, did Casatorres flagrantly invite trouble this time? And why did he do so with comparatively benign subversives, soon after he had dutifully sent more serious rebels to Lima? The corregidor's sudden turnabout earned him a stiff fine (6,000 pesos, later reduced to 4,000) that consumed at least 9,600 yards of the corregidor's textile trade in 1753 (AGN 1752: 43r–76v).[26]

To understand the corregidor's behavior, we must return to the turbulent atmosphere of August–September 1752. On August 12, soon after Juan Santos Atahualpa's invasion, Casatorres drew his bitter lesson: "What is certain is that this problem has the deepest roots, . . . that the biggest enemy is the internal one in the highland Province, secretly favoring the Rebel. If we do not take other measures and precautions, we will be the target of further blows, with danger to the entire kingdom . . ." (Loayza 1942: 210). The simple fact of the matter was that the Indians and mestizos of Andamarca and Acobamba had recognized Juan Santos Atahualpa's authority, and serrano agents had facilitated the Inca's invasion and his escape (AGN 1752: 44r, 46r, 43v). Many persons assumed, moreover, that Juan Santos would soon return in a second invasion (Loayza 1942: 209–10; AGN 1752: 47v–48r). Under these circumstances, authority rested on precarious foundations. Nonetheless, in the last days of August, Casatorres submitted to higher authority by suspending the death sentences of three alleged agent-spies, including the notorious Joseph Campos, and remanded the prisoners and their cases to Lima for final disposition. But this act itself created problems. Casatorres's retreat from a show of strength quickly unravelled the delicate and tattered social fabric: ". . . there began to develop disturbances, with incidents of disobedience . . ." (AGN 1752: 48r; cf. 44v–45r, 48v). During such incidents, moreover, Juan Santos Atahualpa's spirit made itself felt through spontaneous voices "bursting out words in [Quechua] encouraging machination [with] and devotion to the Rebel" (ibid.: 48r; cf. 44v). Anxious to choke off this surge of Indian insolence, and fearful that continued insubordination might lead to a prisoner escape, Casatorres panicked. (See ibid.: 28v, 44v–45r, 48; cf. Loayza 1942: 222, 228, 230.) Suddenly, Indian rumor and insolence demanded that Auqui, Ibarra, and Lamberto *not* follow the earlier trio of prisoners to Lima. They had to be executed—quickly, and in the central highlands, not Lima.

The Andamarca invasion had not only demonstrated Juan Santos Atahualpa's appeal among serranos. It also unsettled the firm grip held by colonial officials on central sierra society. Casatorres had good reason to defy the authority of the criminal judges of Lima's royal audiencia. The executions—conducted with the pomp and solemnity appropriate in a sacred ritual—seemed, moreover, to produce the desired effect: "there has been [afterwards] . . . a different respect, with everything staying quiet, especially the Indians" (AGN 1752: 45r).

Let us turn, finally, to a fifth area of evidence: popular rumors after the abortive invasion of Andamarca. After 1752, Juan Santos retreated from further military conflict and sierra appearances. Now an "invisible" presence, Juan Santos gradually faded from the sierra stage. For a time, however, rumors kept alive the dream of an Inca-led liberation. In the northern sierra of Cajamarca, itself a zone of frequent local rebellions in the mid-to-late eighteenth century (O'Phelan 1978; Espinoza S. 1971, 1960; Golte 1980: 139–53, esp. 151–52), word of an impending liberation broke out in 1753. Indians and non-Indians alike murmured about a general Indian insurrection planned since 1750 (the year of the Lima-Huarochirí conspiracy). By July, Indians discussed a supposed secret agreement by dissident Indian elites to free native society from Spanish rule within six months. Attention focused on a mysterious traveler, said to be an emissary of Juan Santos Atahualpa. "White Cape," as the gray-haired white man wandering north from the central highlands was called, supposedly distributed letters of agreement finalizing plans for a general insurrection to be led by Juan Santos. The commotion led to a general round-up of suspects, and the exile of "White Cape" to Lima for five years (AGN 1753). Three years later, in 1756, Joseph Campos, who had escaped his earlier imprisonment in Lima, reappeared in Andamarca. At the time, rumors spreading in the Jauja region spoke of secret communication between serrano Indians and Juan Santos Atahualpa (AGN 1756: 10v). Several riots actually broke out in Jauja and Tarma in 1755, 1756, and 1757 (O'Phelan 1985: 119, 124–25, 127–30). One wonders if sharpening social tensions inspired rumors of impending liberation, or even if the rumors had a hand in precipitating the riots. In any event, the rumors took on added significance against the backdrop of social conflict and revolt. Briefly, the anxious Jauja authorities wondered whether to repeat the example of 1752 by executing Campos. Another grisly warning to the populace might prevent the "muffled voice running through this said Province" from becoming anything more than rumor (AGN 1756: 10v).

JUAN SANTOS ATAHUALPA AND THE CENTRAL SIERRA: A BALANCE SHEET

Our close review of the evidence has made untenable the marginalization of Juan Santos and the central sierra from the larger history of sierra unrest and mobilization. Serranos constituted a significant minority among the Inca's active following in the central montaña—a fact which facilitated development of an intelligence and organizational network in the highlands. In the sierra itself, authorities contended with betrayal by Indian arrieros and porters drafted to serve on colonial expeditions. The response of Tarma's Indians to the raids and messages of Juan Santos in 1742–1743 suggests that the desertions of arrieros and porters was but a symptom of a more diffuse receptivity to the Inca's plans. Between 1744 and 1750, disturbances in Tarma, Huanta, and Huarochirí proved that the central sierra constituted, in its own right, an arena of social conflict, violence, and Indian mobilization against entrenched authorities. (For Jauja, we may confirm riots as of 1755–1756.) In the cases of Huanta and Huarochirí, we know also that the rebels either explicitly supported Juan Santos, or hoped that he would lead a liberating auxiliary army. In 1752, the welcome accorded by Indians and mestizos to Juan Santos Atahualpa's invasion of the Comas area of Jauja demonstrated that the idea of an Inca-led redemption still held an important grip on the popular imagination. This appeal was all the more impressive in view of the earlier military build-up by colonial officials—a build-up that forced Juan Santos to retreat into the jungle. After 1752, the dream of Inca-Andean resurgence resurfaced in rumors of conspiracy and secret communication not only in Jauja, but in Cajamarca as well.

The evidence has yielded no "smoking pistol"—no major highland insurrection, no single event that by itself proves that Juan Santos Atahualpa could have led such an insurrection. But the totality of the evidence points strongly toward a major insurrectionary threat. The restive peoples of the central sierra constituted, in the mid-eighteenth century, a promising clientele for an Inca-led insurrection. Even the northern sierra, in view of its history of revolt and the rumors of 1753, may have proved fertile ground for such a movement. The words of Friar José de San Antonio (Loayza 1942: 158) on the eve of the Huarochirí revolt in 1750, although hyperbolic, captured an essential truth:

> To see themselves free of so many extreme tyrannies, obligations, and burdens accompanied by cruel violence, many flee to the forests. . . .

> Many of those referred to [i.e., Indians, mestizos, and destitute whites] anxiously await the invasions of the rebel Atahualpa, and if he (God forbid) marched on Lima with two hundred arrow-wielding Indians, one might fear . . . a general insurrection of the Indians. . . .

San Antonio, commissary of the central montaña missions, spoke from experience.

The reality of this insurrectionary ferment explains a curious anomaly in the eighteenth-century sources. After the civil war of 1780–1782, and until this day, it is the "southern" peoples—the Aymara-speaking peoples of Puno, Peru, and the altiplano of Bolivia—who have commanded attention for their bellicosity and history of violent rebellion. In the 1940s, an ethnographic account of the Aymara peoples near Lake Titicaca struggled to explain and qualify their peculiarly violent and defiant reputation (LaBarre 1948: 39–40). A recent textbook mentions the same "warlike and aggressive" reputation (Klein 1982: 15; cf. Valle de Siles 1977: 643, 657). Yet if one returns to eighteenth-century sources written *before* the outbreak of the Túpac Amaru revolution in November 1780, one finds a somewhat different human "map" of renowned troublemakers. Before then, it was the peoples of Huarochirí, Tarma-Jauja, and Azángaro (Puno) who drew attention among colonials for their especially difficult and violent "temperament" (see Cangas 1780: 310–35, esp. 315, 316, 335; *Relaciones* 1867–72: 3:56; Loayza 1942: 169). With the exception of Azangaro, the notorious troublemakers lived in Peru's central sierra.[27] Jauja ranked, in narrow economic terms, among the most lucrative districts available to a corregidor in the eighteenth century (see Macera, in Carrió 1782: 20–21), but as one observer noted, to realize his profits a corregidor would have to overcome "the difficulties posed by the spirit and character of its inhabitants" (Cangas 1780: 315). In view of the central sierra's reputation, Viceroy Augustín de Jauregui's response, in 1780, to the threat of a British invasion becomes readily understandable. Upon assuming office in July, Jauregui improved security by directing arms and munitions not only to strategic points along the Pacific coast, but also to Jauja and Tarma—the key trouble-spots in the sierra (*Relaciones* 1867–72: 3:188–89).

If the central sierra posed a considerable insurrectionary threat, why then did Juan Santos Atahualpa fail to lead a major highland insurrection? This failure constitutes, after all, the most glaring support for the argument that Juan Santos led a frontier insurrection of relatively marginal political importance for the sierra. We should begin with an essential distinction. A subtle assessment of political ferment in the central highlands should distinguish between a rising popular challenge to authority—a challenge, moreover, receptive to the idea of an Inca-led liberation—and the actual circumstances that might or might not transform such a groundswell into reality. We need to distinguish, in other words, between "conjuncture" and "event," and our historical interpretation must operate on both levels of analysis. Our balance sheet must recognize not only the reality of an insurrectionary threat, but also the fact that this threat, although genuine and serious, nonetheless failed to materialize. What forces prevented an increasingly insurrectionary conjuncture from heralding, in fact, the onset of a general insurrection?

An adequate response to such a question would require substantial further research and a separate essay. Several clues, however, may provide the elements of a tentative initial explanation. We should recognize, from the start, the immense difficulty of organizing major Indian insurrection in the eighteenth-century Andes. Recent research casts increasing doubt on notions of "spontaneous" Indian revolts bursting into insurrectionary fire of regional or supraregional dimensions. Major insurrections took years of planning; the conspirators might disagree over details of leadership, including whom to recognize as a new Inca-King; once under way, a territorially extensive insurrection was at best a loosely coordinated set of regional and subregional revolts (see Szemiński 1976: 225–43; Campbell 1981: 677–78, 680–81, 690; O'Phelan 1982, 1979; Zudaire 1979: 79–83; Loayza 1942: 123, 163, 166, 172; Beltrán A. 1925: 54–55; Vargas U. 1966–71: 4:207; Lewin 1957: 118; Cornblit 1970: 11–14; Kubler 1946: 386–87).

The organizational work of insurrection met with two dangerous obstacles: a surprisingly effective network of colonial intelligence and patronage that enabled officials to discover and crush "secret" conspiracies; and a structure of "divide-and-rule" that won the authorities Indian allies and clients once a revolt did indeed break out. Colonial Andean history is littered with failed insurrectionary conspiracies (see Lohmann V. 1946: 89–91; Rowe 1954: 39–40, 45–46; Vargas U. 1966–71: 4:207–8; Carrió 1782: 47–48). The longer it took to organize an insurrection, and the greater the network of those involved, the more difficult it probably was to prevent premature discovery. The prospects of reward, or of vengeance in intranative conflicts, could provide valuable informants to the colonial regime. Even when no informant deliberately betrayed a secret, colonial officials learned of plots through confidences told to Catholic priests during confession. Their familiarity with Indian commoners and their confessional roles enabled priests to perform sensitive "intelligence" and "pacification" functions in colonial life (see Rowe 1954: 46; Lohmann V. 1946: 91; Maúrtua 1906: 12:143).

If a conspiracy was kept secret, or if disturbances did break out, the leaders of revolt contended with divisions that made organization of a "united Indian front" extremely difficult, especially on a regional or supraregional level. Even in the early colonial period, several social forces provided the colonial regime tools with which to contain the threat of Indian resistance. The persistence of ethnic and kin-based rivalries among Indians, the patronage and privileges offered to collaborators, the integration of Indian elites into multiracial "power groups" — all facilitated the rise of a structure of "divide-and-rule" (see Spalding 1974: 31–87; Stern 1982: 92–102, 132–35, 158–59, 163–64; Stern 1983). In the eighteenth century, despite attempts to forge a wider Andean unity, these divisions nonetheless constituted a still potent force. Class lines in provincial Andean society had probably hardened (see Larson 1979: 202–5, 213–14, 220–29; Sánchez-Albornoz 1978: 99–110; Spalding 1974: 52–60; Stern 1983: 35–40), despite the rise of sometimes radical indigenista ideologies among a fraction of the Indian elite (Rowe 1954; Spalding 1974: 187–90; Tamayo 1980: 77–112). Earlier networks of Andean cohesion had eroded or disintegrated, splintering provincial society into smaller, more inward-oriented units of primary identification and cooperation (Spalding 1974: 89–123; Spalding 1984; Stern 1983). At its moments of crisis, the colonial state gained strength from the "divide-and-rule" structure of society. In the northern and southern sierra alike, Indian functionaries helped to quell local disturbances and earned special honors, including military office (Fuentes 1859: 3:279; BNP 1783; cf. Fuentes 1859: 4:99; Loayza 1942: 173). In the Huarochirí revolt of 1750, a Spaniard, Sebastián Francisco de Melo, played on the local "fault lines" (Karen Spalding's term) of provincial society, and on the suspect loyalties of Andean elites, to disorganize the revolt (Spalding 1984: 282–83, 288–89). The civil war that engulfed southern Peru-Bolivia from 1780 to 1782 fractured the Indian elite in complex ways; the upper reaches of the kuraka hierarchy appear, on the whole, to have supported the Crown forces rather than the rebels (see O'Phelan 1982: 477, 480; O'Phelan 1978: 181–82; Campbell 1981: 681–85, 689; Campbell 1979: 10–11). Indian nobles' pride in the Inca past did not, in many instances, preclude conservative loyalty to the Spanish Crown (Burga 1981: 250–52).

Part of the explanation for Juan Santos Atahualpa's failure to lead an insurrection in the central sierra derives, then, from the general circumstances of the eighteenth century. Indian insurrection required considerable organizational work (rather than reliance on near-spontaneous combustion) against difficult obstacles. The balance of forces enabled the authorities to snuff out conspiracies; to crush local revolts before they could spread and gain strength; and to gain Indian allies and armies in the midst of apparent "race war." We should not be surprised to find, therefore, that even when a conjuncture of forces made insurrection increasingly probable, civil war might not in fact break out. Such a conjuncture and failure occurred not only in the central sierra in the 1740s, but also—as was clear to contemporaries—in parts of Peru's central and *southern* sierra in 1776–1777 (Golte 1980: 137–38; Campbell 1978: 100–101; Zudaire 1979: 76–77).

To these general circumstances we should add some particulars from the Tarma-Jauja region. The evolution of the region's indigenous power structure gave the colonial regime added advantages. Since the sixteenth century, the colonial regime consolidated its authority in highland provinces partly by establishing multiracial "power groups" that interlocked elites of indigenous and nonindigenous origin (Stern 1982: 92–102, 158–59, 163–64; Spalding 1974: 31–87; Larson 1979). The success of this strategy certainly varied by region, time period, and strata within the Indian elite. In addition, countervailing tendencies often made Indian-white collaboration an ambiguous, fragile, and internally contradictory affair rather than a straightforward alliance of interest. Most important for our purpose, however, is that the regional interlockings of indigenous and colonial Hispanic power took peculiar and unusually intense form in the Tarma-Jauja area. The weak early presence of the Spaniards, the sixteenth-century alliance of Huancas and Spaniards, the absence of mines but simultaneous proximity to commercial centers such as Lima, Huancavelica, and Huamanga — these idiosyncrasies of the region's early colonial history, along with the astute politics of the kurakas, favored the eventual emergence in Tarma-Jauja of powerful Andean dynasties. The lords of these dynasties were unusually successful at turning Indian-white collaboration to their own advantage, and unusually reluctant, therefore, to attack the colonial power structure. In the central sierra, by the eighteenth century, names such as Astocuri, Apoalaya, and Limaylla stood for powerful regional families whose marriages with one another and with Spanish colonials subjected the region to what was, in reality, a mestizo nobility. These families owned the best haciendas of Tarma-Jauja, dominated the Andean chieftainships and *cofradías* (Catholic lay associations) of the Mantaro Valley, successfully intermarried with Spanish corregidores and officials, and proudly claimed a history of noble Andean descent and loyal service to the Spanish Crown (see Dunbar T. 1942; Celestino 1981; Celestino and Meyers 1981; Espinoza S. 1973a; Espinoza S. 1973b: 230; Arguedas 1975: 80–147).

In Tarma-Jauja, therefore, insurrection led by an outsider such as Juan Santos Atahualpa faced an unusually intense fusion between the colonial regime and the upper reaches of the indigenous power structure. Don Benito Troncoso de Lira y Sotomayor, Governor and Captain of the Tarma-Jauja frontier in 1745, also happened to be the husband of Doña Teresa Apoalaya, a leading chief-matriarch of Jauja since the turn of the century. Her granddaughter, Doña Josefa Astocuri Limaylla, was in turn married to Don Francisco Dávila, a corregidor and kuraka aspirant in Huarochirí (Dunbar T. 1942: 154–56, 172–73 n. 30). Highland kurakas had patronized the Franciscans' missionary work, and acquired lands and cattle in the central montaña region first opened up by the Franciscans, then threatened by Juan Santos Atahualpa (Lehnertz n.d.: chap. 2, 19–20, chap.

5, 33). The upper reaches of the indigenous power structure was in certain respects indistinguishable from the colonial power structure in Tarma-
Jauja. These circumstances imposed especially keen obstacles to insurrection in highland Tarma-Jauja even before the colonial military build-up.
In 1742, Don José Calderón Conchaya, a Tarma kuraka and colonial "field
commander" ("Maestre de Campo"), led an early expedition against Juan
Santos Atahualpa (Loayza 1942: 13). In 1745, Viceroy Manso de Velasco
reported that a loyal high-level kuraka ("cacique principal") had taken
measures to insure "the capture of the said Juan Santos Atahualpa, and
the break-up of his followers" (ibid.: 76). Local rebellion, including riot
against abusive kurakas, could and did take place in the central sierra
of the mid-eighteenth century (Celestino 1981: 23–24; O'Phelan 1985:
127–30; cf. Amat 1776: 10; Mendiburu 1874–90: 7:164; Eguiguren 1959:
1:319). But the would-be organizers of a major insurrection faced unusually
formidable organizational obstacles in Tarma-Jauja.

The policies of the colonials themselves must also figure, finally, in the
explanation of insurrectionary failure. Insurrection was difficult to organize, and especially so in Jauja and Tarma. But the colonials were not
content to take chances. The state's agents used both carrot and stick to
maintain control, and to shift the balance of forces more heavily in their
favor. Recall, for example, the suspension of Tarma's mita to the mines;
the replacement of the needlessly provocative corregidor Alfonso de Santa;
and the framing and deliberately public execution of "spies." Recall, too,
the transformation of the central sierra into an armed camp staffed in part
by trained Spanish troops superior to ordinary provincial militias. (For
the wider context of the military and society, see Campbell 1976, 1978.)
This regional militarization, accompanied in 1759 by further security
measures in the northern sierra of Cajamarca—Huamachuco (Espinoza
S. 1971; Moreno C. 1983: 430–33), altered the balance of military forces
beyond Tarma-Jauja itself. Tarma, in fact, became a staging area for
repression elsewhere in the central-northern sierra. Tarma's fixed troops
earned a reputation as capable veterans of repression, and helped quell
disturbances in Huarochirí in 1750, Huamalíes in 1777, Jauja in 1780, and
Cajamarca in 1794 (Loayza 1942: 171; *Relaciones* 1867–72: 3:36, 53;
Mendiburu 1874–90: 4:193, 196; Silva S. 1964: 99).[28]

The central sierra, by mid-eighteenth century, presented a serious insurrectionary threat to the colonial order. The failure of an insurrectionary *event* to materialize proves neither the absence of an insurrectionary
conjuncture, nor the marginal character of Juan Santos Atahualpa's appeal
in the sierra. The failure of "conjuncture" to materialize as "event" is
testimony, rather, to the difficulties of organizing a full-scale insurrection
in any highland region of the late colonial period; to the especially in-

tense interlock, even fusion, of indigenous and Hispanic power in the Tarma-Jauja region; and to the effectiveness of security measures taken to consolidate colonial control in the central sierra.[29] If this interpretation is correct — if the threat of insurrection was as serious and immediate in the central sierra in 1745, as it was in the southern sierra in 1776-1777 and in 1780 — we must considerably revise the chronological and geographical assumptions underpinning our interpretations of the civil war that engulfed the south in 1780-1782.

THE CENTER-NORTH DURING THE ERA OF TÚPAC AMARU II

Let us turn, then, to the great insurrection. We have already noted the historiographical preoccupation with the geographical boundaries of the war. Except for a brief flare-up in Huarochirí in 1783, the insurrection was confined to southern Peru and Bolivia.[30] We have also seen that the image of a relatively quiescent central sierra, which separated rebellious nuclei in north and south, rests on a mistaken and superficial reading of midcentury sierra politics. More specifically, this view underestimates the repercussions of Juan Santos Atahualpa's redemptive vision in the sierra. But what should we make of the failure of the central sierra, especially Tarma-Jauja, to become engulfed in the violent mobilization that swept over the south in late 1780? Even if we refine the analysis and periodization of unrest in the central sierra, and revise our notions of Juan Santos Atahualpa's impact at midcentury, would we not still have to explain the gap, ca. 1780, between the propensity to rebel in the southern vs. the central highlands? Do not the spatial diffusion and limits of the great insurrection still call upon us to investigate the structural changes that made the south, in contrast to other regions, uniquely vulnerable to violent mobilization?

The problem with these questions is their assumption about the state of our knowledge. They assume that the state of our knowledge about the central sierra, ca. 1780, is more reliable than was the state of our knowledge for the same region, ca. 1750. Yet recent research and new documents demonstrate that *precisely during the era of the great southern insurrection*, the central and northern highlands witnessed a far more complex interplay of rebellion, ideological subversion, and repression than previously assumed.[31] A full-fledged history of politics and unrest in the center-north lies beyond the scope of this essay. (On the north, see O'Phelan 1978; Espinoza S. 1960, 1971, 1981; on the limits of our knowledge of the central sierra, see Celestino and Meyers 1981: 170.) For the purposes of the argument we need only make three points: violent revolt did strike Tarma-Jauja during the Túpac Amaru era; an unfavorable balance of politico-military forces made the transition from rebellion to insurrection especially problematic in Tarma-Jauja; and the center-north, more generally, experienced far greater unrest, violence, and ideological receptivity to an Andean-led revolution during the years 1780–1782 than we have normally acknowledged.

Revolts *did* break out in Tarma-Jauja, the strategic "core" of the central sierra, even as insurrection swept the south. I refer here not to the local rebellions that broke out in scattered parts of Peru – including Jauja, Pasco (Tarma's major mining center), and sites to the south and north – during the early months of 1780. These local revolts, partly a result of the provocations of José Antonio de Areche, Peru's *visitador general*, are well known to historians, and have not played a major role in the interpretation of the Túpac Amaru insurrection. (On the wave of local rebellions in early 1780, and the Areche inspection, see Lewin 1957: 184–85; *Relaciones* 1867–72: 3:39–54; Palacio A. 1946; Mendiburu 1874–90: 1:316–38, 4:193–96, 8:124–25; BNP 1780; CDIP 1971–75: 2-2:148–51, 158; O'Phelan 1978: 74, 106; Espinoza S. 1981.) By July, when Viceroy Guirior left office, order had been restored to the various locales on a case by case basis. The outgoing viceroy assumed that the colonial state would henceforth enjoy a period of calm allowing for a thorough investigation of the causes of local rebellion which would, in turn, prevent their reoccurrence (*Relaciones* 1867–72: 3:40–41, 43). We know, of course, that this self-interested assumption did not hold up in the south. By December, the combined insurrectionary movements led by Tomás Katari and Túpac Amaru II had transformed the political landscape of southern Peru and Bolivia. Not until mid-1782 would "peace" be fully restored.

Equally important for our purposes, however, Tarma-Jauja remained anything but quiescent during the civil war of 1780–1782. The region witnessed riots, land invasions, and the destruction of Tarma's most important *obraje* (primitive textile factory), San Juan de Colpas. Jauja witnessed, during 1780–1781, at least three separate instances of revolt, and the third, as we shall see, is better described as an unfolding process than as an "instance" of rebellion. The first riot – the one described by Guirior in his report in July 1780 – took place in and near Mito,[32] in the southern Mantaro Valley, during the early days of July (see *Relaciones* 1867–72: 3:40, 53–54; AGN 1780: esp. 1r, 6r–7r, 12r; Mendiburu 1874–90: 1:319, 8:125). As in many rebellions of southern Peru and Bolivia, the rebels focused their wrath on the corregidor. Don Vicente de Seneca, Jauja's corregidor and military commander, was "badly wounded" (*Relaciones* 1867–72: 3:53). But Jauja did not settle down in the ways anticipated by Guirior (ibid.: 54, 56). By the closing days of July, wrote Seneca, the Mito revolt had inspired violence elsewhere, especially in Chongos. There, according to several witnesses, a crowd armed with sticks, rocks, and knives lofted a flag of their own on the municipal building. Again, the targets of the crowd suggest resentment of the mercantile distributions manipulated by corregidores and their merchant allies. The crowd threatened to burn down the house of Don Juan de Ugarte, the corregidor's local accounts collector ("cajero"), and to kill Don Francisco Alvarez, a prominent local merchant. Only the pleadings of the local priest and an Indian alcalde dissuaded the rock-throwing rioters from making good on their threats (AGN 1780: esp. 1r–4v, 6v, 10r–14v). The disturbances in Mito and Chongos, although locally serious, appeared not to present a broader or continuing threat. The revolts burned themselves out — apparently — before the outbreak of Túpac Amaru's insurrection in November.

But contemporaries knew better than subsequent historians, perhaps, not to trust in appearances. The most ambitious challenge of all rocked the central sierra precisely as civil war entered its most violent and bitter phase in the south. In Jauja, from January to October 1781, Don Nicolás Dávila, a 22-year-old "pretender" to kuraka status, and Doña Josefa Astocuri, his mother and the widow of a recently deceased kuraka, led a campaign of growing defiance (unless otherwise indicated, see AGN 1781 for the following three paragraphs). Astocuri and her husband, who died in 1781, had once occupied a prominent role in the interlocking Hispanic-Andean power structure described earlier. But a complex intranobility rivalry unraveled the power network, and climaxed with the isolation of Astocuri and her husband from the regional power structure by 1779–1780 (Dunbar T. 1942: 155–61, 173–74 n. 34). The new turn of events converted Astocuri and her son, despite their wealth and conservative background, into leaders of subversion.

Essentially, the two usurped authority in Jauja's Mantaro Valley in alliance with Indian commoners, some Indian alcaldes (municipal officials), and toward the end, some mestizo commoners. By early February, orders disrupting the status quo began to circulate up and down the Mantaro Valley. Dávila and Astocuri advised Indians that they need not obey colonial officials and priests. They ordered Indians not to continue supplying labor drafts (*mitas*), servants (*pongos*), and household necessities such as wood and alfalfa to their erstwhile rulers. And perhaps most serious of all, words were backed by action. The followers of Astocuri-Dávila scandalized public life by breaking into the homes of colonials, especially priests, to kidnap their pongos. Land tenure, too, was subjected to new edicts backed by direct action. The Mantaro Valley region, whose lands and location invited commercial investment and mestizo immigration, suffered from land pressure and competition in the eighteenth century (see Adams 1959: 12–14, 19–21; Arguedas 1975: 94–97, 100; Cangas 1780: 313;

Juan and Ulloa 1748: 3:155–56; Mallon 1983: 37–38; AGN 1781: 8r). Dávila and Astocuri responded to the problem—and built up a following—by issuing edicts redistributing land. As their ambitions escalated, they prescribed a code of fines and corporal punishments for those who dared either to defy the new orders, or to beat Indians. In early months of the disobedience, Don Pedro Nolasco de Ylzarve, Jauja's corregidor and high military officer, hoped to avoid a direct confrontation, "bearing in mind the movements in the *tierras de arriba* [i.e., the lands of southern Peru/Bolivia] and that their threats had reached this province" (AGN 1781: 5r; on "tierras de arriba" as a reference to the southern highlands, see Juan and Ulloa 1748: 3:156; Cangas 1780: 313).

But as authority broke down, the protagonists—whatever their original intentions—moved inevitably toward violent confrontation. Dávila and Astocuri avoided an open challenge to the authority of the King of Spain (even Túpac Amaru II was ambiguous and contradictory on this issue, as were the patriot creoles at the start of the independence crisis). But they proceeded with revolutionary edicts and actions anyway. These ignored the authority of the king's local representatives and of Catholic priests, abolished these officials' customary rights to Indian labor and servants, and redefined the rules of power and property. As a new reality unfolded, Don Nicolás advised his followers "that they did not need to fear anyone," and horrified Spaniards witnessed "the nil subordination of all the Indians, cholos, and mestizos to Royal Justice and to all the Spaniards of this province" (AGN 1781: 6r, 8r). Despite the exaggerated reference to "all" Indians, mestizos, and cholos, what is important is the crumbling of the reality and the expectation of deference that were so central to the traditional social hierarchy. Dávila and Astocuri never proclaimed loyalty to Túpac Amaru II or Tomás Katari. This should not surprise us, if we recall that the Lima-Huarochirí conspirators of 1750 could not agree on the identity of a new Inca-King; that the insurrectionaries of the south were themselves at best loosely coordinated, at worst afflicted by rival allegiances (see Campbell, Chapter 4 in this volume); and that Dávila and Astocuri may have harbored their own ambitions. A failure to challenge the Crown openly, or to proclaim loyalty to southern Andean leaders, made Jauja's defiance no less ambitious or serious. The region's residents knew perfectly well that an insurrectionary tide had swept over the south (see AGN 1781: 5r, 10r; cf. Eguiguren 1959: 1:395, for the case of Huaraz). Just as important, the actions of Astocuri-Dávila struck a messianic chord in the central highlands. Rumor had it, among some followers, that Don Nicolás "would soon be seated . . . on the throne" (AGN 1781: 6r). Or as corregidor Ylzarve explained, the region had been "roused up to a general revolt" (ibid.: 16r). The unfolding conflict climaxed on October 6, when rioters in Jauja stoned the soldiers and citizens assembled by the corregidor to restore order. As Ylzarve explained, his forces had to open fire to defend themselves from the barrage of rocks. But a half hour after their flight, the angry rioters returned with a still larger crowd. Only by opening fire a second time did the corregidor's troops finally disperse the crowd (ibid.: 16r).

Tarma, too, was wracked by disturbances in 1781, but in this case, the details remain frustratingly obscure. What we do know (see Millán de A. 1793: 133-34) is that Indians invaded and destroyed two obraje-hacienda complexes, and a smallish textile workshop (*chorrillo*). The targets of the invaders included San Juan de Colpas, "Tarma's most celebrated obraje" (ibid.: 134). Before the takeover, San Juan de Colpas yielded an annual rent and interest income of 8,800 pesos[33] — a scale implying a huge complex exploiting several hundred laborers at a time. Not surprisingly, Tarma's corregidores had traditionally focused considerable mercantile attentions on San Juan de Colpas, which served as a labor center to which Indians were sent to work off the debts owed on the district's extremely high (Alcedo 1786-89: 4:30) reparto de mercancías accounts. In December 1780, however, the Túpac Amaru revolution suddenly changed the traditional rules. Viceroy Jáuregui, hoping to speed the pacification of the insurrectionary south, abolished the repartimiento de mercancías. In Tarma, the abolition decree backfired. Once Indians learned of the measure, "excited by the desire for liberty, they destroyed the installations [of San Juan de Colpas], and began to take measures to establish themselves [on its lands], constituting a formal pueblo . . . and distributing the lands amongst themselves" (Millán de A. 1793: 134).[34] Similar land invasions destroyed the obraje of Michivilca, and the smaller workshop "Exaltación de Roco." On all three sites the Indians built "pueblos with churches, municipal buildings, and jails" (ibid.).[35]

Our first major point, in evaluating the center-north during the era of Túpac Amaru II, is by now clear. Violent and sometimes ambitious revolts struck Tarma-Jauja, the strategic provinces of the central sierra, precisely as insurrectionary war unfolded in the south. Even after the suppression of the southern insurrection, colonial authority in the central sierra stood on rather shaky ground. Viceroy Jáuregui (1780-1784) reported a riot in Chupaca (southern Jauja region), and ongoing land conflicts simmered in the Yanamarca Valley (just north of the town of Jauja) during 1784-1791. In 1791, the tension forced landowners and colonial land judges to retire to Jauja for safety. (For the above, see *Relaciones* 1867-72: 3:121-22; Yanamarca 1840-42: esp. 575; cf., for Tarma, Eguiguren 1959: 1:339-50.)

To this first point we should immediately add a second: the military balance of forces in Tarma-Jauja during 1780–1782 made it especially difficult for rebels to become insurrectionaries. By this time, we should recall, Tarma-Jauja had become a center of security whose seasoned veterans of repression helped suppress revolts outside and inside their own districts. The speedy availability of regular officers and troops from Tarma, Jauja, and if necessary, Lima, made it relatively easy for authorities to either suppress or isolate quickly rebellions in the central sierra. (For specific examples from the Jauja revolts, for which the evidence is more plentiful than in Tarma, see Mendiburu 1874–90: 8:125, 4:193; *Relaciones* 1867–72: 3:53–54; AGN 1780: 6r; AGN 1781: 6v, 10r, 16r.) In general, it was in the center-north sierra and along the Pacific coast that security was beefed up, in the 1750s and after, to counter the dangers of Indian revolt and British attack. Military governors and troops ruled over Tarma-Jauja; the coastal defenses were reformed; and the sprawling Cajamarca corregimiento district was divided into three corregimientos (Huambos, Huamachuco, and Cajamarca), whose smaller size and Indian militias would make the north more manageable (see Campbell 1978: 60–61; Espinoza S. 1971; BNP 1783: esp. 5v–9v; Espinoza S. 1981: 183).

The balance of forces in the southern highlands contrasts sharply. In the south, authorities ruled over a vast, sprawling territory more isolated from centers of colonial military strength on the coast, and more reliant on rather unreliable provincial militias. Under these circumstances, authorities would find it more difficult to prevent the organization of insurrectionary armies, or the spread of rebellion from one locale to the next. (On the comparative effectiveness of provincial militias and regular troops, see Campbell 1976: 45–47; Campbell 1978: 99, 106–11, 147; Campbell 1981: 676.)

Finally, we should place the Tarma-Jauja experience in the wider context of the center-north. We need not engage here in a detailed analysis of political life and popular unrest in other center-north provinces. Suffice it to say that recent research now casts doubt on earlier assumptions that center-north provinces remained largely uninvolved in or unaffected by the explosion of Andean unrest, violence, and utopias in 1780–1782. The new research is recasting our understanding of two major regions: Cajamarca-Huamachuco, northern sierra provinces overlooking coastal Lambayeque and Trujillo, and Huamanga, the highland region just south of Jauja.

Cajamarca-Huamachuco experienced repeated local rebellions in the eighteenth century (O'Phelan 1978, 1976; Espinoza S. 1960, 1971), but its history of revolt once seemed rather disconnected from unrest in the south. This was the case especially because Cajamarca-Huamachuco appeared quiescent for three years following a local riot in Otusco in September 1780 (see O'Phelan 1978: 72-74). We now know, however, that the Otusco rebellion, unlike the classic village riots studied by Taylor (1979) in Mexico, did not quite burn itself out in several days or weeks; that in January 1781, rumors circulated that an emissary of Túpac Amaru II had arrived on the Lambayeque coast and contacted Otusco's rebels; that to ward off danger, colonial authorities mounted a security campaign to control Indians and castas in and near Lambayeque; and that by April, the volatile mix of rumor and security patrols provoked, in the coastal pueblo of Moche, mass panic and flight. Moche's inhabitants fled to escape soldiers believed to be marching from Lima and Trujillo to quarter the bodies of the locals (Espinoza S. 1981: 169-201, esp. 181-93; for similar fears in Huancavelica in early 1780, and the difficulties of reestablishing order there, see *Relaciones* 1867-72: 3:51-52). We know, too, that Lorenzo Suárez, a chief from Huamachuco, was implicated in the abortive tupamarista revolt in Huarochirí in 1783 (O'Phelan 1978: 71).

Similarly, Huamanga's apparent calm has proved rather deceptive under closer scrutiny. Lorenzo Huertas (1976, 1978) has demonstrated a complex ferment of disturbances, rumors, and repression. Despite several precautions taken, in the closing months of 1780 and in early 1781, to organize small military cuartels and to disarm Indians (Zudaire 1979: 159-60; Huertas 1976: 86-91), riots broke out or nearly broke out in the northern Huamanga district of Huanta during 1781. The disturbances were partly provoked by the reparto de mercancías, and partly by attempts to draft Indians and castas into the army that Huamanga would send to fight Túpac Amaru in Cuzco (Huertas 1976: 93-94). In Chungui, where eastern Huanta descended toward the jungle, the colonials faced a more ambitious challenge. Pablo Challco, a "notorious idolator" (ibid.: 97), publicly proclaimed the coronation of Túpac Amaru II as king in December 1780, and led a movement whose followers—until their final defeat in October 1781—rejected the authority of corregidores and priests (ibid.: 95-102). Earlier that year, in August, a company of Spanish merchants passing through Vischongo (in the Río Pampas zone, considerably south of Huanta) were shocked to stumble upon a large Indian festival celebrating Túpac Amaru II (who was by then dead). The merchants—either armed or accompanied by soldiers—attacked to break up the celebration, but the Indians "rioted" and "took possession of the hills because they were rebels" (ibid.: 95). Even after the final defeat of the southern insurrections, the memory of Túpac Amaru II continued to evoke sympathy and repression. Before his recapture in 1784, Diego Jaquica, an escaped prisoner, native *curandero* (healer), and self-proclaimed relative of Túpac Amaru, wandered through the region and attended public celebrations such as marriages and religious festivals. During his wanderings, Jaquica received respectful treatment as he recounted the epic history of the Túpac Amaru revolution (Huertas 1978: 10-16).

The failure of the great southern insurrections to expand into the center-north is a more complex historical issue than previously acknowledged, and is not reducible to trends in socioeconomic structure that made the peoples of the central or northern sierras either less likely to revolt, or less receptive to messianic and insurrectionary ideas. Not only have we seriously underestimated the repercussions of Juan Santos Atahualpa's movement in the central sierra at midcentury. We have also relied on a data base, when interpreting the regional bases of Andean mobilization in the 1780s, that is profoundly incomplete and misleading (see Map 3). Even in the south, the data base is flawed.[36] The failure of the insurrection in the center-north probably had as much to do with organizational, military, and political matters—some of them outgrowths, ironically, of the very gravity of the crisis in the central sierra at midcentury—as with differences in well-being or rebelliousness rooted in "structural" trends in population, economy, mercantile exploitation, and the like.[37]

Set in the context of recent research on Cajamarca, Huamanga, and Tarma-Jauja, we can no longer dismiss other examples of revolt, insurrectionary ambition, or tupamarista sympathy in the center-north as mere aberrations. Consciousness of the tupamarista project embraced north, center, and south, as did violent revolt itself. As a lampoon in Huaraz (northern sierra) warned on Christmas 1781, shortly before a local rebellion broke out, "if in the lands above [i.e., to the south] there have been two Túpac Amarus [José Gabriel, and his cousin and successor Diego Cristóbal], here there are two hundred" (Eguiguren 1959: 1:395). In the final analysis, the well known Huarochirí revolt of 1783, far from an aberration, fits in well with the larger picture of the center-north during the era of Túpac Amaru II. This was a revolt at once ambitious and visionary in ideological terms, but severely constrained in practical and organizational terms. For high officials hardened by the great southern wars, Huarochirí's was a revolt rather easily isolated and repressed (see Valcárcel 1946: 133-38; Mendiburu 1874-90: 2:252-53; 8:295-98).

Deeply rooted in the political culture of the eighteenth century, the idea of a neo-Inca liberator could resurface even after its time had passed (cf. Flores G., Chapter 7 in this volume). More than a full generation after Túpac Amaru's defeat, neo-Inca messianic ideas still struck a responsive chord in the central highlands. In 1812, during the independence crisis, thousands of Indians invaded Huánuco, the small capital "city" of the province just north of Tarma (see Varallanos 1959: 452-77; cf. Roel P. 1980: 101-6). The Huánuco revolt led the interim intendant of Tarma (an intendancy that included the old corregimiento districts of Huánuco, Tarma, and Jauja in its jurisdiction), Don Ygnacio Valdivieso, to launch a secret investigation to stop possible spillover effects in Tarma and Jauja (see *CDIP* 1971-75: 3-1:121-248, and Dunbar T.'s "Prólogo," iii-xcvii). To Valdivieso's dismay, he discovered a preexisting undercurrent of messianic rumor and threats of violence, and had to take decisive action, including a round-up of ringleaders, to head off possible revolt. In widely scattered parts of Tarma and Jauja, Inca "emissaries" had spread word, as early as May 1811, that an impending change of eras would liberate Indians and do away with Europeans (*chapetones*). That same month, the Buenos Aires patriot lawyer Juan José Castelli, who had led a patriot expedition into Bolivia, declared at the ancient Tihuanaco ruins that the patriot forces would abolish Indian tribute, redistribute land, establish a school system for all, and decree legal equality for Indians (Lynch 1973: 120-24). Castelli's efforts to win a reliable Indian following in Bolivia proved fruitless. From the distance of Tarma-Jauja, however, Indians saw him as a neo-Inca liberator: "they said that the son of the Inca was about to arrive, and that Casteli [sic] was right" (*CDIP* 1971-75: 3-1:124). During the violence in Huánuco in 1812, Indians spoke of the arrival of "King Castelli" or "Castell Inga" (Dunbar T., ibid.: 1).

TOWARD A REAPPRAISAL

If the thesis of this essay is correct, we must embark on a major reappraisal of the chronology, geography, and explanation of Andean insurrection. We have long recognized, of course, that repeated violence in explicit defiance of colonial authority, and the myth of an imminent Inca-led liberation,[38] constituted powerful eighteenth-century forces. Most Andeanist scholars would agree that the rise of revolt and insurrectionary utopias in dynamic relation to one another created, at least in the south in the 1780s, a major crisis of colonial rule.

What has been lost, however, in recent efforts to discern with greater rigor the social and economic bases of insurrection, is an appreciation of the breadth of the crisis and its underlying causes. We have overly narrowed our focus. It is time to reincorporate the more panoramic view of earlier scholars such as Valcárcel, Lewin, and Rowe, without sacrificing our quest for a more precise understanding of timing, geography, causation, leadership, internal contradictions, and so on. (A pioneering start in this direction is O'Phelan 1985). The breakdown of Spanish colonial authority over poor Indians and castas — as manifested by explicit and violent defiance of once accepted authority, and by the rise of new ideologies envisioning a transformed social order — was even graver than we have conceded. Its territorial reach encompassed the northern sierras of Peru as well as the southern territory that became an insurrectionary battle-ground. The crisis of authority included the strategic central sierra districts — Huarochirí, Tarma, and Jauja — that overlooked Lima, the capital city, and that constituted a major gateway between north and south. And the rise of an urgent insurrectionary threat dates back *at least* to the 1740s,[39] and spanned forty years or more before its definitive suppression. To be sure, details of timing, intensity, organizational capacity, and the like varied by region, and this regional variation influenced the outcome of the insurrectionary crisis. But this was a crisis of rule whose proportions approached those which destroyed French colonial rule in Haiti. The gravity and scale of the crisis are all the more striking if one considers the differences in geography and physical environment, repertoire of social control devices (cooption and patronage, repression, counterintelligence, etc.), population density and racial-ethnic composition, colonial experience, and metropolitan politics that gave Spanish colonial rulers great advantage over their French counterparts.[40]

As we search for a more satisfactory explanation of the Age of Andean Insurrection, we will need to revise not only our chronology and geography, but also our methodological tools. We will need to move away from mechanistic approaches to causation that explain the "why," "when," and "where" of insurrectionary mobilization largely in terms reducible to categories of social structure (Cornblit's forasteros), or to rates of economic pillage (Golte's index of peasants' inability to meet reparto demands of corregidores). Methodologically, we need to move in two directions. First, we must pay greater respect to the interplay of structural, conjunctural, and episodic levels of analysis (see Braudel 1958). It is this multiplicity of time scales and causation levels which may help us to understand the erosion of colonial authority, in the long term, over a very wide Andean area encompassing most of Peru-Bolivia; the variations of timing and locale that created "miniconjunctures" within the larger insurrectionary conjuncture of 1742–1782; and the transformation of serious insurrectionary threats, at given moments, into insurrectionary events, aborted revolts or conspiracies, or prevented "nonevents." A second methodological corrective would devote closer attention to the interplay of material exploitation or hardship on the one hand, and consciousness or moral outrage on the other (see Thompson 1971; Scott 1976). It is the moral memory — or myth — of an alternative, Andean-based social order, a cultural memory nurtured and sustained by Andean peoples during an earlier period of "resistant adaptation" to colonial rule (see Huertas 1981; Flores G. 1986; Stern 1982: 187–93, esp. 188), that in part explains why economic pillage led not merely to local revolt, nor even to insurrectionary conspiracies under a Hispanic-Christian millennial banner, but rather to dreams of a great transformation under nativist or neo-Inca auspices.

Our revised methodology need not imply that regional variation is unworthy of investigation, or that the spatial method pioneered by Cornblit and Golte has little to offer. Comparative spatial analysis, if harnessed to a more well-developed data base and a less mechanistic methodology, could yield truly exciting results. Close microanalysis of local districts *within* insurrectionary provinces, for example, might clarify aspects of leadership, social composition, economic interest, and the like that swung a district to support the insurrectionaries or royalists once an insurrection was under way. (See Mörner and Trelles, Chapter 3 in this volume.) Similarly, if we move back to a macrolevel, the particularities of various regions will, in all likelihood, inject important nuances into the larger history of Andean insurrection. In the case of Tarma-Jauja, for example, I suspect that land pressure, a growing population of "Indianized mestizos," and the fluidity of racial boundaries in the plebeian culture of Tarma's mining camps and in Jauja's Indian-mestizo villages, would all loom larger in discussion of the causes and political culture of rebellion than in Cuzco-Puno.[41] Recognition of such variations would undoubtedly illuminate important aspects of the insurrectionary crisis, even if we believe — as I do — that underlying common trends undermined colonial authority in both regions, and created an insurrectionary conjuncture long before the 1770s.

My own hypothesis, subject of course to verification and revision as scholarly research unfolds, is that the changing political economy of mercantile exploitation undermined preexisting strategies and relations of colonial rule and Andean resistance, by the 1730s, across virtually all of highland Peru-Bolivia. The changing relations of mercantile exploitation directly threatened the continuity of colonial political authority, and its rather fragile and partial legitimacy among Andean peasants. During the earlier period of commercial expansion and prosperity in the late sixteenth and early seventeenth centuries, corregidores, judges, and priests could more readily accede to Indian pressure to transform them into "mediating," partly "co-optable" figures of authority. The diverse paths to commercial prosperity open to colonial aristocrat-entrepreneurs and officials, who were divided by their own internal rivalries, allowed Indians a measure of "institutional space" by which to manipulate, bend, or bribe colonial officials and intermediaries to the Indians' own partial advantage. (For a fuller picture of the historical and material basis for such a pattern, the forms of "everyday resistance" it made possible, and the limits of such "resistance," see Stern 1982: 89–92, 114–37; see also Stern 1983.) In the long run, this pattern facilitated the rise of paternal quid pro quos that simultaneously allowed for significant Indian resistance and self-protection from some of the worst depradations, but left intact the structure of exploitation and formal colonial authority. As a practical matter, such quid pro quos between colonial patrons or intermediaries and Indian clients probably afforded greater space for Andean self-protection as time went on, and the earlier success and efficiency of the colonial system unravelled. By the middle decades of the seventeenth century, the Hapsburg model of Andean colonial rule and prosperity perfected by Viceroy Francisco de Toledo (1569–1581) had entered serious decay and revision (see Stern 1982: 114–32, 138–57, 189–92; Cole 1983; Larson 1979). The very ability of Indians to "co-opt" partially figures of paternal authority, and to develop such "co-options" into a major strategy of resistance and self-protection, may also help account for the tendency of peasants to look upon the King of Spain as the ultimate "protector" standing above or outside the local American system. (See Stern 1982: 135–37; Szemiński, Chapter 6 in this volume; for comparative perspective, see Phelan 1978; Taylor 1979.)

By the early eighteenth century, however, the determined efforts of the Crown and of Lima's commercial bourgeoisie to increase the efficacy of mercantile exploitation, in the face of stagnant markets in Andean America and Spain's weakness as an imperial competitor, had effectively destroyed the earlier pattern. Corregidores, after the 1678 "reform" that transformed their posts into speculative ventures auctioned to high bidders in Spain, now found themselves saddled by huge debts as they entered their five-year terms of office. In addition, they now faced a rather stagnant commercial economy whose internal markets expanded mainly through force. The combined pressures of debt and commercial stagnation transformed corregidores into ruthlessly one-dimensional exploiters of Indian lands and labor through the reparto de mercancías system, i.e., the forced distribution of unwanted goods at inflated prices. The Spanish colonial state — allied to Lima's commercial bourgeoisie, committed to a more efficient imperial system, vitally interested in revenues from the sale of corregidor posts to high bidders, and from taxation of a commercial economy expanding by force — would not seriously contemplate reforming the new structure of mercantile exploitation until the political crises of the 1750s and 1770s. In fact, the colonial state had made the political standing of corregidores even more volatile through its considerable efforts, especially under Viceroys Palata (1686–1689) and Castelfuerte (1724–1736), to expand tribute collection, update census counts, and revitalize the *mita*, the institution whereby peasant communities sent rotating drafts of laborers to the mines and other colonial enterprises, or paid monies to hire substitute laborers (see Sánchez-Albornoz 1978: 69–91; Cole 1985: 105–15; O'Phelan 1985: 58–86).

Given these circumstances, and a growing Indian population in need of more lands and productive resources, earlier quid pro quos, strategies of native resistance, and fragile colonial legitimacies all broke down. Corregidores became particularly pointed targets of popular wrath. (For evidence of an emerging crisis in corregidor-peasant relations well *before* the 1754–1780 period highlighted by Golte, see Fuentes 1859: 3:139–40, 277–78; Moreno C. 1977: 171, 227–28 [incl. n. 153], 236–37.) But the new economic pressures on corregidores subjected *all* the collaborators in local power groups to new strains that restricted the possibilities of their partial "co-option" by Indians, and raised the political stakes of such accommodations. Although research on the social and political activities of priests is still in its infancy, the new circumstances of the eighteenth century probably sharpened latent rivalries between priests and corregidores, forced some priests to resort to provocative new fees and land claims to secure their own revenues, and generally eroded the priests' ability to play meaningful mediating roles without directly challenging the authority of corregidores (see O'Phelan 1985: 53–160 passim; Golte 1980: 164–71; cf. Hunefeldt 1983; Cahill 1984). In most instances, priests probably sought to avoid extreme and dangerous outcomes, but the political pressure-cooker sometimes boiled over, converting some priests into sympathetic allies, even instigators, of peasant revolts against corregidores, and others, as in Jauja in 1781, into targets of rebellion (see especially O'Phelan 1985: 53–160 passim). The political crisis sharply affected, too, the ability of Andean chiefs to defend their own legitimacy as "brokers" between peasants and the colonial regime (see Larson 1979).

Future research may find this hypothesis wanting, and would in any event need to supplement it with an explanation of the rise of neo-Inca "insurrectionary utopias" as colonial authority and legitimacy entered into crisis. But however we explain the Age of Andean Insurrection, the severity, breadth, and ideological components of the insurrectionary crisis will raise important issues across time and space. Placed in a comparative Spanish American framework, the contrasts with Ecuador and Mexico are striking. Despite notable revolts in Ecuador (Moreno Y. 1976; Bonilla 1977), a benign Inca myth failed to develop into a powerful political force. What explains the contrasting character of revolt and political culture in Ecuador and Peru-Bolivia? The research of William B. Taylor (1979) on peasant rebellion in Mexico again underscores the particularity of Peru-Bolivia. Villagers rioted repeatedly in the Indian heartland of Mexico in the eighteenth century, but in most cases the rebellions proved eminently containable. The riots, although significant in redressing local grievances, posed little threat to the wider social order. Neo-Aztec ideological motifs, such as they were, blended into the protonational creole ideology emerging in the eighteenth century (Phelan 1960; Lafaye 1976). In Andean Peru-Bolivia, by contrast, local violence and tension repeatedly seemed to threaten possible insurrection waving the banner of a lost — and soon to be restored — native Andean glory. Protonational creole ideology, far from subsuming neo-Inca motifs, found itself in dangerous competition with more "nativist" protonational ideologies. Again, what explains the contrasting character of revolt and political culture in Mexico and Peru-Bolivia?[42]

Once we recognize the particularity of the political culture of eighteenth-century Andean peasants, we encounter further implications across time. In Peru-Bolivia, in the late colonial period, peasants did not live, struggle, or think in terms that isolated them from an emerging "national question." On the contrary, protonational symbols had great importance in the life of peasants and small-holders. Yet these protonational symbols were tied not to an emerging creole nationalism, but to notions of an Andean- or Inca-led social order. Andean peasants saw themselves as part of a wider protonational culture, and sought their liberation on terms that, far from isolating them from an overarching state, would link them to a new and just state. The myth of Castelli as Inca liberator, in the same highland region that also appeared to support more "creole" patriot guerrilla bands during the Wars of Independence (Rivera S. 1958; Mallon 1983: 49–51), should force us to view skeptically the application of assumptions about peasant "parochialism" and "antinational" localism to Andean peoples. The fact that most all native Andean peoples were peasants did not necessarily prevent them from viewing their nineteenth-century destinies in terms linked to a national identity and project. (See Chapters 9 and 10 by Mallon and Platt in this volume; also Platt 1982.) The real issues are how, and to what extent, Andean notions of nationhood gave way to more creole versions of nationhood in the nineteenth century; and to what extent the eventual rise of creole nationality so excluded Andean peoples from meaningful (i.e., partly self-interested) "citizenship" that it forced them into an "antinational" posture.

But we have leaped ahead of our story. The last words belong to an anonymous eighteenth-century songwriter from Cajamarca. Tied to a regional rhythm of life and rebellion so apparently disconnected from the insurrectionary wars raging in the south, our songwriter was nonetheless drawn — upon news of Túpac Amaru's death in 1781 (see Espinoza S. 1981: 193) — to the nearby warm-water springs that once provided relaxation to visiting Incas, and that serve today as a tourist attraction. There, our songwriter could contemplate the profound sense of loss (*CDIP* 1971–75: 2-3:916–17):

At the waters where I awaited
I had come heeding your call,
Feeling within your imminent arrival,
Wondering when you would come.

NOTES

1 See Flores G. 1981: 254; O'Phelan G. 1976: 70–72; O'Phelan 1985: 285–98; Golte 1980: 139–49; Fuentes 1859: 3:277–78; Esquivel y Navia ca. 1750: 1:xlvi–xlvii. Bear in mind that research on local rebellion is far from complete, especially in the Bolivian case. In time, the number of known disturbances may well rise to 200 or more.

2 Although Túpac Amaru was important in Bolivia and northern Argentina, the statement applies better to Peru than to Bolivia, where the Katari name is the leading symbol. It is important to note that the great insurrection embraced *several* insurrections and territorial arenas that were at best loosely coordinated. On Túpac Katari, see Valle de Siles 1977.

3 For these figures, see Vollmer 1967: 247–67; Golte 1980: 42–43; Cornblit 1970: 9. Mörner (1978: 123–25) doubts that such heavy losses were possible, and refers to the relatively light casualties of *ancien régime* wars in general. The cases of Haiti in 1792–1804, and Venezuela in 1810–1821, convince me that Mörner's skepticism may be misplaced.

4 As will become evident in the conclusions and in note 39, one should not view the years 1742 and 1782 as absolute dividing lines rigidly separating insurrectionary and noninsurrectionary periods. Any periodization, if taken too literally, threatens to become arbitrary and misleading. The trends and patterns that distinguish one historical era from another are often discernible and significant shortly before and after an era "begins" and "ends." But this does not make periodization useless or unnecessary, and it does not imply the absence of genuine watersheds dividing one period from another.

5 For yet another twist on the far-reaching reverberations of the Túpac Amaru revolution, see Phelan's (1978: 105–9) comments on the attempt by Colombian dissidents to manipulate fear of the tupamarista insurrection in their own struggle in Colombia (cf. also Loy 1981).

6 A partial exception to this characterization is Rowe's pioneering essay on the "Inca national movement" (1954: 40–47).

7 These two tendencies should not be taken as mutually exclusive.

8 On the origins and importance of the *forasteros*, see Sánchez-Albornoz 1978; Larson 1979: 197–204, 215–26; Wightman 1983; Stern 1982: 126–27, 154–55, 173–74.

9 Cornblit may also be criticized for his rather uncritical acceptance of contemporary stereotypes of the forasteros, and for reliance on theories of mass

and crowd behavior by unintegrated marginals that are at the very least highly questionable. On the latter point, see for examples Rudé 1964; Perlman 1976. Suggestive research on the social relations of forasteros includes Larson 1979; Wightman 1983.

10 The technical problems in Golte's study are substantial enough to require a separate review-essay for their full elaboration. The seriousness of these problems is indicated by the fact that two key statistical bases of his interpretation are rather hypothetical and problematic. The trend in the reparto, which allegedly tripled during 1754–1780, is asserted rather than demonstrated (Golte 1980: 117–18). The evidence cited by Golte demonstrates the prevalence of illegal abuses of the reparto, but not a trend line of the sort he suggests. Yet the alleged tripling of the legal reparto quotas is crucial in the formula measuring the demands placed upon Indians in various provinces (ibid.: 177–78). In addition, the calculation of the "carrying capacities" of the various provinces relies on data from 1792 (ibid., 111–13, 177–78) which may or may not reflect regional variation in "carrying capacities" during the decades preceding the insurrectionary explosion of 1780. To his credit, Golte often warns the reader of the limits of the evidence and the procedures used in his pioneering study. But Golte characteristically then proceeds to ignore his own warnings and qualifications.

11 This does not mean that Juan Santos was unaware of other European peoples such as the English, with whom Juan Santos claimed to have made a political alliance (Loayza 1942: 2; Izaguirre 1922–29: 2:116). The basic data available on Juan Santos's personal biography are repeated in almost all the standard sources, but many of the details of his pre-1742 life remain obscure or unconfirmed (Juaniz 1960 is a fanciful account). Juan Santos had a mestizo appearance (see Lehnertz n.d.: chap. 6, 18–20) despite the identification with Indian society and Inca nobility. He may have been born in Cajamarca (Loayza 1942: 29), was probably Jesuit-educated in Cuzco in the school for sons of native kurakas and nobles, and initially said that the Jesuits could come to teach in his montaña kingdom (ibid.: 4). Contemporaries said that he had made an initial attempt around 1730 or 1731 to organize an insurrectionary alliance among kurakas (see Varese 1973: 179; AGN 1752: 44r), and his critics claimed that he was a criminal fugitive, having murdered a Jesuit during the reign of Viceroy Castelfuerte (1724–1736) and subsequently escaped from prison. Varese (1973: 177–78) intelligently critiques the murder and prison story based on a close analysis of the sources available to him during his research. A document written in 1752 corroborates the prison story, however, although it leaves the murder question unresolved. It refers in a matter-of-fact way to the local corregidor's archival records on Juan Santos Atahualpa's earlier imprisonment by Viceroy Castelfuerte, and his exile to "La Piedra," an island prison off Callao. But it links the imprisonment to Juan Santos Atahualpa's political subversion, and does not mention murder of a Jesuit (see AGN 1752: 47; on "La Piedra" as an island prison, see Armendaris 1725). This documentary finding on Juan Santos Atahualpa's earlier imprison-

ment and escape adds meaning to Juan Santos's own statement in 1742 that "his house is named Piedra" (Loayza 1942: 2).

12 On the reversal of colonial penetration of the frontier, and its long-term legacy, see Mallon 1983: 48–49, 59; Ortíz 1975–76: 1:143; *Mercurio Peruano* 1791–94: 4:28–29 (Jan. 12, 1792); Bueno 1764–79: 46–47.

13 The staffing of corregidor posts by military officers was part of a more general policy trend, but one pursued most assiduously in the districts judged most dangerous (see Moreno C. 1977: 159–65, 140–41).

14 Subsequent to falling upon these criminal cases, I discovered that one had been cited in the overview of late colonial Peru by Tord N. and Lazo G. (1980: 307–8), and another in the overview of women's experience by Prieto de Zegarra (1981: 1:378–80). These authors do not analyze, however, the implications of these documents for the historiography of insurrection.

15 This pattern of escape to the montaña frontier will sound familiar to historians of Afro-American slavery, for whom escapes by rebel "maroons" to interior frontier zones is a topic of great importance (see Price 1979).

16 This interpretation of Juan Santos Atahualpa's political organization and influence is more in line with that of Varese (1973) than that of Lehnertz (n.d.). Despite the value of the evidence in AGN 1752, my comments remain somewhat speculative, and we need further research to corroborate or modify the interpretation suggested here.

17 *One* of the twenty porters remained loyal to the colonials, returned to Huanta after witnessing the episode, and became the source for our knowledge of the porters' betrayal and the Spaniards' fate.

18 See Bueno (1764–79: 139) and Mendiburu (1874–90: 5:272) for references to an incursion that went as far as Canta, a sierra district overlooking the Pacific coast. Even if these references are somewhat exaggerated, they imply an expedition deep into the sierra that risked lines of retreat into the jungle. In later years, the militarization of the central highlands prevented such deep raids.

19 For historical accounts of the 1750 and 1783 revolts in Huarochirí, see Mendiburu 1874–90: 5:172–73, 2:252; Valega 1939: 89; Valega 1940–43: 1:59–60; Rowe 1954: 45–47; Spalding 1984: chap. 9. The 1758 (?) revolt is more obscure, but a brief description is in Carrió (1782: 47–48).

20 Huarochirí, Yauyos, and Canta — western central sierra districts overlooking the Pacific coast — are in Golte's scheme conceded to be more like the "south" in their propensity to rebel (see Table 2.1, p. 42; Golte 1980: 180–81, maps 27–28). It is the more interior central sierra districts — Huánuco, Tarma, Jauja, Angaraes, and Huanta — that are crucial in Golte's interpretation of the central sierra as relatively placid.

21 Lima was an important focal point for growing unrest and ambivalence about the colonial regime by relatively "acculturated" Andean chiefs and nobles, and drew Huarochirí's leading Indians into its social and cultural life (see Fuentes 1859: 4:98–99; Rowe 1954: esp. 42–47; Spalding 1984: esp. chap. 9).

22 Officials writing reports to their superiors, especially viceroys who reviewed

their own rule at the close of their terms in office, were tempted to minimize imminent dangers or unresolved conflicts in order to demonstrate their own competence. An instructive example is the report by Viceroy Guirior on the eve of the Túpac Amaru insurrection (*Relaciones* 1867–72: 3:39–54, esp. 40–41, 43).

23 As we shall see later, Santa was forcibly retired from his duties, reinstalled later, and in his second stint as corregidor, apparently less able to rely on the reparto for a substantial income.

24 Eguiguren (1959: 319) refers to litigation against Severino Yancapaucar, the organizer of one such conspiracy in Tarma, and says that the documentation spans the years 1733–1774. Unfortunately, he does not provide crucial details about the conspiracy or its timing. The prosecutor is one "Don Francisco," and we do know that Don Francisco Obregón purchased the Tarma corregidor office in 1749 (Moreno C. 1977: 94). Whatever the precise timing of the initial charges brought against Yancapaucar, and the collection of formal evidence, it is probable that word of such organizing attempts circulated by the mid-1740s.

25 In actuality, the suspension implied relief from paying the money that Tarma's Indians had paid in lieu of sending mita laborers to the mines (Zavala 1978–80: 3:162).

26 For perspective on the textiles lost to the fine, consider that the amount lost *exceeded* annual textile production in Peru's largest eighteenth-century obrajes (Silva S. 1964: 119–20).

27 It is also worth noting, however, that the central sierra acquired its notoriety *after* 1742, the year that Juan Santos Atahualpa initiated his insurrection. For the "map" of prominent trouble-spots in 1742, see Montero (1742: 31–32).

28 One should recall that this is a list of *known* cases. Other examples have, so far at least, eluded the historical record.

29 I believe that the points just mentioned are both necessary and sufficient to explain the failure of an insurrectionary event to materialize in the highlands. Nonetheless, I should point out that a further relevant variable may be the ideological and strategic thrust of the Juan Santos Atahualpa movement itself. Juan Santos sometimes appears to have sought to minimize violence (see Varese 1973: 183–85, 203; Loayza 1942: 3; AGN 1752: 20v), and to have expected an outpouring of sierra support and sympathy so obvious and overwhelming that it alone would drive the viceroy to accept the coming of an Inca kingdom. During preparation for the Andamarca invasion, Juan Santos apparently planned to "conquer" the sierra by residing in Andamarca three months while highland provinces swung to his cause, and he ordered his chiefs and warriors to concentrate not on killings, but on capture of live prisoners to be integrated into the Inca's swelling ranks. This relatively nonviolent and spontaneous "conquest" of the highlands (one that adequately describes how Juan Santos conquered Andamarca) would presumably suffice to convince the viceroy to abandon Peru (see AGN 1752: 20v). This strategy, if it accurately describes Juan Santos's plans, may reflect a profound spiritual emphasis

within the Juan Santos Atahualpa movement — an emphasis on the healing of wounded spirits in preparation for a just, healthful, and bountiful era, rather than on the organization of armies and political alliances for a direct assault on the citadels of colonial power. Note, in this regard, the striking condolences offered to a frightened mestiza by the three Indians later imprisoned and executed as "traitors." They assured her that she need not worry or cry, "because once she saw their Inca Lord [*Apo Ynga*], he would fill her with comfort [*consuelos*] as had happened to them with their burdens." The Inca would relieve her of all afflictions, pain, and sickness (AGN 1752: 12r). This emphasis on spiritual healing rather than politico-military assault is not unfamiliar to students of millenarian movements, and differs substantially from the military and strategic thrust that would characterize the tupamarista and katarista insurrections in the 1780s.

The problem with the hypothesis outlined here is its highly speculative character, given the skimpy and contradictory state of the evidence currently available. If further research proves this hypothesis to have merit, it could well imply that Juan Santos and his emissaries did not go to great lengths to organize an insurrectionary military assault in the highlands — despite the restiveness and rebelliousness that struck the central sierra in the 1740s and 1750s. More important would be to "spread the word" of an imminent transformation, and of the Inca's benign intentions. This would not suffice to explain why insurrection did not engulf the central sierra anyway, nor would it displace the explanation suggested in the text of the essay. But it would add another element to the obstacles against "conjuncture" materializing as "event."

30   The insurrection actually encompassed the northern parts of present-day Argentina and Chile as well. I use "southern Peru and Bolivia" loosely as a convenient rough reference to the southern Andean highland territory and cultures once associated with the Inca Empire Tawantinsuyu.

31   Actually, Dunbar T. (1942: 160, 176 n. 44) knew of one of the hitherto unexploited documents on the central sierra (AGN 1781), but used it for different purposes that obscured its significance for the history of Andean rebellion.

32   Although the viceroy's official report focused on a pueblo called "Rento," I have been unable to trace the location of such a pueblo, and suspect that a mistaken transcription in the published viceregal report may account for the mysterious reference. In any event, AGN 1780 makes it clear that the first riot was in or near Mito.

33   According to Millán de A. (1793: 134), San Juan de Colpas paid 6,000 pesos in rent and the interest on principals amounting to 56,000 pesos. At a 5 percent interest rate, the standard rate for *obras pías* in the colonial period, the interest income would account for another 2,800 pesos a year.

34   Romero (1937: 148) and Silva S. (1964: 161) were aware of the destruction of San Juan de Colpas, but confused its timing and mistakenly attributed the event to followers of Juan Santos Atahualpa.

35   In a conversation with Don Moisés Ortega of Acolla (north of Jauja) on July 29, 1981, he informed me that further documentation recording violent dis-

turbances in Tarma in 1780–1781 exists in private hands of one of his more distant relatives, but that the owner is unwilling to allow access to the documents. Don Moisés Ortega is a schoolteacher with deep family roots in Acolla and the Yanamarca Valley, and is an extremely knowledgeable historian of the region.

36   Jorge Hidalgo (1983: 127, 130; and personal communication, 1983) has discovered rebellion in the south Andean province of Arica during the Túpac Amaru revolution, but Arica is not included in the rebellious territory mapped by Golte (1980: map 27).

37   For astute comparative comments which further underscore the importance of military matters in the geography of late colonial revolt, see Phelan (1978: 30–31, 99–100).

38   I mean "myth" in a neutral rather than value-laden sense, in the spirit of anthropology and the sociology of knowledge rather than in disparaging terms that assign "myth" to the realm of fiction and fable. It is worth recalling that for brief periods and in some territorities, the myth of Inca-led liberation became an experienced truth.

39   As Rowe pointed out long ago (1954: 37–40), and O'Phelan more recently (1985: 58–92, 275–76), it may be possible to speak of an initial insurrectionary conjuncture as early as the 1730s. Attempts at large-scale insurrectionary organization include Juan Santos Atahualpa's initial efforts in 1730 or 1731 (AGN 1752: 44, 47); the 1737 Azángaro rebellion, part of a conspiracy implicating seventeen provinces (Loayza 1942: 123; Esquivel y Navia ca. 1750: 2:261; Rowe 1954: 39); and the 1739 Oruro conspiracy masterminded by Juan Vélez de Córdoba, which appeared to have organized some Andean support along the Pacific coast if not in the high Bolivian altiplano (Beltrán A. 1925: 54–84; Maúrtua 1906: 12:143; Fuentes 1859: 3:578–80; Lewin 1957: 118–20; Rowe 1954: 39–40; Vargas U. 1966–71: 4:207). The 1730s also witnessed politically significant rebellions in Cochabamba and Paraguay (see Montero 1742: 32, 38–40). Further evidence of political and spiritual ferment as early as Viceroy Castelfuerte's term (1724–1736) involves the case of an Indian forastero who wandered into Puno as a living Jesus of Nazarene—"with a cross on his shoulders and a crown of thorns, barefoot, and with a rope around his neck." The Indian immediately gained a following, and was hailed in processions as his followers carried him into pueblos on their shoulders. Within three days, the local corregidor and militia captured "the Nazarene" and hanged him. (For the entire incident, see Carrió 1782: 39.)

40   This comparative point is not meant to deny the enormous obstacles faced by the Haitian revolutionaries, and the magnitude of their achievement. For a passionate and eloquent study of their achievement, see James 1963. Nonetheless, the factors mentioned in the text made the task of an Indian revolution in Peru-Bolivia more formidable in political and organizational terms.

41   By "Indianized mestizos," I mean mestizos whose language (many spoke Quechua only) and social relations in the countryside made them virtually indistinguishable from "Indians" despite their privileged tributary status as "mestizos." (On late colonial population in Peru, and the disproportionately "mes-

tizo" character of the central sierra, see Vollmer 1967; Browning and Robinson 1976; Celestino 1981: 11–12.) In my own research, I encountered mestizos who needed Spanish interpreters, was struck by the authorities' apparently justified fear that Juan Santos could count on a mestizo as well as Indian following, and was equally impressed by the evident good will and even sympathy (see AGN 1752: esp. 12r) of Auqui, Ibarra, and Lamberto toward the mestizo companions who would lead them to their capture and execution. The prevalence of mestizo in-migration to Jauja's Mantaro Valley, of Indian migration to work in Tarma's and (to a lesser extent) Jauja's mining camps (Haënke 1901: 90), of Indian *arrieraje* (muleteering) and commerce-related mobility, and of individual shifts from "Indian" to "mestizo" categories to gain tribute/mita relief all served to blur social boundaries and distances. In the relatively "cholo culture" of plebeians and peasants in Tarma-Jauja, especially in the mining camps and in the Mantaro Valley, Indians have seemed more "mestizo" than elsewhere, and mestizos more "Indian." For a similar case, see Larson's suggestive discussion of the shift from "Indian" to "mestizo" in late colonial Cochabamba (1983: 173–81).

42 In his comments at the conference upon which this book is based, Friedrich Katz proposed a promising comparative line of analysis, too complex to reproduce in its entirety here. Two key points bear mention in this context, although readers should beware that his comment cannot be "reduced" to these two points alone. First, Mexico experienced an economic boom in the late colonial period, and this allowed for greater reliance on indirect forms of surplus extraction, based on market mechanisms whose political implications differed greatly from the emphasis in Peru on direct taxes such as tributes, forced commodity distributions, and forced labor rights. Second, the evolving memory of the Inca and Aztec traditions took sharply different trajectories in the two culture regions, and effectively precluded the rise of popular neo-Aztec insurrectionary ideology. In the Andes, for example, one would be hard pressed to find, as in Central Mexico, oral traditions recording famine under the native imperial rulers. On the history of neo-Inca utopias, see the splendid essay by Flores G. 1986.

REFERENCES

ACI (Comisión Nacional del Bicentenario de la Rebelión Emancipadora de Túpac Amaru)
1982   *Actas del Coloquio Internacional "Túpac Amaru y su Tiempo".* Lima.
ADAMS, RICHARD N.
1959   *A Community in the Andes: Problems and Progress in Muquiyauyo.* Seattle: University of Washington Press.
AGN (Archivo General de la Nación, Lima, Peru)
1752   "Causa seguida contra Julián Auqui, Blas Ibarra y Casimiro Lamberto . . . por traidores a la Corona. . . ." Sección Real Audiencia, Causas Criminales, Leg. 15, C. 159.

1753   "Causa seguida contra D. Miguel Luis de Cabrera 'por el atroz
        delito de ser convocante, explorador y espía del indio rebelde . . .
        de Tarma.' " Sección Real Audiencia, Causas Criminales, Leg. 16,
        C. 174.
1756   "Causa seguida contra José Campos, vecino de La Concepción . . .
        por espía. . . ." Sección Real Audiencia, Causas Criminales, Leg. 18,
        C. 198.
1780   "Causa seguida contra Paulino Reinoso por 'motor de los tumultos
        habidos en el Pueblo de Chongos. . . .' " Sección Real Audiencia,
        Causas Criminales, Leg. 47, C. 544.
1781   "Autos criminales que siguió Dn. Pedro Nolasco de Ilzarbe, Justicia
        Mayor . . . de Jauja, contra Dn. Nicolás Dávila, . . . contra su madre
        Dña. Josefa Astocuri. . . ." Sección Derecho Indígena, Leg. 17, C. 397.

ALCEDO, ANTONIO DE
1786-89 Diccionario geográfico de las Indias occidentales o América. Biblio-
        teca de Autores Españoles, tomos 205-8. 4 vols. Madrid, 1967.

AMAT Y JUNIET, MANUEL DE
1776   Memoria de Gobierno. Eds. Vicente Rodríguez Casado y Florentino
        Pérez Embid. Seville, 1947.

AMICH, [FRAY] JOSÉ
1771   Compendio histórico de los trabajos, fatigas, sudores y muertes que
        los ministros evangelicos . . . han padecido. . . . Paris 1854. Reprinted
        in Colegio de Santa Rosa de Ocopa, Historia de las misiones de fieles
        é infieles del Colegio . . . de Santa Rosa de Ocopa. 2 vols. Barcelona,
        1883. Vol. 1.

ARGUEDAS, JOSÉ MARÍA
1975   Formación de una cultura nacional indoamericana. Mexico: Siglo
        XXI.

ARMENDARIS, JOSEPH DE [MARQUÉS DE CASTELFUERTE]
1725   "Bando, Lima, 20–VI–1725." In Medina's Biblioteca Hispana-Ameri-
        cana, Roll No. 21, Center for Research Libraries, Chicago.

BELTRÁN AVILA, MARCOS
1925   Capítulos de la historia colonial de Oruro. La Paz.

BNP (Biblioteca Nacional del Perú, Sala de Investigaciones, Lima)
1780   "Expediente . . . sobre los sucesos ocurridos en las Cajas Reales . . .
        de Pasco. . . ." Ms. C394.
1783   "Testimonio de las certificaciones de los méritos al real servicio . . .
        del Crnel. Dn. Tomás Fernández de Segura Cóndor Quispe. . . ." Ms.
        C2859.

BONILLA, HERACLIO
1977   "Estructura colonial y rebeliones andinas." Apuntes 7 (Lima): 91–99.

BONILLA, HERACLIO, AND KAREN SPALDING
1972   "La independencia en el Perú: las palabras y los hechos." In Bonilla
        et al. 1972: 15–64.

BONILLA, HERACLIO ET AL.
1972   La independencia en el Perú. Lima: Instituto de Estudios Peruanos.

BRAUDEL, FERNAND
1958   "History and the Social Sciences." As reprinted in Peter Burke, ed., *Economy and Society in Early Modern Europe*. New York, 1972. Pp. 11-42.

BROWNING, DAVID, AND DAVID J. ROBINSON
1976   "The Origin and Comparability of Peruvian Population Data, 1776-1815." *Bulletin for the Society for Latin American Studies* 25 (London): 19-37.

BUENO, COSME
1764-79   *Geografía del Perú virreinal (siglo XVIII)*. Ed. Daniel Valcárcel. Lima, 1951.

BURGA, MANUEL
1981   "La historia andina a través del arte." *Allpanchis* 15, 17-18: 245-52.

CAHILL, DAVID
1984   "*Curas* and Social Conflict in the *Doctrinas* of Cuzco, 1780-1814." *Journal of Latin American Studies* 16, 2: 241-76.

CAMPBELL, LEON G.
1976   "The Army of Peru and the Túpac Amaru Revolt, 1780-1783." *Hispanic American Historical Review* 56 (Feb.): 31-57.
1978   *The Military and Society in Colonial Peru, 1750-1810*. Philadelphia: American Philosophical Society.
1979   "Recent Research on Andean Peasant Revolts, 1750-1820." *Latin American Research Review* 14, 1: 3-49.
1981   "Social Structure of the Túpac Amaru Army in Cuzco, 1780-81." *Hispanic American Historical Review* 61 (Nov.): 675-93.

CANGAS, GREGORIO
1780   "Descripción dialogada de los Pueblos y Costumbres del Perú." In Simposio sobre la causa . . . 1960: 245-335.

CARRIÓ DE LA VANDERA, ALONSO
1782   *Reforma del Perú*. Prologue and transcription by Pablo Macera. Lima, 1966.

CASTRO ARENAS, MARIO
1973   *La rebelión de Juan Santos*. Lima.

CDIP (Comisión Nacional del Sesquicentenario de la Independencia del Perú)
1971-75   *Colección documental de la independencia del Perú*. 27 vols. Lima.

CELESTINO, OLINDA
1981   "La economía pastoral de las cofradías y el rol de la nobleza india: el valle del Mantaro en el siglo XVIII." *Arbeitspapiere*, No. 25. Bielefeld: Universität Bielefeld.

CELESTINO, OLINDA, AND ALBERT MEYERS
1981   *Las cofradías en el Perú: región central*. Frankfurt/Main: Vervuert.

CHIRIF, ALBERTO, AND CARLOS MORA
1980   "La Amazonía peruana." In Mejía Baca, ed., 1980: 12: 217-321.

CHOY, EMILIO
1976   "Contradicciones y trascendencia de la revolución." In Flores G., ed., 1976a: 259-67.

COLE, JEFFREY A.
1983   "An Abolitionism Born of Frustration: The Conde de Lemos and the
        Potosí Mita, 1667-73." *Hispanic American Historical Review* 63
        (May): 307-33.
1985   *The Potosí Mita, 1573-1700: Compulsory Indian Labor in the Andes.*
        Stanford: Stanford University Press.

CORNBLIT, OSCAR
1970   "Society and Mass Rebellion in Eighteenth-Century Peru and Bolivia."
        In Raymond Carr, ed., *Latin American Affairs*. St. Anthony's Papers,
        No. 22 (Oxford), 9-44. Also available in Spanish in Flores G., ed.,
        1976a: 129-98.

CORNEJO BOURONCLE, JORGE
1954   "El sentido libertario de la revolución de Túpac Amaru." *Revista del
        Archivo Histórico del Cuzco*, 5: 396-411.
1963   *Túpac Amaru. La revolución precursora de la emancipación conti-
        nental*. 2d ed. Cuzco.

DUNBAR TEMPLE, ELLA
1942   "Los caciques Apoalaya." *Revista del Museo Nacional* 11 (Lima):
        147-78.

EGUIGUREN, LUIS ANTONIO
1959   *Hojas para la historia de la emancipación del Perú*. Vol. 1. Lima.

ESPINOSA SORIANO, WALDEMAR
1960   "Protestas, motines y rebeliones de indios, mestizos y españoles
        en Cajamarca, 1756-1821." In Simposio sobre la causa . . . 1960:
        35-36.
1971   "Geografía histórica de Huamachuco, 1759-1821." *Historia y Cultura*
        5: 5-96.
1973a   *La destrucción del imperio de los incas: la rivalidad política y señorial
        de los curacazgos andinos*. Lima: Retablo de Papel.
1973b   *Historia del Departamento de Junín* (volume 1 of *Enciclopedia de-
        partamental de Junín*, Editor Enrique Chipoca Tovar). Huancayo.
1981   "1780: Movimientos antifiscales en la sierra norte de la audiencia de
        Lima y repercusiones tupamaristas en la misma zona." *Allpanchis* 15,
        17-18: 169-201.

ESQUIVEL Y NAVIA, DIEGO DE
ca. 1750   *Noticias cronológicas de la gran ciudad del Cuzco*. Felix Denegri Luna
           et al., eds. 2 vols. Lima.

FEYJOÓ DE SOSA, MIGUEL
1778   "Dictamen . . . sobre que se quiten del todo los Repartimientos a los
        Corregidores. . . ." In Paz 1786: II, 328-357.

FISHER, JOHN R.
1976   "La rebelión de Túpac Amaru y el programa imperial de Carlos III."
        In Flores G. 1976a: 107-28.
1977   *Silver Mines and Silver Miners in Colonial Peru, 1776-1824*. Liver-
        pool.

1979 "Royalism, Regionalism, and Rebellion in Colonial Peru, 1808-1815." *Hispanic American Historical Review* 59 (May): 232-57.

FISHER, LILLIAN ESTELLE
1966 *The Last Inca Revolt, 1780-1783.* Norman, Okla.

FLORES GALINDO, ALBERTO
1976a (Ed.) *Túpac Amaru II — 1780.* Lima.
1976b "Túpac Amaru y la sublevación de 1780." In Flores G. 1976a: 269-323.
1977 "La nación como utopía: Túpac Amaru 1780." *Debates en sociología* 1 (Lima, Feb.): 139-53.
1981 "La revolución tupamarista y los pueblos andinos (una crítica y un proyecto)." *Allpanchis* 15, 17-18: 253-65.
1984 *Aristocracia y plebe: Lima, 1760-1830.* Lima: Mosca Azul.
1986 *Europa y el país de los incas: la utopía andina.* Lima: Instituto de Apoyo Agrario.

FUENTES, MANUEL A., ed.
1859 *Memorias de los vireyes que han gobernado el Perú durante el tiempo del coloniaje español.* 6 vols. Lima.

GARCÍA ROSSELL, CÉSAR
1957 "El separatismo de Túpac Amaru: un análisis de la insurrección de [1780]." *Revista del Archivo Histórico del Cuzco* 8: 92-110.

GOLTE, JÜRGEN
1980 *Repartos y rebeliones. Túpac Amaru y las contradicciones de la economía colonial.* Lima: Instituto de Estudios Peruanos.

HAËNKE, TADEO
1901 *Descripción del Perú.* Lima.

HIDALGO L., JORGE
1982 "Fases de la rebelión indígena de 1781 en el corregimiento de Atacama y esquema de la inestabilidad política que la precede, 1749-1781." *Chungará* 9 (Arica, Aug.): 192-246.
1983 "Amarus y Cataris: aspectos mesiánicos de la rebelión indígena de 1781 en Cusco, Chayanta, La Paz y Arica." *Chungará* 10 (Arica, March): 117-38.

HOBSBAWM, E. J.
1965 *Primitive Rebels: Studies in Archaic Forms of Social Movement in the 19th and 20th Centuries.* New York: W. W. Norton.

HUERTAS, LORENZO
1976 "El movimiento de Túpac Amaru en Ayacucho." In Flores G., 1976a: 83-105.
1978 "Testimonios referentes al movimiento de Túpac Amaru II, 1784-1812." *Allpanchis* 11-12: 7-16.
1981 *La religión en una sociedad rural andina.* Ayacucho: Universidad Naciónal de San Cristóbal de Huamanga.

HUMPHREYS, R. A., AND JOHN LYNCH, eds.
1965 *The Origins of the Latin American Revolutions, 1808-1826.* New York: Alfred A. Knopf.

HUNEFELDT, CHRISTINE
1983   "Comunidad, curas y comuneros hacia fines del período colonial:
         ovejas y pastores indomados en el Perú." *HISLA: Revista Latino-
         americana de Historia Económica y Social* II: 3-31.
IZAGUIRRE, BERNARDINO
1922-29 *Historia de las misiones franciscanas y narración de los progresos de
         la geografía en el oriente del Perú, 1619-1921.* 14 vols. Lima.
JAMES, C. L. R.
1963   *The Black Jacobins: Toussaint L'Ouverture and the San Domingo
         Revolution.* 2d ed. New York: Random House.
JUAN, JORGE, AND ANTONIO DE ULLOA
1748   *Relacion historica del viage a la America meridional.* . . . 4 vols.
         Madrid. Copy used is in the Beinecke Library, Yale University.
1826   *Noticias secretas de América.* London. Copy used is in the Beinecke
         Library, Yale University.
JUANIZ, CONRADO
1960   *El inca ladino, Juan Santos Atahualpa.* Madrid.
KLEIN, HERBERT S.
1982   *Bolivia: The Evolution of a Multi-Ethnic Society.* New York: Oxford
         University Press.
KUBLER, GEORGE
1946   "The Quechua in the Colonial World." In Julian H. Steward, ed.,
         Handbook of South American Indians. 7 vols. Washington, D.C.,
         1946-59. II: 331-410.
LA BARRE, WESTON
1948   *The Aymara Indians of the Lake Titicaca Plateau, Bolivia.* Washing-
         ton, D.C.
LAFAYE, JACQUES
1976   *Quetzalcóatl and Guadalupe: The Formation of Mexican National
         Consciousness, 1531-1813.* Trans., Benjamin Keen. Chicago: Uni-
         versity of Chicago Press.
LARSON, BROOKE
1979   "Caciques, Class Structure and the Colonial State in Bolivia." *Nova
         Americana* 2 (Turin): 197-235.
1983   *Explotación agraria y resistencia campesina: cinco ensayos históri-
         cos sobre Cochabamba (siglos XVI-XIX).* Cochabamba: CERES.
LARSON, BROOKE, AND ROBERT WASSERSTROM
1983   "Coerced Consumption in Colonial Bolivia and Guatemala." *Radi-
         cal History Review* 27: 49-78.
LEHNERTZ, JAY F.
1970   "Cultural Struggle on the Peruvian Frontier: Campa-Franciscan
         Confrontations, 1595-1752." M.A. Thesis, University of Wisconsin-
         Madison.
1972   "Juan Santos: Primitive Rebel on the Campa Frontier (1742-1752)."
         In *Actas y memorías del XXXIX Congreso Internacional de Ameri-
         canistas.* 6 vols. Lima. IV: 111-25.

1974   "Lands of the Infidels: The Franciscans in the Central Montaña of Peru, 1709–1824." Ph.D. diss., University of Wisconsin–Madison.
n.d.   "Land of Infidels: Notes on the Colonial History of the Peruvian Central Montaña (1557–1824)." Unpublished revised version of his Ph.D. diss. provided courtesy of W. Denevan.

LEWIN, BOLESLAO
1957   *La rebelión de Túpac Amaru y los orígenes de la emancipación americana.* Buenos Aires.

LOAYZA, FRANCISCO A., ed.
1942   *Juan Santos, el invencible.* Lima.

LOHMANN VILLENA, GUILLERMO
1946   *El Conde de Lemos, virrey del Perú.* Madrid.
1957   *El corregidor de indios en el Perú bajo los Austrias.* Madrid.

LOY, JANE M.
1981   "Forgotten Comuneros: The 1781 Revolt in the Llanos of Casanare." *Hispanic American Historical Review* 61 (May): 235–57.

LYNCH, JOHN
1973   *The Spanish-American Revolutions, 1808–1826.* New York.

MACERA, PABLO
1977   *Trabajos de historia.* 4 vols. Lima.

MALLON, FLORENCIA E.
1983   *The Defense of Community in Peru's Central Highlands: Peasant Struggle and Capitalist Transition, 1860–1940.* Princeton: Princeton University Press.

MAÚRTUA, VICTOR M., ed.
1906   *Juicio de límites entre el Perú y Bolivia.* 12 vols. Barcelona.

MEJÍA BACA, JUAN, ed.
1980   *Historia del Perú.* 12 vols. Lima.

MENDIBURU, MANUEL DE
1874–90 *Diccionario histórico-biográfico del Perú.* 8 vols. Lima.

MERCURIO PERUANO (1791–1794)
1791–94 Facsimile edition. 12 vols. Lima: Biblioteca Nacional del Perú, 1964–66.

MÉTRAUX, ALFRED
1942   "A Quechua Messiah in Eastern Peru." *American Anthropologist* 44 (Oct.–Dec.): 721–25.

MILLÁN DE AGUIRRE, (DOCTOR DON) MARIANO
1793   "Descripción de la intendencia de Tarma." In *Mercurio Peruano* 1791–94: 8:124–28, 132–49.

MONTERO, VICTORINO
ca. 1742 *Estado político del reyno del Perú.* Madrid. Copy consulted courtesy of P. Bakewell and the University of New Mexico General Library.

MORENO CEBRIÁN, ALFREDO
1977   *El corregidor de indios y la economía peruana en el siglo XVIII (los repartos forzosos de mercancías).* Madrid: Instituto 'Gonzalo Fernández de Oviedo.'

1983   (Ed.) *Relación y documentos de gobierno del Virrey del Perú, José
          A. Manso de Velasco, Conde de Superunda (1745-1761)*. Madrid:
          Instituto 'Gonzalo Fernández de Oviedo.'

MORENO YÁÑEZ, SEGUNDO
1976   *Sublevaciones indígenas en la Audiencia de Quito*. Bonn.

MÖRNER, MAGNUS
1978   *Perfil de la sociedad rural del Cuzco a fines de la colonia*. Lima.

MURRA, JOHN V.
1975   *Formaciones económicas y políticas del mundo andino*. Lima: Insti-
          tuto de Estudios Peruanos.

O'PHELAN GODOY, SCARLETT
1976   "Túpac Amaru y las sublevaciones del S. XVIII." In Flores G. 1976a:
          67-81.

1978   *El carácter de las revueltas campesinas del siglo XVIII en el norte
          del virreynato peruano*. Lima. Copy consulted is held in the Sterling
          Library, Yale University.

1979   "La rebelión de Túpac Amaru: organización interna, dirigencia y
          alianzas." *Histórica* 3, 2 (Lima): 89-121.

1982   "El movimiento tupacamarista: fases, coyuntura económica y perfil
          de la composición social de su dirigencia." In ACI, 461-85.

1985   *Rebellions and Revolts in Eighteenth Century Peru and Upper Peru*.
          Köln: Böhlau Verlag.

ORTIZ, DIONISIO
1969   *Chanchamayo: una región de la selva del Perú*. 2 vols. Lima.
1975-76   *Las montañas del Apurímac, Mantaro y Ene*. 2 vols. Lima.

PALACIO ATARD, VICENTE
1946   *Areche y Guirior. Observaciones sobre el fracaso de una visita al Perú*.
          Seville.

PERLMAN, JANICE E.
1976   *The Myth of Marginality: Urban Poverty and Politics in Rio de
          Janeiro*. Berkeley: University of California Press.

PHELAN, JOHN
1960   "Neo-Aztecism in the 18th Century and the Genesis of Mexican Na-
          tionalism." In Stanley Diamond, ed., *Culture in History*: 760-70.

1978   *The People and the King: The Comunero Revolution in Colombia,
          1781*. Madison: University of Wisconsin Press.

PLATT, TRISTAN
1982   *Estado boliviano y ayllu andino: tierra y tributo en el norte de Po-
          tosí*. Lima: Instituto de Estudios Peruanos.

PRICE, RICHARD
1979   "Introduction: Maroons and Their Communities." In Price, ed.,
          Maroon Societies: Rebel Slave Communities in the Americas (2d ed.,
          Baltimore). Pp. 1-30.

PRIETO DE ZEGARRA, JUDITH
1981   *Mujer, poder y desarrollo en el Perú*. 2 vols. Callao: Editorial Dorhca.

RELACIONES
1867-72   *Relaciones de los vireyes y audiencias que han gobernado el Perú.*
3 vols. Madrid.

RIVERA SERNA, RAÚL
1958   *Los guerrilleros del centro en la emancipación peruana.* Lima: Edición
Talleres Gráficos Villanueva, S.A.

ROEL PINEDA, VIRGILIO
1980   "Conatos, levantamientos, campañas e ideología de la independencia."
In Mejía Baca 1980: 6:9-392.

ROMERO, EMILIO
1937   *Historia económica y financiera del Perú: antiguo Perú y virreinato.*
Lima.

ROWE, JOHN
1951   "Colonial Portraits of Inca Nobles." In Sol Tax, ed., *The Civilizations of Ancient America: Proceedings of the XXIX International
Congress of Americanists* (Chicago). Pp. 258-68.
1954   "El movimiento nacional inca del siglo XVIII." As reprinted in Flores
G. 1976a: 11-66.

RUDÉ, GEORGE
1964   *The Crowd in History, 1730-1848.* New York: John Wiley & Sons.

RUÍZ LÓPEZ, HIPÓLITO
1777-88   *Relación histórica del viage, que hizo a los reynos del Perú y Chile
. . . en el año de 1777 hasta el de 1788. . . .* Ed. Jaime Jaramillo-
Arango. 2 vols. Madrid, 1952.

SÁNCHEZ-ALBORNOZ, NICOLÁS
1978   *Indios y tributos en el Alto Perú.* Lima: Instituto de Estudios
Peruanos.

SCOTT, JAMES
1976   *The Moral Economy of the Peasant: Rebellion and Subsistence in
Southeast Asia.* New Haven: Yale University Press.

SILVA SANTISTEBAN, FERNANDO
1964   *Los obrajes en el virreinato del Perú.* Lima.

SIMPOSIO SOBRE LA CAUSA DE LA EMANCIPACIÓN DEL PERÚ
1960   *La causa de la emancipación del Perú: Testimonios de la época precursora, 1780-1820.* Lima. Publication No. 26 of the Instituto Riva-
Agüero.

SPALDING, KAREN
1974   *De indio a campesino: Cambios en la estructura social del Perú
colonial.* Lima: Instituto de Estudios Peruanos.
1984   *Huarochirí, An Andean Society under Inca and Spanish Rule.* Stanford: Stanford University Press.

STERN, STEVE J.
1982   *Peru's Indian Peoples and the Challenge of Spanish Conquest: Huamanga to 1640.* Madison: University of Wisconsin Press.
1983   "The Struggle for Solidarity: Class, Culture, and Community in
Highland Indian America." *Radical History Review* 27: 21-45.

SZEMIŃSKI, JAN
1976   "La insurrección de Túpac Amaru II: ¿Guerra de independencia o revolución?" In Flores G. 1976a: 199–258.
1980   "Del significado de algunos términos usados en los documentos de la revolución tupamarista, 1780–1783." *Allpanchis* 16 (Cuzco): 89–130.
1982   "La concepción andina de historia: Su influencia en el movimiento tupamarista." ACI: 563–97.
1984   *La utopía tupamarista*. Lima: Pontífica Universidad Católica del Perú.

TAMAYO, JOSÉ ARMANDO
1980   *Historia del indigenismo cusqueño, siglos XVI–XX*. Lima.

TAYLOR, WILLIAM B.
1979   *Drinking, Homicide, and Rebellion in Colonial Mexican Villages*. Stanford: Stanford University Press.

THOMPSON, E. P.
1971   "The Moral Economy of the English Crowd in the Eighteenth Century." *Past and Present* 50 (Feb.): 76–136.

TORD NICOLINI, JAVIER
1974   "El corregidor de indios del Perú: comercio y tributos." *Historia y Cultura* 8: 173–214.

TORD NICOLINI, JAVIER, AND CARLOS LAZO GARCIA
1980   "Economía y sociedad en el Perú colonial (movimiento social)." In Mejía Baca 1980: 5:9–329.

VALCÁRCEL, CARLOS DANIEL
1947   *La rebelión de Túpac Amaru*. Reprint edition. Lima, 1973.
1960   "Finalidad social de Túpac Amaru." In Simposio sobre la causa . . . 1960: 43–46.

VALCÁRCEL, DANIEL
1946   *Rebeliones indígenas*. Lima.

VALEGA, JOSÉ M.
1939   *El virreinato del Perú*. Lima.
1940–43 *La gesta emancipadora del Perú*. 12 vols. Lima.

VALLE DE SILES, MARÍA EUGENIA
1977   "Túpac Katari y la rebelión de 1781. Radiografía de un caudillo aymara." *Anuario de Estudios Americanos* 34 (Seville): 633–64.

VALLEJO FONSECA, JOSÉ A.
1957   "La lucha por la independencia del Perú. La rebelión de 1742. Juan Santos Atahualpa." *Revista del Archivo Histórico del Cuzco* 8: 232–92.

VARALLANOS, JOSÉ
1959   *Historia de Huánuco*. Buenos Aires.

VARESE, STEFANO
1973   *La sal de los cerros (Una aproximación al mundo Campa)*. 2d ed. Lima.

VARGAS UGARTE, RUBÉN
1966–71 *Historia general del Perú*. 10 vols. Lima.

VOLLMER, GÜNTER
1967   *Bevölkerungspolitik und Bevölkerungsstruktur im Vizekönigreich Peru zu Ende der kolonialzeit (1741-1821)*. Bad Homburg.

WIGHTMAN, ANN M.
1983   "From Caste to Class in the Andean *Sierra*: The Seventeenth-Century *Forasteros* of Cuzco." Ph.D. diss., Yale University.

YANAMARCA
1840-42   "Yanamarca vs. Comunidades Concho y Acolla. 1840-1842." Notarial copy of legal suit, in possession of Don Moisés Ortega, Acolla. (Stern consulted notes to this document kindly provided by Florencia E. Mallon.)

ZAVALA, SILVIO
1978-80   *El servicio personal de los indios del Perú*. 3 vols. Mexico: El Colegio de México.

ZUDAIRE, EULOGIO
1979   *Don Agustín de Jáuregui y Aldecoa, virrey interino del Perú (1780-1784)*. Pamplona.

CHAPTER 3

A Test of Causal Interpretations of the Túpac Amaru Rebellion

MAGNUS MÖRNER and EFRAÍN TRELLES

Rural rebellions are often analyzed in terms of "peasant" behavior as related to space. (See Tilly 1976.) With respect to the Andean insurrections of the late eighteenth century, Leon G. Campbell (1979: 25) claimed that the understanding of the socioeconomic bases of the Andean subregions will eventually provide the "principles of variation and evolution of the phenomenon of indigenous revolt." Oscar Cornblit (1970) suggested a striking correlation in the case of the Andean rebellion under Túpac Amaru. It "spread like a wildfire throughout those regions where the proportion of foreign Indians [the *indios forasteros*, landless migrant Indians as opposed to the *originarios*, coholders of the communities] was highest," while it was "easily checked in regions . . . where the proportion of foreign Indians was much lower." Cornblit's observation was a mere conjecture lacking any systematic empirical basis.

In 1978, one of us (Mörner 1978: 109–29) made an attempt to correlate socioeconomic data for the Cuzco diocese, in 1786, with what was known about the various degrees of "rebelliousness" on the provincial level. One of the results was the rejection of Cornblit's generalization with respect to the indios forasteros because their share proved to be strikingly low precisely in the province of Canas y Canchis, the core area of the rebellion. In his book on the *repartos* (forced distribution of goods, described in Stern, Chapter 2 in this volume) and the Túpac Amaru rebellion, Jürgen Golte (1980) took a similar approach. Through tables and maps he attempted to correlate the great rebellion and factors like repartos and tribute.

However, the province level is obviously not close enough to the immediate social reality to serve for the correlation with popular attitudes in an environment characterized by extremely varied ecology and topography. That is why we found it worthwhile to try to analyze the relation, instead, on the parish level, far closer to social reality and the crucial decision-making process. This was possible because the socioeconomic data, already used on the province level, were also available for parishes and annexes. The real problem was that of selecting and documenting criteria for attitudes toward the rebellion on that same local level. What is presented here is merely a preliminary study based on available published documentation only. We devoted much time and effort to the careful screening and weighing of the data for each unit before computerization.[1] We chose to pursue two criteria or models, the first one being the attitude of local, mostly Indian leaders (model L), the other being popular attitudes as shown through collective actions for or against the rebellion (model C). Because, for local populations, the rebellion forced them to choose sides, we discerned rebellious attitudes (+) from loyalist ones (−) without bothering about those who succeeded in remaining more or less "neutral." We also decided to use two different sets of models, one based on very solid information, tied to the parish (restricted = y), the other slightly more generous in terms of the quality of evidence and with annexes being considered equally with parishes (amplified = yy). We were careful only to use the most rigorous methods.[2] Yet our purpose was not so much to advance new causal explanations but rather to test, and possibly reject, previous generalizations based on more impressionistic evidence. We recognized fully that causation in history is always a very intricate matter that cannot be resolved on the basis of quantification only. On the other hand, a quantitative approach has often proved its greatest usefulness by suggesting new avenues of research and the reformulation of old problems. The statement of an old problem in quantitative terms, as attempted here, may therefore quite naturally be followed in the ongoing process of inquiry by very different, qualitative approaches. In fact, one intriguing result of our research would point strongly in that direction.

The main results of our inquiry are presented in the tables to come in a very simple, easily readable way. The following variables have been included:

PI786   Indian population in 1786
PICHI   Absolute growth of Indian population, 1690–1786
SXRTI   Indian sex ratio in 1786 (males per 100 females)
PO786   Non-Indian population in 1786

POCHI   Absolute growth of non-Indian population, 1690–1786
SXRTO   Non-Indian sex ratio in 1786
TT786   Total population in 1786
TTCHI   Absolute growth of total population, 1690–1786
SXRTT   Sex ratio for total population in 1786
INDHA   Hacienda Indians in absolute numbers
INDHAR   Hacienda Indians as a share of Indian total
INDFR   Indios forasteros in absolute numbers
INFRR   Indios forasteros as a share of Indian total
NH786   Number of haciendas in 1786
HCNM   Number of hacienda owners given by name
ATTD   Altitude in meters above sea level

To start with models L (y) and L (yy), Tables 3.1 and 3.2 provide us a series of characteristics of rebel communities as compared to those of loyalist communities. Parishes run by rebel kurakas had, on average, a

Table 3.1. Summary of Model L (y): Leadership Attitudes during the Great War, and Parish Variables, 1786 (restricted model)

Variable	Rebel leadership			Loyalist leadership		
	Sum	n	x	Sum	n	x
PI786	24771	12	2064	32316	13	2486
PICHI	5739	12	478	19350	13	1488
SXRTI	1532	15	102	934	9	104
PO786	3724	12	310	4459	13	343
POCHI	2408	12	200	3403	10	340
SXRTO	1929	15	129	934	9	104
TT786	28495	12	2374	36775	13	2829
TTCHI[a]	8290	12	690	23270	13	1790
SXRTT	1540	15	103	934	9	104
INDHA	468	2	234	3806	7	544
INDHAR	72	2	36	333	6	56
INDFR	115	2	57	980	4	245
INFRR	33	2	16	140	4	35
NH786	54	8	7	132	13	10
HCNM	45	4	11	130	8	16
ATTD	56884	16	3555	43314	13	3321

Key: Sum = total of values observed; n = number of observations; x = average.
[a]In this and Tables 3.2, 3.3, and 3.4, the differences between TTCHI and (PICHI + POCHI) are due to the fact that at times only total change was registered, and at times only the Indians were listed.

Table 3.2. Summary of Model L (yy): Leadership Attitudes during the Great War, and Parish Variables, 1786 (amplified model)

Variable	Rebel leadership			Loyalist leadership		
	Sum	n	x	Sum	n	x
PI786	22582	27[a]	836	32316	16	2019
PICHI	5201	18	289	19350	16	1209
SXRTI	2647	26	102	1136	11	103
PO786	3575	17	132	4459	16	279
POCHI	1872	10	187	3603	12	300
SXRTO	3386	25	135	1401	11	127
TT786	26157	27	969	36775	16	2298
TTCHI	75082	18	421	23271	16	1454
SXRTT	2654	26	102	1141	11	104
INDHA	468	3	156	3811	9	423
INDHAR	122	3	41	364	8	45
INDFR	115	3	38	1069	5	214
INFRR	33	3	11	178	5	36
NH786	61	18	3	135	14	10
HCNM	45	5	9	141	11	13
ATTD	60370	17	3551	50316	15	3354

Key: Sum = total of values observed; n = number of observations; x = average.
[a]Of these, 14 refer to annexes.

considerably smaller Indian population than those of loyalist kurakas (2064/2486).[3] Their demographic growth since 1690, moreover, had been three times less. Table 3.2, corresponding to model L (yy), in which the annexes have been included independently from the parishes, shows the first phenomenon even more dramatically. While the Indian population average for the communities of rebel kurakas was only 836, that of loyalist communities amounted to 2019. Five annexes had been included among rebel villages, and only one among loyalist villages, in restricted model L (y). Logically, the demographic differences between the villages of rebel and loyalist leaders should be more clearly reflected in the amplified model L (yy). Naturally enough, the slow demographic growth in the communities under rebel leadership was above all characteristic of the Indian population. But to a lesser extent, the same was also true of non-Indian inhabitants (187/300). More relevant to the attitude toward rebellion was that in model L (yy), communities under rebel kurakas had on average only 132 non-Indian inhabitants, as compared to 279 in loyalist communities. Clearly, kurakas were freer to join the rebel camp in villages with fewer

"Spaniards."* As far as we know these aspects of our subject did not attract any scholarly attention before. The results are hardly sensational, but they may fit in with an atmosphere of frustration, poverty, and relative freedom from creole or mestizo interference.

Admittedly, our data with respect to hacienda Indians and forasteros are rather scarce, but the trend could hardly be more clear. According to model L (y), the communities of rebel kurakas counted an average of 234 hacienda Indians and 57 indios forasteros, as compared to 544 and 245 respectively in the opposite camp. This may be considered the ultimate proof that Cornblit was wrong as far as the Cuzco diocese is concerned. Logically, the communities of rebel kurakas also include a much smaller total number of "haciendas," classified as such in the 1786 reports: 54 to 132 according to the restricted model (y), 61 to 135 in the amplified model (yy). Our findings do not fit with the stereotype of hacienda serfs rising in violent protest against their landlords. Still, they do harmonize with larger evidence on rural mass risings in Latin America and elsewhere.

The altitude factor provides a rough ecological measure. In such an extremely varied environment as that of Cuzco, this indicator is no doubt somewhat arbitrary; yet, because it refers to the location of the local population center, extremes would tend to be avoided. The communities of rebel kurakas are found to be located on somewhat higher altitudes than those of their opponents (3555/3321 meters according to Table 3.1, and 3551/ 3354 according to Table 3.2). This observation clearly harmonizes with our results on haciendas and hacienda Indians.

When we turn to models C (y) and (yy) (that is, Tables 3.3 and 3.4), we mostly find similarities but also differences from our previous results that invite reflection or require explanation. According to the amplified model (yy), rebel communities were, on average, somewhat smaller than loyalist ones (750/863). However, the restricted model (y) surprisingly exhibits the opposite pattern (2134/1341). A partial explanation, at the least, is provided by the fact that two large rebel centers — Acos and Sangarará — were separated from their numerous annexes only in the ampli-

---

*Editor's Note: Readers should note that judging by Table 3.2, this statement appears to hold true *only* in terms of absolute numbers of "Spaniards" in a given village, not in terms of their relative numbers when compared to the Indian population. (Table 3.1 yields the same qualification.) The contrast seems to be one between a greater influx of non-Indians, in *absolute* terms, into more dynamic and growing communities, with the social networks and controls implied by such an influx; and a lesser pull on the non-Indian population by poorer or otherwise less attractive communities marked by slow population growth. Significantly, however, the impact of a greater or lesser Spanish presence appears to hold true *both* in a relative as well as absolute sense once one turns to collective rather than kuraka attitudes, as given in Tables 3.3 and 3.4.

Table 3.3. Summary of Model C (y): Collective Attitudes during the Great War, and Parish Variables, 1786 (restricted model)

Variable	Rebel communities			Loyalist communities		
	Sum	n	x	Sum	n	x
PI786	27736	13	2134	14751	11	1341
PICHI	7802	13	600	8356	11	758
SXRTI	1956	20	98	895	9	99
PO786	3913	13	301	4476	11	407
POCHI	1838	9	204	3309	8	413
SXRTO	2352	20	118	851	9	95
TT786	31649	13	2435	19227	11	1747
TTCHI	10929	13	840	6169	11	561
SXRTT	1669	20	98	863	9	96
INDHA	1019	5	204	2133	3	711
INDHAR	261	7	37	200	3	66
INDFR	1050	7	150	311	4	78
INFRR	92	7	13	122	2	61
NH786	100	14	7	88	11	8
HCNM	55	13	4	94	9	10
ATTD	57896	16	3619	31992	11	2908

Key: Sum = total of values observed; n = number of observations; x = average.

fied model (yy). A more intriguing contrast between the L and C models refers to demographic growth from 1690 to 1786. In the latter, rebel communities are shown to have experienced greater total demographic growth than their loyalist counterparts: 840/561 according to model C (y), 437/361 according to model C (yy). How should such a striking difference from the L models be explained? It seems to depend simply on the fact that two loyalist communities — Andahuaylillas and Maras — show a very great demographic decline during 1690–1786; they do not figure at all among the communities included in the L models. When analyzing our result, we must always keep each individual case in mind. As a consequence, the contrasts we first observe, eventually tend to become more blurred, but simultaneously occasional contradictory features prove less intriguing.

With respect to altitude, the C models show the same trend as the L models: rebel communities were located higher up. But the difference appears to have been more pronounced: 3619/2908 according to C (y), 3696/3234 meters according to C (yy). It should be kept in mind that in Cuzco the limit between the vertical zone of *suni* and that of *quechua* is at 3300 meters' altitude. In the higher zone, wheat, barley, broad beans, and potatoes are grown, and in the past oca, tarwi, and quinoa as well.

Table 3.4. Summary of Model C (yy): Collective Attitudes during the Great War, and
Parish Variables, 1786 (amplified model)

Variable	Rebel communities			Loyalist attitudes		
	Sum	n	x	Sum	n	x
PI786	27736	37	750	19845	23	863
PICHI	8274	25	331	3666	22	166
SXRTI	3732	37	101	1364	14	97
PO786	3913	37	106	5056	23	220
POCHI	1838	14	131	3649	13	281
SXRTO	4298	34	126	1345	14	96
TT786	31649	37	855	24861	23	1081
TTCHI	10929	25	437	7958	22	361
SXRTT	3725	37	101	1338	14	96
INDHA	1017	11	92	2133	3	711
INDHAR	395	11	35	200	3	67
INDFR	1050	13	81	509	5	101
INFRR	231	13	18	94	4	24
NH786	102	26	4	114	18	6
HCNM	55	13	4	118	14	8
ATTD	62846	17	3696	48508	23	3234

Key: Sum = total of values observed; n = number of observations; x = average.

In the lower quechua zone, maize has been the dominant crop (Gade 1975:
105ff.). Thus, at these altitudes a difference of some 450–700 meters is quite
significant. As a consequence, also, we should not be surprised that the
difference between hacienda Indians in rebel and loyalist communities ex-
presses itself even more clearly in the C models than in the L ones.
According to C (y), the average was 204 in rebel communities as compared to 711; according to C (yy), 92 to 711. On the other hand, the number of haciendas in the two camps did not differ notably.

Beyond the differences that we have noted between the L and C models,
there are at least some common characteristics that distinguished rebel
communities from loyalist ones. The former did appear more marginalized and were smaller. The number of Indians who had settled on the
haciendas was smaller, and the communities were located at higher altitudes. However, to get a clearer picture and draw closer to the geographic
and historical realities it is necessary to analyze our data by glancing at
Map 5 and Table 3.5.

Even a brief glance at the map would then show the concentration of
the rebel foci along the Vilcanota River in Canas y Canchis and Quispicanchis, while resistance was particularly strong to the north of the City

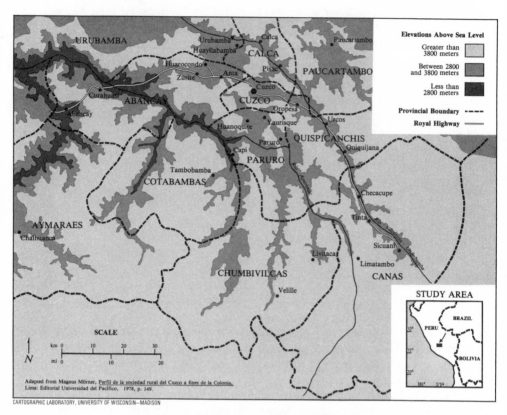

Map 5. The Cuzco Region in 1786

of Cuzco in the "Sacred Valley" of Urubamba. To get a more precise idea of these distributions in space, consider the figures in Table 3.5, derived from restricted models L (y) and C (y). It should be kept in mind that the population figures, based on counts in 1786, may have been somewhat affected by war casualties, at the least with regard to Calca and some districts of Canas y Canchis. In whatever case, polarization between rebel and loyalist kurakas in Canas y Canchis comes through very clearly. With respect to popular attitudes, the evidence underlying the C models reveals that participation for and against was especially widespread in Quispicanchis. In the loyalist camp, apart from the Quispicanchis contingent, people from Paruro were also conspicuous (33.5 percent of loyalists). The general predominance of Canas y Canchis within the rebel camp should lead us to reconsider some of our previous results. Thus, we concluded that rebel communities tended to be located higher up than loyalist ones. One should then not just think of villages lying high up on the mountain slopes.

Table 3.5. Spatial Distribution of Identified Rebels and Loyalists during the Túpac Amaru Rebellion, According to Models L (y) and C (y) and Population Data of 1786

	Absolute numbers	Percentage of Totals Located in:			Percentage of Total Population of:		
		Canas y Canchis	Quispi- canchis	Other Partidos	Canas y Canchis	Quispi- canchis	Other Partidos
Total population, 10 partidos/provinces of Cuzco (excluding the *cercado*)	174,623	16.5	14.8	68.6	–	–	–
Population under rebel kurakas	28,495	50.1	35.3	15.6	48.5	38.8	3.7
Population under loyalist kurakas	36,775	24.7	10.9	64.4	32.7	15.5	19.4
Population of rebel communities	31,649	26.5	50.1	23.4	29.1	27.7	23.5
Population of loyalist communities	19,227	0.0	37.6	62.4	0.0	27.7	10.0

In Canas y Canchis rebel communities, on the contrary, were clustered along the Vilcanota River: on lands that were low in the context of the province. Yet, their average altitude was much higher than in the provinces further north (Orlove 1977: 68–69). Also, the low number of haciendas, hacienda Indians and forasteros was another characteristic of Canas y Canchis. Due to the predominance of the province within the rebel camp, these features were reinforced within the totality of rebel communities as opposed to loyalist communities.

On the other hand, a glance at the distribution in space between rebel and loyalist communities will strengthen recent suggestions made by O'Phelan (1979, 1982), Campbell (1979), and others on the importance of conflict and rivalry between, on the one hand, the family network of Túpac Amaru on the Vilcanota River and, on the other, the aristocratic kurakas of the royal Inca ayllus of the city of Cuzco and along the Sacred Valley. As many as 10.3 percent of the population found by us to live in loyalist communities were inhabitants of the province of Calca. Also, the distribution of rebel populations conforms with the thesis of Juan José Vega (1969), Mörner (1978), and others that muleteering, Túpac Amaru's own profession, helped to launch and expand the rebellion.

The spatial dimension offers other insights as well, less directly related with but yet probably profoundly relevant to the rebellion. There is a document from 1577 giving rather detailed information on the four parts or *suyos* into which the Inca empire was divided. Tom Zuidema and Deborah

Table 3.6. The Four Suyos of the Inca Empire (Tawantinsuyo) and the Attitudes of Cuzco Communities and Leaders toward the Túpac Amaru Rebellion (y models)

CHINCHASUYO		
1. Pucyura	L –	
2. Maras		C –
3. Chinchero	L –	C –
4. Calca	L –	C –
5. Lares	L –	C –
6. Ollantaitambo		C –

Another 5 communities in 1577 (Zuidema and Poole 1982).

Other units from models L and C (y) in the zone:

7. Surite	L –	C –
8. Huarocondo	L –	C –
9. Anta	L –	C –

ANDESUYO		
1. Pisac	L –	

Another 8 communities in 1577 (Zuidema and Poole 1982).

Other units from models L and C (y) in the zone:

2. Taray	L –	
3. Catca	L –	
4. Oropesa	L –	
5. Andahuaylillas		C –
6. Urcos		C –

HANAN SUYO

CONDESUYO		
1. Huanoquite	L –	
2. Paruro		C –
3. Accha Hanan		C –
4. Accha Hurin		C –
5. Capacmarca		C –
6. Colquemarca	L +	C +
7. Livitaca	L +	C +
8. Velille	L +	C +

Another 14 communities in 1577 (Zuidema and Poole 1982).

Other units from models L and C (y) in the zone:

9. Pilpinto	L –	
10. Rondocan	L +	
11. Omacha		C +

COLLASUYO		
1. Quihuares	L +	C +
2. Marcaconga		C +
3. Acos	L +	
4. Sangarará-Acomayo	L +	C +
5. Pomacanche	L +	C +
6. Acopia		C +
7. Yanaoca	L +	
8. Tinta	L +	C +
9. Checacupe	L +	
10. Combapata	L +	
11. Layosupa	L +	
12. Cacha	L +	
13. Pichigua		C +
14. Yauri	L +	
15. Coporaque	L –	

Another 9 communities in 1577 (Zuidema and Poole 1982).

Other units from models L and C (y) in the zone:

16. Pitumarca	L +	
17. Pampamarca	L +	
18. Quiquijana		C +
19. Yarampampa		C +
20. Pueblo Nuevo		C +
21. Huayllque		C +
22. Ocongate		C +
23. Marcapata		C +
24. Sicuani	L –	

HURIN SUYO

Note: "+" signifies rebellious attitudes, and "−" signifies loyalist attitudes.

Poole (1982) have made an effort of reconstructing that division on the map. We include Table 3.6, comparing their results with data from our own restricted models L (y) and C (y). The juxtaposition of the data reveals an extraordinarily high degree of correlation. The ancient Collasuyo, with very few exceptions, emerges as the cradle of the rebellion. As it happens, loyalist Coporaque was the southernmost community and rather isolated from the rest.[4] With all of its communities in the loyalist camp, ancient Chinchasuyo forms the most glaring contrast to Collasuyo. The same applies to the northern part of ancient Condesuyo, including Capacmarca in the south of Paruro. Farther south in Condesuyo, however, rebellious attitudes prevail which are not so hard to explain. Notwithstanding the poverty and roughness of the environment, this latter zone, in 1786 already, had a largely non-Indian population. In the province/partido of Chumbivilcas, mestizos formed 37.5 percent of the total population. In this case, then, links with the Inca past ought to be weak. On the other hand, the people of Chumbivilcas, be they Indian or mestizo, seem to have largely devoted themselves to muleteering. Thus, their prorebellion stance in favor of fellow arriero Túpac Amaru in the beginning of the rebellion is easy to explain. With respect to ancient Andesuyo, our data are rather scarce and barely permit generalizations. Whatever its explanation, we do find a loyalist focus in the corner closest to the city of Cuzco. In the province/partido of Paucartambo no less than about 75 percent of the Indians had settled down on the "Spanish" haciendas. As in the case of Chumbivilcas, it is possible that their links with the Inca past were weaker than in the districts where communities prevailed.

At this stage of our labor we can merely pose the question of why the coincidences with ancient Inca divisions occurred. They cannot possibly be dismissed as mere chance. Much reflection and research will, indeed, be required to resolve that problem. It could be the question of authentic tradition expressing itself in regional consciousness and solidarity. But it may also reflect some aspects of the eighteenth-century Incaic "renaissance" that John Rowe (1954) has discussed. Another possible alternative would be the continued impact of topographical and ecological features on human relationships. Thus, the same factors that determined Incaic boundary lines would still be active in the late eighteenth century. In fact, as shown by Deborah Poole (1982) in her fascinating study on religious sanctuaries in Paruro, the latter were at the same time barter centers between different systems of production and the scenes of interethnic oppositions. At the festival of Pampak'ucho, the maize growers of Paruro and Acomayo met with the cattle breeders of Chumbivilcas. At the festival of Sankha, the cultivating Chillques of Condesuyo met with the Papres shepherds of Collasuyo. We should add that the fourfold Incaic division of the suyos also expressed another divisory principle, that is, the dualism pervading every aspect of the Andean world. The opposition and complementary character of the dichotomy between Hanan-superior and Hurin-inferior gave rise to exceedingly complex patterns (Hocquenghem 1983). Among the suyos, the opposition between Chinchasuyo and Collasuyo was especially intense, and, as it happens, perfectly in line with the pattern of attitudes for and against rebellion we have traced. However, within each suyo, there was apparently also a division between Hanan and Hurin sectors as viewed from the center. The Hanan sectors on the right simultaneously carried superiority and masculinity. Also, every population broke down into Hanan and Hurin ayllus or fragments. As a consequence, there were also kurakas pertaining to the two categories. We may ask ourselves if this principle of division, deeprooted as it was, affected the attitudes of the kurakas and their communities in favor or against the Túpac Amaru rebellion, but we do not venture any answers at this juncture. However, we can notice even today the existence of ritual battles between neighboring communities in the Southern Andes. In the south of Cuzco, such battles were regularly celebrated between, for instance, Langui and Checa, and between the latter and Livitaca (see Skar 1982: 91–102; Alencastre and Dumézil 1953). We cannot exclude the possibility of an impact of such ingrained patterns on the different options pursued by the communities in the course of the Túpac Amaru conflagration. Our discussion about the impact of Incaic boundaries on collective behavior during the great rebellion must conclude here, however, in the same way as we entered it: as a matter of conjecture. Nonetheless, we hope to have advanced scholarly knowledge about the actual division of the rural populations of Cuzco into rebels and loyalists during the great Andean rebellion of 1780.

METHODOLOGICAL APPENDIX

The basis for our characterization of attitudes has been the perusal of all available published sources on the rebellion (above all CDIP 1971–75: 2; and CDB 1982). The sources can be ranged in a decreasing order of confidence, as follows:

(a) Secret rebel reports
(b) Secret authority reports
(c) Reports related to the municipal council (*cabildo*) of Cuzco
(d) Individual opinions.

On principle, references belonging to groups (a) and (b) were considered solid evidence if not contradicted. Information of other origin was only considered solid if backed up by further, strong evidence. In the codification of the data, the norms of the Statistical Package for the Social Sciences (SPSS) were adhered to. The Taurus system of the University of Texas was used. Care was taken to distinguish between the absence of a positive observation as an indicator that the phenomenon is missing, and as an indicator that observations are missing. Also, we used the restricted (y) and amplified (yy) models to make it possible to read the administrative data differently: at the parish *or* annex level only, and as a parish together with its annexes. Our information comprises a total of 226 units with 73 variables each. We already noted in the text that two models were used, L = leadership and C = community action. The division into rebel (+) and loyalist (−) varieties of each model has already been explained, as have the two different sets of models (y) and (yy).

The way in which primary sources and the data of two historians have been used to document our different models is shown below:

Table 3.7. Source Distribution in the Y Models

Model	IR	IA	IRC	OI	SCA	LEV	Total
L +	4	4	1	−	10	−	19
L −	−	5	8	2	6	3	24
C +	17	6	4	−	1	−	28
C −	7	7	4	−	−	−	18
Total	28	22	17	2	17	3	89

Key:	IR	= rebel reports	OI	= individual opinions
	IA	= authority reports	SCA	= O'Phelan Godoy (1979)
	IRC	= cabildo reports	LEV	= Lewin (1957)

We can notice that the treatment of sources is hardly skewed. It is only natural that, for example, the identification of rebel communities (C +) largely rests on rebel reports. Conflicting cases such as Pomacanchis, Acomayo, Combapata, Checacupe, Quiquijana, Taray, Pisac, Langui, and Layo were only given their qualifications after lengthy research, presented in a more detailed Spanish version of this study (see note 1). Our use of the amplified models (yy) may seem somewhat controversial. One of the reasons we use them is in order to give core parishes and annexes the same weight. Another is the need for a simple presentation of statistical complexities, with reference to "nontraditional" statistical material. (See, for example, Diaconis and Efton 1983.) It should be kept in mind that for all our search for precision, we are not interested in absolute quantities as a final result but in relationships such as those between the restricted (y) and amplified (yy) models. If comparable, both gain in veracity. If not, it is necessary to find out if the discrepancies merely follow from codification and calculation methods or are, indeed, substantial. Such changes as can be derived from the structure of the models are especially enlightening in the study of parish-annex linkages. As an example, we can take the Indian population of Sangarará and its annexes (PI786) and population change, 1690–1786 (PICHI), according to the (y) and (yy) models respectively.

Table 3.8. Indian Population of Sangarará: Annexes and Population Change, 1690–1786

	(y)		(yy)	
	PI786	PICHI	PI786	PICHI
Sangarará	3690	2113	1003	553
Marcaconga			1034	553
Yanampampa			266	216
Acopia			680	460
Pueblo Nuevo			707	nd
Total	3690	2113	3690	2113

The correlation between demographic growth and population size comes out very clearly in the amplified version (yy). The tables containing our complete models are included in the more comprehensive Spanish version of our study. Our files with references to documentation for the qualification of the various units were too bulky to include in either version. Colleagues interested may obtain information upon request.[5] Finally, it should be stressed that on the whole our categorization of attitudes rests on data from the end of 1780, at the height of the rebellion after the battle of Sangarará on 18 November. Timing is obviously crucial, but is detailed only in our files. Also, even a parish or an annex may prove too gross a spatial unit to cover adequately the background of political decision making. Yet we can envision no possibility to descend to the level of *parcialidades* but in exceptional cases. A systematic study of kuraka genealogy, however, would permit further elaboration of our models. Historian David Cahill (1984) appears to be at work with this task.

NOTES

1   This is shown in detail in the more comprehensive Spanish version of the present study, "Un intento de calibrar las actitudes hacia rebelión en el Cuzco durante la acción de Túpac Amaru", issued in 1985 as a research paper by the Institute of Latin American Studies (Box 6909, S-10239 Stockholm, Sweden). See also the Methodological Appendix.

2   The authors met at the University of Texas in Austin in early 1983. The study was carried out in collaboration on the basis of correspondence but most of

the research and the entire computerization was made by Trelles. The present paper was written by Mörner. Our thanks are due to the Department of History of the University of Texas for use of their generous computer facilities, and to the organizers and participants of the Meeting on "Resistance and Rebellion in the Andean World, 18th to 20th Centuries," held at the University of Wisconsin-Madison in April 1984, for helpful criticism when the first draft was presented there. At a seminar at the History Department of the University of Cologne, West Germany, and at a "Peruvian Workshop" at the Latin American Center, Liverpool, both in December 1984, the draft was also summarized by Mörner. Some constructive criticism was also received on these occasions.

3   It should be kept in mind that the kurakas were more numerous than our territorial units and that their density (like their degree of control) varied widely. They formed 0.2 percent of all Indian males in Urubamba and Quispicanchis, 1.4 percent in Canas y Canchis and as many as 1.7 percent in Aymaraes in 1786. See Vollmer 1967: 284; Golte 1980: 153-64.

4   In Coporaque, the kuraka Eugenio Sinanyuca — enemy and yet relative of Túpac Amaru — played a crucial role. It is, in fact, more enigmatic that Sicuani followed the loyalist kuraka Simón Callo, notwithstanding its location in the midst of rebel territory and presence of several other, prorebel kurakas. The role of the other principal kuraka, Miguel Zamalloa, a "Spaniard," appears more uncertain.

5   Mörner's address is: Snöhöjdsstigen 10, S-431 39 Mölndal, Sweden; Trelles's address, at present, Percy Gibson 395, Lima 14, Peru.

REFERENCES

ALENCASTRE, ANDRÉS, AND GEORGE DUMÉZIL
  1953   "Fêtes et usages des indiens de Langui (Province de Canas, Département de Cuzco)." *Journal de la Société des Américanistes* 42 (Paris): 1-118.

CAHILL, DAVID
  1984   *"Curas* and Social Conflict in the Doctrinas of Cuzco, 1780-1814." *Journal of Latin American Studies* 16 (London): 241-76.

CAMPBELL, LEON G.
  1979   "Recent Research on Andean Peasant Revolts, 1750-1820." *Latin American Research Review* 14, 1: 3-49.

CDB
  1982   *Colección del Bicentenario de Túpac Amaru.* Lima.

CDIP (Comisión Nacional del Sesquicentenario de la Independencia del Perú)
  1971-75   *Colección documental de la independencia del Perú.* 27 vols. Lima.

CORNBLIT, OSCAR
  1970   "Society and Mass Rebellion in Eighteenth-Century Peru and Bolivia." In Raymond Carr, ed., *Latin American Affairs* (St. Anthony's Papers No. 22), 9-44.

DIACONIS, PERSI, AND B. EFTON
1983   "Computer-intensive Methods in Statistics." *Scientific American* 248,
        5: 116–30.

GADE, DANIEL
1975   *Plants, Man and the Land in the Vilcanota Valley of Peru.* The Hague.

GOLTE, JÜRGEN
1980   *Repartos y rebeliones. Túpac Amaru y las contradicciones de la econo-
        mía colonial.* Lima: Instituto de Estudios Peruanos.

HOCQUENGHEM, ANNE MARIE
1983   "Hanan y Hurin, un modelo de organización y clasificación del mundo
        andino." *Amerindia* 3 (Paris): 3–61.

LEWIN, BOLESLAO
1957   *La rebelión de Túpac Amaru y los orígenes de la independencia de
        Hispanoamérica.* Buenos Aires.

MÖRNER, MAGNUS
1978   *Perfil de la sociedad rural del Cuzco a fines de la colonia.* Lima.

O'PHELAN GODOY, SCARLETT
1979   "La rebelión de Túpac Amaru, organización interna, dirigencia y
        alianzas." *Histórica* 3, 2 (Lima): 89–121.

1982   "Elementos étnicos y de poder en el movimiento tupacamarista,
        1780–81." *Nova Americana* 5 (Torino): 79–101.

ORLOVE, BENJAMIN S.
1977   *Alpacas, Sheep and Men.* New York: Academic Press.

POOLE, D.
1982   "Los santuarios religiosos en la economía regional andina (Cusco)."
        Allpanchis 19 (Cusco): 79–116.

ROWE, JOHN
1954   "El movimiento nacional inca del siglo XVIII." Reprinted in Alberto
        Flores Galindo, ed., *Túpac Amaru II, 1780. Antología* (Lima, 1976),
        11–66.

SKAR, HARALD O.
1982   *The Warm Valley People.* Oslo.

TILLY, CHARLES
1976   *The Vendee.* 2d ed. Cambridge: Harvard University Press.

VEGA, JUAN JOSÉ
1969   *José Gabriel Túpac Amaru.* Lima.

VOLLMER, GÜNTER
1967   *Bevölkerungspolitik und Bevölkerungsstruktur im Vizekönigreich
        Peru zu Ende der Kolonialzeit (1741–1821).* Bad Homburg.

ZUIDEMA, R. T., AND D. POOLE
1982   "Los límites de los cuatro suyos incáicos en el Cusco." *Bulletin de
        l'Institut français des études andines* 11, 1/2 (Lima): 83–89.

CHAPTER 4

Ideology and Factionalism during the Great Rebellion, 1780–1782

LEON G. CAMPBELL

The historiography of Spanish America in the eighteenth century has often been written in terms of the nature and effects of the Bourbon reforms, that complex of political and economic measures usually associated with the reign of King Charles III (1759–1788). This in turn has directly influenced researches into the subject of late colonial rebellion, frequently viewed as a response to these innovations. Seminal works on the "Great Rebellion" of 1780–1782 (Cornejo Bouroncle 1949; Lewin 1957; L. E. Fisher 1966) emphasized that the Bourbon measures designed to increase revenues and centralize political administration also provoked a series of unwelcome changes in the Indian world which produced rebellion on a larger and more serious scale than had ever been witnessed in Spanish America. More recent research into the subject of domestic protest in Andean America has begun to question simple correlations of social and economic dislocation with rebellion in late colonial Peru (see the chapters by Stern and by Mörner and Trelles in Part I) and has also suggested the need for alternative intepretive schemes which extend the geographical focus of these insurrections outward from their presumed center in Cuzco to other areas. In addition, greater attention to changes in Andean consciousness — defined as the self-identifications, cultural meaning systems, interpretations of contemporary society, and aspirations for the future which shaped political behavior — will lead to a better understanding of the origins, nature, and ultimate meaning of Andean resistance and rebellion (Campbell 1979; also chapters by Stern, Salomon, and Szemiński in this volume). This chapter explores the relationship between rebel ideology and the organizational structure of insurrection between 1780 and

1782, and as such is intended as a contribution to the reinterpretation of colonial Andean social movements.

Any reassessment of the Age of Andean Insurrection might properly begin by accepting the broad framework of analysis proposed earlier by John Rowe (1954) and Boleslao Lewin (1957). Although Rowe's now classic analysis of what he termed an Inca nationalist movement implicitly accepts the idea of a unified *Incario*, or area of the former Inca Empire, it constitutes an appropriate concept embracing the several rebellions occurring in areas as far apart as La Paz, Puno, Sorata, Oruro, Cuzco, Arequipa, and Huarochirí, among others. Moreover, the focus on Inca nationalism, which needs further testing as an ideology and organizational strategy, frees the debate from the classic "Western-Hispanic definition of time and place" in which native movements are defined and explained as the indigenous counterparts to creole movements for independence (Lewin 1957; Valcárcel 1970). Under such a construct, the history of Andean America is approached in terms of native mentalities and behavior rather than as simply an aspect of the history of Spain in Peru. At the same time, we need to study the several native rebellions that are comprised in the great insurrection in the context of their specific regional dynamics rather than as part of a more general, unified movement in which rebel leaders worked together under common auspices for similar ends. Freed from defining rebellion in terms of the geographic center of gravity in Cuzco also allows us to consider the degree to which regional rebellions within the insurrectionary mobilization, such as those in Oruro in 1781 and Huarochirí in 1783, do not conform to general patterns of Inca nationalism.

Existing chronological schematics of native revolt and rebellion in the Andean area during the later colonial period also deserve further refinement. Both Golte (1980: 141–47) and O'Phelan (1982: 461–88) have attempted to set down known revolts after midcentury in Peru from the time of that initiated by Juan Santos Atahualpa on the Tarma-Jauja frontier in the 1740s to the few events taking place in the aftermath of the Great Rebellion of 1780. Most of the basic research to date, however, restricts this chronology to events taking place in southern Cuzco and cresting in the rebellion led by José Gabriel Túpac Amaru Inca on November 4, 1780, in Tinta. Under such a schematic, no fewer than 66 revolts, plots, insurrections, *tumultos*, and other miniconjunctures of violence are categorized in terms of a "preparatory cycle" of discontent which eventually produced the major conflagration of 1780. The Great Rebellion itself is divided into at least two phases: a "tupamarista phase," dominated by Túpac Amaru's activities and leadership among the Quechua peoples of southern Peru in 1780–1781, and a "katarista phase," dominated by the activities of the Katari brothers among the Aymara peoples of the Bolivian altiplano in 1781–1782. Despite the fact that fully two-thirds of the area embraced by the Great Rebellion was situated in the *Collado* provinces of Larecaja, Sicasica, Pacajes, and Omasuyos surrounding the sacred Lake Titicaca and La Paz, historians presuming "rational" political and military objectives for the rebels, such as the capture of Cuzco, have neglected the important dimensions of Aymara culture and history in defining the nature and meaning of the Great Rebellion. In effect, the chronology of the Great Rebellion has produced a historiography of Andean protest movements which magnifies events taking place in the southern Cuzco provinces of Canas y Canchis (Tinta), Quispicanchis, and Chumbivilcas during the intensive activity of the six months between November 1780 and May 1781, when Túpac Amaru was executed. This approach marginalizes and diminishes events taking place outside of Cuzco and set within a separate cultural context outside of the former Inca capital.

In a book on Huarochirí, Karen Spalding (1984) has clarified the types and locations of traditional "fault lines" in Andean society, that is, hostilities between individuals, communities, and regions which were only partially and temporarily overcome by norms of reciprocity and exchange. If this well-accepted feature of Andean social history is applied to the social movements under consideration here, any attempt to understand the phenomenon of rebellion must explore the means by which elites and regional groups were able to set aside hostilities in a native society at least as hierarchical and internally differentiated as creole society, and in particular, how rebel leaders unified the Indian masses under their banner.

Early on, John Rowe (1954) explored the possibilities whereby caciques could and did confront Spanish authorities, especially local corregidores, and how certain caciques drew on accounts of prehistory such as Garcilaso de la Vega's *Comentarios Reales de los Incas* (1966), which not only glorified the Inca past, but also, in its late colonial versions, may have even called for rebellion against the Spanish, in order to keep alive the concept of Inca *recuperación*, or recovery of sovereignty (Szemiński 1984: 33). The idea of an Inca recovery, as a manifestation of an organized Inca legacy reproduced throughout the colonial period, is necessarily elusive. Material evidence uniting the Inca order of the sixteenth century to rebel organization in the eighteenth is problematic, imbued as the latter was with three centuries of Hispanic domination. Nevertheless, despite the difficulties of linking eighteenth-century Incaic concepts, organizations, and traditions with continuities from the Inca past, a number of scholars interested in the subject (Gisbert 1980; Wachtel 1976: 169–87; Ossio 1973; Stern 1982; Curatola 1977; Rowe 1954; Hidalgo 1983; Szemiński 1984; Campbell 1985a) are cognizant of the recurring presence, since early colonial times, of belief in an alternative, utopian, Andean social order, sometimes with strong ideological ties to the old Inca order. The question is: how can we relate this Andean belief system to the subject of late colonial rebellion at hand?

In the first place, not since the investigations of Rowe has the subject of eighteenth-century social protest movements been reviewed in the context of an Andean belief system which revived the myth of *Inkarrí*, an ancient Creator who would return to restore justice and harmony, as the legitimizing linchpin of the movement. As Steve Stern has observed in his companion essay in this volume, "colonial Andean history is littered with failed insurrectionary conspiracies" (p. 59). Each of these is of some importance in explaining the process whereby changes in individual perceptions of the state took place, and relationships between classes and ethnic groups were fundamentally altered. Too often the subject of resistance and rebellion focuses narrowly on actual outbreaks of major rebellion such as that of 1780 without judging the broader record of minor, failed resistance against aspects of life under Spanish rule.

The comprehensive approach to the Great Rebellion would thus investigate the Túpac Amaru rebellion as a logical continuation of the rebellion of 1777 led by Tomás Katari, the cacique of Macha, Chayanta in Upper Peru, who, like his counterpart Túpac Amaru, developed a strong local reputation as a defender of his people and challenged local authorities whom he condemned as immoral and unfit to govern prior to taking up arms. In both cases, these leaders left their homelands of Chayanta and Tinta to travel to the viceregal capitals (Buenos Aires and Lima), where they made contact with representatives of the Spanish king but failed to achieve their goals. Subsequently, both returned home professing to have obtained authority in the form of direct orders from the king, whom they saw as a shadowy but benign personage who had authorized them to take action against his corrupt representatives (Lewin 1957: 331–93). Shortly thereafter, these rebels also began to appropriate to themselves the titles of Governor or Inca and to operate more independently. Szemiński's essay in this volume explains the apparently contradictory behavior of the rebels who professed loyalty to the Crown while attacking his functionaries and accepting the mantle of Inkarrí, in terms of a native mentality which viewed the Indies as a separate realm from "Spain." Under these circumstances, a king "over there" (in Spain) could justifiably issue an order against persons "over here" (in Peru). As Szemiński demonstrates, the relationship between God, King, and Inkarrí combined in an ideology so complex that the natives saw no inconsistency in the fact that rebel leaders ordained by the Andean Creator God Wiracocha might accept the mantle of Inkarrí while executing the king's orders also.

Despite the fact that they could find no direct evidence of contact between Tomás Katari in Macha and Túpac Amaru Inca in Tinta, historians such as Lewin and others reported the rebellions as sequential events and attempted to join them despite the fact that the two caciques were residents of different viceroyalties, separated by a distance of 1400 kilometers, and dominated by different cultures (Aymara and Quechua). One (Katari) called for a reduction in tribute levels (CDIP 1971-75: 2:238-40) yet the other (Túpac Amaru) did not make such a suggestion, but instead simply appropriated this exaction for himself as king. Since regional levels of economic hardship varied between the two regions and between social strata (Golte 1980: 176-83; O'Phelan 1983), it would seem that efforts to explain the cogeneration and spread of rebellion might be profitably pursued through the mechanism of native belief systems.

In a recent book on peasant society in early modern France, Robert Darnton (1984: vii) has argued that to understand the sometimes curious behavior of rural people, especially in their dealings with elites, it is necessary to approach human behavior as "a system of meaning rather than a function of the social structure," in an effort to find deeper meanings and continuous patterns for actions that might otherwise appear to be capricious or even irrational. Although the approach is not entirely new, Darnton's emphasis on the roles of myth and symbolism, of ritual and response, and of actions set within belief systems which seem periodically to call for open revolt against authority, thereby giving revolt a cumulative, cyclical character stronger than the individual events themselves, seems to have applicability to the events at hand. Moreover, the author contends that the history of *mentalités*, when reduced to an attempt to measure attitudes by counting (e.g., revolts), has neglected to "read" these cultural objects as a means of understanding the rebel universe and the social dimensions of their beliefs. How might such an investigation be structured?

It is the purpose of this chapter first to explore the relationships between persistent Andean belief systems of the mid-eighteenth century and the spread of rebellion, both as a means of understanding the organization of the movements centered in Cuzco, Sorata, Puno, and La Paz, as well as the meaning of these and other conjunctures of violence. A further purpose is to explore the relationship between rebel ideology, notably the inherently divisive Inkarrí myth, which was predicated on the idea of rule by a crowned Inca noble of Cuzco, and the factionalism which developed between the two major forces in the Great Rebellion—the tupamaristas of Cuzco and the kataristas of La Paz—in an effort to define the limits of ideological unity and to help to explain the meaning of certain aspects of rebel behavior (e.g., the sieges of Cuzco and La Paz) which seem to run counter to "rational" military strategy and warfare. Third, the essay recognizes the profound differences between neo-Inca nationalism as it was expounded by the elitist Túpac Amarus of Cuzco, whose purpose was to unite everyone who was not a "Spaniard," and the radical, populist, and separatist views held by the commoner, indigenous Kataris of Upper Peru, whose ideas were shaped by the strong presence of native community leadership.

This study attempts to relate the factors of Andean ideology and political factionalism, and those of material exploitation and moral outrage within the context of a revived *Incario*, as a guide to future inquiries. My general approach recognizes that Upper Peru was a major, distinctive focus of rebellion, despite the works of Lewin, Valcárcel, and Fisher which have tended to consider the Great Rebellion as emanating and deriving from Cuzco. Writing on the eve of the Túpac Amaru rebellion in Tinta, Visitor General José Antonio de Areche wrote from Lima that by that time rebellion had advanced strongly in Upper Peru and that no fewer than nine provinces, including those of Sicasica, Pilaya, Cochabamba, Paria, Pacajes, Chichas, Lipez, Porco, and Carangas had been affected (AGI 1780). Additionally, I will consider rebellion in Upper and Lower Peru within a context of Andean time, which views temporal change in terms of a series of *pachacutis*, or cataclysms, led by representatives of Wiracocha, the Andean Creator God, who are deemed to have returned to earth to reverse the existing, unjust world order (Szemiński 1984: 50; Gow 1982: 197–223). Using this cyclical context, it is possible to link more comfortably the actions of native rebels beginning with Juan Santos Atahualpa, and continuing with Tomás Katari, Túpac Katari, Túpac Amaru Inca, and Felipe Velasco Túpac Inca Yupanqui, all of whom drew on the traditions and beliefs then prevalent in the Andean world. This concept of Andean time suggests too that the roles played by charismatic native leaders such as Juan Santos Atahualpa, Julián Apasa Túpac Katari, and Túpac Amaru Inca may have been important in fostering the cogeneration of Andean rebellion by reviving the concept of *recuperación*, or recovery, and allowing it to move from the periphery of Tarma and Jauja in the 1740s, to Upper Peru after 1777, and finally to the Cuzco–La Paz corridor after 1780 (Curatola 1977). Thus, the events of 1780 may be less the "logical" culmination of a decade of several (66 or more) local, antifiscal revolts than the continuation of a series of messianic, nativist, neo-Inca protests (Golte 1980: 141–47; O'Phelan 1982: 27). For example, Jorge Hidalgo (1983: 117–38) has demonstrated that as early as 1777, the Indians of Cuzco had not only chosen a king but had planned a general uprising which corresponded to preordained changes in Andean cosmology, and that such

prophecies were commonly known. Visitor Areche contended that he had
been warned as early as 1775 by territorial judges about the possibility
of a pan-Andean uprising planned for 1777, "The Year of the Three
Sevens," which had great, but mysterious significance to the natives (Campbell 1978: 100–1). Some of these prophecies were even published in
chronicles of the times published in Cuzco in 1782 (*Relación de los hechos
mas notables* 1900: 501–32). This chapter develops no "general theory"
to explain the advent of the Great Rebellion; it maintains only that causality
must be determined in its appropriate cultural context.

ANDEAN BELIEF SYSTEMS AND THE SPREAD OF REBELLION

John Rowe (1980) has described the extensive efforts made by Túpac
Amaru after 1770 to secure from the Spanish legal validation of his direct
descent from the Royal Inca line, and demonstrates the efforts which elite
native families made to link themselves to the neo-Inca traditions which
joined them in turn to the Inca past. This and other evidence suggests that
the Great Rebellion was part of a larger effort of cultural recovery, whatever else it might also have signified, and was not, as J. R. Fisher has stated
(1970: 23), a spontaneous and unplanned outburst by Indians driven in
frustration to revolt. The question is: what did Túpac Amaru intend to
accomplish?

An assessment of Túpac Amaru's behavior subsequent to the capture
of the corregidor Antonio de Arriaga on November 4, 1780, suggests that
the rebel chief acted on the calculated risk that he could persuade the inhabitants of southern Cuzco to accept his command in an effort to drive
the Spaniards out of the southern provinces of Tinta and perhaps Quispicanchis where he was aware that discontent was high. Yet this intention
does not explain why this revolt was able to develop into a regional and
eventually a supraregional rebellion unlike, say, community revolts in
Mexico (Taylor 1979). Despite the belief of certain historians of Andean
history and consciousness that the seeds of a protonational Andean identity
were germinating throughout the region at this time (Flores G. 1981: 55–70;
Durand F. 1973), none of them suggest that these sentiments were
sufficiently developed to sustain a rebellion, although Rowe (1954) hints
that this may have been true. Kubler (1946: 350) demonstrates that an
active cult of Inca antiquity had flourished in Cuzco from at least
midcentury, carried on by both creoles, who adopted Inca dress and
furnishings, and caciques, who proudly exhibited the ancient symbol of
the Sun God and of the Incas in public ceremonies. The Bishop of Cuzco
even noted that during the celebration of Corpus Christi and Santiago
the Apostle, Christian deities were dressed in Inca garb (Peru 1980:

2:633–34, 637). Yet can we presume that this nostalgic reaffirmation of Inca glories was strong enough to fuel a major rebellion? More specifically, what sort of a cosmology linking God, the Spanish King, and the Inca might have developed which was capable of sustaining this Andean conception of history and view of the future?

In a series of publications, Jan Szemiński (1976, 1980, 1984, and Chapter 6 in this volume) has begun to suggest ways in which the natives could have developed an ideology which was sufficiently cohesive to counter the divisiveness of Peruvian regional society, which was wary of outsiders and internally divided. His description of Andean society depicts a social world composed of a series of estates in which *españoles* (Spaniards) and *indios* (Indians) often differed little in social terms although widely in terms of their access to economic resources or systems of justice. Szemiński further contends that as the natives' level of dissatisfaction with Spanish colonialism increased during the eighteenth century, rebel leaders found success in helping to foster a conceptual framework which distinguished between Spaniards and Indians on moral grounds as a pretext for action.

In Tarma in the 1740s, for example, Stern has demonstrated (Chapter 2 in this volume) that it was possible for an outsider and possibly even a mestizo named Juan Santos Atahualpa to appropriate the myth of Inkarrí to gain adherents among the Campa tribes of the interior despite the fact that he was opposed by the powerful *caciques gamonales* of the region. Using his knowledge of magic and symbolism, Juan Santos fashioned a legend of invincibility about himself which persisted well after his death and kept alive the hope of a successful Inca liberation movement thereafter.

Clearly the presence of Andean resurrection myths, described by numerous scholars of the Andean area (Wachtel 1976: 291; Ossio 1973: 444; Gow 1982: 197–223), demonstrate that the concept of Inca recovery through the reappearance of a messiah was flourishing by the mid-eighteenth century. Since the Inca had been decapitated by the Spanish in 1572 his body had been regenerating underground, according to legend, leaving open the possibility of eternal reincorporation. Perhaps as important was the fact that the Indians also believed that the Andean crises had also gained attention in Heaven where the Creator God Wiracocha had ordered his followers to take action against those persons who He believed were immoral and rebels against God (CDIP 1971–75: 2:2:321; Peru 1980 1:328–30). The sense that the time for action had arrived is evident in the documents of the time.

Inspection of the course of the Tomás Katari and Túpac Amaru rebellions indicates their appearance as messiahs following a preordained course of behavior with respect to their followers, including the association of their surnames with the Inkarrí myth, the abandonment of their world (Tinta, Chayanta) for the outside worlds of Spanish America (Lima, Buenos Aires), and their triumphant return with creative powers that increased their capability of changing the world (Szemiński, Chapter 6 in this volume).

Both the surname Katari and Amaru refer, in Aymara and Quechua respectively, to serpents, or symbolic representatives of an anthropomorphic "underground" into which the Spaniards had placed the Indians following the Conquest of the sixteenth century (Hultkrantz 1978: 311–19). As John Rowe has demonstrated (1980), Túpac Amaru had drawn on the power of his name in a conscious effort to link himself to the traditions of the last Incas executed in Cuzco by Viceroy Toledo in 1572. The Inca's apparently successful quest for the legitimacy afforded by the Inkarrí legend is acknowledged in the sentence handed down against him by Visitor General Areche in Cuzco in May 1781 (CDIP 1971-75: 2:2:765-78) in which he was convicted as "the vile insurgent José Condorcanqui alias Túpac Amaru and supposed cacique" under his Christian name Condorcanqui of the crime of *lèse majesté*, by impersonation of the Inca-King and other actions "intended to dispossess the [Spanish] King of his realm." So convinced was the court that Túpac Amaru had gained royal status as well as that of symbolic representative of all those natives allegedly held in bondage, that it used the sentence as a pretext to eradicate Inca nationalism. Accordingly, Areche abolished the hereditary position of cacique, the wearing of Inca royal garb, the use of any paintings or likenesses of the former Inca kings, the production of any dramas or spectacles portraying the Incas, or even writings which referred to former splendors (such as Garcilaso de la Vega's *Royal Commentaries*) which kept the idea of recuperación alive. Yet Szemiński in a companion essay in this volume notes that books alone could not do this; rather a general image of history was spread orally and symbolically. Symbols of Inca primacy such as flags or conch shell horns were likewise prohibited and use of the Quechua language was even outlawed (Campbell 1985a).

Despite the powerfully cohesive features of the Inkarrí myth, however, the demonstrated internal dissension within both the Katari and Túpac Amaru rebellions indicates that many segments of native society were immune to the message preached by these caciques or that acceptance of the myth was not sufficient by itself to turn the Indians into rebels. Rather, it might be concluded that the existence of the Inkarrí myth constituted evidence of social fragmentation in areas where the upper reaches of the indigenous power structure remained relatively indistinct from the more pervasive colonial power structure. Although further research on this point needs to be made, this may have been the case in Cuzco, where the indigenous nobility was strongly opposed to Túpac Amaru as an impostor and competitor (Campbell 1981: 681–91). Túpac Amaru's subsequent appointment of new caciques and governors in conquered areas also indicates that his rebellion did not operate entirely within the scope of authority of these native elites, resulting in a war effort which spent considerable time and resources in securing legitimacy. The question then becomes: how did the rebel leaders offset this social fragmentation and how did their commitment to the ideology of recovery affect their movements?

Although there were at least 66 known revolts taking place during the decade 1770–1780, including the 1780 attack against the customhouse in Arequipa (Galdos 1967) and the silversmiths' conspiracy in Cuzco that same year (O'Phelan 1985), these appear to fall generally into the category of almost routine, reformist revolts described by Taylor for Mexico (1979: chap. 4). They were normal outbursts between rulers and ruled and considered by the Crown to be *"cosas de la sierra."* What sets them apart, however, seems to be that events as far removed as the black tax protest in Lambayeque in 1777 (Campbell 1972) and the disturbances in Otusco in 1781 (Stern, Chapter 2 in this volume) seem to have been linked by rumor to the figure of Túpac Amaru, at least an indication that his claim to Inca lineage was gaining notice.

It is at this point that the Tomás Katari rebellion of 1777 in Chayanta must be considered. We know, for example, that Túpac Amaru, as a *cacique arriero*, possessed over 300 mules, maintained direct communications links with Upper Peru through trade routes which he covered between Cuzco and Potosí via La Paz. Although there is no direct evidence of contact between Tomás Katari and Túpac Amaru and in fact katarista efforts to make contact with the tupamaristas in Oruro soon after the revolt had broken out in November 1780 betrayed their mutual ignorance of each other, it is plausible that the Túpac Amarus were at least aware that Tomás Katari was accepted as "an oracle and sovereign" by the people of Upper Peru (AGN 1780; Hidalgo 1983: 122–25), according to Manuel de Bodega, the corregidor of Paria. Although Tomás Katari was apprehended by disloyal Indians and turned over to the Spaniards for execution in January 1781, two months after Túpac Amaru had launched his own rebellion, the people refused to accept that their messiah was dead (Lewin 1957: 739). This would later cause serious problems between the two rebel groups.

During the period following his return from Lima, where he had worked assiduously to gain relief for his people from taxation as well as legal validation to his claim of Royal Inca lineage, Túpac Amaru apparently had begun to get involved in revolts in 1777 in Maras, Urubamba (O'Phelan 1977) and possibly in Huarochirí, where he had contact with caciques of the region (Albó n.d.: 25). Whether Túpac Amaru was also involved in the silversmiths' conspiracy of 1780 is unclear (O'Phelan 1985) but it seems likely that the rebel chief had decided on a course of action and had not simply precipitated "a sudden, unplanned, violent outburst" in 1780 (J. R. Fisher 1970: 23). Yet the question still remains whether the tupamaristas moved the date of their revolt forward to accommodate or even counter the katarista movement in Chayanta. Testimony by Florencio Lupa, the cacique of Macha, Chayanta, boasting of Katari's ability to mobilize up to 30,000 Indians and that the rebel had ideas of invading "Cuzco or Lima" betray the vague knowledge which these Aymara had of the Quechua territories or the equally diffuse notions of "Peru" or "Spain." Yet these rumors may well have served as a threat to Túpac Amaru (Lewin 1957: 376). By 1780, Garcilaso de la Vega's notion of a unified Incario (1966: 391–93) hardly conformed to reality, particularly after 1776 when the creation of the viceroyalty of the Río de la Plata had further divided the Aymara and Quechua as trade routes were altered and each area was redirected toward central governments located along the Atlantic and Pacific coasts. Aymara-speaking inhabitants of the altiplano area surrounding Lake Titicaca preserved proud traditions of having struggled to defend their independence from the Incas of Cuzco (Pease 1978: 81–92; Klein 1982: 15) and, for their part, any rumors of Aymara expansionism were not well received in Cuzco (Lewin 1957: 376).

Thus it seems likely that by November 1780 Túpac Amaru had sufficient reasons to renounce a decade of "working within the system" to secure by legal means his title as *Marqués de Oropesa* and better treatment of his people. The popularity of the katarista movement and the discontent which was becoming manifest within the Indian communities may have convinced the cacique that the time had come to "set the world in reverse" and make things right as had been prophesied (Campbell 1985a; Szemiński 1981: 586–89; Cardenas 1980; Vega 1969: 645–50). As a clear indication that the katarista movement had influenced his decision, Túpac Amaru chose November 4, the feast day of King Charles III, to launch his rebellion, a symbolic event which conveyed to the natives that the objective and subjective factors presaging a *pachacuti* were in place. The fact that the rebel leader was sincere in his loyalties to the Spanish Crown and Church allowed him to mark the birthday by a rebellion against the king's immoral subordinates, specifically corregidor Antonio de Arriaga, who had regularly exceeded the legal limitations of the reparto, both in selling more goods than were allowed, and increasing the total number of collections. Thus focused, the rebellion moved forward by the trial and execution of Arriaga on November 10 in a spectacular and public fashion marking the end of one era and the arrival of another.

During the first month of the tupamarista rebellion, Túpac Amaru gathered around him a close-knit command and staff group composed almost exclusively of family members and trusted insiders, many of them mestizos, whose loyalties were unquestioned (Campbell 1981: 684–89). These commanders were regarded as *hijos*, or sons to the chief and his wife Micaela Bastidas, who served as the rebel comptroller and commandant (Campbell 1985a); they in turn were regarded as "Mother and Father" by their subordinates who called themselves loyal *criados*, or servants of their master (Szemiński 1981: 573–75). Such a command structure underscores the personal, familial nature of the rebellion, and of course a distrust toward outsiders. Such an attitude is similarly expressed in the command structure of the katarista rebellion, the leadership of which passed to Tomás Katari's brothers, Nicolás and Dámaso, following the former's death.

Following the execution of Arriaga, the tupamaristas, under the command of the Inca, moved quickly into the Vilcanota Valley and took control of the obrajes at Pomacanchi and Parapuquio. As they did so, however, Túpac Amaru continued to insist that he had been ordered by the virtuous King of Spain to dispatch his evil representatives, now that the king understood the gravity of the situation in Peru. Thus, the Inca maintained in an edict published posthumously in June that he had received a royal edict ordering him to execute all *puka kunkas*, literally "red necks," a pejorative Quechua term which was common slang for Spaniards (Peru 1980: 3: 949–50). The edict is remarkable because the Inca claimed to be acting on behalf of the king, probably because he had come to realize that the people would not follow without this dual authorization (Szemiński 1984: 19). These dualistic authority symbols, King and Inkarrí, are at the heart of the confusion surrounding the meaning of the Great Rebellion of 1780.

Túpac Amaru's subsequent decision on December 7 to cross the *Raya de Vilcanota* and enter the viceroyalty of the Rió de la Plata on the margin of the Aymara cultures resident in the Collao area surrounding Lake Titicaca is interesting for what it tells us about the relationship between the rebel leaderships. As is well known (Rowe 1954), Túpac Amaru had cultivated close ties with "progressive" creoles in Lima during his residence there in the 1770s, and was as well linked to families in Cuzco, including the powerful Ugarte clan and the creole Bishop Manuel de Moscoso y Peralta, who were also at odds with Arriaga (Campbell 1980). Still another powerful group which the rebel sought to enlist were the caciques, or members of the native nobility, a group of approximately 2300 chiefs whose control over resources and native communities could help to spell the success of the revolt and provide it with additional legitimacy. Moscoso's excommunication of Arriaga may have been interpreted as indicating support for the rebellion by these creole progressives although their subsequent behavior was to demonstrate a fear of mass involvement and unwillingness to commit to the tupamaristas (Campbell 1980: 251–70; Durand 1973: 489–520). At the same time, the rebel's elaborate use of ceremony and ritual in publicly stripping Arriaga of his sash of office and sword, as well as his *bastón*, or authority stick signifying his position as corregidor, dressing the fallen official in sackcloth and ashes and as the penitential habit of the Franciscans, was a visible effort to gain the support of the people also. Witnesses to the event noted that the hanging certified Túpac Amaru's charismatic authority: the people who cordoned off the plaza appeared to be "entranced" and firmly under the sway of the leader (Campbell 1978: 107).

Despite this initial success, Túpac Amaru's earliest edicts are remarkable for their general and unspecific goals of "ending bad government" and removing Arriaga so that the *paisanos* could freely serve their King and Church (Durand 1981: 29–49). Yet with the elimination of Arriaga, the Inca offered no specific means of separating the immoral "corregidores and rednecks," whose very humanity was in doubt, from the more progressive creoles and mestizos whom he hoped to attract. This vagueness of approach allowed for groups to punish their enemies under the auspices of the rebellion and served to frighten many creole and mestizo moderates. Similarly, Túpac Amaru's failure to gain the backing of the powerful *caciques gamonales* of Cuzco, who considered him a provincial upstart, made recruitment in and around Cuzco difficult. Thus, the rebel's decision to march south into Quispicanchis, Lampa, and Azángaro, a route which was to carry him into territories dominated historically by the Colla, Lupaca, and Pacajes peoples who were also the subjects of the katarista rebellion, forced a reevaluation of relationships. The research of Thierry Saignes (1983) makes clear the complicated ethnic structure of the areas but further work will be needed to determine what impact the tupamarista offensive had on these peoples. The fact that Dámaso Katari accepted the authority of "the Inca King Túpac Amaru," who he believed was operating under the orders of "the King of Spain" (CDIP 1971–75: 2:2:549), probably reflects the disorder which the kataristas experienced in the wake of the charismatic Tomás' death on January 15, 1781. Moreover, Dámaso recognized that without the tupamarista presence, the Chayanta revolt would never expand past the local level. Hence, Dámaso sent an emissary to Oruro to make contact with the men of Cuzco (Odriozola 1863: 305–6).

We have only partial evidence concerning Túpac Amaru's motives prior to his sudden return toward Cuzco on December 22, which constituted a strategic pincer movement designed to secure control over this key region of highland Peru. The most notable reason for the foray into Azángaro was of course the tupamaristas' longstanding rivalry with the Choque-guancas, a family which also had claims to Royal Inca lineage and which actively supported the Crown. Perhaps as a show of strength against these caciques gamonales who had resisted his movement and disparaged his lineage, Túpac Amaru's forces burned eleven haciendas and other proper-ties and killed their inhabitants (Campbell 1981: 682–83). Indeed, according to the research of José Tamayo Herrera (1982) the tupamarista offensive into the Collao was marked by considerable violence and banditry and differs markedly with their behavior in the Quechua regions around Cuzco, which was marked by a virtual absence of banditry and destruction (Camp-bell 1983). Such a distinction raises the possibility of factionalism within the movement in the form of punishing disloyalty more severely in Aymara territory. It may also connote different tactics and aspirations between the rebel movements of Upper and Lower Peru.

Although in most cases coercion or co-optation sufficed to reduce ten-sions, sometimes these tactics did not succeed in reducing the factionalism and hostility inherent in Andean native society. Túpac Amaru's scribe, Esteban Escarcena, testified at his trial in Cuzco that the Inca had no direct knowledge of the man they termed "Francisco Catari," yet Escarcena observed that his instinctive reaction was to wage war against this rival unless the latter "agreed to accept a division of the kingdom" (Lewin 1957: 829). Such a statement raises many unverifiable questions, particularly since it was made in the context of a situation where the Katari leadership had accepted the nominal hegemony of this lord of Cuzco, yet at the same time seemed to harbor aspirations of expanding their rebellion outward, perhaps to Cuzco or even Lima, in order to destroy the Spaniards.

Nonetheless, it is clear that however much the Túpac Amarus may have been concerned about the Kataris' continued worship of their departed messiah, their primary problem was to gain support among the powerful caciques of southern Cuzco. This support was only partially forthcoming. In the province of Chinchero, for example, the powerful Pumacahua clan stood out as one of the Crown's staunchest allies; their cacique Diego Mateo Pumacahua was instrumental in securing Spanish victory through his heroic defense of the capital of Cuzco. Deep social fissures in the native world were clarified during and after the rebellion. For example, the tupamaristas initiated the conquest of royalist provinces such as Cocha-bamba by erecting gallows decorated with Túpac Amaru's likeness in the main plaza to remind the residents that the penalty for disloyalty to the Inca was death (Szemiński, Chapter 6 in this volume). Following Túpac Amaru's capture Pumacahua commissioned a painting to celebrate the occasion. The art depicted a puma defeating a snake beneath the benevo-lent gaze of the *Virgen de Monserrat*, Chinchero's patron saint. In the background stood Pumacahua and his wife, both dressed in Spanish garb, affirming their territorial sovereignty. Beneath the painting was inscribed Caesar's dictum: *Veni, Vidi, Vici*, commemorating the defeat of this rival faction, an action which brought the house of Pumacahua renewed respect and power in the reconstruction government of Peru (Gisbert 1980: 214-15).

THE SPREAD OF REBELLION AND THE RISE OF FACTIONALISM

The relationship between rebel ideology and intrarebel political factionalism manifested itself as the rebellion moved out of Tinta and Quispicanchis, provinces where the Túpac Amaru family was socially, politically, and economically well entrenched, and into areas further removed from their homelands where the rebel leadership was required to accommodate groups with whom they had less in common both culturally and economically. The manifold sources of tension within the rebellion have been explored in other writings (Campbell 1985a, 1985b; O'Phelan 1982: 461-86; Lewin 1957: 342-77, 500-537) and need not be reiterated here; the various social groups which made up the rebellion were not natural allies and had to work prodigiously to cooperate in minimal ways. These tensions will be explored in the context of certain politico-military decisions such as the sieges of Cuzco and La Paz which permit insights into the specific causes and effects of this factionalism.

Initial military victories forestalled the divisions which would eventually wrack the rebel offensive. Soon after Túpac Amaru's ceremonial execution of corregidor Arriaga, the rebellion swept into Quispicanchis. There, outside the town of Sangarará on November 18, Túpac Amaru's forces decimated a hastily assembled Spanish militia, shattering forever the myth of Spanish invincibility at arms and providing a dynamic for further expansion of the war (Campbell 1978: 111). Yet even as the tupamaristas sacked the obrajes at Pomacanchis and Parapuquio and distributed cloths and coca to their loyal followers, already creoles were recoiling from the news of 576 deaths in the sanctuary of the church at Sangarará and rumors of cannibalism which reached Cuzco. In response and undoubtedly due to official suspicions about his own role in the conflagration, Bishop Moscoso issued an excommunication of the rebel leadership (CDIP 1971-75: 2:2:275-584; Campbell 1980: 251-70; Durand Florez 1981: 489-520). Such actions may have produced a reorientation in the movement.

By late November, the popular perception of the Túpac Amaru revolt as a movement with strong religious connotations under the leadership of an accepted Inca seems to have been growing. Spanish accounts of rebel forces numbering upward of 60,000 persons blindly loyal to their Inca monarch, when in fact the actual numbers were far smaller, is one indication of this phenomenon (Campbell 1978: 111). Yet another is the cacique's behavior in distributing plundered cloth and coca but keeping part of this trove by right, behavior consistent with Andean norms of interchange and reciprocity (Murra 1975), and also demonstrating Túpac Amaru's ability to give back some of the surplus labor and produce which the Spaniards had been extracting from the people without compensation.

If the emphatic shifts in the actions of Túpac Amaru during the first month of the rebellion were efforts to obtain support, his pronouncements demonstrate an evolution from actions made under royal auspices to ones based on his individual responsibility as the Inca. For example, Durand has observed that there was a pronounced decline in the number of references to the king in the edicts which Túpac Amaru issued to the provinces of southern Cuzco in November and December (Durand Florez 1981: 29–49). Instead, the rebel chief put forth arguments which stressed his own authority as well as a stated desire to incorporate all *paisanos* (compatriots) under his own *bandera* (flag), a subtle ideological shift which signified that Túpac Amaru was now acting as the Inca. Since these correspondences, signed by "Túpac Amaru Inca," were directed to the provincial social groups who had traditionally been loyal to the Crown but who were also restive due to the corruption and maladministration of Peru, it is likely that oral messages conveyed to Indian communities were even more strongly associated with the moral authority of Inkarrí (Hidalgo 1983: 120–21).

Rebel efforts to use Incaic traditions and ideology to offset social segmentation can be seen in numerous ways. Following the Sangarará victory, Túpac Amaru and his wife Micaela Bastidas commissioned a painting which depicted the pair as an Inca-King and *Coya* (Queen), rejecting the plumed tricorner hat and mestizo trappings of earlier days when he labored to achieve legitimate title in the Spanish social order (Gisbert 1980: 208–11; Hidalgo 1983: 117–38; Macera 1975). An orthographic analysis of Túpac Amaru's signature shows that the rebel was cognizant of the need for authority symbols capable of keeping social segmentation in check and favoring coalition (Cardenas A. 1980: 229–32; Aparicio V. 1981: 325–30). Further evidence of the need to prevent disorder was the speed with which the rebels appointed caciques, governors, and military commanders in conquered areas to consolidate the Inca's power (Campbell 1981, 1986). Yet these actions alone were not sufficient to hold provinces in check. First, the governors had the difficult task of distinguishing between creoles, who were not to be harmed, and *españoles*, considered to be immoral, inhuman, and part of the corregidores' faction (Peru 1980: 1:408–9). In certain areas, these commanders asserted that their King had given them the power to "devour" these "leopards, foreigners, apostates, and rebels" who were inhuman and unchristian, leading to acts of violence and even cannibalism (Szemiński, Chapter 6 in this volume). The result was that the rebels had sufficient latitude under their orders to take action against anyone, white or Indian, whom they considered to be *Iskay uya*, a hypocrite (ibid.). Thus the revolt seemed in some instances to accentuate factionalism and disunion by reviving preexisting social conflicts as well as racial animosities.

As the tupamarista rebels moved farther south into the provinces of Lampa, Carabaya, and Azángaro, and later into the regions of Puno, Chucuito, and La Paz following the abortive siege of Cuzco in December and January 1780–1781, the leadership seemed to stress ever more strongly that this was a movement of amarus (serpents), opposed to both the pumas (Pumacahuas) as well as the Spanish *gatos* (filchers) or "rednecks" (Gisbert 1980: 214 ff.; Hidalgo 1983: 128 ff.; Szemiński, Chapter 6 in this volume). As Moscoso moved tactically to close churches and use local priests as informants, so too the rebels moved symbolically, delivering their speeches in Quechua in front of Inca *huacas* (shrines) and cemeteries rather than in Spanish on the steps of Spanish churches, reminding their listeners that they had an obligation to their ancestors to join the struggle. In these weeks, too, the movement seemed to polarize the communities through which it passed, despite the efforts of the leadership to unify the southern sierra.

Spanish reports issued during the initial months of the campaign indicated that numerous españoles, primarily creoles and mestizos, many of them *principales*, or persons of rank and authority, had departed the rebel standard, leaving a residue of peasants to fight under the rebel flag with the Indians (Szemiński 1981: 570–71). Similar defections of mestizos and some creoles were reported in the province of Chumbivilcas, where Túpac Amaru had on November 29 ordered the formation of a militia (CDIP 1971–75: 2:2:308). What was the rebel response to these defections?

Although it is presently unclear whether his followers simply felt that Túpac Amaru *should* be able to revive the dead, it now appears that at some point the Inca accepted the mantle of Messiah bestowed on him by certain of his followers and began to attribute to himself the power to raise the dead. The rebel's words to his confederate Bernardo Sucacagua that persons dying loyal to him "would have their reward" (Peru 1980: 1:456–57) suggests that the rebel saw himself as a Redeemer in principle. Yet Szemiński (Chapter 6 in this volume) also feels that the rebel's stated promise to the wives of his followers to raise the dead in three days also ties his messianism to Christian theology. The natives apparently viewed the Inca as a figure equivalent to Jesus Christ. At the same time, while the rebellion was not overtly anti-Christian, the native belief system accepted Túpac Amaru as a God, Redeemer, and Liberator of the Oppressed. The Inca affirmed this perception by stating that the Spaniards had denied the natives access to their "True God" and that he would nominate persons to show them the truth (ibid.). In response, Indians as far away as Charcas embraced likenesses of Túpac Amaru as their King and Redemptor "without any regard for [King] Charles III" (CDIP 1971–75: 2:2:511). While rumors persisted that Túpac Amaru had taken a crown in Cuzco, in Upper Peru the natives believed that he would accept one in the *Gran Paititi*, an undefined jungle territory where it was believed that the Inca monarchy had survived Spanish domination (AGI 1781; CDIP 1971–75: 2:3:379–88; Szemiński 1981: 573–75, 586).

Given the positive reception accorded to the tupamaristas in the period following the outbreak of violence in Tinta and prior to the appearance of the charismatic Julián Apasa Túpac Katari in Sicasica in March 1781, it is reasonable to believe that the Cuzco rebels sought a permanent presence in the southern Collao provinces to supplant the defections which they had suffered in the provinces of Cuzco. Yet there were difficulties inherent in extending the Cuzco movement into the altiplano provinces around La Paz, where the Colla and Lupaca peoples were proud of their resistance to the Incas' forces before the Conquest (Stern, Chapter 2 in this volume). Hence, while the Inkarrí myth had powerful features which allowed for the extension of the rebellion into Upper Peru, the concept of a Cuzco noble as Inkarrí, one claiming descent, as did Túpac Amaru, from the ancient Cuzco emperor Huayna Capac, and bestowing power upon his family and close associates, became more divisive as it clashed with a virulent form of Aymara nationalism symbolized by the appearance of Julián Apasa Túpac Katari.

Túpac Amaru's decision to dispatch his cousin and trusted lieutenant to Azángaro and then across the Raya de Vilcanota and into Upper Peru has been criticized by modern commentators (Valcárcel 1970a: 143–53; Lewin 1957: 446, 462; L. E. Fisher 1966: 95–96, 104, 125–28) largely because the cacique earlier had received a strong rebuke from his wife and military associate Micaela Bastidas for delaying the attack on Cuzco (Campbell 1985b: 179–81; Peru 1980: 4: 79, 80, 85) which seemed to be "logical" military strategy given the obvious weakness of the city. Yet the fact that Túpac Amaru believed that he "owned" the Cuzco provinces and expected them to fall naturally under his sway is manifest both in his long siege of the city after December 28 and his stated desire to be welcomed there as a Liberator rather than as a military conqueror (Campbell 1983: 147). This interpretation also fails to recognize the equally strong benefits which accrued from neutralizing the royalist caciques of Azángaro and extending the offensive into the Collao, despite the fact that the delay allowed the royalists to move troops from Lima to Cuzco and fortify the city, which ultimately permitted a Spanish counteroffensive to begin in April of the following year.

Túpac Amaru decided suddenly to countermarch on Cuzco on December 20. The plan hardly seems improvised. With a force of 6,000 men, Diego Cristóbal Túpac Amaru returned across the Raya to attack Cuzco from the north, while the Inca led another force to the west of the city, keeping to the high ground above the Apurímac River. A third column completed this pincer movement, led by Andrés Castelo, a creole of Tungasuca who was a trusted commander in charge of the largest rebel force. Military reverses to Diego Cristóbal and Castelo frustrated the rebel plan, which may have been focused on the control of the surrounding provinces of Andahuaylas, which served Cuzco as a granary and source of recruits. Due to strong resistance by the Pumacahuas, Diego Cristóbal was frustrated in his effort to besiege Cuzco while Castelo's force was also seriously reduced.

The well-publicized siege of Cuzco initiated by the Inca on December 28 led to the defection of numerous Indians and a determined offensive by loyal Indians under the command of their corregidores and caciques drawn from the surrounding provinces, with Pumacahua commanding 9,000 forces drawn from the "sacred ayllus" of Cuzco (Albó n.d.: 29–30). With the raising of the siege on January 10, 1781, and the rebels' return to Tinta, the Great Rebellion moved to another phase, one which was centered in the southern provinces near Lake Titicaca. After January, what had begun as a revolt in Cuzco had become a rebellion centered in Alto Peru. No longer a single revolt, the Great Rebellion now included components which were socially and ideologically as different from one another as each was from the Spanish culture which they opposed. These differences were accentuated by the rise of power of Julián Apasa Túpac Katari.

News of Túpac Amaru's march on Cuzco seemed to heighten activity in Upper Peru, as numerous revolts broke out and rumors of a general uprising spread during the public functions accompanying the conclusion of Lent. Yet as the region between La Paz and Cochabamba fermented, Tomás Katari was captured in Aullagas and Túpac Amaru was forced to withdraw from Cuzco to Tinta. Under the command of Tomás' brother Dámaso, 6,000 Quechua and Aymara Indians massed in the environs of La Plata, the capital of the Audiencia of Charcas, to demand the return of Tomás Katari's papers and the release of his confederates, while in Oruro, whites and Indians participated in a brief joint venture to oust the Spanish faction under the control of the Rodríguez family (Cajías

1986). With the defeat of Dámaso and Nicolás Katari outside of La Plata at the end of March by Spanish forces dispatched from Buenos Aires, the Aymara forces directed from Chayanta suffered a temporary crisis of leadership (Albó n.d.: 30–35). This was settled when Tomás Katari's mantle was passed to the charismatic Julián Apasa, who took the name Túpac Katari in a ceremony of reincarnation according to the dictates of the Inkarrí myth. Drawing on Katari's descendance "from the places above and Spain," his namesake preserved the unity of the rebellion and redirected it toward La Paz (Hidalgo 1982: 23; Valle del Siles 1977, 1980).

According to Xavier Albó (n.d.: 36) the appearance of Túpac Katari on the heels of news concerning a crowned Inca of Cuzco gave the movement a new dimension. As the Quechua forces moved north from Azángaro in the months following Túpac Amaru's death in May 1781, mounting victories in Velille, Sicuani, Yauri, Livitaca, and Carabaya gave them control of the provinces of Lampa and Carabaya. These also placed the rebels in a position to gain further successes in the Collado provinces of Larecaja, Sicasica, Omasuyos, and Pacajes, en route to La Paz, yet the presence of two distinct forces caused no small confusion among the citizenry. For example, Albó (ibid.: 36) relates how a miner in Chichas changed his surname to Katari and asserted that he was a "governor and ambassador" of both the Túpac Amarus and the Kataris, not uncommon behavior pending the outcome of the rivalry between caciques. The wily Katari also moved to meet the challenge of Quechua overlordship, amending his earlier assertion of reincarnation to include Túpac Amaru, stating that his authority as expressed in his name (Amaru = Quechua serpent; Katari = Aymara serpent) stemmed from both leaders (Campbell 1986; Hidalgo 1983; Valle de Siles 1977). As he did so, however, Katari established a virtual monarchy in Pampajasi overlooking the city of La Paz, living there with his queen and court, consulting oracles and mawkishly behaving as a sovereign.

During the month of March 1781, Quechua forces from Azángaro cooperated with Aymaras of Chucuito, located south of the Lake Titicaca region which the latter regarded as a sacred area, the womb of the Holy Mother *Pacha Mama*, to force the Spaniards out of the important city of Puno. Yet even here, the closely knit and elitist tupamarista leaders, led by Andrés Ingaricona (plural of Inkarrí, or Inca-King), began to clash with the more popular and radical kataristas (Valle de Siles 1977: 633–77; Albó n.d.: 39), complicating a situation where Indians from Chucuito fought alongside the Spanish defenders of Puno led by the corregidor Joaquín de Orellana while those from the north attacked the city. During the siege of Puno the tupamarista commanders Andrés Quispe and Juan de Dios Mullpuraca made it clear that they accepted orders from

Diego Cristóbal Túpac Amaru alone and did not initially support the kataristas' demands for the abolition of tribute and mita obligations (O'Phelan 1982: 474). The importance of taking Puno, which controlled the trade route between Lower Peru and the silver mines of Potosí demanded cooperation nonetheless.

In the months following Túpac Amaru's capture and execution, apart from wary cooperation during sieges of specific tactical objectives such as Puno in April, little cooperation was observed between the Aymara and Quechua forces vying for control in Upper Peru. In the second siege of the city, for example, the Indians of Carabaya fought alongside the Quechuas while those of Pacajes remained with the Aymaras; natives of Cabanas stood with Orellana and the Royalists (Albó n.d.: 41). For their part, the Túpac Amarus observed the ferocity of popular revolt which they had helped unleash in areas such as Chucuito but made no effort to co-opt it. Indeed, so limited was Túpac Katari's authority when a third siege of Puno was initiated in May that the cacique was obligated to apply for a passport in Chucuito in order to travel to Puno to lend assistance (ibid.: 43). His presence was far less important than the Túpac Amarus' ability to enlist wealthy Aymara Indians from Omasuyos, Larecaja, and Chulumani, which led to the fall of the city. Prior to his departure, Orellana notified authorities in Arequipa that the rebel forces were deeply divided, recognizing either Túpac Amaru or Túpac Katari as their king but never both (Paz 1786: I, 376). In Cuzco, the Spanish judge Benito de la Mata Linares wrote to Minister of the Indies José de Gálvez following Túpac Amaru's death in May informing him of the organizational and ideological differences which separated the tupamaristas, who sought to join everyone not a Spaniard together, and the more radical kataristas, who increasingly had begun to reject alliances outright (AHM 1781).

Diego Cristóbal Túpac Amaru's assumption of power as José Gabriel's "brother" and his refusal to acknowledge Túpac Katari as an Inca precipitated the growing estrangement between the two regional factions (Odriozola 1863: 209–11; Szemiński 1981: 575). Although Diego Cristóbal was careful to recognize the autonomy of Aymara provinces which his forces occupied following his assumption of power, he was equally adamant that they be placed under his flag and that Túpac Katari be accorded no more than tertiary status within the tupamarista chain of command. In an edict published in May, Diego Cristóbal's scribe, Pedro Obaya, who had taken the name Don José Guaina Capac, signed as "Notary Public of the New Conquest" to demonstrate how the tupamaristas regarded the occupation of the Collado provinces (Odriozola 1863: 209–11; CDIP 1971–75: 2:3:96). To underscore the differences between the groups, Diego Cristóbal pointedly referred to Túpac Katari by his

Spanish name of Apasa and offhandedly allowed him the status of viceroy or marquis, while reserving the more intimate term of *hijos* (sons) to his relatives Andrés and Miguel Túpac Amaru and other tupamarista lieutenants. Some of the questions about the extent and impact of this factionalism on the Great Rebellion can be addressed in the siege of La Paz, the climactic event of the rebellion.

As early as March 1781, the kataristas had initiated a siege of the Spanish city of La Paz, being joined there by the tupamaristas under the command of Andrés Túpac Amaru Inca and Miguel Bastidas Túpac Amaru Inca in August. The separation between the two groups was expressed by the rebels' separate military cantonments: the tupamaristas located in *El Alto*, situated 400 meters above the city, on the highway connecting Cuzco to Potosí, while the kataristas camped in Pampajasi on the roadway connecting La Paz with the tropical *Yungas* where Katari had formerly been a purveyor of coca and other goods to the city. These camps not only reflected the physical separation of the two factions, but also symbolized the fact that the katarista organization was governed by representatives of the twenty-four Indian cabildos of La Paz, some of them commoners. The tupamaristas, on the other hand, were under the command of native elites and *ladinos* (Hispanized natives) long associated with the Túpac Amarus in Cuzco.

Conflicts manifested themselves particularly at the leadership levels of the two organizations. The natural antipathy between the kataristas and tupamaristas were accentuated by the youth of the tupamarista commanders in La Paz, Andrés and Miguel Túpac Amaru Inca, although the former had begun a liaison with Katari's sister, Gregoria Apasa, who provided an important yet informal link between the two camps (Campbell 1986). When Andrés Túpac Amaru briefly jailed Katari for insubordination and Katari executed the tupamarista lieutenant Pedro Obaya as a "*ladino*, spy, and outsider" out of defiance, complaining that the tupamaristas refused to treat him with honor and respect (Lewin 1957: 508; L. E. Fisher 1966: 292, 294, 304), it reflected the mistrust which permeated the two organizations, although it is difficult to determine to what degree the rupture affected the war.

On August 28, news was received by the kataristas that José Gabriel Túpac Amaru Inca had died along with all of his sons, giving lie to Andrés' claims of direct lineage, for which the kataristas branded him an impostor (Valle de Siles 1977: 230–31). During the months which passed prior to the arrival of Colonel José de Reseguín and the Spanish forces from Buenos Aires in October, the two camps barely interacted, since by this time Katari had grown more irrational and capricious, ordering anyone who was not demonstrably Aymara put to death and consulting oracles for guidance.

Central to Katari's ideology was to punish all non-Aymara-speaking peoples and usurp their lands, a program repugnant to the moderate tupamaristas who promised to protect the 400 españoles of Sorata from any "treasonous rebels" threatening them with harm (Valle de Siles 1977: 613–24). Thus, the two rebel leaders' methods of countering factionalism, one through a strict appeal to Aymara racial solidarity and the other through the support of all persons opposed to Spanish domination, were themselves inherently divisive. Native communities affected by the rebellion were thus forced to choose between them, as in the case of Sicasica, where members of the *ayllu grande*, all of whom were *principales*, chose to follow the tupamaristas rather than the kataristas, whose ideas they feared as much as those of the Spaniards (Paz 1786: 1:376).

With the royalist entrance into La Paz on October 11 with a force of 7,000 men, whites and mestizos were provided with a second option for their personal protection from the kataristas' capricious racism, distinct from the tupamaristas' fragile ethnic coalition. On October 18, Diego Cristóbal wrote to the royalist Inspector General José del Valle suggesting an independent, negotiated peace, emphasizing that this agreement did not include "Julián Katari, who is independent of this family line" (BL 1781: Azángaro, October 18). While the katarista survivors departed La Paz for the Sanctuary of Copacabana, a shrine to the Virgin of Copacabana located near Lake Titicaca, Miguel Túpac Amaru Inca entered into secret negotiations with Colonel Reseguín on November 3 to bring the war to a close. This treaty allowed for the tupamarista troops to return home without penalty and ultimately resulted in Miguel and Andrés being granted freedom in exile. Túpac Katari, on the other hand, was captured shortly thereafter due to the collusion of Tomás Inga Lipe, a tupamarista colonel and Quechua native of Omasuyos, although it is not clear whether Inga Lipe was acting personally to save himself (Miguel Bastidas Túpac Amaru Inca had allegedly promised Reseguín that he would apprehend Katari and Inga Lipe), or as part of a larger tupamarista bargain in which he was a pawn. At his trial, Katari bitterly accused the tupamaristas of betraying him in order to collect their reward from the Spaniards (CDIP 1971–75: 3:164–80). Xavier Albó (n.d.: 55–58), who has studied the matter from the katarista perspective, notes that the trial court acknowledged that many of the Indians had turned against Katari but feels that existing evidence does not implicate the tupamaristas. On the other hand, the trial court praised Miguel Túpac Amaru for "subjugating" the brutal Apasa and several royalist observers expressed their belief that the "moderate" Túpac Amarus were freed for their part in bringing the rebellion to an end (Valle de Siles 1977: 238–39; CDIP 1971–75: 2:3:146–49).

CONCLUSION

On January 27, 1782, the remaining tupamarista rebels signed the peace of Sicuani, bringing the hostilities of the Great Rebellion to a close although sporadic revolts, quickly suppressed, broke out in Huarochirí and other areas the following year. In July, Diego Cristóbal and the remaining tupamaristas were taken into custody and their leaders tried and executed in an effort to rid the viceroyalty of this influential family although the natives and others sympathetic to the rebellion held out the hope in *pasquines*, or handbills, that their king survived (Baquerizo 1980: 18; Peru 1982: 274): "Our Gabriel Inca lives we swear to him, then, as King because he comes legally and we receive him, all Indians perceive [that] he defends their rights."

This brief overview of the relationship between ideology and organization in the Great Rebellion suggests the need to reevaluate Andean social movements within their proper ideological and cultural context. Historically, and particularly during Peru's sesquicentennial celebration of independence, scholarship has concentrated on the Túpac Amaru rebellion in southern Cuzco to the detriment of other social protest movements occurring concurrently in Upper Peru, Chile, and New Granada (McFarlane 1984; Hidalgo 1982; Moreno Y. 1976). Such a constricted focus omits the fact that the protests and revolts of the mid-eighteenth century were Andean phenomena, involving Quechua and Aymara peoples who viewed their actions as part of a long tradition of resistance and revolt against Spanish colonialism rather than as "precursors" to independence from Spain.

In recent years, the development of Peruvian "New History" (Kapsoli 1984) has begun to emphasize the eighteenth century as a break with earlier traditions, and to view these rebellions as responses to inequitable market forces and protests against onerous forms of colonialism, such as the repartimiento de mercancías, which escalated the exploitation of the Indians' surplus labor and produce (Golte 1980). While such an approach has led to an improved understanding of the structural dynamics and market forces which helped to produce regional protests, these social and economic approaches continue to conceive of the movements themselves within a traditional framework of opposition to Bourbon reformism, and particularly in terms of time series data which correlate the outbreak of revolt with the legalization of the repartimiento in 1754.

Despite this emphasis, Spanish observers and judges acknowledged that the tupamaristas had sought to make a resurrected Incaic concept the legitimizing concept for insurrectionary organization and leadership from above and punished these caciques severely for having done so, to the extent of attempting to eradicate all vestiges of the former Inca Empire (Rowe 1954; Campbell 1985a). The severe punishments meted out to the defendants were only part of a wider group of sanctions directed toward the power of Inca nationalism and mythology, specifically the Inkarrí myth claimed by Túpac Amaru, as by Juan Santos Atahualpa before him and Túpac Katari afterward. According to Hidalgo, it is plausible to believe that Túpac Amaru "received" the mantle of Inkarrí from the people of southern Cuzco well in advance of 1780, and that his counterpart Tomás Katari proceeded under similar "authorization" in Chayanta earlier, both of them commanding a sequence of events linked not only to the excesses of Bourbon absolutism, but also with a vaguely understood mandate to preside over the *pachacuti* or cataclysm which would reverse the existing world order and oust the Spaniards. It is possible that in some instances the masses exceeded the demands of rebel leadership and thereby extended the social dimension of the rebellion.

This view of the struggle is expressed in Túpac Amaru's letter to Visitor General José Antonio de Areche of March 5, 1781, in which he compared himself to the poor shepherd David who sought to free Israel from the Pharaohs by defeating their cruel warrior Goliath (CDIP 1971–75: 2:2:521–31; Klaiber 1982). Although Túpac Amaru could not predict victory, the parable pointed out that it was possible for the disadvantaged to win if they were morally right, and that the result would be that the Spanish State would be forever discredited. As Szemiński's sensitive reading of the massive testimony produced by the Great Rebellion suggests, the rebels accepted the Spanish religion and the authority of the Crown through a complex world view which linked God, King, and Inkarrí into a triumvirate (Szemiński, Chapter 6 in this volume). They were the faithful vassals of the Crown and Church who had arisen only to expel immoral aliens such as the corregidores from their homeland (Peru 1980: 4:347).

While Túpac Amaru's revival of the Inkarrí myth seems to have been accepted in the confines of southern Cuzco, the concept, being based on dualisms within Andean cosmology which afforded status to both Catholic and native religion and secular authority, gave rise to tensions and ambivalence on the part of churchmen, caciques, and native communities, who struggled to align themselves with a movement which sometimes must have seemed a contradiction in terms. Yet, as the rebel leadership struggled with the acceptance of Spanish religion and rejection of Spanish ideology, it depended ever more strongly on the Inkarrí myth as it was understood in Cuzco. Thus, as the tupamarista movement shifted focus toward Upper Peru after the death of the Inca, it confronted an Aymara movement with which it was at variance socially, economically, politically, and ideologically, one based on the exclusion of anyone with white skin rather than a union of *paisanos* and hostile toward the Quechua imperialists. Further research is needed to clarify the nature and extent of this factionalism, and its relationship to the Andean belief systems and oral traditions which have sustained rebellion in Andean America since the times of Inca nationalism.

REFERENCES

AGI (Archivo General de las Indias, Sevilla)
    1780   Audiencia de Lima 1084. José Antonio de Areche to José de Gálvez, Lima, November 3, 1780.
    1781   Audiencia de Cuzco 32. "Autos seguidos . . . contra Ypolito Tupac Amaru." Cuzco, May 17, 1781.

AGN (Archivo General de la Nación, Lima)
    1780   División Colonia, Sección Gobierno, Leg. 93, Exp. 2041. Report of Manuel de Bodega, Paria, October 21, 1780.

AHM (Archivo Histórico, Madrid)
    1781   Colección Benito de la Mata Linares, 55: 84–87.

ALBÓ, XAVIER
    n.d.   "Kataris y Amarus: su actualidad después de 200 anos." Working draft provided by author. La Paz.

APARICIO VEGA, MANUEL JESÚS
    1981   "José Gabriel Thupa Amaro Inga. Verdadero y único nombre del conductor de la 1780." *La revolución de los Túpac Amaru. Antología.* Lima.

BL (Bancroft Library, University of California, Berkeley)
    1781   Documents on the Tupac Amaru Rebellion. Box Z-D.

BAQUERIZO, MANUEL J.
    1980   "La memoria literaria de Túpac Amaru en el Perú." *Tarea* 3 (Lima): 17–24.

CAJÍAS, FERNANDO
    1986   "Objectives of the Indigenous Revolution of 1781. The Case of Oruro." *New World Review* 1 (in press).

CAMPBELL, LEON G.
    1972   "Black Power in Colonial Peru: The 1779 Tax Rebellion of Lambayeque." *Phylon* 33, 2: 140–52.
    1978   *The Military and Society in Colonial Peru, 1750–1810.* Philadelphia.
    1979   "Recent Research on Andean Peasant Revolts, 1750-1820." *Latin American Research Review* 14: 3–49.
    1980   "Church and State in Colonial Peru: The Role of the Clergy in the Túpac Amaru Rebellion in Cuzco, 1780." *Journal of Church and State* 22: 251–70.

1981   "Social Structure of the Túpac Amaru Army in Cuzco, 1780-1781."
        Hispanic American Historical Review 61 (Nov.): 675-93.
1983   "Banditry and the Túpac Amaru Rebellion in Cuzco, 1780-1784."
        Bibliotheca Americana 1, 3 (Miami): 164-80.
1985a   "Crime and Punishment in the Tupacamaru Rebellion in Cuzco."
        Criminal Justice History 3.
1985b   "Women and the Great Rebellion in Peru, 1780-1783," *The Americas* 42, 2: 163-96.
1986   "The Great Rebellion, 1780-1783: A Comparative Study of the Túpac
        Amaru and Túpac Catari Rebellions." *Publications of the Middle
        American Research Institute, Tulane University.* New Orleans.

CARDENAS AYAIPOMA, MARIO
1980   "José Gabriel Tupa Amaro, a propósito de un documento." *Histórica*
        4, 2: 229-32.

CDIP (Comisión Nacional del Sesquicentenario de la Independencia del Perú)
1971-75 *Colección documental de la independencia del Perú.* 27 vols. Lima.

CORNEJO BOURONCLE, JORGE
1949   *Túpac Amaru. La revolución precursora de emancipación continental.* Cuzco.

CURATOLA, MARCO
1977   "Mito y milenarianismo en los Andes: del Takí Onqoy a Inkarrí."
        Allpanchis 10 (Cuzco): 65-92.

DARNTON, ROBERT
1984   *The Great Cat Massacre and Other Episodes in French Cultural History.* New York.

DE LA VEGA, GARCILASO
1966   *The Royal Commentaries of the Incas and General History of Peru.*
        Austin.

DURAND FLOREZ, LUIS
1973   *Independencia e integración en el plan político de Túpac Amaru.*
        Lima.
1981   "La formulación Nacional de los bandos de Túpac Amaru." *La
        Revolución de los Túpac Amaru. Antología* (Lima): 29-50.

FISHER, J. R.
1970   *Government and Society in Colonial Peru. The Intendant System,
        1784-1814.* London.

FISHER, LILLIAN E.
1966   *The Last Inca Revolt, 1780-1783.* Norman, Okla.

FLORES GALINDO, ALBERTO
1976   (Ed.) *Túpac Amaru 1780. Sociedad colonial y sublevaciones populares.*
        Lima.
1981   "La nación como utopía: Túpac Amaru 1780." *La Revolución de los
        Tupac Amaru. Antología* (Lima): 55-70.

GALDOS, GUILLERMO
1967   *La rebelión de los pasquines.* Arequipa.

GISBERT, TERESA
1980   *Iconografía y mitos indígenas en el arte.* La Paz.

GOLTE, JÜRGEN
1980   *Repartos y rebeliones. Túpac Amaru y las contradicciones de la economía colonial.* Lima.

GOW, ROSALIND
1982   "Inkarrí and Revolutionary Leadership in the Southern Andes." *Journal of Latin American Lore* 8, 2: 197–223.

HIDALGO, JORGE
1982   "Fases de la rebelión indígena de 1781 en el corregimiento de Atacama y esquema de la inestabilidad política que la precede, 1749–1781." *Chungará* 8 (Arica): 192–246.
1983   "Amarus y Cataris: aspectos mesiánicos de la rebelión indígena en Cuzco, Chayanta, La Paz y Arica." *Chungará* 10 (Arica): 117–38.

KAPSOLI, WILFREDO, ed.
1984   *Ensayos de Nueva Historia.* Lima.

KLAIBER, JEFFREY
1982   "Religión y justicia en Túpac Amaru." *Allpanchis* 16, 19 (Cuzco): 173–86.

KLEIN, HERBERT S.
1982   *Bolivia: The Evolution of a Multi-Ethnic Society.* New York.

KUBLER, GEORGE
1946   *The Indian Caste of Peru, 1795–1940.* Washington.

LEWIN, BOLESLAO
1957   *La rebelión de Túpac Amaru y los orígenes de la independencia de Hispanoamérica.* Buenos Aires.

MCFARLANE, ANTHONY
1984   "Civil Disorders and Popular Protests in Late Colonial New Granada." *Hispanic American Historical Review* 64 (Feb.): 17–54.

MACERA, PABLO
1975   *Retrato de Túpac Amaru.* Lima.

MORENO YÁÑEZ, SEGUNDO
1976   *Sublevaciones indígenas en la Audiencia de Quito.* Bonn.

MURRA, JOHN V.
1975   *Formaciones económicas y políticas del mundo andino.* Lima.

ODRIOZOLA, MANUEL DE, ed.
1863   *Documentos históricos del Perú en las épocas del coloniaje después de la conquista y de la independencia hasta la presente.* 10 vols. Lima.

O'PHELAN GODOY, SCARLETT
1977   "Cuzco 1777: El movimiento de Maras, Urubamba." *Histórica*, 1, 1 (Lima): 113–27.
1982   "El movimiento Tupacamarista: fases, coyuntura económica y perfil de la composición social de su dirigencia." *Actas del Coloquio Internacional "Túpac Amaru y su tiempo".* (Cuzco): 465–88.
1983   "Las reformas fiscales borbónicas y su impacto en la sociedad colonial del Bajo y el Alto Perú." *Historia y Cultura* 16 (Lima): 113–34.
1985   "The Urubamba Rebellion (1777), the Silversmiths' Conspiracy (1780), and the Great Rebellion of Cuzco (1780): A Comparative Analysis." *Bibliotheca Americana* 3 (Miami).

OSSIO, JUAN M., ed.
1973   *Ideología mesiánica del mundo andino*. Lima.
PAZ, MELCHOR DE
1786   *Guerra separatista, Rebeliones de indios en Sur América*. Luis Antonio Eguiguren, ed. 2 vols. Lima, 1952.
PEASE, FRANKLIN
1978   *Del Tawantinsuyo a la historia del Perú*. Lima.
PERU. Comisión Nacional del Bicentenario de la Rebelión Emancipadora de Túpac Amaru.
1980   *Colección Documental*. 5 vols. Lima.
1982   *Actas del Coloquio Internacional "Túpac Amaru y su tiempo"*. Lima.
RELACION DE LOS HECHOS MAS NOTABLES
1900   "Relacion de los hechos mas notables acaecidos en la sublevacion general fraguada en los Reynos del Peru por el yndio Jose Gabriel Tupac Amaru," *Revista de Archivos y Bibliotecas* 4 (Lima): 501–32.
ROWE, JOHN H.
1954   "El movimiento nacional inca del siglo xviii." *Revista Universitaria* 107 (Cuzco): 17–47.
1980   "Genealogía y rebelión en el s. XVIII: antecedentes de la sublevación de José Gabriel Thopa Amaro." *Histórica* 6, 1 (Lima): 65–85.
SAIGNES, THIERRY
1983   "Políticas étnicas en la Bolivia colonial: siglos XVI–XIX," *Historia Boliviana* 3:1 (La Paz): 1–30.
SPALDING, KAREN
1984   *Huarochirí: An Andean Society under Inca and Spanish Rule*. Stanford.
STERN, STEVE J.
1982   *Peru's Indian Peoples and the Challenge of Spanish Conquest: Huamanga to 1640*. Madison.
SZEMIŃSKI, JAN
1976   "La insurección de Túpac Amaru II: ¿Guerra de independencia o revolución?" In Flores Galindo 1976: 199–258.
1980   "Del significado de algunos términos usados en los documentos de la revolución tupamarista, 1780–1783." *Allpanchis* 16 (Cuzco): 89–130.
1981   "La concepción andina de Historia: su influencia en el Movimiento Tupamarista." *Actas del Coloquio Internacional "Tupac Amaru y su tiempo"* (Lima): 563–98.
1984   *La utopía tupamarista*. Lima.
TAMAYO HERRERA, JOSÉ
1982   "Las consecuencias de la rebelión de Tupac Amaru y la decadencia económica-social del altiplano." *Actas del Coloquio Internacional "Tupac Amaru y su tiempo"* (Lima): 599–608.
TAYLOR, WILLIAM B.
1979   *Drinking, Homicide, and Rebellion in Colonial Mexican Villages*. Stanford.

VALCÁRCEL, CARLOS DANIEL
1970 *La rebelión de Túpac Amaru.* 3d ed. Lima.
VALLE DE SILES, MARÍA EUGENIA DEL
1977 "Tupac Katari y la rebelión de 1781: radiografía de un caudillo aymara." *Anuario de Estudios Americanos* 34 (Seville): 633–44.
1980 *Testimonios del cerco de La Paz. El campo contra la ciudad.* La Paz.
VEGA, JUAN JOSÉ
1969 *José Gabriel Tupac Amaru.* Lima.
WACHTEL, NATHAN
1976 *The Vision of the Vanquished. The Spanish Conquest of Peru through Indian Eyes, 1530–1570.* New York.

PART II

Consciousness and Identity during the Age of Andean Insurrection

Introduction to Part II

It is in the crucible of political crisis and rebellion that people become more conscious of their own latent aspirations and understandings of the world, even as they redefine or perhaps transform them. The connection affects scholarship. The attempts in Part I to reexamine the great insurrection of the 1780s repeatedly underscored just how crucial yet limited is our comprehension of Andean consciousness. The road to an adequate understanding of late colonial world views is long and arduous. The three essays in Part II of this book take us considerably down that road.

Frank Salomon's study of ancestor cults and local riots in Andagua, Arequipa, offers intriguing insights into the political culture of accommodation and revolt that preceded the ascendance of more radical insurrectionary ideologies. The trial documents of Andagua provide rare glimpses of relatively clandestine sides of Andean religious and political life at the local level in the mid-eighteenth century. Used sensitively by a skilled ethnographer, these glimpses illuminate preinsurrectionary folk ideas that lay behind the shifting legitimacy of native Andean leaders at the local level, as well as the colonial regime at large. The Andagua trials document vividly the central role of religious belief systems and ritual practice, particularly ancestor cults, in legitimizing native Andean elites drawn into active entrepreneurship in the mercantile economy.

Salomon's most provocative hypothesis suggests that Andagua's natives developed a concept of correct, orderly Indian-European relations that merged Andean and Hispanic concepts of interethnic relations. From Andean religion they took the notion of the multiplicity of humanity. Andean humanity was divided, subdivided, and redivided again into a structure of oppositional human groupings of varying degrees of inclusiveness. This elaborate series of divisions and subdivisions granted each human segment its own sense of identity and ancestry, while incorporating it into a higher or more inclusive human grouping. Unity between sharply different (or in the idiom of kinship, remotely related) human segments required that one climb the segmentary structure of humanity to a relatively high level, where one encountered the creator-gods and authorities corresponding to more inclusive human groupings. Such Andean notions melded, in Salomon's view, with the plural character of Spanish legal tradition. Medieval law had separated humanity into distinct corporations, each with its own body of legal rights, obligations, jurisdictions, and procedures. Colonial jurists adapted this tradition of plural law to new American realities by distinguishing between law applicable to the "republic of Indians," and that corresponding to the "republic of Spaniards." In Andean eyes, this confirmed that the local Indians and Spaniards of Arequipa represented sharply distinct segments of humanity, subject to distinctive bodies of law, united not directly to one another at the local level, but indirectly, through their common subjection to authority at the viceregal level.

The implication is that the Andagua rebels rioted to defend an Andean moral standard of interethnic relations approved, in their eyes, at the higher levels of the colonial state. This moral standard was indeed compatible with at least certain versions of Thomist rule practiced in earlier colonial times. Colonial officials acquired a measure of legitimacy only to the extent that they were seen as ambassadors of a higher authority, and only insofar as they respected the established etiquettes and customary rights that governed local interethnic relations. In this particular case, the established interethnic practice granted Andagua's natives the right to practice idolatrous ancestor cults on a semiclandestine basis, and had allowed tribute collection to fall into arrears. Salomon's hypothesis complements my discussion (in Part I) of "resistant adaptation" by illuminating indigenous conceptualizations of both the quid pro quos that had once made colonial rule more bearable, and the increased violation of implicit interethnic pacts in the eighteenth century. His notion of the moral basis of interethnic political relations also bears comparison with Platt's analysis (in Part III) of native Andean responses to nineteenth-century liberals in Bolivia.

Local riot to defend a preexisting standard gave way, however, to insurrectionary utopias in the eighteenth century, and Jan Szemiński's essay contributes a remarkable analysis of the language and concepts in play during the war of 1780–1782. Szemiński begins with a deceptively simple question: why did the rebels kill Spaniards? The answer is not nearly as obvious as first appears. The obsession to kill systematically all "Spanish" beings, including children, and the ritual aspects of the brutalities, including bodily mutilations and the denial of clothes and a burial to the victims, are not easily reducible to obvious motives such as vengeance, intimidation, or looting. As Szemiński explores how Andean rebels justified the rites of murder, he draws us into the mental world of the insurrection, and unravels hidden nuances in the meaning of such words as "Spaniard," "King," and "God."

The results are revealing and startling. In Andean rebel eyes, the extermination of "Spaniards," vital to the "moral cleansing" that would usher in a new era, enjoyed the approval of the king of Spain and the Christian God! The insurrectionaries placed the Spaniards in the Andean category of *ñak'aq*, a Quechua term for humanoid beings considered criminal, beastly, and demonic. The human status of such beings was ambiguous, for they stood apart from normal humanity as parasitic antisocials whose own wellbeing was predicated on destroying human life. In the eyes of the insurrectionaries, these Spaniards had rebelled against the king of Spain and the Christian God. Indeed, the mythical "Spain" situated "across the sea," a powerful and distinctive realm distant from the world of humans in America, had no necessary connection to, and in no way legitimized, the colonial "Spain" of Spaniards in Peru. In killing "Spaniards," the insurrectionaries killed traitors and heretics. Szemiński's sensitivity to language exposes the mistaken assumptions behind a common historiographical trap — that which assumes a simple dichotomy between moderate reformist ideology amenable to continued loyalty and submission to the king of Spain (and therefore to colonial rule), and more radical separatist ideology envisioning a fundamental rupture with the colonial past. The trap is a confusing one since the same rebels repeatedly and readily crossed the divide between these positions.

In Szemiński's striking analysis, neither hypocrisy nor contradiction marred the rebels' emphatic assertions of moral sanction for their deeds by the king of "Spain" and by God, and their equally declared insistence that theirs was a war to install a returned Inca-King to govern America in a thoroughly transformed era.

As with many pioneering analyses, Szemiński's study raises more questions than it can answer. As Xavier Albó pointed out in conference discussion, and as Szemiński observes in the introduction to his essay, "Spaniard" constituted a symbolic category, and in practice, the inclusion or exclusion of people in the Spaniard-as-ñak'aq category followed no strict biological or cultural rule. Some Spaniards, particularly creoles, enjoyed exemption from death; some Indian notables and chiefs belonged in the ñak'aq group; creoles and mestizos filled important leadership roles in the Túpac Amaru uprising; and (cf. Campbell, Chapter 4 in this volume), the insurrectionaries themselves divided between a tupamarista tendency more willing to contemplate a multiethnic utopia, and a katarista tendency more inclined to appeal to Aymara racial solidarities excluding even Quechua Andeans (cf. Chapter 4). One key task for future research is to examine the criteria by which people were in practice placed inside or outside the Spaniard-as-ñak'aq category, and the way such practice varied across space and time as the insurrectionary war unfolded.

The other side of the coin is the question of native Andean identity and self-definitions. If it is not always obvious who was considered a "Spaniard" during the civil war, it is also not obvious how the insurrectionaries categorized the remainder of humanity, nor how native Andean groups fit into this larger human world. On what basis did native Andean peoples establish their own positive sense of identity? To what degree did they experience a crisis of identity in the eighteenth century? By what criteria might they incorporate some provincial mestizos and poor creoles into the Andean kingdom to come? And how did particularistic Andean self-definitions, tied to specific gods, landscapes, and ethnic boundaries, become linked to the more universal idea of "Indians" to be unified and liberated by the coming of an Inca-King? Salomon's essay reminds us of the importance of ritual in Andean self-definitions, and at the 1984 conference meetings, Manuel Burga shared research in progress that focuses on the evolution of myth and ritual in the central Andes to trace changing native self-definitions. Burga's research shows that it is misleading to pose the question of Inca-linked identities and utopias in terms that assume simple, direct continuities maintained since the sixteenth century. What he finds instead is that local Andean societies suffered, in the sixteenth and seventeenth centuries, a steady erosion of ritual and mythological connection to the major regional and supraregional deities that had once served to incorporate smaller-scale, more fragmentary identifications of "family" and "community" into wider horizons of identity, interest, and obligation. By the end of the seventeenth century, this religious atrophy had in the main reduced the boundaries of Andean identity and worship to rather narrowly framed ancestor-mummy cults. If Burga's research does not answer all the questions we have about Andean identity in the eighteenth century, it at least enables us to pose the issues more accurately. The question becomes not how Inca-linked identities were maintained and propagated since the sixteenth century, but how, rather, general notions of "Indian-ness" and of an Inca return, accompanied by new forms of memory and ritual, including theatrical reenactment of Inca and conquest themes, came to be grafted onto the otherwise shrinking scale of Andean ritual and mythology, thereby reexpanding the horizons of Andean identification, memory, and cohesion.

Whatever the explanation of the reconstitution and spread of neo-Inca ideas and utopias, these ideas clearly exerted a powerful grip on popular consciousness in the late colonial period. One of the more subtle sides of this phenomenon was the way the Andean utopia might seduce non-

Indians. This Alberto Flores Galindo studies in his sensitive portrayal of Gabriel Aguilar and José Manuel Ubalde, two creole leaders of the curious neo-Inca conspiracy discovered in Cuzco in 1805. In the story of Aguilar and Ubalde's quest to coronate an Inca-King, Flores Galindo detects the remnants of an Andean cultural renaissance so powerful and expansive that it occasionally conquered the imagination of urban creoles and intellectuals. The growing native obsession with Andean glories, traditions, history, and prophecies profoundly influenced the provincial milieus which constituted home for many eighteenth-century creoles and mestizos. Given this cultural influence, and the prophetic and mystical aspects of colonial Catholic culture, even non-Indians could find the idea of a revived Inca kingdom irresistible. In the eighteenth-century world of Peru, Flores Galindo reminds us, the destinies and understandings projected by the native "Andean" side of European-Andean culture could stretch to subsume a diversity of social types: poor indigenous peasant, rich Indian noble, impoverished mestizo, restless creole. We should avoid overstating the point. The quick retreat of most sympathetic creoles from alliance with Túpac Amaru; the killings of creoles by rebel rank and file even when their leaders prohibited the executions; the tension between the more multiracial proclivities of the tupamarista leadership, centered in Quechua Cuzco, and the more exclusivist tendencies of the kataristas centered in the Aymara altiplano — all provide ample warning of the caveats we must make. To the extent that the permeability of cultural and social boundaries reflected day-to-day experiences, it probably varied by region, and perhaps also by strata within racial-ethnic groups.

Nonetheless, the flexibility and reach of eighteenth-century Andean culture is impressive viewed retrospectively, precisely because it would be lost in the aftermath of the Great War. As the nineteenth century unfolded, the world of native Andean preoccupations and identifications shrank to that of the poor indigenous peasant. Had they lived long lives, the aging Aguilar and Ubalde would have found themselves lonely survivors of an almost incomprehensible past.

CHAPTER 5

Ancestor Cults and Resistance to the State in Arequipa, ca. 1748–1754

FRANK SALOMON

Toward the middle of the eighteenth century, the Indian town of Andagua, in the *corregimiento* of Condesuyos de Arequipa, offered a stiff resistance to the colonial tribute regimen. Resistance was not organized in purely political terms, but rather was intimately connected with the persisting cults of mummified ancestors. This chapter proposes to reconstruct the relationship between "idolatries" and antitribute activism through a reading of the 1751–1754 criminal trial of the native leader Gregorio Taco and his allies. The 293-folio trial record is conserved, without any title or classification, in the archive of the Archbishopric of Arequipa, Peru.

Studies of indigenous resistance usually focus on outbreaks of overt revolution, characterized in politics by attacks on colonial authorities and in ideology by "utopian" versions of Andean ideas (Burga and Flores G. 1982). The Andagua papers reveal a situation not polarized to this extreme, and yet already marked by deep popular alienation from colonial institutions which Andean tributaries had earlier tolerated and even helped to administer. Seen from Lima, Andagua's riots and "idolatries" appeared a local scandal attributable to familiar conflicts between city and countryside, Indian and Spanish ethnic groups and estates, and civil versus church governance. They were not taken as a serious threat to the colonial order. But the peculiar, half-revolutionary condition of Andagua thirty years before the great insurrections acquires special interest in hindsight insofar

The author wishes to thank the Fulbright-Hays Commission of Lima for support of the 1982 research underlying this paper. P. Manuel Marzal of the Pontífica Universidad Católica del Perú in Lima kindly pointed me toward the sources, and in Arequipa, Sr. Dante Zegarra of the Universidad San Agustín helped me locate them. Their help is deeply appreciated.

as it helps us imagine with ethnographic clarity the soil in which Andean revolutionism would eventually grow.

The events have several specific points of interest. First, the transformation of the ancestor-mummy cults into foci of rebel factionalism is in itself revealing. In Andean thought as earlier observers had depicted it, ancestral mummies had been literally the incarnation of continuity, and in practice their cults had functioned to reproduce social organization along kinship lines. In clandestinity, the hidden ancestors had symbolized the persistence of communal forms amid deeply compromising colonial conditions. If the cosmological and genealogical order which mummies represented was now seen as a warrant for resistance and not merely for endurance, that is likely to be because worshippers felt their experience in the extracommunal world now violated their basic ideas of right, obligation, and continuity more radically than before. What were these ideas, and with what social processes was the change of consciousness connected? The problem is central, and the case may be useful, for understanding revolt as an endogenous process in the history of Andean societies and not just an automatic, instantaneous response to outside pressures.

Second, the incidents in Andagua, while not openly revolutionary, show that political articulation between Indian collectivities and the colonial regime was suffering damage and erosion. The damage was not just ideological. In practice, Arequipa did become unable to tax or govern at least some of its native territories. Gregorio Taco was able to gain ascendancy not only for endogenous reasons but because the colonial panorama he confronted was riven with more general conflicts which he could exploit and deepen. The "rebels and idolators" of Andagua felt that they were defending a legitimate old order and withholding cooperation from illegitimate pretenders, but the effective force of their actions may have been more innovative than they intended.

The first and second parts of the chapter convey the local context and the events reported in the trial. The third part describes the religious practice of the "rebels and idolators" as a system of beliefs and organizations mobilizing Andagua collectively. The fourth part seeks to juxtapose religious and political data in the context of the above questions.

THE TOWN OF ANDAGUA IN THE EIGHTEENTH CENTURY

Modern Andagua is located at 3,587 m. above sea level in the narrow Valley of Ayo, near Arequipa (IGM 1968). In the eighteenth century such a situation corresponded to the upper margin of tuber agriculture and the lower margin of the semiarid steppe populated by herders (Flores G. 1977: 13, Barriga 1946: 63). Andagua belonged to a heavily indigenous zone whose economy was oriented to the mines of Potosí. In spite of its poor agricultural base, its people included a moderately prosperous sector of native merchants specialized in traffic between the hot coastal valleys, the mine region, and the cities of Arequipa, Cuzco, La Paz, and Oruro (Flores G. 1977: 17, 29). Gregorio Taco, leader of the "idolators" and rebels, belonged to this stratum as did many of his followers.

Toward the end of the century, Antonio Alvarez y Ximénez visited Andagua and described it as a poor and uncomfortable place:

. . . this *doctrina* [native parish] is situated on a short plain, having around it some arid hills, full of thorns, and in inspecting the settlement one sees it to be of ridiculous construction, of uncut stones set over mud foundations, the roofs being of wood with flimsy straw on top, called puna grass; its streets are not badly laid out, but narrow . . . although it has a few arable lands they are not of much use . . . because they are very stony and full of gravel . . . the climate is extremely cold and dry, and much more so in winter, with winds so piercing as to be intolerable (Barriga 1946: 63).

In 1790 it housed 1,606 Andeans and 428 "*españoles*" (ibid.: 60). Despite being heavily involved in long-distance trade and the world mine market, the natives retained local idiosyncrasies in dress (Millones 1975: 63–64) and in language, notably their Quechua-Aymara bilingualism (to which an 1812 report adds the "Coli, Puquina, Isapi, and Chinchaysuyo" languages; ibid.: 47). They developed two commercial specialties: the traffic in distilled liquor from the hot coastal valleys, and the dyeing of wool for export to the highlands (Málaga M. 1981: 74–75; Barriga 1946: 63). For their commercial caravans they maintained considerable numbers of mules. The Andagua natives had the reputation of being self-sufficient, haughty, and very able in their trades, and also, of being incorrigible "witches" and "idolators."

THE EVENTS IN ANDAGUA, 174(8?)–1754

THE CONFRONTATION IN ANDAGUA, 1751, AND THE FIRST INVESTIGATION OF ITS "WITCHES"

In 1751, General Joseph de Arana, Corregidor of Condesuyos de Arequipa, judged the situation in the town of Andagua as intolerable. The chief problem was its stubborn defiance of tribute administration after several years of nonpayment. Two previous corregidores had tried to collect its back tributes, only to find themselves up against an unyielding resistance. Arana travelled to Andagua and called a meeting of the natives (f. 57r–v):

. . . with the greatest friendliness I said to them, "Sons, I have come to make a visit to this town and to see whether you wish to pay the back debts which are on your record"; to which they all replied with disorderly cries, "Even if we were made of money, there would not be any for back tributes; we have all we can do just paying our priest!" Finding myself without sufficient people, I feared some fatal consequence, and accordingly I spoke once more with the same sweetness, saying, "Sons, I do not mean to push you, but this is not the way to free yourselves from the obligation which you are to fulfill in every tax term; and what you may do about it, is to talk to the Viceroy of these kingdoms so that he will order a *revisita* [i.e., revised tax quota inspection] made . . . and the bad reputation you have will be erased." With this they all calmed down and I resumed my journey.

But this success proved illusory. News soon reached the corregidor that immediately after the meeting, Gregorio Taco, ex-cacique of Andagua (f. 245r) and a man known for his leadership in the cults of aboriginal shrines, had renewed the antitribute agitation. On June 2, Arana received a letter from the current interim (i.e., nonhereditary) cacique and governor of Andagua, Don Carlos Tintaya. Tintaya asked the corregidor to send troops to imprison Taco. The corregidor acceded at once, sending Don Bernardo Vera y Vega to Taco's house with thirteen soldiers (f. 1r–v).

They found the "idolator" and his wife Teresa Luychu sleeping drunk after a festival (f. 135v). Caught by surprise, Gregorio Taco shouted furiously at the invaders that no Spaniard from Arequipa could be his judge because he had the protection of the viceroy in Lima. Hearing the shouts, Indian neighbors rang the church bells and ran through the streets "in great numbers, with drums and horns," shouting "Death to the Spaniards!" The women, especially, voiced ethnic hatred ("Even if these moors do not die now, they will die soon") and proclaimed Taco's immunity from Arequipa's jurisdiction ("saying that the corregidor was not his judge and that only the lord Viceroy was his judge"). Although the majority language of Andagua was Quechua, Taco and Luychu cried out in Aymara (f. 10r, 12r). This caused confusion among the soldiers, who thought they heard Taco order his followers to kill Vera y Vega. Amid shouts and music the villagers attacked the invaders hurling stones from their slings. Because of a confusion of identity (later attributed to a likeness of clothing), they thought they had captured the hated corregidor Arana. The soldiers panicked, and barely managed to rescue their commander and escape.

During the following days Arana collected testimony of witnesses about several aspects of Andagua. In the pages of these hearings one can read various points of view, among them that of the Interim Cacique and Governor Don Carlos Tintaya. He expressed disgust at the ignorance of his subjects and their susceptibility to demagogic "idolatry." He reported that Taco's followers had menaced him with loss of office if he meddled with Taco, alleging that their leader was "without a judge at present" and protected by the viceroy (f. 47r–v). According to Tintaya all the Indians accepted unquestioningly the orders of Taco and his well-known *cuadrilla* ("gang").

The "Spanish" residents of Andagua attributed to their Indian neighbors "the utmost haughtiness, with little obedience and less sympathy for the acts of their parish priest" (f. 33r–v). Among Hispanics the town had the reputation of housing innumerable dangerous witches, whose black arts they sincerely feared (f. 14r). Some of the witchcraft acts blamed on natives belong to the European satanist tradition (Silverblatt 1982), including especially those attributed to women. But in general the Hispanic testimonies show a surprisingly full knowledge of Andean religions. Even while categorizing them as "witchcraft," Hispanic witnesses described non-Christian acts of sacrifice and worship with some accuracy.

The *curas doctrineros* (priests of native parishes) in Andagua and nearby villages were not leading accusers in "idolatry" cases. They complained, rather, about the weakness of church and state control over the zones. The priest from San Pedro de Chachas reported that the natives did not go to mass or supply the necessary choristers and sacristans. They lived "in extreme liberty because of being subject to different chiefs, such that it would be appropriate to name one chief and one only" (f. 27r). Their tribute quota records had not been updated. Some wandered from estate to estate to avoid paying tribute. The Andagua priest, Joseph Delgado, maintained that gossip about witchcraft was just a pastime of idlers and drunkards (f. 249r), but public opinion was that he left the "witches" unpunished only because he himself feared them (f. 196r). Delgado repeatedly gave asylum in his house to persons wanted by the civil authorities, among them Gregorio Taco himself (f. 140r). Taco in turn reported enjoying the friendship and trust of his priest (f. 134r).

Having finished the hearings, Arana wrote a memorandum to the higher government of Lima concerning the causes of the evil and possible countermeasures. He attributed the natives' "haughtiness," and their disobedience to civil authorities, to the impossibility of keeping them under scrutiny during their long and frequent expeditions to La Paz and Oruro. To this cause he added two more. One was the recent introduction of distilled liquors. The other was the extralegal leadership of the Taco family, who "dominate with a strange authority due to their being the leaders in deeds of idolatry" (f. 59r–v).

Arana's list of remedies includes drastic measures, such as confiscating the traders' mules and banishing the Tacos. Eventually a reply from the Viceroy Conde de Superunda arrived, with permission to carry out less radical measures. The viceroy and the *fiscal protector de naturales* (public defender for natives) authorized Arana to remove natives from their dwellings "among fields and canyons" and relocate them around the church, to suppress the liquor trade, and to carry out an update of tribute quotas. He also authorized a trial of the main "idolators" (f. 49r–60v).

THE CRISIS OF 1752 AND THE TRIAL OF THE "REBELS" AND "IDOLATORS"

In October of 1752 about fifty armed men under Juan Pablo de Peñaranda, deputized as judge, set out from Chuquibamba to imprison the accused of Andagua. Two caciques of nearby villages took part, together with some Spanish military officers and various mestizos. They were also charged to confiscate salable goods of the accused to satisfy their back tribute debts (f. 61r–63v).

According to one of the caciques, Peñaranda did not abuse the Andagua villagers but, on the contrary, "showed great courtesy and urbanity, as with subjects of a different legal domain [*fuero*]" (f. 103r). Nonetheless, Peñaranda's arrival in Andagua caused "an incredible uproar" among the natives. Later, there were accusations that the soldiers caused the death of a child, an abortion, and the humiliation of several Indian women subjected to "libidinous acts" (f. 69r, 134r, 136r, 158v, 236v, 240r). Still the villagers abstained from violence and the invaders were able to take 24 natives prisoner. Gregorio Taco escaped but his wife was captured. The pro-Spanish interim chief Carlos Tintaya was also imprisoned for failing to collect tributes.

In Gregorio Taco's house Peñaranda found few goods to confiscate. Although Taco owned a large herd of mules, Peñaranda found only a few loads of wool, wine, and coca, and some equipment for muledriving. In Carlos Tintaya's house, the inspectors found small amounts of wool and some Catholic devotional objects. In Matheo Maquito's house larger amounts of goods did turn up, chiefly Andean-style clothing wrapped in packsacks and bags, but altogether the modest finds suggest that the accused had been tipped off and had emptied their houses (f. 63r–64v).

During their stay in Andagua the corregidor's men experienced the first stirrings of a conflict which would paralyze their campaign more and more: enmity between civil authorities and the churchmen responsible for Andean parishes. From the start P. Delgado had shown himself unenthusiastic about the persecutions. Finding his parish up in arms, he approached Peñaranda and threatened him with excommunication unless all the soldiers would voluntarily place themselves under ecclesiastical command. He then dispatched a letter of exhortation to Arana, to which the corregidor replied at once in brusque tones of repudiation (f. 70r–71r).

The opening of the trial brought to light a long chain of antecedents leading to the recent riots. New accusations surfaced that Delgado had let his parishioners practice "witchcraft" because leading "witches" had cowed him with threats of uprisings and hexes (f. 83r, 94v). The cacique of neighboring Chachas said that Andagua's rebellion had a long tradition, that in the past they had assassinated a priest, and that they had always been feared "because they have the custom of attacking the judges and their deputies every time they have been called to account for the payment and satisfaction of the royal tributes" (f. 87r, 94r).

For example, another neighboring chief recalled the failure that the corregidor Juan Bautista Zamorátegui had suffered when trying to enforce tributes against Andagua's tax delinquents; arriving, Zamorátegui found himself alone with the native magistrates, because all the villagers had fled forewarned (some taking asylum in the parish house). The same chief told of taking part in a 1750 attempt at collection, during which Gregorio Taco was taken captive only to be snatched away and turned loose by the "Indian collectivity" (común de indios; f. 101r–v).

Witnesses agreed that "the Gregorio Taco gang" held together around the prestige of its leader. Taco commanded considerable material as well as magical resources; he was the owner of a dye workshop to which various neighbors brought their wool (f. 91v) as well as a mule herd for long-distance trading. But religious and magical issues were the crux. According to his own sayings, he had received this wealth as gifts from the "gentiles" (pre-Christian mummified ancestors) who lived in his family shrine. He recruited members to his group by offering access to these rich deities. Among the most devoted recruits was Ramón Sacasqui, a man who had no affiliation to a local shrine (presumably because he was an immigrant; f. 163r) and lived in extreme poverty, when, in 1740, Gregorio Taco (f. 97r)

taking pity . . . because of the troubles that the said Ramón Sacasqui suffered, went to his house, and said that he felt very sorry to see him [Sacasqui] so poor, and that if he [Sacasqui] wished, he [Taco] would take him to where he had his ancestors [linaje], who gave him everything he needed and rescued him from troubles, [asking] if he [Sacasqui] wished to go and offer worship to them; on account of which advice he [Sacasqui] felt obliged to go with the said Gregorio Taco. And one league above the town of Andagua they arrived at about eight in the evening and they went to the place where the said Gregorio Taco had his shrine [mochadero], and having observed that it was in the form of a cave with a rather narrow door, they entered in and found a seated mummy, to whom Gregorio Taco offered worship. And the said Ramón Sacasqui applauded the shrine, and passing on to another large cave, he found several mummies, and the said Gregorio Taco remarked to him, "These are the ones who give me money and every happiness." . . . Different people go to the said shrines to offer sacrifices of dead llamas, maize beer in little pitchers, and other drinks.

Another man respected as leader of a *facción* ("faction") of "idolators" was Sebastián Tintaya, the father of the interim chief and owner of the mummy shrine called Hasaparco (f. 104r–v, 136v). His Spanish enemies showed the judges a llama-skin packsack full of objects used in native religion, including *mullu* shell, prehispanic statuettes, coca, and maize, which also contained a receipt written to Sebastián Tintaya (f. 117v).

Such men's leadership did not rest, however, on religious or material bases alone. They also served a political function as antitribute leaders. Gregorio Taco had headed the movement for several years. At one point, probably in 1748, he made use of his offices as cacique (f. 150r), presumably interim, and *alcalde mayor* (chief native magistrate; f. 151v) to convene a *cabildo* (council) of "the most prominent" Indians and open discussion of the tribute debt. Many of the councilmen were later to be defendants for "idolatry" (Juan Guanco, "segunda de la otra mitad," i.e., Taco's moiety counterpart; Pascual Lázaro, Matheo Maquito, Diego Cabana Andagua, Pedro Cabana Andagua, Juan Quecaña, Matheo Quecaña, and Benito Andaguaruna). Taco proposed that the tributaries not comply with the corregidor's demands, and that they make a unilateral reduction of five and a half *reales* of tribute, and hand over only what was necessary for the *sínodo* of the priest (f. 124v, 132v, 137r, 144v, 152v, 184r). This policy was received as absolute law by the community and as sufficient justification to defy Spanish civil authority completely.

Gregorio Taco also promoted the idea that the corregidor lacked jurisdiction over Andagua and that its people owed obedience only to the viceroy. In his own confession, he reported having promised the collectivity that he would bring a "judge named by his excellency the Viceroy, a person independent from the corregidor of this province, by the order of his protector Don Agustín de Bedoya Mogrovexo" (f. 178v). On many occasions, according to witnesses, he repeated his orders to withhold tribute pending a new judgment (f. 179v, 180r, 181r).

In October 1752, basing himself on data discovered in the trial, Arana sent a larger force of 150 armed men to capture the resisters, demolish the mummy shrines, and punish ancestor-worshippers. He categorized this task as "extirpation of idolatries," using a phrase common a hundred years earlier but rarely heard since (f. 120r). The force took along Carlos Tintaya and Ramón Sacasqui as prisoner-guides.

Sacasqui took them first to Quisguarani (f. 113r), "an untilled place among the rugged cliffs," where Tintaya pointed out the narrow opening of a cavern. It was reputed to be the "main shrine," whose owner was Gregorio Taco. Another nearby cave was identified as the shrine of Sebastián Tintaya. Inside the main cave, the extirpators found several mummified ancestors surrounded by coca and ceramic flasks of recent design.

The Mercedarian friar Lucas del Fierro exorcised the cave and ordered the natives to take its mummies outside, but, "with the utmost repugnance, and even under coercion of punishment, they scarcely approached the cave." In the end the Indians flatly refused to remove the mummies. "Seeing that not even under the threat of a death sentence would they touch those bodies," the Mercedarian finally had non-Indians destroy the Indian ancestors (f. 112v–13r).

They carried the whole ritual apparatus to Andagua's plaza, where the ancestors were hung from ropes for several days with their liturgical gear. The non-Indians lit a bonfire in the center of the plaza and in the presence of the whole community set the dry mummies aflame (f. 115v–16r). Then they collected the ashes and dropped them into a remote lake. This spectacle caused the natives "deep consternation and melancholy" (f. 112r).

Later the expedition returned to the Quisguarani caves, from which the soldiers removed and burned additional ancestors. They filled the looted shrines with stones and put crosses on the sites (f. 113v). Continuing on to other sanctuaries, they found more ancestors who were burned in the plaza or at their caves (f. 113v) and also a shrine called Pollogchaca in a prehispanic building which they then demolished (f. 114r).

When the destruction of the shrines was complete, Arana and his army took confessions from the accused. They tortured Gregorio Taco by the lash without managing to extract a satisfactory confession (f. 131r). But ten days later Taco made a new and fuller confession in which he said he had held the shrine of Cuyag Mama, "goddess of his lineage," for seventeen or eighteen years. He also said he had been instructed in the belief that "the ancients . . . first and greatest owners of this kingdom" had imposed an everlasting obligation on their descendants to bring sacrifices (f. 131v–32r). Regarding the alleged sedition, he confirmed the story of the Indian council and its unilateral tribute reform but denied being personally responsible for it (f. 132r).

1753–1754: CONFLICTS AMONG THE PERSECUTORS; THIRD INVESTIGATION AND COLLAPSE OF THE PERSECUTION

Toward the end of 1752, discord among the corregidor, the church, and the viceregal representatives became acute enough to hamper the persecution of the Andagua natives. The advocate of the *Audiencia* of Lima intervened by ordering that new confessions be taken in order to satisfy a law which mandated the presence of a fiscal protector de naturales during confession. He also repudiated the trial acts formulated so far because they mixed charges of idolatry with those of tribute nonpayment and thereby illegally crossed the jursidictional boundary between church and state. With the assistance of Joseph de Buenaventura as designated protector, new confessions were taken.

During January 1753, the Arequipa prosecutor asked sentencing of the accused (f. 196r–v, 240r–v) and the protector prepared his response, but the trial advanced more and more slowly for two reasons. For one, the Lima authorities demanded to see the acts (f. 202r); for another, the Ecclesiastical Chapter of Arequipa *sede vacante*, jealous of its authority over spiritual infractions and piqued by the accusation of excessive leniency in the parochial treatment of "witchcraft," began to oppose Arana's continued participation in the prosecution of the "idolators" (f. 207r). During this phase, the Treasurer of the archbishopric, P. Don Joseph Antonio Basurco y Herrera, assumed leadership and dominates the trial record. The chapter named P. Joseph Mogrovejo of Pampacolca as "judge of idolatries" (another seventeenth-century throwback phrase; f. 211r) and delegated the ecclesiastical *promotor* to write an opinion asking lifelong banishment of Gregorio Taco and his fellow "sectarians."

But Arana faced the churchmen with innumerable delaying tactics, continuing to evade numerous letters of exhortation which asked him to hand over the accused and the original trial records even after the higher authorities in Lima had clearly adjudicated the "idolatries" case to the archbishopric (f. 232r–33v). The ecclesiastics did not oppose a continued role for Arana in regard to the riots and tribute nonpayment (f. 211r). But it was obvious that without having the accused physically in his power Arana would never be able to exact tribute payment, and so he remained stubborn in his noncompliance (f. 214r).

The new "judge of idolatries" Mogrovejo travelled to Andagua to carry out a new investigation in May 1753 (f. 244r). Together with P. Delgado he called the collectivity together and exhorted everyone to come and denounce idolators. He also inspected the former shrine sites without finding anything new. Nonetheless, in spite of arriving so late, P. Mogrovejo was able to collect some new data on non-Christian religion (auguries, etc.) because some natives took advantage of his presence to avenge outrages suffered at the hands of earlier informers.

The stalemate between Arana and the chapter lasted through the rest of 1753. The archbishopric complained bitterly of its inability to make Arana turn over the defendants, threatening him with excommunication. Arana argued that the church was impeding the collection of overdue tributes. The interim cacique scarcely acted, confessing himself intimidated by threats from the Indian collectivity. The Lima authorities advised Arana to proceed slowly and gently in the prosecution of tribute delinquents. Toward the end of the year, Arana offered to turn over the accused under the condition that their confiscated goods remain in his power for auction. The church again demanded the banishment of the "idolators" but Arana forbade it lest they again escape tributation.

In 1754 the efforts to punish the resisters and "idolators" collapsed alto-

together, not through any sudden blow, but through a gradual disorganization of the antinative campaign. While Arana and the chapter continued
to wrangle, the situation in Andagua was returning to normal. In February the news arrived that Gregorio Taco's brother and his wife had escaped from prison and that the accused who had not been jailed were
escaping to different places (f. 253r). Other prisoners petitioned for their
liberty adducing ill health or poverty (f. 269r). In May the priest P. Rivero
y Davila reported that Gregorio Taco and his brother were in full liberty
and again organizing trading caravans (f. 288r). A short time later the
chapter received news that the Andagua defendants had returned to their
homes (f. 292r). And in October 1754, Gregorio Taco felt secure enough
to appear in person before the chapter seeking exoneration, claiming to
have been an active member of two *cofradías* (sodalities) and a victim of
false accusations (f. 294r). The chapter admitted his petition, but at this
moment — October 11, 1754 — we lose the thread for lack of further documents. It seems likely that some arrangement between the native leadership of Andagua and the ecclesiastical authority would soon put an end
to the crisis.

ANCESTOR SHRINES, RITUAL LIFE, AND SOCIAL ORGANIZATION IN ANDAGUA, C. 1750

Some of the factors behind the events in Andagua can be understood in
regional terms: attempts at enforcing centralized tax regimes in a setting
historically conditioned by considerable de facto local autonomy; rising
Bourbon-era tensions between church and state; an Indian society in which
the legally mandated colonial chieftaincy and native norms of legitimacy
had come deeply into conflict. But the events also raise questions which
must be answered from the inside of Andagua outward, ethnographically:
why should resistance crystallize around ancestor-cult priesthood and not
some other role? If the jural chieftaincy did not embody the effective
political organization of the community on the eve of the age of rebellion,
what was the effective organization which actually shaped events?

THE ENDURANCE AND FUNCTION OF ANCESTOR WORSHIP

Most students of Andean religion agree that within any local belief
system Andean deities can be considered as points in a system of segment-
ing oppositions that ramify downward from the most cosmic or pan-
Andean numina through regional gods (volcanos, etc.), to origin-shrines
representing self-defined collectivities at descending levels of inclusiveness. Ancestor shrines with mummies manifest the lower, more local

branches of the oppositional tree, corresponding to localized kindreds (Huertas V. 1970). Mummies mediate between people and earth; they are the progeny of earth and reside in the openings of the earth, but they are also the progenitors of living people and apical members of local society. Through their mediation sacrifices go to earth, and wealth comes out of earth.

Cock and Doyle (1979) and others have observed that the upper parts of the system suffered greater erosion in colonial times than the lower ones, and after the major "extirpation" campaigns apical cults almost cease to figure (Marzal 1977). Colonial measures destroying the upper levels of native political leadership also seem to have reduced the number of religious occasions shared among local native groups, heightening the relative importance of ancestor deities and giving scope for their individuality to develop. By 1750 this was the case in Andagua.

Arequipa had lain outside the main path of "extirpation" in the seventeenth century. But about eighty years before the Taco trial, the Archbishop of Arequipa Pedro de Villagómez did organize an "extirpation" campaign in the region. A trial fragment studied by Duviols (1966) and another studied by Wightman (1981) show that the folk religion of the 1750s still resembled earlier beliefs, but that the atmospheric and volcano cults had lost importance (Duviols 1966: 204–5, 207; see also Wightman 1981: 43–45, where the volcano deity Surimana is apparently misidentified as Saramama, and f. 244v of the Taco trial).

Nonetheless, after the Villagómez "extirpations," Andagua enjoyed a long interval of relative religious peace. Carlos Tintaya reported that its people had met no opposition to their clandestine worship, "because [Arana's] predecessors and the priests of the said village have considered this matter as beyond their obligations, letting the cancer spread, and falling naively into the most evident errors, because the said Indians teach their little children to continue on in the same rites." Arana's unforeseen militancy took Andagua very much by surprise, its people never having "seen or heard of any such reform in a great many years, as the Indian men and women of advanced age report, taking the present discovery [of the caves] as a fatal omen" (f. 173v).

Up to Arana's intervention the shrines of the "*linajes*" were the most numerous and vital objects of native worship. Insofar as they represented a society where native leadership existed only at a local level, and indeed one in which colonially legalized native leadership above the kinship level enjoyed little legitimacy, their cogency as "collective representations" seems unique. More interesting than the degree to which mummy worshipers' ideas reflected social self-concept, however, is the question of how their practice organized and reproduced the collectivity. The functioning of religious organization must have been triple: it defined collective "self" and "other" within rigid boundaries; it fostered within the Andean collectivity an economic structure which formed a part of the mining-mercantile system; and it reconciled these two partly contradictory functions by regulating cooperation or resistance vis-à-vis exterior powers indifferent to local concepts of right and obligation.

I suggest that around 1748 Andagua's de facto leaders had shifted from overall policies of cooperation to policies of resistance because they saw direct intervention and tribute enforcement as a threat to the internal constitution of Andagua — a constitution in which advantaged kindreds enjoyed virtual class privilege via their mercantile links, but at the same time exercised their advantage within a local system that made conformity to Andean belief a condition for controlling mercantile resources. The purpose of this section is to sketch that constitution.

ANCESTOR SHRINES AND "FAMILY" ORGANIZATION

Mummy worship formed a seamless web of obligations from hearthside level to the outermost limits of the self-defined collectivity. Witnesses' accounts make it clear that the household (with an undefined degree of extension) formed the atom of religious practice. On Friday nights each household group went separately to a shrine representing the "family" through its ancestors. The word "family" is probably a translation of *ayllu*. Logically one may assume that each ancestor shrine represented a plurality of households composing the unit called "family." Each Andagua person "had" a shrine designated to him or her, and the senior male (or female?) of a "family" was said to be the "owner" of his group's shrine. Apparently he functioned as its chief priest and regulated access to it. The "family" represented by the shrine was conceived of as a permanent corporation.

Witnesses gave remarkably vivid accounts of such shrine visits, and testify to their emotional weight in binding kin together. After dark the worshipers left their homes one by one, to avoid detection, and waited at a certain rock outcrop until all could travel together to the holy place. Only then could they relax the norm of clandestinity, which on all other days forbade conversation about the shrines. At seven years of age children were taken along and formally presented to the ancestors at which time they learned the rules of secrecy (f. 16v–17r).

At the cave mouth the visitors whistled and asked permission to enter. Greeting their ancestors with Aymara invocations (f. 246r), they would then care for their clothing "of ancient design," light llama-fat candles, and set out offerings which always included coca and special red, yellow, and white maize beers (f. 244v; see also Wightman 1981: 44). Each person would talk with his ancestors requesting auguries and favors: a profitable caravan to La Paz, success in learning to weave, etc. (f. 16v–17r). The mummies sat together at tables or in other lifelike attitudes, with coca in their mouths and pitchers of beer in their hands. They wore tailored furs (f. 113r), sandals (f. 115r), and rich multicolored headgear with garlands of grass (f. 115v). The testimonies convey the climate of solemnity and tenderness worshipers felt toward each other and toward their opulent, everlasting forebears.

The ancestors were seen as true owners of the land. A household's descent from them was its claim to local rights, and whatever wealth it possessed was considered as an ancestral gift. Each "family" took its mummy shrine as its corporate symbol, "holding it as a blazon or sign of honor [*timbre o exaltación*] so that others would respect them" (f. 173v). Any aggrandizement of its worship raised the status of its "owners" (Wightman 1981: 43) relative to other corporations.

ANCESTOR SHRINES AND SUPRA-"FAMILY" ORGANIZATION

The corporate kin groups composing Andagua were not self-sufficient. The ancestral shrines were felt to regulate ties of exchange and interdependence among them, and these ties seem to have constituted the major axes of affinity, commerce, and political faction formation. In effect, ties to and through the shrines reproduced the local polity. Jural colonial chiefdom appears weak and specialized by comparison.

In Taco's time the relative standing of "families" and shrines does not seem to have been ordered by any permanent structural scheme of the kinds familiar from Inca studies. The prestige of the Tacos' and the Tintayas' shrines appears more achieved than inherited, rising with the commercial and political fortunes of their leading members. Despite the Andean form of the corporations their relative rank could be defined at least partly in terms of class, and their rivalries in terms of business competition.

It was normal and perhaps mandatory to marry across "family" lines. In arranging a marriage, each household had to invite its prospective son- or daughter-in-law to the ancestral shrine and ask for auguries and permission through the offices of a specialized oracle; a negative answer could annul even a mutually agreeable match. Access to labor apparently also ran through religious channels; Ramón Sacasqui acquired his job as Gregorio Taco's assistant muledriver not by public contract but through an invitation to visit the shrine of Taco's ancestors.

Corporate "families" sought to better their standing by manipulating shrine conduct. They sought to attract more worshipers to their respective mummy caves and provide access to persons whose help would prove valuable. Economic success could be "pyramided" through religious prestige into further success because wealth was understood as the gift of ancestors. Gregorio Taco was able to make almost the whole wool-trading sector a personal clientele by encouraging the conviction that his ancestors held the key to safe caravaneering; he was known to worship "his" shrine, the home of a divine couple called Camag ("Animator" in Quechua, also called Capachica) and Cuyag Mama ("Loving Mother") with rigorous devotion. It became customary for other traders to wait at this shrine for as long as it took to get a favorable augury before setting out (f. 17v–18r, 113v, 115r–v, 129v, 165v). Witnesses felt this advantage to be decisive in establishing Taco as a popular leader. Ties of shrine clientship were extremely strong, both because the parties expected supernatural rewards or punishments for their conduct, and because secrecy made them into mutual hostages.

In the eyes of believers, leaders of important shrines held the collectivity's prosperity in their hands. Their wealth underwrote their prestige both materially and morally, and economic harm would likewise undercut them in both respects. The major shrine priests' role as antitribute activists is understandable as a part of their general role as guarantors of the flow of wealth from the earth to people and back again via the mediation of ancestors: religion and collective self-interest warranted preventing its diversion toward Arequipa.

CONCLUSIONS: ANCESTRY AND THE IDEOLOGY
OF RESISTANCE

The Gregorio Taco faction did not consciously propose a revolution in the sense that Túpac Amaru II's followers eventually would. On the contrary, they considered tribute nonpayment a way of defending what they thought to be an immemorial and correct standard of intergroup relations. What was that standard and to what extent was its defense part of the same historical process which culminated in the great insurrections?

The Andagua defendants expressed a view of correct interethnic relations which drew on both Andean and European sources. Their religion, like other Andean religions, conceived of humanity as having multiple origins. It organized human diversity through the equation of society with landscape (Allen 1981; Rappaport 1982: 95–98), identifying increasingly inclusive segments of humanity ("family," "town," province, ethnic group, etc.) with the increasingly great landscape features that enfolded (or, in Andean myth, engendered) them. The overall scheme is one of segmentary opposition, and its implication is that the more distant or different two human groups are, the higher the point in segmentary structure that unites them.

In connecting this concept with Spanish law, the Andagua defendants superimposed it on medieval legal concepts and on the idea of a "republic of Indians." Older Iberian law had recognized a multitude of *fueros*, or special legal privileges and jurisdictions enabling certain human groupings to be governed by particular statutes and courts even when these contradicted more general laws. Earlier in the colonial era, such ideas had contributed to the widely known concept of a "republic of Indians," that is, a complex, multistate indigenous society which was to exist alongside the "republic of Spaniards" in the New World, and enjoy its own body of laws and rights. In practice, neither the idea of a segregated "republic of Indians," nor its corollary, inviolable and special legal privileges, directly represented reality. But these ideas had enduring appeal to Indians.

The segmented multiplicity of humanity under Andean axioms and its jural plurality under older Spanish ones coincided in Andean thought to form a folk notion of basic colonial law which only vaguely corresponded to codified law but which was nonetheless a potent element of popular ideology. Andagua-area Indians regarded the Spanish of Arequipa as "subjects of another *fuero*," by which they apparently meant members of a distant segment of humanity, and accordingly united to Andagua only by a connection at a high level of spatial and social generality. Indian Andagua and Spanish Arequipa, they felt, held together only at the level representing the whole "Kingdom of Peru" both Indian and Spanish, i.e., the viceroyalty. Andagua's insistence that only the viceroy could judge Taco reflects the idea that viceregal authority reached from Lima to Arequipa and to Andagua through separate lines and that Spanish Arequipa's claims to regional hegemony were illegitimate. Toleration of priests in Andagua, even during the upheavals, suggests that local people accepted the old Church claim to a special warrant for working in all fueros.

By 1750 the Andagua tributaries apparently considered the interventions of Bourbon-era corregidores to be attempts to enforce a very different notion of jurisdiction. Caciques who collaborated with them violated the folk-legal idea of what a native governor should be. Payment of tribute was no longer experienced as representing the folk-legal status of Andagua, and civil officials were no longer seen as legitimate representatives of a higher power but as extortionate emissaries from a neighboring one. When jural chiefs ceased to defend folk-legal rights, Andean priests, whose task was to enforce and interpret sacred flows up and down the hierarchy of people and powers, became the opponents of such sideways misappropriations in secular context (Millones 1979). Among shrine-cult heads, those who had won advantages in the commercial sector would be, by the reasoning of believers, those best equipped to lead resistance because they had themselves best resisted the attack.

Had the Spanish judges sympathized with, or even understood, the Andagua resisters' claims for a pluralist revindication, the resisters might eventually have become reconciled to their condition as tributaries. But in the event their movement seems a step toward the breakdown of the Andean-European *modus vivendi*. It heightened on a local scale the enmity between church and state administrators of Indian affairs; it exposed the weakness of the colonially appointed chiefs in the face of noncompliance; it encouraged panicky fear of Indians among urban Hispanics; and it clearly revealed the inability of royal officers to influence local Indian politics (Salomon 1983). The de facto processes of Andean factionalism were not yet working in the direction of overt revolt, but neither were they working (so the events proved) within the bounds of any shared Spanish-Andean consensus.

What were the effects of losing the ancestors? The trial does not reveal them. As in seventeenth-century cases, insurrection was seemingly not an immediate sequel. From the documents one gets the impression of a return to superficially normal activity, amid a climate of bitterness and tacit hostility. But, given the frustration of folk-legal hopes for equity, and the loss of the shrines which had symbolized connectedness to the past, it is not hard to imagine how these moments could also have opened some minds toward proposals for an overtly radical transformation of the native condition.

REFERENCES

ALLEN, CATHERINE
    1981   "To be Quechua: the symbolism of coca chewing in highland Peru."
            American Ethnologist 8, 1:157–71.
BARRIGA, VICTOR M.
    1946   *Memorias para la historia de Arequipa.* Vol. 2: 1790–1793. Arequipa:
            Establecimientos Gráficos La Colmena S.A.
BURGA, MANUEL, AND ALBERTO FLORES GALINDO
    1982   "La utopía andina." *Allpanchis* 20 (Cuzco): 85–102.
COCK, GUILLERMO, AND MARY EILEEN DOYLE
    1979   "Del culto solar a la clandestinidad de Inti y Punchao." *Historia y*
            Cultura 12 (Lima): 51–73.
DUVIOLS, PIERRE
    1966   "Un proces d'idolatrie. Arequipa, 1671." *Fenix, Revista de la Biblio-*
            teca Nacional 16 (Lima): 198–211.
FLORES GALINDO, ALBERTO
    1977   *Arequipa y el sur andino: Ensayo de historia regional (siglos XVIII–*
            XX). Lima: Editorial Horizonte.

HUERTAS VALLEJO, LORENZO
1970   "Religión indígena colonial en Canta, Chancay, y Cajatambo: Siglo XVII." Tesis para optar el grado de Bachiller en Historia. Universidad Nacional Mayor de San Marcos, Lima.
IGM (Instituto Geográfico Militar)
1968   "Hoja Topográfica 31-R 1:100.000. Orcopamba (Arequipa)." Lima.
MÁLAGA MEDINA, ALEJANDRO
1981   "La industria textil en Arequipa colonial." In Alejandro Málaga Medina, *Arequipa: Estudios históricos* (Arequipa: Publiunsa). Pp. 63–76.
MARZAL, MANUEL
1977   "Una hipótesis sobre la aculturación religiosa andina." *Revista de la Universidad Católica* 2 (Lima): 95–131.
MILLONES, LUÍS
1975   "Economía y ritual en los Condesuyos de Arequipa: Pastores y tejedores del siglo XIX." *Allpanchis* 8: 45–66.
1979   "Religion and Power in the Andes: Idolatrous Curacas of the Central Sierra." *Ethnohistory* 26, 3: 143–263.
RAPPAPORT, JOANNE
1982   "Territory and Tradition. Ethnohistory of the Páez of Tierradentro, Colombia." Ph.D. diss. Department of Anthropology, University of Illinois, Urbana-Champaign.
SALOMON, FRANK
1983   "Shamanism and Politics in Late-Colonial Ecuador." *American Ethnologist* 10(3): 413–28.
SILVERBLATT, IRENE
1982   "Dioses y diablos: idolatrías y evangelización." *Allpanchis* 19: 31–48.
WIGHTMAN, ANN M.
1981   "Diego Vasicuio: Native Priest." In David G. Sweet and Gary B. Nash, eds., *Struggle and Survival in Colonial America*. Berkeley: University of California Press. Pp. 38–48.

CHAPTER 6

Why Kill the Spaniard? New Perspectives on Andean Insurrectionary Ideology in the 18th Century

JAN SZEMIŃSKI

Why were the Spaniards killed during the Túpac Amaru uprising? There were many obvious reasons, but they do not explain the insistence by Spanish sources that in 1780–1782 all Spaniards were killed: *chapetones* (Spanish-born Spaniards), creoles (American-born Spaniards), men, women, and children. Mestizos and sometimes Indians too were killed. In 1974 I first suggested a hypothesis I would later try to prove (Szemiński 1984: 15–57)—that "españoles" ("Spaniards") meant in eighteenth-century Peru Spaniards from Spain; members of the "republic of Spaniards" in America; upper caste; nobility; *qullana* members (i.e., local notables) of Indian communities; persons of Spanish culture; upper class.

Usually the sources do not explain which kind of Spaniard was killed. It is easy to show in every social hierarchy a group called Spaniards, whom the Indians had good reasons to kill. I will try to substitute for detailed analysis of the people killed by the rebels, because data for such analysis are lacking, the image of Spaniards as seen by the rebels. The image may provide a general justification of killings, and not a particular one for individual victims. It is my personal conviction that a general rationale for the killings did exist, because people, in order to kill people, need to show that the killed had lost their human status, or that they never were really human at all.

THE SPANIARD AS EVIL ONE

Many sources show that the Spaniards were believed evil. At the beginning of the insurrection the Inca José Gabriel Túpac Amaru (hereinafter Túpac Amaru) proclaimed his objectives: "to put an end to all Europeans as the main authors" of all evil institutions. At the same time he declared in Quechua "that the time had already come when they should shake off the heavy yoke which during so many years they had suffered from the Spaniards, each day being obliged to endure new duties and pains; that his remedies were to mete out the same punishment to all the corregidores of the Realm, and to put an end to all the Europeans." So "the time did come" and with it the remedy: killing the Europeans (CDIP 1971–75: 2:2:155–56). Several days later Túpac Amaru published the same text as edicts for the provinces of Chumbivilcas and Paucartambo. The culprits were European corregidores and the remedy their extermination, which would reintroduce the order destroyed by the Europeans (CDTA 1980–82: 1:419). The Inca's other edicts and letters (e.g., ibid.: 1:331–489) also condemn the Europeans and speak about the time that has come. Spanish sources confirm the condemnation of the Europeans by Túpac Amaru (ibid.: 1:442; CDIP 1971–75: 2:2:415).

By death to Europeans the Inca's followers meant death to Spaniards. There were rumors that Túpac Amaru had ordered his subjects to exterminate all Spaniards (ibid.: 2:2:532) or even anyone wearing a Spanish shirt (CDTA 1980–82: 1:338). The Inca maintained (and he was believed) that he had received a royal order (*real cédula*) to send to the gallows all the corregidores and *puka kunkas* ("red necks"), a common nickname of the Spaniards (ibid.: 3:945–50).

There are many more mentions of Spaniards killed because they were Spaniards. In all the cases the Inca associated with the "coming of the time" the necessity to kill corregidores and Europeans, while everybody else thought that all Spaniards (i.e., creoles as well as chapetones) should be killed just because they were Spaniards. The conviction preceded the uprising. According to a 1776 Indian testimony, a general Indian insurrection was foretold for 1777. The Spaniards "were to be killed starting with the corregidores, judges, and all other people with white faces or fair-haired, and they should have no doubt because the Cuzco Indians had chosen their king to govern them" (ibid.: 2:229). The testimony enumerates the order of extermination, and shows the criteria: functions and racial characteristics believed to be Spanish. The Spaniard was by nature evil, but why?

THE SPANIARD AS HERETIC

The sources suggest frequently that the Spaniards were believed to be heretics. Many of the documents attributed to Túpac Amaru accuse the corregidores and Europeans of being fearless of God (CDIP 1971–75: 2:2:263), rebels against the king (ibid.: 2:2:272), heretics (ibid.: 2:2:461), apostates condemned to Hell, traitors to their king, and not Christians at all, whose deeds were "perverse impositions," while the Inca's own deeds he considered truly Christian (ibid.: 2:2:461, 463: Túpac Amaru y la Iglesia 1983: 209; CDTA 1980–82: 3:207, 215, 218). In Túpac Amaru's Royal Proclamation the kings of Spain and their officials were called usurpers, criminals and without fear of God (CDIP 1971–75: 2:2:578–79).

The Inca spoke about Europeans, Spaniards from Spain. There was no practical way of distinguishing them from the creoles whose identification with the Spaniards presumed that they too were heretics, apostates, and rebels against the king. The Inca's illiterate, Quechua-speaking audience did not understand his words the same way he did. According to one of the Inca's scribes at Guaro, the Inca told the soldiers and the people "that up till now they had not known God, nor had they understood who He is, because they have respected as God the corregidores, thieves, and the priests, but he was going to remedy this." The same was repeated in many other places (CDTA 1980–82: 5:127–28).

Micaela Bastidas, the Inca's wife, believed that the Spaniards were treacherous and wanted them destroyed (ibid.: 4:9). One of the Inca's governors treated the Spaniards and the mestizos very badly because they were "treacherous and two-faced," "rebels against the Inca," all of whom should be killed on the Inca's orders (ibid.: 3:629–30). At Azángaro, Diego Cristóbal Túpac Amaru (hereinafter Diego Cristóbal) maintained that the Spanish authorities were criminals who did not fulfill royal orders, "foreigners, leopards, and many such others," who caused the Indians to become heretics, and who were apostates in contrast to the true Christians, Diego Cristóbal's followers (ibid.: 2:341–44). Even in a letter to the Lima viceroy, Diego Cristóbal repeated his conviction that the Spaniards were criminals, apostates, and rebels against the king of Spain (CDIP 1971–75: 2:3:127). The Macha leader Tomás Katari repeated nearly the same argument (ibid.: 2:2:244–59). The followers of Julián Apasa Túpac Katari (hereinafter Túpac Katari) accused the Spaniards of killing the king's tributaries without the king's license (Valle de Siles 1980: 103), thereby rebelling against the king. In Copacabana the rebels did not permit the Spaniards to be buried "because all the Spaniards were excommunicates and also demons" (CDIP 1971–75: 2:2:804).

THE SPANIARD AS NONHUMAN HUMAN

If, at least for some of the rebels, the Spaniards were demons, they could not have been accepted as Christians and human beings. An anonymous witness of the Inca's death at Waqay Pata observed that according to the Indians, the Spaniards who were killing the Inca were "inhuman and impious" (CDIP 1971–75: 2:2:776). In La Paz the rebels called the Spaniards devils (ibid.: 2:3:82), while in all the Aymara-speaking region they were called dogs, beasts, and demons, or excommunicates and demons (ibid.: 2:2:804–14).

These references permit us to understand other examples. Micaela Bastidas spoke with horror about the Spaniards (ibid.: 2:2:736). Túpac Katari forbade all Spanish customs and ordered all Spaniards and everybody dressed as a Spaniard to be killed (ibid.: 2:2:802–3). He received dead Spaniards' heads and pierced their eyes (ibid.: 2:2:811). In Tupiza the rebels took the dead corregidor's body from the church and cut his head off (ibid.: 2:2:577). Diego Cristóbal wrote that the Spaniards "always sought out evil for the wretched creoles and Indian notables [*principales*]" (Cornejo B. 1963: 426–31), while the Inca maintained that the corregidores made it impossible for the people "to get to know the true God" (CDTA 1980–82: 2:318). He attributed to the evil Europeans' influence the hostility of the clergy against the rebels. In this way the Europeans wanted to disturb the Christian faith of the people (ibid.: 3:111). A provincial Inca nobleman wrote to Túpac Amaru that the "Spaniards never look at the good treatment they receive from anybody" (ibid.: 3:39).

Treatment of Spanish bodies may be instructive. In Calca province the rebels caught two Spanish brothers, leaders of Spanish troops. They were killed, their blood and hearts were consumed, their tongues cut off and their eyes pierced (CDIP 1971–75: 2:2:471; CDTA 1980–82: 1:200). After the Sangarará battle the rebels took the dead Spaniards' clothes and left naked bodies on the field (CDTA 1980–82: 1:423). Once, during the siege of La Paz, the rebels killed fifty Spaniards, and cut their heads and hidden parts off (Valle de Siles 1980: 107–8). Near Chucuito the rebels painted their faces with the Spaniards' blood, while in Juli they drank their victims' blood (CDIP 1971–75: 1:1:667–68).

Andean tradition condemns cannibalism. If a part of a Spanish body was eaten, either the act must have had a magic meaning or the Spaniard was considered nonhuman. Devilish and beastly status are perfectly compatible, because a beast or a devil is not human. In order to understand whether hearts eaten were "animal" or "human," I searched for every reference to Spanish or other hearts. I found three additional cases. In Juli the

Spanish troops found 71 corpses, among them the bodies of two Juli caciques, their heads in gallows and their hearts extracted by a cut on the left side of the body. A corpse of a cacique's wife was without blood, supposedly drunk by the rebels (ibid.: 2:2:668). During the La Paz siege the rebels caught one of the Spanish officials, cut off his head, legs, genitals, and heart, which they took with themselves with great shouts (Valle de Siles 1980: 94). In Macha province the Moscari Indians killed their cacique, cut his head off, and extracted his heart (Hidalgo L. 1983: 125).

Jorge Hidalgo Lehuede interpreted the last case, using Xavier Albó's data, as a case of a *wilanča* (an offering to Pača Mama, the mountains, and the ancestors). He argued that all cases of heart extractions like the above-mentioned corpses from Juli (according to his data, all of them had the hearts removed) should be interpreted as a wilanča. These wilančas were different from the ordinary wilanča, such as the sacrifice of a llama, because the body or the bones were buried in the case of an ordinary wilanča. The prohibition of burial of the Spaniards served to make sure that the dead Spaniards would not become a *mallki*, a plant of new life which thanks to Pača Mama would be reborn.

Hocquenghem's data (1980–81, 1982, 1983, 1984) and in particular, her interpretation of the images of the condemned (1980–81), prove that such an interpretation is erroneous. The ways the Spaniards were killed were the ways criminals guilty of evil were killed to guarantee that the guilty would not return. An Andean criminal is not buried. Hidalgo Lehuede is right when he says that the dead Spaniard could not become a mallki, that killing him should please the deities, but he is wrong when he says that the victim was an offering to the deities. The Spaniard was a very evil criminal, beastly and devilish.

In pan-Andean beliefs there exists such a criminal, called in Spanish *degollador*, and in Quechua: *pištakuq, nakaq, ñak'aq, qhari siri*. He is frequently identified with the "whites" or mestizos (cf. Ansion and Szemiński 1982; Ansion 1984: 201–8). Such people should be killed by group action, their hearts, tongues, genitals, and eyes destroyed. Modern ñak'aq are considered exporters of human fat for North American and European use. They get the fat killing the Indians. They are antisocials because they destroy human life for their own benefit.*

Editor's Note: Szemiński's discussion of *el degollador* (literally, "the beheader") is based on contemporary field work in Ayacucho, but gains further credence from bits of historical evidence from the same region. As early as the sixteenth century, the region's Indians expressed fear that Spaniards sought their body fat for medicinal purposes. (Cristóbal de Molina, *Relación de las fábulas y ritos de los incas* [1574], as reprinted in *Las crónicas de los Molinas*, Francisco A. Loayza, ed. [Lima, 1943], 79.) And in 1780, Indians in the Huancavelica districts of the greater Ayacucho area rioted against soldiers on patrol because, the

Many a Spaniard saved his life dressing as an Indian. Some had to change their dress on orders of the rebel authorities, but others did so voluntarily. The same applied to the Indians, who had to abandon Spanish dress if they wanted to stay alive (e.g., CDIP 1971–75: 2:1:363; 2:2:474, 505; 2:4:247). Even during peace negotiations, when Miguel Túpac Amaru took two Spanish soldiers to his camp, he treated them very well but obliged them to dress as Indians (Valle de Siles 1980: 172). Sometimes even Indian dress and active participation on the rebels' side did not help. A tupamarista cacique was killed only because he was creole. His killers knew that he had fought on their side (CDTA 1980–82: 1:433–34). In this case, Indian dress was not enough; one needed an Indian face, too.

Rebel authorities (except Túpac Katari) repeatedly prohibited the killing of creoles. In one case, the Indians, in obedience to the Inca's orders not to harm the creoles, decided to catch them with nets, and deliver the creoles to the Inca intact (CDIP 1971–75: 2:3:276).

KILL THE SPANIARD BY THE KING OF SPAIN'S ORDERS

So a Spaniard was human, but beastly and devilish. He was a ñak'aq, antisocial, heretic, recognized by racial and cultural characteristics, evil by nature, doomed to extermination. Killing the Spaniards was associated with the Inca's presence. The various rebel Incas — Túpac Amaru, Diego Cristóbal, Túpac Katari, Tomás Katari and his brothers, Felipe Velasco Túpac Yupanqui, and many others — while killing the Spaniards justified their actions as the Spanish king's orders (*reales cédulas*).

Túpac Amaru was not a fool. He knew perfectly well that no king of Spain would order the Spaniards in Peru to be killed. If the Inca insisted that such orders existed, even in letters directed to the viceroy of Lima or to the Cuzco authorities, he must have had a very good reason to do so. The explanation must be sought in the image of the king of Spain and of Spaniards in Spain, not in Peru, that existed among the inhabitants of the Andes.

I found two sequences of events that illustrate the image of Spain across

---

Indians said, the soldiers were going to behead the Indians. (*Relaciones de los vireyes y audiencias que han gobernado el Perú*, 3 vols. [Madrid, 1867–1872], 3:51.) The oral tradition which associated body fat, medicinal functions, and Spaniards was not invented out of thin air, but very probably based on battle experiences in the sixteenth century. Note this matter-of-fact description by Bernal Díaz del Castillo, the famous chronicler of the Mexican conquest: "and with the fat of a fat Indian whom we killed and opened up there, we salved our wounds, since we had no oil." (*Historia verdadera de la conquista de la Nueva España*, Miguel León-Portilla, ed., 2 vols. [Madrid, 1984], 1, chap. 62, p. 230; cf. chap. 34, p. 149.) There is no reason to doubt that this was a normal practice, given the exigencies of war, in Peru as well as Mexico.

the sea among the Indians. One of them refers to Tomás Katari and Túpac Katari, the other to Túpac Amaru. Boleslao Lewin (1957: 331–93) first called attention to the similarity in the sequence of events in Canas (Cuzco) and Chayanta. He explained it through existence of a conspiracy in which all the leaders of Chayanta and Cuzco had taken part. Hidalgo Lehuede (1983) compared both sequences in order to understand how an Indian Messiah had been born, but he did not show any interest in the image of the king of Spain.

Tomás Katari in a representation to the king argued that it was absolutely impossible that the Great Lord, the most Powerful King of Magnificent Spain and of poor Indians, would permit his representatives in Peru to drink the blood of his poor tributaries (CDIP 1971–75: 2:2:245). Obviously the king in Spain was believed good, only his envoys in Peru were bad or behaved badly. After his return from Buenos Aires, where he had been received by the viceroy, Tomás Katari presented the papers he had been given in Buenos Aires to the La Plata Audiencia (royal high court). He returned to Macha, where he persuaded the Indians that he had been in Spain, where he had kissed the king's feet and informed the king about his Indians' sufferings. He believed and made the others believe that the king had ordered various things in favor of the Indians. Tomás Katari was called "Father" by the Indians (ibid.: 2:2:237–38) and used attributes of power (Hidalgo L. 1983: 124). While Tomás Katari was jailed in Chuquisaca, an Indian in Macha started to say that the Buenos Aires viceroy had diminished the tribute by half, and that the pertinent document was in Tomás Katari's hands. The local governor ordered the Indian arrested, but he was liberated from custody by the Indians who said "that he was the [royal] decree and so could not be jailed" (CDIP 1971–75: 2:2:238).

Neither Tomás Katari nor his followers knew what and where Spain was. The contact with Spain gave special powers, even indirectly: the above-mentioned Indian, linked with Spain through Tomás Katari, became himself the personal embodiment of the royal edict. Later, Katari's brothers requested from the La Plata Audiencia the king's orders they believed their brother had brought (Túpac Amaru y la Iglesia 1983: 220; CDIP 1971–75: 2:2:548). According to Dámaso Katari, they rebelled in order to execute the king's orders and to prepare the land for reception of their Inca-King, Túpac Amaru (ibid.: 2, 2:549). The people did not believe in Tomás Katari's death (Lewin 1957: 739). Hidalgo Lehuede (1983: 128) called attention to the relation between Tomás Katari and Túpac Katari. The latter declared that he had received his mission from Tomás Katari, while his sister maintained that they had received a royal edict which ordered the Europeans killed, the reparto de mercancías abolished, and so on. The executor of all this was Tomás Katari from above and from Spain. Later Túpac Katari said that Tomás Katari came back to life in him.

All the sequence shows that for the Indians, their leaders in Macha and Sicasica included, the Spain from which Tomás Katari acquired his powers had nothing in common with the Spain of Spaniards in Peru. The power that he obtained permitted him to reincorporate himself in Túpac Katari. The same power decreed the death of Europeans in Peru, understood by everybody as death of all Spaniards in Peru. It is not necessary to enumerate all cases when the rebel leaders said they had received the orders of the king of Spain to exterminate the Spaniards, the Europeans, and the corregidores. Anyway, their followers did not doubt that the king had ordered them to kill all puka kunkas (e.g., CDTA 1980–82: 1:406; 3:949). Túpac Amaru even tried to convince the Cuzco clergy that such an order existed (ibid.: 2:318), while Diego Cristóbal did the same with the viceroy of Lima (CDIP 1971–75: 2:3:127). The phenomenon was confirmed by Areche when he sentenced the Inca. According to the sentence, the Inca pretended to act on orders from the king, the Royal Audiencia of Lima, the viceroy, and Areche himself (ibid.: 2:2:768). For some reason the Inca was convinced that the people would follow him if he substantiated his action with the king's orders. The conviction that the king could have ordered such an action must have been general.

Micaela Bastidas also believed in a special relationship between her husband and the king. She confessed that she called him Inca "because she had heard it from her husband, who also said that he would be taken to Spain, and the King would make him Captain General." His portrait, to be sent to Spain and distributed in the Peruvian provinces, showed the Inca with royal insignia (ibid.: 2:2:716–17). The same special relationship is manifested in the beliefs that the king had ordered Túpac Amaru to be taken alive to Spain and not to be killed. Thus Areche and Peruvian Spaniards were rebels against the king of Spain. The same people also believed that the Inca was going to be crowned (CDTA 1980–82: 4:437–38).

According to the priest who had administered the parish of Langui and Layo, where the Spaniards captured the Inca, "when Túpac Amaru came back from this capital [i.e., Lima] to his ancient home . . . I noted the Indians looked at him with veneration, and not only in his village but even outside the province of Tinta; the province, proud with his protection, imagined itself free from the mita obligation" (ibid.: 2:262). The Inca went to Lima in order to get an official recognition of his Inca origins and at the same time he presented in Lima various documents to obtain an exemption from the mita service for the villages of Canas.

The pattern in the case of Túpac Amaru was nearly the same as in that of Tomás Katari. Both went, one to Buenos Aires, the other to Lima, to obtain some privileges for their people. Both returned and were respected as men with special powers. Both came to fight the Spanish administration and argued that they had received the king's order to do so. Their power was transmitted to their followers and collaborators. Katari in Aymara, and Amaru in Quechua, both mean "serpent." The serpent is a member of the Thunder family, a symbol of change and an ancestor of the Incas as earthlings (cf. Hocquenghem 1983; Szemiński 1984: 83–200).

The life of both may be presented in the following way:

(1) The leader is a descendant of ancient rulers, whose forefather was the Sun; his forefathers imposed order in the society in the name of the Sun, just like the Sun who imposes the order in the sky. The leader is also related to Thunder as author of change (Amaru, Katari).

(2) He abandons this world (Kay Pača) identified with his small ethnic group (Canas, Macha), or with Peru (Tawantinsuyu).

(3) He visits the world outside Kay Pača (Lima, Buenos Aires). The world that he visits is associated with the king, with Spaniards and Spain, but also with power and change.

(4) The king, chief of the Spaniards, or the Chief Spaniard gives him power (*real cédula*). The power given is the power to change and reorder the Kay Pača.

(5) He comes back to Kay Pača with power, and uses it to fulfill the orders he received. Fulfilling the orders, imposing order on Kay Pača, consists of castigating those guilty of disorder, and destroying those who govern. Those who govern (corregidores, Spaniards in Peru, their followers) are guilty of disorder, and therefore rebellion.

GOD AS CHIEF SPANIARD

Obviously the king of Spain was a good Christian king, whose power was legitimate, if he could order acts against the Spaniards. In eighteenth-century Peru he was considered a legitimate ruler in the minds of the people (cf. Túpac Amaru y la Iglesia 1983: 152). The Inca's relationship with the king of Spain seems similar to his relationship to God. Túpac Amaru's God is evidently the God of the Bible and the Catholic Church.

In the proclamation issued in Chumbivilcas, the Inca declared that it was his duty to put an end to such great disorder and to stop the offenses against God. The Inca expected that the Divine providence would enlighten him (CDTA 1980–82: 1:419).

There is only one document in which Túpac Amaru uses all his titles: "Don José Primero por la Gracia de Dios Inca Rey del Perú, Santa Fé, Quito, Chile, Buenos Aires, y Continentes de los Mares del Sur, Duque de la Superlativa, Señor de los Cesares y Amazonas con dominios en el gran Paititi, Comisario [y] Distribuidor de la Piedad Divina por Erario sin Par." The document was expertly analyzed by Luis Durand Florez (1974: 141–47, 173–76), who proved that it is not a Spanish forgery. Túpac Amaru is by God's Grace Inca-King of all Spanish possessions in South America. He is also titled Duke of the Superlative where the Superlative is a female being; Lord of the Caesars and Amazons with dominion over the Great Paititi, Comissary and Distributor of the Divine Piety as of a treasure without equal.

Every Christian king is a king by God's grace, but this king was also an Inca by God's Grace, and the God by whose Grace the Incas were kings is the Sun, whose sons they are. Every king is a distributor of Divine Piety. Usually this is only implied by the king's title itself. A Comissary Distributor of Divine Piety suggests a more direct relationship with God, but which God?

My studies of the image of Tawantinsuyu religion as presented by the famed early colonial chroniclers, Don Felipe Guaman Poma de Ayala, Don Joan de Santacruz Pachacuti Yamqui Salcamaygua, and Cristóbal de Molina, and comparison of these data with those collected in twenti-eth-century Ayacucho, convinced me that a Creator-God formed the basis of the Tawantinsuyu pantheon. Depending on the context, his male com-ponent was called Wiraqučan, Pača Kamaq, Inti, etc., while his female component was usually called Pača Mama, the Mother of Time and Space, or Lady World. Today in various contexts she is identified with the Virgin (cf. Mariscotti 1978; Ansion and Szemiński 1982; Szemiński 1983). The female Superlative in Túpac Amaru's full title, is she the Pača Mama?

At one moment Túpac Amaru declared that the cries of the Peruvians reached Heaven, and that is why he, the Inca, ordered in the name of God the Omnipotent many and various things, whose effect would be social and moral health. In many other documents the Inca repeated that he acted with God's Grace and against the people who were rebels against God (CDIP 1971–75: 2:2:321; Túpac Amaru y la Iglesia 1983: 210, 215; CDTA 1980–82: 1:328–30). Sometimes he insisted that God obliged him to act. Having described economic and social causes of the insurrection, the Inca wrote: "All this compelled me to note what is my obligation. As God Our Lord has given me the obligation without taking into consideration my heavy sins, I want to perform a good deed" by killing the corregidor and the Europeans who did not want to accept "my health-giving orders" (CDIP 1971–75: 2:2:463). He argued that thanks to his action the people would be able to know the "true God" (ibid.: 2:2:379), whom they could not truly know during the era of Spanish domination. He, by God's Grace de-scendant of all the Inca kings, accused the government of Peru of intro-ducing unwholesome ways, and the clergy in Peru of forgetting the true

God of Heaven and Earth. He compared the Indians to the Israelites in Egypt and himself to David and Moses. In consequence of his actions, the Omnipotent would be believed and known to the faithful, because his (the Inca's) was the way of the truth (CDTA 1980-82: 2:206, 218, 327; 3:113).

Diego Cristóbal also acted with God's Grace. He was a noble Inca by God's Grace, and in the service of God and king of Spain he accused the Spaniards of inefficient Christianization of the Indies (Cornejo B. 1963: 426-31). He ordered the Christians to adore God and the Most Saintly Mother because by God's favor there came to an end the enslavement of Indians by corregidores. Diego Cristóbal informed the bishop of Cuzco that the kings of Spain had received the obligation to christianize the Indians, but the kingship of the Indies might be withdrawn from them because in the Indies the corregidores did not execute God's will (CDTA 1980-82: 2:354). The same conviction that the Inca and his followers had received a mission from God was expressed in many other documents.

In what system of conceptual references did the rebels invoke the concept of God? Was it Catholic or Andean or both? The rebels repeatedly declared themselves Catholics and Christians. What did "cristiano" mean for an eighteenth-century Peruvian Indian? Today every Peruvian Catholic knows there are ceremonies and rites which it is better that the padre not know about. The difference in conceptual references could be traced through the descriptions of clearly non-Christian rites. There are some such descriptions, but they are so obscure that it is difficult to understand to whom the rite was directed. Another possibility would be to prove the existence of non-Christian priests, but I am unable to distinguish between a native substitute for Spanish Catholic priests and an Andean priest, in contradistinction to Catholic priests. The last possibility is to show that Christian concepts served to cover and legalize Andean images. The references to God and Virgin could serve to demonstrate such a relation, but they may also be perfectly Catholic. As we do not have any detailed historical models of Andean religion, the only possibility left is to show the presence of non-Christian beliefs among the rebels.

In Livitaca, on November 25, 1780, Túpac Amaru told the people that he pardoned all who had fought him with arms, because from now on a new government would start. The Indians saluted him: "Thou art our God and Master and we beg Thee that there be no [Catholic] priests from now on, molesting us." The Inca answered that this could not be, because: "who would absolve us in the matter of death?" (ibid.: 3:76-77). This may be interpreted to mean that in the eighteenth century the clergy and Catholic beliefs were incorporated into Andean religion with a special reference to death. It is also obvious that the people of Livitaca did not feel any need for the presence of a Catholic priest in everyday life.

According to the corregidor of Puno, before a battle an Indian leader told the Spaniards that they the Indians did not consider as their sovereign the king of Spain, only their Inca Túpac Amaru. He added they were going to kill all the Spaniards except the chaplain, whom they wanted to retain in the same function. After the battle, when the chaplain whom they had thought to preserve tried to confess and absolve dying rebels, they died "without taking unto their lips the Lord's sweet name" (CDIP 1971–75: 2:2:407–12). What did they want the chaplain for?

The Cuzco bishop described how Corpus Christi was celebrated in Cuzco by the Incas. They took part in the procession with shields bearing an image of the Sun or of an Inca king. At other opportunities they represented the Child dressed as an Inca king, and "they convince us that they adore the true God only when they see Him dressed like the Incas, whom they believed to be deities." Later the bishop recommended that during the celebrations of Santiago the Apostle (Saint James) the Incas should not be permitted to bring the images of their gentile kings (CDTA 1980–82: 2:633–34, 637). In the sixteenth century, the mummy of any Inca king was called *Illapa*—Thunder. After the conquest, Santiago, the Spanish war god, was identified with Illapa. The bishop knew what he was speaking of. In the celebration, from the Incas' point of view, the Spaniards participated with their images of Thunder, and so did the Incas with their Peruvian Thunders. The Thunder, represented in the sky by Venus, was thought of as the king's brother and at the same time as protector of the king's sons. All the Cuzco Incas, and even all the Inca's subjects, were considered his sons. The bishop did not doubt that Christian ritual was used to cover a corresponding Inca ritual; in a sense, it was the official and legal version of the same ritual.

Túpac Katari invoked God and Virgin in his documents (e.g., ibid.: 3:665). He ordered a chapel built in his camp to celebrate Mass daily. He also used to display a little box that he sometimes put to his ear in order that God speak directly to him (CDIP 1971–75: 2:2:811). During the battle around La Paz, and during the rebels' executions, the rebels died for their Inca king, but they did not want to pronounce the name of Jesus (ibid.: 2:3:147).

The existence of non-Christian rites or beliefs should not be treated as a proof of the existence of two religions. Andean peasants in the eighteenth-century, as today, confessed only one religion. What were its components? It seems that Christian rites and the Mass and the priests were all accepted and considered necessary, but not always necessary. It is also clear that during the revolution a religious transformation took place. The transformation started when God or the king of Spain or both gave a special mission to their representatives in Peru. The mission consisted of exterminating Spaniards in Peru, who were guilty of evil, rebellion, heresy, and apostasy.

THE INDIAN AS CHRISTIAN

The Indians did not feel any necessity for the daily presence of the Catholic Church (e.g., Túpac Amaru y la Iglesia 1983: 133–60; CDIP 1971–75: 2:1:34–35). In 1781 in Yauri, only some 25 out of 8,000 parishioners knew the precepts of the faith; for the rest, the participation in the Mass of their caciques was enough, but everybody took part in the Andean celebrations (CDTA 1980–82: 2:148–49). Túpac Amaru and his followers' declarations of Catholicism are well known. One of them lamented that he had been told that he could not enter the Church or hear the Mass because "all of us are sorcerers" (ibid.: 3:38). The bishop of Cuzco informed Areche nearly two months after the Cuzco rebellion had started that after battle, the Indians loyal to the Spaniards did not want to take anything from the rebel belongings because they considered them excommunicated (CDIP 1971–75: 2:2:383). Priests were sent to the rebels in order to persuade them to surrender but the Indians "blindly and fearless of death threw themselves into battle, and even when badly hurt they never wanted to invoke Jesus' name nor to confess." Túpac Amaru had told them that only those who would not say "Jesus" would revive on the third day (ibid.: 2:1:374). Unfortunately, the source does not mention where such behavior took place. The Inca appears as a personage opposed to Jesus. It does not matter whether he really issued a prohibition against invoking Jesus or not. He himself when tortured called upon Jesus and the Virgin. Why then was it attributed to him that he forbade it?

One of the La Paz defenders wrote that Túpac Katari had an intention to abandon Catholicism and that was why he forbade his followers to pray and to take hats off in the presence of the most holy Sacrament (Valle de Siles 1983: 43). According to Father de la Borda, Katari ordered the Spaniards killed, and their language and customs abandoned. He further ordered that the people, including even priests, who tried to save a Spaniard or Spanish follower should be killed, and that any church serving as an asylum for Spaniards be burned. But two rebel functionaries who did not show respect to Our Lady of Copacabana were executed immediately, and in Túpac Katari's camp there was a chapel and a daily Mass (CDIP 1971–75: 2:2:802–4, 809), even though the rebels killed by Spaniards could not be forced to invoke Jesus (ibid.: 2:3:147). All the elements of the situation among Túpac Amaru's followers are repeated in the case of Túpac Katari's followers.

There are some other, less interesting cases of profanations and religious experimenting (e.g., ibid.: 2:2:693-94). In Caylloma, while killing the Spaniards in a church, the rebels shouted: "The time of mercy is finished, there are no more Sacraments nor God with any power" (ibid.: 2:694). The last case calls attention to what really happened. The rebels believed that something changed in religion, some divinities lost their power, others gained. It seems that for the rebels the presence of an Inca precluded the presence, or power in Peru, of Spaniards and of Jesus. Spaniards were eliminated, but what happened to Jesus?

THE PROPHECIES

I have already tried to prove (1984: 83-158) that the Andean image of history included also a vision of the future. Twentieth-century versions of this vision are commonly known as the Inkarrí myth. The Inca will come back to reorder the world and to put everything in its proper place. The Inca's return is associated with moral cleansing, the destruction of Spaniards and sinners. In 1923, in Cotabambas, an insurrection to restore Tawantinsuyu started with the news that the Inca had appeared. Everyone knew what should be done: the *misti* and the *wiraquča* (mestizos and Spaniards) should be killed (Ricardo Valderrama 1983, personal communication). Since 1978, when I first tried to prove the existence of the Inkarrí myth during Túpac Amaru's insurrection, new documents and studies have surfaced on this theme (e.g., Hidalgo L. 1983). They contain much more data on the prophecies.

Hidalgo Lehuede studied documents about the popular prophecy of 1776, according to which a general Indian uprising would start in 1777 and the Cuzco Indians had already nominated a king to govern them. The Indian nobles who participated in conversations about the uprising communicated the news with the *khipu*, the Inca knots record. The slings were ready, the action should start at 4 o'clock in the morning, just as when the Jesuits had been captured. According to several testimonies, Juan de Dios Orcoguaranca, the principal accused, had affirmed that St. Rosa's and St. Francisco's prophecies were going to be fulfilled, because the kingdom would revert to its previous form. The Catholic religion would be preserved, and an Inca would govern instead of the Spanish king. Orcoguaranca also said that the prophecies were commonly known (ibid.: 120-21). The Indians of Cuzco apparently believed that an Inca would return, exterminate the Spaniards, and conserve Catholicism.

Exactly the same news of an uprising in 1777 was heard in 1776 in

Camaná and Huarochirí. The kingdom would return to its hereditary and legitimate rulers, the Spaniards would be killed, and the insurrection would start in Cuzco, where everybody was ready (CDTA 1980-82: 2:231-32). In December 1776 in Cuzco, an Indian more than 70 years old was jailed because he had sent letters written by another person (he did not know how to write) to the caciques of Maras, Urubamba, and Guayllabamba. One of the letters he himself had given to the wife of the cacique of Maras, "telling her that it had been sent by the Great Quispe Tupa Ynca who had come from Quito." He also explained that the Inca could be found in the Chapel of the Holy Christ of Earthquakes or in a tambo called Montero. In jail he admitted that his name was Don Josef Gran Quispe Tupa Ynca, and that he would be crowned according to the prophecies of St. Rosa and St. Francisco Solano. He believed that the Cuzco Indians were already confederated with those of Collao and Quito. The puka kunkas would be killed, and a special artillery with range of 12 leagues (ca. 60 kilometers) constructed. He had heard the prophecies in chicha beer stores. He believed that, being a descendant of the Incas Wayna Qhapaq and Wiraquča, he—not a Quito descendant of the Inca Ataw Wallpa—should be king. The man who wrote his letters believed him to be a fool and beggar (ibid.: 2:235-43).

The prophecy attributed to Peruvian Catholic saints was obviously commonly known among the Cuzco Indians. An Inca-King would and should reign in Cuzco. According to the most popular version of Inca history, any descendant of Ataw Wallpa should also be a descendant of Wayna Qhapaq and of Wiraquča. Qispe Tupa Inca could not mean the same version of Inca history because it would not give him any preference over Ataw Wallpa's descendants, whose coming to power he was trying to prevent. His attitude suggests that for him a descendant of Ataw Wallpa was not a descendant of Wiraquča and Wayna Qhapaq. Actually, existing theories on the structure of the Cuzco dynasty and lineages do not offer any explanation because they do not permit us to distinguish between the genealogy of Ataw Wallpa's descendants from Quito and Qispe Tupa Inca's genealogy.

Qispe Tupa Inca's arguments suggest that in 1776, in Cuzco, there existed meanings of the word *wiraquča* other than the most obvious. These meanings may have continued the ones known in the sixteenth century, when *wiraquča* could mean any of the following: Wiraqučan—The Wiraquča, the most important representation of God; Wiraquča Runa—the forefathers, ancestors, and the first known humanity considered divine; Wiraquča Inka—the founder of one of Cuzco's lineages; Wiraquča—Spaniard, any white man; Wiraquča Qhapaq—the King of the Wiraqučas or King of Spain. Other meanings, such as cacique, or any founder of any lineage, are also possible. It was Wiraqučan who had created the world and the ancestors of every ethnic group. He sent them to their *paqarinas*, places of origin, and called them from their paqarinas to live on earth, Kay Pača.

In the eighteenth century there existed at least two different meanings of the word written down as "español" or "Spaniard": bad Spaniard in Peru, who should be killed when the Inca comes back, and good Spaniard, in particular the good Spanish King over the sea, the good chief Spaniard. In Quechua, in the eighteenth century and today, the word for Spaniard and any white man is wiraquča. In good Quechua, Spanish King is Wiraquča Qhapaq, but what does this term really mean? What did it mean in the eighteenth century? Wiraquča Qhapaq—King of the Wiraqučas, the most powerful of the Wiraqučas, the chief of the ancestors, must have meant in the eighteenth century: (1) God the Creator, Creator of the World and of the forefathers, and (2) Spanish King across the Sea, not in Kay Pača, but also present in Kay Pača through his representatives. As Kay Pača corresponds more or less to the world inhabited by human beings (i.e., Indians), so both God the Creator and the Spanish King were present in realms beyond Kay Pača.

Wiraquča-Spaniards were people not quite of this world, because their world was over the sea, not here. Here, in Tawantinsuyu, they may be considered out of their proper place.

In the sources referring to the rebellion the word *wiraquča* is nearly absent. I found it used as a cacique's title. The source calls the cacique mestizo and Spaniard, but at the same time member of an ayllu (ibid.: 4:487, 493–95). Did the reference to wiraquča mean here Spaniard or a legitimate descendant of the founders of the lineages of the kuraka?

Qispe Tupa Inca indicated as the first place to find the Inca the Chapel of the "Señor de los Temblores"–Lord of the Earthquakes. Lord of the Earthquakes is a Cuzco image of the Lord of Miracles ("Señor de los Milagros"), called also Lord of Pachacamilla (little Pachacamac). Various scholars have called attention to the fact that Lord of the Miracles occupies today exactly the same place in social and geographical space as old Andean Pača Kamaq. Using data from the Andean chronicler Guaman Poma, I tried to prove that Pača Kamaq (The Soul of Time and Space) is one of the representations of the Andean Creator God (Szemiński 1983). Pača Kamaq is associated with the West, where the Sun goes, with the night; with Ukhu Pača o Hurin Pača, the world of underground or the world below; and with Pača Mama as Mother Earth. He is the author of earthquakes, of all cataclysms, and of all change, and in particular, all irregular change. Pača-kuti, cataclysm or revolution of time and space, was conceived of as any important happening. Small pača-kutis marked periods of individual or family life, great ones divided the pača, the continuum of time and space, into sectors-epochs. In the contemporary Inkarrí myth it is said that the Inca will come back with a cataclysm that exterminates the Spaniards. The Chapel of the Lord of the Earthquakes is really a proper place for a returning Inca. Qispe Tupa Inca's reasoning suggests that the God who gave his obligation to act to Túpac Amaru, Túpac Katari, Tomás Katari and other rebels still had all the characteristics of Wiraqučan and Pača Kamaq. In this respect, the eighteenth-century Christian God, in particular God the Father, was thought of as a Spanish and official version of Andean Creator God. The identification explains also who was a good Christian. Every Indian who kept the rites of his community (*común*) and fulfilled the obligations imposed by tradition and the community exactly as he had been taught by his fathers, was a true Christian. If such were the case, no Spaniard could be a good Christian, and every Spaniard must have been a heretic.

According to the bishop of Cuzco, every Indian desired the return of the golden age of the Incas. The bishop insisted that the prophecies of the Inca's return circulated through printed books, and especially as the consequence of the popularity of Garcilaso de la Vega's *Commentaries* (ibid.: 2:633–37). Printed texts could have influenced the richest and the most educated members of Indian nobility, but in 1780 half of the 24 Electors, the Inca town council of Cuzco, could not sign documents. The 24 Electors were among the noblest and the richest of the Incas. To propagate a general belief books were not enough. Faith in the Inca's return had a basis in general Andean images of history, and it was spread orally. The presence of Peruvian Catholic saints may indicate that the identification of personages of the Inca pantheon with the Catholic pantheon reached a more profound level. It is also possible that some Catholic clergymen did participate in regional conspiracies before the uprising.

Túpac Amaru did know the prophecy. According to an ex-prisoner in Tungasuca, the Inca used to say that "there had come the time of St. Rosa's prophecy when the kingdom would return to the hand of its previous possessors" and that was why he was going to kill all the Europeans. Once he even expressed his surprise that the Cuzco bishop did not know the prophecy (ibid.: 2:380).

Exactly the same prophecy about the return of the kingdom to the hands of its legitimate possessors was repeatedly heard by Father de la Borda in Túpac Katari's presence (CDIP 1971–75: 2:2:810–16). In this case, however, there was no mention of any saints.

It seems that the beginning of the new times was associated with moral cleansing. On November 15, 1780, a witness of the very beginnings of the rebellion declared that he had seen in Parupuqio that "all the Indians able to carry arms carried arms, slings and sables, and they congratulated and embraced each other saying that their sufferings and works had been finished" (CDTA 1980-82: 3:85).

PRIESTS AND GODS

Every tradition, and especially religious tradition, needs some institutionalized transmission. The data on Andean priests who took part in the rebellion are very scarce. It is possible to prove their existence, but it is at this time impossible to find out whether they were distinctively Andean priests, or Andean substitutes for Catholic priests. In nearly all known cases they were illiterate old peasants (ibid.: 3:670, 743-58, 760, 940-49; 4:284-95, 390-99). There even exist descriptions of a Catholic but very unorthodox rebel sanctuary and of an Andean substitute for a Catholic priest (CDIP 1971-75: 2:3:320-22).

If we consider, however, that every kuraka and every Indian leader did have some priestly traits, the picture changes. In the sixteenth century every kuraka represented the ancestors and the founders of the group before his people and before all other powers. He also represented his people before the ancestors. He was an intermediary just like the Inca-King who represented humans among gods and god among humans. (Cf. Salomon, Chapter 5 in this volume.)

There existed a special relationship between Túpac Katari and God, and also between Túpac Amaru and God. Túpac Katari was a reincorporation of Tomás Katari. One of the Indians he ordered to be killed was an incorporation of the Qulla Qhapaq, Colla Kings (CDIP 1971-75: 2:3:168-69). Was Túpac Amaru, too, a reincorporation of somebody?

The most obvious answer is, of course, that he should have been the reincorporation of Thupa Amaru Inca (the last ruler of the neo-Inca state, executed in 1572). There are no documents known that would prove that Túpac Amaru did declare himself a reincarnation of Thupa Amaru Inca. There are, however, numerous documents according to which he acted as Thupa Amaru Inca's descendant. Thupa Amaru Inca had many descendants, but only Túpac Amaru felt himself especially obliged to act in his name. In order to find out whether Túpac Amaru was a special descendant, different from other descendants of the last Inca-King, I tried to analyze the genealogy which he had presented to the Real Audiencia in 1777, according to previous prophecies the year of the Inca's return (Loayza 1946: 5-17).

According to this genealogy, he was a direct descendant of Felipe Thupa Amaro or Thupa Amaru Inca in the fifth degree: Wayna Qhapaq-Manku Inka-Felipe Thupa Amaru Inca-Juana Pillcohuaco-Blas Thupa Amaro-

Sebastián Thupa Amaro–Miguel Thupa Amaro–José Gabriel Thupa Amaro. The fact that he descended from Thupa Amaru Inca's daughter is not significant because there were no known masculine descendants of the Inca. Already all the children of Juana Pillcohuaco were recognized as the Inca's direct descendants (Szemiński 1984: 160–63). Túpac Amaru considered himself Thupa Amaru Inca's grandson in the fourth degree (CDTA 1980–82: 3:201). According to Zuidema (1980: 63, 78), the fourth generation of descendants could intermarry. As an Andean system of kinship is in use today in southern Peru, and there are many indications that it was used in Canas province in the eighteenth century, Túpac Amaru could be considered a repetition of the founder of his ayllu. He occupied in the kinship system the same place as Thupa Amaru Inca in the sixteenth century. This might have been one of the premises that convinced Túpac Amaru to act: he was an Inca-King. It is not possible to know whether he accepted all other consequences. Was he also the Son of the Sun?

The fate of the unfortunate reincarnation of Qulla Qhapaq, executed on the orders of Túpac Katari, seems to indicate that at least among common people Túpac Amaru was considered an Intip Curin, Son of the Sun. Qulla Qhapaq pretended to bring down the Sun from the sky (CDIP 1971–75: 2:3:168). In twentieth-century myths, the Inca tied the Sun his father to a rock called Inti Watana — the instrument of tying the Sun, or the place where the Sun was tied (Ortíz 1973: 131, 140). So Qulla Qhapaq was an Inca and Son of the Sun, but only, as his title indicates, in Qulla Suyu, already occupied by Túpac Katari.

Qulla Qhapaq's story may serve as a proof of Sun worship. The bishop of Cuzco argued that the cult of Santiago was really a worship of the Incas. I interpreted the data as a proof of existence of Thunder worship. Thunder worship exists in Cuzco today. If I have admitted the bishop's evidence in the case of Thunder, I must also accept his affirmations, repeated later by Areche in the sentence against the Inca, that Sun worship also took place (CDTA 1980–82: 2:633–37; CDIP 1971–75: 2:2:771). Túpac Amaru used to wear an image of the Sun made of gold on a golden necklace (ibid.: 2:2:384). The same insignia were used by Túpac Katari (Valle de Siles 1983: 86).

I did not find any evidence of Moon worship although this omission is perfectly explicable by the nature of the sources. As Mariscotti (1978) has shown, the Moon is only a sky representation of Pača Mama. In the same way, the Sun should be treated as a sky representation of Wiraquča–Pača Kamaq. I have shown that Wiraqučan, Pača Kamaq, Illapa, and the dead Inca kings had their official representations: God the Father, the Lord of the Earthquakes, Santiago. Since I did not find any direct proof for Pača Mama worship, it is necessary to draw attention to the presence of any female deities.

The documents frequently mention pairs of Catholic representations, usually composed of a male and a female. The bishop of Cuzco ordered, when the rebellion began, the celebration of a procession with the effigies of the Lord of the Earthquakes (Pača Kamaq) and our Lady of Bethlehem (CDIP 1971–75: 2:2:279). Several years later he described the same celebration as composed of two pairs: the effigies of the Lord of the Earthquakes, the Virgin of Rosary, St. Dominic, and St. Rose of Lima (CDTA 1980–82: 2:420). Diego Cristóbal ordered that "all the Christians should devote themselves to the divine cult adoring the God and the Most Holy Mother" (ibid.: 2:348). These examples may show the presence of Pača Mama. Today the official representation of Pača Mama is the Virgin.

Túpac Katari's order to organize the assemblies on mountain tops (CDIP 1971–75: 2:2:802-4) corresponded to reality. Near Paucartambo the rebels used to assemble for discussions on a mountain top called Apu (ibid.: 2:1:144). Apu — in Quechua "Lord" — is today the title of great mountains considered protectors of many communities or regions. As their cult is general today, there is no need to prove their existence in the eighteenth century. The uprising itself signified preference for the mountain protector as guardian of social and biological life, rather than the churches and the colonial villages established in the sixteenth century. Present-day associations between great mountains and images of Christ may serve to explain why Túpac Amaru was a devotee of the Lord of Tungasuca, his birthplace (CDTA 1980–82: 3:557, 288). Hidalgo Lehuede (1983) called attention to the presence in the rebellion of another element of the traditional Andean pantheon: the ancestors. He argued that frequent mentions of assemblies and proclamations in the cemeteries should be explained as ancestor worship.

THE INCA

In all the data the most important element has been partially present: the Inca, Son of the Sun, reincarnation of Thupa Amaru Inca, representative of God and of the Virgin (Wiraqučan and Pača Mama) on Earth in Kay Pača. It is obvious that he was not an ordinary man. The rebellion, the great change, the pača-kuti, started with the reappearance of the Inca.

The Inca had supernatural powers. In 1978, I argued that the ability to revive the dead was one of his attributes (Szemiński 1984: 159–200). Later, more evidence was published which obliged me to change my earlier supposition that the Inca himself had never attributed to himself the power to bring the dead back to life. There are various testimonies according to which Túpac Amaru publicly said that those who would have died for his cause would be revived three days later (CDTA 1980–82: 3:259–62). According to the bishop of Cuzco, the resurrection was promised by the

Inca on the third day after his coronation in Cuzco (CDIP 1971–75: 2:3:336). One observer maintained that the Inca also forbade his followers to invoke the name of Jesus at the hour of death, if they wanted to be resurrected (ibid.: 2:1:376). All of this may represent a popular amplification of the Inca's words. Anyway, people thought that in order to come back to life, they should not invoke Jesus. The resurrection on the third day is a Christian pattern and may indicate that Inca was perceived as a Tawantinsuyu equivalent of Jesus.

Túpac Katari is said to have persuaded his followers that the king Thupa Amaro would resurrect them five days after the death in battle. Resurrection on the fifth day corresponds to ancient Andean pattern (CDIP 1971–75: 2:3:81). Túpac Katari later denied that he had promised his followers resurrection (ibid.: 2:3:180), but the denial occurred during his own legal confession. He himself was, after all, Tomás Katari reincarnated (Valle de Siles 1983: 48).

According to Huarochirí myths, the resurrection on the fifth day took place in the time of the first, or the most ancient humanity called today the gentiles or mačlu; Guaman Poma called them Wari Wiraquča Runa or Wari Runa (cf. Szemiński 1984: 97–137). This Andean pattern of resurrection may indicate that there existed also a hope for the return of the ancestors. It confirms Hidalgo Lehuede's interpretation of the assemblies and proclamations in the cemeteries. It also indicates that the coming of the Inca represented a new beginning of the human world, comparable to the creation of first generation of Indians, the Wari Wiraquča Runa. Did all the Inca followers become new Wari Wiraquča Runa, founders of new lineages in the brave new world? Túpac Amaru was a new founder of the kings' ayllu. He was associated with Gran Paititi, the place where Incas are said to last even today. Paititi is in the east, where the sun comes from, where everything new should come from (cf. Szemiński 1984: 185–86).

I intended to specify more clearly the image of the Inca among the rebels, but I cannot add anything of significance to what I wrote in 1978. I have found three cases when the Inca was called god, but only one of them is probable, and I have cited it already (CDTA 1980–82: 3:76). According to Father M. de la Borda, the Indians executed Túpac Katari's orders as if he were a real deity (CDIP 1971–75: 2:2:810). Diverse sources indicate that the Inca was seen as an immortal or at least a person that should not and could not be killed. Felipe Velasco Thupa Yupanqui, Diego Cristóbal, and many other rebel leaders maintained that the Inca had not been killed on Waqay Pata; one said he was in Lima, others believed that he was in Gran Paititi. His death was described as death of a being that brings order to the universe (Szemiński 1984: 181–82). In a chicha beer store in Acomayo an Indian "becoming very sad and afflicted, showing it with much cunning said that they were taking the life of the Inca Thupa Amaro on Tuesday . . . while His Majesty ordered him taken alive, and that he did not want his life to be taken; and that is why [Areche], pretending to justify his action, declared that he had received the Inca already dead, and so he was going to send to His Majesty the head only." A conversation about rising against the Spaniards followed later (CDTA 1980–82: 4:347–48). It is worth noting that Túpac Amaru's (i.e., the Inca's) death was interpreted as proof that the Spaniards were rebels against the king of Spain.

It is not necessary to repeat all the titles given to the Inca by his followers: Benefactor of the Poor, Father, Majesty, King, and so on. In the provinces the people believed to represent him were sometimes received kneeling. In one case a Catholic priest used to put the Gospel over the heads of rebel leaders before every action (CDIP 1971–75: 2:2:651). Often the Inca was called Liberator and Redeemer (Lewin 1957: 340). According to the bishop of Cuzco, the Inca's titles were "Liberator of the Kingdom, Restorer of the Privileges, common father of those suffering under the yoke of the repartos" while the people called him Redeemer (CDIP 1971–75: 2:3:332). He was believed invincible (CDTA 1980–82: 5:37). He himself said that he would nominate the leaders that would lead the people by the way of the truth (ibid.: 3:113). He was perceived by the Indians as representing the Indians, Peru, land, and people (Szemiński 1984: 138–39, 178–90). He was also the representation of traditional moral values which should be analyzed separately.

CONCLUSIONS

The rebels had an image of history. The last three epochs of this history were: The World before the Spaniards, The World of the Spaniards, and the World after Inca's return. I have tried to model these epochs (figures 6.1, 6.2, 6.3).

The world created by God the Father and the Most Holy Mother has basically a tripartite structure composed of the sky, the earth, and the underworld, called in Quechua Hanaq Pača, Kay Pača, and Hurin Pača respectively. In every pača there exists a hierarchy of beings who are local representations of God: Sun, Inca, and Jesus (Pača Kamaq). Every male being has its female partner. As the sources referring to the rebellion do not contain any particular data on the image of these hierarchies, I used the simplest version based in equal grade on the information of sixteenth-century chronicles and on twentieth-century myths. The sky hierarchy,

Fig. 6.1. The World before the Spaniards

	Wiraqučan[a] – Paca Mama	
	Dios Padre – La Virgen	
	(God the Father – The Virgin)	

Hanaq Pača[b]	Kay Pača	Hurin Pača
(Higher World)	(This World)	(Lower World)
Inti-Killa	Inka[c]-Quya	Pača Kamaq–Pača Mama
		Jesus
(Sun-Moon)	(Inka-his wife)	(Jesus-Mother Earth)
Caska	Illapa, Amaru	Santiago
(Venus)	(Thunder,	(St. James)
	Serpent)	
Quyllurkuna	Urqukuna	Santukuna
(Stars)	(Mountains)	(Saints)
Kamaqinkuna[d]	Wiraquča Runa,	Wiraqucakuna
	kurakakuna	
("prototypes")	(lineage founders,	(human ancestors)
	caciques)	
?	Willaqkuna	padrekuna
	(Andean priests)	(Catholic priests)
?	Runakuna	Wiraqučakuna
	(Indians)	(Spaniards)

[a]I have no clear idea whether Wiraquča Qhapaq, King of Spain, corresponded to God the Father or to Jesus–Pača Kamaq. Perhaps he was only a king of human ancestors in the Lower World. I preferred to omit him from the diagram. The females, counterparts of every male being, are mentioned only when necessary. There are female stars, saints, and mountains. The composition of the Illapa family (Caska, Santiago, Amaru, etc.) is not well known.

[b]Pača has some other sections, also other subdivisions are possible. I assume that Lima, Buenos Aires, Paititi, and Africa together with Spain form part of Hurin Pača, to which also the night and the dead belong.

[c]Sixteenth-century prayers mention Runa Kamaq, Soul of Man, who guaranteed order in human society. I identified him with the Inca because of the opposition between the Inca and Pača Kamaq–Jesus.

[d]Every being in Kay Pača has a prototype in the sky, possibly identified with a star or a constellation.

as the one that has not changed, served to find the order of entities in other hierarchies (e.g., Venus as sky representation of the Thunder serves also to mark the place of Santiago the Apostle). I am not sure whether the Wiraqučakuna should be marked twice in the Underworld, once as Spaniards and the other one as all human ancestors. Their presence in This World is only a presence of lineage founders identified with the kura-kakuna – caciques, their heirs.

Figure 6.1 explains why the conquest had to happen. In This World there were only the willaqkuna, Andean priests who did not know how to pray and respect Jesus. I assume of course that in 1770–1780 Jesus and Pača Kamaq were completely identified, which might not be completely true. The Inca and the Runas were guilty of neglecting and disregarding Jesus (Pača Kamaq), and all the Lower World hierarchy. It was an offense to God the Father, who punished the Inca and the Runas with the cataclysm of sending the Spaniards. The Spaniards' duty was to punish the Inca and the Runas, and to teach them how to respect Jesus and all the Lower World hierarchy, thereby establishing a proper relationship between the two worlds (figure 6.2).

Fig. 6.2. The World of the Spaniards

	Dios Padre — La Virgen Wiraqučan — Pača Mama	
Hanaq Pača	Kay Pača	Hurin Pača
Inti-Killa	¿Jesus–Pača Mama?	Jesus–Pača Mama ¿Inka-Quya?
Caska	Santiago *Illapa, Amaru*	Santiago ¿Illapa, Amaru?
Quyllurkuna	Santukuna *Urqukuna*	Santukuna ¿Urqukuna?
Kamaqinkuna	Puka Kunka (Spaniards in Peru) *kurakakuna*	Wiraqučakuna
?	padrekuna *willaqkuna*	padrekuna
?	Runakuna	Wiraqučakuna

Note: Italics indicate members of Kay Pača hierarchy who exist but have lost their place in Kay Pača. Question marks indicate Kay Pača Representatives probably transferred to Hurin Pača.

The Spaniards sent by God, in this case by Jesus–Pača Kamaq, came and conquered This World. They introduced their proper ways of respecting Jesus and all the Lower World hierarchy. They punished the Inca and the Runas. They also killed the Inca, and abolished the hierarchy that ruled in This World. They started to rule This World on their own. They killed the Indians for their own benefit. They did not permit the Indians to become Catholic priests, and they forbade proper ways of respecting the sky. So the Spaniards became ñak'aq, antisocials who disrupted social order and offended God by making it impossible for the Christians (i.e., Indians) to respect him properly as Sun or Jesus. As they did not improve and their sins became very great, God decided to punish them and return them to their proper place. Killing the Spaniards in Peru was the simplest way to punish them and send them back to the place from whence they had come. At the same time, order must be restored in This World, and the only one who can and knows how to do it properly is the Inca. The cataclysm started. The Inca came back (figure 6.3).

Fig. 6.3. The World after Inca's Return

	Dios Padre — La Virgen Wiraqučan — Pača Mama	
Hanaq Pača	Kay Pača	Hurin Pača
Inti-Killa	Inka-Quya	Jesus–Pača Mama
Caska	Illapa, Amaru	Santiago
Quyllurkuna	Urqukuna	Santukuna
Kamaqinkuna	kurakakuna	Wiraqučakuna
?	willaqkuna, padrekuna	padrekuna
?	Runakuna	Wiraqučakuna

The Inca's return did not mean a repetition of the pre-Spanish times. His victory and the extermination of the Spaniards would create an equilibrium in the relationship of This World with the Higher World and with the Lower World alike. Both the sky hierarchy and the underworld hierarchy would be properly respected because there would at last be Indian Catholic priests. At the same time the Inca and the kurakas would once more bring order to This World.

The news that an Inca had reappeared obliged every Runa to decide whether this was the Inca for whom everybody was waiting. If he was the Inca, everyone's duty was to follow him and kill the Spaniards, because the pača-kuti, the cataclysm, had come, and the Spaniards' time was up. If, however, he was a false Inca, one should kill him and his followers, because the Spaniards' time would continue. In both cases, the chosen course of action was a religious duty.

If killing the Spaniards during Inca's return was a religious duty, so during every uprising real or supposed Spaniards should be killed. It also means that "everybody" knew how to recognize a Spaniard. In practice, in every village or town, the people knew who was a Spaniard or who was a ñak'aq. At least at the beginning of the movement it was easy to identify the local Spaniards. Once the troops moved to a territory where they did not know the people, however, the lack of criteria must have become significant. Of course, any fair-haired man who spoke Spanish and dressed and behaved as a Spaniard was a Spaniard. Obviously, a dark-skinned Quechua speaker, member of an Indian community, and follower of the Inca was not a Spaniard. Recognition of the persons in between the two extremes, however, depended on local conditions and conflicts. The number of persons recognized as Spaniards probably grew rapidly when the redistribution of wealth started, as always during the construction of a new and moral world. A detailed study of changes in moral values during the uprising may help us to understand how a "Spaniard" was recognized before he was killed. Anyway, every good Andean Christian should kill the Spaniards—thus making the world morally better.

Hidalgo Lehuede (1983) argued that the Inca and Jesus were opposed, the first one associated with life, the other one with death; following the Inca therefore meant rejection of Christianity. I believe it was not so simple. Jesus was the Lord of the Underworld, the Lord of the Dead and of the Night, but at the same time, he was the Lord of Change and of the Beginning. Like Pača Kamaq, Jesus was the Lord of the End and of the Beginning. The Inca's return was, for his followers, possible because Jesus permitted it. The war between the Inca and his enemies was a war among Christians who accused one another of heresy and rebellion. Of course, the real weight of Catholic dogmas and beliefs in Andean religion of the eighteenth century remains to be investigated. Catholic beliefs there were, but to what degree were they important? Were Christian elements merely a series of specialized cults associated only with the Underworld, or were they also present in other aspects of Andean religion?

REFERENCES

ANSION, JEAN-MARIE
  1984   *Demons des Andes. La pensée mythique dans une région des Andes péruviennes (Ayacucho).* Louvain-la-Neuve.
ANSION, JUAN, AND JAN SZEMIŃSKI
  1982   "Dioses y Hombres de Huamanga." *Allpanchis* 19 (Cuzco): 187–236.
CDIP (Comisión Nacional del Sesquicentenario de la Independencia del Perú)
  1971–75 *Colección documental de la independencia del Perú.* 27 vols. Lima.
CDTA
  1980–82 *Colección Documental del Bicentenario de la Revolución Emancipadora de Túpac Amaru.* 5 vols. Lima.
CORNEJO BOURONCLE, JORGE
  1963   *Túpac Amaru. La Revolución Precursora de la Emancipación Continental.* Cuzco.
DURAND FLOREZ, LUIS
  1974   *Independencia e integración en el Plan Político de Túpac Amaru.* Lima.

HIDALGO LEHUEDE, JORGE
1983   "Amarus y cataris: aspectos mesiánicos de la rebelión indígena de 1781 en Cusco, Chayanta, La Paz y Arica." *Chungará* 10 (Arica, March): 117-38.

HOCQUENGHEM, ANNE MARIE
1980-81   "L'iconographie mochica et les représentations de supplices." *Journal de la Société des américanistes* 68 (Paris): 249-60.
1982   "El degollador." Paper presented to the 44th International Congress of Americanists, Manchester.
1983   "The 'beauty' of the dear serpent jaguar, Camak." *Beilage* 1 (Jan.): 4-7.
1984   "Hanan y Hurin, Chantiers." *Amerindia* 9 (Paris): Supplément.

LEWIN, BOLESLAO
1957   *La Rebelión de Túpac Amaru y los orígenes de la Independencia de Hispanoamérica*. Buenos Aires.

LOAYZA, FRANCISCO A., ed.
1946   *Túpac Amaru (Documento inédito del año 1777)*. Lima.

MARISCOTTI DE GÖRLITZ, ANA MARÍA
1978   "Pachamama Santa Tierra. Contribución al estudio de la religión autóctona en los Andes centromeridonales." *Indiana* 8 (Berlin): suplemento.

ORTÍZ RESCANIERE, ALEJANDRO
1973   *De Adaneva a Inkarrí. Una visión indígena del Perú*. Lima.

OSSIO A., JUAN M., ed.
1973   *Ideología mesiánica del mundo andino*. Lima.

SZEMIŃSKI, JAN
1983   "Las generaciones del mundo según don Felipe Guaman Poma de Ayala." *Histórica*, 7:1 (Lima).
1984   *La utopía tupamarista*. Lima.

TÚPAC AMARU Y LA IGLESIA
1983   *Túpac Amaru y La Iglesia, Antología*. Lima.

VALLE DE SILES, MARÍA EUGENIA DEL
1980   *Testimonios del Cerco de La Paz. El campo contra la ciudad 1781*. La Paz.

ZUIDEMA, R. T.
1980   "Parentesco Inca. Sistema de parentesco incaico: una nueva visión teórica." In E. Mayer and R. Bolton, eds., *Parentesco y Matrimonio en los Andes* (Lima). Pp. 57-114.

CHAPTER 7

In Search of an Inca

ALBERTO FLORES GALINDO

To speak of revolutions, to imagine revolutions, to envision oneself in the very heart of a revolution is, in a way, to master the world.

Alejo Carpentier

According to one participant, a conspiracy was put to an abrupt end in Cuzco in the year 1805. Its goal, like that of others which would follow in the Latin American cities of that age, was to storm the military quarters, seize the plaza, and initiate a process which would culminate in the expulsion of the Spaniards. The conventional historiographic account tells us that, in addition to one lawyer, three priests, a councilman, a commissioner of Indian noblemen, and a member of the Indian aristocracy, the mineralogist Gabriel Aguilar and Juan Manuel Ubalde, a member of the *audiencia* (royal high court), figured among the protagonists. In ethnic terms, they amounted to a number of Indians led by various creoles (or mestizos). Those who conceived of and most enthusiastically supported the plot — that is, Aguilar and Ubalde — belonged to the provincial middle classes of that epoch, that social sector which would later seek a protagonist role in the Cuzco revolution of 1814. Up to this point, it seems we are faced with an event which quite naturally inscribes itself in the struggle for independence. But it happens that the conspirators were not contemplating a republican regime; instead, far from any projection into the future, they wanted to restore an earlier order: they were monarchists and they sought an Inca as their king.

The return to the past inspired a revolution. It would remain, nonetheless, among other similarly aborted plans. On the morning of December 5,

This essay derives from a collaborative research effort with Manuel Burga. Translation by Hunter Fite and Steve J. Stern.

1805, Aguilar and Ubalde were hanged in the main plaza of Cuzco (Vicuña M. 1924: 68ff.; BNP 1805: 19ff.). That heterodox interpretation of tradition[1] that they had carried out would be understood still in 1823, when the Peruvian Congress restored the memory of these "insurgents," proclaiming them "national heroes." Some years later, in an account dedicated to these events, Ricardo Palma hesitated to classify his protagonists: were they patriots or were they fools? They opposed the Spanish, but did so according to seemingly preposterous conceptions (Palma 1953: 838). Since this version, traditional history has treated them as a mere footnote to the precursors, uncertain figures who dangle between fiction and reality, "utopians" in the vulgar sense of the word: individuals harboring impossible ideas.[2]

This coolness by historians is not without foundation. In 1780 Aguilar was six years old and Ubalde fourteen. The "great rebellion" of Túpac Amaru, with its violent and destructive aftermath, must have formed part of their childhood recollections. They could not have ignored that throughout the Andean South, haciendas and *obrajes* (textile manufacturing houses) had been ransacked, churches destroyed, in the name of the return of the Inca; that those called *puka kunka* ("red necks") had been shot, and that what had begun as a political revolution was rapidly transformed into an ethnic conflict. Figures such as Aguilar and Ubalde might have been among the eventual victims of those misfortunes. They might have been, for example, among those young children (Spaniards or mestizos) who were hurled from the church towers in Tapacarí. There is sufficient testimony to prove that they were not ignorant of these events. Furthermore, they deemed certain precautions necessary in the event of success: all Spaniards would be rounded up with great celerity and shipped off to Spain, thus avoiding any sort of massacre. This reference, bordering on ingenuity, demonstrates that they were indeed conscious of the risk their plan incurred. Apparently, Aguilar and Ubalde were illustrating that Sartrean tendency to measure the clarity of an idea by the displeasure that it causes.[3]

Perhaps though, without negating the violence unfurled during 1780, historians have exaggerated its impact on the people of that epoch. Luis Durand suggests a carry-over of the tupamarista utopia even into the Cuzco of 1805.[4] What is more, those events ought to make clear that the return of the Inca was not a preoccupation exclusive to the indigenous population. In fact, it seems that the return of the Inca, as an alternative to colonial oppression, was born of the approximation of the Indian and Spanish republics, those two seemingly impassable worlds. A plain biological fact: the increase of the mestizos (22 percent of the population) over the course of the century. Andean culture moved from repression and clandestinity to tolerance and into the public ambits: fiestas and processions exhibited images of the Incas; similar themes appeared on the *keros* (drinking cups), canvasses, and even murals. The reinstallation of the Inca Empire would seem then to constitute a principle of identity: this utopia would not be a product solely of the indigenous sector, but would encompass other social sectors as well.

The approximation of these two republics (Indian and Spanish) followed several routes. At times the creoles and mestizos would opt to express themselves in Quechua, composing *yaravíes* (indigenous folk songs) like "Mariano Melgar" or dramas with Incaic personages in the style of *Ollantay*. On other occasions, the Indian might "employ European elements to better express himself" (Arguedas 1952: 140). But this process of convergence was to be interrupted by the social conflicts which broke loose between 1780 and 1824. The wars for independence over, the shared traditions of the country were superseded by social and ethnic divisions. In what remained of the nineteenth century, the Andean utopia would become a peasant utopia destined to remain confined to rural environs. Aguilar and Ubalde are situated halfway there: in the very center of a period of transition.

We could illustrate this transition in various manners. The theme of the Incas gradually disappeared from creole political discourse. The indigenous aristocracy vanished from the political scenario. Andean symbols went unrecognized in patriotic emblems. The prohibitions established by the Europeans after the defeat of Túpac Amaru (dress, language, art, titles of nobility) have been sufficiently emphasized; it is necessary to add that spontaneous elements made themselves felt in that growing divergence between the two republics. The Indians of the villages of Huancavelica had incorporated the bullfight into their cultural expression; in 1791 an edict attempted to prohibit that "inhumane custom," but proved unsuccussful so that the prohibition against this "heathen" practice was reiterated in 1807.[5] Repression and secrecy once more returned.

Who were our main characters? Their biographies can help us to chart the urban tracks of the Andean utopia. We have indicated three features up to this point, in accordance with other historians: Aguilar and Ubalde were provincial, middle class, creoles. The first two characteristics are sufficiently evident, as we will continue to see. The third, on the other hand, is surrounded by imprecisions. The term "creole" did not exist in official terminology, which, for purposes of census taking and tributes, distinguished only between Spaniards, Indians, mestizos, blacks, and castas (mixed-bloods). To many Limeños, "creole" was a defamatory term, in spite of the fact that writers of such stature as Viscardo and Guzmán,

influenced by their European exile, wanted to salvage the term. In cities
of the provinces like Cuzco, too, it seems to have attained a positive connotation, when compared to pejorative adjectives like *chapetón* or *gordo*.
Face to face with Ubalde or Aguilar, any colonial census taker would have
recorded either Spaniard or mestizo (see Macera 1977: 2:444 ff.).

We know with certainty (thanks to Luis Durand) that Ubalde was born
in Arequipa on May 27, 1766. His family owned lands in Majes by ma-
ternal inheritance. These, perhaps, enabled him to afford an education,
which from early on was under the administration of an aunt. This aunt,
a nun herself, tried consistently to steer him toward the church and clois-
ters. Although she would be unsuccessful, she did manage to instill in her
nephew a great religious preoccupation: he became familiar with the Bible
and hagiography. But it was not simply a matter of the discovery of an
interior mysticism, for it seems that here began as well an intense concern
for the destitute. We find the first traces in Deuteronomy, that exhorta-
tory and prophetic book. The theme of the poor is embodied in the figure
of the slaves—more as example than as reality. I say this because the black
population was slight in the Andean South.

Ubalde went on from Arequipa to Cuzco, where he commenced his
studies of jurisprudence. He carried with him a letter from his aunt, which
would accompany him almost to the scaffold, and which incited him to
remain loyal to the mystical inspiration of his youth. During those years,
he maintained his obsession with reading; we have evidence of his incursions into the world of enlightened thought. He apparently came across
Olavide's *El Evangelio en triunfo (The Gospel in Triumph)*. These new
interests would find propitious surroundings in the libraries of Lima's intellectuals. Once having completed his studies, he practiced law in the
capital city. In 1805, at the age of thirty-nine, he went to Cuzco as a
substitute official of the audiencia. That court of justice had been established only a few years before: the position of deputy counsellor (*teniente
asesor*) would occupy him while José de Reyes, who was away in Spain,
held office (Cornejo B. 1955: 152). From the capital he had returned to
the provinces to initiate his career progression, albeit delayed, in the colonial bureaucracy. He might have had a future. It would be cut short,
however, for in that year he met Aguilar.

Evidently the deputy counsellor of the audiencia was a man of higher
culture than average in the lettered circles of the colony. But his reading
had not eradicated from his mind an obsession with dreams, which he
married with the mysticism of his childhood. If his meeting with Aguilar
proved for his life cataclysmic, this was, among other things, because their
meeting had been foretold or confused with a dream (Vicuña M. 1924:
70). For Ubalde, dreams were not to be forgotten, nor would it have oc-

curred to him that they might have been the language of an inner world; instead he took them for "nocturnal revelations," keys to the future. Lurking here is the belief that there exists something like destiny.

We find these beliefs even more emphatically in Gabriel Aguilar. The younger of the two, he was born around 1774 in Huánuco. We know that he studied mineralogy, and that the range of his intellectual interests was as heterogeneous as it was vast (including cosmography, mechanical arts, and experimental philosophy). Nevertheless, unlike Ubalde, he preferred travel to reading. He passed a while in the *montaña* (tropical eastern slopes descending into the jungle region), reached the Marañon River, visited Chachapoyas. We might have thought him a character comparable to those European voyagers who traversed America in that era. But he travelled neither to explore nature nor to seek out fellow man; instead, his motivation was the pursuit of a kind of interior definition. At nine years old, he had a dream (a revelation), in which he was designated one of the Lord's chosen (*Conato* 1976: 28), an annointed one. He felt himself called toward a greater plan. Wandering the country in search of other signs, he arrived in Lima — watching for and listening to any message. The Convent of the Barefoot Ones ("Los Descalzos"), of the Franciscan Order, was to be an important point on his itinerary: there he contemplated the image of a crucified Christ figure, which, years later, he would believe to rediscover in Cuzco.

He considered joining the Franciscans, but turned in his habit to make way as a pilgrim: ". . . The Lord ordained that he go forward with his cross, abandoning his Fathers, fortune, and comforts" (ibid.: 87). From Lima he set out for the central sierra, where another important stop would be the church of Jauja, where aside from an image of the Lord of Agony (el Señor de la Agonía), he came upon two other Franciscans. Years later he would decide to remain in Cuzco on account of an image of Christ which he contemplated in the church of San Francisco in that city. In his confessions there appears in addition a relationship between poverty and the Franciscans. We note these facts recalling the connection drawn elsewhere between that order and millenarianism.

But let us not jump ahead of ourselves. Before deciding to establish himself in Cuzco, Aguilar traversed the Andean south. Passing through Potosí and Mendoza, heading toward Buenos Aires, he followed the inverse route of *El lazarillo de ciegos caminantes (A Blind Man's Guide)*, by Carrió de la Bandera, which described the itinerary from that southern port up to Lima. On this muleteer's trail, the wanderer would suffer a decisive transformation. Some pampa dwellers mistook him for an emissary of Túpac Amaru, inquired of the latest news from Cuzco, and ended up issuing invitations that "he lead a political uprising" (ibid.: 47). It happens that this traveller resembled any number of others who crisscrossed the Andean footpaths at that time. The historian Lorenzo Huertas (1978: 10), for example, has reconstructed the itinerary of the native Diego Jaquica, a tupamarista rebel in 1780 who was captured and taken toward Lima; in Ica he escaped and went through all the towns on the way to Cuzco, spreading tales of the Incas and indigenous noblemen. In an oral society such as the one of that time, these personalities found ready listeners. The hostelries, inns, and taverns scattered about those extensive routes created an atmosphere well suited for conversations which might easily head toward political themes (Eguiguren 1935: 20). On occasion the public could influence the traveller. Those pamperos, with their inquiries about the tupamaristas, unknowingly guided Aguilar to discover, in the midst of his mysticism, a more earthly route.

Aguilar journeyed to Spain. There was talk of a miracle which supposedly prevented a shipwreck, and also of his possible contacts with Spanish authorities, or rumored conspiracies with the English. Disillusioned with the court, he returned to Peru to carry out travels which would bring him back to Cuzco. He nearly repeated the inverse path of a predecessor: Juan Santos Atahualpa, that student of the Jesuits who abandoned Cuzco and, heading up the jungle rivers, discovered the Gran Pajonal region in the central montaña. Aguilar arrived in Cuzco hoping to find an indigenous woman of peasant origin whom, in accordance with the divine plan, he intended to marry. He was always a tense and tormented man, abandoning his intellectual projects and postponing his hunt for mines in order to meet his supposed destiny. In the verse he composed shortly before his death, he reached the point of defining himself in these terms: "That Gabriel who did live / in continuous suffering" ("Aquel Gabriel que vivió / en un continuo penar"; in Mendiburu 1931: 176).

Some testimonies indicate that Aguilar and Ubalde had met previously in Lima (ibid.). What is certain is that in the imperial city of Cuzco (this phrasing would have had a more concrete significance in the eighteenth century, when the memory of the Incas was not so remote), they developed a friendship based on lengthy discourse. The divine revelations, the dreams, the travels and books, the preoccupation with the poor and with suffering—the experiences of the one and the other began to nurture an idea: to change society by establishing a new order, or rather, the true order. These themes would repeatedly appear throughout the judicial proceedings to which they were both subjected.[6] Shortly after being imprisoned, Aguilar had a vision, which he communicated immediately to Ubalde, according to which "a death sentence would be declared." Faced with this imminent outcome, he decided to recount "all of his revelations,"[7] to speak before his judges rather than conceal his true intentions.

Thanks to this, we can better understand that Andean eighteenth century, if we reexamine the proceedings against them to search for the roots of their beliefs and the central question in any rebellion: what criteria legitimate power and insurrection? We shall see that the Andean utopia of which both conspirators were participants is streaked throughout the oral and written history, the rational and the imaginary, of that society.

For Aguilar and Ubalde, the rejection of the colonial order was justified by two complementary arguments. On the one side lies the notion of "just titles" to govern America, and on the other the tyranny of the king. In the first, we can see in the eighteenth century traces of a theme initiated much earlier, in the sixteenth century, from within the "republic of Spaniards": the preachings of Las Casas on the justification of conquest. The source of the second is clear: St. Thomas Aquinas. The oppressed have the right to rise up in revolt, even to execute their king.

The historian Guillermo Lohmann Villena has followed with characteristic erudition the tracks of Las Casas' influence, which over the centuries touched, within viceregal intellectual circles, personages such as Feijóo de Sosa (1718–1791), Baquíjano y Carrillo (1748–1798), Riva Agüero (1783–1858), and Vidaurre (1773–1841). *La Destrucción de Las Indias (The Destruction of the Indies)* appears in the inventories of three Lima libraries of the eighteenth century. Las Casas proved to be a much-quoted author, expounded particularly by critics of the colonial order (Lohmann V. 1974).

Aguilar and Ubalde proposed to fight in favor of an Incaic monarchy. Two influences seem in turn to have nurtured this idea: Christianity, and the Andean world. Each of these was made manifest by, and confused with, various texts and the voyages and dreams of both protagonists. The written text, as we shall observe with greater precision in the pages to come, was not far removed from oral transmission, nor was reality sharply distinguished from the imaginary. These men did not adhere to the distinctions and borders that we rely upon today.

Apart from what has already been mentioned about the Franciscans and poverty, Christianity implies here the reading of Deuteronomy, those passages of the Bible dedicated to the interpretation of dreams, and finally, the epistle to the Corinthians and the Gospel of St. John. The most precise citations draw upon the latter two references. In St. John the idea that Ubalde seizes on is that "the eternal word illuminates all men who come into this world" (*Conato* 1976: 58; cf. St. John 1:1–18). In this he saw his dreams and revelations justified. When all was said and done, they gave him access to supposed divine plans on the margins of the institutional Church. The enthusiasm of Aguilar and Ubalde for the sacred

word did not seem to extend into a defense of the Church as an institution
(". . . the priests change parishes with the ease with which one abandons
a dirty and worthless shirt"). Able and tempted to enter an order, they
had finally chosen to remain in the world at large. This option was justified precisely in the first epistle to the Corinthians, in which St. Paul refers
to the concept of charity (*la caridad*): "all is believed by virtue of its sin-
cerity" (*todo lo cree por su misma sinceridad; Conato* 1976: 181; cf. 1
Corinthians 13:1–7). This was love placed over faith as the road to salvation. Theirs was a somewhat unorthodox reading of the scriptures; but
it was nonetheless *a* reading of them, since we have been able to match
their citations in the judicial proceedings with the original biblical texts.
We do not know who else may have shared these conceptions or in which
preachers' sermons they might have found encouragement. We can only
indicate that some time before, Túpac Amaru had also turned with fre-
quency to biblical images in his proclamations, comparing, for instance,
the situation in Peru with the oppression of the Hebrews of Israel.

From the union of these readings and his dreams, Aguilar derived his
providentialist and messianic conceptions. Neither Aguilar nor Ubalde considered his biography a product of free will. On the contrary, both felt
themselves called, chosen, designated. They were carrying out a mission.
In the beginning they believed that Aguilar could become the monarch.
But later they discovered a rather obvious point: that to be an Inca, one
must descend from an Inca. In a society organized by estates, such status
rights are inherited. And so began the febrile search for a descendant of
Túpac Amaru I, often confused with Felipe Túpac Amaru, although there
is not the slightest doubt that the reference was to the figure executed by
Viceroy Toledo in the main plaza of Cuzco in 1572. Indeed, it was that
same fellow with whose memory the Inca Garcilaso practically concluded
his *Comentarios Reales*: "And so ended the life of this Inca, the legitimate
heir of that empire by direct male filial descendance from the first Inca,
Manco Cápac" (bk. 8, chap. 9). Legitimacy, at that time, was not solely
a question of divine designation, but also of ascendance and genealogy.
They wanted to reestablish an order by delivering power to its legitimate
holder: the king who had been dethroned. In this enterprise Aguilar and
Ubalde were simple prophets. It was in this manner that Christian forms
(readings, references, conceptions) enveloped Andean projects.

An insurrection is not decided upon by tactical arguments. Notions such
as the correlation of forces, enemies, and allies: these held little importance to Aguilar and Ubalde. They did not reason politically. Their sense
of the times was another one; it functioned by periods and stages. It happened that in 1805 there appeared more than one sign indicating that "the
time had arrived." We can find another evangelical formula repeatedly

in St. Mark, St. Luke, and St. John: "Blessed is he who reads, and those who hear the words of this prophecy, and those who abide by its writings, for the time is coming" (Revelation 1:3). What time? The time of the Indian, while that of the Spaniard would come to an end. Society, as Aguilar and Ubalde perceived it, responded to a dual scheme which at times counterposed Europeans and Americans, at times Indians and whites. Obviously, Aguilar and Ubalde considered themselves closer to the Indians, even though contrary to their own beliefs, the matter was more one of option than of birth.

Were Aguilar and Ubalde exceptional figures? Their declarations did not seem to surprise their judges, excepting that which referred to the dreams and to certain prophecies, considered alibis to extenuate the inevitable punishment. During 1805, Aguilar had conversed not only with Ubalde, but with anyone who might listen in the city of Cuzco and the surrounding villages. It ought not surprise us that the conspiracy was readily revealed, inasmuch as it was completely lacking in the indispensable requirement of secrecy. They disregarded secrecy because they were convinced that the chances for success lay beyond any imposition of human will. In addition, it seems that they easily found an audience for their prophecies. Pablo Inca Roca, an Indian nobleman among the accused, referred to a meeting with Aguilar that took place in the month of June, probably in the parish of San Sebastian: "he called to the one who testifies [i.e., Pablo Inca Roca], and said that the king of Spain had left, and that we were without a king; that the time had arrived for the Incas to reign, and that as he [Roca] was of the Indian caste, he had to be crowned, making sure to behead all the Europeans before anything else" (*Conato* 1976: 170).

The Peru of the eighteenth century seems to have been infused with an "end-of-the-world" atmosphere (Barclay and Santos 1983: 26 ff.). The Inca was awaited. Many testimonies confirm the existence of the so-called mythic cycle of Inkarrí during that century: paintings depicting the beheaded Inca circulated in Arequipa and Cuzco; theatrical representations, inspired by the epic clash at Cajamarca, were performed in the northern country; Juan Santos Atahualpa preached from the jungle that the head of the Inca was in Spain. By then the collective memory had confused the sixteenth-century Incas Atahualpa and Túpac Amaru I: the death of the Inca was staged as if in Cajamarca [site of Atahualpa's death —Ed.], but with characteristics which, according to Garcilaso, surrounded the execution of the last Inca of Vilcabamba [Túpac Amaru I —Ed.] in Cuzco. In the Andean imagination, the Spanish conquest had only just ended in Cuzco in 1572 (Gonzales and Rivera 1982). Two centuries later, it was expected that the Inca would return at any moment. Aguilar believed that more elaborate preparations were unnecessary, since simply to invoke the name of the Inca would suffice to draw the peasants. This central idea formed the backbone of his conceptions.

It is probable, as Federica Barclay and Fernando Santos have suggested, that the expectation of the return of the Inca was closely associated with the physical upheavals which afflicted Peru during the eighteenth century: rains and floods in the south Andes, and a devasting earthquake in Lima in 1746. But it is also certain that the matter must be placed within the interior of an entire indigenous cultural rebirth, which, transcending the peasant world, reached as far as the cities and the intellectuals. A decisive element in this process was precisely the Indian noblemen. At least until 1780, the creoles of Cuzco accepted the use of Quechua in their gatherings (*tertulias*), acquired paintings with indigenous motifs, tolerated the consumption of coca. Aguilar and Ubalde's conspiracy ought to be considered a part of this cycle, even though they appeared, as we have seen, just as these trends were winding down, and the predominant sociocultural tendencies were reversing. There was an anachronistic element in these personages. Creoles such as these had been sought with little success by Túpac Amaru II twenty-five years earlier.

The idea of the return of the Inca must have been engraved in the collective memory of the eighteenth century: it represented the historical consciousness of the conquered populations. But, leaving aside the question of oral transmission, there was one author who inspired this hope: the Inca Garcilaso de la Vega, mentioned various times during the legal proceedings. A number of historians—John Rowe, José Durand, Miguel Maticorena—have underlined the subversive role played by Garcilaso. *Comentarios Reales*, that book of Renaissance history, came to be read much as a pamphlet by figures such as Túpac Amaru, who took as emphatic denunciation the comparison of the Incas and the Romans, the criticisms of Viceroy Toledo, the veiled suggestion that a just and equitable empire ought be reconstructed. Garcilaso turned the Inca era, Tawantinsuyo, into a golden age. The Inca believed that the past could fill a moralizing function by offering models for the present: his historical conception was infected by utopia in the strictest European sense of the word. He was a Platonic historian. The eighteenth-century indigenous elite, which had easy access to Spanish language and to the printed word, understood this inner message of the book; they, in turn, transported it orally to other social sectors. We know that "a work by Garcilaso" accompanied Túpac Amaru in his travels.

But perhaps Garcilaso's catalytic role derived from another aspect of his work, more attributed than real—the role of prophet. Aguilar and Ubalde referred to his prognostications: Garcilaso had foretold the end of the time of the Spaniards, to be displaced by the English. There was even talk of an English fleet anchored off the coast of Africa. The frequent wars between Spain and England, in the late colonial period, would — for those aware of world events — have lent sustenance to this prophecy.

No contemporary reader would discover any evidence of such a prophecy within the pages of *Comentarios Reales*. We are apparently faced with another invention of the oral tradition. But such an interpretation would not be entirely accurate. John Rowe has demonstrated that the edition utilized by Túpac Amaru and the eighteenth-century indigenous aristocracy, published in Madrid in 1723 under the direction of Gonzales de Barcia, included a special prologue elaborated by Don Gabriel de Cárdenas, in which he mentions a supposed prophecy by Sir Walter Raleigh regarding the restoration of the Inca Empire by the English.[8] The mention was made in passing and with a touch of irony, but this prologue was too closely linked with what was, in effect, the epilogue of the book: that passage, which we have already mentioned, referring to the death of Túpac Amaru I. The readers would have invariably related the beginning with the end; everyone reads that which seems of interest. We ought to add that Raleigh was the author of a *History of the World*, written during the same years that Garcilaso composed his work, in which he invited his English readers to fight against Spain, and compared the latter to the most oppressive powers in the history of humanity.

Aguilar and Ubalde may have used that same edition of 1723, but one must mention that in 1800–1801 a new edition was published in Madrid, with an introductory note in which the editor stated: "I confess that it provokes in me nothing less than great wonder that works of this nature, sought after by the sages of the nation, anticipated with great curiosity, lauded, translated and published numerous times by foreigners who are sworn enemies to the glory of Spain, end up becoming so scarce. . . ."

Garcilaso, in his prophetic dimension, had unexpected company: Santa Rosa of Lima. Her prophecy of Lima's destruction still circulates in Peru. The raging blows of the sea flatten Lima, reaching beyond the *Plaza de Armas* [the central plaza — Ed.] to the edge of the city's Indian barrio. During the earthquake of 1746, ". . . the false rumour spread throughout the city that the sea had reached its fringes," and unleashed a veritable panic among the survivors (*Terremotos* 1863: 45–46). There is no allusion to this theme in the judicial proceedings against Aguilar and Ubalde, although Santa Rosa does appear saying that ". . . the kingdom must be returned to the Indians themselves."[9] Originally Santa Rosa belonged to the Spanish colonial pantheon of Catholic saints: an object of religious devotion in Lima, she exalted the practice of flagellation, penitence, and interior seclusion. But eventually she was incorporated into the peasant world as well. The spread of Andean pueblos that took her name bears witness to this process.[10] And while she died on August 24, 1617, over time that date was changed to the 30th of August, which—whether premeditated or by chance—coincided with the death of Túpac Amaru I. This date has also served, in many pueblos of the highlands, as the time to celebrate their principal fiesta. We mention the above solely as a hypothesis, to point out threads that might be helpful in disentangling that dense and knotty matting which constituted mestizo popular culture in the colonial era.

Garcilaso de la Vega's was not the only Andean literature to influence Aguilar and Ubalde. In his own library, Ubalde held a highly valued book called *El llanto de los indios (The Wail of the Indians)*. He devoted great effort to having his friends read and circulate the book, and to protecting it against wear and tear (*Conato* 1976: 32). The author is unknown, but from other references we can guess that it was a work of few pages and small format that denounced injustice and oppression. It was true pocketbook indigenous literature, to be placed among that group of booklets with titles such as the *reclamaciones* ("remonstrances") or *lamentos* ("laments") of Indians. Ephemeral and difficult to conserve, these works held an importance as propaganda and education heretofore undervalued by historians, with the exception of Eguiguren, for whom they came to be "popular catechism . . . heard with appreciation and passion . . ." (Eguiguren 1967: 112). The genre essentially amounted to a form of intellectual production equidistant from the *Mercurio Peruano* and oral culture, and just as difficult to place in bibliographical repositories. Its authors and public were probably members of those intermediate strata in the provinces to which we have already referred.

We have left to the end yet another dimension which figures into the belief system of Aguilar and Ubalde: the European culture of the epoch. Tacitus, Peralta, and Campomanes appear in Ubalde's library; there is particular mention in the trial of the study of the Incas by Abbé Reynal. Curiously, though, he is said to be the author of "political predictions" and hence tied in some way to Garcilaso. *Comentarios* was pamphletized precisely because of the treatment it received from such learned figures as Marmontel. Between 1609 and 1800 seventeen complete or partial editions of the book were published: ten in French, two in English, one in German, and four in Spanish (Tauro 1965). Its tardy fame travelled from Europe to Peru.

It was his encounter with Aguilar and his prophetic temperament that revitalized these readings for Ubalde: "he recalled as much as possible of the many mystic books he had read in childhood and in later years in order to re-evaluate the worth of Don Gabriel." And although Aguilar did not dispose of an equivalent volume of readings, neither was he at the margin of European culture. Without ignoring Aguilar's voyage to that continent, the Bolivian historian Carlos Ponce also finds him accompanying Humboldt in his travels across Peru.

While they were not ignorant of Europe, Aguilar and Ubalde, like Túpac Amaru, found more solid sustenance in traditional Christian thinking or in the cultural products of the Andean world than in the realm of the Enlightenment. The revolution they envisioned, in a manner more evident than in that of 1780, was not in principle destined to question "the bases of Ancient Regime society—stratified, vertical, and hierarchical" (Maticorena 1981: 8). The King and the Monarchy were incontrovertible principles. "In the King resides supreme, temporal power, granted by God" (*Conato* 1976: 173). At issue instead was the matter of exchanging one dynasty (that of the Bourbons) for another (descendants of the Incas). To bring about this change was to execute the divine plan: "God ordained that there would be a great happening in Peru" (ibid.: 61).

The idea of "King," then, was separable from the persona of Charles IV. Important for arriving at this conclusion was the observation of the European scene: the end of a dynasty in France and the recognition by the pope of the new monarch, Napoleon Bonaparte, as "legitimate Sovereign." Bonaparte was the true incarnation of the devil for the colonial elite, but a seemingly positive character in Ubalde's eyes (ibid.: 176). There is some evidence that European events were followed closely. At least from 1791, the "Declaration of the Rights of Man" was already familiar in the Peruvian south (*Declaración* 1955: 76).

The essential element in the vision of Aguilar and Ubalde was its firm anchorage in the Andean utopia—in the return of the Inca and the restoration of an Incaic monarchy. This vision was utopian precisely because it implied an alternative to the colonial order, imaginary and total, a rupture with prevailing conditions; but unlike the European utopias, Andeans developed their model of the ideal society not in the future or in some far-away place, but in the past. And so, their utopia was more a peculiar interpretation of history than an original invention. The ideal community had existed: it was and would be that of the Incas. To describe it one had no need to search for a work which might picture its houses and streets, habits and customs, for these were preserved in daily life (the customs of the indigenous elite) or in oral tradition. Garcilaso came to be a pillar of this collective memory: rather than rely on some architect of the future, the Andean utopia substituted a historian. Like the *yaraví* or the *décimas* [folk song and folk verse respectively—Ed.], the Andean utopia was in reality a creation, a new product. It was neither a prolongation of Andean mental structures rooted in the past, nor the mechanical import of Western concepts. As in the case of other manifestations of that same popular culture — for example, the *retablos* [a form of woodwork sculpture popular in the Andes, and based originally on sculpted altar-pieces — Ed.] — there derived from the union of Western form and Andean content something different from the original patterns.[11]

All the possible differences between the Andean utopia and the European utopias notwithstanding, one would have to concede, nonetheless, coincidences and a certain parallelism in time. As Bronislaw Baczko (1978) has indicated, ". . . the century of Enlightenment is a 'hot' period in the history of utopias — comparable in this respect to the Renaissance or the first half of the nineteenth century." A curious connection remains, though, between the Andean world and Europe, the tracking of which might be the focus of another essay: the enthusiasm on the part of learned Europeans for that which was Incaic, their debates on the nature of the American Man, could reach such distant places as Arequipa, Cuzco, or Huánuco. The Incas had become a familiar theme in French Enlightenment literature. For the utopians, as Raúl Porras notes (1968: 160), Tawantinsuyo was ". . . the model for a contented society under a paternal and communist regime." The concept of the "bon sauvage" found an adequate stage in America. The sources for these conceptions, too, were Las Casas and Garcilaso.

All the passion Gabriel Aguilar and Juan Manuel Ubalde devoted to their common enterprise was displayed by the fortitude with which they marched to the gallows. We have noted several explanations for their demise: excessive confidence in Providence, carelessness regarding necessary secrecy, treason by one of the implicated. One circumstance still remains to be added: the scant bond which they maintained with the Indians. They did not seek to develop it, since they were convinced that the mere mention of the name of the Inca (having found a legitimate descendant) was sufficient for the uprising to explode. But, as one can gather from the trial, this eagerly awaited moment did not come easily. Aguilar transformed his youthful search for individual salvation into a collective undertaking which got confused with the divine plan to find him a woman among the Indians. These objectives notwithstanding, not one "Indian commoner" (*indio del común*) figured among those implicated, which would give the impression that the majority of them were unaware of the dreams of the conspirators. It does not matter if on the day of execution "a large crowd of people" attended. The Indians of Cuzco were not among those people with whom Aguilar or Ubalde had conversed regularly. These mestizo intellectuals of the provinces, who renounced the established order, although they were not themselves Indians, incarnated a feature of Peruvian intellectual circles then and now: their weak social anchorage. This was the socially disconnected intelligence to which Jorge Basadre once referred; or, if we dare rob an image from Martín Adán, an intelligence "come loose."

The case of Aguilar and Ubalde might allow us a final digression on the concept of *lo andino* [literally, "the Andean," or "what is Andean," usually used to refer to an Andean cultural "essence" that has survived intact and sets Andeans apart from non-Andeans—Ed.]. This term has become, among some authors, synonymous with continuity, permanence, reiteration; concepts or mental structures stubbornly perpetuated, unaltered, across the centuries. The Andean quality of a personage is defined in relation to an ideal type: the prehispanic inhabitant. But this image, which shrinks from historical analysis, does not ponder sufficiently the profound transformations that convulsed colonial Andean society. We could rise above discussions that run aground in semantics, if we admit that the content implied in the term "Andean" has varied along with historical conditions. At the end of the eighteenth century, the term widened considerably to include such categories as Indians (both rich and poor), mestizos, and even creoles: it was defined, first, by opposition to the European-born Spanish (that dual vision of society which we saw in our conspirators), and, second, by the assumption of a collective identity which formed around the Andean utopia. To develop these conceptions, one might have drawn on Andean conceptions, or on those learned in the Bible and in Christian preachings. But just as a native Andean man would not stop being such simply because he plows with oxen, tends to sheep, and sows wheat, neither would knowledge of Western culture cut Aguilar and Ubalde off from the same condition. Nevertheless, we will insist for the last time that they be situated within a period of transition. In what remained of the nineteenth century, *lo andino* would shrink, referring only to the peasantry, to the indigenous, and even only to the rural native highlands. Later, in the twentieth century, migration would expand *lo andino*, which spread out over the cities and the ports. The model of what was Andean which inspired Aguilar and Ubalde was not that which had reigned during the sixteenth century; nor was it, however, that which reigns today.

NOTES

1 The idea of the "heterodoxy of tradition" originates in one of the articles by Mariátegui published under the title *Peruanicemos el Perú*. This author pointed out the transforming potential that could have been contained within the Peruvian past, and in this way reclaimed a word like "tradition," which had belonged to the dominant classes.

2 A fairly complete bibliography on the subject may be found in the summary of the Aguilar and Ubalde trial presented by José Agustín de la Puente (1960: 495–525).

3 "I reached the point of thinking systematically against myself, measuring the weight of an idea by the discontent it caused me" (Sartre 1968: 162).

4 Luis Durand is writing a book on the history of Cuzco between the revolutions of 1780 and 1814. For the time being, one may consult his recent article (1983: 187–98).

5 These decrees are Documents C3351 (Año 1791) and D142 (Año 1807) in the Biblioteca Nacional del Perú, Sala de Investigaciones.

6 The Aguilar-Ubalde trial (which we have been citing) has been edited by Carlos Ponce, in La Paz, based on a transcription of the manuscript preserved in the Archivo General de la Nación in Buenos Aires. During the trial, both defendants speak with an unusual clarity, born of the conviction of the correctness of their ideas. They disclose all, even their dreams. See *Conato* 1976.

7 See *Revista del Archivo Histórico del Cuzco*, no. 1 (Cuzco, 1950): 234.

8 See Rowe 1976: 27. This article, originally published in 1954, remains indispensable for anyone concerned with these themes.

9 *Conato* 1976: 117. The Tucumán Congress (1816) had an image of Santa Rosa in its meeting hall, and the liberating army adopted her as their patroness. Cf. Catanzaro 1964: 2; Vargas U. 1959.

10 The name of Santa Rosa appears in such distinct places as Jaén, Chiclayo, Ayaviri, Melgar, Huánuco, etc. (Tarazona 1946).

11 I borrow here some ideas about Andean popular culture from Stastny 1981.

REFERENCES

ARGUEDAS, JOSÉ MARÍA
1952 "El Ollantay. Lo autóctono y lo occidental en el estilo de los dramas coloniales quechuas." *Letras Peruanas* 2: 8.
BNP (Biblioteca Nacional del Perú, Sala de Investigaciones, Lima)
1805 "Expediente relativo al juicio seguido a los conspiradores Aguilar y Ubalde." MS D120. Lima.
BACZKO, BRONISLAW
1978 *Lumières de l'utopie*. Paris: Payot.

BARCLAY, FEDERICA, AND FERNANDO SANTOS
1983   "De la ideología mesiánica a la ideología apocalíptica." *Debate* (Lima, June 20).

CATANZARO, TOMÁS
1964   "El incanato y Santa Rosa en el Congreso de Tucumán de 1816." *El Comercio* (Lima, July 9).

CONATO
1976   *El conato revolucionario de 1805.* Compiled by Carlos Ponce Sangines. La Paz: Municipalidad de La Paz.

CORNEJO BOURONCLE, JORGE
1955   "Pumacahua." *Revista del Archivo Histórico del Cuzco* 6 (Cuzco).

DE LA PUENTE, JOSÉ AGUSTÍN
1960   "Notas sobre la causa de la independencia del Perú." In *La causa de la emancipación del Perú.* Lima: Instituto Riva Agüero. Pp. 495–525.

DECLARACIÓN
1955   "La Declaración de los Derechos del Hombre en Arequipa." *Fénix* 11 (Lima): 76.

DURAND, LUIS
1983   "Juan Manuel Ubalde: la primera conspiración criolla por la emancipación." *Scientia et Praxis* 16 (Lima, January): 187–98.

EGUIGUREN, ANTONIO
1935   *La sedición de Huamanga en 1812.* Lima: Gil.
1967   *Hojas para la historia de la emancipación.* Vol. 3. Lima.

GONZALES, ENRIQUE, AND FERMÍN RIVERA
1982   "La muerte del Inca en Santa Ana de Tusi." *Bulletin del Institut Francais d'Etudes Andines* 11: 1–2 (Lima): 19–36.

HUERTAS, LORENZO
1978   "Testimonios referentes al movimiento de Túpac Amaru II, 1784–1812." *Allpanchis* 11–12 (Cuzco): 7–16.

LOHMANN VILLENA, GUILLERMO
1974   *Tras el surco de Las Casas en el Perú.* Lima.

MACERA, PABLO
1977   *Trabajos de historia.* 4 vols. Lima: Instituto Nacional de Cultura.

MATICORENA, MIGUEL
1981   *Cuerpo político y restitución en Túpac Amaru.* Lima.

MENDIBURU, MANUEL DE
1931   *Diccionario histórico-biográfico del Perú.* Vol. 1. Lima: Enrique Palacios.

PALMA, RICARDO
1953   *Tradiciones peruanas.* Madrid: Aguilar.

PORRAS, RAÚL
1968   *Fuentes históricas peruanas.* Lima.

ROWE, JOHN
1976   "El movimiento nacional inka del siglo XVIII." Orig. pub. 1954. In

Alberto Flores Galindo, ed., *Túpac Amaru II, 1780*. Lima: Retablo de Papel. Pp. 11–66.

SARTRE, JEAN PAUL
1968   *Las palabras*. Buenos Aires: Losada.

STASTNY, FRANCISCO
1981   *Las artes populares del Perú*. Lima: Edubanco.

TARAZONA, JUSTINO
1946   *Demarcación política del Perú*. Lima.

TAURO, ALBERTO
1965   "Bibliografía del Inca Garcilaso de la Vega." *Documenta* 4 (Lima): 393–437.

TERREMOTOS
1863   *Terremotos. Colección de las relaciones de los más notables que ha sufrido esta capital y que la han arruinado*. Lima: Tip. Aurelio Alfaro.

VARGAS UGARTE, RUBÉN
1959   *Vida de Santa Rosa de Lima*. Buenos Aires.

VICUÑA MACKENNA, BENJAMÍN
1924   *La revolución de la independencia del Perú*. Lima: Garcilaso.

PART III

Rebellion and Nation-State Formation: 19th-Century Perspectives

Introduction to Part III

By 1824, American patriots had broken the colonial bond in nearly all of Spanish America, but the creoles who sought to construct new states and nations faced a daunting task. Hampered by a colonial inheritance which divided people by color and class, setting social group against social group; subjected to regional rivalries and loyalties that transformed the legal fiction of "nations" into the reality of civil wars; restrained by the weaknesses of their fledgling states' fiscal and repressive apparata, and by the relatively autarkic economic life of the provinces; imprisoned by their own racism and social fears—creoles who dared contemplate visionary national projects seemed undercut from every quarter. Is it any wonder that for perhaps a half-century the *caudillo* became the classic political figure of Spanish America? The caudillo, a warlord who sought to mold his regionally specific clientele into a personal fiefdom of soldiers, dependents, and tributaries, made little pretense that all adult males were national "citizens" equal before law, and devoted little effort to forging an integrated nation out of district territories. The exceptional caudillos who sought to lay a blueprint for nation-building faced a struggle to control their less exceptional counterparts, and to fashion the machinery of revenue, coercion, and patronage needed to place states on stronger ground. Not until late in the nineteenth century does one commonly find the crystallization of creole ruling groups whose material resources, political organization, and collective self-consciousness enabled them to construct more solid states. And even then, such states often proved fragile under the stress of political violence and war.

Nowhere was the construction of "nations" more problematic than in Andean Peru and Bolivia, countries whose "national question" remains unresolved to this day. Here the legacy of the Great Civil War of 1780-1782 had hardened racial fears and hatreds, bequeathing to the nineteenth-century republics societies profoundly torn by ethnic and class cleavages. The

213

gulf between creole and Indian seemed insurmountable. Here, too, the very geography of extreme and varied mountain environments complicated the task of exerting centralized state control over vast stretches of territory. Economic linkages between regions proved too weak to constitute a countervailing force. The state would have to generate and invest considerable revenue simply to develop the infrastructure of transportation, military force, and bureaucracy adequate to match the centrifugal force of physical, ethnic, and economic balkanization.

Under the circumstances, one would expect to find little basis for nation-state formation, still less for a sense of national consciousness beyond, perhaps, high elite circles. One would expect the rebellions of Indian peasants, outcasts in their own lands, to represent simply an obstacle to the formation of an effective nation-state. In ideological terms, such rebellions would underscore the continuation of divisive ethnic-racial identifications that reduced discussion of national order and cohesion to an elitist rhetoric out of touch with a largely peasant and Indian majority. But the validity of such a conclusion is at least arguable, and the relationship between peasant rebel and creole nation, although tense and conflictual, was also far more complicated than the foregoing description suggests. The essays in Part III explore the arguments and complications.

For the case of Peru, Heraclio Bonilla and Florencia Mallon contribute the latest round in an ongoing debate on the Andean peasantry's historic capacity to forge its own brand of nationalist ideologies and political projects. This debate, whose principal protagonists are Bonilla and Henri Favre on the one side, and Mallon and Nelson Manrique on the other, focuses on Peruvian responses to Chile's invasion of Peru during the War of the Pacific (1879–1883), a war to gain control over the desert nitrates discovered in the border region of Chile, Peru, and Bolivia. For Bonilla, the disastrous experience proved the bankruptcy of the Peruvian "nation," and the strength of divisive colonial legacies that made nineteenth-century "Peru" a string of small parochial worlds torn by ethnic animosities and governed by opportunistic elites. Under the pressure of the Chilean invasion, "Peru" disintegrated into internal warfare. Blacks, Indians, Chinese coolies, and mixed-bloods revolted and pursued their own local vendettas and interests, even when this posture allied them with the Chilean invaders. Not even the dominant class rose to the occasion. The elites gave priority instead to the protection of their lives and property, and to the advancement of their political careers. (The picture meshes well with research in progress by Michael Gonzales, presented at the 1984 conference. Gonzales sees a series of rather parochial peasant uprisings in the nineteenth century as expressions of continuities with the colonial past that fragmented Peruvian society by color and locale. Not until the early twentieth century does one detect a wider peasant challenge assuming regional and even supraregional dimensions.)

The one bright exception in this otherwise dismal canvas was the organization of peasant guerrilla bands by General Andrés Cáceres in Peru's central highlands. This regional experience provided the evidence leading Manrique and Mallon to argue that under some circumstances, Andean peasants proved quite willing to join a multiethnic and multiclass nationalist coalition, and actually forged an authentic, yet distinctive form of peasant nationalism. This example Bonilla finds wanting, partly because he reads the evidence differently, but fundamentally because the region was idiosyncratic—particularly advanced, compared to other highland areas, in its mercantile development and racial mixing—and because Peru's failure as a "nation" fits so well with the theoretical and comparative literature on nationalism. Since the rising bourgeoisie has been the historic bearer of nationalist ideology and national unification, and since its efforts enjoyed the backing of an integrated internal market and strong state, one could hardly expect to find meaningful cohesion or nationalist consciousness in the "Peru" of 1879. Bonilla's challenge to those who postulate that peasants fashioned a "nationalism" of their own is to set the case of the central highlands in a comparative regional context, and to develop a theoretical framework capable of explaining how nationalist forms of consciousness might take hold among peasants in the absence of a well-organized modernizing bourgeoisie, and a consolidated national market.

This challenge Mallon takes up in her expanded study of peasant responses to Peru's crisis. Her work, a comparative regional study of guerrilla warfare in the Departments of Junín (central highlands) and Cajamarca (northern highlands), breaks new ground in several important respects. First, she contributes a new theoretical apparatus that purports to explain why nationalist consciousness may arise among nonbourgeois classes even in largely noncapitalist settings. Her theoretical propositions make the case of the central highlands less anomalous, and provide provocative tools for considering the development of protonational ideologies in colonized areas of the non-Western world. Second, her careful research in the local and provincial documents of two major regions demonstrates that we must take with a large grain of salt the racial hysteria and descriptions of "caste war" so common in more elitist documentation. The collapse of Peru into internecine fighting between superordinate and subordinate classes, and between ethnic or racial subgroupings within the lower classes, turns out under close scrutiny to have been more regionally specific than once thought. In Cajamarca as well as Junín, peasants participated in multiethnic and multiclass guerrilla coalitions against external invaders. Despite important differences between and within the two regions, the guerrilla movements in both areas provide evidence for the kinds of appeals and circumstances that committed Indians and other peasants to link their destinies to populist political coalitions.

Finally, by studying negative as well as positive cases, Mallon deepens our appreciation of the particular conditions that might transform peasant participation in multiethnic defense of the *patria chica*, the local homeland, into a larger national or protonational vision. Only in the case of the central highlands did the process of guerrilla mobilization lead, in Mallon's view, to the development of an authentic nationalist ideology among peasants. Indeed, the Peruvian state as well as the Chilean army constituted external invaders in the context of Cajamarca. In Mallon's analysis, then, the central highlands case remains unique. But the explanation of its peculiarity has less to do with the overwhelming force of a divisive colonial legacy, or with the innate parochialism of peasants in a precapitalist world, than with regional particulars of class, state, and warfare. In both regions, it is misleading to assume that peasant rebellions necessarily implied hostility toward nonpeasants, non-Indians, or the state, or that they expressed the peasants' characteristic inability to conceive of themselves as citizen-participants of a wider, multiethnic "nation" or political structure. As Mallon points out, the colonial legacy itself cuts both ways, in view of the persistent appeal of protonational ideas among Andean peasants in the late colonial period. Looked at in the long term, peasants and villagers in the Andean culture area have from time to time seemed disposed to conceive of their liberation in terms that involve the creation of a state—that is, a new macrolevel political order facilitating or allowing for the confederation of microlevel communities in a common cause or interest. The cruel irony of creole state-building, as analyzed by Mallon, is that an effective national state gained strength by crushing an authentic, but independently fashioned peasant nationalism.

Readers will decide for themselves whether Mallon's central highlands case establishes a form of peasant "nationalism" despite Bonilla's objections. Her essay does demonstrate, however, that the peasant guerrillas of the central highlands forged their own version of a political project, and that their political vision extended outward to reach macrolevel horizons. Whether or not one calls this vision a form of nationalism, it suggests a range of political and ideological possibilities that belies assumptions about peasant or Indian parochialism.

What one needs, however, to draw more rounded conclusions about the relationship between native Andean peasants and the national state is a case study from a more overwhelmingly indigenous region. Indians constituted a majority of the population of Junín, but a small majority by the standards of the "Indian Belt" in southern Peru and the Bolivian altiplano, where Indians commonly surpassed eight- or nine-tenths of a province's total population. Compared to the "Indian Belt," the particular regions of Peru studied by Mallon, like some of the eastern Andean valley systems of Bolivia, included a relatively greater mix of mestizos among their peasants and villagers. What sorts of considerations shaped Andean peasants' responses to the nineteenth-century "nation" and state in regions where the "Indian question" assumed its starkest dimensions? To the extent that native Andeans in these areas built a sense of themselves as participants in state and nation, did such consciousness bear closer resemblance to the more nativist protonational ideologies commonly associated with the eighteenth century? In the oral tradition of southern Peru, for example, accounts of the War of the Pacific state that the peasants, *aided by their Inca*, won the war against the Chilean invaders (Rosalind Gow, communication at the 1984 conference).

These are precisely the sorts of questions analyzed by Tristan Platt in his study of native Andeans and Bolivian Liberals in Chayanta (northern Potosí). Platt seeks to understand the experience that led Andean Indians to participate in the Liberal Revolution of 1899, a participation often viewed in terms of the Indians' manipulation by more sophisticated interests and politicians. His effort to reconstruct the native Andean vision of the political turmoil of the nineteenth century yields an uncommonly penetrating account of the intersection of local political aspirations and alignments on the one hand, and political processes at regional and national levels on the other.

The results challenge several common assumptions. First, Platt demonstrates that native Andean rebellions in Chayanta had less to do with an unbending hostility to the state, than with republican policies that violated the Andeans' historic "pact" with the state (cf. Salomon and Stern, Chapters 5 and 2 in this volume). Andeans understood their own wellbeing in terms that incorporated their own groupings into a wider political order, and they formulated and reformulated their political stance in dialogue with creole laws, policies, and political programs. Their definitions of citizenship and justice diverged from those of creole politicians and rulers, but "citizens" they were, and their justice demanded a vision of the overarching state. As political polarization sharpened in the late nineteenth century, native Andean stances toward dissident mestizos and Liberals ranged from the formation of multiethnic political coalitions to install a Liberal State, to the waging of "race war" to install an Inca Republic.

Second, Platt's ability to set the particular twists and turns of Andean political alignments in the context of the underlying consistency of Andean aspirations makes assumptions about creole-mestizo manipulation of Indians more dubious. In Platt's analysis, the state, its agents, and local mestizos all find themselves pressed, at one point or another, to make concessions to Andean rules of the political game. The line between manipulator and manipulated becomes blurred, and the manipulations take several directions at once. In this scheme, we cannot reduce the explanation of Indian participation in the Liberal Revolution to the political schemes of creoles and mestizos.

Finally, Platt attaches an important qualification to our understanding of protonational ideologies emphasizing the return of an Inca Redeemer. Normally, we think of Inca-led revolution and creole-led republics as mutually exclusive political visions. There is a certain truth to this assumption, and native Andean transitions from Inca-led to creole-led visions of redemption, and vice versa, constitute important historical problems. But Platt's study demonstrates that in the tide of revolt that swept over Bolivia in the 1880s and 1890s, the occasional emergence of "Inca" leaders and more unbending forms of "race war" did not necessarily preclude, even in the short run, Andean commitments to creole-led coalitions to install a Liberal State. One sees in this record not a timeless, once-and-for-all choice between the two irreconcilable visions, but rather an oscillation between them, a mix of pluralist and racist variants within each, and a set of minimal objectives to be defended fiercely in either kind of republic.

Taken together, the essays in Part III provide a striking feel for the tragedy and depth of the "national question" in the nineteenth century. Bonilla's debate with Mallon on nationalism should not divert us from the point on which all three authors agree: the bankruptcy of the "nation" in societies predicated on the oppression of Andean peasants. Nor should we take the studies by Mallon and Platt to deny the importance of localism in peasant political life. Where Mallon and Platt diverge from Bonilla is in their discovery of lost possibilities, aspirations, and commitments. Their research brings into view those Andean rebels and guerrillas who adhered to visions of justice and political order that left room for a *rapprochement* with creole states, and who under some conditions owned up to such visions in political coalitions of national significance. But these ventures proved ill-fated, and Andeans found themselves pushed into an antinational trap irrespective of their political proclivities and services. For by the turn of the century, if not sooner, the creole state-builders, including erstwhile allies and patrons, came round to a policy that crushed dangerous "barbarians" in the name of national order and progress.

CHAPTER 8

The Indian Peasantry and "Peru" during the War with Chile

HERACLIO BONILLA

In an earlier work (1978), I explored the role of the popular classes, especially their ethnic segments, during the war waged between Peru and Chile from 1879 to 1883 for control of the nitrate deposits found in Atacama and on the southern coast of Peru. Those four years of open military confrontation, during which vast regions of Peruvian territory were occupied by the Chilean army, proved exceptionally propitious for the analysis of the limits, nearly six decades after its break with the Spanish metropolis, of Peru's efforts at national construction. The years of war also illuminated the significance of nationhood within the context of the nineteenth century. Based on the pioneering reflections of Henri Favre (1975), the documentation of the British and American consuls, the dispatches of Chilean officials, the correspondence of a number of coastal landowners, and literary testimonies in which realism surpassed imagination, I was able to demonstrate—in the provisional way characteristic of initial versions of an idea—that the participation of blacks, Indians, and Chinese in that conflict arose neither from national nor nationalistic motivations. Rather, their activity did nothing less than expose anew the colonial fissures which the state, now independent, had not managed—probably not wanted—to close.

Since that 1978 article, and in part as a result of renewed debate and

Translation by Hunter Fite and Steve J. Stern. Bonilla's essay is placed before Mallon's (Chapter 9) because it replies to a stage of debate superseded in certain respects in Chapter 9, and because the Introduction to Part III of this book helps provide context within which to situate the Bonilla-Mallon debate. Nonspecialists who nonetheless require further background on some of Bonilla's allusions may, however, find it useful to skim the section on the central highlands in Chapter 9 before reading Chapter 8.

reflection on the so-called national problem in Peru, the role of popular groups in crises such as that of 1879 has inspired many studies, among the latest of which figure those of Nelson Manrique (1981) and Florencia Mallon (1983). The data and reflections incorporated in these works invite us to deepen our knowledge of the relationship between the indigenous peasantry and the national question in Peru during the nineteenth century. For although the findings of both authors suggest a stronger bond with the nation in the case of the peasantry of the central sierra, it nonetheless remains unclear what constitutes an adequate conceptual translation interpreting the peasants' behavior. Equally unclear is whether the national bonds of the peasants in the central sierra extended to other fractions of the peasantry spread across other parts of Peruvian territory. Before entering further discussion of this problem, however, it is helpful to review briefly some of the basic data surrounding the issue.

In 1821, Peru became one of the last colonies to separate from Spain, following a series of ambivalent postures and thanks to the decided military backing of Argentine and Colombian troops. Among the few existing alternatives, this was the compromise which best accommodated the interests of the dominant colonial class (see Bonilla 1981). But the state that emerged was "national" only in the most rhetorical sense. It lacked the means necessary to assert effectively its "sovereignty," let alone to overcome the profound fragility which blocked its effective capacity to acquire national legitimacy. The "state," it is worthy to recall, was the stage from which some forty caudillos sporadically and successively exerted a limited power between 1821 and 1840. With governments whose average duration was a half-year, it was virtually impossible to expect that such a state might provide a basis for the national integration of a former colony.

The economic situation was certainly not much better. The most dynamic sectors of the colonial economy, the mines and coastal agriculture, deteriorated as a result of the disorder introduced by the wars for independence. To the exodus of capital and the destruction of the mechanisms of control and distribution of the indigenous work force, the wars added the physical destruction of agrarian and mining enterprises. The most immediate consequence of this whole process was the decline of the "mercantilization" achieved during the colonial epoch, and the simultaneous shrinkage of established mercantile circuits and regional links. It is this phenomenon to which some historians refer as the "ruralization" and "feudalization" of the Peruvian economy in the first half of the nineteenth century. In political terms this implied the even greater atomization of loyalties and solidarities on the part of peasants. The old articulation of interests and ethnic identifications achieved by important fractions of the

Andean peasantry in answer to colonial domination, gave way in the first half of the nineteenth century to a "balkanization" of the peasants' interests, and the horizons of their consciousness.

On the groundwork of this atomized and fragmented reality, the Peruvian economy reentered the international market with force, by means of the massive exportation from its islands of guano, a product in high demand as fertilizer in the European countrysides. But the nature of the guano export sector (see Levin 1960; Hunt 1973; Bonilla 1974) hardly lent itself to closing the existing internal breaches. Even if the Peruvian state demonstrated great ability to retain ownership of the guano deposits, and managed to reach participation in nearly 70 percent of the yield generated by guano sales (Hunt 1973), the impact of guano on the structure of production in the rest of Peru was practically nil. The guano was extracted from the islands off the southern coast of Peru, its amount declared in customs on the basis of declarations by the shippers. It was consumed on the European market, and its Peruvian proceeds went to the expansion of bureaucracy via public spending, and to the augmentation of internal aggregate demand. As we now know, this expansion of internal demand, far from stimulating production for the domestic market, served the external sector by stimulating the growth of imports. And if the reactivation of certain coastal plantations specializing in the production of cotton, and later sugar, was financed with some capital provided by the guano commerce from the 1850s on (see Burga 1976: 174–82), this type of growth added to the social and economic segmentation of the country. The effective linkages created by the production of cotton and sugar were of little more than regional radius. In terms of trade, since nearly all of the production was destined for the international market, the ties that these regions could generate with the diminutive internal market were quite limited.

Probably the most important implications of the exploitation of guano appeared in the political realm. The revenues generated by guano supported the centralization of capital by groups linked to international commerce, to the large coastal plantations, and to Lima finances—a process through which such groups could reconstitute the material bases of their ascent and consolidate their position through their access to the political mechanisms of the Peruvian state. This was the meaning of *Civilismo*, the movement which organized the Civilista Party in 1871 to promote the interests of those families tied to commerce, banking, and agriculture, and which one year later came to power when Manuel Pardo ended five decades of almost uninterrupted military control of the state. From 1872 until the eve of the war with Chile, the *Civilistas* established the bases of a new type of political control in Peru; but this did not mean that the Civilista

State narrowed the gap that separated the state and civil society. Whether because its dominion was too brief, or because its operation was premised on the explicit exclusion of the subordinate classes, the state of this coastal plutocracy remained as scarcely "national" as the predecessor state controlled by rustic military caudillos.

It is evident that this compressed synthesis of the political and economic process between 1821 and 1879 does not give adequate account of the variations and shadings that existed. But these variants, as we shall see in the case of the central sierra, do not alter the basic outline of the context in which the crisis provoked by the war with Chile erupted.

When the war (the result of Peru's refusal to declare its strict neutrality in the conflict between Chile and Bolivia) exploded, therefore, "Peru" was a fragmented territory in which the dynamic axes of its economy were represented by the plantations of the central and northern coast, by relatively important silver deposits such as those in Cerro de Pasco, and by the nearly exhausted guano deposits. The age of guano was practically over, and the efforts by the Pardo administration to replace guano with nitrates had not yielded the anticipated results. This was a territory, moreover, in which social classes had not reached a defined shape or configuration, and where it was rather the presence of ethnic estates (*estamentos*) of a colonial nature (whites, blacks, and Indians) that was unconcealable. To these groups were added some one hundred thousand Chinese "coolies," the result of the international mobilization of this work force, from the 1840s on, in response to the needs of guano (Stewart 1951). And if it is true that the state, for the reasons given, could not establish a national solidarity between the different classes and ethnic estates, neither did the members of an ethnic estate share a solidarity or common consciousness. Neither "Peruvian" nor "Indian," as generic concepts, held much force in the Peru that went to war with Chile; what mattered instead were segmented ethnic filiations derived from connection to lands or to isolated social entities, and operating under the leadership of a local chieftain.

The military succession of the war is now sufficiently documented in its most significant dimensions (see, for example, Bulnes 1911–19; Basadre 1962–64), and from it I will isolate only those conjunctures which seem to me most pertinent to the problem posed in this study. The essence of Chile's military victory took place between the formal initiation of the war in April 1879 and the decisive battles of San Juan and Miraflores in January 1881, which immediately preceded the occupation of Lima and the fall of the dictatorship installed by Piérola. The Peruvian army and navy had been successively destroyed, sporadic victories and acts of honor on the part of certain Peruvian soldiers notwithstanding, and the Civilista government had ended with rather indecorous conduct by its most prominent leaders. The rapid disintegration of the state and the Civilista government, despite the euphoria and optimism that reigned at the onset, now gave way to open confrontation, in the midst of a national war, between two rival factions of the Peruvian dominant class: the Civilistas and the Pierolistas. On the other hand, the destruction of the Peruvian army — that is, the guarantor of Peru's peculiar political order, and of the subordination of the popular classes — placed the Peruvian landowners in the position of facing the combined threat of the Chilean army and of a general uprising of the popular masses, urban and rural, comprising diverse ethnic estates. If, in spite of this situation, the war was prolonged until the signing of the Treaty of Ancón, in October 1883, this was due to the obstinate resistance that General Andrés Cáceres maintained in the central sierra and in the south of the country, as well as to the promise that the United States would favor a peace with Chile that would not amputate Peruvian territory (Bonilla 1979). And what is of interest here is the problem of Cáceres's resistance and that of the peasant *montoneras* [the peasant guerrilla bands backing Cáceres — Ed.], in order to elucidate the meaning of the peasants' commitment.

After the occupation of Lima and the installation, backed by Chilean bayonets, of the government of Francisco García Calderón, Cáceres arrived in the central sierra with the objective of initiating the resistance to the invading army. To do this, he was counting on the Chilean army's lack of familiarity with the terrain and, above all, on an appreciable contingent of indigenous peasants whom Cáceres hoped to mobilize. The latest investigations by Manrique (1981) and Mallon (1983: 80–122) conclude not only that the caudillo saw his hopes fulfilled during the three years in which he maintained a presence in this region, but also that the peasantry of the central sierra embarked upon an armed mobilization increasingly independent of the framework and military command imposed by Cáceres, and outlasting even the signing of the Treaty of Ancón. Moreover, say both authors, this was not just any type of mobilization. Manrique (1981: 378) refers to the peasants' conduct as *nationalist*, while Mallon (1983: 90–91) tells us that:

Out of this confrontation, they developed both an understanding of national politics and a strong sense of nationalism, though neither would be recognized as such by modern or upper-class standards. Their nationalism, for example, was not a general or symbolic sense of nationhood, but a feeling founded very concretely on their love for their homeland — for the place where they were born, "under the Sun and the earth" — for the land they planted. Thus the Chileans were not enemies because they were Chileans, but because they invaded and destroyed the homeland, the peasants' most precious resource, their source of subsistence and life.

Manrique even thinks that indigenous consciousness did not remain immutable throughout the war, and that three short years, given the acceleration of historical time, were sufficient for the consciousness of the indigenous peasantry to pass through five successive conjunctures: (1) an indifference to the war; (2) a limited loyalty during the Lima campaign; (3) a radical anti-Chilean consciousness rooted in the abuses imposed by the invader in the central sierra, and the formation of a national alliance with the hacienda owners of the region; (4) a "patriotic" consciousness expressed in sanctions against collaborationist *hacendados* ; and (5) an antihacendado class consciousness responding to the antipeasant repression which Cáceres ultimately implemented. In other words, what we have proposed before us here is an experience in which the peasantry of a region is capable, in the context of a foreign occupation, of transcending the limits of its particularistic group consciousness (*conciencia grupal*), and adopts, in a decided manner, a nationalist pattern of behavior (Manrique 1981: 379–80). But the implications of this discovery reach much further. If one supposes that in the Peru of 1879, the class which historically waves the flag of nationalism — that is, the bourgeoisie — did not yet exist, and that when the bourgeoisie constituted itself later, its consolidation as a bourgeoisie came at the cost of rendering itself less and less "national," then it follows that in this kind of context it was the Andean peasantry that had to initiate a peculiar nationalism. This was unfortunately a nationalism truncated precisely because of the absence of that bourgeois class whose cooperation was essential for the promise of this nationalism to become a real possibility. Such proposals are certainly suggestive, but how do we reconcile them with theory, which up to this point has done nothing less than underscore the contrary? For certainly, it does not suffice to revindicate the primacy of practice over theory, as does Manrique, and to say that obviously it is not the reality that is mistaken (ibid.: 381). This is above all insufficient if that reality, reconstructed on the basis of rather unconvincing evidence, can be *read* in a completely opposite manner, and when in the last analysis comparative history, for the experiences it makes available, is the appropriate terrain upon which to ponder the impasses that afflict the linkage of the peasantry with the national question.

Both Mallon (1983: 42–79) and Manrique (1978) have convincingly demonstrated that the central sierra of Peru, and particularly the peasant communities situated along the Mantaro Valley, was a region whose singular characteristics set it apart from other regions even before 1879. By this I mean its greater and very early mercantile tie with Lima, as a supplier of consumer goods; its fairly developed social division of labor, manifested in peasant communities specializing almost exclusively in the production of particular types of goods; and, finally, its advantage due to the relative insignificance of large landed estates as units of exploitation and dominion. These characteristics would have served as the bases for an early process of *mestizaje* [racial and cultural mixing — Ed.] of the indigenous population. These points are important insofar as they provide a very particular connotation to the participation of that region's peasantry during the war with Chile, and insofar as they also make it impossible to generalize findings to other regions more isolated and more indigenous in composition. Now as we have seen, the nationalism of this peasantry had been awakened thanks to the convergence of a double situation: on the one hand, the extortions imposed by the occupying Chilean army and, on the other, the efforts of Cáceres to organize the resistance of the peasantry. The evidences to support Manrique's and Mallon's affirmations are letters interchanged between leaders and recruits and decisions made in campesino meetings. We might ask for the case of the central highlands, as did Lucien Bianco (1967: 257) for China: is hatred the shortest path to the attainment of national consciousness? It is in this context indisputably certain that the oppression imposed by a foreign army on a native population is a very powerful incentive to the resistance and mobilization of the latter group against the "others," and to the framing of such mobilization in a nationalist language. The experience of the Chinese peasantry during the Japanese occupation is an adequate example. But at the same time it is indispensable to recognize that what occurred in the central sierra in 1879 is not comparable in breadth or in duration to that which took place in China beginning in 1937, and that furthermore, even if we set aside these obvious differences, the nationalism of the Chinese peasantry was not born spontaneously. It arose in response to the brutality of Japanese aggression, but also required active agitation of the cadre of the Communist Party (Johnson 1962: 26–27). In the case of the Peruvian sierra, the evidences displayed by those who postulate campesino nationalism do not permit us to establish a clear distinction between the natural peasant reaction to foreign aggression framed in language lent to them by Cáceres, and a more genuine nationalist sentiment or consciousness. Spontaneous "nationalisms" are certainly not very convincing; in this regard it would be of the highest importance to investigate to what the peasants refer when they write or utter words such as *patria* ("homeland"), "country," or "nation."

To mention, on the other hand, a peasant uprising unprovoked by prior aggression, as in the case of Comas, in order to demonstrate a peasant nationalism that did not arise from extortions by the Chilean army (Manrique 1981: 154), serves little purpose when one omits a decisive fact. In a context of war, with communities interwoven among themselves and with continuous displacement of peoples, it sufficed to know what neighboring villages were suffering, without waiting to share the same disagreeable experience, for peasants to begin to mobilize themselves.

It is unclear why it should seem surprising or unusual that campesinos and hacendados of the central sierra formed a common front against the Chilean invaders at the start of the resistance. One might be tempted to say that it is precisely the opposite that would be surprising. For however great the integration of the region with Lima, and however intense the economic changes within it, these processes did not compromise the mechanisms held by the proprietary class to insure the loyalty and discipline of *their* campesinos, who were subordinated directly or indirectly. But it is the rupture of this alliance and the peasant occupation of the haciendas of their former allies that Mallon and Manrique consider yet another evidence of the peasants' patriotism. They tell us, in effect, that hacendados were castigated not for being hacendados but for collaborating with the invader, and in fact various letters allude to this situation. But Manrique himself, pages later (ibid.: 348), recognizes that the distinction between those who were collaborationists and those who were not was "very complicated [given] that merely the residence of the invaders in populated centers directly implicated their inhabitants in the sustenance [of the invaders]." But let us concede for a moment that in spite of it all, such a distinction was possible, and that the peasants proceeded to occupy the haciendas in the south of the Mantaro Valley as a punishment to the pro-Chilean conduct of their proprietors. Nevertheless, it does not require great suspiciousness to interpret such conduct as responding to old grievances, with the additional advantage of camouflaging revenge, in the context of general chaos, under the guise of a moral sanction against dishonorable conduct. In order for the alleged explanation to be more convincing, it would be indispensable to present a more precise reconstruction of the relations established between hacendados and peasants within and nearby the affected haciendas, and to compare these relations with those that prevailed in the haciendas exempted from peasant attacks. It would also have been necessary to allude in a more explicit fashion to a protagonist who almost always remains in the shadows: the peons on the haciendas themselves, and their behavior in the context of the war.

Finally, we are told, as the hacendado class opted in a more decided manner to renounce the resistance in favor of collaboration or a search for peace with Chile at any price (a stage initiated by the energetic demand of the hacendado Iglesias in Montán on August 31, 1882), the peasants of the central sierra proceeded to shed their banner of nationalism, passing instead to an attack against the entire hacendado class, based this time on their respective positions as hacendados and peasants. The proposed shift is certainly captivating, but I confess that I have been unable to detect in the proffered reconstruction of military events the concrete mechanisms that would have made such a transition effectively possible. Without a doubt, it is not surprising that faced with the combined threat of the invading army and the new attitude of their former allies, above all if the latter were physically absent, the peasantry would in its mobilization reclaim and take lands. What remains to be demonstrated more convincingly is that this new behavior would express changed levels of consciousness among the peasantry.

This sui generis peasant nationalism, we are told, dissipated nearly as rapidly as it appeared, even though this time its eclipse is imputed to the absence of an allied class capable of leading nationalism to its full realization. Manrique claims that once the occupying forces disappeared, a peasant movement agglutinated by war began "to become disjoined" (*desagregarse*), to acquire "an increasingly local character" (ibid.: 368). In other words, the peasants were once more atomized. Mallon affirms, in much more analytical terms, that the outcome of the war produced a double situation in the peasant movement of the central sierra, one that derived from the events which occurred during the years of conflict. In the northern part of the Mantaro Valley, where the alliance between hacienda owners and peasants had been more durable, a successful policy of co-optation of the rebels took place, and granted the latter the satisfaction of new district demarcations which could henceforth mediate between peasants' interests and those of the state. But in the south such an arrangement was not possible due to the level of consciousness reached by the peasants of that part of the valley. Instead, as would occur with the federation of districts led by Comas beginning in January 1888, the peasants sought the constitution of regional associations more closely attuned to their own interests. They thereby demonstrated their disposition to support a national-bourgeois platform, had there existed a political party or a class capable and willing to make such a project feasible (Mallon 1983: 101–22). In this historical precocity, therefore, would lie their failure.

Atomized or premature, it hardly matters. The essential lesson of the peasant experience in the central sierra during the war with Chile is precisely that this peasant "nationalism" lacked any solid foundation, and its emergence as a sentiment, although a rapidly dispersed one, corresponded to the incitements of war and the extortions of the Chilean army. Without the material and spiritual bases which effectively forge and make irreversible a national consciousness, once the forces that momentarily soldered a new type of sentiment disappeared, this sentiment also faded away.

All told, the kind of mobilization of peasants that occurred in the central sierra was not duplicated by other fractions of the peasantry within the

Peruvian territory, nor within other regions of the country. In the case of the Chinese "coolies," they instead took advantage of the crisis of 1879 to avenge old and recent grievances (Bonilla 1978: 107–10). In the case of the black peasants in the southern valley of Cañete, the war reopened poorly contained ethnic resentments (ibid.: 109–10). In the case of Cajamarca, the evidence gathered to this point seems to suggest the confrontation of rival bosses with their respective armies in the context of profound social chaos (Dammert B. 1983). The peasant mobilization in the central sierra gave effective support to the resistance led by Cáceres, therefore, precisely because the region and its population were more integrated with Lima. Its peasantry, having participated in more intense mercantile relations, was already the least Indian in the second half of the nineteenth century.

But it is important to reflect now on the content of that mobilization. One of the essential barriers that hampers a correct understanding of the peasants' link to the national question is our complete ignorance of the significance of such concepts as "nation," "homeland" (*patria*), and "country" for peasants who were not only peasants, but also held an ethnic affiliation uneroded by any national attachment. If that blend of sentiments reconstructed by Manrique and Mallon are taken to be the expression of a peasant "nationalism" in the particular cultural context of the Andes, then we may only underline their affirmations. But in this we run the risk of including the most outlandish of such expressions under the concept of "nation"; and it becomes no longer possible to establish an analytical distinction that separates out other loyalties which are not exactly national.

Up to this point, the gross majority of the analyses of the national problem and nationalism have been inspired explicitly or implicitly by the European experience in the nineteenth century. Their point of departure is the recognition that the bearer of nationalism is the ascending bourgeoisie, and that for the realization of nationalism the bourgeoisie can count on an integrated national market and a state capable of transforming its consciousness as a class into a national ideology. But what happens when, as in Peru during the war with Chile, there is neither a bourgeoisie nor a national market, and the state can barely obtain the loyalty of the dominant class? As we have seen, Manrique and Mallon respond that there exists a precapitalist "nationalism," in this case embodied in the peasantry of a privileged region such as the central sierra. Even admitting hypothetically, for the purpose of discussion, that this were true, what in this case constituted the bases for the emergence and the reproduction of this sentiment? And, in the final analysis, to what end did this nationalism point? On these capital questions the authors offer only vague phrases and, in the best of cases, it is their impressions which are given us as the content of the peasants' national consciousness. It is the poetic "love of the land," in Mallon's case, or in the case of Manrique, the confession of doubt that the peasants' nationalism is the same as our own, only to affirm later that the message of the central sierra peasants' nationalism was their quest to "consolidate the autarky and particularisms of the communities" (Manrique 1981: 383, 385). This is nothing other than what anthropologists call tribalism (Sahlins 1968).

In order to deepen the point further, it is perhaps worthwhile now to turn to the lessons of comparative history. "As far as the peasantry is concerned this is, of course, not to say either that no fringe segments of it have been drawn actively into the nationalist movements or that, as nationalism has progressed and established itself, the peasantry has not come to accept it. But in general the rural masses have been indifferent to the new currents or, at the best and belatedly, passive adherents to the nationalist creed" (Emerson 1962: 195). With these words Rupert Emerson summarizes the basic findings of research and testimonies on peasantry and nationalism in Europe, Asia, and Africa available up to the early 1960s. Earlier, in the context of the Second International, Anton Pannekoek wrote: "The peasants are often classified as the loyal and unyielding preservers of nationality. But at the same time Otto Bauer classifies them as tributaries to the nation who have not the slightest participation in the national culture. This contradiction clearly indicates that what is 'national' with reference to the peasantry is something totally distinct from that which constitutes modern nations. Certainly modern nationality emerged originally out of the peasant version, but in spite of this the two are in essence completely different" (1912: 264). I do not have the impression that recent debate and investigations—and this is demonstrated by Arnold's review (1982) of Hardiman's book on the nationalism of the Hindu peasantry— have altered these basic conclusions about the difficulties that stand in the way of the peasantry's assuming an effective national commitment.

When the national integration of the peasantry has been finally produced, moreover, it has been the result of a process entirely different from that presented by Mallon and Manrique for the case of the Peruvian central sierra. In the case of Japan, for example, the national integration of the peasants derived from the efficient role of the nation-state. But, in turn, the action of the state would not have been possible without the existence of favorable preconditions derived from the reforms of the Meiji and Tokugawa periods: feudal systems highly centralized at a regional level; the isolation which permitted racial, cultural, and religious homogeneity; effective intermediaries at the rural community level to receive and implement government policies (Yamasaki 1981). At the other extreme, in the case of France in the last third of the nineteenth century (Weber 1976), it has been convincingly argued that the nation was not an established reality, but a "work-in-progress," and that decisive in the process were the decades between 1880 and 1910. For it was in those years that the construction of roads and railways, and the diffusion of the language of the dominant culture by means of schools and military conscription, which brought such teachings into the home, irreversibly ruptured the isolation of the rural populations of the various regions of France (ibid.: 485–96). In light of this experience, we may only conclude that the national integration of the peasantry in the context of Peru is still, as in so many other cases, an unfulfilled promise.

REFERENCES

ARNOLD, DAVID
  1982   Review of Hardiman. *Journal of Peasant Studies* 10: 119–21.
BASADRE, JORGE
  1962–64 *Historia de la República del Perú*. Vols. 6, 7. Lima: Ediciones Historia.
BIANCO, LUCIEN
  1967   *Les Origenes de la Révolution Chinoise, 1915–1949*. Paris: Gallimard.
BONILLA, HERACLIO
  1974   *Guano y burguesía en el Perú*. Lima: Instituto de Estudios Peruanos.
  1978   "The War of the Pacific and the National and Colonial Problem in Peru." *Past and Present* 81: 92–118.
  1979   "La dimensión internacional de la Guerra del Pacífico." In *Reflexiones en torno a la Guerra de 1879*. Lima: CIC. Pp. 415–34.
  1981   "Estado y clases populares en el Perú de 1821." In *La independencia en el Perú*. 2d ed. Lima: Instituto de Estudios Peruanos. Pp. 13–69.
BULNES, GONZALO
  1911–19 *Guerra del Pacífico*. 3 vols. Santiago.
BURGA, MANUEL
  1976   *De la encomienda a la hacienda capitalista: el valle de Jequetepeque del siglo XVI al XX*. Lima: Instituto de Estudios Peruanos.
DAMMERT BELLIDO, JOSÉ
  1983   *Cajamarca durante la Guerra del Pacífico*. Cajamarca: Obispado de Cajamarca.
EMERSON, RUPERT
  1962   *From Empire to Nation*. Boston: Beacon Press.
FAVRE, HENRI
  1975   "Remarques sur la Lutte des Classes pendant la Guerre du Pacifique." In *Littérature et Société au Pérou du XIXè siècle à nos jours*. Grenoble. Pp. 55–81.

HUNT, SHANE
1973   *Growth and Guano in Nineteenth Century Peru.* Princeton: Woodrow Wilson School.

JOHNSON, CHALMERS
1962   *Peasant Nationalism and Communist Power.* Stanford: Stanford University Press.

LEVIN, JONATHAN
1960   *The Export Economies: Their Patterns of Development in Historical Perspective.* Cambridge: Cambridge University Press.

MALLON, FLORENCIA E.
1983   *The Defense of Community in Peru's Central Highlands: Peasant Struggle and Capitalist Transition, 1860–1940.* Princeton: Princeton University Press.

MANRIQUE, NELSON
1978   *El desarrollo del mercado interior en la sierra central (1830–1879).* Lima: UNA. Mimeo ed.

1981   *Las guerrillas indígenas en la Guerra con Chile.* Lima: CIC.

PANNEKOEK, ANTON
1912   "Lucha de clases y nación." In *La segunda internacional y el problema nacional y colonial.* Mexico City: Siglo XXI, 1978.

SAHLINS, MARSHALL
1968   *Tribesmen.* Englewood Cliffs, N.J.: Prentice Hall.

STEWART, WATT
1951   *Chinese Bondage in Peru.* Durham: Duke University Press.

WEBER, EUGEN
1976   *Peasants into Frenchmen: The Modernization of Rural France, 1870–1914.* Stanford: Stanford University Press.

YAMASAKI, HARUSHIGE
1981   "Integración nacional del campesinado: el caso del Japón." In Celma Agüero, Susana Devalle and Michiko Tanska, eds., *Campesinado e integración nacional.* Mexico City: El Colegio de México. Pp. 132–45.

CHAPTER 9

Nationalist and Antistate Coalitions in the War of the Pacific: Junín and Cajamarca, 1879–1902

FLORENCIA E. MALLON

In 1882 and 1883, while the country was occupied by Chilean troops, the peasants in the central highlands of Peru rose up to defend their homes and fields from the foreign invader. Organized in guerrilla bands on a village basis, they confronted two major Chilean expeditions, often with little more than boulders and slingshots. Much more so than the local landowners—many of whom collaborated with the Chilean occupation forces—it was the peasants of the region who persisted in a war of attrition, serving as the backbone of the La Breña campaign, a national resistance movement organized by Andrés Cáceres in the area between the Mantaro Valley and Ayacucho. By the time the war was over, a combination of landowner collaborationism and increasing peasant autonomy unleashed a class conflict that would not be pacified for nearly twenty years. The issue was, at bottom, that Peruvian landowners had been unable to join with peasants in the interest of national defense, reacting to them as class enemies and preferring to ally with the Chilean invaders. This the peasants saw as a double insult: on the one hand, the *hacendados* were cooperating with the same people who were committing atrocities in the

The research on which this paper is based began as part of my dissertation research, carried out in Peru between 1976 and 1978 under the auspices of the Fulbright-Hays Training Fellowship Program and the Social Science Research Council/American Council of Learned Societies. The data base was subsequently expanded to include the northern highlands, and additional materials on the central highlands were also collected, on a Social Science Research Council Postdoctoral Grant during the summer of 1981. I wish to thank Steve J. Stern and Friedrich Katz for their comments on an earlier draft.

local villages and this made them traitors to the homeland; and on the other, even though the peasants had put their lives on the line defending the region, the hacendados were unable, in the peasants' own words, "to tolerate us as patriotic soldiers" (APJ 1882b).

Meanwhile, in the northern highland department of Cajamarca, two improbable antistate alliances were transformed into bulwarks of national resistance. In the province of Cajamarca, a landowner in rebellion against the Peruvian government joined with peasants from two villages who were resisting taxes and conscription, as well as with merchants of Chinese origin, and fought the Chileans for nearly three years. In the frontier province of Jaén, Indian natives and colonizing merchants joined forces against the Chilean invaders, living off booty stolen from neighboring great estates and resisting payment of the Indian head tax (ADC, passim).

None of these movements was successful in creating a nation-state in its own image, and none of them had that purpose consciously on its agenda. In this sense, it would be unfair to call them national or nationalist. Yet to the extent that they fought against a foreign invader, calling on an alliance of classes to join together in defense of a common interest they termed Peruvian, all three were nationalist movements. To say this, however, stretches the very boundaries of the categories traditionally used to analyze nationalism.

A vast, disorganized, and internally contradictory literature exists on the subject of nationalism and nationalist movements. Some scholars have seen nationalism essentially as a spirit, idea, or belief expressing the unity of a people (Hayes 1966; Kedourie 1960; Kohn 1944). Other writers, especially those in the Marxist tradition, have seen nationalism as the creation of a particular economic system (capitalism) and the dominant class associated with it (the bourgeoisie) (Stalin 1942; Lenin 1968; Davis 1967; Cummins 1980).[1] In a similar fashion some non-Marxist writers, while recognizing the cultural, ideological, and social components of nationalism, have associated it with the modern state and considered it basically a form of politics (Breuilly 1982). Still another tendency among scholars has attempted to put more historical meat on the concept by seeing it as a social movement whose origins must be explained in a similar way to those of other forms of collective action (Smith 1977; Symmons-Symonolewicz 1970, 1981).

Yet despite their many discrepancies, all these approaches to nationalism share two general problems that impede their use to analyze the kinds of movements described above. First of all, whether theories are economically or culturally based—that is, whether they ascribe the development of nationalism to the bourgeoisie and the internal market, or to the development of national identity and the political revolutions of the late eighteenth and early nineteenth centuries — they tend to have a positivist, unilinear view of historical development that by definition assigns no creative role to nonbourgeois classes, pre-Enlightenment politics, or non-Western regions in the genesis of nationalism. Second, whether nationalism is culturally, territorially, economically, or politically rooted, theories tend to see it as emerging "full-blown"; that is, there is no consistent analysis of its *evolution* as a form of consciousness, in actual human experience and conflict, in relation to other forms of ideology or perception, in the context of particular material and political conditions.[2]

This essay constitutes a first and very tentative attempt to establish the kind of dialogue between existing theory and empirical cases that will allow us to move beyond established truths in our understanding of nationalism, nationalist consciousness, and nation formation. Starting from a criticism of all traditional approaches to nationalism, both Marxist and non-Marxist, it seeks to take some halting initial steps in the direction of building an alternate theory. Among the questions it will raise, though certainly not answer, are: the extent to which nationalism or nationalist consciousness can arise in noncapitalist societies; the way that nationalism or nationalist consciousness can vary by class; the extent to which specific forms of nationalist consciousness may, under certain conditions, exist in contradiction to a particular process of national unification; and finally, the extent to which the evolution of nationalism, nationalist consciousness, and national oppression may rest on a set of material relations distinct from, though clearly interrelated with, those that give rise to class relations.

To provide a context for raising these questions, I will start from a relatively unknown 1905 essay by the Russian Zionist socialist Ber Borojov, in which he explores some possible explanations for the relative autonomy of the national question from class relations (1979: 57–87). Societies or social formations, he begins, develop historically in relation to a particular material base — a set of conditions given by their physical location, the specific character of the human and animal population, and their evolving social and historical relationship to nature. These he calls conditions of production, as distinguished from forces or relations of production. Initially, it was the natural and biological conditions of production that were most important; but as people developed greater control over nature, the historical and social conditions of production — including material culture, patterns of interaction among people, traditions, languages, etc. — became more important. It is these conditions of production, then, in their material and cultural forms, that constitute the base for the development of nationality and nationalism. While they clearly interact historically with the mode of production, Borojov argues that they maintain a relative autonomy even as they interrelate (ibid.: 58–61).

In order to understand the evolution of nationalism as a historical process, Borojov distinguishes between two types of relation to the conditions of production, one active and one passive. A people, ostensibly a historically prior category, is a society developing in the same conditions of production but without developing a consciousness of itself as such. A nation, on the other hand, is a people who have already united, in a conscious way, around a common purpose and with a common sense of the historical past. In order for a people to become a nation, they must be involved in some form of national conflict that brings them into contradiction with another people, sharpening their ability to perceive themselves in national terms; in other words, a "national question" must arise (ibid.: 62–64).

When does a national question arise, according to Borojov? When there is a contradiction between the development of the forces of production, and the state of the conditions of production. This may arise in a variety of ways, including a situation in which a society with less favorable conditions of production wishes to appropriate the "better" conditions of its neighbors, or when in the process of growth and development a society needs more room and access to more resources (ibid.: 62–63). Whatever the specific case, it is clear that a "national question" can only arise once there has been *some* development of the forces of production; that is, once societies have moved beyond an initial state of nature. It is also clear that nationalism will develop out of specific and concrete forms of national conflict, in which some groups will attempt to defend and others to conquer particular conditions of production. It does not follow, however, that only with the development of capitalism do we get national conflict or nationalist consciousness.[3] The nationalism emerging with the dramatic economic and political transformations associated with the Enlightenment and the transition to capitalism is certainly a historically powerful one, distinct from other forms; but under the definitions given above there can be other forms and contexts in which nationalism or nationalist consciousness may arise.

In addition to defining nationalism's material base in the conditions of production and providing elements for understanding the historical evolution of nationalism, Borojov also explores the different types of nationalism developed by different social classes. Since each class will have a distinct relation to and interest in a society's conditions of production, he argues, the way in which it will confront and define the national question will also vary. The landowning oligarchy, for example, will associate the defense of their conditions of production with the possession of the land. Workers, on the other hand, according to Borojov, see their conditions of production as basically a place to work that must be preserved and defended. Since each social class has a relation to the conditions of production, each can also develop, at least potentially, a form of nationalism (ibid.: 71–83). And at least by implication, these distinct nationalisms – though each is interested in defending a common set of conditions of production – may at times conflict with each other.

If we apply these general insights on nationalism to the case of Peru during the War of the Pacific (1879–1884), it is possible to make much more sense of the resistance movements that emerged out of the Chilean occupation. To begin with, we should see the war as a moment in which a national question was raised: there was a conflict between two societies over conditions of production, initially over the nitrate-rich southern provinces of Peru. This resulted in the Chilean occupation of its northern neighbor, beginning – depending on the area of the country – sometime between 1880 and 1882. The occupation extended the immediacy of the national question to most areas of Peru, as inhabitants of the country's various regions directly confronted the presence of an invader. Thus the possibility of transforming a people into a nation was created; those who objectively had shared a common set of conditions of production could potentially become conscious of that fact and develop nationalism. The extent to which nationalist consciousness emerged, however, and the actual form it took, depended on the relation of the various classes to the conditions of production, and to each other.

My case studies of the central and northern highlands are an attempt to raise these theoretical questions in a concrete and empirical framework. I begin from several hypotheses, which for the purposes of this discussion will be treated as assumptions. The first is that, despite its existence as an independent country for over half a century, Peru was not a unified nation at the outbreak of the war. Certainly the majority of its people had not developed nationalist consciousness, and the state had been unable effectively to extend its authority over the totality of Peruvian territory. The second hypothesis is that, in the decade before the war, the coastal elite profiting from the guano boom had made a first attempt at national unification (Bonilla 1974). It had taken control of the state apparatuses in Lima and begun negotiations with regional oligarchies over the conditions under which the different economic regions could be integrated into the developing state structure. In all cases, regional oligarchies wanted control of their local conditions of production. What this meant on the ground, however, varied greatly by area, depending both on natural conditions – climate, ecology, mineral wealth – and on previous social, political, and cultural relationships. This negotiation process, while favoring the regional oligarchies, had also affected other social classes, but it had barely begun when it was interrupted by the war.

When the Chilean occupation raised an especially stark national question for most social classes in Peru, therefore, it did so in the context of an interrupted process of national unification. In each region, the nature and relative success of this process naturally had an effect on the way in which people and classes confronted the invasion. So did social and economic structure, ethnic composition, and the prewar balance of class forces. In the end, though a foreign invasion inevitably raised the national question for all those whose conditions of production were affected, the limited amount of national integration in Peru meant that the implications of such a situation were worked out regionally, at the local level, within the conditions most immediately relevant to people's lives.

As we turn to a consideration of regions, it is important to keep in mind that we are juggling a complex and multileveled empirical reality. On the one hand, we are interested in the prewar situation in these areas: the nature of the local economy, society, and culture; the specific character of local conditions of production; and the previous history of class relations and conflict. We are also interested in the nature of each region's participation in the war — when was it occupied? For how long? Finally, we will examine the way in which the specific insertion of a region into the war, when combined with the previous character of local relationships, generated a particular kind of response to the invasion. We will conclude with an analysis of how the postwar pacification was achieved in these areas, and how the 1881–1885 events conditioned the resumption of the process of national unification.

Our story begins, in effect, with the formal defeat of the Peruvian army in the battles of San Juan and Miraflores, on the outskirts of Lima, in January 1881. Dictator Nicolás de Piérola immediately fled into the highlands, vowing to continue the resistance. He set up camp in Jauja, at the northern end of the Mantaro Valley, and named commanders to supervise ongoing campaigns in the central, southern, and northern sections of the country. This set the scene for the development of guerrilla warfare against the Chilean occupation forces, and the Chilean leaders understandably rejected Piérola as legitimate president and negotiator. Meanwhile, as of February 1881, a new government formed in the Lima suburb of La Magdalena. Under the presidency of Francisco García Calderón and with the acceptance of the Chileans, it attempted to negotiate a peace treaty until the inevitability of territorial concessions led to a breakdown in the talks in November of that year. From late 1881 to mid-1882, the Chileans were lost in a sea of quarrelling Peruvian factions, unable to identify the one most likely to advance the peace process. Only in August 1882, when Cajamarcan landowner Miguel Iglesias issued the Cry of Montán, did a faction begin to form that was willing to accept peace with territorial fragmentation. Even then, it would take the Chilean army and the Iglesistas a year and a half of fighting finally to give Iglesias the territorial control and political base from which he could supervise the Chilean withdrawal. Shortly thereafter Andrés Cáceres, leader of the national resistance movement based in the central sierra, rose to challenge Iglesias in a civil war that lasted until early 1886.

Throughout these years, the Peruvian population experienced the destruction of a foreign invasion as well as the violence of civil strife. In every case considered here, they attempted to defend their local conditions of production. Yet the extent to which such attempts became nationalist movements varied greatly from place to place, and depended both on the nature of the war itself and on an area's previous history. It is to the empirical richness of this variation that we now turn.

THE CENTRAL HIGHLANDS, 1879–1902

When Andrés Cáceres first travelled to the central sierra after the Chilean occupation of Lima in early 1881, he set up camp in a rather unusual region of the Peruvian highlands (Map 6). In contrast to other parts of the interior, where the large hacienda had established an overwhelming economic, territorial, and political presence, in the Mantaro and neighboring Yanamarca valleys peasant communities had managed to maintain consistent control over strategic resources. Indeed, during three centuries of colonial rule and fifty years of republican domination, peasants had developed and defended a viable and relatively autonomous form of household economy, village culture, and communal politics. Yet their survival had not depended on isolation or on closing off a corporate unit from the outside world; quite the contrary, villages had historically participated in the commercial economy on their own terms, trading among themselves as well as more broadly, using the resources gained through such trade to reproduce their basic self-sufficiency. And this social and economic style proved successful enough so that, into the 1870s, only forty haciendas existed in the two provinces of Jauja and Huancayo combined, relegated to the less fertile *puna* areas and containing less than a quarter of the region's population (Mallon 1983: 15–41).

The existence of such a dynamic peasant economy became the focus of much conflict in the years immediately following independence from Spain, when a new group of entrepreneurs attempted to take control of the central highlands economy and modernize production. Since peasants had access to means of production in their villages, they resisted the new elite's attempts to make them work in mines or on haciendas, and the regional economy was plagued by labor shortages. Unable in the short run to proletarianize a socially significant portion of the peasantry, mine-

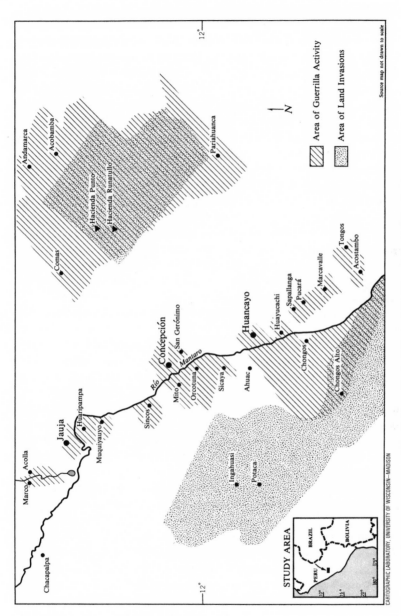

Map 6. Guerrilla Activity and the War of the Pacific: Junín

Area of Guerrilla Activity

Area of Land Invasions

Source map not drawn to scale

N

STUDY AREA

BRAZIL

PERU

BOLIVIA

Chacapalpa

Marco

Acolla

Jauja

Huaripampa

Muquiyauyo

Sincos

Río

Mantaro

Mito

Orcotuna

San Gerónimo

Concepción

Sicaya

Ahuac

Huancayo

Chongos

Huayucachi

Sapallanga

Pucará

Marcavalle

Tongos

Acostambo

Chongos Alto

Ingahuasi

Potaca

Comas

Andamarca

Acobamba

Hacienda Punto

Hacienda Runatullo

Pariahuanca

12°

12°

239

owners, landowners, and merchants all struggled to gain access to workers through patron-client ties or debt relations. The peasants, for their part, tenaciously resisted these attempts, developing their own connections with the commercial sector where possible, using one patron against another whenever they could. In the long run, then, the struggle over labor — who would get access and how — was the crucial class issue in the central sierra during the nineteenth century, pitting elite and peasants against each other in ongoing, though not always overt, conflict (ibid.: 42–79).

In the second half of the century, when attempts at state formation in Peru began to bear their first serious fruits, each class in the central highlands had a different perspective on the local role of the state. From the point of view of the elite, the state should underwrite its control over labor, both through the more effective enforcement of debt relations and by providing an institutional context for greater control over local politics. From the peasantry's perspective, there was a need for greater political autonomy for the villages, and the state should allow for greater independence from the regional centers of landowner, merchant, and mineowner power. Both classes, therefore, were ultimately interested in reorganizing and dominating local political institutions. And it is in this context that the legislation on local government passed in the 1860s becomes most relevant.

According to the Constitution of 1857 and the attendant laws promulgated in the early 1860s, a system of departments, provinces, and districts was created along the old colonial intendancy and parish lines. The districts or municipalities were given authority over law enforcement, revenue collection, and the occasional labor drafts levied for municipal purposes (Peru 1869: 150). Control of the district seat thus became an important local plum in the ongoing conflict over labor; and not surprisingly, the following decades were marked by struggle over where the district boundaries should be drawn. Members of the regional elite in general supported the maintenance of boundaries as they had been, except in those cases where changing economic and demographic realities made effective control within those boundaries unviable. The peasantry, on the other hand, was interested in dividing the larger district units into smaller subdivisions that could bypass existing structures of regional power and decentralize control over revenue and labor. Up until the War of the Pacific, legislation generally favored the regional elite; but there were several cases of villages that had spent substantial amounts of time and money in inconclusive trips to Lima to petition for new districts (Adams 1959: 30; Ortega 1977; SINAMOS 1939: 134–364).

Ultimately, therefore, the central highlands presented contradictory possibilities as the base for a national resistance. On the one hand, participation by significant sectors of the region's population in the economic and political processes associated with attempted nation formation gave them experience with a larger political and economic entity and predisposed them toward perceiving the Peruvian-Chilean conflict in broader terms. On the other hand, the history of regional conflict between classes in the period before the war might make difficult the creation of a multiclass national front. Though Cáceres himself was not aware of it, the way in which he organized and fought the La Breña campaign against the occupation forces between 1881 and 1884, coming as it did on top of the previous decades of change and conflict, would play a crucial role in defining the region's insertion into the ongoing process of national unification in Peru.

In April 1881, however, when the region began to mobilize for direct confrontation with the occupation forces, these deeper contradictions and possibilities were on no one's mind. More important was the organization of a new army, a task to which Cáceres and his supporters dedicated much time and energy. Touring the communities and towns of Jauja and Huancayo provinces, they urged the region's inhabitants, in both Spanish and Quechua, to contribute resources and form guerrilla bands. Relying on smaller merchants, wealthier peasants, and even parish priests with connections to the peasantry, the Caceristas in effect attempted to build a multiclass nationalist front that would be held together through personal and patron-client ties, and by the common threat of a Chilean occupation. The peasantry, organized through intermediaries with prestige at the local level, would constitute irregular forces called *montoneras* (guerrilla bands, as distinct from the bands' soldiers, called *montoneros*) and provide tactical support to Cáceres' regular army, a smaller force made up of more seasoned, urban men. The regional elite, for its part, would be expected to collaborate with material support and as more high-level officers and political officials (Cáceres 1973: 98–114).

At least initially, the alliance seemed to work best in the urban centers. When the Chileans first invaded the central highlands in May 1881, Cáceres enjoyed the support of diverse sectors in the cities of Jauja, Concepción, and Huancayo, including several large landowners who were themselves veterans of the Peruvian defense of Lima a few months before (Valladares 1977; AHM 1918; Moreno de C. 1974: 45–46). But in January 1882, with the arrival of the Chilean colonel Estanislao del Canto at the head of what proved to be an army of occupation, the situation began to change. As Chilean detachments searched the area's villages for supplies to support three thousand enemy soldiers, the peasants began to feel the truly dramatic effects of what it meant to support a hostile army. Taking more kindly to the idea of organizing montoneras, authorities in the region's peasant communities responded by calling town meetings and forming guerrilla bands. Unable to rely on Cáceres' regular army, which had been forced to retreat south with del Canto's advance, the newly organized montoneras independently confronted the Chilean army between February and June, often fighting to the last man (AHM 1918; Cáceres 1973: 99, 104, 134–46; Tello D. 1971: 63–66, 75–76; Bravo G. 1971: 287–91, 671; Manrique 1981: 131–80; APJ 1882a).

By the time Cáceres' regular army was capable of renewed fighting in the area in July 1882, the composition of the nationalist alliance backing it had altered noticeably. The region's peasantry, organized into increasingly autonomous guerrilla bands, fought enthusiastically and successfully in support of the Caceristas. After having managed to dislodge the Chileans from the department of Junín with the peasants' help, Cáceres praised them in a battle report written at the end of July:

The Supreme Government's attention should be especially directed to the spontaneous mass uprising of all the Indians in the Departments of Junín and Huancavelica, with which they have given a most valuable service. This event foreshadows a unanimous movement that will soon transform the nature of the present war (Bravo G. 1971: 667).

Yet what Cáceres failed to point out was that the peasants' very enthusiasm was beginning to fray the edges of his nationalist coalition, especially in the southern section of the Mantaro Valley.

Because the southern region had borne the brunt of the del Canto occupation, landowners and merchants had suffered the exactions and forced contributions of the Chilean commanders in a much more direct way than had their counterparts in the northern part of the valley, around Jauja. To further complicate matters, it was also in the south that the peasant montoneras had organized most successfully and militantly, scoring important partial victories against the Chilean army. Thus it was in the south of the valley that members of the regional elite began seriously to consider the possibility that continued resistance might prove not only futile, but also dangerous. Hoping to protect their remaining assets from their own armed and mobilized peasantry as well as from Chilean reprisals, some collaborated openly with the invasion force. Others remained neutral. In either case, they retired from the Cacerista alliance, forcing the leaders of the La Breña campaign to rely even more heavily on peasant support. And in the heat of battle this reliance, when combined with increasingly direct confrontations between nationalist peasants and collaborationist landowners, would generate greater independence and radicalization among the peasant montoneras (Mallon 1983: 88–89; AHM 1918: 84, 86; APJ 1882b; Manrique 1981: 149–80).

Perhaps most indicative of these developments was the confrontation between the hacendado Jacinto Cevallos and the guerrillas of the southern village of Acobamba. After the montoneros had stopped at his hacienda Punto, northeast of Huancayo, asking for provisions, Cevallos wrote a note to the administrator of his estate in which he called the peasants barbarians and promised revenge. The Acobamba guerrillas, having intercepted the letter, replied to Cevallos in the following words (APJ 1882b):

> Acobamba, Apr. 16, 1882
>
> Capetains [sic] and Lieutenant Govenors [sic]
> To Mr. Civilista Don
> Jasinto [sic] Ceballos [sic]
>
> You would think that under the Sun and the earth they would not know that you were a traitor to the homeland where you were born, well they do know, and we know that you with all your friends traitors to our amiable [sic] homeland are in this province communicating and giving explanations on how they can ruin the Peruvians, to those treacherous Chilean bandits invaders and like you traitors to their homeland. Also you would think that we couldn't grab the communication that you were passing to your Administrator, well we have it in our hands informed of its contents we must tell you: that all the Guirrillas [sic] that are in the valleys of these hills led by the Commander Gonzales Dilgado [sic] are with the express orders of the General Don Andres Abilino [sic] Caseres [sic] and we have orders to punish the deceitful actions of the traitors of the homeland: and you don't put us in the group of the barbarians like you told your Administrator because we with reason and justice unanimously rose up to defend our homeland we are true lovers of our homeland where we were born. I [sic] don't know what people you call miserable and want to revenge yourself over the course of time: don't you think that we until the present cocassion [sic] even though you call us barbarians we still don't walk around committing revenge and other barbarous things, instead we proceed with all loyalty all the Guirrillas even though we know that you are one of the closest associates of the infamous Dr. Giraldez.
>
> It's true that the other day since we passed through your Hacienda after having made an advance across these places to fight those Chilean bandits while we were passing through we asked your administrator to give us about eight cattle for our food to give their rations to two thousand men that are at our command: this is all we have done in relation to your hacienda and you think we have committed barbarous acts, but any hacendado should be able to tolerate us as patriotic soldiers.
>
> God keep you,
>
> [Signed] Mariano Mayta, Lieutenant Governor
> Faustino Camargo, Captain
> Martin Vera, Captain, Lieutenant
> Governor
> Mariano Campos, Lieutenant Governor
> Domingo Mercado

Among the few surviving sources that chronicle peasant participation
in the war from the montoneros' own point of view, this letter is key in
the sense that it documents, on multiple levels, the growth of both class
and national consciousness in the context of a foreign invasion. Reading
between the lines, and establishing a dialogue between the guerrillas' view
of what happened and available chronologies, it is possible to reconstruct
a very rich and complex view of the central highlands resistance. In contrast
to the hacendados, whose connections with the Lima elite had prompted
them to join forces with other regional groups in the disastrous defense
of Lima in 1881, the peasants had not participated actively or autonomously in the war's earlier campaigns. Once the occupation reached the
central highlands, however, it threatened directly and materially their base
of subsistence in the village economy, their conditions of production—
the homeland where they were born. It was at this point that, in their own
words, ". . . we with reason and justice unanimously rose up to defend
our homeland. . . ." Given the nature of the Chilean occupation, as well
as the efforts of the Caceristas to form guerrilla bands, it soon became
clear that the only way the peasants could hope to defend their homeland
against continued exactions and destruction was in an alliance with all
those sharing their concern, all those interested in defending the region,
the conditions of production, from outside invasion. It is upon this base
of shared nationalist interest that the Cacerista alliance was forged; what
held the motley band of priests, regional officials, merchants, landowners,
wealthy peasants and poor *comuneros* together, in addition to complex
and cross-cutting patron-client ties, was a desire to defend their common
conditions of production.

As the occupation proceeded, however, sectors of the regional elite—
especially those in the southern half of the valley—began to discern an
alternative way of defending their conditions of production, namely
through collaboration with the invaders. This new form of defense was
not only more efficient vis-à-vis the Chileans, who were certainly willing
to stop sacking the properties of those who aided them in their task of
pacification, but also with regard to an equally if not more threatening
enemy: the peasant guerrillas themselves. Given the continued autonomy
of the peasant economy in the prewar period and the regional elite's inability to establish unchallenged political control or hegemony in the area,
the two classes did not, in the end, have the same interest in the conditions of production. From the landowners' point of view, and in the context of increasing peasant mobilization and autonomy during the course
of the occupation, it could very well be that the greatest enemy from whom
they had to defend their lands and other property was not the Chilean
army but the Peruvian peasants.

It was at this point that the national vision of each class—that is, the vision of how best to defend the local mode of production from outside interference—began to differ markedly. From the peasants' point of view, the only way to reestablish control and autonomy over the homeland was to ally with other "Peruvians," defined in region-specific but multiclass terms, against the invaders. It is in this context that Cáceres emerges as the symbol of unity around which all can gather and fight—". . . with the express orders of the General Don Andres Abilino Caseres." From the landowners' point of view, however, the best possible solution was the quickest possible peace. By removing the reason for the peasant mobilization, while at the same time forcing the Chilean disoccupation of Peru, such a move would best assure a return to the prewar status quo in the region. In the short run, the only way to accomplish this goal was to collaborate with the Chilean forces in order to hasten the effective enforcement of a peace treaty. As Luis Milón Duarte would explain a few months later when he joined the northern hacendado Miguel Iglesias in calling for immediate peace with territorial concessions, people had done their patriotic duty as long as it was possible; now the task was to redeem and rebuild the country by any means available. And Duarte ended his proclamation with the most direct explanation of why he held the position he did: ". . . my properties have been sacked and burned, as much by the external enemy as by the internal enemies of peace" (Ahumada M. 1891: 8:162).

Perhaps prefiguring an understanding that would become generalized among peasants in the southern Mantaro Valley in the coming months, the Acobamba guerrillas clearly discerned this conflict in April 1882. More than anything else what angered them was that Jacinto Cevallos, a Peruvian landowner, would be more frightened of them, Peruvian peasants, than he was of the Chilean army. For the guerrillas, this fact was symbolized in Cevallos' referring to them as "barbarians." Again and again in their letter to the landowner they returned to this reference, each time opposing their own view of why their presence on Cevallos' property was legitimate: they were not there to invade, sack, or burn, but to demand their rations as part of the Peruvian army. Nowhere is this conflict of vision better encapsulated than in the two concluding phrases of the peasants' letter: "you think we have committed barbarous acts, but any hacendado should be able to tolerate us as patriotic soldiers."

This, then, was the situation Cáceres faced upon his return to the Mantaro Valley in mid-1882: an increasing rift between classes emerging out of the conditions of the resistance itself. And yet the extent to which either landowners or peasants were no longer willing to make common cause in a national resistance varied greatly from one area of the valley to another, depending on local conditions, the balance between the hacienda and the peasant economy, and the extent to which landowners truly saw collaboration as a viable alternative. Thus it was in the southern and eastern parts of the valley, where hacendado properties were concentrated and where mobilization was most intense, that the classes developed violently opposed visions of how to defend their conditions of production. Huancayo, which was the center of the Chilean occupation; the hacendado-dominated city of Concepción; the Comas region where several mobilized villages bordered on the haciendas Punto and Callanca controlled by Jacinto Cevallos; and the western areas of Chongos, Chongos Alto, and Huasicancha, which bordered on several large properties belonging to prominent regional elite families; in all these places class struggle emerged from within the ruins of a nationalist alliance. In the north of the valley, on the other hand, around Jauja, Huaripampa, Muquiyauyo, and north into the Yanamarca Valley communities of Marco and Acolla, the nationalist alliance remained strong. Landowners and merchants in this area, whether because of the less damaging nature of the occupation or because of the closer personal tie some local families had to Cáceres, did not exercise the option of collaboration. As a result, the peasants' vision of a common cause to defend the homeland or local conditions of production was maintained by others as well (Mallon 1983: 93–94).

All of those questions and divisions would become even more important after August 1882, when the northern landowner and ex-Pierolista Miguel Iglesias issued the Cry of Montán, in which he agreed to pursue peace even with the fragmentation of Peruvian territory. By doing so, he appealed to a growing sentiment among landowners in the southern Mantaro Valley, giving them a specific and formal political channel for their new "national" vision. In the months following, as several crucial people in the region declared in favor of Iglesias, Cáceres would be forced to choose between peace under unacceptable conditions and reliance on an increasingly radicalized peasantry. By giving priority to the national war and allying with an increasingly autonomous peasantry, he gave the guerrillas in the south of the valley the legitimacy to engage in class warfare under cover of a national war (Mallon 1983: 95–98; Basadre 1948: 495–96; Cáceres 1973: 183–94; Bravo G. 1971: 673; Ahumada M. 1891: 8:161–62).

Throughout 1883, the battles in the central highlands pitted a Chilean army, led by collaborationist Peruvian guides, against the peasant guerrillas. Though documentary information on these battles is thin, the general picture is one of increasing violence and militance on the part of the montoneras, with at least the tacit acceptance of the Cáceres high command. As long as the peasants supported the Caceristas when needed, it seems, they were left to control the countryside as they saw fit. While this situation did not lead to major confrontations in the Jauja area, where the Cacerista alliance still held fast, in the area around Huancayo and near Comas it had led, certainly by mid-1884, to montonera control, in broad terms, of the major haciendas of the area (Tello D. 1971: 79; APJ 1886a–c, 1887; AHM 1884a, 1885a). Several of the more notable collaborators, including Luis Milón Duarte, had been assassinated under mysterious circumstances (Tello D. 1971: 76, 79; AHM 1918). While the vision of the Chilean high command that this was a war against all whites (Bonilla 1978: 113) is certainly exaggerated, by mid-1884 there was, in the south of the Mantaro Valley and into Huancavelica, a war of the countryside — represented by the peasant guerrillas defending their view of the national resistance — against the city, symbolized by the collaborationist upper class, interested in the quickest possible peace and forced to find refuge under the wing of the Chilean army.

It was at this point that Cáceres once again made a decision that would change the character of the local conflict. When he accepted the Treaty of Ancón in June 1884, he tacitly admitted that the conditions of peace with Chile could no longer be improved. At one stroke, he transformed what had been a national war against a foreign invader into a civil war over control of the presidential palace. In this new context, Cáceres needed effective control of all existing montonera forces in order to make possible his victory against the Iglesista army. He could no longer accept peasant autonomy, nor allow the guerrillas to make their own decisions on military strategy. In the long run, moreover, the hacendados would not constitute the traitors to the national cause they had been previously, but the most powerful and viable dominant class fraction upon which to base an attempt at national reconstruction. Both to reestablish control over the central region and to mend fences with the hacendados, therefore, Cáceres quickly moved against his peasant allies (Basadre 1968–69: 8:448–68; Manrique 1979: 304–5; Manrique 1981: 331–73; Mallon 1983: 99–101; Tello D. 1971: 74–76; Ráez 1898: 21; APJ 1884).

Between July 1884, when he began the civil war against Iglesias, and October 1888, while he was president of the Republic, Andrés Cáceres developed a three-pronged strategy to control the centers of peasant mobilization in the central sierra. The first of these was the incorporation of local villages into the state structure through the creation of independent districts. In October 1886, a scarce four months after he formally became president, Cáceres approved the creation of two new districts in the Mantaro Valley area: Acolla and Muquiyauyo, both near Jauja and both centers of loyal Cacerista guerrilla action upon which he had increasingly counted in the last battles of the war with Iglesias. Interestingly, both villages had engaged in long and ultimately fruitless prewar campaigns for district status: their quick approval by Cáceres thus constituted a "reward" for their loyalty during the La Breña campaign. And in the end, the policy of district creation would most benefit precisely those groups who had helped to mediate between the Caceristas and the local peasantry: the wealthier villagers who, in both cases until well into the twentieth century, would dominate officeholding on the new municipal councils (Mallon 1983: 105–7; Adams 1959: 29–32, 37; Ortega 1977; APJ 1897; Bravo G. 1971: 302; Hutchinson 1973: 29–30; BNP 1888).

Though the creation of districts proved quite effective in integrating communities in the northern Mantaro area into a revamped state structure, predictably it was not successful in the south. Here Cáceres used a judicious combination of selective repression, remobilization, and negotiation, depending on the specific case and initial reaction from the local guerrillas. In Chongos, Chongos Alto, and Huasicancha, for example, he began by executing the three key leaders of the autonomous montonera in July 1884 (Mallon 1983: 100). Once the guerrillas in that area were reorganized under the more dependable leadership of Cacerista notables, they played an important role in confronting Iglesias' 1885 "Pacification Army" (AHM 1884a, 1885a–b). Three years later, Cáceres sent a special commission to this area to hear the peasants' grievances on landowning, thus attempting to use negotiation to reestablish political hegemony (BNP 1889a–c). Only after having used all these other stratagems did Cáceres attempt to use district politics as the coup de grace, though in this case it was negative: he reversed the creation of the district of San Juan in 1891, returning control of the rebellious villages of Chongos Alto and Huasicancha to a municipal council dominated by Cacerista members of the village elite (Samaniego 1978: 52).

The one case where Cacerista repression was not successful was in the region around Comas. Part of the reason for this failure lay in the special qualities of the Comas mobilization. Since the villages in this area, including Acobamba, Canchapalca, and Comas, had served as the vanguard in the resistance to the Chileans, it is hardly surprising that these communities had developed the most independent and active montoneras. Because they were not directly on the most important north-south routes in the conflict, moreover, these same guerrillas had lived off the land without a great deal of interference between 1882 and 1886. When they participated in battles, they did so by moving into the belligerent area, usually the city of Concepción. Otherwise, geography and climate protected Comas itself from repeated incursions, especially during the civil war of 1884 and 1885 (AHM 1884a, 1885a).

By the beginning of Cáceres' presidency, therefore, the peasants of Comas and surrounding villages had developed a rather unique consciousness of their role in the national resistance. Their initial confrontation with Cevallos was followed by a run-in with Cáceres in July 1884, when his prefect sent the villagers a note demanding that they return the cattle taken from the area's haciendas during the La Breña campaign (APJ 1884). Once even Cáceres began to deny them their legitimacy as patriotic soldiers, the Comasinos and their neighbors seemed to have turned inward. Left to their own devices for the next three and a half years, they consolidated their hold over their region and developed a broader vision or project of how their society should be organized. Emerging initially out of the need to defend their conditions of production from the Chilean invasion, this vision had, by early 1888, come fairly close to constituting an alternative national project for their class.

In a letter to the neighboring village of Uchubamba in January 1888, the municipal officials of Comas laid out a proposal for an independent peasant confederation. "The inhabitants of Comas with its *caseríos* [dependent villages or *anexos*] Cochas, Canchapalca, Mucllo, Todos Santos, Runatullo, and those from Punto, Acobamba and Andamarca, have decided to form a confederation or alliance of districts," they wrote (APJ 1888),

in order to defend ourselves and to improve our commerce, industry, education and administration of justice, and we count on a judge from Ica who has already lived a year in Jauja, and who now has decided to come and live among us forever. He has already given us proof of his loyalty to us, and is well known as a reformer. This gentleman is already known in Lima for the articles he has written in the newspapers asking for reform. And we also have other competent people to help us.

If you wish to form a district of our Federal State, you will be free, you will govern yourselves, elect your own authorities, and no one will be able to attack you, without the whole Federal State coming to your defense. In return, you will also be obligated to come with your weapons when we need you. For some time already we have taken up our weapons, we have achieved things, and we will achieve much more very soon. We will know how to contain your enemies if you will join our confederation if you agree send a representative, that is one of your principal citizens to negotiate with us, and everyone will benefit. Those who come should bring a power of attorney so they can contract properly in the name of all of Uchubamba.

This document is striking on many counts. First of all, it makes clear that a fairly sizable amount of territory, including three haciendas and five communities, had de facto constituted an independent social, military, and political entity as of the first months of 1888. The form taken by this entity was a confederation of independent districts, each of which ideally had the autonomy to organize its own economic and political life. The alliance among districts facilitated a common defense, administration of justice, and development of commerce, industry, and education. In keeping with the issues raised in the prewar battle over districts, therefore, the Comasinos and their allies viewed the role of the state (in this case their ideal "Federal State") as guaranteeing local democracy and providing the conditions and financing for local development. The difference was that, coming out of a militant and independent role in a national resistance, they had decided autonomously to implement their vision.

The final fact to emerge from the letter is, perhaps, the most difficult to assess. The authors of the document emphasize the importance of "outside advisors," in the sense of competent experts, in helping them elaborate their project. We will probably never know exactly who these people were — except that they included at least one parish priest (BNP 1896a) and a "judge from Ica." But what is clear is that, even when creating a political structure in their own image, according to their own desires and specifications, peasants needed an alliance with other groups. They needed the intellectual resources and political perspective of other classes. What this meant on one level was that the Comasinos were available to form coalitions with other groups in favor of reform, as long as local democracy and prosperity were emphasized. But in the Peru of the postwar period, where a reconstructed state was still based most strongly on the landowning class, such a reformist coalition proved a historical impossibility (Mallon 1983: 121–22). In the long run, therefore, the Comas confederation was destined to isolation and eventual extinction.

This, however, did not happen during the Cáceres years. After an unsuccessful military campaign to the area in September 1888 and an equally ill-fated attempt at negotiation in January 1889 (BNP 1888–89), the not-so-benign neglect of the Cacerista state gave the Comasinos seven years of breathing space in which to further develop their confederation. Only with the new experiment at national consolidation initiated under Nicolás de Piérola (1895–1899) and his successor Eduardo de Romaña (1899–1903) would a new effort at "pacification" of Comas be undertaken. Even then, it would take two military expeditions and a surprisingly modern counterinsurgency policy — led, symbolically enough, by Jacinto Cevallos himself — to finally break the back of the Comas confederation (BNP 1896a–c; Mallon 1983: 114–20).[4]

With the Pierolista experiment and beyond, the elite generation that had come of age in the fiasco of the War of the Pacific attempted finally to bring to fruition a process of national integration. The economic, territorial, and cultural unification of the country was seen as a precondition for avoiding a repetition of the 1879 disaster. An important policy in this regard was the construction of roads and railroads, which would establish a firm material base for unification. But equally important on a political level was assuring the cooperation of the different regional oligarchies by offering state aid in the solution of their most immediate problems. In the central highlands, this meant not only eliminating the remaining pocket of postwar peasant resistance, but also providing state assistance in labor control and the modernization of the local economy. The death of the peasant republic in Comas in 1902 must be seen in this light. Along with building a road to the jungle, establishing a government office for labor acquisition, and in general facilitating entrepreneurial activity and investment, repression of the Comasinos was part of the state's effort to insure the domination of one class vision over another (Mallon 1983: 125–67). In the process, the state also assured its own consolidation and survival. A national project fundamentally at odds with the one entertained by Comas' peasant confederation had clearly triumphed.

THE NORTHERN HIGHLANDS, 1879–1900

In contrast to the central sierra, where an economically and culturally strong peasant community had placed significant limits on the regional elite's access to labor and political control, in the northern highland department of Cajamarca the regional oligarchy was firmly established in the second half of the nineteenth century. One important explanation for this difference lies in the much weaker peasant communal tradition found in Cajamarca, where even before the Spanish conquest communal structures had been imported from the south through conquest by the Incas, rather than having strong native roots in northern culture. By the time of independence from Spain, even though smallholding villages did exist, they had comparatively little sense of institutional cohesion, communal land, or communal tradition of struggle. Thus the great estate, even while facing opposition to its process of territorial expansion, had not confronted the type of concerted, powerful, and viable communal resistance its counterpart had faced in the central highlands (Deere 1977, 1978; Taylor 1979).

A second factor contributing to hacienda dominance was the lack of economic alternatives available in the regional economy during the nineteenth century. Beginning in the late eighteenth century, the decline of the area's *obrajes* encouraged the local economy to turn in on itself. In quite the opposite way from the central region, where the mining boom of the 1780s reappeared in the 1870s and generated an increasing demand for labor and products, highland Cajamarca in particular seems to have remained an economic backwater in the prewar period. When faced with few alternatives — whether in the form of markets for their surplus production or opportunities for occasional wage labor in mining or other sectors — local peasants had little choice but to turn to the hacienda when in economic need (Taylor 1979: 17–23).

Given the lack of effective weapons available to the Cajamarcan peasantry, conflict between classes in this northern region was an especially unequal contest in the nineteenth century. The hacienda — and therefore the hacendado — was the most powerful social, economic, and political force in local life. The basis for this power was not always direct control over people, but rather a monopoly of the land itself. This is clear from the fact that, while only 30 percent of the department's inhabitants lived on the great estates — which is not all that different from the proportion in the central sierra — the hacienda controlled over two-thirds of the entire land area (ibid.: 14). Thus the majority of the region's inhabitants was dependent on the hacienda for access to resources, even in the cases where they did not live directly on the properties.

Systems of land tenure and population patterns seem to have varied substantially, however, across the various subregions of Cajamarca department (Map 7). In the northern province of Jaén, where the economy had for a long time been based on the commercial exploitation of tropical crops (ibid.: 16, 19), population was still relatively sparse (ibid.: 13). A sizable proportion of the great estates, dedicated mainly to the breeding of cattle and sheep, probably had originally belonged to the Church and then moved to the state-controlled Beneficencia (ADC 1885a). The opportunity to rent these properties attracted entrepreneurs from surrounding provinces, and in the second half of the 1800s Jaén had also witnessed an increase in merchant activity, as traders from Chota province and the departments of Piura and Lambayeque entered the area seeking to buy up supplies of cattle, cacao, coffee, cascarilla, and other products (ADC 1885a–b, 1887). By the immediate prewar period, then, Jaén had undergone a recent commercial expansion. Despite the overall thinness of population in the province, a higher percentage of it was concentrated on haciendas than was usual in the rest of the department: over 40 percent, according to the 1876 census (Taylor 1979: 14). And the dominance of the hacienda was probably associated with the increase in commerce, as more laborers were needed to meet the demand for tropical goods. Certainly local smallholders and peasants perceived it in these terms, generally directing their hostility against "outsiders" from Chota who were associated with large landholding or interprovincial commerce. As we shall see, this association of "outsiders" with the penetration of commercial capital and the expansion of the great estate would have important implications for the type of movement developing during the War of the Pacific.

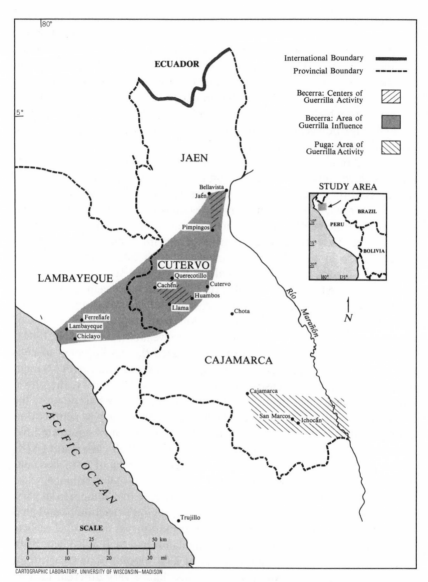

Map 7. Guerrilla Activity and the War of the Pacific: Cajamarca

In contrast to Jaén, the dominance of the hacienda in Cajamarca province, and nearby highland areas, had a relatively long history by the second half of the nineteenth century. In an economy oriented mainly toward cattle and wheat where levels of technique were low, hacendados needed extensive properties in order to maintain their households at a level of consumption acceptable to their class standing. The amount of land they were actually able to bring under production, however, depended on the number of tenants they were able to fix, through a variety of agreements, to their properties. Their overall income depended as well on the amount of labor or product rent they were able to extract through these different agreements. And successful extraction depended, in the last analysis, on the extent to which a landowner was able to back up his or her demands with effective power, that is, on the individual's position within the local political system (ibid.: 27–32).

The need to use extraeconomic means to fix a labor supply, when combined with the territorial domination of the great estate and the historic weakness of the peasant community, created the conditions in Cajamarca for the emergence of a system of private landowner power. By the second half of the nineteenth century, those hacendados who succeeded in extracting rent from their tenants and reproducing their position in local society did so by keeping private armies on their estates and developing patron-client relations with the smallholder villages near their properties (ibid.: 29–30; ADC 1881a–c, 1882a). That such a concentration of authority discouraged overt landowner-peasant conflict and insured continued extraction received negative confirmation from repeated outbreaks of peasant unrest in areas where landlords were weaker (ADC 1881h, 1884a; Taylor 1979: 31–32). This, in turn, encouraged the development of conflict among hacendados, as they attempted to extend and further cement their position at the expense of their competitors. Ultimately, therefore, while there were cases of peasant resistance against the hacendados, the crucial source of conflict in prewar Cajamarca province was competition among landlords, as they attempted to establish the most complete hold over their areas in order to maintain and reproduce their class status (ADC 1881d–g; Taylor 1979: 31–32). It was through this prism of intraclass conflict that the province was integrated into the national resistance.

The final element that helped to define the role of Cajamarca department during the Chilean occupation was the region's reaction to and participation in the prewar attempts at state formation. As mentioned earlier, landowners and peasants in the central highlands had each welcomed, from their own perspective, the involvement of a developing state structure in their internal conflicts. Naturally each class had a very different idea of what the correct state role should be; but the very evenness of the balance of class forces made the state a welcome participant in local politics. In the northern sierra, on the other hand, the existence of an effective system of private landowner power diminished the relevance of state interventions for both classes. From the landlords' point of view, a weak state could only interfere in their successful control of the region. From the peasants' point of view, a state that could not effectively challenge land-owner power only increased the burdensomeness of their existence, especially in the form of taxes and conscription, without giving anything in return. Thus the previous history of class conflict in Cajamarca made it difficult for either class to see the state as a potential ally. Instead, peasants and landowners tended to share a suspicious hostility vis-à-vis the expansion of a state authority they did not think would bring them any benefits (ADC 1881f, i–l; 1881c–d, 1880a–b).

There were, however, intraregional differences. In Jaén, potential class and regional confrontations over the expansion of commercial capital conditioned both classes' views of the state. For peasant smallholders, scattered evidence suggests that they saw state incursions – especially in the form of the *contribución personal* or head tax – as yet another invasion of outsiders that went along with commerce and commercial agriculture (ADC 1880c, 1882b).[5] The Chota landowners, on the other hand, seemed willing to extend commercial agriculture mainly by renting lands through the Beneficencia of Jaén, a state-affiliated charitable organization that got access to funds by administering state properties (ADC 1885a). One could speculate that, when facing a hostile local population in a frontier zone, many hacendados from outside the province were more willing to accept state support than they would have been in their own backyard.

The situation was different in Cajamarca province. There many land-owners defended the sanctity of their properties' boundaries, not allow-ing state officials to cross into their estates while chasing criminals or collecting taxes. Hacendados also hid bandits on their estates in exchange for personal loyalty, and in some cases even protected neighboring peasants who were resisting taxation or conscription (ADC 1880d; 1881b–c, m; 1882a). The peasants, for their part, seemed to prefer a local patron's protection against state exaction to the only available alternative, which was to be taxed by the landlord *and* the state. Only when hacendados competed with each other for influence did the role of the state become relevant. Indeed, the participation of local landowners in factional bat-tles at the national level during the prewar years can best be explained in the context of local intraelite competition (Taylor 1979: 31–32, 74, 82; Manrique 1981: 218–20).

Thus Jaén and Cajamarca provinces each presented a distinct prewar pattern of internal conflict as well as a different relationship to the emerg-ing state structure in Lima. In Jaén, interclass hostility over commercial expansion predisposed outside landowners to accept state aid in extend-ing commercial agriculture, while at the same time it increased peasant resistance to state exactions. In Cajamarca, peasants and landowners both viewed the state with suspicion, preferring the existing status quo to an unclear and disruptive form of change. The only exception seemed to be the weaker landowners who were willing to seek state aid in their unequal battle with their stronger colleagues, thus forcing the political involvement of the more influential Cajamarca hacendados as well. In contrast to the central highlands, then, where a political stalemate between classes made both much more receptive to state involvement, the northern peasants were never open to an alliance with the state. This historically established fact, when combined with the specific insertion of the northern area into the War of the Pacific and the particular reactions of various landowner factions, would generate at least two distinct types of national resistance in Cajamarca department.

When Nicolás de Piérola abandoned Lima to Chilean occupation in January 1881, he established camp in Jauja and divided the country into three large zones of resistance. The northern zone, under the control of Admiral Lizardo Montero, had its headquarters in Cajamarca. In contrast to the northern coastal departments, which had been subject to Chilean invasion and occupation since 1880, Cajamarca seems to have been spared the presence of Chilean soldiers until mid-1882. Even then the actual occupation, while quite destructive, was short-lived (Basadre 1968–69: 6:272–80, 406–11; Manrique 1979: 277–78; Lynch 1883–84: 2:94–100). This did not mean, however, that the political conflicts among Peruvians generated by the war and the occupation did not have a significant impact in the highland department. Indeed, both of the major resistance movements that developed in the region had their origins in intraelite battles over how best to deal with the Chilean occupation of the country.

Only a few months after he became commander of the northern zone, Montero named Manuel José Becerra subprefect of Chota province (ADC 1881n). Apparently not a member of the highest landowning elite, Becerra nevertheless seems to have participated in the prewar commercial boom in Jaén, travelling to that province in search of commercial opportunities.[6] During the early part of the war, he had fought as a lieutenant colonel in the fourth division of the Northern Army organized by Miguel Iglesias (AHM 1880). Once the formal battle was lost in 1881, Becerra enthusiastically supported the option for continued resistance as represented by Montero and Piérola. In a letter to the prefect of Cajamarca, he expressed his pleasure at knowing that the leader of the northern zone had pledged to continue the war. "For my part," he continued, "I offer you, in the name of all the towns in my province, that we will leave no stone unturned in our efforts to save the homeland, no matter how long the war turns out to be, and no matter what the sacrifice" (ADC 1881n).

There were those with different ideas, however. Shortly after the Chileans refused to recognize Piérola and supported the formation of a new government based in the Lima suburb of La Magdalena and headed by Francisco García Calderón, political agitation began in Chota, especially around the city of Bambamarca, for recognition of the García Calderón government and immediate peace negotiations. By the time Becerra became subprefect, several outbreaks of violence had already occurred (ADC 1881o). Yet it would only be in the latter part of 1881 and the beginning months of 1882 that these events would take on greater meaning.

In November 1881, encouraged by the energetic intervention of U.S. special envoy Stephen Hurlbut and hoping to achieve peace without territorial concessions, Lizardo Montero recognized the government of García Calderón. With the president's exile to Chile that same month, however, a junta governed until early December, when Montero himself succeeded to the presidency. By early February 1882, Montero had passed his position as a commander of the northern region to Miguel Iglesias, a landowner from Cajamarca province who had been in retirement on his estate since the Peruvian defeat in Lima one year before (Manrique 1981: 219; Basadre 1948: 492–96; Manrique 1979: 294–97; Basadre 1968–69: 8:344–57). The combination of Montero's "defection" to the García Calderón camp and Iglesias' appointment to commander generated wild rumors in Chota. It was even said that a battalion was headed for the province to force payment of war contributions and install a new pro-Magdalena government. The Chota notables who had supported continued resistance considered this an insult to their nationalist credentials, vowing to take up arms against the battalion. In a desperate letter to the prefect, Becerra explained that he was unable to influence public opinion to the contrary, urging that the government reconsider and not allow the army to advance. "It is neither patriotic nor just to bloody the soil of a brother population," he explained (ADC 1882e). Yet his plea seems to have fallen on deaf ears; by May 1882 he was on the run in the province of Jaén, pursued as a rebel by government forces (ADC 1882f).

From May 1882 until his death in 1885, Becerra led a guerrilla movement that repeatedly eluded both occupation and government forces. Operating mainly along the commercial routes tying the jungle to the coast, especially in the provinces of Chota and Jaén, Becerra's montonera was instrumental in preventing collaborationist forces—most notably Miguel Iglesias—from establishing full control in the northern highlands. Yet in contrast to the image commonly presented in the literature, Becerra's rebellion was not simply that of a landowner faction unhappy with the individuals in power.

Though a complete assessment will have to await future research on the area, it seems that Becerra and the other leaders of his movement were from an intermediate stratum of Chota merchants, small landowners, and village notables who, while apparently profiting from the prewar boom in Jaén, were never fully incorporated into the local elite (ADC 1880e, 1881p, 1885c; BNP 1883). Even a cursory placement of the montonera's operations on a map makes clear, moreover, that its long-term survival depended on the knowledge of trade routes and resources previously amassed by its leaders. There were two main areas of operation. One centered in Bellavista district, in the jungle area of Jaén province, connecting west to Jaén itself and then further west across the highlands to the commercial center of Olmos, on the way down to the coast in the department of Lambayeque. The town of Pimpingos, south of Jaén and en route to the commercial centers of Chota and Cutervo, was also in this first general area (ADC 1884i, e, d, m; 1885e–h, c). The second base formed a rectangle whose northern, eastern, southern, and western angles were the towns of Querecotillo, Huambos, Llama, and Cachén respectively. Located much further south in the Chota-Cutervo highlands, nearly halfway between Chota and the coastal commercial entrepôts of Ferreñafe, Chiclayo, and Lambayeque, this second guerrilla stronghold was based in the towns from which many of the regulars in Becerra's band originally came (ADC 1884g, b–c, j–k; 1883a; 1885i).

By basing itself in areas familiar to the members of the band, due to previous trade and family connections, Becerra's montonera was able to survive through a combination of stealing and marketing commercial goods, and of seeking the protection of local village notables whom they knew personally. Indeed, local authorities or prominent citizens in the towns and villages through which Becerra passed played a crucial supportive role, providing information, commercializing stolen goods and acquiring arms, recruiting additional men (ADC 1883a; 1884i, b, e, d; 1885g, i, c). In the final analysis, then, Becerra's montonera operated not as a landowner's army based on the haciendas, but as a merchant's army based in the small towns and commercial routes of the region.

Though led by merchants and small landowners, the montonera had a much more varied base of support. On one side were the large hacendados, mainly from the western corner of Chota and into the department of Lambayeque, who provided crucial commercial connections to the coast. On the other side were the peasant and even Indian populations who provided the fighting men and, particularly in Bellavista, the resources and logistical support for a hideaway when government pressure was high. Taken together, this wide variety of contacts and environments was ideal for the survival of a small guerrilla force. Near the coast, influential landowners and others served as a conduit through which flowed booty in exchange for arms and ammunition (ADC 1884g; 1885c, f, h, j). In Chota a base among smallholding peasants and petty merchants provided fighters, occasional refuge, additional commercial connections, and intelligence on troop movements (ADC 1884g, b-c, j-k; 1885i; 1883a). And in Jaén, Bellavista was the largest producer of cacao in the province, directly on the Marañón River, yet difficult to reach if travelling overland from west to east — all characteristics making it an excellent refuge from armies based in the highlands (ADC 1887, 1888). The question remaining, though, is how Becerra was able to keep such a broad and varied coalition together at all. In order to answer it, we must turn to an examination of the movement's internal social dynamics.

It is easiest to hypothesize about the interests Becerra shared with his fellow merchants. Involved in the attempt to commercialize tropical products before the war, these traders had nevertheless found themselves in competition with much more established landowners and entrepreneurs. They must have been highly gratified by the modified and selective forms of banditry in which the band engaged to finance itself, involving theft of commercial cargoes on the roads of Jaén and ultimately the expulsion of large landowners from the province along with the destruction of Jaén's Beneficencia (ADC 1884i, d, m; 1885e, h, c, b). This type of operation allowed them a legitimate way to revenge themselves on their economic competitors, perhaps even the fantasy that after the war they might take over the more profitable routes. Certainly they would have chuckled had they read the desperate report submitted by Jaén's subprefect from his hideout in Cutervo in 1884, when he explained that Becerra, his father-in-law Manuel Vílchez, and other leaders had made it impossible for any merchants from Cutervo or Chota to trade in the province except under threat of violent death (ADC 1884d).

Becerra's connections with hacendados are certainly more difficult to explain, given his movement's hostility to the prominent landowners in Jaén and Chota. The fact that his landlord connections were outside these two provinces, in or near the coastal departments of Piura and Lambayeque, helps to explain part of the contradiction. So does the fact that separate commercial routes connected Jaén to those coastal areas — in particular through the strategic center of Olmos — and that it was not necessary to go through the Chota strongholds. But most important of all, the two groups were united in a common antistate sentiment. For the merchants, the state represented collaboration with the enemy and the local landowning class. For those hacendados supporting Becerra, the state represented an unwelcome interference in their lives. In this context it is interesting to note that José Mesones, Becerra's strongest hacendado ally, had been involved in a major altercation with local authorities in 1880 when these had attempted to draft men from his hacienda (ADC 1880f, 1885h).

An antistate sentiment also united Becerra with his peasant supporters. As we shall see in more detail below, many highland villagers had experienced the earlier part of the war as a violent incursion of the Peruvian state, most notably in the form of taxes and conscription. For the Indians and peasants of Jaén, the prewar commercial penetration and the increasing presence of the state had meant one and the same thing: a challenge to their subsistence from the outside. Becerra was able, through astute populism, to unite these sentiments into a powerful movement against the collaborationist Peruvian government and the foreign invader (ADC 1884e, d; 1885d). His most powerful weapons in doing so were his attacks on prominent highland landowners, his opposition to the head tax, and the fact that he fought with a volunteer army. And one must not forget his sense of theater: there is no image more telling in this regard than the description of Becerra riding into one of his strongholds in Jaén province, appropriating two hundred receipts for the head tax, and tearing them up in the central plaza to general applause (ADC 1884e).

Becerra's movement was thus a motley coalition of rebellious hacendados, ambitious merchants and local notables, and dispossessed or pauperized peasants. What kept them together was a variety of antistate feelings that had emerged, for different reasons within each group, in the prewar and early war period. Yet in what sense can we consider this movement to be nationalist? Certainly in terms of the initial perceptions or feelings involved, we cannot. People joined Becerra to defend themselves from the incursions of the Peruvian state against its own people in the form of head taxes, war contributions, and conscription, rather than because they wanted to defend their homes against a foreign invader. If some specific leaders, such as Becerra himself, were motivated at least in part by a desire to resist the Chileans, this did not a nationalist movement make. The irony of it all would be that, once the Peruvian state began to collaborate with the Chilean army, and especially once Chilean forces made incursions into the highlands, Becerra's montonera became nationalist almost by default.

What is most interesting about Becerra's movement is that it shows us how a previous history of class and ethnic conflict and of relations with a state can condition the extent to which nationalism emerges in the context of a foreign occupation. The very weakness of the state in the area before the war meant that, during a national emergency, its efforts to collect resources and raise an army resulted in violence and aggression against the peasantry's conditions of production. It was the Peruvian state itself, then, that first acted as a foreign invader in the northern highlands. In reaction to this, a multifaceted alliance emerged among a series of groups and classes: antistate landowners and peasants, Indians resisting commercial penetration, and merchants attempting to marginalize larger land-owners from the profits of Jaén's commercial boom. Both Becerra's as-tute political sense and their common antigovernment position kept them together for the duration: but after his death in 1885 and Cáceres' triumph over Iglesias, there was no common vision or project to bind them any longer. Indeed, in the postwar confusion it would be the differences among them that would float to the surface (ADC 1886).

While sharing some similarities with Becerra's movement, the second major center of resistance against the occupation and the collaborationist Peruvian government was located in a very different part of Cajamarca and composed of very different people. Led by José Mercedes Puga, a prominent hacendado from southern Cajamarca province, this movement started later and had more of a base on highland haciendas. It began as a response to Miguel Iglesias' political actions in the period between Au-gust and December 1882, and involved political differences and personal rivalries between the Puga and Iglesias families that dated back to the prewar years.

Iglesias and Puga had confronted each other over issues of local power for years before the war, becoming legendary rivals in the province of Cajamarca. In the 1860s and 1870s, they had lined up on opposite sides of the emerging national factions, more for local than ideological reasons, with Iglesias becoming a Pierolista and Puga a Civilista (Taylor 1979: 81–82; Manrique 1981: 218–20). When Piérola organized the defense of Lima in late 1880, therefore, it is hardly surprising that Iglesias was called upon to organize the northern army, while Puga apparently sat on the sidelines and dragged his feet in contributing to the defense effort (AHM 1880; ADC 1882g). Puga was even further alienated from the political process when Montero named Iglesias his successor in the north; but it seems that the Chilean invasion of Cajamarca in mid-1882 and the forced contributions they placed on the local population began to change Puga's mind. This was especially true given the rather lukewarm defense of the region organized by Iglesias (Manrique 1981: 219–22; Basadre 1968–69: 8:408–11). Thus when Iglesias issued the Cry of Montán, and even more important when he organized a constituent assembly in Cajamarca to legitimate his role as national leader, Puga decided to act. As of Decem-ber 1882, there are references to his participation in a growing rebel move-ment directly to the south of Cajamarca city, in the area between the dis-tricts of San Marcos and Ichocán and the city of Cajabamba (Basadre 1968–69: 8:410–12; Manrique 1981: 222; ADC 1882h–i, 1883b). Once again in contrast to its established image in the literature, however, Puga's mon-tonera was not composed mainly of his direct dependents or hacienda peons.

Ichocán and San Marcos, both centers of rebel activity, were villages with a history of resisting taxation and conscription. In July 1880, for example, the governor of Ichocán district was attacked by a group of two hundred women and fifty men, armed with stones and sticks, as he attempted to lead a group of conscripts out of the area (ADC 1880a). During the following year, the authorities encountered major resistance in attempting to tax or draft the local population, often returning from their missions with hands empty. In some cases, people simply retired to the hills; in others, the local habitants—mainly the women—took it upon themselves to defend prospective conscripts by attacking the officials (ADC 1881q–r). In San Marcos as well there was violent resistance against local authorities, especially with regard to taxation. In October and November 1882, government representatives had major confrontations with local citizens while they tried to charge the contribución personal (ADC 1882j–n). The most serious incident occurred on October 25, when over five hundred women and men ambushed the governor and his force, shooting at them and attacking them from the surrounding hills (ADC 1882j).

Local reaction was understandable given the methods used by the government. Forced conscription, it seems, was quite common. Soldiers entered the villages breaking down doors in the middle of the night and taking people off at gunpoint. The result was usually that the rest of the population fled the villages, hiding out on the punas or in caves, fearing a repetition of the attack (ADC 1881s). It is of course hard to gauge, on the basis of existing documentation, what proportion of conscripts was taken violently; but correspondence to the prefect's office is full of letters from individuals begging that recruits taken by force be set free (ADC 1880b, g).

Under conditions such as these, with the Peruvian state perceived as the most direct enemy by many villagers, the stage was set for an alliance with several hacendados in San Marcos and Ichocán districts who had also been dragging their feet when faced with draft or war contribution requests (ADC 1881i, 1882g, 1881t). They had hidden possible recruits and criminals within their properties, ignoring official orders to turn men over to local authorities (ADC 1880h, 1881c, 1882a). Since government representatives apparently needed a special warrant to enter haciendas (ADC 1881b), protecting individuals within the borders of large estates was quite effective. As of the last months of 1882, it seems that landowners in San Marcos and Ichocán districts, most notably the owner of hacienda la Pauca, José Mercedes Puga, were extending protection within their borders to all peasants resisting state exactions (ADC 1882a).

Puga had a longstanding relationship with the inhabitants of Ichocán and San Marcos. As was true in many other parts of Cajamarca, these two villages did not have enough land, especially pasture. Many individuals therefore rented lands from Puga, ostensibly as part of an ongoing relationship of patronage and clientele (ADC 1882a, 1883c). This preexisting relation, combined with a common antistate position generated by wartime incursions, formed the glue that held the montonera together.

The other important component of Puga's movement was a sizable proportion of the urban Chinese population, particularly from the city of Cajamarca (AHM 1884b; ADC 1883d). It is difficult to know at this point why they joined; perhaps because they feared being associated with the coastal Chinese who had rebelled against the hacendados and joined with the Chileans, perhaps because their extensive commercial relations in the province had brought them into conflict with members of the anti-Puga faction (ADC 1881u; 1882o; 1880i). Whatever the reasons for their participation, Puga seems to have trusted the Chinese members of his montonera implicitly. In addition to acting as his spies in Cajamarca city (ADC 1883c), it was mainly the Chinese montoneros who escaped with him across the Marañón River when he knew he was being pursued by a superior force in November 1884 (ADC 1884n).

When we look beneath the surface, it is clear that Puga's montonera was much more than a group of his peons fighting under his orders. The second major resistance movement to appear in the department of Cajamarca was a complex alliance of landowners, retainers, village peasants, and urban Chinese. As in the case of Becerra, what seems to have held them together was a common antistate sentiment, though the reasons for it were understandably different in each case. The village peasantry had experienced the Peruvian state's efforts to raise funds and men for the war as a foreign invasion, as an attack on their conditions of production. They had therefore risen up to defend themselves against the outside threat. They had been able to count on the aid of a powerful landowner faction which, for reasons of its own, was also opposing state efforts at taxation. The end result was a powerful and relatively unified montonera that was quite effective in confronting the collaborationist Peruvians as well as the occupation forces. In a similar way to Becerra, however, it only became a nationalist movement because its local enemies ended up collaborating with the foreign invader.

Yet no matter how diverse, Puga's montonera was still hacendado-dominated. This made it quite different from Becerra's movement. The most important hideouts in times of trouble, for example, were on Puga's properties. The haciendas were also the storage place for stolen cattle, and the most effective battle sites (AHM 1883a–d; BNP 1885). And in the end, Puga's own motivations were highly colored by his ongoing conflict with fellow hacendado Miguel Iglesias, probably more so than by an abstract sense of or commitment to a national interest. This was also true of those who fought against him, such as Francisco Baldomero Pinillos, an hacendado from Santiago de Chuco who had been involved in border conflicts with Puga before the war. Pinillos became a rabid Iglesista, leading his own men into battle against Puga's forces and perceiving the entire conflict in localistic terms (BNP 1885).

In the end, neither Becerra's merchant montonera nor Puga's hacienda-oriented movement developed what can be seen as a nationalist vision. Both were diverse coalitions of people, held together by an antistate sentiment that in a particular conjuncture prompted them to fight on the nationalist side; but in neither case did events lead them in the direction of elaborating a national project. When the war was over, therefore, and especially after the defeat of Iglesias, fighting in the area unravelled into a confusion of bandit and landowner factions. The confusion was further increased by Puga's and Becerra's deaths in 1885 (BNP 1885; ADC 1885b). Into the early 1890s, it seemed impossible for the Cacerista state to establish control in the region (BNP 1886, 1892, 1895a). It would only be under Nicolás de Piérola, and the post-1895 government of national reconstruction, that the department of Cajamarca was returned to a semblance of order. As was the case in the central highlands, Piérola's bid for power would be supported by the traditional landowning oligarchy eager to reachieve the prewar status quo (BNP 1885b, d–f; 1889d); but what that meant in the north was quite distinct from what it meant in Junín.

Though they had rejected state intervention in the years before the War of the Pacific, by 1895 most members of the landowning oligarchy in Cajamarca were forced to admit they needed some kind of relationship with the state structure. Even if they had not faced an autonomous and militant peasant movement of the kind existing in the central highlands, the disorganization and destruction of the Chilean occupation and subsequent civil strife had badly shaken their economic and political control (Taylor 1979: 86, 177–79). The situation was further exacerbated by the fact that, after 1890, the increasing demand for labor on the coastal sugar plantations threatened to drive a wedge in their monopoly of highland labor power (ibid.: 86–87, 103–5). When Nicolás de Piérola returned to the presidential palace in 1895, then, he was welcomed warmly by many traditional landowning families in Cajamarca who viewed him as a savior come to reestablish their position in local society (BNP 1895c–e, g; 1896d; 1889d). Yet even as they welcomed the state into their areas, landowners in Cajamarca developed a very different relationship with it than did their counterparts in the central sierra.

While in the central highlands the post-1895 state played a strongly interventionist role to favor the hacendados in a relatively even class conflict, in the north it tended to underwrite or rebuild a system of private landowner power. This was possible in part, of course, because of the relative weakness of independent peasant mobilization in the area. It was also possible because the prewar history of class relations had given the landowners a strong territorial and political base from which to work. The end result was an hacendado-state relationship that looked a great deal more like traditional *gamonalismo* (rule by landed oligarchs) than it did in the center of the country. In exchange for sanctioning the continued privatization of power in the countryside, the government was assured collaboration from local landlords. And the deal seemed to work to a great extent. Although the army did periodically have to participate in repressing the banditry endemic to such a system (Taylor 1979: 106–15; Gitlitz 1980), until the 1960s the police were not allowed to penetrate the borders of the great estates in highland Cajamarca (Montoya 1981).

CONCLUSIONS

The case studies of the northern and central highlands provide us with an empirically rich and complex view of each region's participation in the War of the Pacific. By following each case through to the postwar attempts at national reconstruction and unification, we can also trace the impact of local events before and during the war on the particular form taken by state expansion in each area. Several things are clear from such an analysis. First, that the prewar history of people's interaction with their conditions of production, as well as the previous nature of class conflict, set the parameters within which resistance movements developed and gave them their specific character. Second, that the events of the war itself — the nature and length of occupation, the attitude of local elites vis-à-vis the Chileans, and the actions taken by the Peruvian state at the local level — also conditioned the type of resistance movement and whether or not it developed nationalist consciousness. And finally the proof of the pudding, so to speak, was in the postwar process of national unification. While the destruction of the war itself and subsequent difficulties with re-establishing political control certainly disciplined regional oligarchies into perceiving their need for state support, the particular nature of the state-regional landowner pact varied according to the patterns of power and conflict already established by previous events. Perhaps a quick overview of each region, with these questions in mind, can best clarify these points.

In the northern highlands, the lack of a strong peasant community combined with the powerful territorial presence of the hacienda to yield an unequal class conflict in the prewar years. Except in the northern province of Jaén, where landowners welcomed state aid in attempting to dominate commercial production against the resistance of intermediate merchants and local smallholders, most hacendados in the department of Cajamarca did not see the advantage to participating in a process of national unification. The peasants in the area were also leery of the state, since it did not have the strength to counter landowner power and would simply graft a new set of obligations onto those already owed to local powerholders. As a result, the prior attempts at state formation in the northern sierra were ineffective; hacendados participated in national politics only as an extension of local factional conflicts.

When the war came, Cajamarcans experienced it first as an incursion of the state against their conditions of production. This was true because the very weakness of state influence in the region forced government officials to raise by force the money and men needed for the war effort. When combined with the weak and sporadic presence of the Chilean invaders, this meant that, for many people, the main contradiction during the war years continued to be the oppressive presence of the Peruvian state. Building on this common antistate feeling, Chota merchants and Cajamarcan landowners each developed a multiclass montonera which, even while fighting on the nationalist side, never developed nationalist consciousness.

In addition to not developing nationalist consciousness, these montoneras also maintained their multiclass nature. Once the war was over, therefore, despite the high levels of conflict, the local oligarchy did not face a strong class challenge. Able to rebuild the status quo from a position of relative strength, hacendados in Cajamarca participated in the process of national unification on the basis of receiving state aid to reconstruct and reproduce a system of localized and privatized landowner power.

The situation was quite distinct in the central highlands. In the prewar period, a dynamic and relatively autonomous peasant community had been able to resist elite efforts at labor acquisition and maintain control of important agricultural resources. Given the stalemate in class conflict, both peasants and landowners welcomed the participation of the state in local politics during the 1860s and 1870s. By the time of the war, both classes were attempting to use the process of state formation to their advantage, especially through the manipulation of municipal law in the struggle over local labor and revenue.

In contrast to the north, the early war did not produce an antistate reaction in the central highlands. Eager to strengthen their connections to the state, central sierra landowners organized two battalions to fight in Lima. Medium-sized merchants and even wealthy peasants seem also to have volunteered (Valladares 1977; AHM 1918; Bravo G. 1971: 654–58). When the local population felt the war's incursion into their conditions of production, then, it was in the form of a Chilean occupation of the region, rather than forced conscription or taxation by the Peruvian state.

Thus the prewar and wartime events in the central sierra set the conditions for the development of nationalist consciousness. The intensity of previous class conflict, however, militated against the maintenance of a single nationalist vision. So did the protracted and destructive occupation of the area by Chilean troops. For the landowners, the final result was an attempt to defend their conditions of production against both Chileans and Peruvian peasants by seeking peace at any price. For the peasants, whose resistance to the Chileans was based in their communities and increasingly autonomous from outside control, the outcome was the development of an independent peasant nationalism which, depending on the specific part of the central highlands, was more or less hostile to the landowning class.

When the war was over the dominant landowners in the area, mainly concentrated in the southern part of the Mantaro Valley, had lost control of their properties to a hostile and nationalist peasant class. In the area around Comas, where the movement reached its ultimate logical conclusion, an independent peasant confederation with an elementary national project survived into the twentieth century. Faced with such a strong class challenge, the regional oligarchy in the central sierra did not have the basis for independent power that would have allowed a pact with the post-1895 state similar to that developed in Cajamarca. Instead, they participated in the process of national unification in exchange for state repression of the peasantry and assistance in labor control.

In 1888, at a fundraiser given by Lima's schoolchildren to collect money to ransom Tacna and Arica from the Chileans, Manuel González Prada spoke on a theme often repeated in his writings about the War of the Pacific. Peru was not defeated by the Chilean army, he insisted, but mainly by its own lack of freedom. "I am talking, Gentlemen," he explained, "of freedom for everyone, and principally for the less fortunate. The real Peru is not made up of groups of creoles and foreigners who inhabit the strip of land between the Pacific Ocean and the Andes; the nation is made up of the Indian multitudes spread along the eastern slopes of the mountains" (1915: 78). In this speech, González Prada raised a question that would reappear again and again among Peruvian intellectuals, especially in the first decades of the twentieth century. If Peru was not yet a unified nation, upon whom should this unity be based? For many, in a more or a less romantic way, the unity was to be based on the Indian masses who composed the broad majority of the country's population. Often, however, the vision of how to accomplish this goal remained frustratingly fuzzy, with little sense of who those Indians were or what their view of or interest in a nation might entail (Arguedas 1975, Degregori n.d., DESCO 1981, Flores G. 1981).

This consistent lack of clarity among intellectuals is particularly ironic in view of how long a history protonational traditions have had in the Andes. As is clear from other contributions to this volume, the dream of an indigenous, pan-Andean nation was nurtured among the folds of the colonial social formation, reemerging in numerous forms—not only with the Túpac Amaru rebellion—until well into the nineteenth century. And it is in this context that the experience of the Comas peasantry between 1881 and 1902 takes on its greatest meaning. While we would have to compare the Comasinos to peasants from more heavily indigenous regions in order to weigh the ethnic factor more completely, certainly the Andean tradition of reemerging protonationalism, in which the Comasinos also shared, provided a framework that facilitated the emergence of a certain nationalist perspective. In combination with the harshness of the Chilean invasion in the central highlands and the resilience of their own local communal institutions, the Andean tradition provided the Comas peasants with the resources to fashion their own particular vision of the nation.

Yet we should not overemphasize the uniqueness of the Comas case. While the Comasinos' historical experience with nationalisim is striking and distinct, it is certainly not the only case historians have found in Latin America. My own research on the states of Morelos and Puebla in Mexico (in progress), as well as the work of Leticia Reina (1980) on the Sierra Gorda and the state of Veracruz, have begun to explore cases in which peasants, often though not exclusively in the context of a foreign invasion, begin to formulate their own alternative visions of how the nation should be organized. One culmination of these visions for Mexico would be found in the Zapatista program during the 1910 Revolution (Womack 1969).

For each case, however, the specific set of conditions under which peasants lived would yield a particular form of nationalist consciousness. The Comasinos formed theirs in reaction to a Chilean invasion that attacked them in their very homes, building off a protonational Andean tradition, and in the context of a resistance movement organized by communities and given a great deal of local autonomy. Despite their continuing existence in a precapitalist economy, therefore, the Comasinos were indeed able to develop nationalism. Yet their particular brand of nationalism, emerging as it did from their relation to the conditions of production, had a peasant base. It envisioned a society in which local autonomy would nurture local prosperity, without landowner oppression or state exactions, and where a larger confederation could handle commerce, infrastructure, and a common defense. It recognized the need for alliance with other classes, and for help from leaders who had a broader political preparation and vision. Indeed, throughout the war and postwar periods it called out for coalition with other classes that, given their common relation to the conditions of production, would be willing to ally with the peasantry in the defense and construction of a nation.

Yet it is here that the development of nationalist consciousness came into conflict with the process of national unification. Once the war was over, the easiest and most viable class base for reconstruction was the landowning oligarchy. A peasant program for reform, for nation-building, was fundamentally at odds with such a base. Given the regionalization of class formation and class conflict before the war, and the diverse wartime experiences of the various regions, there were no allies in other parts of the country who might have collaborated in constructing a different nation-building coalition.

When the Comas peasants stood up in 1888, along with their parish priest and a judge from Ica, and waved their alternative national program, no one was ready to listen. In the next decades, when intellectuals would recognize the desirability, even the urgency, of constructing a nation based on the needs of the majority of the population, the Comasinos would no longer be in a position to do anything about it. Even today, one hundred years after the Comas coalition began and long after Peru had undergone an effective process of national unification, the challenge of basing national unity on the needs of the majority remains unmet. Understanding the alternative national visions of groups like the Comasinos, then, as well as the conditions that facilitate or impede their development, should constitute an initial step in finally meeting that well-worn challenge.

NOTES

1 A somewhat different approach within Marxism, best symbolized by Rosa Luxemburg, has recently received renewed attention. See especially Davis 1978 and Luxemburg 1976.

2 In addition to the sources already cited, an overview of the literature is presented in Smith 1973. Some more recent sources have reproduced the "top-down" bias in the literature on nationalism and nation formation by either avoiding the role of the popular classes altogether, or by seeing them only as passive recipients of change coming in from the outside. See, respectively, Tilly 1975 and Weber 1977. Even the literature on non-Western nationalism or anti-colonialism tends to see it as an ideology imported from the West through local

bourgeoisies. For recent critiques, see Davis 1978; Deeb 1973; Hardiman 1981; Mallon 1981; Manrique 1981. Yet the critiques have not presented a convincing alternative theory of the nature or genesis of popular nationalism (Arnold 1982).

3　It is here that I part company with Borojov's analysis (1979: 67–69), since it does not follow from his own logic that nationalism can only develop with the rise of capitalism and of the bourgeoisie as a class.

4　The assessment of Cevallos' counterinsurgency campaign is based on twenty-six documents found in the APJ. They are listed in Mallon 1983: 117–20, footnotes 107–23.

5　Much of this evidence is indirect, such as the fact that the nonpayment of the *contribución* becomes a big issue in the rebellious villages of Chota and Jaén provinces (ADC 1884b–d), and that one of the *montonera* tactics for gathering support is to tear up the receipts for the Indian head tax (ADC 1884e).

6　He and members of his family had connections both in Chota and Jaén provinces during the 1870s and 1880s. By 1886 Santos Vílchez, Becerra's brother-in-law, was firmly established as the leader of the "outsider" faction in the district of Bellavista, something that meant, most probably, a prewar presence in the area (ADC 1886). And in 1881 Vílchez had been postulated as a candidate for municipal office in Cutervo district, province of Chota, which also manifested his connections there (ADC 1881p). Finally, by 1880 it seemed a fairly established practice for local notables active in the municipalities of Chota to travel to Jaén on commerce (ADC 1880e).

REFERENCES

Abbreviations　ADC　　　　Archivo Departamental de Cajamarca
　　　　　　　　AHM　　　　Archivo Histórico-Militar (Lima)
　　　　　　　　APJ　　　　Archivo Prefectural de Junín (Huancayo)
　　　　　　　　BNP　　　　Biblioteca Nacional del Perú: Sala de
　　　　　　　　　　　　　　Investigaciones
　　　　　　　　SINAMOS　Archivo de Comunidades, Oficina Regional de
　　　　　　　　　　　　　　SINAMOS (Huancayo)

ADAMS, RICHARD N.
1959　　A Community in the Andes: Problems and Progress in Muquiyauyo. Seattle: University of Washington Press.
ADC
1880a　　"Oficio del Gobernador Santos G. Cobán al Prefecto." Distrito de Ichocán: July 18. Gobernadores del Distrito de Ichocán, 1856–99.
1880b　　Una serie de solicitudes de diferentes personas al Prefecto del Departamento, protestando el enrolamiento de hombres en el ejército. Varios lugares y fechas. Particulares, 1880–89.

1880c "Oficio del Gobernador de San Felipe al Subprefecto de Jaén." April 29. Subprefectura de Jaén, 1880–89.

1880d "Oficio del Gobernador Manuel María Lazo al Prefecto." April 8. Gobernadores del Distrito de San Marcos, 1854–99.

1880e "Oficio del Subprefecto Eulogio Osores al Prefecto." June 20. Subprefectura de Chota, 1880–89.

1880f "Oficio del Subprefecto Eulogio Osores al Prefecto." May 25. Subprefectura de Chota, 1880–89.

1880g "Solicitud de María López, indígena de Cajabamba." July 20. Particulares, 1880–89.

1880h "Oficio del Gobernador Manuel María Lazo al Prefecto." April 8. Gobernadores de San Marcos, 1854–99.

1880i "Dn. Juan Chavarria con Dn. Luis Maradiegue, sobre entrega de dos caballos." Cajamarca: May 19. Corte Superior de Justicia, Causas ordinarias, Legajo No. 54.

1881a "Carta del hacendado Daniel Silva Santisteban al Subprefecto de la provincia." Hacienda Chonta: April 21. Particulares, 1880–89.

1881b "Oficio del Gobernador José Gastañaduy al Subprefecto." n.d. Gobernadores del Distrito de San Marcos, 1854–99.

1881c "Oficio del Gobernador José Gastañaduy al Subprefecto." December 13. Governadores del Distrito de San Marcos, 1854–99.

1881d "Circular del Prefecto P.J. Carrión al Subprefecto del Cercado." Sept. 1. Prefectura, 1880–85.

1881e "Oficio de Manuel María Arana, hacendado de La Laguna, al Subprefecto." Cajamarca: January 22. Particulares, 1880–89.

1881f "Resolución del Jefe Superior del Norte, comunicado por el Prefecto Tadeo Terry al Subprefecto del Cercado." Oct. 19. Prefectura, 1880–85.

1881g "Decreto del Prefecto Tadeo Terry sobre la solicitud de Dn. Carlos Montoya Bernal, apoderado de María Arana." Oct. 15. Prefectura, 1880–85.

1881h "Oficio del Subprefecto Manuel B. Castro a las autoridades de su dependencia." Sept. 22. Subprefectura de Cajamarca, 1880–85.

1881i "Oficio del Subprefecto Manuel Castro al Prefecto." Oct. 28. Subprefectura de Cajamarca, 1880–85.

1881j "Oficio del hacendado Francisco Arana al gobernador de Chetilla." Caraden: Aug. 16. Particulares, 1880–89.

1881k "Oficio de la hacendada Norverta Villavicencio." Sacas: Dec. 28. Particulares, 1880–89.

1881l "Oficio de Francisco A. Lizarzaburu, hacendado de Yaden, distrito de Cascas, al Prefecto de Cajamarca." Trujillo: Dec. 10. Particulares, 1880–89.

1881m "Oficio del Prefecto Leonardo Cavero al Subprefecto del Cercado." May 13. Prefecturas, 1880–85.

1881n   "Oficio del Subprefecto Manuel J. Becerra al Prefecto, acusando recibo de la copia del oficio de Montero." May 22. Subprefectura de Chota, 1880–89.

1881o   "Oficio del Subprefecto Domingo Lacerna al Prefecto." April 30. Subprefectura de Chota, 1880–89.

1881p   "Terna para gobernador del distrito de Cutervo, presentada por Manuel A. Negrón." Chota: March 28. Subprefectura de Chota, 1880–89.

1881q   "Oficio del Gobernador Cobrán al Subprefecto." Sept. 18. Gobernadores del Distrito de Ichocán, 1856–99.

1881r   "Oficio del Gobernador Cobrán al Subprefecto." Dec. 12. Gobernadores del Distrito de Ichocán, 1856–99.

1881s   "Oficio del Gobernador Accidental Lucas Carrera al Subprefecto." Sept. 2. Gobernadores del Distrito de Ichocán, 1856–99.

1881t   "Oficio del Gobernador Lizardo Zevallos al Subprefecto." June 26. Gobernadores del Distrito de San Marcos, 1854–99.

1881u   "El asiático Wing-Walon con Don Justiniano Guerrero sobre cumplimiento de un contrato." Cajamarca: Oct. 15. Corte Superior de Justicia, Causas ordinarias, Legajo No. 58.

1882a   "Oficia del Gobernador Manuel Rubio al Subprefecto." May 15. Gobernadores del Distrito de San Marcos, 1854–99.

1882b   "Oficio del Subprefecto de Jaén al Prefecto." Pucará: Dec. 10. Subprefectura de Jaén, 1880–89.

1882c   "Oficio del Subprefecto Pajares al Prefecto." Oct. 13. Subprefectura de Cajamarca, 1880–85.

1882d   "Oficio del Subprefecto Guillermo Serna al Prefecto." Jan. 21. Subprefectura de Cajamarca, 1880–85.

1882e   "Oficio del Subprefecto Manuel J. Becerra al Prefecto." Feb. 4. Subprefectura de Chota, 1880–89.

1882f   "Oficio del Subprefecto J. de la R. Salgado al Prefecto." May 20. Subprefectura de Jaén, 1880–89.

1882g   "Oficio del Subprefecto Serna al Prefecto." Feb. 19. Subprefectura de Cajamarca, 1880–85.

1882h   "Oficio del Gobernador Hilario Padilla al Subprefecto de Cajamarca." Nov. 23. Gobernadores del Distrito de San Marcos, 1854–99.

1882i   "Oficio del Gobernador Manuel Rubio al Subprefecto de Cajamarca." Dec. 28. Gobernadores del Distrito de San Marcos, 1854–99.

1882j   "Oficio del Gobernador Manuel Rubio al Subprefecto." Oct. 25. Gobernadores del Distrito de San Marcos, 1854–99.

1882k   "Oficio del Gobernador Manuel Rubio al Subprefecto de la provincia." Oct. 12. Gobernadores del Distrito de San Marcos, 1854–99.

1882l   "Oficio del Gobernador Manuel Rubio al Subprefecto de la provincia." Sept. 20. Gobernadores del Distrito de San Marcos, 1854–99.

1882m   "Oficio del Gobernador Manuel Rubio al Subprefecto de Cajamarca." Oct. 27. Gobernadores del Distrito de San Marcos, 1854–99.

1882n   "Oficio del Gobernador Manuel Rubio al Subprefecto de Cajamarca." Oct. 31. Gobernadores del Distrito de San Marcos, 1854–99.

1882o   "D. Manuel Rubio con el asiático Colorado sobre pago de cantidad de soles." Cajamarca: Jan. 11. Corte Superior de Justicia, Causas ordinarias, Legajo No. 62.

1883a   "Oficio del Subprefecto J. de la R. Salgado al Prefecto." Pucará: April 1. Subprefectura de Jaén, 1880–89.

1883b   "Oficio del Gobernador Manuel Rubio al Subprefecto." Jan. 25. Gobernadores de San Marcos, 1854–99.

1883c   "Oficio del Alcalde Pedro W. Zevallos al Prefecto." Ichocán: July 31. Alcaldías de los distritos de Cajamarca, 1855–99.

1883d   "Solicitud de Francisco Deza, asiático, al Prefecto del Departamento." Cajamarca: Dec. 7. Particulares, 1880–89.

1884a   "Oficio de la Abadesa del Convento de Religiosas Descalzas Concebidas de Cajamarca, al Prefecto." Oct. 28. Particulares, 1880–89.

1884b   "Oficio del Subprefecto de Chota al Prefecto del departamento." May 12. Subprefectura de Chota, 1880–89.

1884c   "Oficio del Subprefecto de Chota al Prefecto del Departamento, transcribiendo oficio del gobernador del distrito de Llama." May. Subprefectura de Chota, 1880–89.

1884d   "Oficio del Subprefecto de Jaén al Prefecto." Cutervo: Oct. 15. Subprefectura de Jaén, 1880–89.

1884e   "Oficio del Subprefecto de Jaén al Prefecto." Cutervo: Sept. 7. Subprefectura de Jaén, 1880–89.

1884f   "Oficio del Subprefecto de Chota Timoteo Tirado al Prefecto." Jan. 7. Subprefectura de Chota, 1880–89.

1884g   "Oficio del Subprefecto de Chota Timoteo Tirado al Prefecto." Feb. 6. Subprefectura de Chota, 1880–89.

1884h   "Oficio del Subprefecto Accidental de Chota al Prefecto." Feb. 13. Subprefectura de Chota, 1880–89.

1884i   "Oficio del Subprefecto de Jaén al Prefecto del Departamento." Cutervo: n.d. Subprefectura de Jaén, 1880–89.

1884j   "Oficio del Subprefecto de Chota Timoteo Tirado al Prefecto." Bambamarca: May 26. Subprefectura de Chota, 1880–89.

1884k   "Oficio del Subprefecto de Chota al Prefecto del Departamento." Dec. 18. Subprefectura de Chota, 1880–89.

1884l   "Oficio del Gobernador del Cercado de Jaén al Prefecto." July 28. Gobernadores de los Distritos: Jaén, 1855–98.

1884m   "Oficio del Subprefecto de Jaén al Prefecto." Cutervo: Nov. 3. Subprefectura de Jaén, 1880–89.

1884n   "Oficio de Gregorio Relayze, Prefecto del Departamento de Cajamarca en comisión y Comandante General de la 4ª División, al Prefecto Accidental de Cajamarca." Cajabamba: Nov. 16. Prefectura, 1880–85.

1885a   "Marjesí de las Rentas de la extinguida Beneficencia de la Provincia de Jaén presentada por el Subprefecto Baltazar Contreras," Caja-marca: March 15. Subprefectura de Jaén, 1880–89.

1885b   "Solicitud de Manuel Collazos al presidente de la República Miguel Iglesias," Lima: Nov. 3. Particulares. f. 1.

1885c   "Oficio del Subprefecto de Jaén Baltazar Contreras al Prefecto." Sept. 10. Subprefectura de Jaén, 1880–89.

1885d   "Oficio del Subprefecto de Chota al Prefecto." Jan. 4. Subprefectura de Chota, 1880–89.

1885e   "Oficio del Subprefecto de Jaén al Prefecto." Cutervo: Feb. 6. Sub-prefectura de Jaén, 1880–89.

1885f   "Oficio del Subprefecto de Jaén al Prefecto." Cutervo: Feb. 14. Sub-prefectura de Jaén, 1880–89.

1885g   "Oficio del Subprefecto de Chota al Prefecto." Mar. 27. Subprefec-tura de Chota, 1880–89.

1885h   "Oficio del Subprefecto de Jaén al Prefecto." Cutervo: May 13. Sub-prefectura de Jaén, 1880–89.

1885i   "Oficio de Baltazar Contreras al Alcalde Pedro Ceballos." Cutervo: May 25. Particulares, 1880–89.

1885j   "Oficio de Nicolás Tellos, Hacienda Llaucan, al Prefecto del Departa-mento." Nov. 18. Particulares, 1880–89.

1886   "Informe del Subprefecto Arróspide al Prefecto." Jaén: Oct. 11. Sub-prefectura de Jaén, 1880–89.

1887   "Informe del Subprefecto Arróspide sobre la provincia de Jaén," May 2. Subprefectura de Jaén, 1880–89.

1888   "Observaciones del Subprefecto Miguel Arróspide sobre el Presupu-esto para 1889." Apr. 16. Subprefectura de Jaén, 1880–89.

AHM

1880   "Organización del Ejército del Norte dictada por el General Miguel Iglesias." Lima: Jan. 3. Collección Vargas Ugarte, Legajo 54.

1883a   "Oficio del Comandante en Jefe de las fuerzas del Norte al Ministro de Estado en el Despacho de Guerra y Marina." San Marcos: De-cember. Correspondencia General, Paquete 0.1883.1.

1883b   "Oficio del Comandante en Jefe de las fuerzas del Norte al Ministro de Estado en el Despacho de Guerra y Marina." Cajamarca: Dec. 9. Correspondencia General, Paquete 0.1883.1.

1883c   "Oficio de José Mercedes Puga a Recavarren." Hacienda Huagal: July 18. Collección Recavarren, Manuscritos, Cuaderno No. 10: pp. 72–73.

1883d   "Oficio del Jefe de las fuerzas expedicionarias al distrito de la As-unción." Cajamarca: May 6. Paquete 0.1883.2: Ordenes Generales y Correspondencia.

1884a   "Oficio del Prefecto de Junín Andrés Recharte al Ministerio de Guer-ra," Huancayo: Dec. 10. Paquete 0.1884.6: Prefecturas.

1884b   "Oficio del Comandante en Jefe de las fuerzas del Norte al Ministro de Estado en el Despacho de Guerra y Marina." Cajamarca: Jan. 6. Correspondencia General, Paquete 0.1883.1 [sic].

1885a   "Oficio del Prefecto Relayze al Oficial Mayor en el Despacho de Guerra y Marina, transcribiendo el oficio del Subprefecto de Huancayo." Cerro de Pasco: Feb. 2. Paquete 1885 s/n.

1885b   "Parte del Coronel Eduardo Jessup, Comandante General de la Primera División, al Comandante General en Jefe del Ejército del Centro." Huancayo: May 12. Paquete 0.1885.2.

1918   "Memorias sobre la Resistencia de la Breña del Teniente Coronel Ambrosio Salazar y Márquez (Escrita por su hermano Juan P. Salazar)." Huancayo.

AHUMADA MORENO, PASCUAL

1891   *Guerra del Pacífico (Documentos).* 8 vols. Valparaíso: Imprenta de la Librería del Mercurio.

APJ

1882a   "Acta del pueblo de Sincos ofreciendo tomar armas en defensa de la honra Nacional." Apr. 11.

1882b   "Oficio de los guerrilleros de Acobamba a Jacinto Cevallos." Apr. 16.

1884   "Prefecto del Departamento al Gobernador del Distrito de Comas." Huancayo: July 31.

1886a   "Juan E. Valladares al Ministro de Gobierno." Huancayo: June 7.

1886b   "Ministerio de Gobierno al Prefecto del Departamento de Junín." Lima: Aug. 3.

1886c   "Juan E. Valladares y otros al Prefecto del Departamento." Huancayo: Aug. 10.

1887   "Oficio de varios vecinos de Comas al Prefecto del Departamento." Jauja: Sept. 9.

1888   "Autoridades de Comas a las autoridades de Uchubamba." Comas: Jan. 25.

1897   "Informe de la Subprefectura de Huancayo al Prefecto del Departamento." Huancayo: Feb. 17.

ARGUEDAS, JOSÉ MARÍA

1975   "Razón de ser del indigenismo en el Perú." In Angel Rama, ed., *Formación de una cultura nacional indoamericana.* Mexico City: Siglo XXI Editores.

ARNOLD, DAVID

1982   "Review of David Hardiman, *Peasant Nationalists of Gujarat." The Journal of Peasant Studies* 10, 1: 118–21.

BASADRE, JORGE

1948   *Chile, Perú y Bolivia independientes.* Barcelona–Buenos Aires: Salvat Editores, S.A.

1968-69 *Historia de la República del Perú,* 6th ed. 17 vols. Lima: Editorial Universitaria.

BNP

1883   "Oficio N° 3: Prefecto de Cajamarca Miguel Pajares, al Director de Gobierno." Cajamarca: Doc. No. D3712.

1885   "Nota dirigida por el Prefecto y Comandante General del Departamento de la Libertad D. Z. Relayze adjuntándole documentos relativos a la invasión de la provincia de Huamachuco por el caudillo Dr. José Mercedes Puga." Trujillo: Mar. 29. Doc. No. D3710.

1886 "Memoria que presenta el Prefecto de Lambayeque, Crel. Federico Ríos, al Ministro de Gobierno, Policía y Obras Públicas sobre el estado del Departamento a su mando." Chiclayo: Apr. 26. Doc. No. D3980.

1888 "Nuevo Personal de los Concejos Distritales, Junín." June. Doc. No. D6954.

1888-89 "Parte oficial sobre la expedición a Punto." Doc. No. D11466.

1889a "Oficio de Emiliano Carvallo al Director de Gobierno." Tarma: Mar. 10. Doc. No. D12846.

1889b "Comisión especial del Supremo Gobierno, Decretos sobre Potaca y Chongos Alto vs. Antapongo, Chupaca vs. Aliaga." April. Doc. No. D8207.

1889c "Nueva petición de Chongos Alto sobre linderos con Antapongo," May 13. Doc. No. D12844.

1889d "Oficio de Piérola al Presidente del Comité Departamental de Trujillo, José María de la Puente." July 3. Archivo Piérola: Copiador No. 16, 1889-90: Correspondencia Oficial y Particular, Norte.

1892 "Memoria del Subprefecto de Cajamarca, Tomás Ballón, al Prefecto del Departamento." Cajamarca: June 3. Doc. No. D5156.

1895a "Notas sobre el envio de una expedición a Gorger con el fin de capturar a Román Egües García y Cia." Cajatambo: Dec. 17. Doc. No. D7611.

1895b "Cartas de Nicolás Rebaza y Santiago Rebaza Demóstenes, de Trujillo, felicitando a Piérola y communicándole ser partidarios fervorosos de él. . . ." Mar. 28. Archivo Piérola: Caja (Antigua) No. 41: 1892-95.

1895c "Carta de Vicente González y Orbegoso a Piérola." Hacineda Motil: April 12. Archivo Piérola: Caja (Antigua) No. 41: 1892-95.

1895d "Carta de Rafael Villanueva a Piérola." Cajamarca: Apr. 13. Archivo Piérola: Caja (Antigua) No. 41: 1892-95.

1895e "Carta de José María de la Puente a Piérola." Trujillo: July 13. Archivo Piérola: Caja (Antigua) No. 45: 1895.

1895f "Carta de Isidro Burga a Piérola." Cajamarca: June 17. Archivo Piérola: Caja (Antigua) No. 45: 1895.

1895g "Oficio de Isidro Burga a Cruz Toribio Ortiz." May 29. Archivo Piérola: Caja (Antigua) No. 45: 1895.

1896a "Oficio del Prefecto del Departamento de Junín al Director de Gobierno, adjuntándole el acta suscrita por los vecinos del pueblo de Comas y oficio del cura-párroco del lugar." Tarma, Nov. 6. Doc. No. D5048.

1896b "Pacificación de Comas y Acta de Adhesión al Supremo Gobierno." Tarma-Jauja: Nov. 21-23. Doc. No. D5051.

1896c "Pacificación de Andamarca y acta de adhesión al Supremo Gobierno." Tarma-Andamarca: Nov. 23. Doc. No. 5046.

1896d   "Carta de José María de la Puente a Piérola." Trujillo: Jan. 29. Archivo Piérola: Caja (Antigua) No. 53: 1895-97, Correspondencia sobre varios asuntos, ff. 141-42.

BONILLA, HERACLIO

1974   *Guano y burgesía en el Perú.* Lima: Instituto de Estudios Peruanos.

1978   "The War of the Pacific and the National and Colonial Problem in Peru." *Past and Present* (November): 92-118.

BOROJOV, BER

1979   *Nacionalismo y lucha de clases.* Mexico City: Cuadernos de Pasado y Presente, No. 83, Siglo XXI Editores.

BRAVO GUZMÁN, ADOLFO

1971   *La segunda enseñanza en Jauja.* Jauja: 2d ed.

BREUILLY, JOHN

1982   *Nationalism and the State.* New York: St. Martin's Press.

CÁCERES, ANDRÉS A.

1973   *La guerra del 79: Sus campañas (Memorias).* Lima: Editorial Milla Batres, S.A.

CUMMINS, IAN

1980   *Marx, Engels, and National Movements.* New York: St. Martin's Press.

DAVIS, HORACE B.

1967   *Nationalism and Socialism.* New York: Monthly Review Press.

1978   *Toward a Marxist Theory of Nationalism.* New York: Monthly Review Press.

DEEB, MARIUS

1973   "The 1919 Popular Uprising: A Genesis of Egyptian Nationalism." *Canadian Review of Studies in Nationalism* 1, 1: 106-19.

DEERE, CARMEN DIANA

1977   "Changing Relations of Production and Peruvian Peasant Women's Work." *Latin American Perspectives* 4, 1-2 (Winter and Spring): 48-69.

1978   "The Development of Capitalism in Agriculture and the Division of Labor by Sex: A Study of the Northern Peruvian Sierra." Ph.D. Diss., University of California, Berkeley.

DEGREGORI, CARLOS, et al.

n.d.   *Indigenismo, clases sociales y problema nacional.* Lima: Ediciones CELATS.

DESCO

1981   *Problema Nacional, cultura y clases sociales.* Lima.

FLORES GALINDO, ALBERTO

1981   *La agonía de Mariátegui.* Lima: DESCO.

GITLITZ, JOHN S.

1980   "Conflictos Políticos en la Sierra Norte del Perú: La Montonera Benel contra Leguía, 1924." *Estudios Andinos* 9, 16: 127-38.

GONZÁLEZ PRADA, MANUEL
1915   *Páginas Libres*. Madrid: Biblioteca Andrés Bello.
HARDIMAN, DAVID
1981   *Peasant Nationalists of Gujarat: Kheda District, 1917–1934*. New Delhi: Oxford University Press.
HAYES, CARLETON J. H.
1966   *Essays on Nationalism*. New York: Russell and Russell.
HUTCHINSON, WILLIAM B.
1973   "Sociocultural Change in the Mantaro Valley Region of Peru: Acolla, a Case Study." Ph.D. Diss., Indiana University.
KEDOURIE, ELIE
1960   *Nationalism*. London: Hutchinson.
KOHN, HANS
1944   *The Idea of Nationalism*. New York: The Macmillan Co.
LENIN, V. I.
1968   *National Liberation, Socialism and Imperialism*. New York: International Publishers.
LUXEMBURG, ROSA
1976   *The National Question: Selected Writings*. Ed. Horace B. Davis. New York: Monthly Review Press.
LYNCH, PATRICIO
1883–84   *Segunda Memoria que el Vice-Almirante D. Patricio Lynch presenta al Supremo Gobierno de Chile*. 2 vols. Lima: Imp. de la Merced.
MALLON, FLORENCIA E.
1981   "Problema nacional y lucha de clases en la Guerra del Pacífico: La resistencia de la Breña en la Sierra Central, 1881–1886." *Allpanchis* 17–18: 203–31.
1983   *The Defense of Community in Peru's Central Highlands: Peasant Struggle and Capitalist Transition, 1860–1940*. Princeton: Princeton University Press.
MANRIQUE, NELSON
1979   "La ocupación y la resistencia." In Jorge Basadre et al., *Reflecciones en torno a la Guerra de 1879*. Lima: Francisco Campodónico-Centro de Investigación y Capacitación. Pp. 271–331.
1981   *Campesinado y Nación: Las guerrillas indígenas en la guerra con Chile*. Lima: C.I.C.-Ital Perú S.A.
MONTOYA, RODRIGO
1981   Personal conversation with the author. Lima, July.
MORENO DE CÁCERES, ANTONIA
1974   *Recuerdos de la campaña de la Breña (Memorias)*. Lima: Editorial Milla Batres S.A.
ORTEGA, MOISÉS
1977   Interviews and conversations with the author, throughout the year. Acolla, Peru.
PERU
1869   *La Constitución y leyes orgánicas del Perú dadas por el Congreso*

de 1860: "Ley orgánica de municipalidades," Capítulo 1, Artículos 7–9. Lima: Imprenta del Estado.

RÁEZ, NEMESIO A.
1898   *Monografía de la Provincia de Huancayo.* Huancayo: Universidad Nacional del Centro del Perú (2d ed., n.d.).

REINA, LETICIA
·1980   *Las rebeliones campesinas en México (1819–1906).* Mexico City: Siglo XXI Editores.

SAMANIEGO, CARLOS
1978   "Peasant Movements at the Turn of the Century and the Rise of the Independent Farmer." In Norman Long and Bryan R. Roberts, eds., *Peasant Cooperation and Capitalist Expansion in Central Peru.* Austin: University of Texas Press. Pp. 45–71.

SINAMOS
1939   "Expediente sobre la reivindicación del molino de propiedad comunal." cc205 (Marco).

SMITH, ANTHONY D.
1973   *Nationalism: A Trend Report and Bibliography.* The Hague.
1977   (Ed.) *Nationalist Movements.* New York.

STALIN, JOSEPH
1942   *Marxism and the National Question. Selected Writings.* New York: International Publishers.

SYMMONS-SYMONOLEWICZ, KONSTANTIN
1970   *Nationalist Movements: A Comparative View.* Meadville, Pa.: Maplewood Press.
1981   "Some Observations about the Comparative Approach to Nationalism." In Michael Palumbo and William O. Shanahan, eds., *Nationalism.* Westport, Conn.: Greenwood Press. Pp. 60–66.

TAYLOR, LEWIS
1979   "Main Trends in Agrarian Capitalist Development: Cajamarca, Peru, 1880–1976." Ph.D. thesis, University of Liverpool.

TELLO DEVOTTO, RICARDO
1971   *Historia de la provincia de Huancayo*, Huancayo: Casa de la Cultura de Junín.

TILLY, CHARLES (ed.)
1975   *The Formation of National States in Western Europe.* Princeton: Princeton University Press.

VALLADARES, HERNÁN
1977   Interview with the author. Huancayo, June 3.

WEBER, EUGEN
1977   *Peasants into Frenchmen: The Modernization of Rural France.* London: Chatto and Windus.

WOMACK, JOHN, JR.
·1969   *Zapata and the Mexican Revolution.* New York: Alfred A. Knopf.

CHAPTER 10

The Andean Experience of Bolivian Liberalism, 1825–1900: Roots of Rebellion in 19th-Century Chayanta (Potosí)

TRISTAN PLATT

"I, Telésforo Mendoza, tributary Indian of the Provincial capital of Chayanta, declare that your higher authority should instruct your subalterns to provide us with all the guarantees that the Fundamental Charter of the State offers to every person living in this country called Bolivia. The Indian race constitutes the potentiality of this country, because it is owner of its lands since time immemorial. Besides cultivating these lands, whose production sustains all the residents of Bolivia, this race attends to stock-rearing and the transport of merchandise; and it is this race that lives buried in the entrails of the mountains as miners: this is the race that constitutes the strength and wealth of this country of injustice. . . . I have come from far away to demand justice from you, Señor Presidente, whose goodness and honor are known throughout Bolivia. . . . Señor Baptista, I and those of my race demand justice, justice, nothing else but justice; justice which you have the duty to give us."

Signed for the plaintiff, *alcalde* of Puraka
Ayllu, by Plácido Serna. La Paz, 6/11/1893

INTRODUCTION

The Bolivian Revolution of 1899, whose most obvious consequence was the transfer of the seat of government from Sucre to La Paz, represents the climax to a renewed crescendo of popular uprisings that had already

In this article I have made use of materials collected during a project sponsored by the Instituto de Estudios Peruanos (IEP) on *Mining and Economic Space in the Andes, 16th–20th centuries*. Earlier drafts were presented at the University of Wisconsin, the London Institute of Latin American Studies, and the Oxford Centre of Latin American Studies. I am grateful to all those who enriched the final version, and in particular to Olivia Harris and Steve Stern for their detailed comments.

begun before the end of the War of the Pacific (1879–1883). Since the pioneering study of Ramiro Condarco Morales (1965), it has been clear that the mobilization of the Indian communities was a crucial factor in the victory of General Pando's Liberal Party over the Constitutionalist government of President Severo Alonso (1896–1899). Yet the autonomy of Indian objectives within this nineteenth-century "popular front," emphasized by Condarco Morales, has often gone unheeded in later historical treatments of the theme. Alipio Valencia Vega (1973), for example, attributes the conflict to the rivalry between the "mining capitalism" of La Paz and Sucre's "feudal estates" (but see Rivera 1978); while Herbert Klein (1982) posits an underlying competition between northern tin miners and southern silver miners. Neither of these hypotheses is wellfounded, even at the level of the creole leadership; both suggest that Indian participation was subject to the manipulations of Liberal politicians who had "gone beyond the traditional rules" (ibid.: 163).

A different element is introduced by José Fellman Velarde (1970: 289–95), who perceives a struggle between La Paz "middle classes" (the Liberals) and Sucre "ruling classes" (the Constitutionalists) — read, approximately, mestizos and creoles (Anderle 1982). Here Liberal mestizos from the North are supposed to have stimulated an "instinctive reflex" in defense of land among the Indians (who only then, like some vast quagmire, would begin to engulf the unfortunate southern troops) by holding out the carrot of land reform. Embattled by a common enemy identified with the great estate owners of the Constitutionalist oligarchy (here Fellman Velarde draws close to Valencia Vega), it was the middle classes who were able to articulate the "instinctive" yearnings of the Indian masses to find "freedom" as private smallholders amid the burgeoning ranks of a hegemonic petty bourgeoisie. The 1899 Revolution can thus be presented as a frustrated anticipation of the 1952 Revolution directed by Fellman Velarde's own MNR (Nationalist Revolutionary Movement), and the Land Reform decree of 1953 as the triumphal climax to a secular popular aspiration.

This heady mix of vulgar Marxism and mestizo nationalism also distorts certain essential facts. Land privatization was an old creole policy, traceable at least as far back as Bolivar's "dictatorial decrees" of 1825, whose implementation had been seriously attempted under Ballivian (1841–1847) and Melgarejo (1864–1870), before reappearing as the main objective of the "First Agrarian Reform" of 1874. I have elsewhere shown that the same liberal ideology can be detected in the "Second Agrarian Reform" of 1953, which also aimed *in practice* at the consolidation of a "petty commodity" regime of peasant smallholdings (Platt 1982a, 1982b). The evidence from Potosí suggests that it was precisely this objective of

state policy that aroused suspicion and resistance among Indian groups
(*ayllus*). Fellman Velarde's interpretation can therefore be recognized as
a political misreading of a fundamental motive behind Andean rebellion.
It also disguises the fact that, in many areas, agrarian tension had been
generated as much by the encroachment of mestizo smallholdings on ayllu
lands, as by the expansion of the great estates.

Although in the province of Chayanta (Map 8) most mestizos did end
up in the Liberal camp, and were indeed driven into alliance with the
Indians in opposition to the Constitutionalist regime, creole silver miners
and landed oligarchs were not absent from the Liberal leadership. Hence
Fellman Velarde is equally unconvincing when he attributes the reasser-
tion of creole hegemony after 1899 to Constitutionalist infiltration of an

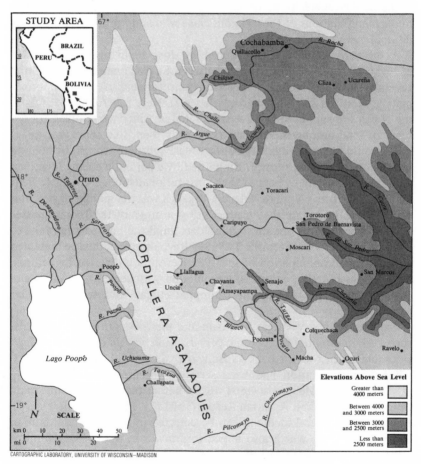

CARTOGRAPHIC LABORATORY, UNIVERSITY OF WISCONSIN–MADISON

Map 8. The Chayanta Region of Northern Potosí

ideologically pure Liberal Party. A simpler explanation would point to the healing of a rupture between two creole factions confronted with the specter of race warfare. As Pando himself put it to Alonso in peace proposals dating from March 4, 1899, "No one can be unaware of the damage that is being done by this fratricidal war; to which may be added, inevitably, that threatened by the caste war that is upon us, impelled by the Indian race itself . . ." (cited in Condarco M. 1965: 295).

There can be little doubt that the Liberal Party tried successfully to exploit the growing contradictions in the nineteenth-century social order, harnessing to their cause forces that soon appeared uncontrollable, and obliged therefore to embrace their vanquished rivals in order to regain control over the Indian "barbarians" that threatened to overturn the creole vision of "civilized" society. But the problems that remain are immense. What was the reality of the mestizo-Indian alliance that Fellman Velarde's account considers so natural? How can it be reconciled with the constant antagonism between these castes over land and local authority? Given that the roots of the Andean movement predate the founding of the two creole parties, how was a convergence achieved between these two forces originating at opposite poles of Bolivian society? Can mestizos be considered "political brokers" between the Indians and the Liberal leadership, and what was their relation with the emerging Indian leadership? How were the different Indian groups, riddled with factionalism, able to overcome their squabbles and fuse into a coherent movement of rebellion?

To answer these questions it is necessary to insist on the importance of an anthropological view from the roots. Students of Andean rebellion have seldom tried, for example, to distinguish between the institutions and representational systems specific to each ethnic group or region, which offer a filter through which changes in state policy and in wider cultural and economic currents are perceived and analyzed. Hence the need to integrate ethnographic perspectives with the documentary evidence in order to detect the mechanisms guiding alliance and conflict in the ayllu-dominated countryside of Chayanta.

One element in Andean-colonial belief systems has received preferential treatment: the Inca-Rey myth, and the widespread Indian hope for their King Inca's "Second Coming" (Ossio 1973; Szemiński 1982). But future studies must distinguish between those readings of "history" characteristic of each region involved in rebellion, as expressed in the changing corpus of their myths (*cuentos*) and rituals (*costumbres*). For example, we still await an analysis of the transformations of the Inca myth between three main foci of the 1780s rebellion: Tinta, Omasuyos, and Chayanta. New questions arise concerning Dámaso Katari's invocation of Túpac Amaru as his Inca-Rey (Lewin 1967: 535), when we observe that, today, the staff of authority (*vara*) borne by the moiety kurakas of Macha (the Katari ethnic group) is called the "royal child" (*rey niño*) of the Inca and his fertile mate (*t'alla*); that the moiety system itself is thought to have originated with the rising of the Inca (and Christian) Sun; that the stones slung between moieties or neighboring ayllus during disputes over land are also called "incas"; that the union between stones and mud that sustains the construction of a new couple's house is also phrased as a meeting between the Inca and his mate (Platt 1976). Did the same name inspire identical symbolic functions in Omasuyos or Tinta? Did the Inca "speak" everywhere the same language?

The Inca, and even the Cult of the Sun, reappear in Chayanta in the 1880s as agglutinating symbols imported from the North. Although we are still unable to propose such an interregional diversity of "readings," the data cited suggest for Chayanta that his name was associated with the origins and reproduction of certain basic social institutions: authority, moieties, ethnic territories, households, justice. In the 1780s, Túpac Amaru would naturally represent the restoration of a "just order" that had been obstructed by Bourbonic abuses (O'Phelan 1985). At independence this function could be contested by republican Citizenship only insofar as the latter was compatible with a restored "pact" with a paternalist State (Platt 1982a). The Inca would only offer a brief political alternative as liberal ideas of "national integration" unleashed a yet more radical assault upon the structure of regional society.

For as the century advanced, fiscal policies aimed at abolishing tributary statuses, atomizing collective units of landholding to establish a land market, creating a new land tax (*predial rústico*) based on the Napoleonic *Catastro* (land register), were all combined with monetary revaluation which increased real tributary values. The tenuous protectionist dikes, which had encouraged Indian reentry into a reviving internal market, were overwhelmed by the rising Free Trade tide, which sought to incorporate Bolivian consumers and raw materials into the oceanic rhythms of a world market. In resisting the First Agrarian Reform, the ayllus were rejecting the most visible of a series of "modernizing" tactics, developed by a creole oligarchy anxious to complete the process of "primitive accumulation" that had preceded the success of its European models. "It is neither Muñoz nor Melgarejo," wrote a pamphleteer (Anónimo 1871), "who has invented the sale of communities; for Muñoz and Melgarejo are the last to sell, because only in Bolivia (to civilization's horror) did communities still exist."

We shall begin by examining the terms of insertion of the Republican ideal into the persisting fabric of Andean-colonial society during the early years prior to the fall of Ballivian in 1847. The problems of the tribute system in Chayanta also illuminate recurring features of local organization. In particular, the moiety collectorships (*recaudadores*) were reestablished under the Republic in the hands of mestizos and whites, who since the Andean defeat of the 1780s had appropriated the product of collective labor in ethnic "common lands" (*comunes*). We shall note Indian efforts to gain control of these collectorships, whose recuperation by the early years of the twentieth century represents one of the most striking features of the emerging ethnohistory of Republican Potosí.

THE FIRST CRISIS OF THE REPUBLICAN TRIBUTE SYSTEM, 1825–1848

The idea of abolishing the Andean ethnic groups, with their hierarchy of reversionary rights and corporate nature, was a policy of enlightened liberalism, designed to transform Indian tributaries into propertied Citizens, subject to the same tax system as all other Bolivians. The bitter conflicts of the second half of the century originated, therefore, in this generous but ethnocidic vision of the creole architects of Independence. On December 22, 1825, following Bolivarian policy, Sucre decreed the replacement of the tribute system by a new direct tax (*contribución directa*) to be levied on all productive capital. The first Catastro of Chayanta was accordingly carried out in 1826 by the Potosí miner José Eustaquio Gareca. This was a register of all "capitalists" (in the terminology of the period) and their means of production. It included owner-occupied houses in the towns, mines and the mineral-processing plant, small traders and saleswomen, artisans and mining employees, as well as various categories of rural property. Indian lands, together with the common lands, were registered apart from other holdings, which were divided into owner-cultivated, rented, and squatters (many of these in the Indian commons).[1]

The separation of Indian lands and commons from lands belonging to other castes was reinforced by the continuing reality of the tribute system: a new Law of December 27, 1826, exempted Indian tributaries from payment of the new land tax, because of the established legitimacy of what the Indians saw as their "single native contribution" (*única contribución de naturales*). In 1827, this argument was used by several ayllus of Chayanta Province to demand a further exemption from the new tax levied on their other property, in particular their houses in the old Indian towns where artisans had their workshops (AHP PDE 80). In 1829 it reappears in ayllu claims to be exempted from the sales tax (*contribución indirecta*) on Indian produce, such as cereals and dessicated potato: "not even the tyrannic Spanish government could fail to exempt us from the *alcabala* on flour," protested the Indian attorneys (*apoderados*) of the Sakaka ethnic group. Emphasizing their eagerness to identify the Republic's interests with their own, but regretting their incapacity to pay due to "the imponderable labors, losses, desolations, and calamities experienced during the revolution," the petition insisted that their production could only stretch to "furnishing our subsistence and the satisfaction of our tribute, or single contribution, and our other duties as Religious Citizens" (ANB MH t.16 no. 22).

The word "citizen" in a text that reaffirms the special treatment to be accorded to Indians, while criticizing the "tyrannic" nature of Spanish rule, must raise queries as to the meaning of the word in Andean discourse. The same question occurred to créole administrators, struck by a new Indian recalcitrance. "The Indians are not as obedient as they were," observed the provincial governor of Chayanta in 1830: "accustomed to the abuses of the Spanish government, they coldly receive our orders, which are based on the honor, maxims, and principles of the Republican State. . . . Our only recourse is to imprison them . . . and hope for civilization to become generalized among the Natives of the Country" (AHP PD 78 no. 80). Incomprehensibly, Indian "citizens" seemed to be defending the tributary policies of Spanish "indirect rule."

In fact, the demand for tributary status together with exemption from new taxation is coherent with the view that Chayanta Indians were intent on collectively renegotiating their terms of coexistence with the centralized state power. Here must be noted their willingness to consider the restoration of the other pillar of the Andean-colonial "pact": the *mita* service in the Potosí silver mines (Saignes 1985a, 1985b). In 1826, some 1000 Indians[2] appear to have presented themselves to Gareca, as he was carrying out the Catastro in the valleys of Chayanta, saying "that their only wish was to return to the ancient service of Potosí, since only since its suspension had they known the effects of misery" (ANB MH t.16 no. 22).[3] And in 1830–1831 we find 350 Indians from Porco Province arriving at Potosí to collaborate with the "voluntary mita" introduced by President Santa Cruz: they only withdrew their labor once it became clear that the extralegal practices associated with the Bourbon regime (Tandeter 1980) were also reemerging (AHP PD 91 nos. 35 and 62; PD 109 no. 7). This confirms that, for the Indians, "citizenship" meant freedom from the reimposition of late colonial "abuses," under the guarantees provided by republican legality; but it was not incompatible with what they considered the *equitable principle* of the Tributary State, based on their right to dispose collectively of their ayllu lands in exchange for the labor prestations and tribute they provided.

This position appeared to some creole authorities as resistance to the Republic as such, attributable to the lack of "enlightenment" (*ilustración*) that afflicted a caste unprepared for "real" (i.e., liberal) freedom. If the

Indians wished to be treated as legal minors, it only remained to hasten their "maturity." Hence the "re-Indianization" of the Andean population after Independence cannot simply be blamed on creole economic interests (as is often assumed): equally important was the Andean defense of an alternative model of state-community relations.

THE EARLY REPUBLICAN TRIBUTE SYSTEM IN CHAYANTA

The importance of the Indian tribute for early Republican finances is well known: until the 1850s, it represented between 26 and 52 percent of total government revenue (Sánchez A. 1978), and Chayanta provided some 47 percent of Potosí's whole tributary income (ANB MH t.22 no. 19). The amounts budgeted were taken from the tribute census (*revisita*) in force, which was in theory updated every five years. However, the money actually collected was always less than the amount expected; and even the sums delivered could be advanced by the provincial governor rather than collected from the Indians, particularly when the treasury demanded anticipated payment. For the governor's most important function at this time was to assume responsibility for delivering his province's tribute to the treasury on demand. If the Indians were unable to pay up on the nail, the governor would have to seek sources of credit or lose his property guarantees (*fianzas*). Credit could be sought through his business agent in Potosí, or local mining companies in Aullagas (Colquechaca) could issue credit notes (AHP PD 422 no. 20). But the most important resources available to the governors was their control over the fiscal intermediaries that lay between themselves and the Indian tributaries.

Here we confront that rupture between Republican legislation and customary practice which was a recurring feature in Bolivian regional society. President Santa Cruz had retained certain elements of "Napoleonic" public administration in his tributary Law of September 28, 1831: in particular, he had assigned 1 percent of all monies collected to the corregidores of the local canton (generally based on the rural parish). In fact, however, there was no necessary correspondence between the ethnic groups and the cantons: some cantons contained members of two or more ethnic groups, and some ethnic groups straddled several cantons (Platt 1982a). How, then, was the 1 percent remuneration to be allocated?

The problem was clearly explained in 1838 by the governor, Pedro Diez Canseco (AHP PD 286 no. 40):

. . . the tribute collection is in the hands of the corregidores of cantons with only one ethnic group [*parcialidad*], and where there are two or more it is necessary to name private recaudadores to help with the collection. This occurs in Chayanta where there are six groups, in Aymaya where there are two, in San Pedro where there are two, and in Pocoata and Macha, where there are also two. . . .

The six parcialidades of the town of Chayanta are the two triads of Laymis, Puracas, Chullpas (Laymi parish), and Chayantakas, Sicoyas, Carachas (Chayantaca parish) (Harris 1978a). In Aymaya were to be found the Aymayas and Jukumanis (Godoy 1981). Pocoata and Macha were the names of two towns called after two great ethnic groups, each divided into the two moieties of Alasaya ("Upper Half") and Majasaya ("Lower Half") (Platt 1976, 1978). All of these groups had lands on the high puna and in the warm valleys, according to the regional expression of Andean vertical organization (Murra 1972). Finally, San Pedro, a purely valley canton, embraced two lowland ethnic groups—the Awkimarkas and the Qhänas—who were under constant pressure from non-Indian townsfolk in the canton capital. Although the valley lands of the Chayantakas and the Sicoyas are also located in San Pedro, these were considered to belong to the tributaries of the puna.[4]

But a list of recaudadores and their ethnic groups available for 1835 shows an even more complex situation: corregidores could often be recaudadores, even when their cantons were inhabited by more than one parcialidad (AHP PD 201 no. 29). In Macha, for example, Felipe Neri de Vazquez was at once corregidor, recaudador of Alasaya, and justice of the peace—an overbearing concentration of local posts, as the Majasayas of Macha were quick to point out during an intermoietal dispute in 1834 (AHP PDE XXXVI). In Moscarí and Sacaca, the corregidor was also recaudador for the whole canton, although the Sakaka ethnic group was also divided into two moieties, each with valley lands in distant cantons (Acasio and Quirquiavi). The corregidor of Chayanta itself was recaudador for the Chullpas in 1835, while one of the other Chayanta recaudadores was responsible for both Laymis and Carachas (one from each of the local parishes). And in 1838 Governor Diez Canseco himself proposed two efficient recaudadores as corregidores of Pocoata and Pitantora (AHP PD 286 no. 128). The conflict between the two administrative systems was thus resolved at the local level on an ad hoc basis, which allowed the governor to strengthen his control over the tribute-collecting process.

Other evidence allows us to enrich our picture of the recaudadores' social personae. Juan Martín Flores, for example, recaudador of the Chullpas in 1835, as well as being corregidor of Chayanta was a local merchant, and in 1855 reappears forming a society for collecting the first fruits (*primicias*) in the valley cantons of San Pedro and Micani (AHP EN 234 ff.49r-51v). Christóval Fernández, recaudador of the Jukumanis in 1835, resurfaces in 1843 as a gold miner in Amayapampa (Chayantaca parish) (ANB MH t.94 no. 35). In 1842 the governor names as recaudador of the Chayantakas the son of the aging colonial silver miner Juan José de la

Rua, whose longstanding links with Chayanta (Buechler 1981) included the ownership of most of the Amayapampa gold mine, which he offered as guarantee for his son (AHP EN 367 f.125). Rafael Sotomayor, recaudador of the Carachas and Chullpas in 1850 (AHP PDE 3372), belonged to an influential mining family in the town of Chayanta, and frequently collected tithes and twentieths throughout the province in the 1840s (see, e.g., ANB MH t.103 no. 44). All these represented merchant and mining interests in the provincial capital, which in 1844 was still — with Sacaca and the Aullagas mining camp — the richest and most populated canton in the province (ANB MH t.98 no. 36). But in remoter cantons, it was probably the local landed interest that acted as recaudadores, such as Juan Bautista Gareca, "farmer" (*labrador*) of Acasio in 1850; or José Manuel Daza, recaudador of the Awkimarkas in 1848 and another important provincial tithe collector; or Benigno Oporto, corregidor of Moscarí in 1835 and recaudador of the same canton in 1829, 1835, and 1850.

These, then, were the sort of men who had replaced the hereditary Andean aristocracy at the head of the ethnic groups. How did they set about collecting the tribute from their Indians? In the nineteenth century, the old method of charging half the tribute at two semestral ceremonies named after the solstices at Christmas and Saint John's Day was still flourishing (it in fact persists to this day). But the exact dates varied from one ethnic group to another according to details of the local economic calendar. From May till August, puna households would transfer to the valleys to ensure supplies of local produce. As Governor Berdeja explained in 1843 (AHP PD 422 no. 71):

. . . the customs which distinguish this province from others are not arbitrary: the time for tribute payment depends on the double residence [*doble domicilio*] which forces each individual to move from one climate to another, according to their work schedule. Even between the communities [parcialidades] some make their payments at different times, according to the distance of their respective valleys, or the location of the markets where they expend their products; so that the Chayantakas, for example, celebrate their *cabildos* on San Roque's Day (August 16), while the Sicoyas can only do so at Rosario (October 23). . . .

These differences between Chayantakas and Sicoyas, and by implication other groups as well, represent the fiscal dimension of what Harris (1982) has termed the "ethnic economy" of each.

Further details are provided in Governor Diez Canseco's account of 1838 (AHP PD 286 no. 42):

. . . the Indians of Chayanta Province only pay their tribute at certain ceremonies, presided over by the collector, which they call cabildos; and as their dwellings are scattered all over this territory, it is necessary to counter their indolence with some enticement that can attract them, unite them, and extract the tribute from them. Such are the fiestas of San Pedro, Micani, Carasi, Torotoro, Moscarí, San Marcos, and Guaycoma, which are celebrated in the valley cantons during the months of June and July: in these months the last cabildos are celebrated to complete the tribute for Christmas. Such too are the fiestas of Chayanta, Pocoata, Macha, and other puna towns, which are held in the months of October and November, when the last cabildos are celebrated to collect the Saint John tribute. . . .

Although highland produce, such as fresh or dessicated potato, was sold in local mining centers when demand was sufficient, in 1838 we are told that most of it went on family subsistence and "in the exchanges which the inhabitants of Cochabamba come to make with their respective products" (ibid.). The tributary money was expected to come principally from sales of lowland grains and flour: only in moments of extreme dearth would the Indians' "savings"—livestock—be broken into (ibid.; also AHP PD 25 no. 192). Hence the close relation between seasonal migration patterns and the timing of the cabildos. The complexities seem to derive from the fact that the valley cantons harbored a small permanent population occupied with the day-to-day care of the crops, just as in the highland cantons a certain number of households, particularly those with small children (Harris 1978b, Platt 1982b), would not be able to take part in the journey to the valleys. So while most of the Christmas cabildos could be celebrated in early March or "after Carnival" (AHP PDE 837-a), some remnants would have to be completed among the resident valley population. Equally, although most of the Saint John cabildos could be held in the valleys, where the recaudadores would be present with the bulk of the highlanders among the valley-dwellers, a small residue of nonmigrants would have to be finished off on the return to the puna.

The whole calendar was regulated by reference to the Catholic fiesta cycle, although differences between ethnic economies meant that the province would be marked by a constant pulsation of fiesta dates, with particularly dense clusters around key periods in the agricultural and fiscal calendars. The cabildos were presided over "in each ayllu by the recaudador, his Indian deputies [segundas], and their subsidiary collectors, the mayores and jilanqus": each of these correspond to different levels within the segmentary organization of the ethnic groups. But they were indeed festive occasions, for without the "chicha, food, and coca provided by the recaudador and the ayllu chiefs [principales], there is no human power that can wrench from them a single half-real of contribution" (AHP PD 809 no. 62). Thus their semestral contribution had to be wheedled from the Indians through shows of generosity from the representative of the state.

On the other hand, the recaudadores enjoyed a series of privileges: each ethnic group offered its recaudador "a doorman [*pongo*] and a maid [*mitani*] who, according to the practices of each town, come for their turns every few weeks or months." Moreover, the Indians also provided collective labor in the common lands of their group, sowing, tending, and harvesting the crops for the recaudador "with coca as their only remuneration" (ibid.). According to another source for 1847, those Indians who wished could offer instead a measure of potatoes, wheat, and oats (*semaneras*), "so that the collectors have their commons sown and harvested free, and with seed also provided by the tributaries" (ANB MH t.113 no. 11). Each Indian had also to provide a chicken for the collectors at each semestral ceremony (Aymara *apaca* = "little extra"), and each local community chief (*jilaqata*) serving under the collector had to pay him a peso at each ceremony "for the hire of mules" (ibid.).

It should be emphasized that only the highest category of Indian tributaries, the *originarios*, in fact provided their recaudador with labor in the commons (AHP PD 809 no. 62). But just as the recaudador offered fiscal confirmation of their own rights to land, so the originarios were the source of the cultivation rights enjoyed by lesser tribute categories, such as the *agregados* and the "marginals" (Aymara: *wit'u jaqi*; Spanish: *forastero*), from whom the originarios in their turn received some labor services and other small favors (Harris 1978b; Godoy 1981; Platt 1982b). The privileged relationship between the recaudador and his originarios was therefore replicated in the relationship between each originario and his dependents. With regard to his parcialidad, each recaudador could consider himself a sort of mini-*hacendado*, although his "demesne" was in fact the common land, originally designed to serve the interests of the collectivity; similarly, each originario held extensive lands from which he could make "grants" to his dependents, although here it was the originario's prior right as a "commoner" that had to be questioned if the dependents felt the need to consolidate their holdings.

Now the common lands had in fact shrunk drastically since late colonial times, though, as Table 10.1 shows, they were still distributed between high potato and barley lands and low cereal fields. By comparing the lands corresponding to the Laymis with the commons claimed by their mestizo lord, Don Valerio Mariño, in 1797, we can observe the scale of the contraction following the invasion of mestizo squatters. In 1797 the Laymis worked 50 *ollas* of maize for their recaudador (as against 4 ollas in 1847), as well as 50 *cargas* of potatoes (which fell to 10 by 1847) and 46 cargas of barley (a mere 2 cargas in 1847) (ANB Minas t.129 no. 16). Yet even in the mid-nineteenth century, the commons were still the principal attraction of the post. Indeed, it was because of the services in the commons, "and not for the petty fee of 1 percent offered by law, that the re-

Table 10.1. Common lands registered by Chayanta ayllus in 1847

Ayllu	Location	Area (in volume of seed)	Produce
Chullpas	Opposite the town of Micani	2 ollas	Maize
	Puna lands	11 cargas	Potatoes
	Puna lands	1½ cargas	Barley
Puracas	Lands of Saychani and Arapani in Carasi	5 ollas	Maize
	Lands of Calacala	10 cargas	Potatoes
	Puna lands	1½ cargas	Barley
Laymis	Lands of Tomata and Guaripampa in Micani	4 ollas	Maize
	Puna lands	10 cargas	Potatoes
	Puna lands	2 cargas	Barley
Chayantakas	No Maize-lands	—	—
	Puna lands	7 cargas	Potatoes
	Puna lands	1 carga	Barley
Sicoyas	Lands of Achacomallku in San Pedro	2 ollas	Maize
	Puna lands	8 cargas	Potatoes
	Puna lands	1½ cargas	Barley
Carachas	Lands of Umapampa, Suarani, Cuñurani, and Pocoatillo in Micani	8 ollas	Maize
	Puna lands	12 cargas	Potatoes
	Puna lands	3 cargas	Barley
Totals		21 ollas	Maize
		58 cargas	Potatoes
		10½ cargas	Barley

Source: ANB MH t.116 no. 30. *Razón de los terrenos sobrantes de la provincia de Chayanta,* f.25r–v.: "Relación jurada que presenta el Corregidor que subscribe de los terrenos que con nombre de Comunes se conocen en las seis Parcialidades que tiene esta Capital. . . ." Chayanta, 25/8/1847.

caudadores bind themselves to deliver the tribute when the governor demands it" (AHP PD 809 no. 62; cf. ANB MH t.120 no. 35). Tribute collection before the customary cabildo dates was constantly the aim of a Departmental Treasury on the verge of bankruptcy; and there are signs that, if the governor defended the recaudadores' rights to the commons as the only solution to this problem, it was in exchange for personally disposing of the 1 percent assigned to the local collectors by Santa Cruz's 1831 Law.

THE TRIBUTE SYSTEM AND LAND REFORM UNDER BALLIVIAN

Between 1831 and the fall of Santa Cruz in 1839, the tribute system just described was able to coexist with legislation that kept a discreet silence over the juridical status of the recaudadores' privileges (*adehalas*). Distracted by the Confederational Wars after 1835, Santa Cruz was in no position to disrupt the ambiguous bases of fiscal income, and state prosecution of land reform was postponed as long as the war lasted. But the erosion of ayllu commons and tributary lands continued at the local level: when in December 1840 José Eustaquio Gareca was again commissioned to check the land-tenure situation in Chayanta, he reported a confused picture. Unofficial sales of rural and urban lots had been countenanced by the governors themselves, and buildings erected on them by the illegal "purchasers"; the parishes held lands without title; other parcels had been granted to demobilized soldiers; some mestizos had acquired cultivation rights as dependents of Indian originarios, while others had settled in the common lands. In these circumstances the government in 1841 ordered the status quo to be left undisturbed pending the registration of all lands eligible for state reclamation as falling within the boundaries of the colonial territorial districts, or *repartimientos* (ANB MH t.85 no. 20). However, José Ballivian assumed the presidency before the new register could be completed.

In 1843 the project was revived, and a census (*visita*) decreed of all "uncultivated and surplus lands" (*terrenos baldíos y sobrantes*) belonging to the old repartimientos. At the same time, the "Law of Enfiteusis" declared the tributaries mere tenants of state lands, which the state was also authorized to sell by Law of October 17, 1844. The main lines of state policy are clear: first the ethnic groups were to be reconstituted to the boundaries they had held at independence; then their lands were to be sold off by the state, if necessary to the Indian tributaries who occupied them. The legal basis was thus established, both for Melgarejo's sale of communities in the 1860s, and for the First Agrarian Reform decreed in 1874. But while the first part of the program could naturally be supported by the ayllus, it also defined the aims of nontributary squatters as the acquisition of titles to their de facto possessions.

One category of "empty lands" could be excluded from this policy, according to the provincial governor in 1846–1847. These were the highest puna lands, subject to lengthy rotation cycles, which the Indians "enjoy collectively with the name of *manta*. . . . These are cultivated both by originarios, and by agregados and forasteros, except that the last two categories enjoy less than the first, and the forasteros least of all . . ." (ANB MH t.116 no. 30. *Razón de los terrenos sobrantes de la provincia de Chayanta*, ff. 8r–v, 12r–v).

A second category, in which both ayllus and the state were directly interested, were those individualized parcels at the lower puna levels and in the valleys, which had passed into the hands of nontributaries, with a corresponding defraudation of fiscal rights. The government's proposal was that these lands should be reincorporated into the ethnic groups, and their possessors converted into tributaries. While some mestizos accepted the change, it was indignantly rejected by the regional elite in the towns of Macha, Pocoata, and Sacaca. The reason offered was the financial burden of the tribute (now legally a "rent" on state property), though equally important must have been a change of status that might make them subject to the Indian tribute system. Their pressures for outright purchase were being considered by the government at the moment that Ballivian was ousted by Velasco, and finally replaced by the Belzú regime with its open support of communal property.

But the most disputed category affected by the new legislation were the common lands enjoyed by the recaudadores with the labor of their originarios. In 1844 the land inspector (*visitador*) reported the interest of some "entrepreneurs" (*empresarios*) in constructing flour mills in parts of the commons; other townsfolk asked to be registered as tributaries in the same lands (ANB MH t.96 no. 21). These probably represent the same social groups that had previously been content to squat in the commons, and the government viewed their case favorably provided the needs of land-hungry Indians were met first. An important modification of the colonial regime was thus introduced: the repartimientos were to be reconstituted by maximizing the number of tributaries in each, even at the expense of the traditional commons. Tribute income could thus, it was hoped, be raised to its highest level, at the same time as the preconditions for the future regime of peasant smallholdings was established. Here state policiy came up against the unofficial bases of the existing tributary system.

The status of the commons became the subject of debate from another angle also. In the early 1840s, we find the first indications that the recaudadores were beginning to exploit their position beyond the level of customary prestations recognized by traditional practice. With the number of commons available on the decline, new methods were found of "squeezing" the tributaries. Hence the denunciation presented in 1842 by the Jukumanis of their recaudador, Pedro Gamón, for collecting tribute money from unregistered Indians "for his own pocket" (AHP PDE 1902 and 2358).

The initiative came from José Zenteno, tributary of the Jukumani ayllu Cuico, who protested that Gamón had charged him tribute while he was serving as mayor of the posting house (*tambo*) of Morochaca—a post Zenteno considered qualified him for exemption. At his instigation, the justice (*juez de letras*) of Chayanta prepared a suit against Gamón, for which it was necessary to consult the provincial governor over the legal basis of the recaudadores' privileges in the commons. The case was passed to the departmental prefect, and thence to the president of the Republic. Both considered that the cause of the abuses lay in the failure to implement Santa Cruz's original Law of 1831. It appeared that, while the ethnic recaudadores continued to enjoy their unofficial privileges, the governors had been taking the full 4 percent assigned to the provincial administration in the annual budget, instead of leaving 1 percent for the use of the recaudadores. In vain the governor protested that the existing system was the only way of ensuring efficient delivery of the tribute: all he received was a rap over the knuckles, and instructions to ensure that the corregidores collected the tribute in exchange for the 1 percent they were endowed with by law.

This result roused the governor's fury against Zenteno, and in 1844 he summed up his activities as follows (AHP PDE 2358):

It is enough to say that Zenteno has been one of those influencing the auxiliary collectors, named by custom within the communities, not to pay their own contribution. . . . He has told the Indians that they are under no obligation to provide pongos and mitanis for the governors and priests. He has taken it on himself to harvest the crops corresponding to the recaudadores in the little commons of his community. And finally he has headed a rabble when this authority pronounced on the matter, for which he was held prisoner for three months.

By harvesting the commons, Zenteno seems to have been completing his denunciation of Gamón by abolishing the bases of his authority, although we cannot be certain whether this meant that he was constituting himself as recaudador or recovering the commons for his own and other tributaries' use. But his opposition to the provision of services, and his support for auxiliary collectors' exemption from tribute during their term of office, are elements that reappear in Indian demands later in the century. Although the governor was able to get Zenteno condemned to a year's army service "to preserve order and calm among the communities," his example was followed by other ethnic groups, also eager to replace the alien recaudadores with collectors drawn from their own ranks (AHP PD 526 nos. 30 and 32).

Governmental opposition to the commons developed, therefore, both through support for their distribution among new tributaries, and by attempting to implement Santa Cruz's tributary legislation of 1831. The matter came to a climax in the last year of the Ballivian regime. In 1847 the fiscal attorney (*revisitador*) found a white recaudador in Moromoro still enjoying his access to the local commons. Probably to persuade a group of land-rich agregados to accept their conversion into originarios (an advantageous move for state finances, since originarios paid 2 pesos 6 reales more annual tribute than agregados), the attorney promised that all the services owed by originarios to their recaudador would be abolished. Simultaneously, he proposed that the recaudadores should now be chosen exclusively from among the Indians. The measure received instant support from the government (ANB MH t.120 no. 35); it was indeed entirely coherent with the aims developed during Ballivian's presidency. Only in 1848 would the trend be halted, as the new regime set itself to defend the bases of fiscal income and reconfirm the access of the white and mestizo recaudadores to the privileges they had traditionally enjoyed (ibid.).

Nevertheless, the Ballivian government was of crucial importance for the future of the agrarian question. For the first time, Republican legislation had been encouraged to "engage" the social reality of Chayanta, and, in spite of clash and contradiction, had thrown to the fore the issues that would recur time and again. Two of these stand out: the Andean defense of the traditional system, but directed by Indian collectors who might be prepared to forego the colonial privileges of their posts; and the dogged expansion of a regime of private smallholders into ayllu lands, sometimes accepting tributary status, but with the long-term aim of individualized consolidation. Perhaps even more striking is the fact that both currents could adduce legal backing for their positions, located within the subtly ambiguous framework of creole legislation. Was the space between them so great as to preclude a settlement? Any such convergence was blocked by the resurgence of the non-Indian recaudadores, a regional elite less interested in the abolition of the commons than in utilizing the remaining legitimacy of the old Aymara lordships for strengthening their role as the mini-hacendados of regional society.

INCAS AND CITIZENS: THE LEGALITIES OF REBELLION, 1870–1900

With the presidencies of Belzú (1848–1855), Linares (1857–1861), and Melgarejo (1864–1870), echoes of these three tendencies reappear sequentially. Belzú brought new life and closer regulation to the old tributary regime: his prohibition of anticipated tribute collection in 1853, though largely ignored in practice, prefigured a solution to one Indian complaint at the end of the century. Linares, on the other hand, forbade the exaction of unpaid Indian services by regional authorities. Though it too never got beyond the statute book, his Law of 1858 was at one with Ballivian's own policies, and was also invoked by Indian representatives during conflicts shortly before the 1899 revolution.

Finally, Melgarejo unleashed the practical implications of the other facet of Ballivian's legislation, launching a sale of tributary lands on an unprecedented scale. Indian resistance was violent. In Macha the town came under siege from "an immense multitude of ferocious Indians who occupied the surrounding hills," although their main target was the parish priest Dr. Martin Castro (Barnadas 1978), whose enthusiasm for Melgarejo, enlightened liberalism, and agrarian reform continued to arouse hostility till the last years of the century (AHP PD 1298 no. 32; AHP PD 2257 no. 69). Elsewhere in Chayanta, the result was the consolidation of tributaries' tenure at a price later contemplated (as stamp duty on title deeds) by the First Agrarian Reform of 1874. Lands lost were revindicated for the ayllus (and the state) by Morales (1871–1872) (Grieshaber 1977), although in a few areas around San Pedro and Sacaca some non-Indian squatters were able to consolidate their "purchases" outside the ayllu regime (AHP PD 1379 nos. 90, 125, and 129).

THE EMERGENCE OF THE FREE TRADE ECONOMY IN CHAYANTA

Melgarejo's assault also coincided with a new crisis in the provincial economy. The chaos of the early Republican years, when overproduction and a general lack of coin threatened to paralyze Indian sales (AHP PD 25 no. 192; AHP PDE 837-a), had been temporarily solved by Santa Cruz's issue of a debased coinage for internal circulation, which reestablished the preconditions for Chayanta's late colonial trade with southern Peru (Anónimo 1860:7). From the mid-1840s, the export of grains and flour to La Paz, the Yungas, and Puno had become the ayllus' main source of tributary coin (Platt 1982a). Melgarejo's reciprocal trade treaties with Chile and Peru opened up the northern markets to imports of Chilean grains, cutting short Chayanta's brief bonanza. Although Peruvian grain traders still came south to Chayanta (no doubt because only there could they get rid of their antique Bolivian coins), this traffic finally seized up with the outbreak of the War of the Pacific (AHP PD 1760 nos. 124 and 127; Platt 1986).

At the same time the growth of silver mining in Colquechaca (Mitre 1981), on the high puna frontier between the Macha and Pocoata ethnic groups, created a new axis for the regional economy. Breaking out of almost twenty years' slump in the 1860s, production was reorganized in 1878 with the foundation of the *Compañía Colquechaca* (whose shareholders included Aniceto Arce and Gregorio Pacheco). In 1882 it was producing

15–20,000 marks of pure silver per month; but struggles with the water that constantly threatened to invade the lower levels forced a damaging diversion of labor to the pumps. Profits collapsed, unpaid wages accumulated, and the only solution seemed to be the merger, completed in 1892, with other local companies, in particular the immensely successful *Compañía Aullagas*. This had been founded in 1884 by the Chichas magnate Jacobo Aillón, and struck rich deposits of ruby silver (*rosicler*) almost immediately.

This change was the regional expression of a wider transformation in the Bolivian economy, as native capital — first commercial and later extractive — began to merge with powerful foreign sources. The new growths were grafted onto the old order, utilizing or displacing those mechanisms of surplus production characteristic of the Tributary State. In the long run, the process would lead to the relative marginalization of the Indian communities, while mining taxes soon replaced the tribute as the state's main fiscal support (ibid.; Platt 1982a).

Colquechaca's growing population, estimated in 1885 at almost 2000 mine workers and over 10,000 souls, constituted a new market with a monthly circulation of some 140,000 Bs. (AHP PD 2020 nos. 51 and 75). But although its icy heights were supplied with the produce of all the surrounding ecologies (*El Industrial*, Sucre, 26. 3/7/1878), the conditions of entry into this market were stringent for the Indians. Their old cash crop was under squeeze from imported grains. Their old supply niche providing fuel and transport for the mines was increasingly taken over by the companies themselves, who expropriated ayllu reserves of peat and *yareta* and transported crude ore from mine to refinery in mule-drawn carts. Foreign commercial houses formed local distribution points for imported consumer goods. Moreover, the center's "main source of all articles of prime necessity" was Cochabamba (AHP PD 2312 no. 12). Even when the Indians could find buyers for their products, they were often paid with clipped, forged, or obsolete coins (pesos), or fragments of bank notes, due to the scarcity of small change in Colquechaca (*El Tiempo*, Potosí, I.43. 7/11/1885; AHP PD 2095 no. 1; AHP PD 2198 no. 31).

The monetary crisis during the last decades of the century had a major impact on the Indian tributaries. It was prepared by Melgarejo's issue of debased coinage in a Free Trade context, and was confirmed by the 1872 Law legalizing the exportation of uncoined silver. Although this was a precondition for the influx of foreign capital, it also reduced drastically the amount of raw material available to the Potosí mint. In 1877 the government announced the official depreciation of the debased coinage, and thereafter set itself the objective of receiving the tribute in the scarce new coinage (bolivianos). When this was converted into the old coinage which continued to predominate in Chayanta's commercial transactions the result was a tributary increase of 25 percent. Although bank notes had begun to circulate alongside the depreciated coins in the 1870s (AHP PD 1675 no. 13), the collapse of the Bank of Potosí in 1895 (four years before the Revolution) rendered its notes valueless and killed confidence in the notes of other banks (AHP PD 2652 nos. 46 and 73).

The growth of the Free Trade economy thus began to undermine the bases of the state-ayllu "pact." The same erosion can be observed in the provision of refurbished communications between Colquechaca and the major cities. Traditional labor prestations on the roads, bridges, and posting houses (*La Industria*, Sucre, 7.729. 23/4/1887) were reorganized from 1889 into a new *corvée* (*prestación vial*) which affected Indians and mestizos alike: both castes resisted (including those puna Indians whose vertical holdings made them liable for service in both zones) (AHP PD 2252 nos. 69, 81, and 99). New postillions were required with the reconstruction of the road to Cochabamba, which wound down from Colquechaca through Pocoata territory, reaching the Río Grande at Tacarani, where a basket on ropes (*oroya*) ferried travellers and merchandise across the ravine to Moscarí and San Pedro (AHP PD 2312 no. 12). To the south, the roads to Potosí and Sucre also required additional posting houses, with new obligations for the Indians of Macha and Moromoro (AHP PD 1419 no. 61; AHP PD 2060 no. 1). And in 1891 the timber posts for the new telegraph line between Colquechaca and Potosí were grudgingly brought up from the valleys of Micani and Carasi by Macha and Pocoata migrants returning to the puna, while the Moromoro Indians insisted that they had been obliged to provide posts for the line to Sucre without payment (AHP PD 2382 nos. 75 and 81; AHP PDE 8171). Thus, even the construction of Colquechaca's communications system meant stretching the extent of Indian prestations beyond the recognized margins.

THE CONTENT OF AGRARIAN REFORM, 1881–1899

It was in this changing economic context that the government began to implement a radical transformation of Chayanta's land-tenure patterns. Behind the attempt lay the old liberal objectives of the Republican state: the reconstitution of the colonial repartimientos prior to their atomization into a multitude of privately owned smallholdings, subject to the new land tax along with all other properties to be listed in the Napoleonic Catastro. But the policy was not clothed in the rhetoric of "modernization," as part of a policy of rural "development" parallel to the revitalization of Colquechaca's mining industry (de la Riva 1885).

The administration of the reform was placed in the hands of two land commissions (*mesas revistadoras*), one for each of the provinces into which the old province of Chayanta had been divided since 1877.[5] To the north lay the new Charcas Province, with its capital in the valley town of San Pedro. To the south were confined the remaining cantons of Chayanta Province, with its capital in the boom town of Colquechaca. In Charcas, the ethnic groups of Sacaca and Chayanta (town) continued to enjoy access to puna and valley lands within the same province, but in Chayanta both Machas and Pocoatas found their valley lands had been assigned to Charcas. The ensuing clash of jurisdictions, and the Indians' fear that they might have to pay for two sets of titles, meant that the land commission for Chayanta had to descend to the interprovincial border and register the Indians' valley lands through agents sent over the border (AHP PD 1997 no. 18; AHP PD 2506 s/n various; AHP PD 2552 no. 41).

Though also called a revisita, the procedure of the commissions was completely different from that of the old quinquennial census of Indian tributaries. This had been based on demographic evidence brought by Indians and local authorities to the desks of the fiscal attorneys, who would only carry out site inspections in specific cases of conflict (Platt 1982a). The new approach involved the precise measurement and valuation of each holding by a surveyor, who was expected to make scale drawings in order to establish productive capacity (Carnero 1980). This was to provide the basis for the new tax. Meanwhile, even the stamp duty on title deeds varied accordingly. The standard rate proposed by Decree of February 22, 1883 was 10 Bs. for originarios and 5 Bs. for dependents (agregados and forasteros) with cultivation rights, although increases were authorized up to 20 Bs. where greater extensions of land were involved. The four members of each commission were to be paid with money received from the sale of title deeds. Finally, although the new tax was to be postponed until the commissions could complete their work, the receipt of new titles made the Indian liable to pay tribute in bolivianos instead of pesos (Sanchez A. 1978).

Indian resistance to this legislative package was immediate and widespread. "We don't want this revisita," Puraka and Laymi Indians told the surveyor of their valley lands in 1883: "give us the old one which didn't touch our lands, for we are their owners whatever you may do" (AHP PD 1919 no. 96). In 1885, the Sakaka Indians carried off the surveyor's theodolite as "war booty" (AHP PD 2035 no. 15), while the commissioner for Charcas Province (AHP PD 2015 no. 25) explained to the prefect that

. . . one reason for Indian exasperation is the charge of tribute in bolivianos, for, having been told that the purpose of measurement and evaluation is the establishment of an equitable tax on the basis of production, and having seen that on the contrary their contribution is increased, they declare that the whole business is a trick. . . .

The same year the Pocoata Indians erupted against the operations of the Chayanta commission, forcing the suspension of activities and claiming that therefore they could not be asked to pay in bolivianos. The finance minister had to agree that, "if they have not received the benefits of the registration law [*ley de exvinculación*] (though through their own fault)," they would have to go on paying in pesos (AHP PDE 7205). Obviously, such a decision encouraged Indians to avoid both the increased tribute and the cost of title deeds by refusing to collaborate with the commissions.

Resistance to the stamp duty had been foreseen in 1881, when a law offered the option of collective titles *pro-indiviso*, with a reduced quota to be paid by each beneficiary. This was an unsatisfactory palliative, as the Chayanta commissioner pointed out (de la Riva 1885), insofar as it defeated the long-term aim of reform. Although some collective titles were issued, these were later taken as sufficient reason for repeating registration on an individual basis, with the result that those affected found themselves obliged to pay stamp duty twice (AHP PD 2656 no. 18). Moreover, as successive uprisings forced the resignation of commissions, new ones were appointed who would even repeat registration of ayllus whose members had already received individual titles. While this practice increased the commissions' income, it also "set fathers against sons" in Sacaca, where different individuals received titles to the same lands (AHP PDE 9229). How is this situation to be understood?

The problem is directly related to the position of agregados and forasteros, both within the ethnic groups and in relation to the new agrarian legislation. The issue which confronted Indians and commissioners alike was whether marginal dependents with cultivation rights should be considered as "having" land or not. The first possibility would make them eligible to receive title deeds at a cost proportionate to the value of land occupied. This had been contemplated in the Decree of 1883. In the second option, the land cultivated would be included within the originario's title: dependents would then be classified as landless, and exempt, under the Decree of 1874, from all tribute obligations save the head tax (Sanchez A. 1978).

But the crude polarity of liberal concepts of "possession" could not cope with a subtler range of social statuses concealed beneath the word "forastero." I have elsewhere suggested that, in the nineteenth century as today, these categories did not necessarily refer to "immigrants" from outside the ethnic group, as has traditionally been assumed (Platt 1982a). This can now be confirmed for the Moromoro ayllus, where alien settlers were mingled among local forasteros with the name of *mostrencos:* these were "placed in the same tribute category as the forasteros" by the recaudador, who then pocketed their tribute as part of his privileges (AHP PD 1919 no. 100). Where, then, did the local forasteros come from? Some may have been descendants of previous immigrants, who had inherited cultivation rights and the associated obligations (in Moromoro, services to the Church, as well as to the originario commoners). Others would be junior members of overgrown descent groups, who had been squeezed out of their family lands to resettle in the unoccupied margins of less populated descent groups. As in the case of true aliens, one means of access to land could here be marriage with the daughters of originarios without male heirs (Platt 1982b). They would then become "in-laws" to the landholding group (Spanish, *yerno*; Aymara, *tullga*), such as have been identified among seventeenth-century forasteros (Saignes 1985b). Finally, today junior members of Macha descent groups, settled in available land on the margins of their originario father's cultivated plot, have been found to be classified as forasteros or agregados, pending the succession of one of them to the father's originario status (Platt 1982b).

It is the last situation that appears relevant for understanding the internal conflicts of Sakaka descent groups. In 1882, we find that "the sons of tributaries, exempt from tribute, refuse to pay the head tax saying that they will replace their fathers or other dead tributaries . . . as their successors [*próximos*]" (AHP PD 1865 no. 32). This suggests that forasteros (exempt from tribute but liable to head tax) could be located within the category of a tributary's heirs. If such dependents were issued titles by a later commission to lands which an earlier commission had included within their fathers' holdings, the result would indeed be to "set fathers against sons."

The ambiguous status of dependents was resolved in different ways according to the demographic situation within each ethnic group. In Chayanta town, for example, Laymi originarios in 1886 denounced their recaudador, accusing him (among other things) of "collecting tribute from Indians who have no lands" (AHP PDE 7324). Is this a case like the mostrencos of Moromoro? An alternative interpretation presents itself if we examine the tributary composition of the Laymis in the last census of 1877. Here, the Laymis are divided into a strong block of originarios (approximately 38 percent), a more numerous block of agregados (62 percent), and no forasteros at all (ANB Revisitas no. 217). More probably, then, Laymi originarios had decided to oppose the fragmentation of their "original" holdings by refusing to admit the consolidation of their own kin as agregados. This is supported by the denunciation in 1893 of a later recaudador for seeking to "increase state tribute income" by "charging all young Indians the sum of three pesos four reales"—the semestral tribute of an agregado (AHP PDE 8277).

The Macha situation was different again. The 1877 tribute lists show a tiny originario population (1.5 percent), a substantial block of agregados (32.5 percent), and no less than 66 percent represented by forasteros. Here, clearly, it was the forasteros (whatever their origins) that had the deciding voice. In 1885, we find them continuing to pay the tribute, in spite of their legal exemption, "so as not to lose the lands they occupy" (AHP PD 2015 no. 11). The following year the Indian authorities of both moieties sent a petition to the president of the Republic, in which they pointed out that, since in Majasaya there were only two originarios and in Alasaya only four, the forastero majority did in fact possess lands, and should be allowed to continue paying tribute (AHP PDE 7287 and 7323). In 1885 and 1889 the Machas rebelled against measurement of their lands and the consequent obligation to pay the tribute in bolivianos. But neither were they prepared to admit reclassification of the forasteros as agregados, since this too meant an increase in tribute payments (AHP PDE 9495 and 9512). A similar situation can be observed among the Pocoatas, who in 1897 appear resisting the collectors' efforts to wrest the additional tribute from forasteros who refused to become agregados (AHP PDE 8902).

Common to all these situations is the problem of the relation between kinship and fiscal categories. But whereas young Sakaka heirs refused to be categorized as forasteros, the Laymis opposed their transformation into agregados. In Macha, on the other hand, most forasteros cultivated "in the margins" of agregado holdings, and the emphasis was on their *right* to continue paying the old forastero tribute in order for their holdings to be recognized. Such varied situations may warn us against generalizations concerning the political behavior of specific tribute categories (Cornblit 1970; but cf. Mörner 1978), if fiscal terminology is not first dissolved to reveal the social and kinship bases of Indian society at the level of each ethnic economy (Wachtel 1978; Harris 1982).

The greatest political blunder in the First Agrarian Reform was probably its attitude to mestizo squatters. These continued to be regarded as illegal occupiers of state lands. Already in 1882 the Sacaca mestizos rebelled against the Charcas commission, "for not leaving them the properties they usurped from the state, for which reason they even instigated the Indians toward a general uprising" — at this early date, without success (AHP PD 1865 no. 14). But with time this policy offered a solid basis for an Indian-mestizo alliance. In Pocoata and Macha, mestizos attempted to defend themselves by claiming descent from the Indians who in 1646 had been granted colonial titles to the lands surrounding the towns (originally founded as part of Toledo's Indian resettlement program) (AHP PD 2492 s/n; Platt 1982a n.87). But their claim was considered unproven, and in 1896 Pocoata mestizos allied with neighboring ayllus to take the town and drive out the Chayanta land commission (AHP PD 2656, no. 10).

At the same time, the 1874 Decree had proposed the exemption of Indians from all "forced services"; and although it could be argued (e.g., de la Riva 1885) that the Indians offered their labor willingly, any excesses could be resisted by invoking the law. Further, in 1888 Aniceto Arce resolved that the recaudadores should be Indians, thereby reinstating the objectives originally proposed by Ballivian. These reforms were naturally resisted by authorities who profited from the status quo, leading them to invoke the old argument from legitimacy to stir up the ayllus against the commissions (AHP PD 2123 s/n). Here again was a basis for an alliance between ayllus and townsfolk. But increasingly we find these elements being incorporated into specific ethnic programs: the Laymis in 1886 (AHP PDE 7324), the Moromoros in 1892 (AHP PDE 8171), and the Sakakas in 1896 (AHP PDE 9229) all demanded the Indianization of the collectorships and the abolition of "forced services."

The First Agrarian Reform was a contradictory affair, which in practice threatened to dismantle the bases of the regional society that had reconstituted itself in the early years of the Republic and had survived the passing interruptions posed by Ballivian and Melgarejo. Indians and mestizos could agree on the chaos introduced into their respective systems of landholding, although stealthy mestizo advances (Platt 1982a) could still cause friction between them. On other issues, however, they were opposed. Apart from growing disagreement on the tribute system, with its associated prestations of Indian labor in the commons, Indians found no support from mestizos in their resistance to monetary reform: the local townsfolk were probably better placed to take advantage of the growing Free Trade economy, and in any case few of them paid tribute. The creation of the anti-Constitutionalist front was thus an erratic process, capitalizing on a generalized dissatisfaction felt by diverse — and sometimes opposed — interest groups, each of which would attempt to maximize its strategic advantages in the aftermath of the revolutionary upheaval.

THE PHASE OF INDIAN COORDINATION, 1870–1888

Between 1881 and 1888 the new provinces of Charcas and Chayanta developed their resistance on separate stages, in spite of attempts at coordination between 1883 and 1885. To the north, Sacaca, Moscarí, and Chayanta (town) learned to work in harmony, in spite of differences in the timing and nature of the provocations suffered by each. Here, too, we can detect the recurring influence of events on the distant altiplano around La Paz. In the south, Macha and Pocoata formed a separate focus of rebellion, supported by the Indians of Aymaya on the frontier with Charcas, and more distantly by the Moromoros in the valleys descending toward the national capital of Sucre.

Our understanding of revolutionary organization must start from an appreciation of regional social structure in the prereform years. The vertical distribution of ethnic groups between puna and valleys formed a segmentary system that in certain circumstances could take precedence over the Napoleonic division into cantons, and even provinces, predetermining the general form of political alliances. This system is characterized by the fusion/fission principle: local groups within an ayllu may squabble over land claimed by each, but will merge to defend shared interests against threats from other ayllus. Equally, all ayllus within a moiety may unite to beat off attacks from an opposing moiety, or both moieties fuse to confront rival ethnic groups, bringing together at the point of conflict distant residents from up and down the vertical space. Today, the tensions generated during these terrific battles over land (*ch'ajwas*) may spill over into ritualized exchanges of balanced violence (*tinkus*), which are still celebrated in the streets and squares of rural towns during fiestas on locally honored saints' days (Platt 1976). Andean traditions of ceremonial warfare are a crucial (and much neglected) aspect of Andean rebellion (but see Salomon 1982; Szemiński, Chapter 6 in this volume).

Mestizo apprehension over these tumultous events is related to the danger that, as spirits grow more exalted, warring groups may fuse against a common enemy. Two reactions are possible. One is to try and remain "above" the conflict, and attempt to impose a solution. The second is to throw themselves into the conflict on the side of the Indian group that dominates their canton, or with which they have other close ties. This choice may even become one between two aspects of mestizo consciousness: in the first option, they distance themselves from the "barbarian" Indians, and draw toward the "civilized" creole lawgivers; in the second, they merge with the Indian dynamic and develop their participation in accordance with its rules.

A paradigmatic case can be observed during the 1870s, when a feud reverberated up and down the vertical frontier between the Macha and Pocoata ethnic groups. In 1874, Miguel Santander, a creole gold panner from Pocoata, was acting as corregidor in Macha. When he proposed a legal solution to the conflict, he was immediately denounced by the Machas for complicity with the Pocoatas: it was assumed he was supporting "his" Indians. The Machas were in turn supported by a local lawyer, and by one of their recaudadores, who had his eye on the post of corregidor and could thus acquire Indian approval for his efforts to oust the intruding *pocoateño* (AHP PD 1509 no. 18).

The following year the feud broke out again, further down the frontier in Surumi. The corregidor of Surumi sided with the Machas, denouncing the Pocoatas for aggression under the leadership of the neighboring corregidor of Chayala—a Pocoata valley canton (AHP PD 1522 no. 10). According to the 1877 tribute lists, Surumi contained 118 Macha tributaries to only 31 Pocoatas, which no doubt helped the corregidor of Surumi to decide his divided loyalties (ANB Revisitas no. 217). But a few days later the corregidor of Chayala sent in his report of the Macha counterattack: "under the leadership of the corregidores of Chayrapata [a neighboring Macha canton] and Surumi, and their justices; the Indians are committing a thousand iniquities, killing, sacking, destroying crops, and Señor, the ferocity of these caribs [i.e., "cannibals"] leads them to commit excesses. . . ." The Macha victory was supported "by all their *cholada* [i.e., mestizos], sounding their horns . . ." (AHP PD 1533 no. 11).

In October 1876 the battle was renewed, "with many wounded and two dead," including the servant of Miguel Santander, caught in the cross-fire of his master's divided affiliations (AHP PD 1598 nos. 54 and 55). But efforts by the provincial authorities to restore order risked setting off a united Indian resistance. In 1878, the subprefect wrote that "a multitude of crimes" had been committed by Machas and Pocoatas along their shared frontier. Two commissioners sent to control the situation were driven out by "more than 4–5,000 armed Indians barricaded behind the crags": they suffered injuries and lost their mules and supplies (AHP PD 1678 no. 26). Here both Indian armies seem to have merged (in a neat example of segmentary fusion) to get rid of the representatives of government before resuming their own internal dispute.

The imposition of ethnic loyalties upon caste solidarity suggests that, in the absence of state recognition, mestizos had been obliged to come to terms with the loyal ayllus to protect their rights to land. By offering legal and physical support, they could gain some local tolerance for what the state considered their "usurpations." In these circumstances, the corregidores became local ethnic patrons rather than the lowest rung in the Napoleonic administrative structure. Hence the land commissions' difficulties in finding local authorities to collaborate with a reform that not only attacked their own interests, but was also rejected by the Indian "clients" (e.g., AHP PD 1976 no. 21).

The alliances that began to form in Chayanta Province against the progress of reform were thus articulated by the segmentary structure of ethnic groups. But in the early stages, mestizos fought shy of an open alliance with Indian rebellion. As well as battling against Machas on their southern frontier, the Pocoatas were also locked into a dispute with Jukumanis to the north. In 1871 they had combined with their Condo neighbors, on the other side of the interdepartmental frontier with Oruro, as well as with their kin in the Chayala valleys, to hold back the enemy. Such, at least, was the version of the corregidor of Pocoata: for the corregidor of Aymaya, it was the Pocoatas who were to blame (AHP PD 1379 no. 22). Yet in 1885 we find Machas, Pocoatas, Aymayas, and Condos all united to force the suspension of the commission's activities in Pocoata, even threatening to invade Colquechaca itself (AHP PD 2020 no. 71). The reasons for the uprising were the conversion of forasteros into agregados (AHP PD 2015 no. 11), the cost of title deeds, and tributation in bolivianos. Two Indian recaudadores, Diego Apaza and Ciprián Ramírez, emerged to take the tribute in pesos direct to Potosí, ordering their supporters to withhold payment in bolivianos to the official recaudadores in Pocoata (AHP PD 2020 no. 16). But Pocoata mestizos sided neither with the commission ("except for a few local creoles") nor with the Indians. Aware of the threat against their own holdings, they could scarcely fail to observe the parallel dangers of Indian rebellion (de la Riva 1885; AHP PD 2015 nos. 19 and 23).

In Charcas Province, there are signs from the start of greater antagonism between Indians and townsfolk, probably due to the consolidation of mestizo holdings in ayllu territory following the Melgarejo episode. In Moscarí, more than anywhere else, we hear complaints against large landowners as well as small, whose advances already caused threats of rebellion in 1879 (AHP PD 1723 no. 73). In Sacaca, the first insurrection of 1882 was organized entirely by mestizos, while the Indians refused their invitation to participate (AHP PD 1865 no. 14). In 1883, the Indians even revolted "against the townsfolk" to avoid tributation in bolivianos (AHP PD 1915 no. 93) and the conversion of unlisted dependents into agregados (AHP PD 1915 no. 25). In 1884, ayllu authorities ("*ylancos*") of Sacaca and Micani supported the subprefect in continuing the non-Indian recaudadores, with one day's labor annually from each ayllu (AHP PD 1967 nos. 59 and 67). But the recaudadores immediately attempted to collect in bolivianos, and an alliance was formed between the ethnic groups of Sacaca, Chayanta (town), and Moscarí, threatening to kill a particularly abusive Laymi recaudador, Dionisio Arancibia (AHP PD 2035 nos. 54 and 99).

By 1885, then, both provinces had developed equivalent programs. In Chayanta, the initiative had come from the Indians, while in Charcas the mestizos had made the first move. In Chayanta the mestizos kept a low profile in 1885, while in Charcas they had already become a target by 1883. One Sakaka leader, Manuel Salas, working from his ethnic group's puna and valley cantons, was inspired by the success of the Pocoatas and their allies, and attempted to coordinate the movements in both provinces (AHP PD 2015 no. 24; AHP PD 2035 no. 61). His success was hampered on the puna by the emerging antagonism between Laymis and Jukumanis over the new interprovincial boundary, and Laymi hatred of their recaudador was increased by the fact that he was also corregidor of Aymaya (AHP PDE 7184).

An easier movement toward interprovincial unity could develop in the valleys, where the interdigitation of ethnic plots meant that distant puna groups might there find themselves neighbors. A case in point is that of Laymis and Purakas (Charcas Province), separated on the puna from Pocoatas and Machas by the intervening lands of the Jukumanis (Chayanta Province), but settled alongside them in the warm valleys of Carasi and Torotoro. Already in 1883 Laymis and Purakas had found their wavering resistance to the surveyor's activities strengthened from their neighbor's puna headquarters (AHP PD 1919 no. 97):

The contagion has come from the neighboring province of Chayanta. Among various communities resident there but with lands in this province, there are in Carasi two fractions belonging to the ferocious hordes of Machas and Pocoatas, who (as is well-known) have for ages been in open conflict with the law and the authorities. It is these that have managed to subject the Indians of this region, who are of gentler character and were about to be reconciled with the reform. It is clear, Señor, that a coalition is being formed throughout the province to resist the reform.

Acting through their colonies in Carasi, Machas and Pocoatas had "sent agents" (AHP PD 1919 no. 98) to strengthen collective resistance in the shared lowland canton. The convergence of interests in Carasi was probably a key aspect of the interprovincial coordination achieved in 1885, with the Indian-dominated regions of Macha and Pocoata setting the pace.

By blocking the advance of reform in Pocoata, the Indians of Chayanta Province had achieved their objectives. Only in Moromoro, where the commissioners had been able to complete their work (de la Riva 1885), would solitary protests continue against tributation in bolivianos, the continuation of "forced services," and (a complaint rarely heard in the region at this period) the abuses of tithe collectors (*La Industria*, Sucre, 6.652. 13/8/1886). Between 1885 and 1888, therefore, the initiative passed to Charcas Province. In a rapid process of radicalization, the Sakakas took up contacts with the Aymaras of La Paz hoping to coordinate an interregional rebellion (AHP PD 2089 no. 6) "against the white race" (AHP PD 2058 no. 3). In 1886, Pedro Gabriel assumed the role of provincial subprefect, deposing the ayllu authorities (*ylancos*) loyal to the white subprefect and naming others in accord with Indian aims (AHP PD 2088 no. 125). Angry protests against tributation in bolivianos followed the failure of an uprising planned for Candelaria (February 2), while the loyalty of the National Guards, rapidly conscripted to quell the revolt, could not be counted on "as they are in contact with the Indians in their agricultural relations" (AHP PD 2089 no. 15). The land commission continued its policy of converting heirs into tributaries (AHP PD 2089 nos. 62 and 66), and in 1887 we find mestizo squatters and recaudadores (eager to regain Indian services in the commons) beginning to take sides with the Indians (AHP PD 2123 s/n).

But when the uprising finally came in February 1888, it was again an affair with overtly racial overtones. Sacaca was surrounded by 3,000 Indians armed with slings, sticks, and knives, threatening fire and slaughter and demanding the head of the land commissioner (AHP PD 2207 no. 23). The Indians were led by N. Willka from Guaicho (La Paz), who ". . . took the title of heir of the Incas, stirring up the Indians with promises to restore the Cult of the Sun, reestablish the rules of his race in all branches of public administration, and get rid of the white race . . ." (AHP PD 2201 no. 16). Although the white subprefect beat off the besiegers, killing more than fifty Indians and wounding many more, the National Guard was disbanded without capturing the Inca, and the operations of the commission were temporarily suspended (ibid.; AHP PD 2201 no. 66).

The radicalism of Andean revolt in Sacaca is clearly to be related to the greater strength of the townsfolk opposition, and to the continuation of the commissions while they were suspended in Macha and Pocoata. The crucial contact with La Paz will need further research. But in 1888 a new element appeared on the provincial scene: the May elections. In Sacaca the event was orchestrated from the Liberal Party headquarters in Colquechaca (AHP PD 2201 no. 104), and it introduced a new dimension into the problem of interprovincial coordination. The appearance of Liberal Party slogans in the mouths of Macha Indians during the uprising of 1889 clearly marks the beginning of the next phase in the process.

THE EMERGENCE OF THE LIBERAL FRONT, 1888–1899

The Liberal Party set up its branch headquarters in Colquechaca in 1887 (four years after the Constitutionalist Party had set up its own), following *vivas* for its national leader, Eliodoro Camacho, during the miners' Carnival that year (*El Tiempo*, Potosí, 5/3/1887). The president, vice-president, and others on the committee were all shareholders and board members of the prosperous *Compañía Aullagas*, although Party cadres were also incrusted in the administration of the ailing *Compañía Colquechaca*: one of these, Nicolás Lora, even invited Pando to use Colquechaca as his base for the premature coup of 1890 (*La Industria*, Sucre, 10/7/ 1890). Although support for the Liberal Party also emanated from the tin miners of Llallagua-Uncía, Pastor Sainz and Dulfredo Campos (AHP PD 2324 no. 7; AHP PD 2652 no. 47; AHP PD 2798 s/n; AHP PD 2841 s/n; AHP PDE 8348), it is obvious that Klein's (1982:161–64) attempt to reduce the opposition between Constitutionalists and Liberals to a rivalry between silver miners and tin miners lacks foundation.

Colquechaca quickly became known as a hotbed of Liberalism at all levels of its turbulent society (AHP PD 2312 no. 72). Following the elections of 1888, Fructuoso Ramos, future Liberal prefect of Potosí and Party organizer in both provinces, seized the subprefecture and began collecting Indian tribute to fill Party coffers (AHP PD 2198 no. 97). Such an opportunity for propaganda helps explain the shouts of ¡viva Camacho! among the Machas and their allies in 1889 (AHP PD 2257 no. 61). But although Colquechaca Liberals were in touch with emerging cells among the rural town elites, who in turn recruited support among local mestizos and Indians (AHP PD 2252 nos. 29 and 69), there were also direct contacts between Indian miners and the countryside. Although the composition of Colquechaca's workforce is not yet known in detail, there were sufficient local Indians in it to produce a labor shortage when they migrated to the valleys in May or June (AHP PD 1926 no. 85; cf. AHP PD 2200 no. 55 for Llallagua-Uncía), or joined the annual pilgrimages to such great shrines as Quillacas (Lake Poopó), Surumi, and Panacachi (AHP PD 2599 no. 95). Nearby Indian hamlets were swallowed up by the expanding town (AHP PD 2020 no. 47), and Colquechaca's religious calendar would draw in rural visitors from a wider area. Such a web of communications between workforce and ayllus, facilitated through kinship links with seasonal workers, helped project the Liberal caudillos as national leaders, rather than mere elite figures.

The Macha uprising was a direct response to the appointment of a new land commission for Chayanta Province in 1888 (AHP PD 2198 no. 74). In January 1889 the commissioner was informed of an imminent uprising "on the fiesta of Candelaria . . . of this canton's Indians with those of Pocoata, in combination with those of Sacaca" (AHP PD 225 no. 1). Agitators from Pocoata and Sacaca were said to be combing the Macha hamlets in groups of twenty, threatening all who collaborated with the commission with death. A petition sent to Potosí asking for the suspension of reform led the subprefect to call a halt to the commission's activities, pending the prefectural decision (AHP PD 2225 nos. 3, 4, and 6). But by March the commission was back in action, and the Indian uprising began on the twenty-fourth, when the loyal ylanco of Majasaya, Mariano Sayali and his wife Juana Colque, defected to the commission in Macha town, with news that the Indians of Macha, Pocoata, and Aymaya were gathered on the heights of Chacarani and intended "to exterminate the town under the shadows of the night." Led by Mariano and Domingo Achu, from the Macha hamlet of Coacani, the rebels burned the defectors' house (AHP PD 2257 no. 59), and on April 1 occupied the town. At the same time the subprefect, preparing to march to Macha from Colquechaca, found rebellion in the ranks of the National Guard, while "the plebeian and completely Liberal people" of the town besieged the subprefectural residence and the barracks (AHP PD 2257 no. 66). When he finally arrived in Macha, the Indians retired to the surrounding hillsides, whence they yelled *¡viva Camacho!*, and threatened to kill the commission and sack Colquechaca (AHP PD 2257 nos. 61 and 65). Though dislodged by gunfire from the remaining National Guardsmen, they quickly agreed to repeat the uprising on the fiesta of the Holy Cross (May 3), celebrated with ritual battles (*tinkus*) in Macha and Pocoata. The subprefect was forced to leave twenty Mauser rifles with the non-Indian recaudadores of Pocoata, fifteen rifles in Macha, and distribute troops at key points throughout the province, in order to control the situation (AHP PD 2257 nos. 80 and 83).

Inter-provincial coordination was again incomplete, although both ethnic groups and Liberal leaders were now working toward the same end. The Sakakas had been awaiting the Macha uprising at Candelaria (AHP PD 2252 no. 10), and seem to have been disconcerted by the delay. The Liberal politician Fructuoso Ramos sent a secret envoy to the town of Chayanta, but he found the National Guard had already been mobilized (AHP PD 2252 nos. 28 and 29). Nevertheless, the evident strength of popular opposition in both provinces must have encouraged Pando to base his coup attempt of 1890 in Colquechaca.

Between 1890 and 1897, Indians and mestizos in both provinces were finally driven into each others' arms, in part through Liberal Party agitation, but more decisively by the Constitutionalist insistence on renewing the land commissions. In Chayanta Province no commission was appointed until 1893. Meanwhile, Machas and Pocoatas resisted attempts to collect the agregado tribute from forasteros, provoking the renunciation of various recaudadores (AHP PD 2312 no. 44). Their petitions to the government were busily supported by two lawyers from Macha town, J. M. Orellana and Pedro Saavedra, whose letters to the recaudadores and Indian authorities, as well as inter-ayllu correspondence, were collected by the subprefect (unfortunately without sending them to Potosí) as evidence of subversion by Liberal "penpushers" (*tinterillos*) (AHP PD 2374 no. 111).

The first steps of the new commission were cautious. The commissioner complained to the finance minister when the subprefect tried to collect the tribute in bolivianos, forcing yet again a reversion to pesos (AHP PD 2490 no. 74). Since the Indians resisted paying for another set of title deeds, the commissioner turned his attention to the mestizo squatters. He suggested that his team's salaries should come from 50 percent of the auction value of all "usurped" lands (AHP PD 2492 s/n). Mestizo reaction was foreseeable: finding themselves now under direct attack, they joined ranks with the Indians in resisting the reform (AHP PD 2490 nos. 12 and 49). This process culminated in the third rebellion of Pocoata in 1896, when mestizos also encouraged Machas and Pocoatas to help stop the activities of the Charcas commission in the neighboring province (AHP PD 2656 nos. 10 and 42).

Meanwhile in Charcas the new commissioner, who took office in 1895, was none other than a member of the old Andean aristocracy, José María Ayaviri, whose ancestors had been hereditary lords of Sacaca (AHP PDE 9229; cf. Espinoza 1969). Now well acculturated to the mores of progress, he represented part of a Constitutionalist elite in Sacaca, where (according to the Indian attorney there, Julian Gabriel) the priest was father-in-law to the subprefect and to Ayaviri, while the subprefect was father-in-law to the local judge and Ayaviri was compadre to the recaudadores. From this tight little power bloc, Ayaviri demanded that an army squadron be sent from Oruro to support (in his own words) "his authority so repudiated by the Indians, and even by the townsfolk, who exploit the services and ignorance of the aboriginal peasantry . . ." (AHP PD 2584 nos. 12 and 34). At the same time the subprefect denounced agitators "from a single family, refractory to any system of order," who were stirring up Indian resistance to the commission and even to the tribute itself, in order to protect their own possession of "vast tracts of unregistered communal land" (AHP PD 2652 no. 30). Factionalism among the local elite, with two groups competing for control of ayllu land, is here expressed as inter-Party friction between Liberal squatters and the dwindling nucleus of Constitutionalist authority.

Once again, greater social tensions in Charcas Province led to more radical forms of confrontation. In 1896 the future "general attorney of the two provinces," Juan Coyo (AHP PDE 9348), arrived from Chayanta (town) to discuss terms with the Sacaca Liberals. It was agreed to oppose not only the commission, but even *the tribute itself* for all who had received new title deeds, and to work for a general uprising (AHP PD 2652 nos. 30, 33, and 41). In the midst of the crisis provoked by the collapse of the Bank of Potosí, the presidential elections were held in which Severo Alonso won by the narrowest of margins: agents sent from Colquechaca and Llallagua helped raise Liberal riots in Sacaca (AHP PD 2652 no. 47). And a few months later the land commission came flying back from Moscarí, with an Indian uprising on its heels, supported not only by local squatters but by 4,000 Indians arriving from Macha and Pocoata (AHP PD 2652 nos. 79 and 82; AHP PD 2656 no. 33). The coordination between the two provinces was at last a reality.

It is important, however, not to draw the political frontiers more clearly than they were in reality. While Liberal agitators, as well as Juan Coyo, could appeal to the abolition of the tribute as an obvious Indian ideal, the lower Indian leaders, as well as the tributaries themselves, were still worried about the new land tax that would follow the Catastro. In August 1896 we hear of Indians going in front of the commission in Sacaca, "advising them not to accept measurement, threatening them not to take out titles if their lands had already been measured, arguing that the operations of the commission are valueless, exaggerating that they will be charged Catastro even on the number of children in each family, and that the old revisita should return instead of the present land commission . . ." (AHP PD 2656 no. 32). Although a leader such as Julian Gabriel could contemplate the Catastro as a possible solution to the chaos let loose in Indian land-tenure, it is probable that most Sakakas would prefer the tribute to any unknown future tax that might follow on payment of title deeds. The safest tactic was not to collaborate with the commission.

On the other hand, although we hear of corregidores and recaudadores stirring up the Indians so as to retain their "forced services," the Constitutionalists here seem to have struck a responsive note among the Indians. Complaints against non-Indian recaudadores multiply toward the end of the century. Forced by their superiors to collect the tribute in bolivianos, their legitimacy crumbled among the tributaries; as their access to Indian services was slowly withdrawn, their efforts to retain their old hierarchy became abusive. Commons were further eroded, with the connivance of the commissions (AHP PD 2656 no. 39), and some recaudadores took to forcing "sale" of livestock at nominal prices for resale in the mines of Colquechaca and Llallagua (AHP PDE 7324; AHP PD 2382 no. 32; AHP PDE 9229).

At the same time Indian leaders emerged from below to replace the discredited authorities. In 1886 the Laymis had demanded the replacement of Dionisio Arancibia by Julian Leiva "our old collector," invoking the law to demand that the subprefect should work through "an *ilacata* or *segunda* from our ayllu, who cannot abuse us as a member of our race" (AHP PDE 7324). The phrase should be interpreted as the contemporary form (Demelas 1980) of an old political argument (Platt in press). Tributaries had always struggled for responsiveness to their interests even from the old hereditary lords. With these replaced by non-Indians even more abusive than their predecessors, collective efforts were now directed toward the "democratization" of the fiscal system, not through an expansion of state power (as in the Napoleonic model), but by proposing individuals subject to ayllu consensus as local recaudadores and corregidores (AHP PD 2020 no. 16; AHP PD 2035 no. 54; AHP PDE 9512; AHP PD 2645 no. 18). This meant (in the case of Machas and Pocoatas) reasserting their

control over their cantons which had been questioned by state intervention through the land commissions, and extending upward in the fiscal
hierarchy that direct control already exercised over lower Indian authorities (AHP PD 1870 no. 95; AHP PD 2257 no. 59; etc.). Within this program, many groups now refused to permit the rebirth of a discredited
system, and demanded that their nominees be paid a percentage of tribute
monies, rather than receiving "forced services" from their ayllus. To this
was added another demand: exemption from tribute during their term of
office for all Indian authorities and postillions—a position clearly anticipated by José Zenteno in the 1840s (AHP PDE 6108, 7324, 8171, 8902,
9229, etc.).

It is this depth and consistency in the Indian position (even allowing
for local variations and disagreements) that make it impossible to attribute their mobilization to mere "manipulations" from above. In constant
dialogue with the creole legislation, the Indians ended up selecting those
elements in the proposals of both Parties that coincided with a position
formulated before either existed. Their political rapprochement with other
sectors was that of a majority in search of a place in the Republican sun:
real discrepancies were postponed as growing state violence clarified the
revolutionary frontiers. In 1897, Indians and townsfolk in Sacaca were
celebrating the national fiestas in August, when the soldiers of the "Junin,"
stationed there since Ayaviri's troubles the year before, opened fire on the
people, killing four and wounding some seventy. Military requisitioning
of forage, services, and women had aroused local resentment, and the
soldiers, already jittery, were egged on by the fiscal agent Teófilo Lozada.[6]
Whether by accident, provocation, or Liberal design, the remaining legitimacy of the Constitutionalists in Charcas Province was dissolved (AHP
PDE 9106, 9113; AHP PD 2725 s/n).

With the disappearance of the Inca Willka from Sacaca in 1888, the
radical Andean project seems to subside beneath the rising banner of the
Liberal Party. Not until 1896 do we find a new reference to an interprovincial coalition of "the savage race" with the aim of "asserting itself over
the white race" (AHP PD 2656 no. 42), although this possibility cannot
have disappeared from the backs of people's minds. How had the Party
managed to co-opt the Inca?

The Liberal Party was not explicitly identified with any one set of concrete interests: its members and sympathizers were distributed through
every social class and caste. Such a heterogeneous membership meant
heterogeneity of appeal, and it was loaded with conflicting aspirations
whose incompatibility would not become apparent until the revolutionary "moment of truth." The Party offered a catholic mirage, a reflection
of existing society with the Constitutionalist "taint" removed, a mirror

in which all who looked might hope to see themselves whole. To this extent, it could be seen as the latest in a long line of Andean movements that aimed to restore a "just order" that had been betrayed, to realign a social project that had become distorted. This discourse could seduce supporters of a whole range of positions, from the March of Progress to the Tributary State, from a Bonapartist Presidency to a Sunborn Inca, from a Liberal Citizenry to an Indian.

On the other hand, we have just seen that the Indian movement could engage the Liberal Party without renouncing its immediate objectives. The demand for fiscal justice, expressed by the Laymis as "moralization through Indianization," would be the same within a Liberal as within an Inca state. The difference was that, through dialogue with the Liberal Party, the process of "Indianization" could not be projected beyond the level of the recaudadores and corregidores, leaving open the higher echelons for mestizos and creoles. In the Inca Republic, however, the process could be extended up to the subprefecture (Pedro Gabriel in 1886) and the cupola itself (Inca Willka). The transition in Charcas Province from Pedro to Julian Gabriel, from N. Willka to Juan Coyo, seems to represent a reversion, at the level of the leadership, from the second to the first objective.

1899: REVOLUTION AND THE REEMERGENCE OF RACISM

Both projects had their pluralist and their racist variants. Liberal Republicanism contained an ethnocidic component in its very universalism (Platt 1984), which could easily acquire a genocidic extension (Rivera 1984). Equally, the assertion of Indian hegemony over "the white race" could be extended to "getting rid of the white race" altogether. The Inca version of racism simply held up a mirror to the Liberal version (Mannoni 1969), which in turn felt horror at finding its own "Social Darwinist" theories of social evolution (Demelas 1980) inverted to its disadvantage.

A vivid expression of the ambiguity inherent in Indian adoption of Liberal slogans can be seen in their adoption into that most "Indian" of contexts: territorial disputes over land (*ch'ajwa*). In March 1899, at the height of the Revolution, the loyalist corregidor of nearby Urmiri (Porco Province) wrote to the last Constitutionalist prefect in Potosí (AHP PD 2837 s/n):

Last February 13, at 2 P.M., our *Segunda* Carlos Morales was assassinated. The Caguayos did it. Apart from the homicide, 10 were seriously wounded and are convalescing. Treacherously the traitors told us to abstain, so my community went to check our boundary stones without any offensive weapons. But the Caguayos were waiting for us with slings, sticks, knives, and clubs, 100 of them — and with the further circumstance of ¡*viva Pando!* It wasn't just the Caguayos, but the Cultas too; and they want to take over our pastures, which according to documents from the time of the king were bought by our ancestors. . . . And they say they are of another department, that the authorities of Potosí have no authority over them.

In this interethnic confrontation, *¡viva Pando!* flies across the border like a stone from a sling (let us recall that, in Macha, such stones are called *incas*). For the loyal Urmiris, the shout hurts like an offensive weapon. Moreover, the land concerned lies on the frontier between revolutionary Oruro and a loyal fraction of Potosí: interethnic boundaries had lent their fluidity to interdepartmental limits, and both coincided with the point of political rupture at the national level. Turning the tables on the Urmiris thus becomes for the Caguayos part of a wider inversion of the existing order which — in Andean as in Liberal discourse — should usher in a new age of "justice."

Further north, however, the autonomy of the Indian objectives had already become plain. On March 1 the figure of the Indian leader from Sicasica (La Paz), Z. Willka, had replaced that of Pando in the minds of the ayllus of Mohoza, as they proceeded to sacrifice and consume parts of 120 Constitutionalist soldiers (Condarco M. 1965: 280–91). On the same day in Charcas Province, Juan Coyo left Chayanta (town) and descended to the valleys where, supported by Chayantakas, Qhanas, Awkimarkas, and the Moscarí ayllus, he joined with Liberal townsfolk to take San Pedro on March 17 (AHP PDE 9348). A few days later, Machas and Pocoatas, together with local mestizos and (probably) a detachment of northern Indians, rose up to isolate and storm Colquechaca — without success (AHP PD 2835 s/n various; AHP PD 2839 s/n various). Both forces then converged on Tacarani, where the rope-bridge had been cut, leaving two companies of Alonso's Fifth Batallion unable to cross the river in spate. Under attack not only from the Indians but also from Llallagua tin miners, the Constitutionalists were able to cut their way back to Sacaca. But the subprefect wrote from Colquechaca that "in the skirmish of Tacarani fragments of soldiers have been found, who were probably mutilated by the Indians in the heat of the battle" (AHP PD 2839 s/n various; AHP PDE 9348). These extensions of *ch'ajwa* norms (such as we have already met with during the Macha/Pocoata feud of 1875) into the revolutionary arena would trigger off the Liberal clampdown on the "barbarian" allies of "civilization," as the Constitutionalist resistance faded away.

All over the region, Indian mobilization was quickly reclassified as "rebellion" by incoming Liberal authorities. The two new subprefects demanded military support to "crush and pacify uprisings" in their respective provinces (AHP PD 2839 s/n; AHP PD 2841 s/n). In Carasi, the townsfolk killed one Indian and wounded fourteen others with guns distributed by the Liberal corregidor. When the Machas and Pocoatas tried to sue them and get the corregidor changed, the subprefect first received the defendants' gifts of sugar cane, eggs, fish, corn beer, and grape alcohol, before whipping the plaintiffs and disallowing their candidate. Further, the Pocoatas' lawyer, Dr. Osvaldo Abastoflor, who had been wounded fighting the Constitutionalists and had saved Carasi from Indian invasion (due to his personal links with their leaders) (AHP PDE 9243), was now outlawed as an "agitator" of "cannibals" (*antropófagos*) after being freed from arrest by his still rebellious clients in Tacarani and Moscarí (AHP PD 2841 s/n).

Here, racist polarization was extreme. The collapse of the intercaste front following the *ch'ajwa* with the Constitutionalists was confirmed when it became clear that the Indians meant to reincorporate squatters' lands into the ayllu regime. Though consistent with existing legislation, this was not why private farmers had fought for the Liberal Party. Under the leadership of Juan de Dios Jarro, the Indians took over farms and divided the harvests and lands among themselves. With support from some mestizos, they refused to pay their tribute, sending representatives to the new government to demand fulfilment of previous Liberal promises. With the main road to Colquechaca virtually in their hands, and the postillion service suspended, the Indians of Moscarí and Micani conspired to sack the towns and declare war on "the white race." From the other side of the gulf, one estate owner called the rebels "communist savages" — a neologism whose blanket dismissal of collective forms of property (both rural and industrial) would resound in the Liberal phrasebook for many years to come. The subprefect of Charcas, too hawkish to recognize the legal foundation for the Indian position, warned the government that "the savages could be about to consummate an act more horrific than Mohoza" (AHP PD 2841 s/n various; AHP PD 2894 s/n various).

We do not yet know how the situation in Moscarí and Pocoata was resolved. But the presence of some mestizo support, and that of lawyers such as Abastoflor, should not be reduced simply to "agitation" from self-interest. Cash payments by ayllus to their legal representatives (*derramas*) could be extracted deceitfully, but they could also correspond to real services rendered, as we have seen. More suggestive is the reference in July 1899 by the subprefect of Chayanta Province to the "division of the Liberal Party in this province into two completely 'personalist' groups" (AHP PD 2841 s/n). It is tempting to relate this division to two styles of approaching the task of reconstructing intercaste client relations under Liberal hegemony. Hardliners, like the subprefect of Charcas, may be contrasted with others whose greater responsiveness to Indian demands could permit them to reestablish some degree of legitimacy. The interplay of both styles would be an essential feature of the uneasy political truce that permitted the consolidation and further expansion of private smallholdings, with government support, between 1900 and the next regional explosion in 1927.

But it would be wrong to conclude that the results of Indian mobilization were so "derisory" that it should be interpreted as nothing more than a jacquerie (Demelas 1985). Rather, all participants in the Revolution ended up jostling to expand into that part of the regional political space that had constituted its immediate objectives. Attempts to reconstruct the system of intercaste relations could not disguise important changes. Within the rural world, mestizos could now count on state support for their efforts to consolidate their holdings. But the Indians were successful in taking over control of the tribute collection process — and until 1930 the tribute continued to represent up to a fifth of total departmental income (Platt 1982a). Liberal prefects in Potosí were impressed with the punctualitiy of semestral deliveries "in spite of the suppression of the recaudadores, who have been replaced by persons named from among the commoners themselves with the title of *curacas recaudadores*." While the possibility of continued access to recognized services in the commons will need further research, it seems that the Indian collectors now began to retain a percentage of tribute monies as their remuneration. Some even took it on themselves to update the tribute lists, though without yielding copies to treasury officials. Fiscal control by departmental authorities became impossible, since the Indians were also able to force the suspension of land commissions in 1902, which would not return until after the Second Agrarian Reform of 1953.

It is clear that, in spite of economic crisis and growing pressure from private property, the ayllus entered the twentieth century with a substantial increase in fiscal autonomy. The temporary renewal of their "pact" with the state had become possible on the basis of proposals originally conceived under the Ballivian regime. Internal contradictions in creole legislation had reflected the incapacity of the state to impose its model of Citizenship on an alien reality. Beyond all the rhetoric of "civilization" and "savagery," these contradictions reemerged at the end of the century, as each sector backed up argument with force to advance its claims. Old tensions were increased, but the contenders were still too evenly matched for any definitive resolution to occur in 1899.

CONCLUSIONS

We have seen how the 1899 Revolution stands at a climax in the secular confrontation by which enlightened liberalism attempted to dismantle Bolivia's Andean-colonial inheritance, in the name of a historicism oriented toward universal progress through the expansion of private property, capital accumulation, and free trade. Agrarian reform had been implicit in the Bolivarian premises of independence. But although Melgarejo's assault on the communities is commonly taken as the model of creole intentions, we have here preferred to emphasize the Indian experience under Ballivian, as a crucial antecedent for understanding the barely masked conflicts within the Liberal Party's "popular front."

We have insisted throughout on the importance of approaching Andean rebellion through the institutional bases of Indian rural society. In Chayanta, the segmentary system combines with the "archipelago" settlement pattern to establish a social framework for the dynamics of alliance formation. At the same time, the function of the Catholic fiesta-cycle as an economic and ritual calendar is extended, with its associated customs of ceremonial warfare, to cue the organization of rebellion in time and space. On the other hand, differences in the balance between tribute categories must be examined in relation to kinship, inheritance patterns, and tribute within each ethnic group. Rather than leaping to conclusions about the political predispositions of forasteros, we have preferred to emphasize the variety of situations disguised by the term, with a corresponding diversity in the precise nature of ethnic protest.

In the same way, the problem of leadership has been approached through the hierarchy of Indian authorities in charge of tribute collection. Ayllu control over the lower levels has been contrasted with subprefectural nomination of non-Indian recaudadores until the Revolution. The breakdown in this system's legitimacy led to the eventual appearance of Indian collectors subject to ayllu consensus. Preenlightenment pressures toward "democratization" from the Indian tributaries could thus dispute the model proposed by liberal Republicanism.

Land problems, though real, were essentially an aspect of the fiscal debate: both converged in the reconstitution of the old repartimientos. Indian fiscal authorities could thus naturally assume the defense of territory. Some would become attorneys (apoderados) to their ethnic group (following a pattern already established by the Katari brothers in the 1780s), though we know little of the mechanisms favoring the extension of certain leaders' jurisdictions (such as Juan Coyo). Legal counsel was also available from non-Indian lawyers in the local towns (sneered at as "penpushers" by government authorities): these could form a component in the erratic alliances between Indians and mestizos. Although such men could acquire influence, there is little reason to suppose that manipulating leaders and "agitators" necessarily led the mass of the Indians by the nose. Protests against agrarian reform emerged initially from the tributaries themselves, and leaders had to build on their critical support.

The presence of an Inca leadership in the 1880s has been analyzed, not as a "messianic dream," but as a natural mirror to creole hegemony within a common "Republican" model. It represents an extension of local ayllu efforts to control fiscal administration, by simply projecting the Indianization policy toward the dominant levels in the state apparatus. Pluralist and racist variants can be detected in both Inca and Liberal Party rhetoric, but to dismiss the Inca as a *coquecigrue* (Demelas 1985) is to substitute creole attitudes for analysis. The appearance of the Inca, with a subprefect at his right hand, represents a specifically nineteenth-century transformation of an old symbol of Andean statecraft. His promise of Indian hegemony has repeatedly found supporters among the ayllus at conjunctures when no source of redress is visible within the existing social hierarchy.

Precisely this absence seemed to have been rectified by the emergence of the Liberal Party. But renewed racist polarization was an inevitable consequence of the creole decision to join hands against the "barbarian" threat to "civilization." Moreover, by supporting mestizos in their efforts to consolidate their holdings, Party leaders were able to drive a wedge between the Indians and their ambivalent allies. They could not know that they had taken on board a "Trojan Horse," which would finally erupt in the faces of the creole oligarchy during the mestizo drive to national hegemony in the wake of the Revolution of 1952.

NOTES

1 Only a summary of this source, for Chayanta Province, has yet been located although we know the *Catastro* was carried out in all Potosí provinces. If the originals can be found, they will prove an invaluable source for the study of early Republican rural society.

2 The source cited in fact gives 10,000 as the number of aspiring *mitayos*. But in the 1832 *Manifiesto* of the *Tribunal General de Minería* (ANB MH t.29 no. 9) we hear of 1000 Chayanta families willing to provide *mitayos*, which seems a more realistic number.

3 I have elsewhere analyzed the legal and religious connection perceived between *mita* service and communal prosperity, as the basis of the *mita*'s legitimacy within the Colonial "pact" (Platt 1983).

4 This assignment of valley lands to highland tributary groups explains the governor's otherwise curious statement that the valley cantons of Carasi, Micani, Guaycoma, Chayrapata, Chayala, San Marcos, and Surumi were without Indian tributaries (AHP PD 286 no. 40). Cf. Platt 1982a: 47–48.

5 Since the presidency of Achá, subprefects had replaced governors and Linares' *jefes políticos* at the head of the provinces.

6 Teófilo Lozada is a mysterious figure: an ally of Juan Coyo in 1896 (AHP PD

2652 no. 41), proposed as Secretary to the land commission in July 1897 (AHP PD 2713 s/n), the following month he sparks off the Sacaca massacre. Was he a Liberal Party *agent provocateur*?

REFERENCES

Abbreviations: AHP Archivo Histórico de Potosí
ANB Archivo Nacional de Bolivia
EN Escrituras Notariales
MH Ministerio de Hacienda
PD Prefectura Departamental (Correspondencia)
PDE Prefectura Departamental (Expedientes)

ANDERLE, ÁDÁM
1982 "Conciencia Nacional y Continentalismo en América Latina en la Primera Mitad del Siglo XX." *Acta Historica*. Acta Univ. Szegediensis T. 73. Szeged-Hungary.

ANÓNIMO
1860 *Opúsculo sobre la Moneda Boliviana que Circula en el Perú. . . .* Lima: José Daniel Huerta.

ANÓNIMO, UN VECINO DE CHAYANTA
1871 *La propiedad de las tierras de originarios y la injusticia de las ventas de ellas.* Sucre.

BARNADAS, JOSEP
1978 "Martin Castro (un clérigo boliviano combatiente combatido)." *Estudios Bolivianos en Homenaje a Gunnar Mendoza.* La Paz.

BUECHLER, ROSE MARIE
1981 *The Mining Society of Potosí, 1776–1810.* Syracuse University: Department of Geography.

CARNERO, NADIA
1980 *Mapas Campesinos de Bolivia.* Lima: Seminario de Historia Rural Andina. Universidad Mayor de San Marcos.

CONDARCO MORALES, RAMIRO
1965 *Zárate, el Temible Willka.* La Paz: Talleres Gráficos Bolivianos.

CORNBLIT, OSCAR
1970 "Levantamientos de masas en Perú y Bolivia durante el siglo dieciocho." *Revisita Latinoamericana de Sociología* 6.1. Buenos Aires.

DE LA RIVA, NARCISO
1885 *Informe del Revisitador de tierras de origen de la provincia de Chayanta.* Sucre.

DEMELAS, MARIE-DANIÈLE
1980 "Darwinisme à la créole: le darwinisme social en Bolivie (1870–1910)." *Pluriel* 20.
1985 "Jacqueries indiennes, politique créole." *Caravelle* 44. Toulouse.

ESPINOZA, WALDEMAR
1969   "El Memorial de los Charcas." *Cantuta*. Chosica.

FELLMAN VERLARDE, JOSÉ
1970   *Historia de Bolivia. Tomo II: La Bolivianidad Semifeudal*. Cochabamba: Los Amigos del Libro.

GODOY, RICARDO
1981   "From Indian to Miner and Back Again: Small-scale Mining in the Jukumani Ayllu, Northern Potosí, Bolivia." Ph.D. thesis, Columbia University.

GRIESHABER, ERWIN
1977   "Survival of Indian Communities in Nineteenth-Century Bolivia." Ph.D. thesis, University of North Carolina.

HARRIS, OLIVIA
1978a   "De la symétrie au triangle: transformations symboliques au nord du Potosí." *Annales ESC* Année 33, nos. 5–6.
1978b   "El parentesco y la economía vertical en el ayllu Laymi." *Avances* 1. La Paz.
1982   "Labour and produce in an ethnic economy, Northern Potosí, Bolivia." In *Ecology and Exchange in the Andes*, ed. David Lehmann. Cambridge University Press.

KLEIN, HERBERT
1982   *Bolivia: The Evolution of a Multi-Ethnic Society*. Oxford University Press.

LEWIN, BOLESLAO
1967   *La rebelión de Túpac Amaru*. Buenos Aires: Sociedad Editora Latinoamericana.

MANNONI, OCTAVE
1969   *Clefs pour l'imaginaire ou l'autre scène*. Paris: Seuil.

MITRE, ANTONIO
1981   *Los patriarcas de la plata*. Lima: Instituto de Estudios Peruanos.

MÖRNER, MAGNUS
1978   *Perfil de la sociedad rural del Cuzco a fines de la colonia*. Lima: Universidad del Pacífico.

MURRA, JOHN
1972   "El 'control vertical' de un máximo de pisos ecológicos en la economía de las sociedades andinas." *Visita de la Provincia de León de Huánuco en 1562, tomo II*. Huánuco: Universidad Nacional Hermilio Valdizán.

O'PHELAN, SCARLETT
1985   *Rebellions and Revolts in Eighteenth Century Perú and Upper Perú*. Lateinamerikanische Forschungen 14. Böhlau Verlag Köln Wien.

OSSIO, JUAN, ed.
1973   *Ideología mesiánica del mundo andino*. Lima.

PLATT, TRISTAN
1976   *Espejos y Maíz: temas de la estructura simbólica andina*. La Paz: Cuadernos de Investigaciones CIPCA no. 10.

1978   "Mapas coloniales de Chayanta: dos visiones conflictivas de un solo paisaje." *Estudios Bolivianos en Homenaje a Gunnar Mendoza*. La Paz.

1982a   *Estado boliviano y ayllu andino*. Lima: Instituto de Estudios Peruanos.

1982b   "The rôle of the Andean *ayllu* in the reproduction of the petty commodity régime in Northern Potosí (Bolivia)." In *Ecology and Exchange in the Andes*, ed. David Lehmann. Cambridge University Press.

1983   "Conciencia proletaria y religión andina: *qhuya runa* y *ayllu* en el Norte de Potosí." *HISLA* 2. Lima.

1984   "Liberalism and Ethnocide in the Southern Andes." *History Workshop Journal no. 17*. London: Routledge and Kegan Paul.

1986   *Estado tributario y librecambio en Potosí (siglo XIX). Mercado indígena, proyecto proteccionista y lucha de ideologías monetarias*. La Paz: HISBOL.

in press   "Pensamiento político Aymara." In *Cultura y Sociedad Aymara*, ed. Xavier Albó. UNESCO–Siglo XXI.

RIVERA, SILVIA

1978   "La expansión del latifundio en el Altiplano boliviano." *Avances* 2. La Paz.

1984   *Oprimidos pero no vencidos*. La Paz: HISBOL-CSUTCB.

SAIGNES, THIERRY

1985a   "Notes on the Regional Contribution to the *Mita* in Potosí in the Early Seventeenth Century." *Bulletin of Latin American Research* 4, 1. London: Pergamon Press.

1985b   *Caciques, Tribute and Migration in the Southern Andes: Indian Society and the 17th-Century Colonial Order*. Institute of Latin American Studies Working Paper No. 15. London.

SÁNCHEZ ALBORNOZ, NICOLÁS

1978   *Indios y tributos en el Alto-Perú*. Lima: Instituto de Estudios Peruanos.

SALOMON, FRANK

1982   "Chronicles of the Impossible: Notes on Three Peruvian Indigenous Historians." In *From Oral to Written Expression: Native Andean Chronicles of the Early Colonial Period*, ed. Rolena Adorno. Syracuse University.

SZEMIŃSKI, JAN

1982   *Los Objetivos de los Tuparamistas*. Academia de Ciencias de Polonia. Warsaw: Ossolineum.

TANDETER, ENRIQUE

1980   *Trabajo Forzado y Trabajo Libre en el Potosí Colonial Tardío*. Estudios CEDES 3, 6. Buenos Aires.

VALENCIA VEGA, ALIPIO

1973   *El Pensamiento Político en Bolivia*. La Paz: Editorial Juventud.

WACHTEL, NATHAN

1978   "Hommes d'eau: Le problème uru (XVI–XVII siècles)." *Annales ESC* Année 33, nos. 5–6.

PART IV

Political Dilemmas and Consciousness
in Modern Andean Revolt:
Bolivian Case Studies

Introduction to Part IV

Since the late colonial insurrectionary war, whenever Andean revolts have broken out of the mold of localized peasant uprisings, Andean peoples have forged their political strategies and consciousness in relation to two basic poles: one which pursues a multiethnic praxis, defines enemies narrowly, and envisions a just political order on terms that accord a prominent, perhaps hegemonic, place to creole allies and leaders; another which stresses Indian autonomy, construes most non-Indians as real or potential enemies, and accords a decisive role to the Indianization of national power and leadership. These two poles define a basic dilemma, or tension, of Andean political life. If Andean peoples sometimes appear to partake of both poles at once, as in Túpac Amaru's recruitment of creole and mestizo leaders to wave the banner of an Inca kingdom, or if Andean peoples have sometimes appeared to oscillate rather than choose between poles, as in the swings between Inca- and Liberal-led rebellion in Bolivia during the 1880s and 1890s, it is not because the tension does not exist. Such actions indicate, perhaps, that each pole is too restrictive, that the negations implied by either choice exact too strong a cost, that the basic political contradiction cannot be wished away. The necessity of a multiethnic practice, suited to the realities of power and citizenship in a multiracial society, does not erase the necessity of independent Andean organization and strength, suited to the realities of racism and betrayal in a neocolonial order.

For Andean peoples, the twentieth century brought new twists to this basic dilemma. Revolutionary agendas, populist politics, and radical critiques of a corrupt and backward *ancièn regime* redefined national politics in the twentieth century and created for the first time serious drives, from within the creole-mestizo world, to transform society in ways that might incorporate indigenous revindications into the very core of national progress and reform.

The new scheme did not burst forth rapidly and of a piece. Nor did it imply uniformity among the radicals and reformers, themselves divided between Marxist agendas emphasizing class struggle and socialist revolution; populist appeals to anti-imperialism, antifeudalism, and the construction of a reformed capitalist order; and ambiguous stances that simultaneously favored specific social reforms, such as the abolition of servile labor obligations on haciendas, while failing to challenge the landed oligarchy as such. Creole and mestizo projects for national transformation took shape in fits and starts against the backdrop of several conditioning influences. First, there were the independent mobilizations and revolts of native Andean peoples. In much of highland Peru and Bolivia, the great wave of effective republican hacienda expansion occurred late, in the closing decades of the nineteenth century and early years of the twentieth. The revival of the Bolivian mines and their food markets, the expansion of wool exports from southern Peru, and the growth of Peru's cities and mining camps all made such expansion attractive, and the work of governments to modernize transportation and the army, and to promote hacendado interests, turned the attractive into the possible. By the 1920s, the great landed estates had locked their iron grip over lands controlled by indigenous communities during much of the nineteenth century. A cycle of major indigenous revolts erupted, with special intensity from 1916–1917 on into the 1920s. These rebellions, like their counterparts in Bolivia in the mid-1940s and early 1950s, and in Peru in the late 1950s and early 1960s, constituted important reference points for national political debates.

Second, the political consequences of capitalist transition created the kind of ferment that placed oligarchical politics on the defensive. The rise of trade unions and labor militancy; the growth of cities and rural-to-urban migration; the emergence of a *petit bourgeois* strata, including professionals and a reform-minded intelligentsia, relatively disconnected from oligarchical patronage and control; the roller-coaster cycles of prosperity and depression in key export sectors — all contributed to the leftist critiques, political parties, and mass actions that made the game of oligarchical rules trickier to play without resorting to repression, populist political styles, or both. But these expedients could also backfire, simply feeding into political polarization.

Third, specific crises provoked the turning points that galvanized key political sectors, especially the military, into organized antioligarchical action. The revolts of Andean peoples and the challenge of labor, creole radicals, and the Left had already made themselves felt during the 1920s. It was not by accident, for example, that *indigenismo* came of age as a powerful intellectual and political movement in the Peru of the 1920s, nor was it by chance that the same period produced Peru's two great radical mentors: Víctor Raúl Haya de la Torre and José Carlos Mariátegui. Yet once the promise of these years fizzled, Peru would have to await a crisis which combined national political scandal with military soul-searching and fresh memories of peasant struggle and guerrilla war to produce, finally in 1968, a modernizing revolution serious enough to attack the highland oligarchy. In Bolivia, the turning point came earlier. Bolivia's bloody and humiliating defeat to Paraguay in the Chaco War (1932–1935) thoroughly discredited the old political order, revitalized the Left, and set the stage for the experiments with "military socialism," populist pacts, and worker-peasant mobilization that culminated, in 1952, with the victory of the National Revolutionary Movement (MNR). The MNR, a populist coalition pushed to the left in 1952–1953 by armed mine workers and Indian peasants, had no choice but to submit to the nationalization of the tin mines and the expropriation of the highland haciendas.

The timing, particular coalitions, and rhetoric of revolutionary politics varied greatly between Peru and Bolivia. But at bottom, native Andean peoples in both countries had to consider whether the rise of sympathetic patrons and allies, including leftist revolutionaries, within the changing creole polity significantly altered the terms of their old political dilemma. When creoles and mestizos attacked the oligarchical order, when populist politicians might court Indians, when new historic alliances became available to promote basic Andean revindications, how should native Andean peoples respond? Did the new scheme of politics render obsolete the historic tension between "national" and "nativist" versions of political destiny? If the new scheme did not dissolve the tension, did it at least change the relative appeal of the two "poles" of Andean politics in a lasting way?

These questions set the context for the two essays in Part IV. Each essay explores the perceptions, dilemmas, and choices of Andeans in the fluid world of modern Bolivian politics. Together, they illuminate the experiences and circumstances that lent legitimacy to *both* poles of Andean politics amid the dramatically shifting political landscape of the twentieth century.

The essay by Dandler and Torrico explores what we may call a "paternal pact" between Andean peasants in Ayopaya (Cochabamba) and President Gualberto Villarroel, leader of the ill-fated military-MNR coalition government (1943–1946) that experimented gingerly with Andean revindications. The field work by Dandler and Torrico, part of a collaborative project with Cochabamba peasants seeking to recover their own history, provides an unusually vivid picture of the agrarian conflict and mobilization that constituted an important prologue to the 1952 revolution. Dandler and Torrico give us the "eyes" we need to see the clandestine leadership networks the peasants relied upon to build an agrarian movement despite the repression, surveillance, and isolation that buttressed the hacienda regime. Their account of local persecution of peasant organizers corrects the kind of hindsight that dismisses the first National Indigenous Congress, held in 1945, as an ineffectual and largely rhetorical activity that evaded a bold stand on agrarian reform. The charge is "true," but misses the point. Dandler and Torrico demonstrate that in its time, and for all its limitations, a national convention to press indigenous claims to citizenship, cement a political pact with the nation's president, and revamp the structure of labor, usufruct rights, and landowner privileges on the haciendas constituted a challenge sufficiently great to unleash the hacendados' organized fury and resistance. The hacendados attempted to block the national meeting, and *did* succeed in rendering national decrees impotent at the local level. Dandler and Torrico's account allows us to appreciate why merely to hold the Congress, in the Bolivia of 1945, constituted a difficult political achievement.

Moreover, their close attention to specific leaders underscores the way peasant leaders took initiatives that forced Villarroel's hand. It was Luis Ramos Quevedo, peasant leader, who manipulated Gualberto Villarroel, Bolivia's President, into publicly committing the government to sponsor the National Indigenous Congress. This perspective illuminates the tensions that developed as all parties sought to bend the terms of their alliance and as the unfolding contradictions led to the ultimate irony: the selective repression of peasants by their government patrons.

Perhaps most unusual, Dandler and Torrico provide striking material on peasant interpretations of their pact with Villarroel. The peasants' and Villarroel's own words point to a highly paternalistic and personally sealed reciprocity that fused the destinies of national leader and Andean peasantry into one. Granted the dignity of citizenship — a citizenship sponsored by a president who spoke Quechua, mixed and ate with Indian delegates, and issued decrees attacking the landed oligarchs — the peasants owed Villarroel their loyalty and obedience. Granted the peasants' backing, the embattled president owed the peasants a pledge to pursue their welfare with the zeal of a father protecting his children. Villarroel needed, in fact, all the backing he could get by 1946. His government had mixed fascist tendencies and brutal repression of competing political parties to its right and left with more progressive revindications of peasants and tin miners. The end result was many enemies, including not only the landed oligarchy, but parts of the labor and university movements. The urban crowd of La Paz rejoiced when it hanged him on July 14, 1946. But Dandler and Torrico make it possible for us to understand the loyalty of those peasants who stood by Villarroel to the bitter end. We are not surprised to discover that the peasants of Yayani gathered in their church, the women dressed as widows, to mourn the president's execution. If Dandler and Torrico's tight focus on one paternal pact does not uncover the whole of modern Andean political consciousness, it at least unlocks the door to one important side of it — the pursuit of a just place in the paternal sun of multiethnic populism.

Other doors are opened in Xavier Albó's study of the rise of the katarista movement among the Aymara people of the altiplano, and as a force to be reckoned with in national politics. The kataristas have sought to break with the tendency to subsume Andean revindications under the political umbrellas wielded by paternal patrons with priorities of their own. At one point or another, these patrons have included labor and political parties of the revolutionary left, as well as civilian and military populists. Self-consciously ethnic in its language and symbols, the katarista movement has stressed the combined struggles against ethnic-national domination and class exploitation; the importance of independent political agendas and organization enabling Andeans to enter pacts on a contingent basis, as equals; and the identification of the contemporary quest for Andean liberation with that led by Túpac Katari in the insurrection of 1780. Strictly speaking, the rise of katarismo, and the concomitant crumbling of earlier Andean peasant pacts with populists and the military, date back only to the 1970s. But this is too narrow an approach. For Albó succeeds in elucidating the fuller meaning of the katarista movement by setting its story in the double context of a lucid narrative of political relations between Andean peasantries and Bolivia's political parties, the military, the labor movement, and the state since the 1940s; and a sweeping overview of several centuries that casts illuminating light on the regions and issues prominent during the last forty years.

The results are important on several counts. Within an internally plural world of Andean regions and peoples, we are able to understand more clearly the regional and ethnic boundaries of Andean pacts with the state, even at the time of those pacts' greatest strength. In Albó's analysis, the Quechua valleys of Cochabamba and the Aymara altiplano of La Paz become partly real, partly symbolic expressions of two poles in Andean politics. More important, Albó gives us tools with which to begin mounting an explanation for Cochabamba's comparative receptivity to external influences and multiethnic coalitions, and La Paz's firmer conviction that Andeans gain strength by turning inward and avoiding multiethnic entanglements leading to illusion and betrayal.

At the same time, these regional contrasts apply only up to a certain point. Albó's narrative exposes Andean political experiences common to both regions that pushed Andeans to search for greater autonomy. On the one hand, populist pacts with the state degenerated, under military rule, into the crudest sort of paternal authoritarianism and repression. It was in Cochabamba that Andean peasants mounted the fiercest opposition to President Bánzer's austerity package, in 1974, and it was in Cochabamba that the military responded by firing on the peasants. On the other hand, to suggest that the katarista founders began with a clear emphasis on Andean political autonomy, or that they have stood apart from ongoing experimentation with political coalitions and umbrellas, would grossly distort their political experience. The kataristas built their sharpening sense of ethnic political identity and strategy in direct relation to all-too-familiar experiences of humiliation and powerlessness at the hands of patronizing allies and sponsors on the Left.

Finally, Albó demonstrates that Andean peasants responded to the failure of paternal pacts with strategies more complex than a simple swing from the pole of multiethnic politics to the pole of nativist independence. Albó sees in the katarista movement an attempt to achieve a new synthesis superseding old dichotomies: a refusal to consider class and ethnicity as mutually exclusive priorities of struggle; a determination both to expand peasant autonomy vis-à-vis the state, *and* to demand participation in and shared governance with the state; an effort to develop an independent indigenous politics not to withdraw from collaboration with non-Indians, but to achieve the first-class citizenship needed to negotiate on a new basis the collaboration of native Andeans with workers, state, and nation. The katarista attempt at creative synthesis of elements drawn from antagonistic poles actually corresponds well, in Albó's view, to the preference of Andean peasants to avoid the traps set by overly rigid oppositions. Even as the katarista movement, for example, gained organizational and ideological strength among various Aymara peoples, as voters the Aymara peasants pursued a pragmatic electoral strategy favoring old-line candidates with a "real" chance to win. Perhaps, Albó reminds us, Andeans apply to politics the strategy they bring to agriculture. If Andean peasants characteristically insure against harvest failure by cultivating several crops in a variety of highland microenvironments, why not play several political "cards" at once to insure against the failure of any one of them?

Two other participants in the 1984 conference provided significant evidence of the effort by Andean peasants and political leaders to turn antithetical choices into complementary strategies in a difficult political landscape. Víctor Hugo Cárdenas drew on his own experience in the katarista movement to present powerful and eloquent testimony of the katarista effort to transcend conventional formulations that lock Andean peoples into a fixed (and futile) stance on one side of a great divide. To have to choose between "class" and "ethnicity" as *the* organizing principle of political action, for example, forced Andean peasants either to subsume their struggles under a working class framework that, practically speaking, placed the peasants in a position to suffer manipulation, humiliation, and betrayal at the bottom of the Left's political ladder; or to retreat into extreme Indianist postures that readily degenerated into racism, manipulation by right-wing patrons, or the suicide of political isolation. For the case of Peru, Rosalind Gow drew on extensive field work and historical research in Cuzco and Puno to argue that Andean peasant ideology has in this century proved far too flexible and adaptive to shifting circumstances to fit consistently in the mold either of separatism and withdrawal, or multiethnic collaboration and political integration. In her analysis, the core ideology of Andean revolution — *Tawantinsuyu* — rises above the poles of practical politics by referring not so much to particular political strategies of the moment, as to the *moral* qualities of social relations in times of the Inca Empire ("Tawantinsuyu") and in the transformed era to come. In practice, the ideology of *Tawantinsuyu* has justified behaviors ranging from "race war," to silent withdrawals from "external" creole worlds, to participation in multiethnic projects of reform and revolution.

In the dialectic between Cochabamba and La Paz, Albó finds a modern reincarnation of the older political tension between the revolutions of Túpac Amaru and Túpac Katari. In the katarista movement of Bolivia, Albó finds that the leaders, events, and issues of the great insurrection of 1780 have in some way burned themselves into the consciousness of contemporaries, providing them the irresistible symbols that energize people to act in social movements. In my own experience in Ayacucho, Peru, in the late 1970s, few could escape that sense of the past's immediacy, its tangible presence and urgency in the polemical world of contemporary life. For in the Andes, past, present, and future merge in the unfolding saga of survival, resistance, and revindication.

CHAPTER 11

From the National Indigenous Congress to the Ayopaya Rebellion: Bolivia, 1945–1947

JORGE DANDLER AND JUAN TORRICO A.

The objective of this chapter is to identify those organizational initiatives by the peasantry during the 1940s which seem to us important for understanding how that rural sector participated in the intense political dynamics and mobilization associated with the crisis of the state and society preceding the Revolution of 1952. Undoubtedly, the 1940s were a period of great consequence for Bolivia. In the aftermath of the Great World Depression and the Chaco War, the 1940s witnessed the formation of mass parties, the consolidation of important unions for mine and factory workers, and the definition of goals and revindications at odds with the oligarchic state. It was as well a decade of great struggles, massacres, and repression in the countryside, mines, and cities. All of these processes form part of a concentrated history of struggle and mobilization prior to the Revolution of 1952. The crisis of the state was manifested precisely through events such as those we will analyze in this essay.

We will focus on two episodes: the National Indigenous Congress of 1945, and the peasant rebellion of Ayopaya, in Cochabamba in 1947. The Congress was a great national event, the culmination of various regional congresses and other organizational efforts of the peasantry. The rebellion was a regional event, perhaps a parochial one, but like other rebellions which occurred during the 1946–1952 sexennium prior to the April revolution, it revealed that the hacienda system was no longer hegemonic.

We searched in diverse areas of Cochabamba for peasants who had served as delegates to the National Indigenous Congress.[1] The peasants

---

Translation by Hunter Fite and Steve J. Stern. A previous version of this chapter appeared in Spanish in Dandler and Calderón 1984: chapter 4.

not only recalled the names of their delegates, but also described to us the significance of the Congress and the Villarroel administration: it was the first national congress of peasants, and President Villarroel abolished servitude on the haciendas. We were able to interview a number of delegates who offered a more detailed account of their participation in the Congress, and the manner in which the *patrones* (landowner bosses) attempted to obstruct all attempts at organization. Any delegate was automatically labelled an "agitator" or "ring leader" by the landowners, and many were expelled from the haciendas even during Villarroel's government. In some haciendas, previously organized *campesinos* (peasants) demanded the fulfillment of the law. But the vast majority of landlords refused to enter into negotiations with the peasants, manipulating instead the local authorities to repress any campesino demand. During the course of our field work, people spoke to us of a great rebellion in the province of Ayopaya, which took place early in 1947, just six months after the death of President Villarroel. The patrones had reintroduced the system of servitude, and were attempting to repress any vestiges of organizational autonomy or peasant leadership. In Ayopaya we interviewed many participants and witnesses to the uprising.

The Congress of 1945 and the rebellion of Ayopaya are two events ingrained in the historical memory of the peasantry. These events, like many other such events, have nonetheless not yet received much explicit attention in written form. And according to those peasants of the old generation who endured the hacienda system and struggled so much, the Congress, the rebellion, and similar events are already distant and difficult-to-understand events to the new peasant generation born since the Agrarian Reform.

This chapter attempts to synthesize the history of both events as part of a collective investigation initiated with the peasants themselves about their own history. We present the study as a narrative that attempts to integrate the observations and perspectives of the campesinos themselves. We keep notes and bibliographic references to a minimum in order to simplify the presentation.

THE HIGHLANDS OF AYOPAYA

In the Cochabamba region one observes a great historical heterogeneity of agrarian situations. The central valleys of Cochabamba witnessed a long process of formation and decomposition of the hacienda system. Larson's historical study (1983) demonstrates that during the colonial period, there developed in the valleys a hegemonic hacienda system tied directly to the commercialization of agricultural, livestock, and artisanal products for the mines of Potosí. In the late colonial period, with the decline in silver mining and the contraction of the colonial market, the commercial and productive dynamism of the haciendas deteriorated. Increasingly, the *hacendados* (hacienda owners) turned into rentier landlords, while at the same time sectors of the peasantry developed a strengthened position as direct producers for the market. Decades before the Agrarian Reform, there already existed in some rural settlements small peasant proprietors (*piqueros*), independent of the haciendas. There was also an accentuated process of subdivision within the haciendas and diverse forms of tenancy, from *colonato* (labor-based tenancy) to forms of leasing and labor "in partnership" with a proprietor. In Ucureña, in the *valle alto* ("upper valley"), for example, at the Monastery of Santa Clara, a hacienda where serfdom and colonato were still maintained, the peasants organized a union during the 1930s to demand the right to rent and later to buy plots within the hacienda. In the lower valleys, the hacienda no longer monopolized the use of its own lands, and one could observe the growing strength of small-scale agriculture, on plots both in and outside the hacienda (Dandler 1969).

In contrast, in the province of Ayopaya (see Map 9) the hacienda exerted its nearly hegemonic domination over property in land, production, and peasant labor until the implementation of the Agrarian Reform in 1953. There the haciendas were large and extended over a wide range of ecological zones, from river banks as low as 1,700 meters above sea level, to high lands up to 4,000 meters above sea level. This in turn facilitated quite diversified production. In the decades prior to the Agrarian Reform, there developed a stronger tendency on the haciendas to increase the scale of potato production for markets in the city of Cochabamba, the mines, and the cities of the altiplano. Morochata and Independencia, the two principal pueblos, resembled more closely villages such as Achacachi (northern altiplano of La Paz), Sorata, Coroico, or Chulumani (Yungas region of La Paz), than the villages in the valleys of Cochabamba. That is to say, they served less as centers of commercialization than as centers of hacienda domination and services; indeed, a large share of production bypassed these towns for direct wholesale marketing in the *tambos* (roadside outlets) and urban centers. The majority of landholding families chose not to reside in these towns: the great hacendados of Ayopaya lived in the city of Cochabamba or in villages and other properties in the valleys. Morochata and Independencia were the seat of middle-class proprietors, hacienda administrators, town "citizens" (*vecinos*), and provincial officials who lived off the hacienda system and the exploitation of the peasantry.

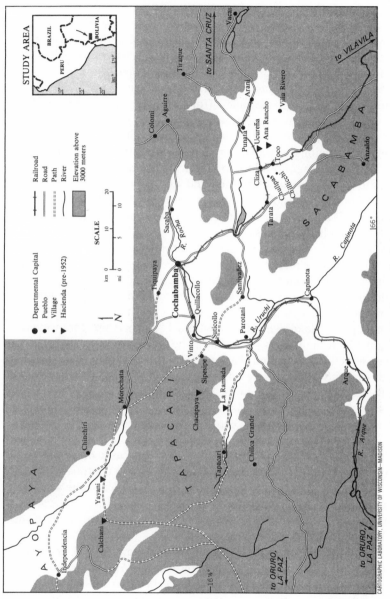

Map 9. Ayopaya in the Greater Cochabamba Region

337

In the mountains of Ayopaya, as in the other high zones of Cochabamba, the peasants were *laris* or "Indians of the estates" (*indios de es-
tancia*), culturally and socially differentiated from those in the valleys. In
the high zones, the campesinos were monolingual Quechua speakers, and
the few schools in existence had been established only recently in the 1940s.
The social and economic distance between the people of the towns (*gente
del pueblo, vecinos del pueblo*) and the laris was much greater in the
mountains than it was in the valleys (for further details see Dandler 1971).

The system of servitude, too, was more brutal and traditional than in
the valleys. A range of gratuitous services prevailed in the high zones,
among them: colonato, usufruct rights in lands granted in exchange for
labor and the return of produce to the hacienda; *mitanaje* and *pongueaje*,
domestic services provided by men and women at the big house of the
hacienda or at the residence of the patrón; and *cachas*, the gratuitous
transport of the hacienda's products to a pueblo or city on the campesinos' own mules or llamas.

Ayopaya was a zone of intensive agriculture where labor was not abundant. For this very reason the rigidity of labor control and the colonato
system more or less embraced the entire peasant population. Under these
conditions, the *colonos* (serfs tied to the colonato system) did not have
the alternative of becoming independent of the hacienda by renting or
buying a plot of land. The aforementioned "partnership" arrangements,
fashionable in the valleys, were rare. The expulsion of a colono, or its
threat, served as control mechanisms over the work force. In some haciendas colono escapes were common. Fugitives sought work in other
haciendas, in the mines, or in the villages and haciendas of the valleys.
The haciendas of Ayopaya, on the other hand, were engaged in the continuous recruitment of poor or expelled peasants from other more remote
haciendas, nearby mountain regions, or from the valleys of Cochabamba.
During the Chaco War (1932-1935), there were cases of colonos who
escaped from haciendas to enlist in the army. But in contrast with other
zones of the country, few colonos from Ayopaya joined the war, since
the hacendados succeeded in imposing their own priorities on the government, thereby avoiding the conscription and subsequent reduction of their
work force.

One large hacienda which became an important site of peasant resistance shortly before the Agrarian Reform was Yayani, owned by the
Monastery of Santa Teresa (Carmelite Order) and rented out under contract for three generations. The property was donated to the monastery
by an owner of other properties in Ayopaya and the Cochabamba region.
It is significant that, according to the documents of the hacienda, during
the War for Independence (1814-1825) the property of Yayani could no

longer be managed by the hacendado who rented it, because of the turbulence and ongoing guerrilla warfare in the zone commanded by the patriot
Lanza. Ayopaya constituted one of the *republiquetas* ("little republics")
of Independence, an area where guerrillas fought against the Spanish
regime for fifteen years (see Mendoza 1982). The contract and legal re-
strictions on the property of Yayani remained unaltered after the founding of the Republic. In the period of interest to us, exploitation was extreme and, according to the peasants, the patrones and administrators
intensified servile obligations and exactions in order to increase the commercial yield of their properties.

THE AWAKENING

Toward the end of the 1930s, as a result of the great political and social
crisis brought about by defeat in the Chaco War, the advent of the nationalistic military governments of Busch and Toro, as well as the surge
of new political currents, the peasantry in Ayopaya and other regions found
some echo of its search for justice:

We noticed that things were changing during the Busch administration, when
periodicals and various individuals published articles and pamphlets speaking in
favor of the campesinos. Once when we were transporting potatoes by mule over
to the house of the patrón in Vinto, some friends read to us from the papers about
the education decrees. But the patrón whipped us for talking with other peasants
near the railroad station. It was very difficult to apprise ourselves of Busch and
his decrees and promises because the patrones and administrators did not want
us to talk with anyone from the valley or village. . . . It was also prohibited for
us to read newspapers at the hacienda. Very few colonos knew how to read anyway, so we had to talk with people from the valley. In Morochata the people treated
us like *pongos* [servants] and animals. After everything, [in spite of] what we heard
about these decrees and promises, no one helped us, and, by order of the patrón,
we were treated more cruelly than ever. . . . But by this time we were beginning
to defend ourselves like men.

According to an ex-hacendado whom we interviewed,

The peasants, emboldened by a government that offered them promises and people who promoted indigenous schools, political lawyers, and union proselytizers,
and even resentful hacienda administrators and majordomos, began to rouse the
colonada [the mass of colonos] against the patrones.

In various haciendas of Ayopaya in 1940 and 1941, the peasants issued
judicial demands against the patrones and administrators of the haciendas.
The campesinos readied themselves in an organized way, initiating clandestine conversations with lawyers and later insisting that the provincial

judges proceed with the formalities of holding trials and the corresponding hearings, that they listen to and interrogate plaintiffs, witnesses, and accused, that they file the *expedientes* (legal dossier of documents), and that they abstain from emitting a biased judgement.

The peasants from one hacienda in Ayopaya brought suit against the patrón (the documentation of which we found in the Archivo Judicial de Independencia) for excesses within the servitude system and abuses of young girls who served as "mit'anis" in the main house of the hacienda; a long expediente contains detailed declarations taken from dozens of women and colonos regarding their many obligations and punishments.

In the hacienda of Yayani, the campesinos of the *suyo* (section) of Tirita filed a suit in 1940 against the overseer and patrón based on a labor-related incident: a peasant was viciously assaulted by the overseer and threatened with death. His workmates defended him and interposed themselves to avoid further problems. The entire group and the assaulted man were imprisoned in Cochabamba. Other peasants, among them Hilarión Grájeda (the victim's brother), went to the city to defend them and free them from the police. This incident served to establish contact with some lawyers and leaders of manufacturing and printing unions. Grájeda and other peasants presented a formal complaint at the Ayopaya court (filed as a criminal suit by the peasants of Yayani, April 24, 1940, in the Juzgado de Instrucción Penal de Ayopaya, Sección Independencia):

Since our youth we have been colonos and servants of the proprietor of the Yayani estate, for whom we have always reserved the utmost respect and consideration. But, not content with our servile attitude and taking advantage of our condition as natives, which we are, he commits all kinds of crimes against our persons and the little property we have. So it is that with frivolous pretexts and without our having provided any justifiable motive, he violently takes from us the animals which are exclusively ours, and furthermore, commits abuses and exactions which now make intolerable our situation as colonos on that property. May it be added to the aforementioned that the overseer . . . apparently on the instruction of his patrón, the proprietor, commits all classes of abuse on our persons and other colonos from the same estate, going so far as inflicting blows upon us and whipping various people, such as [names] and others. He even went so far as to set fire to the hut of [woman's name].

It is probable that only after 1940 did peasants, relying on the support of a few lawyers in the city of Cochabamba, "dare" to file suit against patrones. It is significant that in these trials, the judicial authorities adhered to the formalities, serving summonses and taking written accounts of the interrogations of the plaintiffs, witnesses, and accused. In the case cited, the trial ended formally in March 1946; the first judge abstained from intervening in the case, and another took it over, only to conclude that the evidence against the accused was insufficient.

From the moment they initiated these judicial complaints, the peasants involved themselves in an open conflict with the administrators and patrones of Ayopaya. Some were expelled from the hacienda or persecuted for various years. In the Yayani case, Grájeda and his group of plaintiffs arranged to carry out the suit in Independencia and Cochabamba City, gaining legal protection to absent themselves periodically, and avoiding expulsion from the hacienda.

The expectations of the peasants of Ayopaya increased with the ascent of Colonel Gualberto Villarroel to power in 1943, with the aid of a coup d'etat sponsored by the *Movimiento Nacionalista Revolucionario* (MNR; "Revolutionary Nationalist Movement"). Grájeda and a small nucleus of collaborators from Yayani, as well as some *alcaldes de campo* (hacienda leaders) and neighbors, began to make contact with other leaders in the highlands, altiplano, and valleys. Some of these travelled extensively through the rural areas to make contact with other peasant leaders and recently named governmental authorities. For the peasants of Ayopaya the relationship established initially with several peasant leaders from other zones was important.

Luis Ramos Quevedo was the son of a small proprietor in Chacapaya, in the high zone of the village of Sipe Sipe in Quillacollo province (Cochabamba). He distinguished himself as the general secretary and principal agent of the National Indigenous Committee. With other leaders he organized various regional congresses, and from the first months of the Villarroel government he dedicated himself to the promotion of a National Indigenous Congress, among other goals. The peasants of Ayopaya remember him as the "Rumi Sonk'o" ("heart of stone") for his great capacity as a leader and his daring. According to informants, "upon the death of his father, his brother offered him two of five hectares of land, which he refused, since he preferred to struggle for the peasants." An ex-administrator of the hacienda Chacapaya recalls that in the early 1940s, he organized peasants from this and other haciendas, together with Dionisio Miranda, whom we shall discuss further on. Ramos Quevedo maintained relations with lawyers, political leaders, and miners, and it is likely that he had developed an extensive network of contacts in Tapacarí, Quillacollo, and Ayopaya before the advent of the Villarroel government. In 1939, for example, he had taken the initiative to meet with President Quintanilla to request measures on behalf of the peasantry, but according to Ramos, it was only Villarroel who listened to the peasants (*La Razón*, December 8, 1944). The peasants of Yayani recall his visits to them on various occasions, affirming his longstanding friendship with Grájeda. The Villarroel government extended him credentials and support for his efforts to organize a National Indigenous Congress. A few weeks following an interview held by the president, the minister of government (Colonel

Edmundo Nogales), and others with Ramos Quevedo and other peasant leaders, there appeared in various rural districts leaflets summoning the National Indigenous Congress in December 1944, and including a photograph of the interview with the authorities. This came as a surprise to Villarroel and Nogales, as the government had expressed only its interest, but had not yet come to a resolution. This demonstrates that the initiative to hold the Congress did not come from the government itself. A few months before the Congress took place, Ramos was disempowered because of accusations of excesses that he had committed on some haciendas, and for charging the peasants quotas to cover the cost of the event (in itself not a crime, since the Indigenous Committee had approved this). He did not assume any post in the Congress, nor was he heard from in the years that followed.

Dionisio Miranda was a colono of the hacienda Chacapaya (the same locale of origin of Ramos Quevedo). Miranda was known in the province of Tapacarí and in the *valle bajo* ("low valley") of Cochabamba as a fighter for the peasant cause. He formed part of the National Indigenous Committee and later, during the National Indigenous Congress, was elected its vice-president. It was through Miranda that Grájeda and other leaders in Ayopaya established contact with Ramos Quevedo and Luis Bustamante (whom we will discuss later). A few months before the Congress, Miranda, Grájeda, Julio Carrasco, and Nicolás Carrasco (Julio's father) were all jailed in Cochabamba and sent to La Paz. Miranda had made various visits to Ayopaya before the Congress, and afterward he accompanied the labor inspector to assure the enforcement of the decrees that liberated peasants from the servitude system on the haciendas. Miranda had also made a name for himself in a suit filed against a patrón for the repression which occurred in Sipe Sipe in 1943, and left two peasants dead and others wounded (*La Calle*, December 16, 1944; interviews with various informants).

Luis Bustamante was another outstanding leader and adviser. He was a vecino of the pueblo of Sipe Sipe, and from the 1930s maintained close relations with the peasants of Tapacarí, Ayopaya, and the valle bajo. He had contact with diverse political and union leaders of the MNR and the POR (*Partido Obrero Revolucionario*; Revolutionary Workers' Party); he had worked previously in the mines of Oruro and the city of La Paz. Bustamante distinguished himself after the revolution as a union organizer and adviser of the peasants. He was one of the founders of the Departmental Federation of Campesinos in August 1952 in Sipe Sipe (for more details see Dandler 1971). He died of the miners' disease (*mal de mina*) around 1954.

Antonio Alvarez Mamani was one of the most important and persecuted leaders of the 1940s. Hailing from the northern altiplano, he spoke Quechua, Aymara, Callawaya, and Spanish. (Some say he was Callawaya in origin, but of this we are not certain.) He was involved in the organization of various regional congresses, especially in La Paz. According to the peasants of Ayopaya, Alvarez Mamani frequented that zone during the reign of Villarroel and maintained contact with them after it: "He would arrive disguised as an Indian to the most remote points of Ayopaya. He made contact with our leaders. We held meetings with him and Grájeda about the injustices of the patrón and how we ought to organize ourselves" (interview with Julio Carrasco). At the Regional Congress of Laja (February 7, 1945), he was elected the general delegate from the La Paz region to the National Indigenous Congress (*La Calle*, February 21, 1945). Nevertheless, he was marginalized shortly before the Congress, perhaps for being a leader who escaped the direct control of the government, as in the case of Ramos Quevedo. During the sexennium of repression (1946-1952) that followed the fall of Villarroel, Alvarez Mamani worked in clandestinity, denouncing the repression suffered by peasant leaders, and facilitating some organizational continuity in the countryside. He maintained contact with Grájeda and other leaders of Ayopaya during this time, a matter we shall discuss in further detail later. After the MNR government came into power in 1952, Alvarez Mamani did not hold any union office.

Another important leader, but one unknown in Ayopaya until after the National Indigenous Congress, was *Francisco Chipana Ramos*, a young peasant hailing from the community of Challapa, in the province of Camacho (La Paz). During his adolescence he worked as a servant for a family in La Paz, "who personally taught me to read and write and later sent me to a school" (interview with Chipana Ramos, *Los Tiempos*, May 13, 1945). He fought in the Chaco War, became the messenger for Captain Germán Busch (who later became president), fell wounded, and was taken prisoner by the Paraguayans in the last year of the war. During the Busch regime, he got involved in various undertakings on behalf of the peasants, securing Busch's support through the Office of Indigenous Education, whose head was the teacher Elizardo Pérez (founder of the teacher training school Warisata in 1928). Hence he had relationships with *indigenista* ("Indianist") teachers as well as union leaders, the latter given stimulus by the recently created Ministry of Labor and its minister, Waldo Alvarez (a factory militant). Upon the inauguration of the Villarroel government, he became a person trusted by the leadership of the MNR, and collaborated with the effort to develop contacts in the countryside. He was elected president of the National Indigenous Congress in 1945.

Through these peasant leaders and other contacts, Grájeda and his collaborators from Ayopaya were introduced to government authorities,

including even President Villarroel — who came from the valle alto of Co-
chabamba and spoke Quechua himself — and the minister of government,
Colonel Edmundo Nogales. In this period (late 1943 and early 1944), the
National Indigenous Committee was constituted — under the auspices of
the Villarroel government, but organized under the initiative of Ramos
Quevedo and other leaders.

The committee consisted of about fifteen peasant representatives from
around the country. Grájeda was a member; his work included not only
the representation of Ayopaya, but various assignments at the departmental level for Cochabamba. Each member of the committee held an
official credential extended by the presidential office, and signed by Villarroel. This act in itself was very important, we were told by various peasant leaders, for no previous government had ever granted this type of
official status to an action undertaken by the peasants themselves. This
meant that Grájeda and the other members of the committee could count
on official support to travel and absent themselves from the haciendas for
long periods, in order to attend to procedures in defense of the peasants,
and to organize and promote the announced National Indigenous Congress. In this manner, the committee played a crucial role as coordinator
and promoter; aside from pushing for the collective organization of the
peasantry, it succeeded in relating peasant leaders from diverse regions
not only with one other, but also with national authorities, union leaders,
printers, miners, factory workers, and others.

The committee rapidly forged an ample network of contacts with local
leaders in the communities and haciendas. It is significant to note that
there had always been local leaders — the *jilakatas* of communities, and
the alcaldes de campo and *kurakas* of haciendas; the committee managed
to convert itself into an articulating institution at the supra-local level,
something the system of hacienda domination had always repressed. But
this time, at least during the Villarroel regime, such a mechanism could
count on official support and legitimacy. In the case of the haciendas, the
alcaldes de campo and kurakas were men not necessarily loyal to their
communities, and the committee therefore sought to identify those local
leaders with the organizational capacity, tact, or courage necessary to elude
control by the patrones. In various local meetings, members of the committee promoted, at times openly and at times surreptitiously, the election
of local base leaders (*líderes de base*) as delegates to the Congress. According to the convocation of the National Indigenous Congress, each
canton of the altiplano, valleys, and mountains (*serranías*) should elect
two delegates, one from the haciendas and the other from the communities; in the eastern tropical region of Oriente, two delegates were to be
recruited from each province. In their assemblies, the peasants prepared

reports and resolutions on the specific abuses of authority, obligations on the haciendas, and necessities such as schools and transport, characteristic of each zone.

All this activity relied on the backing of Villarroel and the MNR, which shared power. At the same time, organizations such as the Miners' Federation and the departmental Worker-Union Federations participated as well. The government and these unions aided the efforts of the National Indigenous Committee to organize various regional congresses that preceded the National Congress; in La Paz, for example, congresses were held in Laja (in February 1945), Kollana (April), and Cañaviri (May). President Villarroel attended the first and the third, as did various cabinet ministers and members of the diplomatic corps. In both of the preliminary events, Villarroel manifested his interest in measures to eliminate serfdom (*servidumbre*) on the haciendas, to establish salaried labor and just wages, and to take other steps to alleviate the peasants' situation (*La Calle*, February 21, 1945; *Los Tiempos*, November 19, 1943; Reinaga 1952: 29–33). The regional congress held in Sucre on August 6–7, 1944, with backing from the departmental prefecture and the Chuquisaca Worker-Union Federation (*Federación Obrera Sindical de Trabajadores de Chuquisaca*), produced a manifesto of eighteen demands, among them the following (as summarized in *Los Tiempos*, April 5, 1945):

Creation of a National Indigenous *Patronato* ["patronship], support by the state for indigenous literacy, abolition of pongueaje, recommendation to the National Legislature of the creation of an Agrarian Code, the restitution of provincial attorneys-general, the creation of Juridical Offices in the cities to attend to indigenous affairs free of charge, general reinspection of lands to establish the legality of titles to the land of communities and *latifundios* [large haciendas], review by a special committee of the trials brought against haciendas by communities for the expropriation of lands . . ., appointment of Inspectors of Indigenous Labor by the Minister of Labor, creation of sanitation brigades to attend to the rural population, etc.

Similar resolutions resulted from congresses held in La Paz, Oruro, Cochabamba, and Tarija during 1944 and the first months of 1945 (data proportioned by Domingo Castellón, ex-leader of the Cochabamba Worker-Union Federation, and by newspapers of the period).

The peasant question and especially the call for a National Indigenous Congress gave rise to an intense political debate. In the National Legislature, the MNR presented a preliminary plan for an Agrarian Statute based on expositions already presented at the Constitutional Convention of 1938. The PIR (*Partido de Izquierda Revolucionaria*; Party of the Revolutionary Left) — opposed to the Villarroel government, principal rival of the

MNR in the battle for popular support, and the organization that would align itself with parties on the right to overthrow Villarroel in July 1946 — also struggled to be the voice of peasant demands. We must also take note of two additional political groupings which defined positions on the agrarian question. On the one hand, there was the "Radepa" (*Razón de Patria*; "Cause of the Fatherland"), a brotherhood of young soldiers who had studied in Italy in the late 1920s and participated in the Chaco War. This group supported Villarroel, and its frank sympathies with fascism involved the government as a pro-Axis party in an international controversy; nevertheless, Radepa also included in its statute of principles a statement favorable to changes in the countryside. In like manner, the political effervescence of the Villarroel period yielded an "Indian" party organized by Fausto Reynaga, then a deputy of the MNR in the Legislature. This party called itself the National Agrarian Party (PAN; *Partido Agrario Nacional*; also called *Asociación Nacional Bolindia*).

What were the positions of the MNR, PIR, Radepa, and PAN (Bolindia) with respect to the "indigenous problem" and the agrarian question? Without attempting an exhaustive analysis, we will summarize some aspects essential to establish the context of political debate during the period in question. The MNR produced a manifesto in 1942 (see Cornejo 1949: 147–51), in which the peasant problem was characterized as the provision of a definitive solution to the "Indian" problem through cultural and educational integration, the expropriation of unused land on large and unproductive latifundios, and the elimination of serfdom on the haciendas by introducing an Agrarian Code or Statute to regulate labor relations in the countryside. Radepa did not go beyond these positions. The PIR, a party more decidedly Marxist, elaborated a "Program of Principles" in 1941 which took a clearly defined position on an agrarian reform "designed to liquidate the unproductive feudal estates, to abolish the servitude of the Indian, to convert indigenous communities into agricultural cooperatives." Their program also included "education on a vast scale . . . [and] intensive instruction of reading and writing to the Quechua and Aymara Indians in their native tongues . . ." (extracted from ibid.: 233–76; on the position of the MNR, see ibid.: 147–51; for that of Radepa, see Candia A. 1957: 21; Dandler 1971: chapter 3; Romero 1971: 45–46).

The National Agrarian Party was of slight militance, but nonetheless took a more defined position on the recognition of ethnic autonomy. The PAN was founded in June 1941 in Tiawanaku as a product of the radicalization which had occurred within the MNR, and as a response to the lack of clarity with which the leftist political parties handled the pluricultural character of the country and its majority population. In its "Tiawanaku Proclamation" the PAN declared (*El País*, December 12, 1945):

Bolivia was, is, and must be Indian. Bolindia is Indian Bolivia, for the Indian is the majority in Bolivia. Ninety percent of all Bolivians are Indian. The PAN will make sure the earth belongs to he who makes it fruitful with his sweat. The indigenous problem is neither an ethnic nor a cultural one; it is economic and social, and not political. Bolivia will be great when the Indian is free.

The Revolutionary Workers Party (POR; *Partido Obrero Revolucionario*) also took part in the agrarian debate and the proselytization in the countryside; it reinforced ties between miners' unions and the peasantry in certain regions. Nevertheless, as noted in a previous study (Dandler 1971), the POR was bound up for a long time by a dogmatic attitude that underestimated the autonomous capacity of the peasantry to mobilize itself, and, perhaps mechanically, subordinated the peasants to a proletarian vanguard.

The organizational activity in the countryside and the political debate on the peasant question flourished during the Villarroel regime. Without a doubt, the Villarroel government and the MNR expressed an attitude of change and awareness on the campesino issue. This did not imply, however, the absence of a certain ambiguity, in part because the government was weak and still vulnerable to a strong power bloc articulating the interests of the big miners, the landed oligarchs (*latifundistas*) and the financial sector. The departmental and national *Sociedades Rurales* ("Rural Societies," organizations of the great landowners), the political parties of the Right, and a powerful antigovernment press comprised of established major newspapers mounted a strong campaign against the government. Villarroel was accused of being an irresponsible demagogue and agitator of the peasant class, whose government threatened to destroy the property of "civilized" Bolivians (*La Razón*, May 11, 1945). Other articles reminded readers of the Túpac Amaru rebellions, the siege of La Paz perpetrated by Túpac Katari, the Willka Zárate rebellion, and other historical events that demonstrated the capacity of the indigenous peoples to mobilize themselves if precautions were not taken (ibid., April 24, 1945).

In the National Legislature, debate also surfaced on the fact that while each citizen had the right to move freely or hold meetings, in the case of the "natives," the right was prohibited. Representatives of the MNR and the PIR exposed the existence of regulations which, for example, prohibited the movement of "natives" along certain streets and plazas of La Paz and other cities. The president of the National Legislture—Dr. Franz Tamayo, a well-known intellectual—declared: "The existence of such dispositions, which go beyond the frontiers of iniquity, constitutes a shameful disgrace [*una vergüenza*]" (*El Diario*, October 30, 1944).

On various occasions, at the request of Luis Ramos Quevedo and other members of the National Indigenous Committee, the Ministry of Government had to send circulars to departmental and provincial authorities, affirming this constitutional right of peasants as citizens; these were intended to guarantee the organization of the National Indigenous Congress, but they were not necessarily heeded.

If it is true that the government sponsored regional congresses and the announced National Congress, at a provincial and local level the "state" was in the hands of hacendados and townspeople tied to *gamonalismo* (rule by local bosses and oligarchs). In fact, the local "state" remained to a great extent at the margin of effective control by a "transitory" national government such as Villarroel's. In this context, for the peasants to hold meetings in one or another hacienda, in remote cantons, and to discuss the organization of a regional congress, the National Indigenous Congress, and related matters was to the patrones an unacceptable challenge. The campesino "ringleaders" and "agitators" were persecuted, expelled from the haciendas, and jailed or physically abused with the consent of the local authorities. The leaders of the National Indigenous Congress often acted clandestinely, holding meetings in isolated places at night. There they helped to elaborate the demands and complaints of the peasantry, establishing the bases for wider peasant organization and unity. But they had to confront not only the hostility of the provincial authorities, the patrones, or hacienda managers, but also the fear of the peasants themselves (interview with Julio Carrasco, leader of Yayani and collaborator with Grájeda):

During our activities, we had to be very careful with the people whom we permitted to participate in our meetings. Beforehand, one had to go through a special ceremony, in which we swore before Grájeda and other leaders never to reveal what was heard or spoken; but there was always some squealer [*soplón*] among us who would tell the administrator or some relative what we had talked about. Almost always, the day after a meeting, the administrator would know that we had gathered or that someone had visited us from the outside. . . .

FROM PEASANT INITIATIVE TO GOVERNMENTAL CONTROL

We would like now to retrieve a crucial interpretive thread. While the realization of preparatory congresses and contacts for the National Indigenous Congress received formal backing of the government, at least until the first projected date (December 1944) of the Congress, it was the National Indigenous Committee, under the leadership of Luis Ramos Quevedo, that undertook a great deal of the initiative. As all this activity came to life — crystallized first in a series of massive meetings and regional assemblies (where the MNR, labor unions, and even the PIR certainly fought for a leading role), and later erupting into various incidents and conflicts, including work stoppages, "misunderstandings" spread by peasants who exceeded the instructions of the National Indigenous Committee, and an intense campaign of exaggerated accusations launched by the patrones and the Bolivian Rural Society (*Sociedad Rural Boliviana*) against the government for permitting the activity of agitators – the government decided once and for all to take greater control of the Congress. First, the government ordered the postponement of the Congress until February 1945. Then in January it announced a second postponement until May. In order to insure that this postponement was not just a stratagem for letting the Congress die quietly, Ramos Quevedo held an interview with President Villarroel at the end of January, and obtained the promise that the Congress would definitely occur on May 10.

Second, a short while later, difficulties with Ramos Quevedo arose, and at the initiative of members of the National Indigenous Committee, authorities such as Colonel Nogales judged him beyond governmental control. Meanwhile, the antigovernment press intensified its campaign questioning the Congress and scratching up whatever local detail might magnify its reports and give indication of rural agitators, peasant rebellion, and lack of discipline precisely during harvest time. Thus was Ramos Quevedo "caught" stirring up the peasants in different zones: in various parts of Oruro on March 7 (*La Razón*, March 8, 1945), in the province of Quillacollo on March 20 "agitating with extremist slogans" the peasants of the Chacapaya and Uchu Uchu haciendas (ibid., March 24, 1945). In the latter incident, at the request of departmental authorities, Nogales was made to travel in reaction to the complaints of the patrones. The result was that, justifiably or not, Nogales formally stripped Ramos Quevedo of his authority, denying that he had ever been an agent of the government, but claiming rather that "he had only been entrusted with the mission of organizing indigenous representations for the Congress" (*Los Tiempos*, March 20, 1945).

These and other incidents before the Congress brought Ramos Quevedo into disgrace. There is also later notice that he was imprisoned (*Los Tiempos*, March 25, 1945). But we suspect that the real motive was the government's decision, in March, to subordinate strictly the activities and role of the National Indigenous Committee under the direction of a governmental Steering Committee presided by Dr. Carlos Morales Guillén. The government justified the call for a National Indigenous Congress and the making of decisions on the agrarian question as a method of channelling and "controlling" a growing wave of rural agitation helped along by other political groups and even peasant leaders. As Minister Nogales put it after the Congress: "the Indigenous Congress has not been, as argued crudely, the source of the current disturbances. The process of indigenous agitation began around 1941 . . ." (*El País*, December 12, 1945). He also maintained

that at no time was the agitator Luis Ramos Quevedo invested with official representation, and that it violated the good faith of the President of the Republic to get him to pose with [Ramos Quevedo] and a group of natives for a photograph, on the basis of which he has speculated ably, collecting quotas in the hundreds of thousands of pesos. On account of these shenanigans, Ramos Quevedo was detained and later transported to Beni, from where he managed to escape to Brazilian territory.

There are also indications that hostilities surfaced between the government and the peasant leader Antonio Alvarez Mamani, due probably to the marginalization of Ramos Quevedo, among other reasons. In a declaration to the press before the National Indigenous Congress, Alvarez Mamani resigned as general delegate of La Paz, adducing a list of reasons, among which figured the following (*La Calle*, March 20, 1945):

For disagreeing with the organizers of the Congress who took into account only indigenous agriculturalists, when . . . all natives of the republic should be taken into account: from those who reside along Lake Titicaca and live off fishing, to the herbalists and *kallawayas* [doctors]; as well as those who work in the roundups on the cattle ranches [in Oriente], [and] those who are buried in the mines. . . .

In a later declaration, Alvarez Mamani requested the further postponement of the Congress until July 1945, citing problems of organization, resources, and guarantees for the delegates. He also objected to the detention of Luis Ramos Quevedo as a "subversive agitator, with no one to take his place" (ibid., April 10, 1945). A few days later, a concerted campaign of accusations was launched against Alvarez Mamani (ibid., April 13, 1945):

A dangerous mestizo is acting as representative of the natives to the Congress. The District Attorney requests that Antonio Alvarez Mamani be restricted from congressional activities on account of his abominable precedents. . . . [H]e recently published a manifesto and just directed an extensive memorial to the President regarding the congressional activities. . . . The District Attorney says that the aforementioned delegate does not belong to the indigenous class, since even his last name reveals his mestizo status; the same has problems pending with the Courts for various crimes . . . in different areas of the department. He therefore cannot and should not become the voice of the entire indigenous element of La Paz. . . . The exclusion of Alvarez Mamani from all indigenous activities is suggested, preventing if at all possible his contact with the native masses whom he deceives and tries to represent for iniquitable purposes.

We note these declarations as the antecedents — probably unfounded — of certain official measures which induced his isolation as a defender of the peasantry. During the Villarroel regime itself, he was confined to the island of Coati (*Libertad*, November 20, 1946), a prison which would gain notoriety from 1946 to 1952. His official marginalization and even imprisonment did not affect his dedication to the struggle, as we shall see later, upon examining the persecutions of 1946–1952.

As was to be expected, many obstacles were placed in the way of the Congress. When the definitive date finally drew near, the minister of government and other authorities had to exert great efforts to pacify conflicts — for example, "sit-down strikes" — initiated not necessarily by the peasants, but in many haciendas by the patrones themselves and by the political opposition. In spite of reiterated governmental statements and instructions intended to guarantee the peasants' freedom of movement, it was impossible to prevent the patrones from taking reprisals against or denouncing what they themselves saw as "the indigenous awakening." It was precisely because the entire situation had escaped official control that the government tried from January 1945 to intervene more strongly in the peasants' undertaking. As we shall see later, what occurred before and especially after the Congress already exceeded all possibility of governmental control. An economic and social crisis of grand proportions was spreading in the countryside in 1943–1946, at the same time that an intense mobilization of the popular sectors took place in the mines and cities, and the government found itself less and less capable of effecting change in the face of oligarchical interests and power structures which were hardly open to negotiating.

THE NATIONAL INDIGENOUS CONGRESS

The Congress was inaugurated on May 10 at the Luna Park sports coliseum in La Paz, with more than one thousand campesino delegates in attendance. The Congress elected a directorate, naming Francisco Chipana Ramos president, Dionisio Miranda vice-president, and Desiderio Cholina the general secretary. The three represented the Aymara, Quechua, and Oriente constituencies respectively.

Four commissions were organized around various issues, to consider reports and develop resolutions for approval in the Congress. One newspaper (*La Calle*, May 11, 1945) characterized the inauguration of this event under the title "A Seemingly Unusual Event":

Yesterday the official inauguration of the first Bolivian Indigenous Congress took place, attended by the entire executive branch and the national army, represented by its highest directive and technical bodies, as well as the diplomatic corps and other organizations of elevated significance in the national life. There were, likewise, military honors . . . and the classic twenty-one gun salute. . . . Such a display of solemnity and grandeur for the inauguration of a congress of natives must have appeared unusual and inexplicable to many people — something which denotes the upset of all that is customary and silently accepted as normal. The reserve is explicable, and lies [in the fact] that recently there has been imposed a transformation in the manner of appraising the social phenomena of the country. . . .

At the inaugural session, President Villarroel referred to the effort extended by his government (ibid.; emphasis added):

[The government] wants to help you to live better, to have a good house and clean clothes, nutritive food and care for the sick. Similarly, it will help to insure that your labor brings higher yields through the use of new methods. . . . [T]he government will educate campesino children . . . the living conditions of our people cannot be elevated unless we do this with the peasantry, the mass majority, the base of our economy. This, enunciated so simply, is [in fact] complex and slow to be realized, and in more than one hundred years of republican life, governments have systematically postponed its solution.

. . . [T]he campesino is as much a son of this flag as any man of this land, and must be treated like a son by the government: he will be protected, he will have schools, he will have guarantees, but he will also be obligated to work, loyally fulfilling his debts and obligations. . . . [R]emember that he who works will be respected and protected. . . . *[T]oday begins the work of the government that will watch over you like a father caring for his sons. The abuses will end.* . . .

. . . [L]isten to my words, think about what I tell you, and respond like honest men to the effort which we will put forth for you, and when you return to your lands as the notables [*principales*] [and] caciques that you are, *I will entrust to you the duty to watch over the labor and the peace of all, and with this assignment, I make of you my representatives and the persons responsible to me for this mandate.* . . .

Francisco Chipana Ramos, the president of the Congress, responded (ibid.):

that the indigenous people are assembled thanks to President Villarroel . . . that the government has trusted in them, and they therefore ought to trust in it . . . that the nation needs labor and peace, and that everything makes one think that the hour of redemption has arrived for the indigenous people . . .

The Minister of Labor, Germán Monroy Block, mentioned that while 174 laws relating to the peasantry had been issued since the founding of the republic, not a single government had carried them out, and that the Villarroel administration "wants to avoid this continuance of errors." He also mentioned that the legislature had promulgated laws and social projects for workers in the mines and factories, and that now, in a second stage, they could secure identical laws and benefits for all the peasant workers of the country. . . . [T]o define the rights of workers signifies democracy. . . . [T]o listen to some to the detriment of others is called oligarchy.

Hernán Siles Zuazo, representing the MNR, declared as one of his party's principle postulates that "the land should belong to those who work it, [and] although many years will pass before this leap . . . I believe that this Congress is the first step" (ibid.).

The deliberations of the Congress and its commissions proceeded with intensity. A large number of reports, lists of abuses, and draft resolutions were presented by the peasant delegates. It is significant that most of the government's impulse focused not on the problem of land and property, but rather on labor relations and servitude. The president of the steering committee, Carlos Morales Guillén, introduced projects to abolish pongueaje and mitanaje, and to regulate other personal services, and these were presented to the Congress at its close on May 15. These decrees had been approved by the ministerial cabinet the preceding day. Their content was important and merits lengthy citation:

. . . The services of pongueaje and mitanaje are abolished. . . . The authorities, whether administrative, judicial, ecclesiastic, provincial, cantonal, etc., are prohibited from obliging natives, colonos, community members, or pueblo or city residents to perform gratuitous services. . . . All service must be voluntarily performed and justly remunerated. . . . Those authorities who infringe upon this disposition will be sanctioned with the revocation of their positions. . . . The pongos and mitanis presently serving [in the houses of the patrones] are authorized to return to their dwellings. . . .

As to the regulation of personal services:

While the agrarian labor code is being created, the lending of the campesino's services will be regulated as follows: (1) the colonos will not be obligated to [perform] chores not specifically related to cattle and crop raising, without previous consent and just retribution; (2) personal or domestic services . . . will proceed in force subject to prior agreement on remuneration and in any case to the contrary, with the intervention of the nearest political authority . . .; (3) the colono is the absolute owner of his harvest, and may sell it freely on the market . . . the loan of mules, carrying containers, the delivery of lambs, wool, birds . . . and other tributes may not be exacted by proprietors for free, or as remuneration under the heading of cattle herbage and pasturing fees . . . in any case, payment will be at the going rate . . . it is also prohibited to demand of the colonos any contribution, in money or in kind, for the payment of cadastral taxes or rent. . . .

At the same time, it was also specified that

. . . if, falsely alleging these dispositions or following ends of political agitation, the peasants fail to fulfill the obligations inherent in tasks truly related to cattle or crop raising with prejudice to production, upon the verification of the minister of government and provincial authorities, they will be sanctioned with isolation from the property on which one is colono and sent, along with the entire family, to the government colonies which will be organized by the minister of agriculture; in these cases public penal action may be taken against the instigators or agitators who, in addition to being sent also to the government colonies, will be responsible for the damages and the corresponding penal sanctions. . . . [T]he collection of "ramas" [quotas] in money or in kind is also prohibited; the instigators or agitators who are denounced by the authorities will be obligated to the restitution of the sums . . . plus the payment of a fine. . . .

As for the proprietors of haciendas and their administrators, "whatever person vexes or employs violence against the peasants will be sanctioned," and natives seeking to redress land grievances "shall present their complaints in the Offices of Gratuitous Defense of Native Peoples."

SELECTED TESTIMONIES

As was mentioned earlier, in Ayopaya, the expectations of some sort of change began during the presidency of Lieutenant Colonel Busch; the peasants, however, did not gain benefits from this. When Grájeda and others from the *suyo* (section) Tirita of the Yayani hacienda initiated a suit in 1940 against the patrón and the overseer, they were persecuted. And so it was that Grájeda and others established contacts with lawyers of the MNR and the PIR, and with Luis Bustamante (interview with José Grájeda, brother of Hilarión, April 21, 1969):

[T]he lawyers wrote the briefs for us. . . . [F]or this reason they wanted to take us to the island of Coati from then on. . . . [W]e have suffered a great deal in order to pursue these litigations, because . . . we had no money for food, and we had to make our journeys by foot . . . because besides all this when we got a ride on a train, they would take us prisoner, and that is why this great man Luis Bustamante from Sipe Sipe . . . collaborated with us in our complaints and brought us before other gentlemen. . . .

According to the peasants of Yayani, once Villarroel took office, their hopes gained strength; Grájeda and other campesinos from various haciendas intensified their contacts and travels. At the same time, they continually confronted many obstacles, as they could no longer rely on guarantees within the hacienda, nor on the support of the provincial authorities. As the date of the National Indigenous Congress drew near, diverse localized conflicts broke out on various haciendas of the province. To a great extent, these conflicts developed as the result of meetings held among peasants, steps taken by leaders like Grájeda to organize the Congress, and strikes initiated by the peasants themselves on various haciendas.

During this period, in December 1944, José and Hilarión Grájeda, Julio Carrasco, his father Nicolás, Dionisio Miranda, and others were confined to the island of Coati on Lake Titicaca. Carrasco says: "at the time [the main authorities] did not tell us that we had been taken prisoner for laying claim to the land nor for [demanding] abolition of [labor] services, but they said that we were thieves . . ." (interview, April 21, 1969). The prisoners were freed thanks to the efforts of Luis Bustamante, deputies of the MNR, and others. According to Carrasco and José Grájeda (brother of Hilarión), they conversed in February 1945 with President Villarroel and Luis Ramos Quevedo, head of the National Indigenous Committee. Villarroel, they say, put them at ease, telling them to return to their haciendas without resentment of the outrages meted out by lower authorities, and to await the realization of the Congress in May.

These facts demonstrate that the organization of the Congress, already postponed two times, ran into obstacles which even the government could not control. Nevertheless, an intense relationship was forged between Villarroel and the peasants who believed in him. As one informant recalled (interview with Leonardo Alavi, Grájeda's stepbrother, Tirita, October 8, 1981), Villarroel made them pledge their allegiance to him:

he made us swear before all the rebel leaders . . . so that not even he could relinquish the search for [just] law in favor of the campesinos. . . . "I must bequeath the decrees . . . if they kill me, well that law they will not cause to be lost . . . if they kill you, others must come forward to take up the defense" . . . because of that pledge, neither could we relinquish the search [for justice]. . . .

In May, the different delegates mobilized themselves to arrive in La Paz in various manners. Some went by train from the station of Quillacollo and Vinto; others, however, journeyed by foot from Ayopaya to La Paz, an eight-day trip fraught with fear that the provincial authorities might capture them on the road. Other delegates were deceived by the hacienda administrators themselves, as in the case of Esteban Cruz, who was dispatched to tend to a task in Morochata (the province capital), where he was captured and confined for four months with other peasants who shared the same misfortune (interview with Cruz and others, 1968). Upon arrival in La Paz, many delegates still encountered difficulties. Some of them did not have the proper credentials to attend the Congress, since they had evaded the provincial authorities who, in accordance with instructions, were to have provided them with this documentation. This problem made it difficult for them to gain lodging set up by the government in the Calama barracks.

The National Indigenous Congress, for those peasants with whom we have spoken, was an extraordinary experience. For many of them it was their first visit to the capital city of the country; they met with hundreds of campesinos of diverse regions and languages; and they shared the same assembly roof with the president and other authorities. Carrasco and others presented long lists of the abuses which had been committed in the haciendas. In the debates and speeches, the delegates learned that peasants in other zones of the country confronted similar situations. Never before had they experienced such a massive and openly public discussion of their problems — in the presence, moreover, of governmental and political authorities whose attendance demonstrated they were on the peasants' side. In our conversations with them, the peasants described in minute detail numerous experiences which they had lived during the Congress. What most impressed us in these conversations was their identification with Villarroel, his speeches and the interviews held with him. The decrees eliminating pongueaje and mitanaje came as a surprise.

The event culminated with a huge official party, held in a field behind the General Cemetery, where Villarroel and other authorities welcomed the peasants in a festive atmosphere, with military bands, food, and drink. As one ex-delegate recalls (interview with José Flores, ex-delegate from Ayoma baja, province Nor Chichas, Potosí, February 9, 1968):

. . . there were some campesinos who had feathers on their heads, others blew their conch trumpets [*pututus*]. . . . [T]he President spoke always in Quechua . . . as did other ministers. . . . [T]his fiesta lasted until nightfall because there were army bands who played so that the peasants would dance. . . . [A]t times I could hardly believe that the president was among us, eating the same as we did, the same as other gentlemen. . . .

Gregorio Loayza of Yayani, another delegate to the Congress, who arrived at the event late after walking six days in the company of Feliciano Coca, an excombatant of the Chaco War from the hacienda of Yayani, recalls that at the farewell to the delegations, President Villarroel drank from a single glass with Hilarión Grájeda and bid them to be careful upon their return to the haciendas.

The delegates' return to their places of origin was indeed laden with difficulties at the hands of local authorities and hacendados. Many were arrested at the Oruro station, and reentry onto the haciendas themselves was furtive. In Ayopaya, as in other places, the delegates proceeded to hold meetings with the peasants to recount the experience and communicate the decrees. In most cases, the meetings were not open, since the patrones and administrators intimidated the peasants with the threat of arrest. In Yayani, for example (interview with Segundo Pérez, May 18, 1981), when we returned from the Congress, they [the administrators] were waiting for us, ready to grab [i.e., arrest] us. . . . [I]n light of this, we communicated only among ourselves, gathering people together bit by bit, telling them in this way and that. For this reason, the patrones or renters [of the hacienda] were watching us, waiting for a chance to seize us, and they called us "these wandering ringleaders" [*estos cabecillas caminadores*], they did not recognize our [authority] . . . they hated us completely. . . .

The majority of the peasants of Yayani were curious to find out about the Congress, but for fear of the reprisals of hacienda authorities, they visited the delegates in their homes by night (interview with Gregorio Loayza, July 15, 1969).

And so began a period of delays, negotiations, and visits by departmental authorities; as was to be expected, in a short while conflicts broke out. On the one hand, the patrones did not observe the dispositions; they persecuted the "ringleaders" or utilized whatever stunts they could to evade the fulfillment of the decrees. On the other hand, the campesinos themselves attempted to protest in various ways to make their demands heard, and entered into passive resistance and work stoppages. Finally, the authorities recently named to carry out Villarroel's decrees and others already established (corregidores, subprefects, etc.) did not fulfill their assigned functions on behalf of the peasantry. For example, controversy arose in Yayani between administrators and campesinos over the work tasks on the hacienda, which later paralyzed labor until the director of the Cochabamba Office of Campesino Defense and Dionisio Miranda (the vice-president of the National Indigenous Congress) arrived on the scene. But this did not lead to a stable agreement between the peasants and the hacienda. According to an ex-majordomo of Yayani (interview, June 4, 1969):

the peasants clung to the decrees of Villarroel, but the authorities did not enforce them, for once they went out commissioned to resolve some peasant conflict, it happens that as soon as they left the city, they were bribed by the proprietors, so that they always came out . . . against the peasants.

Undoubtedly, these situations generated greater distrust of departmental authorities and greater resentment toward patrones and administrators. Hence, labor relations did not reach a *modus vivendi*; instead the uncertainty and tension deepened. Moreover, according to peasants of Yayani and neighboring haciendas, the hacendados and administrators managed to maintain certain obligations with a mere change of name. For example, they substituted the name "mulero" ("mule-boy") for "pongo" (native servant).

As in many regions of the country, in the department of Cochabamba, and especially in the province of Ayopaya, "sit-down strikes" proliferated, occurring intermittently for the year following the Congress and until Villarroel was overthrown on July 21, 1946.[2] In some cases, there were clashes between peasants and public security troops. For example, in La-chiraya, a hacienda near Yayani and ten kilometers from Morochata, a huge groups of peasants from different haciendas gathered around May 21, 1946; they were confronted by a detachment of rifle-bearing soldiers, who left three campesinos dead and a number wounded (interviews with various witnesses, corroborated by the press; see for example, *Los Tiempos*, May 22, 1946). It was during this period of conflict at Lachiraya that various peasant leaders were arrested and sent to Chimore, a secluded prison camp in Chapare (an eastern frontier zone of the Cochabamba region).

In the first half of 1946, the conflicts on the haciendas of Ayopaya intensified. Minister Nogales arrived in Morochata early in May to ob-serve the happenings first hand and to explain the scope of Villarroel's decrees to a gathering of peasants, whom he urged to reach nonviolent agreements with the patrones. Increasingly, the supposed blame for the labor stoppages and conflicts fell on the backs of the peasants. Witnesses in Yayani and bordering haciendas attest to the fact that the police pres-ence in the zone was nearly permanent; in this context, the authorities assumed a posture increasingly explicit and in favor of the proprietors.

Our interviews with witnesses from other zones confirm how difficult it was for the campesinos to enforce Villarroel's decrees. For example, an ex-corregidor of Vitichi (Nor Chichas province, Department of Potosí) recalled:

The peasants of this region went on just as before, both in their work and in their services at the patrón's house. . . . Of course there were some small changes of name in the services. What were known before as "pongos" were now called "muleros," and they changed the name of the "mitanis" to "ovejeras" [shepherds] . . . so when they would come to one of the landowners' houses in this pueblo, they would say to the men "mulero mantachu jamunqui" ["have you come as a mulero?"], and to the women they would say "ovejera mantachu jamunqui?" ["have you come as an ovejera?"] . . . This was the only change; their obligations were the same as before. . . .

REPERCUSSIONS

We will now proceed to analyze briefly some events that stand out as the consequence of the measures decreed by the Villarroel government and of peasant rebelliousness. Increasingly, the government found itself on the defensive, faced with a phenomenon of popular mobilization in the countryside and consolidation of the opposition. What broke out in the countryside was one of the principal factors contributing to the overthrow of the regime, and the brutal hanging of the president in the Plaza Murillo in July 1946.

With the Congress over and two unprecedented decrees issued, an extraordinary and intense conflictual process was unleashed in the countryside. The delegates who had attended the event were the carriers of a message: we are no longer pongos nor mitanis, we must no longer be exploited, we no longer work for free. At the same time, the government was giving instructions to the departmental and provincial authorities, and hastily assembled a National Directorship and Offices for the Gratuitous Defense of Natives. Meetings, debates, negotiations, and verbal confrontations with the administrators and patrones rang out in each hacienda, and in many, the peasants refused to settle for promises, postponements, or negotiations. The hacendados tenaciously opposed any change whatsoever, subjecting the peasants to lengthy negotiations, official procedures, visits to authorities, review of the peculiarities of labor in each location, and so on. As was to be expected, the majority of local and provincial authorities also declined to collaborate with the governmental dispositions.

The peasants themselves, moreover, entered into conjectures on the reach of the decrees. For example, within a month of the Congress, an intense mobilization developed in Tarija around disputes over rental contracts (a matter not clarified in the decrees or regulations), and around a question which the government sidestepped during the Congress: the question of land and the latifundio system. The campesinos of Tarija organized a departmental congress to clarify the coverage of the National Indigenous Congress and to develop objectives which went beyond those achieved to date. One of the principal conclusions of that congress was that the indigenous problem could not be addressed without touching the land question. The latter implied declaring that "the land belongs to the one who works it" ("la tierra es del que la trabaja"). The government attempted to pacify the latifundistas by saying that the demands of the Tarija peasants were erroneous (*La Calle*, June 16, 1945). As innumerable conflicts arose on different properties, and a process of "sit-down strikes" spread over Tarija, the prefect (*La Razón*, July 10, 1945)

gathered the subprefects together to explain to them the limits of the [National] Indigenous Congress, recommending that they reject the petitions for the distribution of lands, arrest the agitators, and attend to the reclamations of the patrones, as well as the workers, in the manner prescribed by the laws.

Two months after the Congress, President Villarroel declared that (*La Calle*, July 27, 1945)

. . . the indigenous problem is not one specifically of lands, but rather of regimen. For, while we have more than enough land, what is needed is to organize the social and economic management of the Indian, to whom it is necessary to provide sufficient capacity to become an active element of the national economy. . . . [W]e might distribute lands to them in the long run, we have an exceses, but meanwhile, it will be more advisable to move toward a cooperativist-type organization for the exploitation of land by the native.

Once the government took up the question of the elimination of hacienda servitude, it could not really leave aside the question of land. It found itself increasingly entangled in the debate, assuming a defensive position. At the National Legislature, the legislators spend months discussing an Agrarian Code without managing to ratify the supreme decrees approved by the Cabinet in May 1945. On August 15, the hacendados held their third Rural Society of Bolivia Congress in Cochabamba, in which they affirmed the right to hold private property, and took an inflexible stand toward the changes in the labor system. The minister of agriculture, Major Jorge Calero, in a frank concession, proposed measures to guarantee and define the peasants' obligations to the patrones, in order "to avert the advance of an indigenous revolt, encouraged and instigated by political elements adverse to the current regime" (*La Razón*, August 17, 1945).

A few months later, in December, a peasant uprising took place in Las Canchas (Potosí) which the government itself had to repress. Controversy and accusations commenced between the MNR and the PIR. The newspapers that month were filled with stories of conflict and confrontation: a sit-down strike on the haciendas of Aiquile (Cochabamba), one of whose "ringleaders" was said to have claimed descent from the Inca Emperor Atahualpa, and to have given himself the title of Inca; a threatening massing of peasants near Sorata (La Paz), leading to the arrest of about ten leaders; the capture of patrones as hostages by peasants during hacienda work stoppages in Capinota (Cochabamba); revolt on the hacienda Churitaqa (Chuquisaca province, east of Potosí), whose 2,000 Indians killed the administrator and attacked two towns; an indefinite strike on the haciendas of Tiraque (Cochabamba), pending the forging of an agreement on the labor regime (*El País*, December 11, 19, and 29, 1945; *La Razón*, December 12, 19, and 20, 1945; *El Diario*, December 13, 1945; *Los Tiempos*, December 30, 1945). This is but a small selection of many episodes that testify to the magnitude of the process of conflict and confrontation which shook the countryside. The latifundista organizations took ready advantage of such events to intensify their campaign against the government.

The majority of conflicts stemmed from negotiations about the labor system, and were not the "uprisings" adduced by the rightist press. These were not rebellions or uprisings as such, but rather processes of concerted mobilization and organization, of "sit-down strikes" in response to the intransigence of hacendados, and the inability of the government to intervene in the making of concrete agreements.

This surprising official weakness was rooted in the presence of local and regional "states" which undermined every centralizing and pro-indigenous effort by the national "state." In reality, what developed was a formidable avalanche of opposition forces within as well as without the Villarroel regime itself. During the first six months of 1946, the government grew increasingly defensive. Faced with a growing wave of work stoppages in the countryside, the government proved impotent, unable to clarify and impose solutions to the labor conflicts on the haciendas. The local and departmental authorities identified rebel "ringleaders" as the culprits responsible for the restlessness. In reality, in countless rural areas, the peasants and their leaders ended up as orphans, bereft of effective governmental support. It is symbolic that Chipana Ramos, the very president of the National Indigenous Congress, was arrested and tried by provincial authorities in May 1946 in the altiplano of La Paz, and that the central government could not defend him. The same situation had occurred many times before with leaders of lesser significance. In effect, from the most recondite corners of the country, a punitive and conspiratory campaign was developed and politically coordinated, culminating in July with the destruction of Villarroel.[3]

With Villarroel gone, the peasants now found themselves totally deprived of all defense. The patrones decided to impose order. They proclaimed that the Villarroel decrees no longer existed, in spite of the fact that the Monje Gutiérrez government (which lasted one year and, calling for elections, sought to take a "civilized" attitude) attempted weakly to confirm their validity. But this was no longer a time of negotiations and work stoppages in the countryside, but rather one of strong repression and a succession of peasant uprisings. In the following pages we will limit ourselves to examining some testimonies in the countryside regarding the death of Villarroel, and one of the various rebellions that characterized the *"sexenio"* — that is, the six years of social struggles and repression which preceded the April insurrection of 1952.

TESTIMONIES IN THE COUNTRYSIDE ON THE DEATH OF VILLARROEL

The repression in the countryside was harsh. In each zone of the country and in every hacienda, an attempt was made to roll back every advance gained during the Villarroel period. One informant (interview with an ex-corregidor of Vitichi, November 12, 1968) told us the following, for example, about what happened in the province of Nor Chichas in the department of Potosí:

After the Congress, many patrones complained about their colonos, saying that they refused to work and to fulfill their old obligations . . . guaranteeing that this would not last, and that when the change would come, the peasants would rue what they were doing, and they made good on this, for when Villarroel died, they doubled the obligations of all those who had attended the Congress, and others they even kicked off the haciendas . . . and these campesinos wandered about, a sorry sight, until the Agrarian Reform was declared, because not a single hacienda would have them, saying that they were ringleaders who fomented laziness, but when the Agrarian Reform arrived, their lands in the haciendas where they had lent their services were returned to them.

An ex-delegate from the same zone (interview with José Flores, ex-hacienda Ayoma Baja, February 9, 1968) related his own personal suffering:

When President Villarroel died, for many of us peasants who attended the Congress in La Paz, there also came upon us the suffering imposed by the patrones as well as their administrators. . . . [F]or this reason, we had to abandon our lands so as not to go on suffering. . . . [S]ome who were already old died of the hardship because on other haciendas they did not want to take us upon learning that we had been in that Congress, and they said to us: "this one is lazy and that is why he makes himself an agitator among the Indians. . . ."

In the *valle alto* (high valley) of Cochabamba, the reaction to the death of Villarroel took diverse forms. In Muela (the birthplace of the president) and in other places, homages were observed. In Ucureña, on the other hand, where the peasants were in this period involved in a lawsuit against the Monastery of Santa Clara and other landowners for the possession of lands (Dandler 1969), an ex-delegate related that Villarroel's decrees did not have much significance, compared to that in the mountains (*serranías*) where the elimination of pongueaje by itself signified an important achievement for the peasants (interview with Ernesto Claros, October 1969). Furthermore, in the province of Cliza, many peasants had identified with the PIR. When this party helped to overthrow Villarroel, they hoisted a red flag in the municipality of Cliza as a signal of joy which did not cease to provoke the campesinos and townspeople identifying with the MNR and Villarroel (interview with Germán Vera Tapia, June 5, 1969).

In Yayani (Ayopaya) and bordering haciendas, the death of Villarroel set off an intense chain of events. Grájeda and Carrasco, who found themselves attending to official matters in La Paz on behalf of a school, watched helplessly the hanging of Villarroel in the Plaza Murillo. According to Carrasco, the euphoric urban mob cheering the PIR terrorized any campesino who crossed its path. Grájeda and Carrasco fled the city terrified, arriving at Yayani after several days of anxious travel to find the peasants assembled in the church, the women dressed in mourning, the crowd drunk with sorrow and rage (interview with Carrasco, corroborated by others, April 21, 1969). Other witnesses told us that the administrator approached them and said: "the thief, just like you, has died . . . that man was condemned by his chicanery [*a ese hombre la trampa le ha cargado*]." Upon hearing this, "we said among ourselves . . . if our father has died, we too will die; either they will be finished, or we will . . ." (interview with Esteban Cruz, in the presence of Natilio Pérez and Francisco Campero, April 21, 1969).

THE AYOPAYA REBELLION

Upon the death of Villarroel, gratuitous labor services were reimposed with greater force at Yayani and neighboring haciendas. The "ringleaders" who had been delegates to the National Indigenous Congress were persecuted; some, like Hilarión Grájeda and Nicolás Carrasco, abandoned the hacienda, but remained hidden in the same zone. Others stayed on the hacienda, enduring abuse so as not to lose their land and to maintain contact with the rest of the peasants. The clandestine leaders (Grájeda and others) intensified their contacts with political and labor leaders, who were also forced to act in secrecy and to regroup their opposition forces. From the first months of the "sexenio," the MNR—even though many of its principal leaders were in exile—managed to maintain a certain continuity of organization through clandestine cells. But it was the Miners' Federation, led by Juan Lechín, that took up the vanguard of the resistance. As the repression in the countryside had commenced during the Villarroel period itself, the National Indigenous Committee and the network of contacts among peasant leaders quickly fell apart. Nevertheless, they attempted to regroup,[4] under the shelter of political and labor organizations. There were attempts made to organize a National Agrarian Federation, with the support of the COB (*Central Obrera Nacional*; National Workers' Central). In Cochabamba, an incipient Departmental Agrarian Federation did not manage to establish itself. Feliciano Coca and Esteban Cruz, who represented Yayani in the federation, confirmed to us that this organization had barely achieved its formal constitution when there arose conflicts and a wave of repression tied to the uprisings in Ayopaya and other provinces. Nevertheless, in La Paz, the Departmental Agrarian Federation achieved a stronger coherence and base built on beginning attempts to form peasant unions to push for negotiations between campesinos and patrones on the haciendas. At this time (1947), the government was categorical in prohibiting all attempts at unionization, arguing that the Constitution only allowed for the unionization of wage workers.

During this period, the POR and the MNR formed an alliance in resistance. On the other hand, the PIR, which collaborated in the fall of Villarroel, now found itself losing all popular support, suffering a massive desertion by militants who joined the ranks of the MNR and POR. These two parties did not participate in the national elections held in 1947. Enrique Hertzog (leader of PURS, the Socialist Republican Union Party) was elected president with the aid of a coalition of various conservative groups. In those elections, the PIR managed to place representatives in the Legislative Chamber, allying itself in the initial months with the new government. When the PIR joined the opposition and, among other objectives, attempted to take up the agrarian question once again and to regather political support in the countryside, it exposed its nearly total failure. In this context and during the succeeding years of the "sexenio," the MNR established itself as the party with the most popular support.

On February 4, 1947, six months after the overthrow of Villarroel, a major uprising exploded in Ayopaya; it lasted a week (until February 10) and was strongly repressed by police forces, army troops, and reconnaissance planes. We will first outline, in schematic form, some of the more significant facts, then proceed to analyze testimonies and explanations offered by the peasants themselves, and lastly review some of the consequences they later suffered.

A great mass of organized campesinos from the four suyos or sections of the hacienda Yayani congregated on the night of February 4, and attacked the big house of the hacienda with dynamite. In the house were the son of the patrón, Major Carlos Zabalaga, and Lieutenant Colonel José Mercado, who had been residing at the hacienda by police order. (Both were members of the group "Radepa," which had supported Villarroel.) Upon attempting to escape, Mercado was beaten to death; Zabalaga managed to escape barefoot, along with others from the hacienda administration. The peasants sacked the hacienda house, taking with them some tools, arms, and provisions. That same night they went on to the hacienda Lachiraya, where they were joined by peasants from this and other haciendas. The following day they continued on to Parte Libre, Puncachi, and Quiriquiri, haciendas bordering on Yayani. Then they climbed to higher lands to reach the haciendas of Moyapampa and Llajma. All these haciendas they attacked and ransacked. In Llajma they killed the proprietor, José María Coca. On the third day they went on to the hacienda Charapaya, located near Calchani, adjacent to the province of Tapacarí. From the third day on, army and police forces from the city of Cochabamba and from Oruro mobilized into action intended to encircle the insurgents from various strategic locations. They also used reconnaissance planes, although these were not very effective during the first days due to bad rainy-season weather. The insurgents disbanded after the third day; the majority retreated to their places of origin, while another contingent, led by Grájeda and others, continued the attacks on other haciendas and recruited peasants encountered on the way. Later, part of this contingent went off toward Leque and Challa, at the intersection of the Cochabamba-Oruro highway, for the purpose of gaining reinforcements in Oruro. About twenty campesinos, including Grájeda, were captured in Challa and taken to Oruro. Others, who took a different route, got as far as Oruro, where, a few days later, they too were captured.

In Ayopaya itself, it took the troops a week to control the rebellion, in part because of the difficulties of transport and the bad weather. Simultaneously, as a result of the displacement of rebel peasants from Ayopaya, campesinos of nearby Tapacarí joined the rebellion and attacked some haciendas in the high ranges of that province. Elsewhere, the month of February witnessed the spread of rebellions and looting on haciendas of the altiplano of Oruro and La Paz. These were also forcefully repressed by the army and police of those departments. In declarations to the press, the ministry of defense revealed "that the principal decision was to order the bombardment of subversive concentrations [*focos*], if necessary" (*La Razón*, February 9, 1947).

Let us review, now, some observations by the rebel actors themselves which help to elucidate events and motives.[5] On February 3,

Grájeda arrived along with the miner Gabriel Muñoz and a woman [Lorenza Choque—Ed.]. . . . [S]he read some pamphlets that night. . . . [W]e leaders had a meeting with them and with other campesinos of the hacienda. . . . [T]his meeting was held in a cave. . . . [T]here was also a man who was a soothsayer [*adivino*] there and he read the coca. . . .

[H]e told us that all would go well but "be careful." . . . [D]o not confront them face to face, but from afar, and take great care, because they are watching you just to take you prisoners. . . . [T]he patrones, too, will have their punishment. . . . [T]he words of this man came true. . . .

The next day, beginning in the early hours,

the people went off toward Mulu Falda [near Tirita, a suyo of Yayani], the place where the miner Muñoz distributed dynamite to those who knew how to use it, but mostly he used it because he was a miner and knew how. . . .

. . . we had only pillories, hoes and shovels [*palas*], rocks, and sticks. . . . [L]ater, we got shotguns and rifles on the haciendas, but we hardly used them. . . .

. . . the woman said that if we didn't fight now and get rid of the patrones, we would all die, and our families would lose their lands and die of hunger . . . [S]he told us that the moment had arrived to defend the president [Villarroel]. . . .

. . . as we swore before the Congress at La Paz, Villarroel said that he was prepared to die for us, and now we are ready to die for him. . . . [W]e all loved Villarroel like a father. . . .

That night, "close to midnight, we attacked the main house." Later, when they went on to other haciendas, the group made arrangements that peasants would not attack their own haciendas, so as to avoid being identified. "The main thing we looked for in the hacienda houses were guns and food to keep on going."

The soldiers got as far as Lachiraya, the hacienda located at the end of the highway path and in the bed of the Morochata River; from there, the ascent into the higher lands of Yayani and other haciendas became more difficult. There were no confrontations with the soldiers. Seeing the military force which was approaching them, most of the campesinos sought refuge in the high lands, leaving the women and children in the houses. When they arrived at Yayani, the soldiers and police removed the women, children, and their animals from their houses and gathered them in the patio of the hacienda. There they threatened to take away the livestock if the women did not produce their husbands. And so many fugitives surrendered, and were immediately taken captive, interrogated, and physically abused in order to get their testimony. Since Hilarión and José Grájeda, Julio Carrasco and his father Nicolás, and others were not available, the soldiers burned the houses of these families. They captured Donata and Fortunata Carrasco, mother and sister respectively of Julio Carrasco, and later imprisoned them in Cochabamba along with other peasants. Donata was with a child, and she remained in jail with the boy for six years. During the military occupation of the hacienda, many women suffered physical abuse and rape. The troops also used the insurgents' produce and livestock for their own sustenance. Part of this livestock was sold to purchase other products like sugar, rice, and other foodstuffs. As many rebels did not surrender, the troops had to dress up in the clothing of the peasants and go up into the higher lands. Then, when fugitives in need of food approached to ask for help, they were captured.

The peasants of Ayopaya who were captured in Oruro and nearly one hundred others (from the haciendas Yayani, Lachiraya, Quiriquiri, Parte Libre, Punacachi, and others) were imprisoned in the Cochabamba City jail; shortly thereafter the proprietors (Zabalaga, Achá, Coca, and others) filed a criminal suit against them which included charges of homicide.

As mentioned earlier, two groups of peasants set out from Llajma and Charapya toward Leque and Challa (department of Oruro). One — with

Grájeda at the head — was taken captive in Challa. Another group of about fifty — with the miner Gabriel Muñoz and his wife Lorenza Choque at the head — reached the outskirts of the city of Oruro, where the two leaders said that they would enter the city by themselves to make contacts, and that later, the peasants should secretly make their way to the home of the couple. When some of the campesinos arrived at the house, they found only Choque:

> . . . since I was familiar with Muñoz's house, I and other peasants went together. . . . [V]arious others were there . . . but since a telegram reached [the authorities] before we got there, stating that there was an insurrection at Yayani, the police were already searching for all the peasants who had come to Oruro, in other words some of us went directly to the police [i.e., were taken prisoner]. . . . [T]hey told us that we had killed all the patrones . . . [W]e arrived at Muñoz's house at night, but did not find him, because the newspapers were already looking for him. . . . [T]hat night we slept in a house; the following day we left by night, one by one. . . . [S]ome of us made it to Caracollo some thirty kilometers away at the intersection between the La Paz and Cochabamba roads, and others of us were caught while still in Oruro. . . .

> . . . there were campesinos who made it to Oruro, and, terrified, never returned to the hacienda. . . . [T]hey left their wives and children, who later also left, surely to join up with them. . . .

The police took preliminary statements from those captured in Challa and Oruro. Those caught in Ayopaya also had to submit to interrogations, in the city of Cochabamba. In the majority of cases, especially those of "ringleaders," the authorities tortured their prisoners, employing even electrical shock to get them to confess and to divulge the names of all the participants. As one victim recalled,

When they put me at the spot [*puesto*] for the current, I broke out in a cold sweat and for that while I could have sold my father and my mother no matter how untrue. . . . [S]ince then, I've lost all fortitude [*me he vuelto sin fuerzas*] . . .

One peasant, Macario Luna of Yayani, died in the police jail as a result of the beating he received. As is customary in the police jails, the authorities did not feed the prisoners, leaving it to the families to look after them. Once the interrogations were completed, more than one hundred accused were held in preventive detention; the campesinos from Yayani numbered forty-three, and included a number of women.

During these detentions and later, when the trial began, the peasants had to make real sacrifices in order to get a defense attorney. The few lawyers who came forward to defend the peasants did so for personal benefit, and most demonstrated little perseverance, since the resources peasants could mobilize were slight, the trial long, and the atmosphere hostile to the defense. Not a single political or university group openly involved itself in their legal defense, given the repressive character of the "sexenio." Among the few lawyers who stood out in the defense were Germán Vera Tapia and Celestino Franco, who also served as the defendants' guarantors, thereby enabling the prisoners to gain passes allowing them to leave to work for money to supplement their food. During the trial, the district attorney assigned lawyers to many campesinos, and these attorneys took up the defense mechanically, without great conviction. Siding with the patrones, the local and national press generally branded the peasants criminals; few were the articles or editorials calling for reflection on the social causes or the system of exploitation which might have sparked a rebellion of the magnitude of Ayopaya's. One may affirm that during the "sexenio" it was difficult, perhaps impossible, for a peasant to obtain official justice. The regime intended to defend privilege at all costs.

In Yayani, while the trial went on (1947 to early 1952), the hacienda owners imposed greater overwork on the men and especially on the women whose husbands were in jail; on various haciendas, especially Yayani, the work force declined because of the massive detention of peasants and the flight of others. For those who remained, the various hacienda obligations continued in force, with greater intensity, without any attempt to reformulate the labor relations. (Recall the nearly permanent presence of police forces during this period.) The excesses motivated one fugitive "ringleader" and Luis Bustamante to obtain an interview with the Minister of Labor, at the risk of their arrest (*La Razón*, June 16, 1947):

In a visit to the Minister of Labor, Julio Carrasco and Luis Bustamante, the indigenous delegates from the hacienda Yayani, stated to the Minister that the police force commissioned after the insurrection has exceeded its function of controlling the activities of the natives and ensuring the tranquility of public order, having committed a series of abuses and violences against the natives, and that as a result of these acts, there exists a state of violence between the natives and the hacienda.

The peasants who remained on the hacienda had to endure the rigors of the work there for lack of an alternative. In some cases, the wives and children of defendants were forced to relocate to marginal, higher lands. In others, the administrators obligated the women to abandon the lands assigned in usufruct to their husbands and take up with another man.

The documents of the trial contain lengthy testimonies of the accused, plaintiffs, and witnesses. The latter consisted mostly of peasants, who, for fear of reprisals, found it necessary to testify against their comrades. There are also detailed police and military reports which verified damages.

The contents of the evidence and the tone of the judicial proceedings weighed unfairly against the campesinos. The accused like Grájeda, Illanes, the Carrascos, and other rebel leaders and participants did not have evidence or witnesses presented in their favor. In reality, the entire trial served primarily as a punitive lesson to the peasantry by the hacendados and authorities.

Keeping in mind the prevailing sociopolitical context when the trial took place, it is not surprising that the defense of the peasants was weak. The plaintiff proprietors focused on three basic arguments against the accused: (1) the great peasant mass was deceived by "bandit" leaders, and (2) incited by foreign elements such as miners and politicians who began to indoctrinate the peasant leaders during the Villarroel regime; (3) the government and the authorities had to impose order and control on the peasantry to prevent economic problems and a decline in the production of goods contributed by the haciendas to the country. The governmental authorities who delivered reports to the courts on the rebellion also agreed with these three principal arguments. The defense lawyers and accused peasants, for their part, presented the following three arguments: (1) the great peasant mass was innocent, and (2) the "ringleaders" were deceived by outsiders and by political groups; but (3) it ought also be considered that grave problems of injustice and abuse existed on the haciendas, that the peasants were encouraged that Villarroel and his decrees would liberate them from servitude, and that the patrones would not yield, nor the authorities collaborate in the fulfillment of these measures.[6]

Thus it was that the allusion to the miner Muñoz arose and became permanent. Tried and sentenced to capital punishment in absentia, he came to personify the deceit and the agitation: *the cause of the rebellion.* No authentic evidence was presented in the judicial proceedings that any political or labor organization participated directly in the rebellion. Nor did such groups intervene in the legal defense of the peasants, probably for fear of being incriminated. The strategy of the various defense attorneys was not to enter into a political or social polemic with the plaintiffs, nor to emphasize the internal causes which provoked a peasant rebellion against the patrones. Instead, they basically accepted the terms of legal discourse imposed by hacendados and authorities, for the purpose of maneuvering a less drastic sentence for the accused.

The trial commenced on February 14, 1947, in the second penal court of the district of Cochabamba. A large majority of the peasant prisoners remained in jail for around six years while the trial went on. On August 15, 1949, the fifth penal court passed sentence on 132 peasants. Nineteen, mostly from Yayani, among them Hilarión Grájeda, Pedro Soto, Francisco Illanes, Gregorio Loayza, and Julio Carrasco and Gabriel Muñoz in absentia, were to suffer capital punishment. The other 113 accused were given eight years of imprisonment (see *El País*, September 21, 1949). The judgement was appealed to the district supreme court, which confirmed the death penalty only for Grájeda and Muñoz.[7] Four months after the April Revolution, the MNR dictated a decree (July 22, 1952) which granted total amnesty to all persons who had been involved in strikes, uprisings, or other acts of social protest during the "sexenio." The doors of the prison opened for the Ayopaya offenders, and they returned to their haciendas. Grájeda, Miguel Carrasco, Francisco Illanes, Pedro Soto, and others had already managed to escape from their cells during the revolution or "civil war" of 1949 (an unsuccessful struggle of the MNR and popular forces against the government of Urriolagoitia). Nevertheless, shortly thereafter, some of them had been newly captured (Grájeda, Miguel Carrasco), while others remained fugitives. It is significant that these leaders rapidly involved themselves after April 1952 in the organization of unions which would form an important contingent of the Departmental Federation of Campesinos of Cochabamba in August 1952 (see Dandler 1975).

WHY THE REBELLION?

In many of the testimonies contained in the trial, one can appreciate the desperation the peasants experienced because Villarroel's decrees could not be fully enforced. This, and Villarroel's death, led them to a profound questioning of their position. This was confirmed by the many conversations which we had with peasants of Yayani and bordering haciendas. We will attempt here to synthesize the principal causes and motivations of the rebellion, and to base this reflection directly on conversations with the actors themselves and other witnesses.

The zone of Ayopaya was characterized by the intense and hegemonic dominance of the hacienda. This was accentuated in the 1930s and 1940s by the imposition of extra work due to the hacienda's more commercialized orientation to consumer markets for various crops, especially potatoes, in the urban and mining centers. The proprietors of that epoch did not introduce new modes of compensation to their labor force, but simply intensified the servitude system and reinforced their administrative staffs by employing, as in Yayani, more supervisory personnel.

It was in this regional context that the government of Villarroel had a special effect on the expectations of the campesinos. A leadership and incipient organization emerged on various haciendas, and focused on a central revindication which found echoes at the level of many labor, political, and governmental organizations: the problem of uncompensated obligations and serfdom on the hacienda. In contrast with other zones, like the valle alto (Ucureña), where the peasants had been unionized since 1936 and were soon involved in a fight for the ownership of land, the peasants of Ayopaya did not reach the point of proposing a redistribution of land. Nor did there exist in the province of Ayopaya indigenous communities such as those in Tapacarí, the Norte de Potosí (i.e., Chayanta), or the altiplano, where peasants held some sort of territorial space of their own from whence to unite around claims against the expansion of the hacienda, governmental measures to privatize communal property, and other exactions (see Chapters 10 and 12 by Platt and Albó in this volume). For the peasants merely to question the prevailing labor system on the haciendas, and to have this backed by a wider process of mobilization and debate (the National Indigenous Congress) and legitimated by a governmental decree abolishing gratuitous services on the haciendas — in Ayopaya, this *was* a significant step.

The campesinos lived this period intensely. Theirs was a hope that grew and solidified in the process of participation by delegates and leaders, who in every locale reiterated a hope confirmed by contacts with governmental authorities. This hope, as expressed by many leaders, was embodied in the figure and pledge of a president who for the first time addressed them directly and convened them as brothers and fellow citizens. The right to remunerated labor and to be free of arbitrary dispossession by the patrones were claims which Villarroel expounded as rights of citizenship historically postponed, but now to be enforced by his government. The relationship with Villarroel was conceived by the peasants as a *pact of reciprocity*: Villarroel and his government committed themselves to help the peasants, in exchange for the peasants' support and commitment in a hostile atmosphere which pitted them all against the patrones. The countless experiences of persecution, the interminable negotiations, and the systematic opposition by the patrones and local authorities only served to reinforce the peasants' organization and resolve, as evidenced in the "sit-down strikes" which broke out after the National Indigenous Congress. If we add to this experience the violent overthrow of Villarroel and the crushing of any reformist effort during the "sexenio," the peasantry was left, as one campesino put it, "naked before the patron . . . so that they would not have to recognize any change, but could rather exploit us more. . . ."

As in other regions where hacienda dominion was acute, the peasants of Ayopaya suffered the renewed vigor of landowner attacks after the Villarroel administration was overthrown. The restitution of servitude and the persecution of their leaders exacerbated their sense of impotence and isolation, in the context of general repression of the popular movement during the "sexenio." Campesinos from various haciendas who were involved in the rebellion described their dilemma in the following manner in a statement to the press shortly after the rebellion broke out (*El Pueblo*, February 8, 1947; emphasis added):

We have gathered in this city [La Paz], making the journey by foot from our districts, sent by about three hundred colonos from the region and their respective families.

The motive of our commission is to present before the Supreme Government the grievances of our counterparts, demanding guarantees . . . that are the cause for the most inhumane treatment and exactions.

All the laws and protectionist measures sanctioned by the Indigenous Congress of the last regime proved worthless. [The patrones] were authorized to revive the old customs, the pongueaje, the mitanis . . . the contributions in kind.

In many cases they appropriate our products, saying that the plots they grant us in recognition of personal services, should be [worked on a 50 percent sharecropping basis] or "in partnership."

Finally, to insure our submission to this new order of things, they have told us that they are authorized to use the whip if we do not want to serve willingly, and that the new government has even supplied them with arms and munitions, to get respect, they never tire of showing their arms and munitions. . . .

We come to you, Mr. Minister [of Labor] to request that you take our complaint before the Honorable Government Junta and that it . . . makes known to all the indigenous peoples, currently on a war footing, that the laws subsist, that the new regimes will not forget us, but lend us their support and, finally, that they summon and sanction the evil patrones . . . *that they investigate the causes of the insurrections and revolts, and that they point to those who are sowing anarchy.*

This was a desperate outcry for legal guarantees and state support for the decrees of Villarroel. But with or without rebellion, the prevailing system of domination had no reason to accept such petitions. It was only through a profound political transformation—the April Revolution of 1952 and the agrarian mobilization immediately following it—that a qualitative change came about for the peasantry.

Why did Yayani become the principal center of the rebellion? A number of conditions were important to understand the rebellion, among them the existence of a rental system somewhat anomalous for the period, and a rigid system of servitude and exactions. The hacienda was under contract by the Monastery of Santa Teresa to rent the property to one family for "three lifetimes." The contract was signed in 1817. The second "lifetime" ended with the death of the hacendado in 1894. Then the Monastery refused to recognize the third "lifetime," which motivated a six-year trial that ended in 1900 with victory by the renting family of a third extension.[8]

We found no evidence of this type of contract anywhere else in Ayopaya, or in other regions of the country. According to ex-administrators and ex-majordomos of the hacienda, the labor problems dated back to the 1920s, and resulted largely from exactions and abuses imposed by the patrón. This situation culminated in a suit filed in 1940 against a major-domo and the patrón.

In the 1940s, the peasants could foresee the end of the lease of "three lifetimes," since the patrón was old; nevertheless, their fears augmented as the patrón's son began to affirm his presence by initiating productive projects on the hacienda and by cultivating ties with tenant patrones who had signed sublet contracts since the beginning of that decade. In other words, the campesinos feared that a possible "fourth lifetime" might be added to the rental contract. All this collective reflection on their situation occurred precisely in a wider context — the political atmosphere generated by Villarroel — which stimulated expectations of change. The government promoted an effort to transform labor relations. When Villarroel died and the landowner in Yayani imposed the restitution of servitude, as other patrones had done, he faced a peasantry more alert, combative, and organized than before 1943, disturbed by one retreat and fearful that the contract, instead of running out, might be extended for another generation.

There remains the issue of leadership. In Yayani one leader, Hilarión Grájeda, stood out, and surrounded himself with a nucleus of collaborators in that locale and distinguished himself more generally in the zone. Furthermore, he was one of those Ayopaya leaders who cultivated relationships with peasant leaders from other regions through his participation in the National Indigenous Committee. He also knew some of the outstanding political figures of the period. According to his ex-collaborators, Grájeda had problems with the patrón in 1927 and was expelled for a time.[9] Later, in 1940, he acted as the principal plaintiff in a criminal suit against an overseer and the patrón. He did not know how to read, he understood little Spanish, he picked up a bit of Aymara, "but as he was intrepid, he just came in and made himself understood." His personal qualities singled him out as an authority respected among the campesinos. According to Julio Carrasco, one of his ex-lieutenants:

Hilarión was like an energetic father, very strict, and at times he punished us like his children. But we admired him and feared him because he knew how to talk, how to organize us, and he was constantly going off to La Paz to converse with government people and others, always in search of help. . . .

Before the Villarroel regime, Grájeda went with other campesinos, at the suggestion of a lawyer, to the National Archive in Sucre, where he hoped to find some document related to the lands of Yayani providing evidence with which to question the legal origin of the property. We do not know whether Grájeda found any clue. Nevertheless, he later consulted with lawyers about the three-lifetimes contract, about which the campesinos were fully aware.

The factors outlined — general conditions of the hacienda system in the province of Ayopaya, peasant identification with President Villarroel, advances and retreats regarding the labor system on the hacienda, local repression during the "sexenio," and specific conditions of the hacienda Yayani — sufficed to generate a peasant rebellion of almost provincial stature. During the years before the rebellion, the campesinos of Yayani and other haciendas became involved in an effort to change their servile situation; the traditional system of exploitation had intensified during the last two deceases as a result of the greater commercial orientation of the haciendas. The peasants did not explicitly raise the problem of the possession or ownership of lands. Even the National Indigenous Congress and the government of Villarroel evaded this question. The peasants of Ayopaya centered their principal claim, rather, on the problem of unpaid services on the hacienda and the insecurity of their usufruct rights in land, a condition which subjected them to the whims of the patrones, renters, and administrators. The National Indigenous Congress was in this context a significant innovation, since it allowed for the peasants to organize themselves, to express publicly their situation, and to find a sympathetic echo in a government providing evidence that it favored them. The results included decrees abolishing servitude on the hacienda and regulating the security of usufruct rights, and the establishment of a political discourse that considered the peasants citizens with dignity and rights. It was a discourse born in the trenches of the Chaco War; the peasants had been a majority contingent and had fulfilled the greatest obligation required of a citizen. It was the political groups of popular orientation and the military nationalists who took note of this fact. In this way, the agrarian question became a central preoccupation of the effort to transform society and the state. On agrarian matters, the political discourse focused on the educational integration of the "native" during the 1930s; in the 1940s it focused on the problem of servitude; only after the Revolution of 1952, and by means of a peasant mobilization, did there crystallize action directly around the land and its redistribution.

During the Villarroel regime, a "thick" process of popular mobilization took place in the mines, cities, and countryside. This was an offensive of the popular sectors which shook up a system of oligarchical domination whose hegemony was in the midst of decomposing. The organizational process that began in the countryside and the changes achieved in the area of labor relations – however incipient they may have been – proclaimed the end of a traditional order. The rebellion of the hacendados commenced during the Villarroel regime, and was consolidated with the president's death and the succession of regimes that characterized the "sexenio" before the April Revolution. On one and another hacienda, the landowners' rebellion meant taking vengeance on that peasantry which had dared to introduce a discourse on citizens and the just remuneration of labor. The uprisings of the peasants of Ayopaya and many other regions of the country were responses that made of this the last great rebellion of the hacendados.

NOTES

1 During the Villarroel regime, the press was filled with reports, editorials, and details of even the most localized happenings related to the agrarian question. This reflected the suspiciousness of the rightist opposition press. On the other hand, there existed newspapers like *La Calle* (pioneering newspaper of the MNR directed by Carlos Montenegro and Augusto Céspedes), which contains a wealth of information on social issues, and where excellent reports and commentaries on the issue may be found. These sources are indispensable in placing events, names, and debates. Nevertheless, we have carried out exhaustive field research based on interviews with campesino leaders and other persons close to the events. Our quotations from newspapers, therefore, are not based on casual selection from these sources.

2 The Cochabamban press reports strikes and troubles at Yayani and other haciendas of Ayopaya especially during the months of April, May, and July, 1946.

3 The PIR, which had developed a more integral, if doctrinary, perspective on the agrarian problem, joined the forces of the right to overthrow the Villarroel administration, and with this sealed its political suicide. The explanation of its leader, José Antonio Arze, is significant (*La Razón*, August 10, 1945):

   . . . in the social aspect, the overthrown government promised to solve the problems which bear on our proletariat of the mines and rural areas. Of course, we know that it did nothing to improve the living conditions of those sectors . . . and the indigenous class, the only thing it gave them was a picturesque congress, the fatal consequence of which was the "Las Canchas" massacre. So it had to be that, from the very start, the sole objective of those campaigns was to win over voters and militants.

4 The following letter from Antonio Alvarez Mamani to Hilarión Grájeda is indicative of the contacts maintained between campesino leaders and their attempts to regroup in defense of their interests:

   I have come here [Vinto, Quillacollo province, Cochabamba] to reach an agreement with all the delegates, and in case you want to continue with this, we need a central office in Cochabamba for everyone.

[The letter continues with an enumeration of necessary expenses such as the purchase of a second-hand typewriter, telegrams, the rental of a room, and a secretary's salary; it also proposes that for the next meeting, all the compañeros carry adequate identification.]

. . . the new President of the Republic is a leader of the conservative Liberal Party, and we can only rely on six legislators who are miners; there is much struggle ahead. I need an immediate response from the delegates and from you [Vinto, January 13, 1947; written by hand; letter provided courtesy of Grájeda's widow].

As the rebellion in Ayopaya occurred at the beginning of February, there was no time to formulate any concrete response to Alvarez Mamani's letter.

5   We would like to note here that, upon arriving in Ayopaya, we were already equipped with general information about the rebellion and the subsequent criminal trial, based on interviews with some ex-administrators and lawyers, and newspaper clippings we had gathered regarding the agrarian question in the 1940s. We arrived at Yayani after making a number of previous contacts and attending a campesino meeting in the Lachiraya zone. At this conference, the motive for our presence was explained, and by nightfall we reached Yayani by mule, accompanied by various union leaders of the area. After a number of days of making contact with some ex-delegates and ex-"ringleaders" from Yayani to the National Indigenous Congress, we held a collective meeting with them and with authorities from the area. There was a profound initial distrust of us, justified by the persecutions they had suffered, the possible reprisals, and because of the existent political context (during the Barrientos regime there were cases of ex-hacendados who attempted to recuperate lands). In a ceremony attended by the corregidor, we took an oath (having brought along a legal document stating our purpose and commitment) that we were carrying out an investigation for the purpose of disseminating a historical event, and we clarified that there was no possibility of a new trial or legal recriminations against them, since the supreme amnesty decree (April 1952) was still in effect. That is, the information gathered would not be used against them. It was very clear that the rebellion, the trial, and above all, their identification with Villarroel formed part of a collective historical memory. They judged it appropriate that we, as investigators, should ask them all sorts of questions, in order that the result would be a publication, disseminating the facts and their experiences, as an example of the campesinos' struggle to liberate themselves from exploitation, years before the Revolution of 1952 and the Agrarian Reform. They also felt the need to transmit their experience so that the new generation, including their own children and grandchildren, would be able to know it, as the majority already did not appreciate what had been sacrificed to obtain the freedom and lands from which they now benefit.

6 In the testimony of Grájeda:

I have been a colono of Yayani for many years. Because of the abuses committed by the patrón . . . against the colonos of said estate, they named me as their representative to protest these abuses. By virtue of that delegation, I have acted as a leader of the aforementioned estate, and have also travelled on various occasions to the city of La Paz to meet with government representatives in order to obtain the modification of certain customs in the obligations of the colonos in service to the hacienda; but not once did I even have even so much as the idea of distributing the patrones' lands . . . nor did anyone inculcate those ideas in us. . . .

The only antecedents and motives which induced us to commit the crimes for which we are being tried were none other than the outrages we have suffered from the patrones, who have wanted, at any cost, to make a joke of the benefits that the last decrees expedited by the Villarroel administration granted us . . . [pp. 10, 15, cuarto cuerpo, trial against the campesinos of Yayani and other haciendas, Archivo Judicial de Cochabamba].

7 The Supreme Court of the district of Cochabamba (August 20, 1951) confirmed the death penalty of Grájeda and Muñoz; sentenced 82 persons to ten years in prison (including Pedro Soto, Gregorio Loayza, Julio Carrasco, Natilio Segundo, León Pérez, and others, mostly from Yayani); three persons to seven years and six months in prison (Lorenza Choque, wife of Muñoz; Donata Pérez de Carrasco and Miguel Carrasco, mother and brother of Julio Carrasco); and absolved 49 persons for lack of evidence, with the obligation to reimburse the state and the plaintiff proprietors all costs occasioned by the trial (information extracted from the expediente of the trial about Yayani and other haciendas, Archivo Judicial de Cochabamba).

8 Dates extracted from the Agrarian Reform expediente appropriating the hacienda Yayani (Ayopaya), Consejo Nacional de Reforma Agraria (1956).

9 Unfortunately, when we arrived in Ayopaya for the first time in April 1968, Grájeda had died six months earlier, at age 72. When we returned in 1981, his tomb still stood out among all the others, and once a year, on All Saints Day, the campesinos cleared it of weeds and still offered their respects. When the Revolution of 1952 came about, he became the leader of the peasant union of Yayani, headed the demand for expropriation of the hacienda, and in 1957 personally distributed the property titles to all the campesinos of Yayani.

REFERENCES

CANDIA ALMARAZ, ALBERTO
1957   *Razón de Patria ante la historia*. Cochabamba: Imprenta Pelikan.

CORNEJO, ALBERTO
1949   *Programa político de Bolivia*. Cochabamba: Imprenta Universitaria.
DANDLER, JORGE
1969   *El sindicalismo campesino en Bolivia: cambios estructurales en Ucu-reña (1935-52)*. Mexico: Instituto Indigenista Interamericano; 2nd ed., La Paz: Centro de Estudios de la Realidad Económica y Social (CERES), 1984.
1971   "Politics of brokerage, leadership and patronage in the campesino movement of Cochabamba, Bolivia (1935-52)." Ph.D. diss., University of Wisconsin–Madison.
1975   "Campesinado y reforma agraria en Cochabamba (1952-53): dinámica de un movimiento campesino en Bolivia." La Paz: Centro de Investigación y Promoción del Campesinado (CIPCA). Mimeo.
DANDLER, JORGE, AND FERNANDO CALDERÓN, eds.
1984   *Bolivia: La fuerza histórica del campesinado*. La Paz and Geneva: Centro de Estudios de la Realidad Económica y Social (CERES) and United Nations Research Institute for Social Development.
LARSON, BROOKE
1983   *Explotación agraria y resistencia campesina en Cochabamba: cinco ensayos históricos (siglos XVI-XIX)*. La Paz: CERES.
MENDOZA, GUNNAR
1982   *Diario del Tambor Vargas*. Mexico: Siglo XXI.
REINAGA, FAUSTO
1952   *Tierra y Libertad: La Revolución Nacional y el Indio*. La Paz: Ediciones Rumbo Sindical.
ROMERO, HUGO
1971   "Integración y politización en una sociedad compuesta." *Aportes:* 32-49.

CHAPTER 12

From MNRistas to Kataristas to Katari

XAVIER ALBÓ

INTRODUCTION

Two centuries ago, from March to October of 1781, the city of La Paz was blockaded by a ring of thousands of Aymaras. Headed by Julián Apasa, who called himself Tupaj Katari, the siege was one of the most important episodes in the great Indian uprising in the late colonial period. A few years ago, in December of 1979, the *gente decente* ("respectable folk") of La Paz felt a panic which revived, perhaps unconsciously, the collective memory of that famous blockade. The peasantry — still *la indiada* ("the Indian mass") in the words of the gente decente — initiated a general blockade that isolated La Paz and other cities as part of a protest against certain economic measures.

The 1979 blockade, like another more recent one in April of 1983 and many other manifestations of a powerful peasant movement, had also been an initiative of the Aymaras. Their most militant sectors like to call themselves "kataristas," in memory of, and as testimony to the ideological and historical link with, the hero of 1781. Their principal leader, Jenaro Flores, comes from a community in the region of Sicasica close to Katari's birthplace, and more recently the birthplace of katarismo. There is an evident continuity at least in the memory of this people, a memory awakened in the last few decades.

Nonetheless, in the two hundred years that have gone by there have been events and structural changes worthy of consideration. The Spanish colonial era against which the original Katari fought came to an end. The mining *mita* (forced labor drafts), the tributes, and the *reparto de mercancías* (forced distribution of goods), which had constituted the principal

---

Translation by Lianne Werlein-Jaén and Steve J. Stern.

areas of struggle, were done away with. The new Bolivian state undertook a series of "agrarian reforms" in 1825, 1874, and most notably in
1953, which attempted to modernize agriculture, erasing from the map
the traditional communities or ayllus (i.e., lineage groups within communities), proposing in their stead the private ownership of land, and foment-
ing the integration of the entire rural populace into the rest of the society.

How to explain, then, this continuity? Is it only a matter of a superficial
symbolic similarity, or does it touch something deeper? Despite the strong
advance in our current knowledge about the great uprising of 1780–1782,
we are still far from a coherent and definitive vision of what really happened during the uprising, especially from the perspective of its Indian
protagonists. In another study, as yet unfinished, I seek to understand
better the variegated role which the Aymaras played, as a first step toward
tracing the great arc between 1780 and 1980.[1] But the scope of this essay
is much more limited: I will concentrate only on the final curve of the
arc. The most distant and distinct point in relation to the uprising of 1780
is perhaps the agrarian revolution which took place in Bolivia in response
to the Agrarian Reform of 1953. But what catches the eye is that after
the reform and the lethargic two decades that followed, the Bolivian peasantry has begun to agitate once again in a manner reminiscent of that
distant Katari of the colonial period. This new awakening toward the future
through a reencounter with the past, quite visible in the evolution from
1953 to 1983, will constitute the topic of this essay. The continuity and
contrast between two moments — Ayopaya, 1947 (studied by Dandler and
Torrico in Chapter 11) and contemporary katarista ideology — will be better understood in light of the evolution presented here.

HISTORICAL ANTECEDENTS

After the two wars for Independence — the "Indian" one, which was frustrated, and the "creole" one, which triumphed — and before the crucial
Agrarian Reform of 1953, one can distinguish two distinct phases regarding the problem of the peasantry and peasant movements. These phases
are demarcated by the Chaco War (1932–1935).

After Independence, and for various decades, the rural situation in the
new republic of Bolivia in fact prolonged the colonial situation against
which the Amarus and Kataris had fought. But beginning in 1866 with
Melgarejo, and especially after the consolidation of the new oligarchic
state of conservatives and liberals in 1880, the "liberal" program advo-
cated by Bolívar began to become a reality. The dominant elites believed
that the solution to their problems lay in adopting the principles of liberalism. In agriculture, a precondition was the individual ownership of land,

so that land could enter without hindrance into the magical world of supply and demand. This would lead it more easily into the hands of those most apt to make it productive. The practical effect for the traditional owners of the land, the communities, was dispossession. Practically all of the peasant uprisings from the middle of the nineteenth century up until the Chaco War were marked by the communities' desperate defense of their lands. Their uprisings invariably ended in massacres carried out by the armies at the service of the landowning oligarchy. Another characteristic of the period was that the new groups which emerged within the dominant oligarchy initially sought the backing of the angry *comuneros*, promising to defend them in exchange for the communities' support of their quest for power. However, once a new group came into power, it continued with the dispossession practiced by its predecessors. In another work, I have caricatured this pattern, repeated at least three times in sixty years, as "la misma chola con otro sombrero" ("the same *chola* wearing another hat").[2]

The second phase, after the Chaco War, witnessed an obvious shift of objectives, protagonists, and allies. Although the desperate defense by the communities continued, what came to the fore was the struggle of peons on some deteriorating haciendas, such as the ancient estates in the valleys of Cochabamba, where the leadership of Ana Rancho/Ucureña surfaced.[3] Initially the peasants fought to better the conditions of life within the haciendas without questioning the validity of the regime itself. But little by little, they began to raise the destruction of the system itself, in the slogan "the land is for those who work it." The other novelty of this period was the intimate bond between the struggle of the hacienda peons and that of the new political parties which emerged out of the national crisis created by the Chaco War. It was evident to the leaders of these new groups that the old oligarchic state no longer worked. All of them suggested that there needed to be a "revolutionary" change which should include, among other items, the incorporation of the Indian into the public life of the country. For this reason they began to call the Indian a "peasant," and the Indian-peasant problem was incorporated into the parties' programs. Before, opposition groups within the oligarchy took advantage of communal discontent merely to find allies of the moment. Now, by contrast, the incorporation of the hacienda serf and a more or less radical agrarian reform became integral parts of the political project of these parties. For example, the efforts made by the Villarroel/MNR government to begin the massive organization of peasant unions, taking advantage of the discontent that already existed in many haciendas (as Dandler and Torrico explain to us in detail in Chapter 11 of this volume), were well known. From this phase onward the communities, the protagonists of every rural movement from the colonial times of Tupaj Katari until the Chaco War, faded into the background: they had either been destroyed and transformed into haciendas, or they had been squeezed into a corner, reduced to 22 percent of the lands for which census data are available.[4] In this sense the focus of this new phase shared with the previous one the conviction that the communities were only relics of an already surmounted past.

FROM THE MNR TO THE MILITARY-PEASANT PACT (PMC): 1952–1969

The phase which followed was really the consolidation and triumph of the previous one, the product of the MNR's coming to power in 1952, its enactment of the Agrarian Reform in 1953, along with complementary measures such as universal education and suffrage, and the MNR's continuation in power for twelve years. All of this was part of a capitalist and partly statist modernization program which included (1) the nationalization of the main source of foreign currency, the mines of three great oligarchs now converted into the large state enterprise COMIBOL; (2) the amplification of the political and economic base of the nation to include all Bolivians – in practical terms, the Indians' incorporation into the market, the electoral process, and the educational system; and (3) the extension and diversification of the agricultural-geographical frontier through the opening of new roads to the east, where new productive possibilities were opened up in oil and agribusiness. As Silvia Rivera (1983: 130) has summed it up, with the new program of the MNR,

The country of Indians governed by Lords would disappear with the revolution. The lords would turn into democrats and bourgeoisie and the Indians into citizens, integrated into an independent and egalitarian sovereign state, founded on the solid ground of the internal market, and the recovery of the export economy by the state. The Indian would also disappear in the process of *mestizaje*, Hispanization of language, migration, and the parcelling out of the communities.

The participation of the peasantry in this project was massive. In its initial stage one could even call it decisive. It is not even clear that the MNR wanted to get very far in its practical projects of agrarian reform. Its previous stands on this subject were more ambiguous than those of the other "revolutionary" parties of the time, the PIR (*Partido de la Izquierda Revolucionaria*; Party of the Revolutionary Left) and the POR (*Partido Obrero Revolutionario*; Revolutionary Workers' Party). But, on the other hand, the MNR did take much more seriously the expansion of its base throughout the countryside: it was the most populist of the three. Immediately after the coup/revolution which carried the MNR to power on April 9, 1952 (with very little peasant participation), it created a Ministry of Peasant Affairs whose principal function was to expand the governing party's ties throughout the countryside, through the creation of its *own* peasant unions.

One of the areas that was given priority was Cochabamba. As demonstrated in Dandler and Torrico's chapter, the MNR had done solid work there in the past, demonstrating already the contradictions of its populist focus. On the one hand, it instigated the well-known rebellion of Ayopaya in 1947, but at the same time, it checked initiatives from below in order to channel popular impulses toward its own objectives: it wanted a new peasant participation, but it wanted the MNR to remain in the driver's seat. But in 1952, in the *valle alto* ("high valley") of Cochabamba, the MNR was forced into the passenger's seat. A group of peasant unions had been struggling there for sixteen years with the support of another of the new parties, the PIR.[5] The heart of this group, led by José Rojas and Crisóstomo Inturias among others, was in the forementioned hamlet of Ucureña. They imposed on the MNR their leaders—quickly ratified on a national level in exchange for loyalty to the MNR—and later an agrarian reform which was swifter and more radical than the one conjectured by the MNR. In the face of governmental indecision, they began by taking over the haciendas on their own, and thanks to these de facto actions, the MNR government ended up deciding in favor of agrarian reform. This decision soon turned into an essential political tool of the governing party, assuring it the support and the vote of this majority sector. If one can speak of peasant initiative in certain parts of Cochabamba, it is also evident that in most of the country the reform was launched by the government, although the state did not always manage to keep the grass roots, once mobilized, under its control.[6]

The peasant movement was massive and relatively monolithic during the first years, when with the government's support it fought to acquire land and to expel the landowners. There were many regional variants in this process which we need not outline here. But, with greater or lesser radicalism, the mobilized peasants had no doubts about the legitimacy of taking over the land, nor about the good intentions of the MNR, the first government to have given them the green light—if not the fuel—to carry out this process.

Several problems became acute once the peasants owned (albeit without any legal deeds) their land. New objectives for collective struggle did not surface immediately. Since the MNR was interested above all in winning over the peasants, the normal practice was that the unions and their leaders were more successful the more they tied themselves to direction by the MNR. When the question of land was no longer a motivating force, and in the traditional communities, where there had never been hacendados, subsidized food coupons became another of the MNR's instruments to attract peasant leaders, thus establishing new forms of political clientelism. In this fashion, the strong dependence of peasant unions on the government was consolidated. As Rivera (ibid.) points out, the peasantry's initially active subordination little by little became a passive subordination: in exchange for favors received, the peasantry supported the MNR in times of crisis, as in the various attempted coups by the Falangists, the ever-present ghost of the former landowners. But at the same time the peasants expected all from the government: subsidized food, schools, even political-union posts, the latter also a source of another series of small personal gains. During this period many divisions arose within the peasant organizations, divisions which in time led to serious conflicts and killings between peasants. Especially serious were those in Cliza/Ucureña, Achacachi/Warisat'a, and in the Norte de Potosí. But even in these cases, none of the conflicting factions questioned the legitimacy of the MNR government. The conflicts either consisted of struggles for power between local caciques over which the government had little control (especially in valleys of the Norte de Potosí), or else they mirrored parallel conflicts within the government between different factions of the MNR. For example, certain factions were Guevarists or Lechinistas, while others continued to support the more numerous followers of Paz Estenssoro or Siles. But all were MNRistas to the core.

The MNRista scheme for a dependent alliance between the government and the peasantry worked during the twelve years that the MNR was in power in practically all of the rural regions of the country, albeit with different intensities. It was weakest in peripheral areas where the landowners were more steadfast and, in some cases, remain so today. On the other hand, it was strongest in those areas most influenced by centralized power. In the east, with its abundant land and the opening of a new locus of capitalist development, the process was very different from that of the Andean areas.

Within the more central Andean regions linked to the state, the MNR's populist model took root most in those areas long dominated by the hacienda, as in Cochabamba or Achacachi. It was there more than elsewhere that the MNR, first as a party and later as the government, seemed to the *colonos* (serfs) a superior and powerful ally, a new and to a certain extent unexpected one, with which to fight and eventually defeat their most visible enemy: the landowners. With this victory, the colonos' dependence on the government was strengthened, as well as the government's search for populist support among the peasantry. Already in 1943–1947, during the Villarroel government, and in the evolution of locales such as Ayopaya, the first indications of this pattern had appeared. Dandler and Torrico demonstrate in the previous chapter the preponderant, although not exclusive, role that the haciendas had played. These authors are prompted to speak of a "pact of reciprocity" between Villarroel and those peasants, most of them colonos, to confront the landowners and their allies together, if only in the search for better labor relations. But in this pact Villarroel was already seen as "a father who cares for his children," to use his own words, spoken at the National Indigenous Congress of 1945. After 1952, with or without bottom-up struggles depending on the region, the MNR, the absolute ruler of the government, organized the countryside, distributed land, installed universal suffrage, inaugurated schools, and favored the most faithful. With this, its image as a benevolent superior was consolidated in the countryside.

Nonetheless, in the regions dominated by the communities rather than haciendas, this dependent relationship, although present, did not penetrate as deeply. First of all, communal organization had been strong in these regions for a long time, and needed only limited adjustment to the "union" structure. Second, the relationship with the government had long been governed by another scheme, more clearly dual, joining community-ayllu and the state. This was a kind of "contract," certainly unequal, in which greater distances were maintained; the community paid various tributes and as a result the state respected its relative autonomy (Platt 1982). Third, the struggle to regain land barely came into play in the communities, which meant that the MNR's "benevolent paternalism" was embodied in less essential benefits.

When in 1964 General Barrientos swept aside the MNR and initiated eighteen years of military regimes, one of the political pillars of the new regime was the so-called *Pacto Militar-Campesino* (PMC; "Military-Peasant Pact"). Behind the apparent rupture with the MNR, there was a surprising continuity in the populist style relation between the government and the peasantry. Let us try to explain this continuity. Its point of departure was the now well-rooted scheme of passive subordination of the peasantry to the MNR. In addition, Barrientos had been an MNRista military man, and had played an important role in the relations between that party and the peasantry. His role had been especially crucial during the Ch'ampa War, that is, the conflict and shootings between the peasants faithful to Cliza and those tied to Ucureña, in the very same area of Cochabamba where the peasant movement and the Agrarian Reform had been born. That conflict had already become chronic and was aggravated when each band joined with one or another leader or sector of the also divided MNR. The war had already claimed more than one thousand lives when Barrientos pacified the Valley.[7] Under these circumstances

Barrientos and his military men appeared as the "saviors" in a no-win situation.

It was then, with the MNR still in power, that a *Pacto Militar-Campesino Anticomunista* ("Military-Peasant Anti-Communist Pact") was sealed in Ucureña. "Communism" was considered the culprit behind all those fratricidal struggles between unions whose leaders had been reduced to political clients of one or another of the factions within the MNR. Barrientos and his military forces, on the other hand, were viewed as the new redeeming fathers, and as the revivers of the MNR's revolutionary process. When Barrientos ascended to power soon thereafter, many sectors in the countryside initially held reservations. But this background of events, and the personal charisma of this Cochabamban military man who made generous use of populist tactics, assured the success of the transition. Barrientos spoke Quechua, drank *chicha* beer, hopped to any corner of the countryside in his helicopter, lavished small gifts, gave subordinate official posts to loyal peasants, and, with the motto of exchanging rifles for ploughs, set up the Armed Forces' Civic Action and Community Development Program ("Desarrollo de Comunidades y Acción Cívica de las Fuerzas Armadas"). All this was especially successful in the valleys of Cochabamba where the MNR's populist-clientelist project had also been most successful. In this way the full and passive subordination of the peasantry to an authoritarian regime was in reality the culmination of a long populist process — not its negation. What the PMC actually negated was the old-style dual contract of ayllu/state. Barrientos, "the people's General," became in addition the "supreme leader of the peasantry." It seemed as though the peasant movement had been given its final blow, and that the Agrarian Reform, with its grants of small parcels to peasant families, had achieved its soporific effect. When Ché Guevara's guerrillas appeared in Ñancahuazú in 1967, there was even a "Barrientos regiment" formed by Cochabamban peasants to fight against "those Communists."

The capitalist modernization process initiated by the MNR on April 9, 1952, proceeded during Barrientos's rule (1964–1969). But the illusion of creating a new "nationalist" bourgeoisie, free of international dependence, had already given way to a strong dependence on the United States during the MNR's last years. In that sense, Barrientos, a creation of the United States, was also the culmination of an earlier process. The interests and priorities of the development model which was adopted were in fact contradictory to those of the popular sectors which the populist stand seemed to support: they fomented the development of a new bourgeoisie — owner, in turn, of the new state — which could only consolidate itself at the expense of the aforementioned popular sectors. The contradiction had surfaced most notably, during the MNR's times, in the confrontation between the state/COMIBOL and the miners: the state (and the corrupt managers of COMIBOL) foisted social costs on the miners' shoulders. With Barrientos this confrontation—promoted by the capitalist managerial logic of the U.S. advisors—reached its peak with the lowering of already nominal salaries, the elimination of the company stores, the white massacre (i.e., the massive dismissal of personnel), and finally, the red massacre—the Night of San Juan. Throughout this confrontation Barrientos sought as a counterweight the support of the peasant organizations, which were more subordinate and unquestioning since they depended not on salaries, but on patron-client favors. Barrientos provoked what Siles had attempted in 1959: a confrontation between peasants faithful to him and the miners, although he, like Siles, achieved no more than a distancing between the two groups. In any case, he did succeed in getting the peasantry and its "unions" to adhere to the PMC and to recognize him as the peasants' "supreme leader."[8]

Before continuing any further, let us pause a moment to review quickly the important sectors that comprised (and still comprise) the peasantry since that time, toward the end of the 1960s. Most of the peasantry remained in the traditional *collas*, or native Andean areas, with especially important concentrations in the departments of La Paz (approximately one-third of the total), Potosí, and Cochabamba. Of these colla peasants, the majority continued in a primarily subsistence economy, especially with regard to their daily food, although they participated partially in the market, especially in nonfood items. This partial insertion into the market was becoming a new source of differentiation within each community (Kelly and Klein 1981). The second sector, also from the same colla regions, was the transitional peasantry, which had a stable participation in the market, but which involved itself partially in subsistence activities. The central valleys of Cochabamba, among others, could be considered part of this sector, although they were rapidly advancing toward a total incorporation into the market, especially through complementary, nonagricultural activities. Finally, the third peasant sector, comprising perhaps 20 to 25 percent of the total, was already totally immersed in the market economy, living exclusively from the sale of its products. This was the case primarily in warm areas well connected to the market centers: for example, Yungas since long ago; and more recently, the new areas of colonization opened during the final years of the MNR.

In addition to this small-scale peasant agriculture, there developed the new agricultural enterprises based on large capital investments and on mainly temporary hire of labor, provided precisely by the impoverished peasants of the subsistence and semisubsistence sectors. In remote traditional areas, in the big cattle-raising haciendas, and in the rubber estates of the east, there still persisted a relatively stable force of peons subject to landowner *patrones*.

PIONEER EFFORTS AT RUPTURE (1969–1971)

Nonetheless, the consolidation and domestication achieved by Barrientos did not represent the final gasp of the peasant movement. The fraud of his paternal pact was already visible to the eyes of certain peasant groups during his government's last years.

The first contesting group was the *Bloque Campesino Independiente* (Independent Peasant Bloc).[9] The cause was Barrientos's attempt, following the suggestion of North American fiscal advisors, to tax peasants on the area of land to which they had consolidated or received title. There were protests nearly everywhere, to the point that even those leaders most loyal to the general resisted following him on this issue. The protests climaxed in the altiplano of La Paz and Oruro, where perhaps the greatest land surface was possessed by peasants, but where land was rather unproductive. This was the opportunity for many of the former leaders, who had been displaced during or even before Barrientos (especially those who had maintained ties with various leftist, anti-Barrientos parties), to come together and form the Bloque Campesino Independiente. Some of them had maintained their links with the grass roots—for example, near the mining districts—but most had lost that contact. They became dissident voices, precursors of the unions' independence. However, these voices did not represent clamor of the peasant masses—these, despite their rejection of the tax, remained true to Barrientos—and neither did they find an echo in those masses.

Barrientos died in a mysterious helicopter accident while he was making one of his usual visits to peasant communities. Soon thereafter followed the rapid succession of governments of Siles Salinas, Ovando, and Torres (1969–1971) characterized by the country's shift to the left, Ché's posthumous impact. Except for Siles, the other presidents were military men, but they were more concerned with "gaining" the loyalty of the emerging urban, working-class left than with ingratiating themselves with the peasantry: this sector's support was taken for granted. In this sense, the government's tutelage was less devastating. At the same time, one could say that the leftist working-class sectors, which gained strength within the government and even formed the Popular Assembly as a popular alternative to the Congress did not make winning over the peasantry a priority either. They either considered the peasants too closely identified with the military right, or took too dogmatically the metaphor of the amorphous and passive "sack of potatoes" used by Marx to describe the French peasantry of the 18th Brumaire.

Nevertheless, this period of relative openings and of growing popular effervescence provided a propitious environment for the incubation of new sociopolitical developments in the peasant sector. First of all, the Bloque Campesino Independiente gradually consolidated itself. It established its headquarters in a room given over to them by the *Central Obrera Boliviana* (Bolivian Workers Central; COB), the powerful confederation of all the urban unions, now beginning again to play an important role.[10] The Bloque Campesino was clearly "independent" of the government, but it followed the old scheme of dependence vis-à-vis the COB and several of the parties its leaders represented. The Bloque's public communiqués in the press and in the radio were becoming more and more frequent and better known. However, its relationship with the peasant masses did not improve significantly. The Bloque was more the COB's and certain leftist parties' peasant voice, than it was an organic representative of the peasant masses. It was never able to overcome the elitist nature of its inception.

The second area in which the PMC was broken was in various colonization frontier regions. This important episode of the Bolivian peasant movement has not yet been studied in detail, but there are several factors which without a doubt must be taken into account in order to understand it. Barrientos had taken special care to win over the colonizer sector. Given that many of the colonies were consolidated in his time, this was the sector in which the general could best supplant Víctor Paz as the "godfather" who gave land to the poor peasants. On the other hand, the colonization programs, which were formally promoted with the help of the United States and other international agencies, allowed more than anywhere else for the establishment of a new paternalistic relationship between the state and the peasantry. The "unions" were formally banished in the most controlled and planned "supervised colonization" programs. Instead of forming unions, the peasant colonizers were to form "community assemblies," "cooperatives," and other organizations more closely related to production. The government, in turn, was to be the provider of lands, credit, and technical support to those modern pioneers on the agricultural frontier. On the other extreme of the spectrum, various leftist parties and sectors interested in winning over the peasantry had also reached the conclusion that the colonizers structurally constituted the sector in which it would be the easiest to establish a bridgehead: they were more linked to the market and in closer contact with the dominant system's contradictions through the issue of prices, and the contrasts with capitalist agro-industrial development of the Oriente (the eastern territory). The colonizers were also seen as those peasants most open to any kind of innovation since they had been able to break with their original homelands. Even Ché had thought for a while to establish his guerrilla "foco" in the area of colonization. In other words, the colonization phenomenon attracted political forces on one side and another.

During the conflicts about the land tax, Barrientos also had to confront protests in his favored colonization area, the north of Santa Cruz, but he was able to dodge them airily with his Quechua and his eloquence. Nonetheless, the same governmental patronage which promised more than it delivered and controlled more than it aided, was finally responsible for creating a growing discontent among the colonizers, especially in the supervised colonization projects. This discontent was taken advantage of in several ways by the antimilitary political sectors, especially after Barrientos's death, in 1969 and 1970. Thus, in the spontaneous colonization of Caranavi there came into being a worker-student-peasant pact, and a renowned road blockade, organized to protest low prices, achieved the expulsion from the area of an officialist leader. In Santa Cruz, the *Unión de Campesinos Pobres* (Union of Poor Peasants; UCAPO) — promoted by the PCML, a communist party following a Maoist line — came into being and organized the seizure of several ranches. These and other local initiatives crystallized in February 1971 in the new *Federación Nacional de Colonizadores* (National Federation of Colonizers), which was clearly independent of the government and formed primarily by peasants from the supervised colonies in order to channel their complaints to the *Instituto Nacional de Colonizadores* (National Colonization Institute).

The third attempt came about in the Aymara altiplano. It was born with many more theoretical ambiguities, but also with more roots in the masses. It is what in practice later jelled under the name of *katarismo*. It is worthwhile that we consider its inception in more detail.

KATARISMO IS BORN

As Jean Pierre Lavaud (1982) says, the phenomenon of katarismo would not have been conceivable had the Agrarian Reform, and the other phenomena it unleashed, not occurred first. Its maximum proponent, Jenaro Flores, was eleven years old when the Reform decree was signed in Ucureña. But, in addition, katarismo essentially transcends the schemes and horizons of the rose-tinged MNR peasant movement. "We are no longer the peasants of 1952" is one of this new movement's favorite slogans, and it must be taken seriously.[11]

The origins of katarismo lie in the city of La Paz rather than in the countryside, but its protagonists are students from the rural areas, above

all from the province of Aroma, that is, the old Aymara bastion of Sicasica. Its first proponent, Raimundo Tambo, comes from none other than
Sullkawi (Ayo Ayo), the very community where Julián Apasa, the Tupaj
Katari of 1781, was born. During the 1960s, before and after the Barrientos government, many of these students attended the same Villarroel
secondary school and there they founded the Fifteenth of November
Movement (the date of Tupaj Katari's immolation in Peñas).[12] Aside from
the still much alive rhetoric of the MNR Revolution, these students were
also influenced by Fausto Reinaga, the prolific and marginalized writer
and self-publisher of Indianist themes, and the founder of a more symbolic than real Indian Party.[13] But more than anything else, this handful
of students created an identity based on their own experience as peasants
and Aymaras in the face of the city's challenges. When some of them,
along with others of diverse backgrounds who joined them, reached the
university, they formed the MUJA: *Movimiento Universitario Julián
Apasa* ("Julian Apasa University Movement"). Their studies were diverse:
law, dentistry, economics, etc. At first, they were only a group which attempted to express its members' preoccupations. But toward 1965, their
main leader had returned to the countryside and began to take on leadership roles within the only peasant organization in existence: the official
one, linked consequently to the PMC and to all of the flaws associated
with subordinated unionism. Significantly, Tambo acted from the start
on a regional level, without having previously gone through the ordinary
communal levels of the organization. This was not a strange jump for
people with urban experience.

Five years younger than Tambo, Jenaro Flores had had a comparable
trajectory: he was born in the community of Antipampa, close to Sicasica; he went to the same school, although in inferior courses; he also went
to the university, but dropped out early on due to a lack of funds. It is
said that he eventually worked at the electrical plant during his stay in
the city. He participated in the aforementioned movements without yet
playing a directive role. Married to another "resident" (peasant migrant)
from another province, he returned to his community. During that time
a group from the University of Wisconsin (contracted by CIDA) and from
the Bolivian government's National Agrarian Reform Service were con-
ducting case studies in various rural regions of the country. One of the
communities that was chosen was precisely Antipampa, and the comunero
Jenaro was chosen as one of the research assistants. This experience allowed him to learn more about rural issues, at the same time that he experienced firsthand the discrimination faced by the Aymara "pongos" (i.e.,
servants) of those official functionaries. On a local level, he learned his
own community's reality perhaps better than anyone else. Soon after the

project was finished, Jenaro was chosen "secretary general" of his community, a year-long position which all community landowners tend to hold at one time or another, a type of mandatory and reciprocal communal service. The peculiar thing is that Flores, who had been absent in the city for a few years, reached this position without having first held the series of prior posts normally demanded.

Flores' meteoric rise began right away: a few months after his appointment in the community, he was elected executive secretary of his subcentral; in another few months he reached that position at the central level (encompassing all of the province of Aroma), beating his old veteran friend, Raimundo Tambo. Flores likes to remember that this did not lead to resentments or factions, but ended rather in an embrace of the two contenders followed immediately by their close collaboration. Almost immediately, in March 1971, he was named executive secretary of the Departmental Congress for all of La Paz. To emphasize the change of focus, the new board added the consonants "TK" to the traditional acronym of the Federación Departamental de Trabajadores Campesinos de La Paz (Federation of Peasant Workers of the Department of La Paz; FTCLP), to stand for its new last name, Tupaj Katari. In little more than a year, Flores had climbed four of the organization's levels. One must remember that these union elections did not in any instance—not even on a national level—have the rigor of a secret vote by all delegates, and only by delegates. They demonstrated, rather, the ability to attract and mobilize sectors, in great measure geographical, on the basis of the image the candidate was able to project and of the connections of those who supported him. One must not discard as a hypothesis the possibility that his experience with the National Agrarian Reform Service—not only as a source of personal prestige and as a life experience, but also as a catapult from the government circles linked to Torres' leftist administration— might have influenced this initial ascent.

What made this new group led by Flores and Tambo different from earlier ones? Formally, nothing. It was one of the many changes of leadership within the schemes and dependencies of always. The new team was able, for example, to establish very good relations with the prefect of La Paz, José María Centellas, who was very loyal to President Torres. These connections, in addition to the ones with the "gringos," allowed them to get donations and services efficiently. But there was also a new style which was young and fresh and a content that was not "officialist." Youth manifested itself, for example, in the emphasis Jenaro Flores (a robust sports enthusiast) gave to soccer championships in all the different levels he worked in. Soccer, as well as being recreational, proved to be an excellent opportunity for the leaders to interact on a social level. Greater radicalism manifested itself in a regional debate about prices for which Flores was given the title of "communist" by the intermediaries. But its maximum expression was the thrust given to land invasions on some haciendas consolidated under the Agrarian Reform. This was something unheard of in the altiplano since the Agrarian Reform in the MNR's finer days. The most talked about case was that of Qollana, a mechanized hacienda famous for its cheeses. But support was also provided in cases in regions as distant as Chuma, in the valleys to the north of the department, where the Agrarian Reform had arrived late and feebly. The workers' traditional May Day march in La Paz brought to light another facet of the movement. A large peasant group marched, cheering Tupaj Katari and displaying his picture. The pictures of the president, General Torres, which had been handed out before the event, remained hidden underneath ponchos.

Together with these changes in the union organization, two other institutions came into being in La Paz. They were two more expressions of the same dynamic, and they held close ties to the same leadership. In 1969, the *Centro Minkha* ("Minkha Center"; *mink'a*: one of the forms of Andean reciprocity) was established. It was composed primarily of peasants who had had the opportunity to become professionals, many of them through scholarships to go abroad, acquired through their connections to state offices. Among the founders were Mario Gabriel (Jenaro Flores' brother-in-law) and Mauricio Mamani (an Aymara from Irpa Chico), for years William Carter's co-investigator, and a member also of the Wisconsin/CIDA/SNRA team, and therefore with connections to Flores. This cooperative institution wanted to be a type of advisory service by and for peasants. But over the years, it suffered a series of problems on account of inexperience and of not knowing how to draw the line between personal and administrative use of funds.

At the beginning of August 1971, another idea which had been toyed with for a long time was carried out: the creation of the so-called *Centro Cultural Tupaj Katari* ("Tupaj Katari Cultural Center"). Many ideas still topical today were already present in this project: on an economic level, to better prices by eliminating middlemen, and even to seek the self-financing of peasant organization; on a social level, to have a place to meet and a means of mass communication; on a cultural level, to reaffirm one's own value. In its name was again the memory of Tupaj Katari. The project solidified on account of an agreement between the group from Aroma, along with other altiplano provinces, and Alberto Méndez, the director of the radio station of the same name, who saw this alliance as an important route for commercial expansion.

In a parallel fashion, and on the whole unconnected to the happenings in La Paz, something else was going on in the neighboring department of

Oruro,[14] also Aymara and in the high altiplano. In this region, even more arid than the northern altiplano, the protests against Barrientos's land tax were also strong and led to the convocation of a general departmental meeting in which soldiers dressed as peasants surprised and locked the participants inside the local church. But in Oruro the main leaders of this protest did not pass over to the Bloque Independiente, but remained, like the kataristas of La Paz, in a certain sense tied to the primary and practically unique organizations of local peasants. From this pattern Macabeo Chila emerged as the principal departmental leader. In contrast to the kataristas, Chila had had more contact with leftist political parties, whose language he had assimilated in a coherent way. The historico-cultural dimension deepened in him and his people through a rather indirect route: the INDICEP (and to a certain extent, CEDI) popular training centers which the Oblatos fathers (of French Canadian background) directed in the city of Oruro. The origins of these religious men made them especially sensitive to the region's cultural and linguistic issues. Some colorful posters with the figures of Tupaj Katari and his wife Bartolina Sisa had a great impact in all the countryside. In addition, INDICEP turned over the ownership of Radio Bolivia and of the Quelco Press to the union by agreement with local peasant organizations. This event was a great stimulus leading the kataristas in La Paz to search for a way into Radio Méndez.

On August 2, 1971, a new milestone was reached. The government had called and financed the Sixth National Peasant Congress in Potosí, which was to elect the new officials of the *Confederación Nacional Campesina* ("National Peasant Confederation"). Delegates, generally people who questioned the situation very little, came from all over the country. Potosí was also the forum in which the diverse tendencies noted up until now would make themselves known. In this sense, it was the least officialist of the officialist peasant congresses. UCAPO, the Bloque Campesino, and even Reinaga's Indian Party all circulated flyers. But the central issue was the election of a new secretary general, and on this matter the struggle was mainly between the old style, represented by the old Barrientistas of the PMC and supported above all by the chief of the Cochabamba garrison, and the new style, represented mainly by the kataristas from La Paz, and supported among others by the prefect of that department. Chila also ran, but he was only supported by Oruro. The other groups mentioned, by concentrating their strategy on new organizations rather than on the one that had existed up until then, really did not stand a chance of being elected; at best they could infiltrate. Earlier, the kataristas had sent emissaries to different departments in order to win the support of other delegations. In Potosí it first won the presidency of the Congress, which fell upon Raimundo Tambo, and later Jenaro Flores, who in this way culminated his vertiginous ascent. Thus innovation had reached the heart of officialism, but did not break with it.

Before closing this period, we will briefly analyze the relationship between the ascending katarismo and the traditional Left, which at this point was pressuring Torres' government so much, mainly through the Popular Assembly. As was mentioned, this Left was not interested in massively incorporating the peasantry. It had other priorities and tactics. In the Popular Assembly, of 218 delegates only 23 were assigned to the peasants, and of these few were really delegates from the bottom up. The only peasant organizations recognized by the COB, and consequently by the Popular Assembly, were the *Federación de Colonizadores* (the "Federation of Colonizers"), closer to the grassroots, and the Bloque Campesino Independiente, further removed from a popular base. In Potosí there was a discussion about what attitude the peasantry should take toward the Popular Assembly, but opinions were not uniform. In the assembly the question of greater peasant participation was never introduced for the reasons already noted: the peasants were neither trusted nor given priority. Perhaps it is valid to add that at that time, the katarista leadership did not much trust the "communists" in the Popular Assembly either; nor did they give priority to a possible link with the COB.

A few days after the Potosí Congress, on August 19–21, 1971, Bánzer's military coup swept away all of these innovations, and unified through undifferentiated and brutal repression all those groups who had sought agreement without reaching it.

BÁNZER AND THE AWAKENING OF THE GIANT, 1971–1978

Bánzer in his first phase dispersed all of the groups and their leaders. Many of the leaders had to spend more or less long periods in exile, and there they had the opportunity to broaden their horizons, get to know other groups, and polish their positions, as would be seen as they returned to the country. But inside the country there was a return to the crudest and most militaristic form of the PMC, which also lost the credibility Barrientos's charisma had given it.

Of those initiatives that preceded the coup, only Minkha and the Tupaj Katari Cultural Center survived openly. But the former became entangled in its own administrative problems, and failed to play a major role. The Cultural center, on the other hand, gained fortitude thanks to its daily program and occasional festivals on Radio Méndez; the radio spread the idea and the group. New peasants arrived daily to the program to make themselves "partners" (*socios*) through modest contributions that created a social fund of $20,000 (U.S. dollars). This money bought shares in another program (Radio Progreso) in order to guarantee two entire days per week of broadcasting in Aymara.

This cultural cover made possible other organizing and mass educational activities. During Torres' ephemeral government, a monument to Tupaj Katari had been erected in Ayo Ayo with the president's attendance. Since then this has been the locus of massive peasant gatherings each November 15. Even up until today this event has not been taken over by the officialist sectors. On July 30, 1973, on the eve of the official "Indian Day" celebrated each August 2,[15] Minkha, the TK Center and two other peasant student and teacher associations signed the Tiwanaku Manifesto, the first attempt, still embryonic but nonetheless historic, to systematize katarismo.

The year 1974 brought a return to explicitly political activities. In 1972 Jenaro Flores had already returned, more radicalized, from his exile in Chile, and he lived clandestinely in the countryside. Early in 1974, an economic program decreed by Bánzer which, as usual, placed most of the social cost on the peasantry, sparked one of the worst crises between his government and the peasantry. This time, the initiative returned, after many years, to Cochabamba. The three main highways which link the country through this city were blockaded by thousands upon thousands of peasants in numerous places, especially in the valle alto. As in the case of Aroma in 1970, a young directorate had recently assumed control of the officialist organization (the only one in existence) in Punata, the main city of the valle alto. The blockade was in part supported by a military sector which opposed Bánzer and by the Christian Democrats, who had been active in the countryside of that region for some time. But the initiative was above all popular and massive. One of the major blockades was in Tolata, next to the turn-off to Cliza-Ucureña. There, dialogues took place with the military, and the president's presence was requested, but all this was brutally interrupted by a group of armored trucks which opened fire and left a toll of almost 100 dead. There were deaths at three other points along the blockade within a distance of 200 kilometers. These mournful events have gone down in history as *la Masacre del Valle*, the Massacre of the Valley.[16]

Although they had not taken the initiative, the Aymara peasantry joined forces with this action, and also blocked the La Paz–Oruro–Cochabamba route, precisely in Aroma province. There the initiative came from peasant students originally from La Paz, and to a certain extent it was the Aymara peasantry that learned the political lesson best: the Military-Peasant Pact led to bloodbaths. The following year there was a new provincial congress in Colquencha in order to renovate the Aroma leadership. The kataristas believed that, as in 1970, the time had come to take over. But the officialists, now protected by the dictatorial regime, resisted this with bullets. There was one death, and the government cancelled the TK Cultural Center's activities and also froze its funds. Activity and contact had to go underground: those from different regions took advantage of officialist congresses to meet and to hold secret meetings. During such activities of the period, there were relatively intense contacts with one of the underground opposition parties. But no formal alliances were forged between the kataristas and the political parties. Unfortunately, during this time Raimundo Tambo disappeared from the scene, victim of a truck accident.

Thus we reach Bánzer's last phase, toward 1977, in which he and other Latin American dictators, pressured by U.S. President Carter's human rights policy, had to open the door to democracy. Bánzer called elections, but tried to manipulate them in his way, without allowing political amnesty, nor full independence to the unions. During this period, it was the kataristas who were among the first to defy openly the decadent military government. On November 15, there was the traditional gathering in Ayo Ayo, presided over this time by the local bishop, who talked about the right to organize. Among others was distributed a pamphlet entitled "What Every Peasant Movement in Bolivia Should Know," which in twelve concrete points attacked head-on Bánzer's pseudo-opening. In his speech, Jenaro Flores, drawing on a phrase which oral history attributes to Tupaj Katari, summed up as follows: "today Tupaj Katari has returned in millions of people."[17]

In the following weeks, similar documents circulated in different peasant regions in La Paz. Finally, in a clandestine press conference on December 14, Jenaro Flores and his staff formally announced that from then on they would repudiate the officialist National Confederation and that they, the legitimate representatives chosen by the Potosí Congress of 1971, would reassume leadership. In that same month began the historic hunger strike carried out by four women miners, who were joined by more than a thousand followers throughout the country, including eight kataristas. Bánzer had to give in and grant total amnesty and freedom to the unions. Coinciding with the last days of the hunger strike, the kataristas accomplished no less than a clandestine Departmental Congress in the small community of Qullana Norte. Soon after, they began to organize other provincial congresses, not without the opposition of the military, who resisted losing their old rural fief. Finally, in March, the national congress met and consolidated the total triumph of katarismo. Jenaro Flores was named executive secretary of the *Confederación Nacional "Tupaj Katari"* (CNTK; "National Tupaj Katari Confederation"). Second in charge was Macabeo Chila, the old Oruro leader who was by now fully integrated into katarismo.

FROM THE ELECTIONS TO SILES, 1978–1984

We cannot attempt to reconstruct here the entangled sequence of events, partisan alliances and counteralliances, and conflicts between peasant leaders and pseudo-leaders during the next five years (1978–1982), which witnessed three general elections, six bloody coups, and a total of thirteen presidents.[18] For the purpose of our analysis we shall limit ourselves to reviewing the attitude taken by the increasingly consolidated katarista movement and organization toward the other peasant organizations, the political parties, and the COB.

PEASANTS AND PARTIES

The first two go very much together. Each time there was a new election — and there were three in three years (1978, 1979, and 1980) — acronyms and top-down leaderships (*cúpulas*) of the peasant unions would begin to proliferate. The most significant parties all sought the peasants' support through the conquest — ideological or monetary — of a few leaders.

In these cases there was never lacking one or several groups linked to the old officialism and its PMC. Nonetheless, the peasant vote increasingly repudiated the military candidates (and the pact) on the three occasions. The only exception was in the first electoral contest, when the military candidate Bernal opposed the dauphin, Pereda Asbún. In 1978 Bernal won important peasant support in Oruro (explicable because it was his native region) and more significantly, in Cochabamba. This success could have been circumstantial — based on the assumption that the military might not accept a nonmilitary candidate's triumph. But in addition we must remember that Bernal had collaborated closely with Barrientos in the valley's pacification after the Ch'ampa War at the end of the MNRista period, and in the following stage when the PMC still seemed credible. The Cochabamban vote in this case demonstrates that not even the Massacre of the Valley in 1974 had entirely dispelled the idea that there might be military friends of the peasantry: it had only achieved the distinction between good and bad military men. In contrast, in the rest of the country the repudiation was radical and absolute.[19] Cochabamba and Oruro joined the majority current in the next elections. This was the pact's absolute requiem. When, during the intervals of military government by coup, there was an attempt to revitalize the scheme, there were always some opportunistic leaders ready to collaborate. But, with very few exceptions, they were automatically branded as traitors and "burned" in the eyes of their base constituencies.

In general, the other top-down peasant leaderships (appendages of political parties) would come into being on the eve of an election only to disappear once it was over. In that sense, they were not any more representative. But there are two cases which merit a more detailed analysis: the peasant branch of the "Chinese" PCML (along with the MNR of Paz), and the peasant branch of the UDP (*Unidad Democrática Popular;* "Popular Democratic Unity"), which won the elections and finally gained power.

As will be remembered, the pro-Chinese communist party was behind the UCAPO movement in the colonization areas in 1971. Exile led to a closer alliance between this group and sectors of the old Bloque Campesino. In addition, as a result of the opening in 1978, the PCML had strong influence in the COB, and succeeded in binding together and leading a *Frente Revolucionario de Izquierda* (FRI; "Leftist Revolutionary Front"). The FRI was more radical than Siles's UDP, which had assumed the role of main civilian opposition. Realizing its slim chances of triumph, the FRI chose a symbolic candidate, the Cochabamban Casiano Amurrio, who came accompanied by another symbol, the miner Domitila Chungara. But the electoral public is more pragmatic than symbolic and the FRI got very few votes.

New alliances were formed for the following elections. In the world at large, China and the United States had come together against the Soviet Union; in the Bolivian branch of this world, the PCML and the MNR of Paz Estenssoro[20] (the United States's civilian card) joined against the UDP and Siles, supported by the Muscovite PC. But with this alliance the "Chinese" party, and those peasant groups which supported it, were "burned" in the eyes of the rest of the Left. Despite their previous militance, valuable peasant leaders of the 1970s were trapped in this game of international interests, relegated to mere appendages on the margin of the grass-roots bases. Only a few of them, in the colonization zone to the north of Santa Cruz where UCAPO had been born, maintained popular support.

Katarismo survived unscathed from this first pounding, but not so much the next time, during the 1979 elections. For the reasons indicated above, in this second round the MNR of Víctor Paz, united with the PCML, made its most serious attempt to get power. It put into gear all of its machinery to win the peasant vote, attempting to "capture" key leaders, even among the katarista ranks. Depending on the region and the people, their methods emphasized speeches, money, or the promise of congressional positions. To all this was added the doubts of the kataristas as to what attitude to take with the UDP, given the independent attitude this front took toward katarista proposals. It is possible that in some instances there came into play the typical peasant astuteness of playing several cards (just as the peasants plant different crop species in different seasons and microclimates). In any event, in this second electoral campaign the CNTCB-TK

and katarismo did not take an official position. Katarista leaders, moreover, differed in their postures. Some openly supported the UDP of Siles,
others the MNR of Paz; many, including Flores, did not align themselves.
The final effect for katarismo was the loss of some important figures, such
as Macabeo Chila and Mario Gabriel, who from that point on faded from
the political scene, "burned" by their choice in favor of Víctor Paz, who
had included them in his list of delegates.

The other case of interest is the game between the peasant organization
and the triumphant UDP, made up mainly of the alliance between Hernán
Siles Zuazo's MNRI (*MNR de Izquierda*; "MNR of the Left"), the MIR
(a young leftist party with strong European Social Democrat influences),
and the PC (of Muscovite tendencies). In the first elections in 1978, which
coincided with the kataristas' honeymoon with the MIR, Jenaro Flores
formally supported the UDP. Of relevance was the still vital loyalty of
peasants at the grass roots to the MNR that had decreed the Agrarian
Reform. Siles was the expression of that MNR, especially in the Aymara
countryside of La Paz. Paz Estenssoro had "burned" himself there on account of his alliance with Bánzer in 1971.[21] Nonetheless, at a gathering
for candidate Siles in Achacachi, Jenaro Flores stressed in front of him
the circumstantial nature of that support: it was only temporary, until
such time as the peasants had their own adequately prepared candidates.
This initial rapprochement was lost in the two following elections. The
main reason was that the peasants felt they were being treated with too
much paternalism and authoritarianism by the UDP, or by the parties that
comprised it. The peasants were not really taken seriously. At the same
time, the UDP's leaders considered that the katarista candidates did not
take their obligation to the party very seriously. Specifically, Siles's MNR,
accustomed to the subordination of the peasantry that had prevailed between 1952 and 1964, was not quick enough to realize that this new generation "was no longer the peasantry of 1952." The UDP then tried to do
the same as other parties and organized its own peasant appendage, called
the *Confederación Campesina Julián Apasa* (CCJA; "Julián Apasa Peasant Confederation"). The CCJA was given over to the veteran MNRista
and ex-peasant, Zenón Barrientos. But in the long run this electoral leadership faction had the same short life as the others.

TOWARD THE KATARISTA PARTY

In short, experiences like these tended to draw the organized peasantry
to katarismo in the growing conviction that their organization should preserve greater independence not only from the military, but also from the
rest of the parties, right or left. This did not lead the peasants to reject
the idea of a party in itself, but to toy with a new idea: the formation
of new parties which would truly express peasant interests.

In truth this conviction or preoccupation had been around for some time. Its first expression had been Reinaga's symbolic Indian Party—although it was devoid of Indians and not talked about for long. Later, in the Peasant Congress of 1977, there had already been leaflets put out by the so-called *Movimiento Indio Tupaj Katari* (MITKA; "Tupaj Katari Indian Movement"), written by the most "Indianist" groups within the movement. Their thesis was centered on the idea that the root of all problems was the Spanish conquest of the Andean "Indian" peoples, and that it was therefore totally useless to ally themselves with any party made up by the successors of those invaders. The electoral bid in 1978 presented the opportunity to discuss things in depth. In April of that year, there were heated discussions among kataristas, and the result was the most explicit formulation of the different tendencies that had been incubating in the movement. The first split was that of the MITKA, which formed its own party and launched its own presidential candidate on the terms described above.

Much more closely linked to the CNTCB-TK was the other party born in the same conjuncture, the *Movimiento Revolucionario Tupaj Katari* (MRTK; "Tupaj Katari Revolutionary Movement"). It shared with MITKA the idea that the conventional political parties did not have a program that really responded to the needs of the peasantry, and that it was therefore necessary to form a party that would do this. It seems that one of the main instigators of this idea was Macabeo Chila, the katarista leader with the most experience and training among leftist parties, but Flores and other high leaders of katarismo soon took it over. In this sense, one could argue that the CNTCB-TK was the peasant trade union branch of katarismo, and the MRTK aspired to become its political branch, hoping to go beyond its peasant base alone, while guaranteeing that the peasants' perspective would be satisfactorily integrated into its program.

In reality, the mere decision to found a party is not enough to assure its existence as an organic and ideologically coherent entity. The history of the MITKA and the MRTK show how difficult it is to reach that point of consolidation. During the third election of 1980, MITKA had already subdivided into two parties, MITKA and MITKA-1 (following the typical evolution of the "big" parties), each with its own candidate. Later, the Indian Party (not Reinaga's, which has practically disappeared) and other groups broke off. The divisions surfaced not so much from ideological conflicts, but out of struggles for leadership and for access to the aid funds provided by North American and European Indianist organizations. One of those conflicts occurred in the last CISA (*Consejo Indio de Sudamérica*; "South American Indian Council") in Tiwanaku in 1983.

The MRTK has emphasized more the sociopolitical problem, an emphasis reflected by its acronym ("R" for revolutionary, instead of "I" for

Indian). In this sense, it does not exclude but rather gives a certain priority
to class analysis. For this reason, it is also more pragmatic about the possibility of establishing alliances with other parties. Thus, in 1978, it formally
united with the UDP. In 1979 — as was noted — it split into one sector that
followed the UDP and another allied to Víctor Paz's MNR (an alliance
about which little was heard after the elections). In 1980, the main sector,
led by Jenaro Flores, followed the lead of the sindicalist branch, which
was already part of the COB, and formally supported Lechín's indecisive
candidacy. (Lechín would present himself one day, and withdraw the next.)
Since then, the MRTK, which at one point in time was also called the MKL
(*Movimiento Katarista de Liberación*; "Katarista Liberation Movement"),
has been working on its own identity. The problem was expressed suc-
cinctly as the need to see and solve the country's problems "with both eyes":
that is, to see them both as a problem of exploited social classes, and as
a problem of oppressed nations (peoples, ethnic groups) within a common Bolivian State.

Neither the MITKA nor the MRTK (when it participated on its own
with Lechín) had even partial electoral success. In the Lechín-MRTK case,
one could seek an explanation in the candidate's calculated indecision to
participate. In all cases, the lack of funds and of a well-established political machine undoubtedly weighed heavily. But in addition one must remember that the peasant, and the majority of the populace, votes prag-
matically for someone who has a real possibility of getting into power
and bettering the voter's lot somewhat. There are few merely "symbolic"
voters. And up to this point, it has to be recognized, these parties, off-
shoots in one or another form of katarismo, were simply "symbolic": an
institutional expression of lack of confidence in the other parties' real
commitment to the peasantry, especially the Aymara peasantry, and an
affirmation of that sector's desire also to gain political power and thereby
change the present situation.

KATARISMO, THE COB AND THE "CONFEDERACIÓN ÚNICA"

When in 1977 and 1978 there developed the struggle for a democratic
opening (*apertura*), the diverse documents produced by the kataristas emphasized their solidarity with the miners, workers, and other exploited
groups, and recognized the COB as well as the unifying organ of all the
workers in the country. The katarista leaders made numerous efforts to
be accepted into the heart of the COB. But those attempts clashed directly
with the opposition of certain party interests, especially those of the
PCML, hegemonic within the COB. This party preferred to keep the control it had over "its" peasants — especially Casiano Amurrio — within the
central organization. To that end, it argued that the only peasant unions

to be recognized within the COB should continue to be the Bloque Campesino Independiente ("Independent Peasant Bloc," now renamed a "Confederation"), and the Federación de Colonizadores ("Federation of Colonizers," also promoted to a "Confederation"). A document sent by the new directorate chosen by the Peasant Congress of May 1977 to the National Congress of Miners expressed the desire for unity and the frustration caused by these blocs within the "Bloc":

> The CNTCB-TK is with you, our miner comrades. The miners' struggle is also our struggle. . . . We are still not members of the COB despite our anti-imperialist and revolutionary political and sindical behavior; despite the work done in these last seven years of harsh repression; despite our reorganization of the peasant movement and our rejection of the Military-Peasant Pact; despite our having taken the initiative to unite and work together with the Federation of Miners and the COB. . . . We are still not members of the COB because it seems they prefer "peasants" who are unrepresentative and manipulated by some party.

At first, Lechín — the head of the Confederation of Miners and of the COB since their foundation — and other leaders shared in a certain mistrust of the peasants, whom they continued to treat as "children." But the relationship improved, in part because of the diversification of tendencies within the COB as exiles returned, and in part because the kataristas were gaining prestige for their debates with the COB and for their actions, which evidenced their authenticity as peasant representatives. This was the state of affairs at the time of the COB's Fifth Congress in May 1979, to which the kataristas were invited, along with member organizations. This congress marked the loss of hegemony by the PCML — by this time allied to Paz Estenssoro — which withdrew with its followers.

In order to decide which organization should represent the peasantry, the COB's new directive decided to convoke a congress for peasant unity. The body that came out of this congress would be the legitimate representative. That congress took place at the end of June. The CNTCB-TK, the Julián Apasa Confederation (peasant appendage of the UDP), and the truly independent sector of the Independent Peasant Confederation, all attended. The Confederation of Colonizers participated as "fraternal delegates," but their full incorporation was not a topic of discussion, given their regional peculiarities and specific problems. Out of this came one organization: the *Confederación Sindical Unica de Trabajadores Campesinos de Bolivia* (CSUTCB; "Unified Sindical Confederation of Peasant Workers of Bolivia"), with Jenaro Flores as its first executive secretary. The decision to unite was easy. The name took longer to decide on since the loss of the name of Tupaj Katari was painful to the kataristas. But the name was accepted in the interests of universality. The name of Tupaj

Katari remained attached to that of the La Paz Federation, and this hero's image continued to appear in all the literature of the new CSUTCB, affiliated with the COB.

At the end of the same year, there was a military coup which aborted after fifteen days, thanks especially to the resistance of the COB and its new members, the peasants of the Confederación Unica. The president of the Parliament, Lidia Gueiler (who had ties to Paz's MNR), assumed power. One of her first moves was to enact a package of economic measures suggested for some time by international financiers. Once again, the social cost was to fall mainly on the peasantry, without making any amends in their favor. The CSUTCB complained to no avail, for which reason it was decided to call for the general blockade to which we alluded in the introduction of this chapter. This situation sparked frictions between peasant/katarista leaders of the CSUTCB, and the COB's labor leaders. The latter were against the blockade, first because there was an economic conflict of interests between wage workers and peasant producers. The economic package had damaged the purchasing power of the former, for whom the compensatory measure freezing the prices of basic necessities was therefore desirable. By contrast, for the peasants the freeze meant that the price of their products—which is the small producer's monetary income, or "salary"—did not go up while the price of transportation, agricultural inputs, and all else that they had to buy with money, went up substantially. In the second place, the workers believed that it was a dangerous time—after a just neutralized military coup—to pressure the new government. To the peasant leaders they said in no uncertain terms that they would not permit the blockade. The peasants informed them with equal forcefulness that they had decided to carry out the blockade, and explained their reasons. They insisted that they needed the rest of the COB workers' support. Significantly, the main mediator within the COB, who understood the peasants' stance and effectively explained it to the rest, was a veteran anarcho-sindicalist. The blockade was in the end carried out, with special intensity in the department of La Paz, and even secured a forty-eight hour solidarity strike by the workers. An alliance had been forged in which workers and peasants treated and respected each other as equals.

The blockade had economic causes. But there were also ideological ones: it spoke to a strongly felt need to establish the peasants' own identity and presence. Behind the more technical demands, such as the lowering of the new price for gasoline (which was achieved), lurked a demand never expressed formally but nevertheless central: to have the peasants respected and listened to in reality, as first-class citizens, by the government, the country, and even by the workers. The issue of ethnic and historic identity was present as well. In the Copacabana church, near the Peruvian border, a large group of visitors (half travellers, half smugglers) had been trapped by the blockaders. They communicated with La Paz by radio and colored their story most dramatically. The case of these "pilgrims" was given utmost importance by the "emergency radio chain" formed by all of the city's radio stations (it was the first in Aymara in the country's radio history). The Red Cross mobilized itself and went to Jenaro Flores to beg for compassion for these poor travellers who had already been waiting for four days. Had he no heart? The katarista leader replied: "We have been waiting for four hundred years!"

We must limit ourselves to giving only a summary "flash" of the most significant events which occurred in the following years. In January 1980, a National Congress of Peasant Women formed the female branch of the CSUTCB under the name of *Federación Nacional de Mujeres Campesinas de Bolivia "Bartolina Sisa"* (FNMCB-BS; "Bartolina Sisa National Federation of Bolivian Peasant Women"; Bartolina Sisa, wife of Tupaj Katari, joined him as a militant in the uprising of the eighteenth century). Special branches for the seasonal cotton and sugar cane harvesters were also formed. In July 1980, General García Meza launched his "narco-military" coup, assaulting an emergency meeting of the COB leadership by surprise. The main leaders were arrested and one was killed. Jenaro Flores, who was at the meeting, had left to make a phone call and therefore escaped and became the top leader of the clandestine COB: this was another first in Bolivian history. Months later, working in this capacity, he was found and shot by paramilitary men; he has remained paralyzed since. Nonetheless, even before the fall of the four military governments which succeeded each other, he presided over the general meeting in which the CSUTCB publicly reconstituted itself. Since then, the CSUTCB has continued to solidify its organizers.

An important aspect of the most recent past had been the CSUTCB's struggle to maintain its sindical independence, even during the democratic period which followed the ascension of Siles and his UDP to power at the end of 1982. The new government respected the CSUTCB and Flores' indisputable leadership, hallowed now by his history of resistance and martyrdom. But it attempted to put its own people in key positions, using any means to this end. The conflict in various congresses, and especially at the National Congress in July 1983, was impassioned and not free of blows. But sindical independence was successfully defended.

Another development, deserving of specific study in its own right, was the search for new objectives once the old dependencies on the military and the government were destroyed. In April 1983 there were new blockades demanding the implementation of a series of concrete (and in some cases conjunctural) requests which remained unfulfilled. Of greater importance was another project mentioned since 1979, but put into effect only after 1982, when the CSUTCB came back above ground: the elaboration of a Fundamental Agrarian Law (*Ley Fundamental Agraria*) which would replace the historical Agrarian Reform Law of 1953 (see CSUTCB 1984). Because of the issues it raised, and its very existence, the project presupposes the total rupture of that umbilical cord to the MNR established thirty years earlier.

PATHS FOR ANALYSIS

Of the many themes of theoretical and practical importance suggested by the evolution of the Bolivian peasant movement during the period under review, we have selected several of special significance.

MOTIVATIONS AFTER THE AGRARIAN REFORM

It is always said that peasant movements revolve around the problem of access to land, and that once that objective is reached, they die out. Until recently, the Bolivian case seemed to confirm this belief. Klein (1982: 235), for example, concluded that "the Indians became a relatively conservative political force . . . indifferent if not hostile to their former urban worker colleagues." The experience of the most recent years, however, has shown that this is not always the end point. What have been the motivations that have reawakened the anesthetized giant?

The great majority of specific and localized mobilizations have been related to issues of taxes and prices affecting agriculture's products, inputs, or necessary services such as transportation. In all such cases, what is involved is both the articulation of the peasantry with monetary circuits, as well as the weaknesses of that articulation. That is why modifications in the terms of trade injure the fragile peasant economy quickly and easily. It should not be forgotten that the two most important protest mobilizations—the blockades of 1979—occurred in the colla areas only partially inserted into the market in response to new price levels, and that both occurred also in that part of the agricultural cycle when the peasantry is short of food and cash. This means well after the big harvest (approximately April–May), but before the early harvest (February)—that is, when the peasants are most likely to turn to their scarce monetary resources even to buy food.

But what has glued together a great, systematically organized movement of increasingly national dimensions was a negative objective: to break with the Military-Peasant Pact. The military dictatorships served, then, as coagulants for the movement, and came to create a crisis in the pattern of filial dependence established with so much effort by the MNR.

Finally, even after the Agrarian Reform, where there have still been land problems, these have continued to be a singularly important motivation. UCAPO initiated its mobilizations in the east with the occupation of cattle ranches. The kataristas initiated their "new style" with the invasion of "medium-sized" properties established by the Agrarian Reform. Most recently, the CSUTCB (1984) has given very high priority to its new project, the proposed Fundamental Agrarian Law, which seeks to substitute and surpass that of the MNR in 1953. This new law mainly focuses on the land issues, but sees the question no longer as one of gaining or losing access to land, but as part of a more sweeping set of issues encompassing the entire productive process and the relationship with the state.

ORGANIZATIONAL FORMS

The main question at this point is why UCAPO or the Independent Peasant Bloc were less successful than katarismo or the CSUTCB. There are two answers, one related to organization, and the other to ideology.

On an organizational level, UCAPO and especially the Bloc came from the outside. Their godfathers were nonpeasant organizations (political parties, the COB), and some of their leaders, especially those of the Peasant Bloc, no longer lived in the communities. Furthermore, in their initiatives the goal was to establish another organization, parallel to and in competition with that which was already in existence in the community, and somewhat coterminous with it. On the other hand, katarismo came from within. Its leaders were members of the communities (even when they had left temporarily to study), and their intention was only to occupy key positions within that sindical organization which was almost inherent in the community and which had, to a great extent, taken as its basic "cell" the communal organization in existence since time immemorial. One must remember that the so-called sindical organization in the rural areas of Bolivia has really fused two functions: it is the communal organization at its minimal level, and it is a "federation of communities" pursuing more "sindical" revindications at higher levels. There are other elements which need to be analyzed, such as the fact that almost all the key leaders had important experiences outside the community, and that their passage through the bottom levels of the community infrastructure has often been atypical, since they passed very rapidly to the higher levels, where their extracommunal experiences were more functional. But we cannot delve more deeply into this complex theme at this point.

On an ideological level, the answer is similar. Although UCAPO and the Bloc arose out of deeply felt motivations (such as resistance to new taxes, and the appropriation of new lands), for both these organizations these conjunctural grievances served above all as bait. Their global program was to a certain extent dictated from the outside, by nonpeasant godfathers. Both organizations wielded urban and international leftist rhetoric well, and thereby impressed their national audiences. But this did not always achieve the same result with peasant audiences. Katarismo, on the other hand, did not have the same level of sophistication, but what it said more closely echoed what was said in the communities, even if it sounded "reformist" or "incoherent" to urban observers. The praxis of a permanent relationship with the grass-roots base counted for more than the conceptual coherence of the discourse, as evidenced by the evolution of leaders in one or another tendency.

Following this line of analysis, it is understandable that certain of the Bloc's sectors gained strength to the extent that they fused with grass-roots katarismo through the new CSUTCB. Likewise, UCAPO moved closer to the heart of the peasant base to the extent that it changed and became integrated with the Federation of Colonizers, whose organizational characteristics were closer to those of katarismo, albeit in another environment with its own specific issues.

NEW RELATIONSHIP TO THE STATE

In the discussion of motivations we have pointed to an objective—the elimination of the Military-Peasant Pact—which had already demonstrated, albeit in a negative way, a relationship with a particular type of state on terms totally antithetical to those established by the MNR. Once this objective was achieved, the best indicator of the new type of relationship to the state (which was no longer dictatorial, or military, but constitutional) is to be gained by analyzing some aspects of the Fundamental Agrarian Law project elaborated by the CSUTCB (1984). Two apparently contradictory tendencies emerged simultaneously from this project, but they in fact reflected two complementary tactics.

The first tendency has been that of winning autonomous terrain in the face of a state considered inefficient, if not allied with the capitalist sectors (agro-industry, exporters, etc.). This has been the only type of state the peasantry has known in the last few decades through diverse governments, including several which have linked this negative image to their godfather, the MNR.[22] Another expression of this trend is the contemporary peasant movement's insistence on creating new parties, on having its own legal projects emphasizing the communities' autonomy and expansion, or creating peasant corporations to channel resources without the state's tutelage. To a certain extent, this tendency could be considered to be in line with the type of relationship which Tristan Platt (1982; Chapter 10 in this volume) has pointed to between ayllu and state: a theoretically symmetrical, although subordinate, relationship regulated by an implicit contract between an autonomous body (the ayllus) and the state. The peasant project, then, appears to point to a plurinational state.

The second tendency seeks full participation in the state as a means of controlling the government. The Fundamental Agrarian Law project also reflected this trend from its inception since it proposed a law drawn up by peasants for ratification in the parliament. Certain proposals of the project also demonstrate this tendency: peasant cogovernance of several state bodies, and joint management of state agricultural and ranching enterprises by state and peasantry. The influence of the miners' model of shared management of the great state mining enterprise is evident in both cases.

In the peasants' eyes the first tendency is more realistic given their lived experiences. The second one demonstrates the realization that they will continue to need a state, but that it will be favorable only if the peasantry has decision-making power within it. It is a step toward a more popular state, one that is more "their own."

THE COMPLEMENTARITY OF CLASS AND ETHNICITY

Many analysts as well as practical militants have tended to present a class analysis and an analysis based on ethnicity/nationality as disjunctive alternatives. The former prevails among those who take sociology and political science as their points of departure. They tend to see the problem of ethnic or cultural identity as "racism" or as a dead end. The second analysis, by contrast, is more common among those who come out of anthropology and history.[23] In addition, some of these people tend to view the class vision as "foreign ideas." Both of these tendencies have prevailed, with greater or lesser force, in various manifestations of the peasant mobilization studied in this essay. UCAPO and the Independent Peasant Bloc, more closely tied to the urban political parties, emphasized almost exclusively the class component. At the other extreme, the various MITKA and Indian parties, often linked to other First World groups, underlined the ethnic contradiction as fundamental. But neither the one side nor the other has achieved a massive rooting in the peasantry.

In practice, the peasant movement that has achieved massive mobilization does not make these theoretical distinctions: its ideology is nurtured strongly by both fountains, since both are an integral part of the peasant experience. At most, the movement makes distinction according to regions. The class question weighs most in those regions most inserted into the market, like the colonization zones, while the ethnic discourse has greater force in the Aymara altiplano. What does not arise in any case is the dichotomous view that considers the other position "dangerous" when in fact the "other" is part of the peasants' own motivation. The 1979 road blockade was perhaps one of the opportunities in which this synthesis of components was most clearly felt. The cause of the blockade was clearly a problem of a class nature: a new economic package which particularly

affected the interests of the peasant class. There was even a great deal of
effort to achieve a peasant-worker alliance, that is, an alliance of the labor-
ing classes. But at the same time the discourse used throughout the blockade was rich in ethnic allusions, such as the allusion to four hundred years
of waiting without being heard. This synthesis is probably the ideological
key to katarismo, especially in the Aymara region.

THE SHIFT OF HEGEMONY FROM COCHABAMBA TO LA PAZ

From 1936 until the end of the MNR era, the initiative for peasant
mobilizations definitely came from Cochabamba. In the following years,
there was no longer a clear hegemonic center. Some of the initiatives derived from the altiplano; others seemed to develop a center in the colonization areas; Cochabamba seemed to regain the initiative in the 1974
blockade. But recently, in the important developments and events of the
last decade, the initiative and hegemony of the peasant movement came
from the Aymaras of the La Paz area, and specifically from the province
of Aroma. To some this change is disconcerting, since these Aymaras, who
persist in a subsistence economy with a great deal of consumption of their
own food crops, and who in addition still preserve much of the old communities, seem to be going against the historical tide. The Cochabamban
agricultural sector had led the movement precisely because of its higher
level of modernization, and its receptivity to new ideas. If leadership had
to leave Cochabamba, the obvious outcome should have been that it pass
over to the eastern colonization regions, the areas most open to new ideas,
and most exposed to the market's contradictions. The latter would be the
most probable stimulant to mobilization when there no longer existed a
grave problem concerning access to land. This was the scenario expected
by the UCAPO Maoists, many of the workers, the university students
linked to Caranavi, and Ché Guevara's group. Leadership, however,
neither remained rooted in Cochabamba, nor shifted to one of the colonization regions. Instead, it passed on — or more precisely, returned — to
the Aymara altiplano of La Paz. What factors can explain this process?

This historical-structural contrast between the Cochabamban valleys and
the La Paz altiplano is clear and comes from way back. Since pre-Incan
times, the nuclei of the ayllu or *jatha* populations were preponderant in
the *puna*, that is, the high altiplano. The Cochabamban valleys were merely
appendages held by the puna ayllus, an area where people from different
places converged and mingled to gain access to maize, hot peppers, and
other resources. The people of the valley developed no identity of their
own. The Incas took advantage of this situation and founded one of the
most ambitious state projects in the central Cochabamba Valley: grain
cultivation by *mitma* (permanent colonizer) and possibly *mit'a* (rotating

laborer) groups from various parts of the vast empire, Tawantinsuyu. Included by this new policy were the ayllus of the Aymara "nations" of the puna (Wachtel 1981). With the arrival of the Spaniards, this situation facilitated the early formation of haciendas in large expanses of the Valley, while the ayllus—now more shrunken and territorially fixed—continued to be concentrated in the high altiplano. In addition, the Potosí mining phenomenon affected the two regions differently throughout the colonial period. The altiplano, with its ayllus, was the permanent terrain of *mitayo* laborers (i.e., drafted peasants on temporary duty), who constantly crisscrossed the area in journeys toward Potosí. Cochabamba, on the other hand, because dominated by Spanish haciendas, was exempt from the mita, but rather received escaped mitayos, who became *yanaconas* (serfs) on the haciendas. The owners of the latter lived off the splendor of Potosí, where they sold their grain (Larson 1981). All of this led to a potentially explosive dualism, or polarization, between Aymaras and Spaniards in the altiplano, while the Cochabamban valleys were more tranquil and accommodating to change.[24]

Toward the end of the Spanish colonial period, and in the republican era, the decline in mining brought with it the decline of many Cochabamban haciendas, and with this the increased importance of small agriculturalists. But these lacked the ancestral altiplano experience of solid communal organization, and were therefore more exposed to the whims of fashion and innovation. The altiplano, by contrast, increasingly experienced the opposite phenomenon: the aggression of new hacendados toward the ayllus or communities, creating another explosive situation. Hence, after the period of crisis and national reexamination which followed the defeat in the Chaco War, there remained in La Paz remnants of resistant communities contending with encroaching haciendas, while in Cochabamba what was left were decaying haciendas losing ground to encroaching groups of small landowners. These, as in the past, were open to what was new—in this case, innovative ideas and political parties, such as the PIR and the MNR.

Only during this new conjuncture did the Cochabamban peasantry snatch away the insurrectionary leadership which had until then been rooted in the ayllus of the altiplano, and the Chayanta region (el Norte de Potosí). The new type of "modernizing" peasant movement (facilitating the transition from archaic haciendas to small, individually owned properties) was now centered primarily in Cochabamba. And the Cochabamba mobilizations, unlike the rebellions of the puna, were built in good measure on the basis of an intimate relationship to nonpeasant power, expressed first in the revolutionary political parties, and later, in the "revolutionary" government of one of the parties. Local developments, brought about at first by the Inka Wayna Qhapaq, and later by the Potosí market, were once again linked to the experience of a good relationship with external forces. The Aymara altiplano experience, by contrast, had been that they had had to fight together against the Spanish/creole *q'ara* ("rednecks") and that although the latter might pretend to be a friend, the story always ended with betrayal.[25]

This historical flash demonstrates why the model of populist revolution, very much linked to a project of the state, was more digestible in Cochabamba. The model also exerted appeal in the altiplano, but there, significantly, regional hegemony during this period centered in Achacachi, the "Cochabamba" of the altiplano on account of its long history of haciendas as well as its other characteristics. In any case, the impact of the MNRista model was only skin deep. As a consequence, when this model began to wear out and degenerate into the Military-Peasant Pact, the Cochabambans continued to consider it credible for a longer period of time (even after the Massacre of the Valley), while the Aymaras more quickly discarded it. Among the latter there revived the ancient historical memory of their ethnic and class struggles—such as the Katari rebellion in 1780, the resistance against patrones led by Zárate Willka in 1899, or the uprisings of Machaca, Guaqui, Pucarani, Chayanta, and so many others in this century.

The divergent evolution of the two cases also led to two distinct forms of organized peasant resistance. In Cochabamba this force sprang from a weak communal tradition and tended toward new unions linked to a great extent to the government apparatus or to diverse factions within the governing party. This syndical dependence also existed in the altiplano of La Paz during the MNR and PMC periods. But at the root of every local union was the community with all its historical strength and depth, and behind that, the ayllu. This was true even in the haciendas, many of which were of recent formation in the nineteenth and twentieth centuries, and which were in many respects composed of what Silvia Rivera calls "captive communities" under a patrón. It is not surprising, then, that with the deterioration of the model of dependence on the MNR-PMC, the Aymara communities had greater organizational reserves with which to reemerge as a force to be reckoned with.[26]

CONCLUSION

And so it is that we have arrived at the final stretch of the great arc: from the kataristas of 1980 to the Katari of 1780. In response to the question we asked ourselves at the beginning of this essay, it is evident that the Katari/katarista nexus, spanning across two hundred years, has an ideological element: a unifying and mobilizing historical memory. But the discussion just concluded has led us to detect deeper structural factors that explain this continuity in the high Aymara puna.

Other parallels linking 1780 and 1980 are intriguing. The contrast between the Quechua peoples of Cochabamba and the Aymaras of La Paz are reminiscent of the now increasingly understood differences (see Campbell, Chapter 4 in this volume) between the Amarus of Quechua Cuzco, a region of flourishing haciendas on the main road (*camino real*) to Potosí, and the Kataris of the altiplano ayllus. The Amarus seem to be precursors of the MNR's "populism" in their insistent praxis of systematic alliance with mestizos and creoles. The Kataris are undoubtedly the originators of the stance of the kataristas, who discover their class solidarity *in* their ethnic identity, and who are less inclined to make the aforementioned alliances. In 1780, the communities played a decisive role, more so than any other kind of population settlements including Indians. In the katarismo of the 1980s the community is again the key engine. Paradoxically, the Agrarian Reform of 1953, despite its advocacy of individual ownership of property, at the same time reinforced this community cell by "liberating" those communities once "captive" within the haciendas.

In his controversial but quite suggestive book about rebellions and repartos in 1780, Jürgen Golte (1980) proposed the hypothesis that the great revolt had strength mainly in those regions where there was the greatest disproportion between monetary demands to pay tributes and repartos, and the labor effort needed to satisfy them—that is, in those provinces that, while articulated strongly to the wider economy and society, had maintained internally a mode of production more oriented toward subsistence. Could there be here too a parallel with the revolutionary potential of the La Paz altiplano in 1980?

These are a few of the reflections and questions raised by the dynamics of Aymara peasant life in Bolivia during the last several decades. We have in this essay limited ourselves to hacking open a trail (*machetear una brecha*) with more daring than precision. Without a doubt, the open path holds many more surprises and lessons for anyone who chooses to pursue it.

NOTES

1 See Albó (1984), although that version should be considered superseded on account of access to new documents, such as those of the *Colección Documental del Bicentenario de la Revolución Emacipadora de Túpac Amaru*

(Lima). We hope to present an amplified and updated version in the near future.

2　See Albó and Barnadas (1984), which is a preliminary effort to demonstrate the historical evolution of the Bolivian peasantry, on a popular level, with the most important bibliography in Spanish. On a more formal level, see Rivera (1979, 1984), and Huanca L.'s new thesis (1984) on the historical question of the Andean ayllu. It includes new statistical data about land expulsions in La Paz which complements the work of Grieshaber (1977, 1980). The following rebellions have been studied up to the present: Willka Zárate—1899 (Condarco M. 1965); Jesús de Machaca—1921 (Choque 1979); Corocoro—1911 (Flores 1979). The most important revolt about which there are still no available studies is the one of Chayanta in 1927, although Abraham Lupa and René D. Arze have already accumulated important material on it.

3　Studied above all by Dandler (1969, 1971). See also Antezana (1960) and Dandler (1984) on this period.

4　According to the 1950 Agricultural and Livestock Census which only covered part of the national rural territory. It is estimated that around 1825 the communities still occupied two-thirds of the rural areas.

5　Initially the PIR had had a more radical agrarian platform, but it lost credibility in 1947 when it allied with the right-wing PURS to topple Villarroel. This gaffe by the PIR facilitated Ucureña's transition to the MNR.

6　About the MNR era as a whole, see Malloy (1970) and Mitchell (1971), although neither concentrates on the peasantry, about which there is still no definitive study for this period. See, however, Kohl (1969). For the early years, see the press summary by Antezana and Romero (1973). Cochabamba has been studied by Dandler (1969, 1971, 1984). Achacachi, in the altiplano of La Paz, has been studied by Albó (1979a) and the Norte de Potosí by Harris and Albó (1975).

7　Dandler contributes a chapter on the Ch'ampa War in Calderón and Dandler (1984); the war was also analyzed in a very preliminary way by Antezana (1960).

8　There is still no comprehensive study about the relationship between Barrientos and the peasantry. Brill (1966) analyzed Barrientos's rural program in a study that appears to have been financed with CIA funds (cf. Mitchell 1971). In addition, in the United States, the RISM (Research Institute for the Study of Man, New York) has on microfiche the field work studies done for the Peace Corps around 1965, with important details regarding the peasant reaction to Barrientos's coup and the first few months of his military government.

9　At present, the only essay about the Independent Peasant Bloc is that done by Lavaud (1981).

10　When the COB was founded in 1952, the new peasant unions formed an integral part of the organism. Later on the COB gradually turned into the working class's organization, increasingly distanced from the MNR, whereas the peasant organization remained allied to the government party, and therefore practically broke away from the original organ. Nonetheless, there was always a faction of the peasantry that remained close to the MNR's leftist sector (transformed into PRIN around 1962), and that maintained regular ties with the COB. Some of its members, like Enrique Encinas of the valle bajo of Cochabamba, and Paulino Quispe (Wila Saco) of Achacachi, have been the thread connecting the initial period, the Independent Peasant Bloc, and recently, the CSUTCB, always within the COB. Paulino Quispe, despite being Aymara, had already accompanied the MNR in Ayopaya in the 1940s.

11 The literature about katarismo is growing. Javier Hurtado's thesis, still in progress [as of 1984 — Ed.] is the most in-depth study. I am grateful for access to his rough drafts, especially for the initial period of katarismo through 1971, and for practically all of the information about Oruro. Other less lengthy essays are those by Rivera (1983), Lavaud (1982), Le Bot (1982), and the pertinent parts in Iriarte and the CIPCA group (1980), Albó (1979a, 1979b), and Alcoreza and Albó (1979). For this summary I have also consulted my collection of peasant documents for 1970–1984.

12 Tupaj Katari was actually executed early on November 14, according to the documents of his sentencing and Castañeda's diary (1781) of the La Paz siege, which confirms that the hero's head arrived in La Paz on that date.

13 Fausto Reinaga is the descendant of an hacendado from the Macha region (Potosí). He participated in the organization of Villarroel's National Indigenous Congress in 1945. His most complete and significant work dealing with this period is *Revolución India* (1970). Reinaga's son Ramiro, after a militant period in the Communist Party, has turned into one of the main theorists of the "Indianist" line represented by MITKA. See above all his book *Tawantinsuyu* (1978).

14 Javier Hurtado is the only one who has studied katarismo in Oruro.

15 On August 2, 1931, the first Indian school in Warisat'a (La Paz) was inaugurated, and since then, "Indian Day" has been celebrated on that date. Twenty-two years later, the Agrarian Reform was decreed in Ucureña (Cochabamba) on the same date.

16 About the Massacre of the Valley, see the official report (Justicia y Paz 1975), which has been published again on various occasions; Laneuville's analysis (1980); and the thesis of Edith Gutiérrez, still in progress (Cochabamba).

17 Oral tradition has it that Julián Apasa died saying "I will return turned into millions."

18 See the last charts in Iriarte and the CIPCA group (1980).

19 Alcoreza and Albó (1979) has abundant material about the peasantry's anti-military sentiment during the 1978 elections.

20 After the 1978 elections, Paz Estenssoro's MNR first attached the suffix "Alliance" (MNR-A), and later "Historic" (MNRH).

21 With the help of their allies of the PCML who had gone into the zone earlier as the UCAPO, Paz's MNR has remained stronger in the region of Santa Cruz North (*el Norte de Santa Cruz*). In various elections, it has been strongest in the peripheral regions, mainly in the East, where the peasantry was less critical in distinguishing recent evolutions within the MNR.

22 That is, Bánzer's regime, initially supported by the MNR of Víctor Paz; and more recently, the UDP, presided by Hernán Siles and his MNRI.

23 The recent analyses by Lavaud (1982) and Flores (1984) are "representative" of the first tendency. Rivera (1983) and Barnadas (1983) give more weight to the latter.

24 The relative tranquility of the Cochabamban countryside during the Kataris' general uprising in 1780–1781 is noteworthy. Popular urban sectors had rebelled thirty years earlier, with Alejo Calatayud, in protest of fiscal measures. But in 1780–1781 the main rebellious region was Tapacarí, where the traditional communities were still predominant. In the valle alto, which would later become the birthplace of the 1953 Agrarian Reform, there were some uprisings on the part of the *indiada* ("Indian mass") which were quickly suffocated by the "*mozos*" [male youths, presumably non-Indians—Ed.] from the pueblos.

25 On this subject see Rivera's stimulating analysis (1983).

26 Up until the time of this writing (the end of 1984), katarismo has preserved its hegemony within the CSUTCB, the national peasant movement's organization. Under this leadership, the CSUTCB has achieved a number of victories, among them, for example, the inclusion of the agricultural workers under the General Labor Law; the transfer of an important stock of tractors to the peasant organizations, rather than to elitist groups; and a better quota of power within the Bolivian Workers' Central (COB). Nonetheless, in the last two or three years, a new tendency somewhat counterposed to katarismo has taken on strength within the peasantry, a phenomenon which demonstrates the permanent vitality of the Bolivian peasant movement. This is the so-called *Movimiento Campesino de Bases* (MCB; "Peasant Base Movement"), which came out of the lower regions, whose characteristics are notably different from those of the Aymara altiplano, the center of katarismo. In the MCB are rural cultivators much more conflicted by the contradictions of the market and capitalism, for whom the ethnic problem is minor or nonexistent, and whose roots in a historical tradition are weak. The present coexistence of the katarista tendency and the MCB is a partial expression of the diversity of issues in play in the Bolivian countryside. But the analysis of this new situation would require another essay.

REFERENCES

ALBÓ, XAVIER
  1979a   *Achacachi, medio siglo de luchas campesinas.* Cuaderno de Investigación CIPCA, no. 19. La Paz.
  1979b   *Khitipxtansa, quienes somos. Identidad localista étnica y clasista en los aymaras de hoy.* 2d ed. La Paz: CIPCA and Instituto Indigenista Interamericano.
  1984   "Etnicidad y clase en la gran rebelión Aymara/Quechua: Kataris, Amarus y bases, 1780–1781." In Calderón and Dandler 1984: 51–118.

ALBÓ, XAVIER, AND JOSEP M. BARNADAS
1984   *La cara campesina de nuestra historia*. La Paz: UNITAS.

ALCOREZA, CARMEN, AND XAVIER ALBÓ
1979   *1978: El nuevo campesinado ante el fraude*. Cuaderno de Investigación CIPCA, no. 18. La Paz.

ANTEZANA E., LUIS
1960   *La lucha entre Cliza y Ucureña*. Pamphlet with place and publisher unidentified.

ANTEZANA, LUIS, AND HUGO ROMERO
1973   *Historia de los sindicatos campesinos*. La Paz: Consejo Nacional de Reforma Agraria.

BARNADAS, JOSEP M.
1983   *Au/ctos de fe*. Cochabamba: Historia Boliviana.

BRILL, WILLIAM H.
1966   "Military civic action in Bolivia." Ph.D. diss., University of Pennsylvania.

CALDERÓN, FERNANDO, AND JORGE DANDLER
1984   (Eds.) *Bolivia: La fuerza histórica del campesinado*. Cochabamba: CERES and United Nations Institute for Social Development.

CASTAÑEDA, D. F. DE
1781   *Diario de los principales sucesos acaecidos en los asedios o cercos que padeció esta ciudad de La Paz por los indios desde el dia 15 de marzo, hasta el dia 15 de noviembre del presente año de 81*. José Rosendo Gutiérrez, ed. La Paz, 1879.

CONDARCO MORALES, RAMIRO
1965   *Zarate, el temible Willka: Historia de la rebelión indígena de 1899*. La Paz. (A second enlarged edition was published in 1983.)

CSUTCB (Confederación Sindical Unica de Trabajadores Campesinos de Bolivia)
1984   *Ley Agraria Fundamental*. La Paz.

CHOQUE, ROBERTO
1979   "1921. Sublevación y masacre de los comunarios en Jesús de Machaca." *Revista Boliviana de Antropología* 1: 1–32.

DANDLER, JORGE
1969   *El sindicalismo campesino en Bolivia: los cambios estructurales en Ucureña*. Mexico City: Instituto Indigenista Interamericano.

1971   "Politics of leadership, brokerage and patronage in the campesino movement of Bolivia (1935–1954)." Ph.D. diss., University of Wisconsin–Madison.

1984   "Campesinado y reforma agraria en Cochabamba (1952–53): Dinámica de un movimiento campesino en Bolivia." In Calderón and Dandler 1984: 201–39.

FLORES, GONZALO
1979   "Una indagación sobre movimientos campesinos en Bolivia: 1913–1917." Mimeo ed. La Paz: CERES.

1984   "Estado, políticas agrarias y luchas campesinas: Revisión de una década en Bolivia." In Calderón and Dandler 1984: 445–545.

GOLTE, JÜRGEN
1980   *Repartos y rebeliones: Túpac Amaru y las contradicciones de la econo-
        mía colonial.* Lima: Instituto de Estudio Peruanos.
GRIESHABER, ERWIN P.
1977   "Survival of Indian Communities in XIX Century Bolivia." Ph.D.
        diss., University of North Carolina, Chapel Hill.
1980   "Survival of Indian Communities in Nineteenth-Century Bolivia: A
        Regional Comparison." *Journal of Latin American Studies* 12: 223–69.
GUTIERREZ, EDITH
n.d.   Thesis in preparation on la Masacre del Valle.
HARRIS, OLIVIA, AND XAVIER ALBÓ
1975   *Monteras y guardatojos. Campesinos y mineros en el Norte de Potosí.*
        Cuaderno de Investigación CIPCA, no. 7. La Paz.
HUANCA LAURA, TOMÁS
1984   "La desestructuración de los espacios socio-económicos andinos en
        el Altiplano lacustre: Agresión colonial y resistencia comunitaria."
        Thesis in sociology. La Paz: UMSA.
HURTADO, JAVIER
n.d.   "El origen, desarrollo y carácter del movimiento Tupaj Katari." Ph.D.
        thesis in progress, Free University of Berlin.
IRIARTE, GREGORIO, AND THE CIPCA GROUP
1980   *Sindicalismo campesino, ayer, hoy y mañana.* Cuaderno de Investiga-
        ción CIPCA, no. 21. La Paz.
JUSTICIA Y PAZ
1975   *La masacre del Valle, enero 1974.* La Paz.
KELLY, JONATHAN, AND HERBERT S. KLEIN
1981   *Revolution and the Rebirth of Inequality: A Theory Applied to the
        National Revolution in Bolivia.* Berkeley: University of California
        Press.
KLEIN, HERBERT S.
1982   *Bolivia: The Evolution of a Multi-Ethnic Society.* New York: Oxford
        University Press.
KOHL, JAMES
1969   "The Role of the Peasant in the Bolivian Revolutionary Cycle, 1952–
        1964." Ph.D. diss., University of New Mexico, Albuquerque.
LANEUVILLE, DIEGO
1980   *Movimiento campesino en el Valle Alto de Cochabamba.* Cocha-
        bamba.
LARSON, BROOKE
1981   *Explotación agraria y resistencia campesina.* Cochabamba: CERES.
LAVAUD, JEAN PIERRE
1981   "Les paysans boliviens contre l'Etat: du refus de l'impot unique a
        l'opposition aux 'decrets de la faim' (1968–1974)." *Cahiers des Amer-
        iques Latines* 23: 141–72.
1982   *Indianité et politique: le courant Tupac Katari en Bolivie.* Document
        de Travail. Paris: ERSIPAL.

LEBOT, YVON

1982   "Etrangers dans notre propre pays: Le mouvement Indien en Bolivie dans les années soixante-dix." In *Indianité, ethnocide et indigénisme en Amérique Latine.* Toulouse: GRAL: 155–63.

MALLOY, JAMES

1970   *Bolivia: The Uncompleted Revolution.* Pittsburgh: University of Pittsburgh Press.

MITCHELL, CHRISTOPHER

1971   "Reformers as Revolutionaries: The Tragedy of Bolivia's Movimiento Nacionalista Revolucionario, 1952–1964." Ph.D. diss., Harvard University.

PLATT, TRISTAN

1982   *Ayllu andino y estado boliviano.* Lima: Instituto de Estudios Peruanos.

n.d.   "Pensamiento político Aymara." Forthcoming in Xavier Albó, ed., *Raíces de América: el mundo Aymara.* Mexico: UNESCO–Siglo XXI.

REINAGA, FAUSTO

1970   *La revolución India.* La Paz: Partido Indio de Bolivia (PIB).

REINAGA, RAMIRO. See Wankar.

RIVERA, SILVIA

1979   "Medio siglo de luchas campesinas en Bolivia." In *Ultima Hora.* Edición especial "Bodas de Oro." La Paz, April 30, 1979.

1983   "Luchas campesinas contemporáneas en Bolivia: El movimiento 'Kataista,' 1970–1980." In René Zavaleta, ed., *Bolivia Hoy* (Mexico: Siglo XXI): 129–68.

1984   *Oprimidos pero no vencidos: Luchas del campesinado Aymara y Quechua de Bolivia de 1900 a 1980.* La Paz: El Tigre de Papel.

WACHTEL, NATHAN

1981   "Los mitimas del valle de Cochabamba: La política de colonización de Wayna Capac." *Historia Boliviana* (Cochabamba) 1: 21–57.

WANKAR (Ramiro Reinaga)

1978   *Tawantinsuyu. 5 siglos de guerra qheswaymara contra España.* La Paz (Chukiapu): MINKHA.

Index